D0923403

WITHDRAWN
UTSA LIBRARIES

CASES ON PRIVATE
INTERNATIONAL LAW

CASES ON PRIVATE INTERNATIONAL LAW

BY

J. H. C. MORRIS, D.C.L., F.B.A.

OF GRAY'S INN, BARRISTER-AT-LAW
FELLOW OF
MAGDALEN COLLEGE, OXFORD
UNIVERSITY READER IN
CONFLICT OF LAWS

FOURTH EDITION

OXFORD
AT THE CLARENDON PRESS
1968

Oxford University Press, Ely House, London W. 1

GLASGOW NEW YORK TORONTO MELBOURNE WELLINGTON
CAPE TOWN SALISBURY IBADAN NAIROBI LUSAKA ADDIS ABABA
BOMBAY CALCUTTA MADRAS KARACHI LAHORE DACCA
KUALA LUMPUR HONG KONG TOKYO

© OXFORD UNIVERSITY PRESS 1968

FIRST EDITION 1939
SECOND EDITION 1951
REPRINTED LITHOGRAPHICALLY 1956
THIRD EDITION 1960
FOURTH EDITION 1968

PRINTED IN GREAT BRITAIN

TO
M. J. M.

PREFACE TO FOURTH EDITION

TWELVE new cases and four new statutes have been added to this edition, and seventeen old cases and one old statute have been omitted in order to make room for them. The decision of the House of Lords in *Indyka* v. *Indyka* presented me with my most serious editorial problem, for it is probably the most important case in our subject to be decided in this century, yet the report of the case in the Weekly Law Reports runs to fifty-five pages (and will run to more in the Law Reports), and all of their Lordships said different things. To print only one judgment would have been to give a misleading impression, while to print all five in full was clearly out of the question in the space at my disposal. So I compromised by printing one judgment in full (that of Lord Pearson) and snippets from all the others. But even with this drastic editing the case occupies some twenty-two pages in the book, so I had to prune and scrape wherever I could to make room for it. Even so I am sorry to say that this edition is some eighteen pages longer than its predecessor.

Perhaps I may be allowed to confess that the omissions which gave me the greatest pleasure were those of *In re Marshall* (1957) and Lord Kingsdown's Act 1861, while those which gave me the greatest pain were *Wood* v. *Wood* (1957) and *Loucks* v. *Standard Oil Co.* (1918).   J. H. C. M.

Magdalen College
Oxford
25 November 1967

CONTENTS

PART I. INTRODUCTION

CHAPTER 1. CHARACTERIZATION AND THE INCIDENTAL QUESTION

CHAPTER 2. RENVOI

CHAPTER 3. PENAL AND REVENUE LAWS

CHAPTER 4. PROOF OF FOREIGN LAW

CHAPTER 5. DOMICILE

CONTENTS

PART II. FAMILY LAW

CHAPTER 6. MARRIAGE
Section A: Formalities

Section B: Capacity to Marry

Section C: Polygamous Marriages

CHAPTER 7. MATRIMONIAL CAUSES
Section A: Divorce

Section B: Nullity of Marriage

CONTENTS

Chapter 8. LEGITIMACY, LEGITIMATION, AND ADOPTION

Section A: Legitimacy

Section B: Legitimation

Section C: Adoption

PART III. LAW OF OBLIGATIONS

Chapter 9. CONTRACTS

Section A: Doctrine of the Proper Law

Section B: Capacity

Section C: Discharge

CONTENTS

Section D: Illegality

CHAPTER 10. TORTS

PART IV. LAW OF PROPERTY

CHAPTER 11. IMMOVABLES

Section A: Distinction between Movables and Immovables

Section B: Jurisdiction

Section C: Choice of Law

CHAPTER 12. TRANSFER OF TANGIBLE MOVABLES

CONTENTS

CONTENTS

Section C: Wills of Movables

Section D: Powers of Appointment

PART V. FOREIGN JUDGMENTS

CHAPTER 19. FOREIGN JUDGMENTS

Section A: Jurisdiction

Section B: Finality of Judgments

Section C: Defences

Section D: Direct Enforcement

PART VI. LAW OF PROCEDURE

CHAPTER 20. JURISDICTION TO STAY ACTIONS

CHAPTER 21. SUBSTANCE AND PROCEDURE

TABLE OF CASES

(The leading cases reported in the book are italicized, and the page on which the report begins is printed in darker type)

TABLE OF CASES

TABLE OF STATUTES

TABLE OF BOOKS REFERRED TO

BAR   *Private International Law* (Gillespie's Translation) (2nd ed. 1892).

BEALE   *Treatise on the Conflict of Laws* (1935).

CHESHIRE   *Private International Law* (7th ed. 1965).

COOK   *Logical and Legal Bases of the Conflict of Laws* (1942).

DICEY   *Conflict of Laws* (8th ed. 1967).

FALCONBRIDGE   *Essays on the Conflict of Laws* (2nd ed. 1954)

FOOTE   *Private International Law* (5th ed. 1925).

GOODRICH   *Handbook of the Conflict of Laws* (4th ed. 1965).

GRAVESON   *Conflict of Laws* (5th ed. 1965).

LORENZEN   *Selected Essays on the Conflict of Laws* (1947).

READ   *Recognition and Enforcement of Foreign Judgments* (1938).

RESTATEMENT   *American Law Institute's Restatement of the Conflict of Laws* (1934).

WESTLAKE   *Private International Law* (7th ed. 1925).

WOLFF   *Private International Law* (2nd ed. 1950).

PART I

INTRODUCTION

Chapter 1

CHARACTERIZATION AND THE INCIDENTAL QUESTION

The court does not necessarily characterize rules of foreign law in the same way as their nearest equivalents in English law.

In re Cohn [1945] Ch. 5 (Chancery Division)

A MOTHER and daughter, Mrs. Cohn and Mrs. Oppenheimer, were German nationals domiciled in Germany but resident in England. They were killed in an air raid in London as a result of the same explosion, and it could not be proved which of them survived the other. Mrs. Oppenheimer was entitled to movable property under Mrs. Cohn's will if she survived Mrs. Cohn.

UTHWATT J.: ... There is a difference between the law of England and the law of Germany regarding the presumption which is to be made about the order of the deaths in the circumstances stated. The law of England, by s. 184 of the Law of Property Act 1925, prescribes that, where two or more persons have died in circumstances rendering it uncertain which of them survived the other or others, 'such deaths shall (subject to any order of the court), for all purposes affecting the title to the property, be presumed to have occurred in order of seniority, and accordingly the younger shall be deemed to have survived the elder'. The Civil Code of Germany makes different provision. In the first book of the German Civil Code, headed 'General Principles', the first chapter of the first part deals with 'Natural Persons'. Article 20 contained in that chapter provides that, if several persons perish in a common danger, it is presumed that they have died simultaneously. On July 4, 1939, this was replaced by the following article:—'If it cannot be proved that of several deceased persons or persons declared dead one has survived the other, it is presumed that they have died simultaneously.' It may be observed in passing that the date of the widening of the scope of art. 20 affected by the amendment is of interest to the general historian. Under German law Mrs. Oppenheimer can benefit under the will of Mrs. Cohn only if she (Mrs. Oppenheimer) was the survivor of the two.

It was argued by Mr. Danckwerts, on behalf of those interested in Mrs. Oppenheimer's estate, that the first question which the court was called on to ascertain was whether or not Mrs. Oppenheimer survived Mrs. Cohn; that, in ascertaining that fact, the method of proof was determined by the lex fori (the law of England)—a general proposition which cannot be disputed; and that, when once it was shown that it was uncertain which of them survived the other, s. 184 of the Law of Property Act 1925 came into operation as part of the lex fori compelling the court to draw the inference or proceed on the footing that Mrs. Oppenheimer survived Mrs. Cohn. It was, according to his argument, only after reaching that point, that one turned to the law of the domicile.

In my opinion, this argument is not well founded. The law of the domicile, namely the law of Germany, is alone relevant in determining the effect of the testamentary dispositions of movables made by Mrs. Cohn, the basis on which the movables are to be administered, and the facts which it is necessary to ascertain to administer that estate. If, for instance, under the law of Germany, it was not necessary for the efficacy of the disposition in her favour that Mrs. Oppenheimer should survive Mrs. Cohn, but was only necessary that she should survive either Mr. or Mrs. Cohn, no inquiry as to survivorship such as is here being made would have been necessary. The question of survivorship is, in fact, opened up by the provisions of German law as to inheritance and is formally not: 'Did or did not Mrs. Oppenheimer survive Mrs. Cohn?' but 'Is the administration of Mrs. Cohn's estate to proceed on the footing that Mrs. Oppenheimer survived Mrs. Cohn or on the footing that she did not?' The purpose to which the inquiry as to survivorship is directed must be kept in mind. The mode of proving any fact bearing on survivorship is determined by the lex fori. The effect of any fact so proved is for the purpose in hand determined by the law of the domicile. The fact proved in this case is that it is impossible to say whether or not Mrs.

2

Oppenheimer survived Mrs. Cohn. Proof stops there. Section 184 of the Law of Property Act 1925 does not come into the picture at all. It is not part of the law of evidence of the lex fori, for the section is not directed to helping in the ascertainment of any fact but contains a rule of substantive law directing a certain presumption to be made in all cases affecting the title to property. As a rule of substantive law the section is relevant where title is governed by the law of England. It has no application where title is determined by the law of any other country.

In re
COHN.
—
Uthwatt J.

I turn now to consider the law of Germany in relation to the facts proved, unhampered by s. 184 of the Law of Property Act 1925. In my view, the provision contained in the article of July 4, 1939, is part of the general substantive law of Germany and not part of its law of evidence. Its terms and the place in which the repealed article dealing with the same general subject-matter was to be found make that clear. That rule of law has to be applied, inter alia, as part of the Law of Inheritances, contained in the German Civil Code. Predicating of Mrs. Oppenheimer that she is presumed to have died simultaneously with Mrs. Cohn, it is clear that Mrs. Oppenheimer was not a person living at the time when the succession to Mrs. Cohn's estate opened, and that, accordingly, having regard to arts. 1922 and 1923 of the German Civil Code, the defendants, Mrs. Freudenthal and Siegfried Cohn, take Mrs. Cohn's movable estate.

APT *v.* APT [1948] P. 83 (*post*, p. 62)

OGDEN *v.* OGDEN [1908] P. 46 (*post*, p. 77)

In re MALDONADO [1954] P. 223 (*post*, p. 444)

HUBER *v.* STEINER (1835) 2 Bing. N.C. 202 (*post*, p. 522)

The court may apply a foreign rule of the conflict of laws to determine some question which incidentally arises in the course of deciding the main question.

SCHWEBEL *v.* UNGAR (1963) 42 D.L.R. (2d) 622

(Ontario Court of Appeal)

SCHWEBEL
v.
UNGAR.

The defendant was born in Hungary. In 1945 she married Joseph Waktor in Hungary according to the rites of the Jewish faith. Joseph Waktor was domiciled at that time in Hungary. Shortly after the marriage they both decided to leave Hungary and go to Israel. They

3

were in several refugee camps in Europe and finally in one in Italy in the course of their efforts to get to Israel. While in the camp in Italy, and while still domiciled in Hungary, they were divorced by a gett (an extra-judicial Jewish divorce). A few weeks later, in December 1948, they both arrived in Israel. This divorce was not recognized as a valid divorce by the law of either Hungary or Italy but it was recognized as such by the law of Israel.

The defendant then lived in Israel for seven and a half years with her parents. She then came to New York and Toronto to visit relatives, and while in Toronto she met and married the plaintiff in April 1957.

The plaintiff petitioned for a decree of nullity on the ground that Joseph Waktor was still alive at the date of the plaintiff's marriage to defendant which was therefore bigamous. McRuer C.J. granted a decree, holding that Joseph Waktor and the defendant had never lost their Hungarian domicile of origin.[1] The defendant appealed.

The judgment of the court (MacKay, Kelly, and McLennan JJ.A.) was delivered by

MACKAY J.A. (after stating the facts, and holding that Waktor and the defendant acquired a domicile of choice in Israel before the defendant's second marriage): One of the requirements for a valid marriage in Ontario is that the parties entering into the marriage have the status of single persons and the question here is whether the personal status of the defendant was that of a married or single person at the time she entered into the marriage contract with the plaintiff in 1957.

If we determine the question by asking, (1) What was her domicile at that date? and (2) What was her personal status under the law of her country of domicile? the answer clearly is that she was domiciled in Israel; her status was that of a single person and therefore her marriage in 1957 was a valid marriage.

On the other hand, if we say her status in Israel is one based on the recognition by the law of Israel of a divorce obtained in another country where she was not domiciled and that divorce was one not recognized as valid by the law of her country of domicile at the time it was obtained, should we say: 'The status you claim of being a single person is valid only in Israel and cannot be recognized in Ontario.' In other words, should our enquiry as to personal status

[1] 37 D.L.R. (2d) 467.

extend beyond the simple enquiry as to what was her status under the law of her country of domicile at the date of her marriage in 1957 in Ontario? Do we accept that law as establishing her status in Ontario?

(After quoting from *Le Mesurier* v. *Le Mesurier*,[1] *Armitage* v. *A.-G.*,[2] *Mountbatten* v. *Mountbatten*,[3] *Har-Shefi* v. *Har-Shefi* (No. 2),[4] and Dicey's Conflict of Laws,[5] the learned judge continued): The decision in the present case turns on the marital status of the defendant at the time of her marriage to the plaintiff. To determine that status, I think our enquiry must be directed not to the effect to be given under Ontario law to the divorce proceedings in Italy as at the time of the divorce, but to the effect to be given to those proceedings by the law of the country in which she was domiciled at the time of her marriage to the plaintiff in 1957, namely, Israel, a domicile that she retained until her marriage to the plaintiff was actually performed, or, to put it another way, the enquiry is as to her status under the law of her domicile and not to the means by which she acquired that status. To hold otherwise would be to determine the personal status of a person not domiciled in Ontario by the law of Ontario instead of by the law of that person's country of domicile. This would be contrary to a basic principle of private international law and would result in the social evil referred to by Lord Watson in the *Le Mesurier* case of a person being regarded as married in one jurisdiction and unmarried in another. If Waktor or the defendant, after arriving in Israel, had attempted to obtain a divorce, any such application would have been rejected on the ground that the marriage had already been dissolved. If in any proceedings in the courts of Israel the defendant's status had been called in question, it would undoubtedly have been held that her status was that of a single person; if the defendant had married while in Israel, the marriage being valid according to the law of Israel should be recognized as valid in Ontario. It seems to me that the legal result should not be different because the marriage took place in Ontario. . . .

In the present case the Waktors were divorced in a country in which they were temporarily resident but not domiciled and by whose laws the divorce was not recognized as a valid divorce, nor was it recognized as such in the country of their domicile of origin.

SCHWEBEL
v.
UNGAR.
Mackay
J.A.

---

[1] [1895] A.C. 517; *post*, p. 114. [2] [1906] P. 135. [3] [1959] P. 43.
[4] [1953] P. 220. [5] 7th ed. (1958) pp. 223–5, 249, 256, 307.

5

SCHWEBEL
v.
UNGAR.

Mackay
J.A.

In this respect this case differs from any reported case I have found. It was, however, recognized as valid by the laws of the country in which they later became domiciled and I think must be regarded as an exception to the general rule that a divorce is not valid under the law of Ontario when it is not recognized as valid by the laws of the country of the domicile of the parties at the time it was obtained. This is so because the defendant subsequently, before coming to Ontario, and before she acquired a domicile in Ontario by her marriage to the plaintiff, acquired a domicile in a country by whose laws the divorce was recognized as a valid divorce. . . .[1]

Appeal allowed.

[1] This judgment was upheld on appeal to the Supreme Court of Canada: 48 D.L.R. (2d) 644.

Chapter 2

RENVOI

When a rule of the English conflict of laws refers to the 'law' of a foreign country, the reference sometimes means the 'whole' law of the foreign country, including its rules of the conflict of laws, in which case the English court will decide the case as nearly as possible as it would be decided by a court in the foreign country.

In re ANNESLEY [1926] Ch. 692 (Chancery Division)

THE testatrix, a British subject who had lived in France since 1866, died in 1924. By clause 2 of her will (made in the English language and form) she gave pecuniary legacies to friends and servants. By clause 4 she gave the residue of her property on trust for sale and out of the proceeds to pay an annuity and a trust legacy. By clause 5 she gave the ultimate residue to one of her two daughters absolutely. By clause 8 she declared that it was not her intention to abandon her English domicile of origin and that she had made no application under Article 13 of the French Civil Code (since repealed) for permission to establish her domicile in France. As the testatrix left two children surviving her, by French domestic law she could only dispose of one-third of her movable property. The testatrix by her will purported to dispose of the whole of her movable property.

RUSSELL J. (after deciding that on the facts the testatrix was domiciled in France at the date of her death, notwithstanding the declaration in her will and her failure to comply with Article 13, continued):

I accordingly decide that the domicile of the testatrix at the time of her death was French. French law accordingly applies, but the question remains: what French law? According to French municipal law,[1] the law applicable in the case of a foreigner not legally domiciled in France is the law of that person's nationality, in this case British. But the law of that nationality refers the question back to French law, the law of the domicile; and the question arises, will the French law accept this reference back, or renvoi, and apply French municipal law?

[1] Evidently a slip for 'French private international law' (*Ed.*).

7

Upon this question arises acute conflict of expert opinion. Two experts took the view that the renvoi would not be accepted, but that a French court would distribute the movables of the testatrix in accordance with English municipal law. One expert equally strongly took the view that a French court would accept the renvoi and distribute in accordance with French municipal law. I must come to a conclusion as best I can upon this question of fact upon the evidence after considering and weighing the reasons given by each side in support of their respective views. It is a case rather of views expressed by the experts as to what the French law ought to be, than what it is. Although there is in France no system of case law such as we understand it here—the decisions of higher courts not being binding upon inferior tribunals—yet I think I must pay some attention to the fact that this question of renvoi has at different times come for consideration before the Cour de Cassation, the highest court in France, and each time with the same result—namely, the acceptance of the renvoi and the application of the French municipal law. It is true that the Cour de Cassation is quite free to take the opposite view on a future occasion, but it has never done so. I refer to the cases which were discussed and expounded before me—namely, the *Forgo* case in 1882, and the *Soulié* case in 1910. In the former case, a decision of the Cour de Cassation, the renvoi was accepted, and French municipal law was applied to the disposition of the estate of a Bavarian national domiciled de facto in France (but not domiciled there according to French law), because according to Bavarian law the law of the domicile or usual residence was applicable. The *Forgo* case gave rise to grave differences of opinion among French jurists and was followed by many conflicting decisions in lower courts, some favouring the 'Théorie du Renvoi', others against it. The matter again came under the consideration of the branch of the Cour de Cassation entitled Chambre de Requêtes, one of whose functions is to decide whether or not an appeal to the Cour de Cassation should be allowed to proceed. That was the *Soulié* case, in which the court below had held that French municipal law governed the succession to the movable property of an American subject who had died in France with a de facto domicile in that country. The Chamber declined to allow an appeal to the Cour de Cassation to proceed. This decision, coming as it did after the grave differences of opinion which resulted from the *Forgo* case, strikes me as of great importance. As is pointed out in a note to the report in Clunet, it shows that the Supreme Court persists with energy in its former view, notwithstanding the views of text-writers to the contrary.

In these circumstances, and after careful consideration of the evidence of the experts called before me, I have come to the conclusion that I ought to accept the view that according to French law the French courts, in administering the movable property of a deceased foreigner who, according to the law of his country, is domiciled in France, and whose property must, according to that law, be applied in accordance with the law of the country in which he was domiciled, will apply French municipal law, and that even though the deceased had not complied with art. 13 of the Code.

The result is that as regards her English personal estate and her French movable property the testatrix in this case had power only to dispose of one-third thereof by her will.

Speaking for myself, I should like to reach the same conclusion by a much more direct route along which no question of renvoi need be encountered at all. When the law of England requires that the personal estate of a British subject who dies domiciled, according to the requirements of English law, in a foreign country shall be administered in accordance with the law of that country, why should this not mean in accordance with the law which that country would apply, not to the propositus, but to its own nationals legally domiciled there? In other words, when we say that French law applies to the administration of the personal estate of an Englishman who dies domiciled in France, we mean that French municipal law which France applies in the case of Frenchmen. This appears to me a simple and rational solution which avoids altogether that endless oscillation which otherwise would result from the law of the country of nationality invoking the law of the country of domicile, while the law of the country of domicile in turn invokes the law of the country of nationality, and I am glad to find that this simple solution has in fact been adopted by the Surrogate's Court of New York: *In re Tallmadge*.[1]

Certain other subsidiary questions arise. In consequence of the restrictions on the power of the testatrix to dispose of her property, the legacies bequeathed by the will cannot be paid in full. The will, in my opinion, is so worded that the pecuniary legacies given by clause 2 of the will must be paid in full before any of the sums

---

[1] (1919) 181 N.Y. Supp. 336.

mentioned in clause 4 of the will are set apart or paid. These last mentioned sums must if necessary abate rateably.

In re Ross [1930] 1 Ch. 377 (Chancery Division)

Janet Anne Ross, a British subject domiciled in Italy, died in 1927 leaving movable property in England and Italy and immovable property in Italy. She left two wills, one in English and the other in Italian. By her English will she gave the residue of her property in England to her niece, the defendant Caroline Waterfield, absolutely. By her Italian will she appointed her grand-nephew Aymand Waterfield heir of her movable and immovable property in Italy, subject to a usufruct in favour of his mother Caroline Waterfield during her life. Neither will left anything to the plaintiff, who was the testatrix's only son. The plaintiff claimed a declaration that he was entitled, notwithstanding the testamentary dispositions of his mother, to one moiety of her movable and immovable property in Italy and one moiety of her movable property in England as his legitima portio under Italian law.

Article 8 of the Italian Code provided that succession, whether under an intestacy or under a will, was regulated by the national law of the deceased, whatever the nature of the property. Article 9 provided that the substance and effect of testamentary dispositions were deemed to be governed by the national law of the testator.

LUXMOORE J.: . . . I will deal first with the movable property. Both the plaintiff's and defendants' counsel agree that by English law, the succession to movable property wherever situate is governed by the law of the domicile, in this case the law of Italy. In Italy, as in most of the European countries, the law refuses to recognise domicile as governing succession and other personal rights, and accepts the law of the nationality as the governing law. . . . The parties are agreed that 'the law of the domicile' governs the succession to the movable property. The dispute which arises between them and which I have to determine, is what is meant by 'the law of the domicile'. Does the phrase, so far as the English law is concerned, mean only that part of the domiciliary law which is applicable to nationals of the country of domicile (sometimes called 'the municipal law', or 'the internal law'); or does it mean the whole law of the country of domicile, including the rules of private international law, administered by its tribunals? If the former contention is correct, then the

English court, in deciding a case like the present, is not concerned to inquire what the courts of the country of domicile would in fact decide in the particular case, but what the courts of the domicile would decide if the propositus, instead of being domiciled in the foreign country, was also a national of that country. Whereas if the latter view is the correct one, the English court is solely concerned to inquire what the courts of the country of domicile would in fact decide in the particular case. In my opinion the latter is the correct view, as laid down by the English decisions, and there is no decision that has been quoted to me in argument or that I have been able to discover which supports the former view, though there is a dictum in the most recent case dealing with the question, which expresses approval of that view. I refer to the dictum of Russell J. in *In re Annesley*.[1]

The argument against the view that the law of the country of domicile means the whole of the law of that country, including its rules of private international law, is based on a claim that if this be the meaning of the expression 'the law of the domicile', then logically the meaning of the expression 'the law of the nationality' must also mean the whole of that law, including its rules of private international law; and it is said that if this be the true rule, the English court, in effect, has to say—I am putting the argument in the concrete form applicable to the case before me—the Italian law provides that the law of the nationality (the English law) is to be the governing law on the basis that the domicile of origin is English; but as the English law considers the law of the domicile to be the governing law, there is a further reference back from it to the Italian law as the domiciliary law, the logical result being an endless oscillation backwards and forwards from one law to the other, the English court sending the case back according to the English doctrine of domicile to the Italian court, and the Italian court sending it back again to the English court according to the Italian doctrine of nationality, and so on ad infinitum; the result being the establishment of what has been called by some of the text-writers a 'circulus inextricabilis'. The circle can only be cut if and when one or other of the opposing systems of law—to use once more a phrase adopted by the text-writers—'accepts the renvoi'.

Is this argument well founded? Indeed, does it arise at all? It does not in fact arise if the true view of the English court is that, by the

---

[1] [1926] Ch. 692 ; *ante*, p. 9.

phrase 'the law of the country of domicile' is meant that law which the courts of the country of domicile apply to the decision of the case to which the rule refers. If this is the correct view, the English courts in deciding the case 'accept the renvoi'. Let me illustrate what I mean by a reference to the question before me. It is admitted on both sides that the English court must adhere to the rule that, Janet Anne Ross having died domiciled in Italy, the distribution of her movable property must be governed by the law of Italy. On the proposition with which I am dealing this means the law which the Italian courts would hold to be applicable to the case of Janet Anne Ross, she being a British subject with an English domicile of origin. If because of her nationality the Italian courts hold that her movable property ought to be distributed in accordance with English internal law as applicable to English nationals domiciled in England—then the English courts will distribute this property in exactly the same way as if Janet Anne Ross was in fact at her death domiciled in England. If, on the other hand, the Italian courts should hold that her movable property should be distributed in accordance with the internal law of Italy applicable to Italian nationals, then the English courts will distribute Janet Anne Ross's movable property in accordance with Italian internal law. In other words, the English court will endeavour to ascertain what the Italian courts would in fact decide with regard to that part of Janet Anne Ross's movable property as might come under the actual control of the Italian courts.

My attention has been called in the course of the argument of this case to a number of authorities, and I have also considered a number of other decisions. In my view the general trend of the authorities establishes that the English courts have generally, if not invariably, meant by 'the law of the country of domicile', the whole law of that country as administered by the courts of that country, and with the exception of the dictum already referred to, there is no case to the contrary.

(His Lordship reviewed the authorities and continued:) In my opinion the present case must be decided in accordance with the law of Italy, as that law would be expounded in the Italian courts. If the Italian court had in fact dealt with the matter there would be no necessity to inquire into the law, and it would be my duty simply to follow the decision. Since there is no decision by the Italian court, I am bound to ascertain how the Italian court would decide the case from the evidence of those competent to instruct me. I am glad to say that the Italian lawyers who have been called on both sides are unanimous in this conclusion, that if the case fell to be decided in the Italian courts, it would be held that the testamentary dispositions of Mrs. Janet Anne Ross were valid, and provide for the total disposition of her property in Italy; and that in no circumstances would the Italian court recognise any right on the part of the plaintiff to any part of her property as legitima portio, as it would have done had Mrs. Janet Anne Ross been an Italian national.

. . . This disposes of the case so far as the movables in Italy are concerned. The position as to the immovable property in Italy seems to me to stand on a different basis. It is true that the law of Italy provides, by arts. 8 and 9 of the Code, that the succession to movable and immovable property is governed by the law of the nationality of the deceased owner, yet the English law has never suggested that the law of the domicile has anything to do with the succession to immovables. On the contrary, it has always recognised that the lex situs governs the succession to immovables, and the lex situs must necessarily be the law of the country where the property is situate, as it would be expounded by the courts of that country; and domicile cannot under any circumstances have any bearing on the case. But to some extent the theory of the renvoi may apply, for the law of England refers the question of succession to immovables to the lex situs (in this case the law of Italy), and the lex situs (the Italian law) refers the case to the law of the nationality, and this might mean the law of the nationality including the rule relating to the lex situs, and once again the circulus inextricabilis would be constituted. But in my view the lex situs must, for the reasons I have already stated with regard to the meaning to be placed on the phrase, 'law of the domicile', be construed in the way the courts of the country where the immovables are situate would themselves determine. On this basis the expert evidence is clear that the Italian courts would decide the succession to the immovable property in the same manner as the English court would determine it if the immovable property in question belonged to an Englishman and was situate in England.

. . . In the result the plaintiff has failed to substantiate either of his claims in this action, and I therefore dismiss it with costs.

In re ASKEW [1930] 2 Ch. 259 (Chancery Division)

By an English marriage settlement made in 1893 on the marriage of John Bertram Askew, a British subject then domiciled in England, it was provided that if John Bertram Askew should marry again he might by deed or will revoke in part the trusts of the husband's trust fund and might appoint that part upon such trusts for the benefit of any child of such subsequent marriage as he might think proper.

John Bertram Askew separated from his wife, and acquired a domicile of choice in Germany prior to 1911. In June 1911 a German court made a decree dissolving his marriage. In 1912 he married Anna Askew in Berlin. In January 1911, before the divorce, a daughter named Margarete Askew had been born to Anna Askew in Switzerland and she was acknowledged to be the daughter of John Bertram Askew.

By deed poll dated in 1913 John Bertram Askew purported to revoke part of the trusts of the husband's trust fund under the settlement of 1893 and to appoint that part to Margarete Askew absolutely.

The trustees of the settlement took out a summons for the determination of the question whether the power of appointment had been validly exercised in favour of Margarete Askew by the deed poll of 1913.

An affidavit by a German lawyer, accepted by all parties as correct, stated as follows: 'A general principle of German law is that the law of the country of which the father at the time of the marriage is a national governs the question of legitimation per subsequens matrimonium. I am informed and believe that John Bertram Askew was an Englishman. Therefore English law would be applied by the German court in deciding the question. (I am informed that the English law refers the question back to the law of the domicile, in the present case German law.) The German court would in these circumstances first have to decide whether to apply the municipal law of England only, or also the principles of international private law as interpreted by the English courts. The rule followed by the German court is that both the municipal law and the rules of international law, as interpreted by the English court, are to be applied. The German court therefore accepts the renvoi. There is no general statutory rule of German law as to which municipal law in the case of renvoi as in the present case is to be ultimately applied. The question has, however, been decided by numerous decisions of the Reichsgericht, the court of the highest instance in Germany. These decisions are to the effect that in a case where the German law provides that the law of the nationality is to govern a question and the law of nationality refers to the law of domicile and the domicile is German, the German court is to apply German municipal law. *In re* ASKEW.

'I am therefore of opinion that the German court would hold that according to German law Margarete Askew was legitimated by the marriage of her parents notwithstanding the fact that her father at the time of her birth was still married to a woman other than her mother and that by reason of the legitimation the child Margarete Askew has become issue of the marriage between John Bertram Askew and Anna Askew née Wengels.'

MAUGHAM J.: There is no doubt that, if German local law were applicable, the subsequent marriage of the parents of the defendant Margarete Askew would effect her legitimation, and that although she was born before the divorce, which was not made absolute until July 27, 1911. The trustees are naturally desirous of the protection of the court in relation to the question whether the power of appointment in question was validly exercised by the deed poll, and for this purpose it is necessary to determine whether the defendant Margarete Askew, though born out of wedlock during the continuance of a previous marriage, is, having regard to her father's domicile, legitimate. It is admitted that the Legitimacy Act 1926 would not have had that effect, having regard to the fact that John Bertram Askew was married to his first wife when the defendant Margarete Askew was born.[1]

The question of legitimation of a child by the subsequent marriage of its parents in a foreign country (apart from the provisions of the Legitimacy Act 1926, s. 1, sub-s. 2, and s. 8) appears at first sight to be well settled. Dicey (Rule 137, Case I, in his Conflict of Laws) states the result of the decisions thus: 'If both the law of the father's domicile at the time of the birth of the child and the law of the father's domicile at the date of the subsequent marriage allow of legitimatio per subsequens matrimonium, the child becomes or may become legitimate on the marriage of the parents.' The authorities cited are *Udny* v. *Udny*;[2] *In re Wright's Trusts*;[3] *In re Grove*,[4] and they bear out the proposition. Now, John Bertram Askew was admittedly domiciled in Germany both at the date of the birth and at the time of the subsequent marriage. But what is the meaning of the phrase 'the law of the father's domicile'? Does it refer to the

---

[1] As to this, see p. 249, *post*.   [2] (1869) L.R. 1 Sc. & Div. 441 ; *post*, p. 39.
[3] (1856) 2 K. & J. 295.   [4] (1888) 40 Ch. D. 216.

municipal law or local law of Germany, or does it refer to the whole of the laws applicable in Germany, including the views entertained in Germany as to the rules of private international law? There is no doubt that Dicey means the latter (see his Interpretation of Terms, Definition II); but in my opinion it is very doubtful whether the courts who have dealt with the matter did not mean the former. The so-called doctrine of renvoi, which has been so much discussed by jurists of recent years, had not been formulated in earlier days; and those who look at the statement of the foreign law in the earlier cases (see, for example, *In re Wright's Trusts* and *In re Grove*) will find that the foreign law as stated was the local or municipal law, and that no evidence was adduced as to the rules of private international law applied in the foreign country. It would seem that rules of private international law, not being founded on custom or statute, but being based upon considerations of justice and what is called 'comity', ought to be the same in all countries, though it is now well known (contrary to the belief entertained by Lord Westbury: see *Udny* v. *Udny*) that they are not. I am convinced that sixty or seventy years ago it never would have occurred to lawyers who were proving, say, the law of Italy (or France) in relation to the succession to an Englishwoman dying domiciled in Italy (or France) to depose (first) that the Italian (or the French) law gave a son a legitima portio; (secondly) that foreigners domiciled in Italy (or France) were deemed to retain their personal law; (thirdly) that he was informed that according to English law an English testator had a free power of disposition; and (finally) that, accordingly, by an application of Italian (or French) rules of private international law, the son had not (or had) a right to a legitima portio. It is on evidence of this kind that English courts have now to decide cases relating to the succession to movables belonging to British subjects who die domiciled abroad, and other cognate matters. It may be added that there is generally an acute conflict of expert opinion as to the foreign law, which has to be proved afresh in each case. Foreign jurists and foreign courts take from time to time varying views on the subject of renvoi. The result is not always satisfactory. It may, then, be useful to consider the question from the point of view of principle before dealing with the four modern authorities which must, I think, guide me in the matter.

    I will take the case of John Doe, a British subject, who goes to a foreign country, the Commonwealth of Utopia, and there acquires a permanent home without any intention of returning to his native land. He does not care to become a naturalised Utopian, and he does not trouble to fulfil the legal formalities which Utopia requires before legally admitting him to a Utopian domicile. Now the State of Utopia is one which (I assume) has adopted what is called the principle of nationality for foreigners, including those who have permanently settled in the realm, and it accordingly applies their national law in all questions relating to their status, capacity, and the succession to their surplus assets and the like. The first question that arises is whether in these circumstances John Doe in an English court can be said to have acquired a Utopian domicile. Clearly this depends upon the true meaning to be attached to the word 'domicile'. Until the decision of the House of Lords to be referred to later, this was at least doubtful; but it is now, I think, finally settled that in an English court John Doe must be taken to have been domiciled in Utopia, because domicile is a pure question of fact and does not in any true sense connote a legal relation. In English courts, English law must be applied; and by that law all these matters must be decided, at any rate prima facie, by the lex domicilii, that is, in the case under consideration, by the law of Utopia, and not the less that the courts of Utopia attach no importance in such a case to the lex domicilii. Now the second question arises—when the English courts refer the matter to the law of Utopia as the lex domicilii, do they mean the whole of that law, or do they mean the local or municipal law which in Utopia would apply to Utopian subjects? In order fully to appreciate this matter, it is necessary to answer the question, how comes it that an English court applies to John Doe the system of law of Utopia to which he does not owe allegiance? The answer must be that, in the view of an English court, John Doe, by acquiring a permanent home in Utopia, has attracted to himself the system of personal law which Utopia would apply to him, and it may be added that this would be in accordance with his presumed intention. Moreover, questions of private international law, in the absence of statute, depend largely on the historical views and the opinions of jurists which have been adopted in our courts; and it is the fact that, for some hundreds of years before the nineteenth century, continental and British jurists alike were practically united in the view that there existed in the world a number of civil societies based on domicile in the sense that the status and capacity of the members of those societies were governed by the lex domicilii, whatever their nationalities might be.

In re ASKEW.
—
Maugham J.

In France, Italy, Germany and elsewhere a different principle—namely, that of nationality—has gradually been introduced and now prevails; but in the British Empire, including as it does within its area so many distinct systems of law, the old doctrine is retained, and domicile is still the criterion in our courts of the personal law. If the law of Utopia had taken the same view as the English courts and applied to John Doe the Utopian local law, there would of course be no difficulty whatever. But since the jurists of Utopia have adopted the principle of nationality as governing the question of his personal law, the result is that, when the English court makes an inquiry as to the Utopian law, the first answer may be that Utopia prima facie applies to John Doe the law of England. It is, I think, a misunderstanding of the problem to suggest that this leads to a deadlock. Like others before me, I have spoken of the lex domicilii as applying to John Doe; but it should not be forgotten that the English court is not applying Utopian law *as such*, and the phrase is really a short way of referring to rights acquired under the lex domicilii. The inquiry which the court makes is, of course, as to Utopian law as a fact, and one to be proved in evidence like any other. The inquiry might accurately be expanded thus: What rights have been acquired in Utopia by the parties to the English suit by reason of the de facto domicile of John Doe in Utopia? For the English court will enforce those rights, though, I repeat, it does not, properly speaking, enforce Utopian laws. It is evident that, so stated, the question involves this. Have the parties acquired rights in Utopia by reason of the personal law of John Doe being English local law or Utopian local law? There is this alternative and no other. It is apparent that there is no room here for a deadlock, and that the circulus inextricabilis is no better than a (perhaps amusing) quibble.

The English judges and the foreign judges do not bow to each other like the officers at Fontenoy. The English court has to decide a matter within its jurisdiction according to English law in the wide sense, and if the matter depends on foreign domicile it is only necessary to prove certain facts as to rights under the foreign law. It is therefore, I think, clear that, when we inquire whether John Doe has acquired rights in Utopia by Utopian law, we must mean by the whole of the laws of Utopia including any views of private international law which may be deemed to give him rights (or subject him to restrictions), though an Englishman settled in that land. A final question may sometimes remain—namely, whether the lex domicilii is one which the English courts can recognise. If it is (as it nearly always is), we have only to ascertain what the lex domicilii in the wider sense is. I will add that I am not aware of any satisfactory definition of the term renvoi; but it will be noted that, if I am right, an English court can never have anything to do with it, except so far as foreign experts may expound the doctrine as being part of the lex domicilii. . . .

In re
ASKEW.
—
Maugham J.

(His Lordship discussed the cases of *In re Johnson*,[1] *Casdagli* v. *Casdagli*,[2] *In re Annesley*,[3] and *In re Ross*[4] and the evidence of German law and continued:) For the reasons given above I hold that in an English court the lex domicilii in the wide sense must prima facie apply, and, this being a law which the English courts will recognise, the conclusion is that the defendant Margarete is a legitimate child of John Bertram Askew in our courts and that the power of appointment was effectively exercised in her favour.

I think it proper to add that in my opinion it is unsatisfactory to find that, upon the evidence adduced in the two cases of *In re Annesley* and *In re Ross*, the courts were bound to hold that, although both in France and in Italy the national law of the de cujus is held to prevail, yet, owing to a divergence on the theoretical question of renvoi, the property and capacity of an Englishman domiciled in Italy is held to be a matter of (local) English law, whilst the property and capacity of an Englishman domiciled in France is held to be a matter of (local) French law. Nor is there any certainty that a contrary result will not be reached upon the evidence adduced in the next two cases which arise as to persons dying in France and Italy respectively. Those who have any acquaintance with the extensive literature that has appeared on the Continent on the subject of renvoi and the great diversity of view that exists would not be surprised to find that the legal decisions in France and Italy, where legal decisions are not binding as authorities to be followed, had changed in their effect. An Englishman domiciled de facto in France can have no certainty that his personal law is the municipal law of France, nor can he be sure if he crosses the frontier and becomes domiciled de facto in Italy that the municipal law of England will become his personal law. It may be added that views which seem strange to an English lawyer are entertained on these matters in some Eastern countries and also in some of the States in South

---

[1] [1903] 1 Ch. 821. [2] [1919] A.C. 145. [3] [1926] Ch. 692; *ante*, p. 7.
[4] [1930] 1 Ch. 377; *ante*, p. 10.

America; and in those countries the result of acquiring a domicile must be very doubtful. I cannot refrain from expressing the opinion that it is desirable that the position of British subjects who acquire domiciles in countries which do not agree with our views as to the effect of a foreign domicile should be made clear by a very short statute. There is much to be said for the 'simple and rational solution' suggested by Russell J. in *In re Annesley*; but whether the municipal law of the foreign country or the municipal law of England is to be held applicable in British courts in these cases, it is clearly desirable that the matter should be certain and should not be held ultimately to depend on the doubtful and conflicting evidence of foreign experts.

Note A: CHARACTERIZATION, THE INCIDENTAL QUESTION AND RENVOI

THESE subjects appear at the beginning of this book because that is the logical place for them, the place they would occupy if the English conflict of laws were ever codified. But the student is strongly advised to postpone detailed consideration of them until he comes to the end of the subject, because they are very difficult topics. Moreover, they are topics about which more can be learnt by reading textbooks and articles than by studying cases. This is especially true of Characterization, because *Re Cohn* (*ante*, p. 1) is one of the very few English cases in which the court even mentions the problem. One aspect of the problem of characterization can be profitably studied in connexion with chapter 21, *post*, p. 522. The following books and articles are recommended for study: Cheshire, pp. 39–73; Beckett, 15 B.Y.B.I.L. 46 (1934); Dicey, pp. 19–71; Falconbridge, pp. 50–263; Lorenzen, pp. 19–135; Cook, pp. 211–51; Robertson, *Characterization in the Conflict of Laws*; Griswold, 51 Harv. L.R. 1165 (1938); Gotlieb, 33 Can. Bar Rev. 523 (1955). Most of these discussions emphasize the relation between the problems. A detailed treatment is outside the scope of this book, but something must be said about the nature of the problems and the various solutions which have been propounded.

(1) *Characterization*

The nature of the problem can best be understood from some examples. (i) A Frenchman under 21 marries an Englishwoman in England without obtaining the consent of his parents as required by French law. The French and English conflict of laws rules agree that the formalities of marriage are governed by the law of the place of celebration (English law), and also that the husband must have capacity to marry by his personal law (French law). But this does not solve the problem until we know what is the nature of the French rule about parental consents: is it a rule relating to formalities (in which case it will not apply to a marriage in England)? Or is it a rule relating to capacity to marry (in which case it will apply to the marriage of a Frenchman)? This is a question of characterization: and the problem is to know by which law, French or English, the characterization of the French consents rule is to be governed. See *Ogden* v. *Ogden* (*post*, p. 77). (ii) An action is brought in England on a promissory note made in France after the expiry of the period fixed by the French (but not by the English) statute of limitations. By the English rules of the conflict of laws, questions of substance are governed by French law as the lex causae, questions of procedure are governed by English law as the lex fori. By English law, the statutes of limitations affect procedure, but by French law they affect substance. See *Huber* v. *Steiner* (*post*, p. 522).

Four principal solutions of the problem have been suggested:

(*a*) Characterization should be governed by the lex fori. The forum should characterize rules of its own domestic law in accordance with that law, and should characterize rules of foreign law in accordance with their nearest analogy in its own domestic law. This is in substance what was done in *Ogden* v. *Ogden* and *Huber* v. *Steiner*. The main objections to this view are (i) that to argue by analogy from a rule of domestic law to a rule of foreign law is to indulge in mechanical jurisprudence of a particularly vicious kind, and may result in the forum seriously distorting the foreign law, applying it in cases where it would not be applicable and vice versa; and (ii) that the view breaks down altogether when there is no close analogy to the foreign law in the domestic law of the forum.

(*b*) Characterization should be governed by the lex causae, that is, the appropriate foreign law. This is in substance what was done in *Re Maldonado* (*post*, p. 444). This view is open to even more serious objections. In the first place, it is arguing in a circle to say that the foreign law governs the process of characterization before the process of characterization has led to the selection of the foreign law. Secondly, if there are two potentially applicable foreign laws, why should the forum adopt the characterization of one rather than that of the other?

(*c*) According to a third view, the problem can be solved by distinguishing between primary characterization, a matter for the lex fori, and secondary characterization, a matter for the lex causae, the difference between them being that primary characterization precedes, and secondary characterization follows, the selection of the proper law. The objections to this theory are too numerous to mention here, but perhaps the chief one is that its advocates are not even approximately agreed on what for them is the crucial point, namely, where the line is to be drawn between primary and secondary characterization. It seems that the same situation can be made to appear as a case of either primary or secondary characterization by simply formulating it differently without any change of substance. It is significant that the author of this theory seems to have abandoned it: see Cheshire, pp. 39–53.

(*d*) A fourth view is that the process of characterization ought to be performed in accordance with the principles of analytical jurisprudence and comparative law. The objections to this theory are that there are very few principles of analytical jurisprudence and comparative law of universal application; and that while the study of comparative law is capable of revealing differences between domestic laws, it is hardly capable of resolving them. For instance, comparative law may reveal that statutes of limitation are sometimes treated as procedural and sometimes as substantive, or that

21

parental consents to marriage are sometimes regarded as affecting formalities and sometimes as affecting capacity: but how can comparative law determine how these matters should be characterized in a conflict of laws case?

Determination of the connecting factor. It is settled that for the purposes of an English conflict rule, the question where a person is domiciled must be determined exclusively by English law: *Re Martin (post,* p. 450); *Re Annesley (ante,* p. 7). There is no reason to doubt that a similar rule would be applied to other connecting factors such as place of contracting, place of performance, place of wrong, or situs of things. It is a matter of dispute whether this problem should be regarded as a question of characterization or as sui generis.

Question. In *Re Cohn (ante,* p. 1), was the court characterizing s. 184 of the Law of Property Act 1925 and article 20 of the German Civil Code, or was it characterizing the presumption of survivorship in the abstract?

Problems. (a) What would have been decided in *Re Cohn* if the court had held that s. 184 was substantive and article 20 procedural, or vice versa?

(b) An action is brought in country F for breach of a contract governed by the law of country X after the relevant periods of limitation fixed by the laws of F and X have both expired. By the law of F, the statutes of limitation are substantive, by the law of X, they are procedural. Will the action succeed?

(2) *Incidental Question*

This problem arises in the following way. Suppose that the forum is considering a main question which has foreign elements, in the course of which a subsidiary question, also having foreign elements, incidentally arises. Suppose that by the conflict of laws rules of the forum the main question is governed by the law of a foreign country. Should the forum's conflict of laws rules or those of that foreign country determine the law which is to govern the subsidiary question? The classic example is that of a testator domiciled in France who gives movables in England to the children of A. The main question is one of succession to movables, governed by the law of the testator's domicile, in this case France. A subsidiary question arises as to the legitimacy of one of A's children. Should the English or the French conflict of laws rules determine what law governs this question?

The writers who have discussed the incidental question are sharply divided in opinion. Some think it should be governed by the foreign conflict rules, on the ground that the question is not the abstract question, is the child legitimate? but rather, is the child entitled to succeed under T's will? Others think it should be determined by the conflict rules of the forum, on the ground that since the subsidiary question is ex hypothesi capable of arising in its own right (otherwise it would not have its own conflict rules), to hold otherwise might compel the forum to decide that the child is illegitimate in one set of proceedings and legitimate in another set of proceedings arising in a different context.

Reported cases raising the problem of the incidental question are extremely rare, but an instance is afforded by *Schwebel* v. *Ungar (ante,* p. 3). The main question there was the capacity of the defendant to marry the plaintiff, which was governed by the law of her domicile, that of Israel. The subsidiary question was the validity of the divorce. The court applied the Israeli conflict rules and not its own to determine this question. The result is very controversial: see 43 Can. Bar Rev. 363, 374–80; 27 M.L.R. 727; 14 I.C.L.Q. 659.

(3) *Renvoi*

The nature of this problem can also best be understood from an example. Suppose a British subject dies intestate domiciled in Italy, leaving movables in England; and that by the English conflict of laws rule, succession to movables is governed by the law of the domicile (Italian law), but by the Italian conflict of laws rule, succession to movables is governed by the law of the nationality (English law). Which law, English or Italian, will regulate the distribution of the English movables? Three solutions have been suggested:

(*a*) *The internal law theory.* The English court should distribute the movables in accordance with domestic Italian law, disregarding the factors which render the situation a conflict of laws situation for the Italian court: that is, disregarding the British nationality of the intestate and the English situation of the movables. This theory has been recommended obiter by Russell J. in *Re Annesley* (*ante*, p. 9) and by Maugham J. in *Re Askew* (*ante*, p. 20), on the ground that it is 'simple and rational', but was rejected in *Re Ross* (*ante*, p. 10) after a comprehensive review of the authorities.

(*b*) *The partial renvoi theory.* The English court should 'accept the renvoi' from Italian law and apply English domestic law, disregarding the Italian domicile of the intestate. This theory has been adopted in a number of celebrated continental cases (e.g. *L'Affaire Forgo*, 1883, and *L'Affaire Soulié*, 1910), but it is not the current doctrine of the English courts.

(*c*) *The total renvoi theory.* The English court should decide the case as it would be decided by the Italian court: if for any reason that court would apply English domestic law, or if for any reason that court would apply Italian domestic law, the English court should do likewise. This theory was applied in *Re Annesley* (*ante*, p. 7), *Re Ross* (*ante*, p. 10), and *Re Askew* (*ante*, p. 13), and up to a point those cases are reinforced by a dictum of the Privy Council in *Kotia* v. *Nahas* [1941] A.C. 403, 413, and by the decision of Wynn Parry J. in *Re Duke of Wellington* [1947] Ch. 506; affirmed on other grounds [1948] Ch. 118. One has to add the qualification, because the Privy Council was sitting on appeal from a Palestine court and dealing with the Palestine, not the English, conflict of laws; and because no two writers are in agreement as to what the *Wellington* case decided, or even what the issue was in that case: see Mann, 11 Mod. L.R. 232; Falconbridge, pp. 229–32; Morris, 64 L.Q.R. 265; Jennings, 64 L.Q.R. 321; Cheshire, p. 70.

How this theory works in practice can best be seen by comparing *Re Annesley* and *Re Ross*. In *Re Annesley*, the Judge looked first at French law (lex domicilii); finding that it referred to English law (lex patriae) and would accept the reference back to French law, he applied French law. In *Re Ross* the Judge looked first at Italian law (lex domicilii and lex situs); finding that it referred to English law (lex patriae) and would not accept the reference back to Italian law, he applied English law. What would happen if the foreign law adopted the same theory of renvoi as the English court must remain a mystery. 'With all respect to Maugham J. (*ante*, p. 18) the English judges and the foreign judges would then continue to bow to each other like the officers at Fontenoy' (First Report of the Private International Law Committee, Cmd. 9068, para. 23 (3)). Whatever theory of renvoi is adopted by the foreign law, the result often depends on 'the doubtful and conflicting evidence of foreign experts' (*ante*, p. 20) and so is completely unpredictable.

INTRODUCTION

The crucial question is whether the English cases lay down a rule of universal application in the conflict of laws, or whether they must be confined to questions of succession, title to foreign land, and status. In view of the difficulties discussed by the writers, and the thousands of cases in which the foreign domestic law has been applied without reference to the foreign conflict of laws, the former would appear to be the preferable view. 'Much of the discussion of the renvoi doctrine has proceeded on the basis that the choice lies in all cases between its absolute acceptance and its absolute rejection. The truth would appear to be that in some situations the doctrine is convenient and promotes justice, and that in other situations the doctrine is inconvenient and ought to be rejected. . . . In all but exceptional cases the theoretical and practical difficulties involved in applying the doctrine outweigh any supposed advantages it may possess. The doctrine should not therefore be invoked unless it is plain that the object of the English conflict rule in referring to a foreign law will on balance be better served by construing the reference to mean the conflict rules of that law' (Dicey, pp. 62–63).

The Hague Draft Convention of 1951. In October 1951 an international Conference on Private International Law approved a draft Convention containing the following provision: 'When the state where the person concerned is domiciled prescribes the application of the law of his nationality, but the state of which such person is a citizen prescribes the application of the law of his domicile, each contracting state shall apply the provisions of the internal law of his domicile.' It will be observed that this provision only purports to resolve conflicts between the law of the nationality and the law of the domicile, and not (for instance) conflicts between the law of the nationality and the law of the situs (cf. *Re Ross, ante,* p. 10, as to the immovables). It represents a concession by the advocates of the nationality principle to the advocates of the principle of domicile. But the price of the concession is that domicile should be defined to mean 'habitual residence'. Since this is not the meaning of domicile in English law, considerable amendment of the English law of domicile would be needed before the United Kingdom could become a party to the Convention. See Cohn, 71 L.Q.R. 562. Because of the difficulties which have been found in amending the law of domicile (see *post*, p. 52), the Private International Law Committee no longer recommend that this country should adhere to the Hague Convention in its present form (Seventh Report, Cmnd. 1955 (1963), paras. 13–17).

Chapter 3

PENAL AND REVENUE LAWS

English courts will not enforce the penal laws of foreign countries. What is a foreign penal law is a matter to be decided by the English court.

HUNTINGTON *v.* ATTRILL [1893] A.C. 150 (Privy Council)

Appeal from the Ontario Court of Appeal

THE judgment of their Lordships (Lords Halsbury, Watson, Bramwell, Hobhouse, Morris, and Shand) was delivered by

LORD WATSON: The appellant, in June, 1880, became a creditor for money lent to the Rockaway Beach Improvement Company, Limited, which carried on business in the State of New York, being incorporated pursuant to Chapter 611 of the State laws of 1875. Sect. 21 of the Act provides that: 'If any certificate or report made, or public notice given, by the officers of any such corporation, shall be false in any material representation, all the officers who shall have signed the same shall be jointly and severally liable for all the debts of the corporation contracted while they are officers thereof.'

The respondent was, in June, 1880, a director, and in that capacity an officer of the company within the meaning of the statute. On the 30th of that month he, along with other officers of the company, signed and verified on oath, as prescribed by sect. 37, a certificate setting forth that the whole capital stock had, at its date, been paid up in cash.

In the year 1883, the appellant instituted a suit against the respondent before the Supreme Court of New York State for the unpaid balance of his loan to the company, alleging that the certificate contained representations which were material and false, and that the respondent had incurred personal responsibility for the debt as provided by sect. 21. The respondent defended the action; but, a verdict having been found against him, the court, on the 15th of June 1886, gave final judgment, ordering him to pay to the appellant the sum of $100,240.

Having failed to recover payment, the appellant, in September, 1886, brought an action upon his decree in the Common Pleas Division of the High Court of Justice for the Province of Ontario, where the respondent resided. The only plea stated in defence was to the effect that the judgment sued on was for a penalty inflicted by the municipal law of New York; and that the action being one of a penal character ought not to be entertained by the courts of a foreign state.

Mr. Justice Street, who tried the case, being of opinion that the enactments of sect. 21 were strictly punitive and not remedial, dismissed the action with costs. The judges of the Appeal Court were equally divided in opinion, the result being that the appeal taken from his decision was dismissed. The Chief Justice (Hagarty) and Mr. Justice Osler were of opinion that the statutory remedy given to the appellant as a creditor of the company being civil only, and not enforceable by the State or by the public, was not a penal matter in the sense of international law. Mr. Justice Burton was of the same opinion, but held himself precluded from giving effect to it for reasons which he thus explains: 'The courts of the State of New York have placed an interpretation upon this particular statute in which I should not have agreed; but those decisions are the law of the State of New York, and with that we are dealing. I am of opinion, therefore, that on that undisputed expert testimony this is a penal statute there, and the judgment obtained upon it cannot be enforced here.' In the conclusion thus stated, Mr. Justice Maclennan expressed his concurrence. But the learned Judge, in that respect agreeing with the Court of First Instance and differing from the other members of the Court of Appeal, held that the enactment was in itself undoubtedly penal, inasmuch as it was 'passed in the public interest, providing a punishment for an offence', and that 'it makes no difference that what it exacts from the offender is given to persons who are ordinary creditors of a company in payment of their respective debts'.

Their Lordships cannot assent to the proposition that, in considering whether the present action was penal in such sense as to oust their jurisdiction, the courts of Ontario were bound to pay absolute deference to any interpretation which might have been put upon the Statute of 1875 in the State of New York. They had to construe and apply an international rule, which is a matter of law entirely within the cognizance of the foreign court whose jurisdiction is invoked.

Judicial decisions in the State where the cause of action arose are not precedents which must be followed, although the reasoning upon which they are founded must always receive careful consideration, and may be conclusive. The court appealed to must determine for itself, in the first place, the substance of the right sought to be enforced; and, in the second place, whether its enforcement would, either directly or indirectly, involve the execution of the penal law of another State. Were any other principle to guide its decision, a court might find itself in the position of giving effect in one case and denying effect in another, to suits of the same character, in consequence of the causes of action having arisen in different countries; or in the predicament of being constrained to give effect to laws which were, in its own judgment, strictly penal.

The general law upon this point has been correctly stated by Mr. Justice Story in his 'Conflict of Laws', and by other text-writers; but their Lordships do not think it necessary to quote from these authorities in explanation of the reasons which have induced courts of justice to decline jurisdiction in suits somewhat loosely described as penal, when these have their origin in a foreign country. The rule has its foundation in the well-recognized principle that crimes, including in that term all breaches of public law punishable by pecuniary mulct or otherwise, at the instance of the State Government, or of some one representing the public, are local in this sense, that they are only cognizable and punishable in the country where they were committed. Accordingly no proceeding, even in the shape of a civil suit, which has for its object the enforcement by the State, whether directly or indirectly, of punishment imposed for such breaches by the lex fori, ought to be admitted in the courts of any other country.

Their Lordships have already indicated that, in their opinion, the phrase 'penal actions', which is so frequently used to designate that class of actions which, by the law of nations, are exclusively assigned to their domestic forum, does not afford an accurate definition. In its ordinary acceptation, the word 'penal' may embrace penalties for infractions of general law which do not constitute offences against the State; it may for many legal purposes be applied with perfect propriety to penalties created by contract; and it therefore, when taken by itself, fails to mark that distinction between civil rights and criminal wrongs which is the very essence of the international rule. The phrase was used by Lord Loughborough and by Mr. Justice

27

Buller in a well-known case (*Folliott* v. *Ogden*[1] and *Ogden* v. *Folliott*[2]) and also by Chief Justice Marshall, who, in *The Antelope*[3] thus stated the rule with no less brevity than force: 'The courts of no country execute the penal laws of another.' Read in the light of the context, the language used by these eminent lawyers is quite intelligible, because they were dealing with the consequences of violations of public law and order, which were unmistakably of a criminal complexion. But the expressions 'penal' and 'penalty', when employed without any qualification, express or implied, are calculated to mislead, because they are capable of being construed so as to extend the rule to all proceedings for the recovery of penalties, whether exigible by the State in the interest of the community, or by private persons in their own interest.

The Supreme Court of the United States had occasion to consider the international rule in *Wisconsin* v. *The Pelican Insurance Company*.[4] By the statute law of the State of Wisconsin, a pecuniary penalty was imposed upon corporations carrying on business under it who failed to comply with one of its enactments. The penalty was recoverable by the commissioner of insurance, an official entrusted with the administration of the Act in the public interest, one half of it being payable into the State Treasury, and the other to the commissioner, who was to defray the costs of prosecution. It was held that the penalty could not be enforced by the Federal Court, or the judiciary of any other State. In delivering the judgment of the bench, Mr. Justice Gray, after referring to the text-books, and the dictum by Chief Justice Marshall already cited, went on to say: 'The rule that the Courts of no country execute the penal laws of another applies not only to prosecutions and sentence for crimes and misdemeanours, *but to all suits in favour of the State* for the recovery of pecuniary penalties for any violation of statutes for the protection of its revenue or other municipal laws, and to all judgments for such penalties.'

Their Lordships do not hesitate to accept that exposition of the law, which, in their opinion, discloses the proper test for ascertaining whether an action is penal within the meaning of the rule. A proceeding, in order to come within the scope of the rule, must be in the nature of a suit in favour of the State whose law has been infringed. All the provisions of municipal statutes for the regulation

---

[1] (1789) 1 H. Bl. 135.   [2] (1790) 3 T.R. 734.   [3] (1825) 10 Wheat. 123.
[4] (1888) 127 U.S. 265.

of trade and trading companies are presumably enacted in the interest and for the benefit of the community at large; and persons who violate these provisions are, in a certain sense, offenders against the State law, as well as against individuals who may be injured by their misconduct. But foreign tribunals do not regard these violations of statute law as offences against the State, unless their vindication rests with the State itself, or with the community which it represents. Penalties may be attached to them, but that circumstance will not bring them within the rule, except in cases where these penalties are recoverable at the instance of the State, or of an official duly authorized to prosecute on its behalf, or of a member of the public in the character of a common informer. An action by the latter is regarded as an actio popularis pursued, not in his individual interest, but in the interest of the whole community.

The New York Statute of 1875 provides for the organization and regulation of corporations formed for the purpose of carrying on all kinds of lawful business with the exception of certain branches therein specified. It confers rights and privileges upon persons who choose to form a trading association, and to become incorporated under its provisions, with full or with limited liability; and, in either case, it varies and limits the rights and remedies which, under the common law, would have been available to creditors of the association, as against its individual members. On the other hand, for the protection of those members of the public who may deal with the corporation, the Act imposes upon its directors and officers various stringent obligations, the plain object of which is to make known, from time to time, to all concerned, the true condition of its finances. Thus they are required (sect. 18) to publish an annual report stating the amount of capital, the proportion actually paid in, the amount and nature of existing assets and debts, the names of the shareholders and the dividends, if any, declared since last report; and (sect. 37) to certify the amount of capital stock paid in within thirty days after payment of the last instalment. In both cases the consequence of the report or certificate being false in any material representation, is that every director or officer who vouched its accuracy becomes, under sect. 21, liable personally for all the debts of the corporation contracted during his period of office.

The provisions of sect. 21 are in striking contrast to the enactments of sect. 34, which inflicts a penalty of $100 upon every director or officer of a corporation with limited liability, who authorizes or

INTRODUCTION

HUNTING-
TON
v.
ATTRILL.
—
Lord
Watson.permits the omission of the word 'limited' from its seal, official publications, or business documents. In that case, the penalty is recoverable 'in the name of the people of the State of New York by the district attorney of the county in which the principal office of such corporation is located, and the amounts recovered shall be paid over to the proper authorities for the support of the poor of such county'. It does not admit of doubt that an action by the district attorney would be a suit in favour of the State, and that neither the penalty, nor the decree of a New York Court for its amount, could be enforced in a foreign country.

In one aspect of them, the provisions of sect. 21 are penal in the wider sense in which the term is used. They impose heavy liabilities upon directors, in respect of failure to observe statutory regulations for the protection of persons who have become or may become creditors of the corporation. But, in so far as they concern creditors, these provisions are in their nature protective and remedial. To use the language of Mr. Justice Osler, they give 'a civil remedy only to creditors whose rights the conduct of the company's officers may have been calculated to injure, and which is not enforceable by the State or the public'. In the opinion of their Lordships, these enactments are simply conditions upon which the Legislature permits associations to trade with corporate privileges, and constitute an implied term of every contract between the corporation and its creditors. . . .

Appeal allowed.

Nor will English Courts enforce foreign revenue laws.

GOVERN-
MENT OF
INDIA
v.
TAYLOR.GOVERNMENT OF INDIA *v.* TAYLOR [1955] A.C. 491 (House of Lords)

The Delhi Electric Supply and Traction Co. Ltd. was incorporated in the United Kingdom but carried on business in India. In 1947 it sold the whole of its undertaking to the appellant, the Government of India, for the sum of 82, 11, 580 rupees. This sum was paid to the company in India and remitted to England a few days later. In 1949 the company went into voluntary liquidation in England and the respondent was appointed liquidator. The Government of India claimed to prove in the liquidation for the sum of 16, 54, 945 rupees which consisted of Indian capital gains tax on the sale of the company's undertakings. The liquidator rejected this claim and Vaisey J. and the Court of Appeal (Evershed M.R., Jenkins and Morris L.JJ.) held that he was entitled to do so.

VISCOUNT SIMONDS: My Lords, I admit that I was greatly surprised to hear it suggested that the courts of this country would and should entertain a suit by a foreign State to recover a tax. For at any time since I have had any acquaintance with the law I should have said as Rowlatt J. said in *King of the Hellenes* v. *Brostrom*:[1] 'It is perfectly elementary that a foreign government cannot come here— nor will the courts of other countries allow our Government to go there—and sue a person found in that jurisdiction for taxes levied and which he is declared to be liable to in the country to which he belongs.' That was in 1923. In 1928 Tomlin J. in *Re Visser*,[2] after referring to the case of *Sydney Municipal Council* v. *Bull*,[3] in which the same proposition had been unequivocally stated by Grantham J., and saying that he was bound to follow it, added: 'My own opinion is that there is a well-recognised rule, which has been enforced for at least 200 years or thereabouts, under which these courts will not collect the taxes of foreign States for the benefit of the sovereigns of those foreign States; and this is one of those actions which these courts will not entertain.' My Lords, it is not seemly to weigh the pronouncements of living judges, but it is, I think, permissible to say that the opinions of few, if any, judges of the past command greater respect than those of Lord Tomlin and Rowlatt J., and what appeared to one of them to be a 'well-recognised rule' and to the other 'elementary' law cannot easily be displaced.

My Lords, the history and origin of the rule, if it be a rule, are not easy to ascertain and there is on the whole remarkably little authority upon the subject. I am inclined to agree with the Court of Appeal that the early cases of *A.-G.* v. *Lutwydge*[4] and *Boucher* v. *Lawson*,[5] to which some reference was made, do not give much help. It is otherwise when we advance a few years to the age of Lord Mansfield C.J. That great judge in a series of cases repeated the formula 'For no country ever takes notice of the revenue laws of another.' See *Planché* v. *Fletcher*,[6] *Holman* v. *Johnson*,[7] and *Lever* v. *Fletcher*.[8] It is true that Lord Mansfield was not directly concerned with the case of a foreign power suing in an English court to recover revenue, but with the validity of a contract made abroad where the seller was not implicated in smuggling operations which contravened the revenue laws of this country or with the rights of insurers where a

GOVERN-
MENT OF
INDIA
v.
TAYLOR.
—
Viscount
Simonds.

---

[1] (1923) 16 Ll.L.R. 190, 193.   [2] [1928] Ch. 877, 884.   [3] [1909] 1 K.B. 7.
[4] (1729) Bunb. 280.   [5] (1736) Cunning 144.   [6] (1779) 1 Doug. 251, 253.
[7] (1775) 1 Cowp. 341, 343.   [8] (1780) (unreported).

GOVERN-
MENT OF
INDIA
v.
TAYLOR.
—
Viscount
Simonds.

ship which had cleared for Ostend went direct to Nantes thereby affecting the customs dues payable abroad. But in each case he could not have reached his conclusion but for the fact that he applied the rule that no country ever takes notice of the revenue laws of another. Where Lord Mansfield led, Lord Kenyon C.J. followed, though he was not a judge who followed blindly. I agree with the learned Master of the Rolls that it is clear from such cases as *Clugas* v. *Penaluna*,[1] *Bernard* v. *Reed*,[2] and *Waymell* v. *Reed*[3] that Lord Kenyon accepted without qualification the broad rule which Lord Mansfield had formulated. I pass over a number of cases where the question was as to the admissibility of documents made in a foreign country and not stamped according to the law of that country, pausing only to remind your Lordships that in *James* v. *Catherwood*[4] Lord Tenterden (then Abbott C.J.) said: 'This point is too plain for argument. It has been settled, or at least considered as settled, ever since the time of Lord Hardwicke that in a British court we cannot take notice of the revenue laws of a foreign State.' The learned Chief Justice went on to apply the rule in a manner that may not have been justified, but that does not detract from the importance of his unqualified assertion of it.

Here, my Lords, is a formidable array of authority. It is possible that the words 'take notice of' might, if applied without discrimination, lead to too wide an application of the rule; for as Lord Tomlin pointed out in *Re Visser*, there may be cases in which our courts, although they do not enforce foreign revenue law, are bound to recognise some of the consequences of that law, and for this reason the terms of Lord Mansfield's proposition have been criticised. But in its narrower interpretation it has not been challenged except in the three cases mentioned earlier in this opinion and in them it was unequivocally affirmed.

Nor does the matter rest there. For Sir Andrew Clark, who argued the case for the appellant with equal vigour and candour, admitted that he knew of no case in which a foreign State had recovered taxes by suit in this country nor of any case in any foreign country in which the government of this country had done so. And in this connexion it is worthy of note that, as my noble and learned friend, Lord Somervell of Harrow, has by his independent researches

[1] (1791) 4 T.R. 466.   [2] (1794) 1 Esp. 91.   [3] (1794) 5 T.R. 599.
[4] (1823) 3 Dow. & Ry. K.B. 190.

discovered and will presently tell your Lordships, this same rule is stated in at least one French text-book of high authority.[1]

The matter is carried one step further by the fact that the rule appears to have been recognised by Parliament. For I see no other reason for the exclusion from the advantages of the Foreign Judgments (Reciprocal Enforcement) Act 1933 of a judgment for 'a sum payable in respect of taxes or other charges of a like nature or in respect of a fine or other penalty' (s. 1 (2) (b)), except that it was regarded as axiomatic that the courts of one country do not have regard to the revenue laws of another and therefore will not allow judgments for foreign taxes to be enforced.

It may well be asked, then, upon what grounds this appeal is founded. I think that counsel relied upon two main grounds, first that Lord Mansfield's proposition, which I have more than once quoted, extended to revenue law a doctrine properly applicable only to penal law and (I think it must be faced) that Lord Mansfield was wrong in so extending it and everyone who has since followed him was wrong: and secondly that, whatever may have been the rule in the past, there ought to be and is a trend towards a mitigation of the rule, particularly as between States which are united by the bonds of federal union or by such looser ties as bind the British Commonwealth of nations.

My Lords, these seem to me frail weapons with which to attack a strong fortress. The suggestion that Lord Mansfield's proposition was too wide was supported partly by the fact that in *Huntington* v. *Attrill*[2] the proposition was somewhat more narrowly stated, as it was also in the case of *A.-G. for Canada* v. *William Schulze & Co.*[3] In those cases the question was of enforcement of a penalty imposed by a foreign State and the observations of the court were directed to that question. This seems to me an inadequate reason for challenging a wider statement in regard to a different subject-matter. Further, upon the assumption which must be made, that the decision in *Huntington* v. *Attrill* was correct, it was conceded that it must cover not only a penalty strictly so-called but also any tax which could be regarded as penal or confiscatory. This seems to me to create a difficult task of discrimination, which is not made easier by the test suggested by counsel. 'If a tax', he said, 'is the sort of tax which is recognised in this country, it is not penal.' I am little disposed to

GOVERN-
MENT OF
INDIA
v.
TAYLOR.

Viscount
Simonds.

---

[1] Pillet, *Traité de Droit International Privé* (1924), s. 674.
[2] [1893] A.C. 150; *ante*, p. 25.   [3] (1901) 9 S.L.T. 4.

GOVERN-
MENT OF
INDIA.
v.
TAYLOR.
—
Viscount
Simonds.

introduce so nice a refinement into a rule which has hitherto been stated in terms that are easy to understand and to apply. . . .

The second branch of the argument for the appellant was directed to showing that in the United States of America there had been in certain States a disposition to relax the rigidity of the rule, and counsel was able to point to certain cases not cited to the Court of Appeal where the courts of one State had admitted and enforced claims for revenue by another State, notably in the States of Missouri and Kentucky. And reference was made also to the fact that in the 1948 supplement to the well-known 'Restatement' some doubt was cast upon the rule (Conflict of Laws, s. 610). But it was conceded that this was not the trend in all States, the States of New York and of Delaware continuing to apply the old rule. My Lords, I do not think it necessary to occupy your time by an examination of the American cases. I am ever willing to get help from seeing how the law, which is our common heritage, has developed on the other side of the Atlantic, but a development which is not universal, and is in any case confined to relations between State and State within the Union, can have no weight in determining what the law is in this country.

Finally, it was urged that, whatever might be the position as between this country and a foreign country, it was not the same as between different members of the British Commonwealth, including those members which, though within the Commonwealth, do not acknowledge the sovereignty of the Queen. For such a distinction there is no authority and I can see no reason. If such a change is to be made, it is not for the courts to make it. It will be the task of Governments and perhaps of Parliaments. I do not think that it will be an easy task.

(His Lordship proceeded to hold that s. 302 of the Companies Act, 1948, which provides that in a voluntary winding-up the liquidator is bound to discharge the liabilities of the company, did not assist the appellant, because the word 'liabilities' did not include an obligation to pay foreign taxes.)

LORDS MORTON and REID concurred. LORDS KEITH and SOMER-VELL delivered judgments to the same effect.

Appeal dismissed.

Note. Although English courts will not *enforce* foreign penal or revenue laws, they frequently *take notice* of them. Thus in *Regazzoni* v. *Sethia* [1958]

A.C. 301, the Indian Government had, as a political protest against the treatment of Indians in South Africa, prohibited the shipment of jute from India to South Africa. By a contract the proper law of which was English, made between the plaintiff, who resided in Switzerland, and the defendants, merchants in India, the defendants agreed to sell a quantity of jute bags to the plaintiff, who (as the defendants knew) intended to reship them to South Africa. Both parties knew that this was illegal by Indian law. The defendants repudiated the contract. It was held that the plaintiff could not recover damages. Lord Simonds said (at p. 322): 'It does not follow from the fact that today the court will not enforce a revenue law at the suit of a foreign State that today it will enforce a contract which requires the doing of an act in a foreign country which violates the revenue law of that country. The two things are not complementary or co-extensive. This may be seen if for revenue law penal law is substituted. For an English court will not enforce a penal law at the suit of a foreign State, yet it would be surprising if it would enforce a contract which required the commission of a crime in that State.' Lord Keith said (at p. 328): 'I agree with the view entertained by some of your Lordships and by all the Lords Justices in the Court of Appeal that the proposition that "no country ever takes notice of the revenue laws of another" is too widely expressed.'

Chapter 4

PROOF OF FOREIGN LAW

Foreign law is a question of fact for the Judge to be proved by expert evidence.

LAZARD BROTHERS AND CO. *v.* MIDLAND BANK [1933] A.C. 289

(House of Lords)

BEFORE the Bolshevik Revolution in Russia in October 1917, the Banque Industrielle de Moscou (hereinafter called the Moscow Bank), a Russian bank, kept current accounts with the Midland Bank Ltd., and at the end of 1917 these accounts were in credit to an amount exceeding £300,000. At the same time the Moscow bank were indebted to Lazard Brothers & Co., bankers in London, in a sum which, though large, was less than that owed by the Midland Bank to the Moscow Bank. Both these debts were English debts, payable in England and governed by English law.

On 27 October 1930 Lazard Brothers & Co. obtained an order from Branson J. in Chambers for leave to issue a writ against the Moscow Bank and to serve notice thereof at Moscow by sending it by registered post to the Moscow Bank. In pursuance of this order Lazard Brothers & Co. issued a writ against the Moscow Bank claiming the sums owing to them, and sent notice of it by registered post to Moscow. On 24 November 1930 judgment in default of appearance was given for Lazard Brothers, who on 28 November 1930 received a letter from the Soviet Embassy returning the notice of writ and stating that it could not be delivered because the Moscow Bank had gone out of existence during the Revolution of October 1917.

On 12 December 1930 Lazard Brothers obtained a garnishee order nisi against the Midland Bank attaching all debts owing from the Midland Bank, the garnishees, to the Moscow Bank, the judgment debtors, to answer the judgment of 24 November. On the same day a copy of this order was sent by registered post to the Moscow Bank, but the envelope was returned marked 'Unknown'.

On 20 January 1931 a garnishee issue was directed between Lazard Brothers as judgment creditors and the Midland Bank as garnishees, the issue being whether the garnishees were indebted to the judgment debtors, the Moscow Bank. Roche J. made an order absolute that they were so indebted. His judgment was reversed by the Court of Appeal on the ground that the Moscow Bank had ceased to exist as a juristic person before 1930 and that therefore the writ and judgment, and consequently the garnishee proceedings, were null and void.

The judgment creditors appealed.

LORD WRIGHT: ... The Industrial Bank was a corporation established by an Act of the Tsar; but the governing authority in Russia, as recognised in the English courts, is now and has been since October, 1917, the Soviet State. Soviet law is accordingly the governing law from the same date in virtue of the recognition de facto in 1921 and de jure in 1924 by this country of the Soviet State as the sovereign power in Russia. The effect of such recognition is retroactive and dates back to the original establishment of Soviet rule which was in the 1917 October Revolution, as was held by the Court of Appeal in *Luther* v. *Sagor*.[1] The question, therefore, is whether by Soviet law the Industrial Bank was at the date of the issue of the writ in this action, that is on October 27, 1930, an existing juristic person. What the Russian Soviet law is in that respect is a question of fact, of which the English court cannot take judicial cognizance, even though the foreign law has already been proved before it in another case. The court must act upon the evidence before it in the actual case. The recent enactment, s. 102 of the Supreme Court of Judicature (Consolidation) Act, 1925, which provides that this question of fact must be decided by the judge alone instead of by the jury, if there be a jury, expressly treats the question as depending on the evidence given with respect to the foreign law. No earlier decision of the court can relieve the judge of the duty of deciding the question on the actual evidence given in the particular case. On what evidence of the foreign law a court can act has often been discussed. The evidence it is clear must be that of qualified experts in the foreign law. If the law is contained in a code or written form, the question is not as to the language of the written law, but what the law is as shown by its exposition, interpretation and adjudication; so in effect it was

---

[1] [1921] 3 K.B. 532 ; *post*, p. 373.

LAZARD
BROTHERS
& CO.
v.
MIDLAND
BANK.
—
Lord
Wright.

LAZARD
BROTHERS
& CO.
v.
MIDLAND
BANK.
—
Lord
Wright.

laid down by Coleridge J. in *Baron de Bode's Case*;[1] in the *Sussex Peerage Case*,[2] Lord Denman stated his opinion to the same effect as he had done in *Baron de Bode's Case*. He said that if there be a conflict of evidence of the experts, 'you (the judge) must decide as well as you can on the conflicting testimony, but you must take the evidence from the witnesses'. Hence the court is not entitled to construe a foreign code itself: it has not 'organs to know and to deal with the text of that law' (as was said by Lord Brougham in the *Sussex Peerage* case). The text of the foreign law if put in evidence by the experts may be considered, if at all, only as part of the evidence and as a help to decide between conflicting expert testimony. . . .

(His Lordship reviewed the evidence of Soviet law and came to the conclusion that the Moscow Bank had by Soviet law ceased to exist long before 1930, although in *Russian Commercial and Industrial Bank* v. *Comptoir d'Escompte de Mulhouse*[3] the House of Lords had held that a Russian bank had not been dissolved by the same Soviet decrees as were in issue in this case.)

LORDS BUCKMASTER, BLANESBURGH, WARRINGTON OF CLYFFE, *and* RUSSELL OF KILLOWEN concurred.

Appeal dismissed.

[1] (1845) 8 Q.B. 208, 266.   [2] (1844) 11 Cl. & F. 85, 116.   [3] [1925] A.C. 112.

Chapter 5

DOMICILE

*If a domicile of choice is abandoned, and a fresh domicile of choice
is not acquired, the domicile of origin revives.*

UDNY *v.* UDNY (1869) L.R. 1 Sc. & Div. 441 (House of Lords)

APPEAL from the First Division of the Court of Session in Scotland.

Colonel Udny, of Udny in the county of Aberdeen, was born in
1779 at Leghorn (where his father was consul) with a Scottish domicile of origin. In 1797 he became an officer in the Guards. In 1802 he
succeeded to the family estate. In 1812 he married, retired from the
Army, and took a leasehold house in London, where he resided for
thirty-two years, paying occasional visits to Aberdeenshire.

In 1844, having got into pecuniary difficulties, he broke up his
establishment in London and moved to Boulogne, where he remained for nine years, occasionally, as before, visiting Scotland. In
1846 his wife died.

Some time after the death of his wife Colonel Udny formed at
Boulogne a connexion with Miss Ann Allatt, which resulted in the
birth of a son (the respondent) in Surrey in 1853. Colonel Udny
married Miss Ann Allatt at Ormiston in Scotland in 1854, and the
question was whether the respondent had become legitimate per subsequens matrimonium.

The Court of Session decided that Colonel Udny's domicile of
origin was Scottish, that he had never altered or lost it, notwithstanding his long absences from Scotland; and that therefore the
respondent, though illegitimate at his birth, was legitimated by the
subsequent marriage of his parents. Hence this appeal.

LORD WESTBURY: The law of England, and of almost all civilized
countries, ascribes to each individual at his birth two distinct legal
states or conditions; one by virtue of which he becomes the subject
of some particular country, binding him by the tie of natural allegiance, and which may be called his political status; another, by
virtue of which he has ascribed to him the character of a citizen of

39

some particular country, and as such is possessed of certain municipal rights, and subject to certain obligations, which latter character is the civil status or condition of the individual, and may be quite different from his political status. The political status may depend on different laws in different countries; whereas the civil status is governed universally by one single principle, namely, that of domicile, which is the criterion established by law for the purpose of determining civil status. For it is on this basis that the personal rights of the party, that is to say, the law which determines his majority or minority, his marriage, succession, testacy, or intestacy, must depend. International law depends on rules which, being in great measure derived from the Roman law, are common to the jurisprudence of all civilized nations. It is a settled principle that no man shall be without a domicile, and to secure this result the law attributes to every individual as soon as he is born the domicile of his father, if the child be legitimate, and the domicile of the mother if illegitimate. This has been called the domicile of origin, and is involuntary. Other domiciles, including domicile by operation of law, as on marriage, are domiciles of choice. For as soon as an individual is sui juris it is competent to him to elect and assume another domicile, the continuance of which depends upon his will and act. When another domicile is put on, the domicile of origin is for that purpose relinquished, and remains in abeyance during the continuance of the domicile of choice; but as the domicile of origin is the creature of law, and independent of the will of the party, it would be inconsistent with the principles on which it is by law created and ascribed, to suppose that it is capable of being by the act of the party entirely obliterated and extinguished. It revives and exists whenever there is no other domicile, and it does not require to be regained or reconstituted animo de facto, in the manner which is necessary for the acquisition of a domicile of choice.

Domicile of choice is a conclusion or inference which the law derives from the fact of a man fixing voluntarily his sole or chief residence in a particular place, with an intention of continuing to reside there for an unlimited time. This is a description of the circumstances which create or constitute a domicile, and not a definition of the term. There must be a residence freely chosen, and not prescribed or dictated by any external necessity, such as the duties of office, the demand of creditors, or the relief from illness; and it must be residence fixed not for a limited period or particular purpose, but general and indefinite in its future contemplation. It is true that residence originally temporary, or intended for a limited period, may afterwards become general and unlimited, and in such a case so soon as the change of purpose, or animus manendi, can be inferred the fact of domicile is established.

The domicile of origin may be extinguished by act of law, as, for example, by sentence of death or exile for life, which puts an end to the status civilis of the criminal; but it cannot be destroyed by the will and act of the party.

Domicile of choice, as it is gained animo et facto, so it may be put an end to in the same manner. Expressions are found in some books, and in one or two cases, that the first or existing domicile remains until another is acquired. This is true if applied to the domicile of origin, but cannot be true if such general words were intended (which is not probable) to convey the conclusion that a domicile of choice, though unequivocally relinquished and abandoned, clings, in despite of his will and acts, to the party, until another domicile has animo et facto been acquired. The cases to which I have referred are, in my opinion, met and controlled by other decisions. A natural-born Englishman may, if he domiciles himself in Holland, acquire and have the status civilis of a Dutchman, which is of course ascribed to him in respect of his settled abode in the land, but if he breaks up his establishment, sells his house and furniture, discharges his servants, and quits Holland, declaring that he will never return to it again, and taking with him his wife and children, for the purpose of travelling in France or Italy in search of another place of residence, is it meant to be said that he carries his Dutch domicile, that is, his Dutch citizenship, at his back, and that it clings to him pertinaciously until he has finally set up his tabernacle in another country? Such a conclusion would be absurd; but there is no absurdity and, on the contrary, much reason, in holding that an acquired domicile may be effectually abandoned by unequivocal intention and act; and that when it is so determined the domicile of origin revives until a new domicile of choice be acquired. According to the dicta in the books and cases referred to, if the Englishman whose case we have been supposing lived for twenty years after he had finally quitted Holland, without acquiring a new domicile, and afterwards died intestate, his personal estate would be administered according to the law of Holland, and not according to that of his native country. This is an irrational consequence of the supposed rule. But when a proposition supposed to be authorized by one or more decisions involves absurd results, there is great reason for believing that no such rule was intended to be laid down.

In Mr. Justice Story's Conflict of Laws (the last edition) it is stated that ' the moment the foreign domicile (that is the domicile of choice) is abandoned, the native domicile or domicile of origin is reacquired'. And such appears to be the just conclusion from several decided cases, as well as from the principles of the law of domicile.

In adverting to Mr. Justice Story's work, I am obliged to dissent from a conclusion stated in the last edition of that useful book, and which is thus expressed, 'The result of the more recent English cases seems to be, that for a change of national domicile there must be a definite and effectual change of nationality.' In support of this proposition the editor refers to some words which appear to have fallen from a noble and learned lord in addressing this House in the case of *Moorhouse* v. *Lord*[1] when in speaking of the acquisition of a French domicile, Lord Kingsdown says, 'A man must intend to become a Frenchman instead of an Englishman.' These words are likely to mislead, if they were intended to signify that for a change of domicile there must be a change of nationality, that is, of natural allegiance. That would be to confound the political and civil states of an individual, and to destroy the difference between patria and domicilium.

The application of these general rules to the circumstances of the present case is very simple. I concur with my noble and learned friend that the father of Colonel Udny, the consul at Leghorn, and afterwards at Venice, and again at Leghorn, did not by his residence there in that capacity lose his Scotch domicile. Colonel Udny was, therefore, a Scotchman by birth. But I am certainly inclined to think that when Colonel Udny married, and (to use the ordinary phrase) settled in life and took a long lease of a house in Grosvenor Street, and made that a place of abode of himself and his wife and children, becoming, in point of fact, subject to the municipal duties of a resident in that locality; and when he had remained there for a period, I think, of thirty-two years, there being no obstacle in point of fortune, occupation, or duty, to his going to reside in his native country; under these circumstances, I should come to the conclusion, if it were necessary to decide the point, that Colonel Udny deliberately chose and acquired an English domicile. But if he did so, he has

[1] (1863) 10 H.L.C. 272.

42

certainly relinquished that English domicile in the most effectual way by selling or surrendering the lease of his house, selling his furniture, discharging his servants, and leaving London in a manner which removes all doubt of his ever intending to return there for the purpose of residence. If, therefore, he acquired an English domicile he abandoned it absolutely animo et facto. Its acquisition being a thing of choice, it was equally put an end to by choice. He lost it the moment he set foot on the steamer to go to Boulogne, and at the same time his domicile of origin revived. The rest is plain. The marriage and the consequences of that marriage must be determined by the law of Scotland, the country of his domicile.

UDNY
v.
UDNY.

Lord
Westbury.

LORDS HATHERLEY, CHELMSFORD, and COLONSAY delivered judgment to the same effect.

Appeal dismissed.

A domicile of origin is retained until a new domicile of choice is acquired. A domicile of origin cannot be lost by mere abandonment.

BELL v. KENNEDY (1868) L.R. 1 Sc. & Div. 307 (House of Lords)

BELL
v.
KENNEDY.

Appeal from the Second Division of the Court of Session in Scotland.

Mr. Bell was born in Jamaica of Scottish parents domiciled in Jamaica. He was educated in Scotland but returned to Jamaica in 1823 soon after attaining his majority. In 1828 he married in Jamaica. In April 1837 he left Jamaica for good and went to Scotland, where he lived with his mother-in-law and looked around for an estate on which to settle down. Owing to the bad weather and to the high price of land he became dissatisfied with Scotland and undecided whether to settle there or in England or the south of France. On September 28th, 1838, his wife died and the question was: Where was he domiciled on that date? The Second Division of the Court of Session held that he had become domiciled in Scotland.

LORD WESTBURY: What appears to me to be the erroneous conclusion at which the Court of Session arrived is in great part due to the circumstance, frequently lost sight of, that the domicile of origin adheres until a new domicile is acquired. In the argument, and in the judgments, we find constantly the phrase used that he had abandoned his native domicile. That domicile appears to have been regarded as if it had been lost by the abandonment of his residence in Jamaica.

Now, residence and domicile are two perfectly distinct things. It is necessary in the administration of the law that the idea of domicile should exist, and that the fact of domicile should be ascertained, in order to determine which of two municipal laws may be invoked for the purpose of regulating the rights of parties. We know very well that succession and distribution depend upon the law of the domicile. Domicile, therefore, is an idea of law. It is the relation which the law creates between an individual and a particular locality or country. To every adult person the law ascribes a domicile and that domicile remains his fixed attribute until a new and different attribute usurps its place. Now this case was argued at the Bar on the footing, that as soon as Mr. Bell left Jamaica he had a settled and fixed intention of taking up his residence in Scotland. And if, indeed, that had been ascertained as a fact, then you would have had the animus of the party clearly demonstrated, and the factum, which alone would remain to be proved, would in fact be proved, or, at least, would result immediately upon his arrival in Scotland.

The true inquiry, therefore, is—Had he this settled purpose, the moment he left Jamaica, or in course of the voyage, of taking up a fixed and settled abode in Scotland? Undoubtedly, part of the evidence is the external act of the party; but the only external act we have here is the going down with his wife to Edinburgh, the most natural thing in the world, to visit his wife's relations. We find him residing in Scotland from that time; but with what animus or intention his residence continued there we have yet to ascertain. For although residence may be some small prima facie proof of domicile, it is by no means to be inferred from the fact of residence that domicile results, even although you do not find that the party had any other residence in existence or in contemplation.

I take it that Mr. Bell may be more properly described by words which occur in the Digest; that when he left Jamaica he might be described as 'quaerens, quo se conferat, atque ubi constituat domicilium.'[1] Where he was to fix his habitation was to him at that time a thing perfectly unresolved; and, as appears from the letters which your Lordships have heard, that irresolution, that want of settled fixity of purpose, certainly continued down to the time when he actually became the purchaser of Enterkine. But the punctum temporis to which our inquiries are to be directed as to Mr. Bell's intention is of an earlier date than that. The question is, had he any

[1] D. 50, 1, 27.

44

settled fixed intention of being permanently resident in Scotland on the 28th of September, 1838? I quite agree with an observation which was made in the Court of Session, that the letters are the best evidence in the case. To those letters your Lordships' attention has been directed, and whether you refer to the language of the wife's letters, or look exclusively at the language of the husband's letters written to his familiar friends or his relatives whom he had left in Jamaica, it is impossible to predicate of him that he was a man who had a fixed and settled purpose to make Scotland his future place of residence, to set up his tabernacle there, to make it his future home. And unless you are able to shew that with perfect clearness and satisfaction to yourselves, it follows that the domicile of origin continues. And therefore I think we can have no hesitation in answering the question where he was settled on the 28th of September. It must be answered in this way; he was resident in Scotland, but without the animus manendi, and therefore he still retained his domicile of origin.

LORDS CAIRNS, CRANWORTH, CHELMSFORD, and COLONSAY delivered judgment to the same effect.

Appeal allowed.

BELL
v.
KENNEDY.
———
Lord
Westbury.

Stronger evidence is required to prove the abandonment of a domicile of origin than the abandonment of a domicile of choice.

RAMSAY *v.* LIVERPOOL ROYAL INFIRMARY [1930] A.C. 588

(House of Lords)

RAMSAY
v.
LIVERPOOL
ROYAL
INFIRMARY.

Appeal against an interlocutor of the First Division of the Court of Session in Scotland affirming an interlocutor of the Lord Ordinary (Lord Mackay).

George Bowie, whose domicile of origin was Scottish, but who had lived the latter part of his life in Liverpool, died in Liverpool on 5 November 1927, leaving a holograph will dated 7 August 1927, which was valid by the law of Scotland but was not valid by the law of England.

This action was brought by the respondents, the residuary legatees under the will, against the appellant, the testator's sole next of kin, for a declaration that the testator's domicile at the date of his death was Scottish.

The Lord Ordinary held that the defender had failed to prove that the testator had changed his domicile and granted the declaration.

RAMSAY
v.
LIVERPOOL
ROYAL
INFIRMARY.

Lord
Thankerton.

and the First Division (the Lord President, Lord Blackburn (doubting but not formally dissenting), and Lord Morison) affirmed his decision.

LORD THANKERTON: My Lords, the deceased George Bowie died in Liverpool, on November 5, 1927, aged 82 years and unmarried. Originally employed as a commercial traveller in Glasgow, he gave up that employment about 1882, and did no work for the rest of his life. About 1891 or 1892 he came to Liverpool, where a brother and sister were already settled, and resided in Liverpool for the remaining thirty-five or thirty-six years of his life. His domicile of origin was Scottish, and the question in the present appeal is whether he still retained that domicile at his death, or was then domiciled in England.

George Bowie left a holograph will, which was made by him in Liverpool, on August 7, 1927. That will is valid according to Scottish law and invalid under English law. The appellant, as next of kin, maintains that George Bowie died domiciled in England and that the will is invalid. The respondents are the residuary legatees under the will, and maintain its validity on the ground that George Bowie retained his Scottish domicile.

Admittedly the appellant undertakes the burden of proving that George Bowie acquired an English domicile animo et facto; his long residence established the factum, but there remains the question of the animus. It seems clear on the authorities that mere length of residence by itself is insufficient evidence from which to infer the animus; but the quality of the residence may afford the necessary inference. For instance, the purchase of a house or estate coupled with long residence therein and non-retention of any home in the domicile of origin, might be sufficient to prove the intention to acquire a new domicile. But the long residence of George Bowie in Liverpool is remarkably colourless and suggests little more than inanition.

George Bowie went to Liverpool to live on the bounty of his brother Alexander, and, during his residence there, his means of existence were supplied by that brother and his sister Isabella. He received a legacy of £1,000 from the former and succeeded to the latter's whole estate on her death in 1920. He lived in lodgings until 1914, when he went to live with his sister Isabella, then the only other surviving member of the family, in a leased house, where he lived till his death. With the exception of family ties, he appears to have had few, if indeed any, ties either in Scotland or England.

Apart from residence, the evidence bearing on animus is vague and indecisive. It is not certain whether he knew that his will would be invalid in England, but he named his cousin, a Glasgow writer, as trustee, and he directed that his residuary bequests, of one-fourth each to three Glasgow infirmaries and one Liverpool infirmary, should be given anonymously as from a 'Glasgow Man'. He told people that he was proud to be a Glasgow man, and received a Glasgow weekly newspaper. With his sister Isabella's estate he became owner of a tenement property in Glasgow, which he desired to sell, but a bad market prevented its sale, and he retained it till his death. There is some evidence of his declining on one or two occasions to move to Glasgow and to visit Glasgow, but until 1912 he was dependent on his brother's bounty, and after 1912 it is probable that his disinclination was owing to the inertness of age and indifferent health. He was buried in Liverpool, but that was alongside of his brother Alexander and three sisters in ground for which Alexander had paid.

I am unable to find in this case sufficient evidence of a definite intention on the part of George Bowie to abandon his domicile of origin and to acquire a new domicile. The law on this subject is well fixed; the difficulty is found in its application to oft varying combinations of circumstances. The present case appears to me to be directly affected by the opinions (a) of Lord Westbury in Bell v. Kennedy,[1] where he says: 'Although residence may be some small prima facie proof of domicile, it is by no means to be inferred from the fact of residence that domicile results, even although you do not find that the party had any other residence in existence or in contemplation'; (b) of Lord Chelmsford in Udny v. Udny,[2] that 'in a competition between a domicile of origin and an alleged subsequently-acquired domicile there may be circumstances to shew that however long a residence may have continued no intention of acquiring a domicile may have existed at any one moment during the whole of the continuance of such residence. The question in such a case is not, whether there is evidence of an intention to retain the domicile of origin, but whether it is proved that there was an intention to acquire another domicile'; and (c) of Lord Macnaghten in

RAMSAY
v.
LIVERPOOL
ROYAL
INFIRMARY.

Lord
Thankerton.

[1] (1868) L.R. 1 Sc. & Div. 307; ante, p. 44.
[2] (1869) L.R. 1 Sc. & Div. 441, 455; ante, p. 39.

Winans v. *Attorney-General*,[1] where he states: 'Such an intention, I think, is not to be inferred from an attitude of indifference or a disinclination to move increasing with increasing years, least of all from the absence of any manifestation of intention one way or the other.' This last opinion appears to apply exactly to the circumstances of George Bowie's residence in Liverpool.

Accordingly, I am of opinion that the appellant has failed to prove the intention on the part of George Bowie to acquire an English domicile, and that the appeal fails.

LORDS BUCKMASTER, DUNEDIN, and MACMILLAN delivered judgment to the same effect.

Appeal dismissed.

During the subsistence of a marriage the domicile of the wife is the same as, and changes with, that of the husband.

ATTORNEY-GENERAL FOR ALBERTA v. COOK [1926] A.C. 444
(Privy Council)

Appeal from a judgment of the Supreme Court of Alberta reversing a judgment of Walsh J.

In November 1921 the respondent obtained in Alberta a decree of judicial separation from her husband, both spouses being at that time resident in Alberta.

In 1922 the respondent instituted in Alberta a suit for divorce on the ground of adultery and cruelty; she obtained an order for substituted service on her husband.

Walsh J. found that the husband had not lost his domicile of origin in Ontario. He dismissed the suit on the ground that the court had no jurisdiction, as the wife was not competent to acquire a domicile separate from that of her husband.

The Appellate Division allowed the wife's appeal and made a decree dissolving the marriage.

The judgment of their Lordships (Lords Cave L.C., Haldane, Dunedin, Shaw, Phillimore, Blanesburgh, and Merrivale) was delivered by

LORD MERRIVALE: . . . The competency of the wife's suit for divorce depends, first, upon her power during her marriage to

Margin notes: RAMSAY v. LIVERPOOL ROYAL INFIRMARY. Lord Thankerton. A.-G. FOR ALBERTA v. COOK.

[1] [1904] A.C. 287, 291.

48

acquire domicile in Alberta, her husband not being domiciled there, and, secondly, upon the jurisdiction of the Supreme Court of Alberta at her instance to change the matrimonial status of her husband. . . .

A.-G. FOR
ALBERTA
v.
COOK.

Lord
Merrivale.

Propositions of law in respect of domicile were advanced on the respondent's behalf to this effect: that the identity of the domicile of a wife with that of her husband is a legal fiction or presumption of law; that domicile depends upon the capacity in law of individuals to choose a permanent home; and that when this capacity exists in a wife by reason of judicial separation, and has in fact been exercised, the rights arising from domicile result in her favour. The mode of giving effect to such rights must, it was argued, be matter of procedure for the tribunals of the State within which domicile has been gained. A separate contention was raised upon the construction of the statute, the Matrimonial Causes Act 1857, under which the separation here in question was decreed.

The contention that husband and wife may be domiciled apart and may resort to different jurisdictions and different codes of law to seek thereunder dissolution of the marriage between them appears to challenge directly the rule laid down in *Le Mesurier* v. *Le Mesurier*[1] in 1895, and affirmed in the House of Lords in *Lord Advocate* v. *Jaffrey*,[2] that matrimonial status is governed by the law of domicile of the parties. In the former case the rule was stated by Lord Watson to be that 'the domicile for the time being of the married pair affords the true test of jurisdiction to dissolve their marriage'. In the latter it was epitomized by Lord Haldane in these words: 'Nothing short of a full juridical domicile within its jurisdiction can justify a British Court in pronouncing a decree of divorce.' Both pronouncements are declaredly founded on a principle which was stated in the judgment of Lord Penzance in *Wilson* v. *Wilson*:[3] 'The differences of married people should be adjusted in accordance with the laws of the community to which they belong and dealt with by the tribunals which alone can administer those laws.' The decision in *Le Mesurier* v. *Le Mesurier* does not deal with the case of spouses judicially separated, and that case is expressly reserved for future decision in the opinions of the noble and learned Lords who decided *Lord Advocate* v. *Jaffrey*. The judgment delivered by Lord Watson in *Le Mesurier's Case*, however, brings inevitably into view the fact that divorce obtainable under different systems of municipal

[1] [1895] A.C. 517; *post*, p. 114.   [2] [1921] 1 A.C. 146.
[3] (1872) L.R. 2 P. & M. 435, 442.

law by spouses living in separate jurisdictions is irreconcilable with the existence of any axiom in private international law that there is in the case of every marriage one sole jurisdiction in which dissolution of the marriage tie can be decreed.

It was common ground in this case that the rule propounded on behalf of the respondent has not been heretofore laid down by any express judicial decision which binds this Board. The decision under appeal was arrived at upon examination of conflicting opinions, some of them declared by distinguished judicial persons, and others expressed by eminent jurists. These opinions have received the consideration to which they are entitled. . . .

Underlying the English rule as to a wife's domicile is a principle of the common law, uniformly declared during six centuries before 1857, and not dependent upon any maxim of the civilians, whatever may have been its origin. Four citations may be made, which set forth this rule: 'Vir et uxor sunt quasi unica persona';[1] 'Le baron et sa feme ne sont forsque un person en ley';[2] 'The husband and wife are one person in the law;[3] 'By marriage husband and wife are one person in law'.[4]

The rule thus declared was not a fiction or presumption which, within the competence of the tribunals concerned, might control procedure, but must be disregarded upon questions of substantive right. It was of unquestioned operation under the common law to an extent which is only partially indicated by the instances comprised under the title Baron and Feme in the 'Table' annexed to Coke's First Institute. By this rule the wife's property was disposed of and her jurisdictional status ascertained, and it determined her situation as to domicile. . . .

Singular anomalies must arise in respect of the causes for divorce —strictly limited and carefully defined in the Act of 1857—if upon the true construction of the clauses relating to judicial separation a wife who is judicially separated is thereby qualified to choose an independent domicile. A husband may be, and sometimes has been, a suitor for judicial separation for cruelty or for adultery. Assuming ss. 25 and 26 to have the suggested effect with regard to domicile, it would seem to follow that a guilty wife judicially separated may by virtue of domicile acquired in a foreign jurisdiction become entitled

---

[1] Bracton, *De Legibus Angliae*, lib. v, c. 25, s. 10.
[2] Littleton, *Tenures*, s. x, 168, 291. [3] Coke, *Institutes*, I. 112a.
[4] Blackstone, *Commentaries*, I. 442.

to cite her husband to answer there a suit for divorce upon grounds sufficient by the local law but unknown in the law of his domicile. The marriage of British subjects would thus become liable to dissolution by authority to which they owe no obedience.

The contention that a wife judicially separated from her husband is given choice of a new domicile is contrary to the general principle on which the unity of domicile of the married pair depends; divorce a mensa et thoro gave no such right; and the statute of 1857 was not framed with that intention and does not effect that purpose.

Under British law one of the effects of marriage is to give to the spouses a common domicile—the domicile of the husband. Within the jurisdiction thereby arising, and by the marriage laws to which the spouses are there subject, the claims of either of them to a decree of dissolution of marriage ought to be determined. In so far as British tribunals are concerned it is a requisite of the jurisdiction to dissolve marriage that the defendant in the suit shall be domiciled within the jurisdiction. In such cases actor sequitur forum rei. This is the true effect upon the present proceedings of the rule laid down in *Le Mesurier* v. *Le Mesurier*.

Appeal allowed.

A.-G. FOR ALBERTA v. COOK. — Lord Merrivale.

NOTE B: THE DOMICILE OF MARRIED WOMEN

IT is settled that in no circumstances can a married woman have a domicile different from that of her husband. The result has been severely criticized: see Dicey, p. 114; Graveson, pp. 176–7; Read, pp. 202–16; Willis, 14 Can. Bar Rev. 7; and Falconbridge, pp. 729–33. It has been described as 'The last barbarous relic of a wife's servitude' (*Gray* v. *Formosa* [1963] P. 259, 267); contrast Cheshire, p. 167, who maintains that the rule 'rests upon solid reasoning'. In divorce it has produced a total denial of justice to deserted wives, and has had to be reversed by legislation (*post*, p. 116). Since the middle of the nineteenth century American courts have held that, at least for some purposes (and this includes divorce), a married woman may acquire or retain a domicile different from that of her husband. In New Zealand, a wife is now allowed a separate domicile for purposes of matrimonial causes (Matrimonial Proceedings Act 1963, s. 3).

In 1954 the Private International Law Committee recommended that a married woman judicially separated from her husband should be able to acquire a separate domicile (First Report, Cmd. 9068). In 1956 the Royal Commission on Marriage and Divorce recommended that a wife who is living separate and apart from her husband should be entitled to claim a separate English domicile for the purposes of the matrimonial jurisdiction of the English courts (Cmd. 9678, paras. 819–26, 894). In 1958 a Bill was introduced in the House of Lords which gave effect to the first of these recommendations, and other proposals of the Private International Law Committee for the reform of the law of domicile. At the Committee stage an amendment was carried which gave a wife the right to establish a separate domicile for all purposes. But the Bill was successfully opposed on behalf of the foreign business community in this country on the ground that it might make it harder for them to prove that they were not domiciled in the United Kingdom, and so might make them liable to pay United Kingdom income tax on the income of their foreign investments. A second, modified Bill failed to allay their fears and the matter was again referred to the Private International Law Committee. In their Seventh Report (Cmnd. 1955 (1963), paras. 24, 25) the committee thought that 'serious legal difficulties' would be created if wives were allowed a separate domicile, and that such a rule 'simply would not work'. And there the matter rests.

The committee's conclusions have been vigorously criticized (see M. Mann (1963) 12 I.C.L.Q. 1326, 1332–9). There can be no doubt that the present law is capable of working great hardship. Suppose, for example, that an Englishwoman marries a foreigner. The marriage breaks down, and the parties agree to part. So far as jurisdiction is concerned, the wife could get a divorce after three years' ordinary residence in England under s. 40 (1) (b) of the Matrimonial Causes Act 1965 (post, p. 116). But she might have no grounds; or divorce might be against conscience. The result would be that, so long as the husband is alive, not only can she not remarry, but also she cannot adopt a child in England (not even her own child) because she is domiciled abroad: Adoption Act 1958, s. 1 (1) (post, p. 238).

Since the decision of the Court of Appeal in De Reneville v. De Reneville [1948] P. 100 (post, p. 160), it has been possible to formulate more precise rules as to the domicile of women whose marriages are void or voidable. If the marriage is voidable, the domicile of the woman is, by operation of law, the same as that of the man until the marriage is annulled by the decree of a court of competent jurisdiction. This is quite logical, for until the marriage is annulled the marriage is valid and produces the usual legal consequences of marriage. On the other hand, if the marriage is void, the ceremony produces no legal consequences whatever, and therefore the woman does not as a matter of law acquire the domicile of the man. She may of course do so as a matter of fact if she lives with him for a substantial period in the country of his domicile (as in Von Lorang v. Administrator of Austrian Property [1927] A.C. 641, post, p. 185), just as a mistress may acquire the domicile of the man with whom she lives (as in Re Luck's Settlement Trusts [1940] Ch. 864, post, p. 227). But if the woman never lives with the man in the country of his domicile (as in Ogden v. Ogden [1908] P. 46, post, p. 77), or only for a short period (as in Mehta v. Mehta [1945] 2 All E.R. 690, and MacDougall v. Chitnavis, 1937 S.C. 390), she does not acquire his domicile: and dicta to the contrary in Ogden v. Ogden (post, p. 77) and Von Lorang's Case (post, p. 193) must now be regarded as overruled.

If the reason why the marriage is void is that the woman is already married to someone else, then so long as her first husband is alive she will not acquire the domicile of the man with whom she went through the second ceremony, no matter how long she lives with him in the country of his domicile: Re Cooke's Trusts (1887) 56 L.T. 737.

DOMICILE

What is the effect of the husband's death on the domicile of his widow? If immediately prior to his death the parties were living together in the country of his domicile, the widow retains that domicile until she changes it: she does not automatically revert to the domicile she had before her marriage (*In bonis Raffenel* (1863) 3 Sw. & Tr. 49; *Re Wallach* (1950) 66 T.L.R. (1) 132). But if the wife was living apart from her husband in another country with the intention of remaining there indefinitely, she gets a domicile there immediately on his death (*Re Cooke's Trusts* (1887) 56 L.T. 737; *Re Scullard* [1957] Ch. 107).

PART II

FAMILY LAW

Chapter 6

MARRIAGE

Section A: FORMALITIES

The formalities of marriage are governed (in general) by the lex loci celebrationis.

BERTHIAUME *v.* DASTOUS [1930] A.C. 79 (Privy Council)

APPEAL from a judgment of the Court of King's Bench for Quebec affirming a judgment of the Superior Court, District of Montreal.

The judgment of their Lordships (Viscount Dunedin, Lord Warrington of Clyffe, Mr. Justice Duff, and Sir Lancelot Sanderson) was delivered by

VISCOUNT DUNEDIN: In 1913 the respondent, a French Canadian of the Roman Catholic faith, being then a girl seventeen years of age who had just graduated from a convent in a small town in Montreal, went on a trip to Europe with her father. She there met the appellant, a member of a Quebec family and also of the Roman Catholic faith, who had been living in Paris for several years. He proposed to her, and she accepted. The appellant asked the respondent to make the necessary arrangements, and she called on the curé of the parish where her fiancé had been residing and where she was then temporarily residing. The curé informed her that there were certain civil formalities to be gone through and that he would celebrate the marriage. She asked her fiancé to attend to the civil formalities, and he took her to the British consulate where certain papers were signed and a certificate issued which was given to her fiancé. After that the

55

parties proceeded to the church, the certificate was handed to the curé, who then proceeded to celebrate the marriage according to the form of the Roman Catholic Church. The parties lived together as husband and wife until the year 1926, when on returning from an absence from home the respondent discovered that the appellant had been guilty of infidelity and had introduced a mistress into their home. The respondent then applied to the Court in Paris for a divorce. That Court before proceeding further demanded the exhibition of a civil certificate of marriage. This the respondent was unable to produce. She then discovered that the certificate which her fiancé had procured at the British consulate was only a notice of intended marriage, and that the officiating curé had carelessly omitted to notice that it was not a certificate of marriage. As a matter of fact he had exposed himself to severe penalty by celebrating the religious ceremony without the production of a certificate. As no certificate of marriage could be produced—none such ever having been in existence—the Court declined to proceed with the case for divorce. The respondent then raised another action in the French courts, craving a judgment 'pour faire statuer le mariage', and craving alternatively that if the marriage was declared void it should be held that she had contracted it in good faith and was entitled to a declaration of civil effects in her favour. The appellant appeared and denied the jurisdiction, he having still retained his Canadian domicile. This plea was sustained and the action dismissed. The respondent then raised the present action in the Superior Court of the Montreal district. The action sought a declaration of marriage, decree of separation, a dissolution of the communauté des biens—the marriage having been without a marriage contract, communauté des biens would ensue—and a judgment for alimony. Damages were also claimed, but that claim was departed from. Alternatively a declaration was sought that as the respondent had been in good faith, the marriage was a putative marriage and in terms of article 164 of the Civil Code produced civil effects. The case depended before Loranger J. who held the marriage valid, pronounced a decree of separation, dissolved the community of goods and granted a decree against the appellant for an alimentary allowance of $1,500 a month. On appeal the Court of King's Bench by a majority upheld the judgment. Bernier J. dissented, and held that the marriage was null and that a null marriage could not be a putative marriage. The present appeal is from that judgment.

Their Lordships are unable to agree with the judgment under appeal. If there is one question better settled than any other in international law, it is that as regards marriage—putting aside the question of capacity—locus regit actum. If a marriage is good by the laws of the country where it is effected, it is good all the world over, no matter whether the proceeding or ceremony which constituted marriage according to the law of the place would or would not constitute marriage in the country of the domicile of one or other of the spouses. If the so-called marriage is no marriage in the place where it is celebrated, there is no marriage anywhere, although the ceremony or proceeding if conducted in the place of the parties' domicile would be considered a good marriage. These propositions are too well fixed to need much quotation. They were laid down long ago in England in the well known case of *Dalrymple* v. *Dalrymple*[1] and in *Scrimshire* v. *Scrimshire*,[2] approved by Lord Stowell in *Ruding* v. *Smith*.[3]...

Now in the face of the facts set forth in the narrative above given, and these facts were found by all the judges of the courts below and are amply borne out by the evidence, it is clear that under international law there was no marriage in this case. The law of France is peremptory. There must be a civil ceremony of marriage, and if that has not taken place any religious ceremony is an idle performance so far as the law is concerned....

(His Lordship proceeded to hold that as there was good faith on the part of the respondent, the marriage, though null, was capable of producing civil effects, including the right to alimony, under article 164 of the Quebec Civil Code, and that the case should be remitted to the court below to determine its amount.)

Appeal allowed.

BERTHIAUME
v.
DASTOUS.

Viscount
Dunedin.

Retrospective legislation in the locus celebrationis validating a formally invalid marriage will be given effect to, even though the parties are domiciled in England at the date when it takes effect.

STARKOWSKI *v.* ATTORNEY-GENERAL [1954] A.C. 155
(House of Lords)

STARKOWSKI
v.
A.-G.

Henryka Juszczkiewicz and Richard Urbanski were born in Poland with a Polish domicile of origin. In 1944 they moved to

---

[1] (1811) 2 Hagg. Cons. 54.   [2] (1752) 2 Hagg. Cons. 395.
[3] (1821) 2 Hagg. Cons. 371.

STARKOWSKI
v.
A.-G.

Kitzbühel in Austria but remained domiciled in Poland. They were both Roman Catholics and anxious to be married in a church by a priest. Owing to the German occupation of Austria there were difficulties in their way and the priest at Kitzbühel at first refused to marry them, but when the Germans were driven out there was much confusion and he eventually agreed to do so on 19 May 1945, when they went through a ceremony of marriage according to the rites of their Church in the parish church at Kitzbühel. In June 1945 a daughter Barbara was born to them.

Henryka and Richard arrived in England in the autumn of 1946 and became domiciled here. In 1947 they separated. In March 1949 Henryka gave birth to a son Christopher of whom Michael Starkowski, a Pole domiciled in England, was the father. On 11 February 1950 Henryka went through a form of marriage with Michael at the register office in Croydon.

Christopher, suing by his mother as next friend, petitioned for a declaration under the Legitimacy Act 1926 and section 17 of the Matrimonial Causes Act 1950[1], that his parents were lawfully married and that by that marriage he became legitimated.

By the German marriage law in force in Austria on 19 May 1945 a religious ceremony did not constitute a valid marriage since a civil ceremony was required. On 26 June 1945 the Austrian Government promulgated an Order (No. 31) enacting that religious marriages celebrated between 1 April 1945 and the date of the decree should be valid as soon as they were registerd in the Family Book kept by the registry office. By some oversight the religious ceremony between Henryka and Richard was not registered until 18 July 1949. Before that date the law of Austria would not have regarded the parties as married, but after that date it would have regarded them as having been validly married on 19 May 1945.

Barnard J. and the Court of Appeal held that Christopher was not legitimated because the marriage of his parents was void, his mother being at that date validly married to Richard. The petitioner appealed.

LORD TUCKER: My Lords, counsel for the Attorney-General, in supporting the judgments of the courts below, submitted that the case was governed by the well-established rule of private international law that, so far as formalities are concerned, the validity of

---

[1] Now s. 39 of the Matrimonial Causes Act 1965

marriage is governed by the lex loci celebrationis, and he cited the well-known passage to this effect in the speech of Lord Dunedin in *Berthiaume* v. *Dastous*[1] and other authorities to the like effect.

Counsel for the appellant did not dispute this principle, but contended that an equally well-established rule of private international law was applicable to the facts in this case, viz., that the courts of one country will not recognize the extraterritorial effect of a foreign statute on the status of a person not domiciled in, or the subject of, the legislating State.

The problem is whether a foreign validating Act with retroactive effect dealing with the form of marriage but with consequential effect on the status of persons domiciled outside the legislating country should be treated as a law concerning the formality of marriage or as a law affecting status.

My Lords, at one time I felt some doubts whether on its special facts this case did in truth involve a conflict between these two principles, having regard to the fact that at the date of the coming into force of the validating Order of June 26, 1945, Henryka and Richard were still resident within the jurisdiction of the country where they had gone through the marriage ceremony, and the registration of the marriage was merely an administrative act which should have been carried out immediately after the ceremony but which happened to have been delayed until the parties had left and acquired a fresh domicile elsewhere. On consideration, however, I have reached the conclusion that the date of registration is the material date in this connexion, and that the position is the same as if Order No. 31, having immediate retroactive effect without the necessity for registration, had been enacted on July 18, 1949.

Which, then, of these two conflicting principles should your Lordships—in the absence of authority—apply to this case? Whichever is chosen must inevitably result in hardship to one or other of the children whose legitimacy is in question.

My Lords, I feel little doubt that it is the former that should prevail and be regarded as an exception to the latter, or rather, perhaps, that the latter should be interpreted as referring to laws directly affecting status as distinct from those which deal with form and only have indirect or consequential effect on status. What influences me most in reaching this conclusion is that there is no field of legislation which has been so fruitful of retrospective validating legislation in

[1] [1930] A.C. 79; *ante*, p. 57.

this country as that of marriages invalid for lack of some requisite formality. Your Lordships were referred to more than fifty of such statutes between 1780 and 1939. Seventeen of these Acts deal exclusively with marriages outside the United Kingdom in territories or portions of territory regarded for certain purposes as notionally British soil and generally apply only where one or both of the parties is a British subject, but the remainder deal with marriages in the United Kingdom and in no single instance is the validity made to depend upon the domicile of the parties at the date of marriage or at the date of the Act. The legislature of this country has clearly assumed competence to pass legislation validating informal marriages contracted here irrespective of domicile or nationality. It would seem to be in accord with comity and with principle that our courts should recognize the validity of similar foreign laws dealing with an aspect of marriage, viz., formality, which has always been recognized as governed by the lex loci celebrationis.

There are other reasons for accepting this view, the most cogent of which are, I think, as follows: (1) Since a marriage, even if valid by the law of domicile, is regarded as invalid if not in conformity with the law of the place of celebration, it would seem illogical if this same law cannot retrospectively cure the invalidity. (2) The legislature of the place of celebration is more likely to be cognizant of the informality and accordingly more likely to afford the necessary statutory relief.

A number of authorities were cited in argument and several of them are referred to in the judgments of the courts below. None really deal with the problem which now arises for decision for the first time. It is, however, satisfactory to find that in the case of *Luna* v. *Godin*[1] the French courts accepted the principle of private international law which Barnard J. and the Court of Appeal considered applicable. . . .

With regard to the case of *Lynch* v. *Provisional Government of Paraguay*,[2] where it was held that succession to property in England of a deceased foreigner is governed by the law of the place of his domicile at the time of his death, and that no subsequent retrospective legislation would be recognized as affecting the distribution of his personal property in England, I agree with the observation of Barnard J. that that case decided that the relevant date was the time of death, whereas in the present case the relevant date is that of the

[1] (1881) 10 Clunet 621.   [2] (1871) L.R. 2 P. & M. 268.

second ceremony and that consequently the decision is one which

would have been of more assistance to the petitioner if the second ceremony had preceded the registration of the first marriage.

Re Luck's Settlement Trusts[1] was a case where the Court of Appeal, by a majority, held that, as the father of an illegitimate child, born in California, had not acquired a domicile of choice in California at the date of the child's birth, a declaration of adoption, after he acquired domicile and which by Californian law was effective to legitimate the child as from birth, could not be recognized by the courts in this country. In that case it was not disputed that the law of domicile had to be applied, but the question was whether domicile at the date of the child's birth or domicile at the date of the declaration of adoption was to be looked at. In the course of the majority judgment, however, there are passages in which Lord Greene M.R. and Luxmoore L.J. assume that no provision of foreign law will be recognized here as effective to change the status of a person not domiciled in the foreign country at the time, except perhaps where the law of the country in which such person is domiciled would itself recognize such foreign law. The language was used with reference to laws expressly directed to the alteration of status, and the court was not concerned to express any view as to the indirect effect on status of foreign law dealing with the formalities of marriage which have always been recognized as being within the province of foreign law. I do not, therefore, consider that any real assistance is to be derived from that case.

It was further contended by the appellant that in any event there was no evidence that Henryka had consented to the registration of the marriage and insufficient evidence that she had consented to marry in that she knew that the ceremony was invalid by Austrian law.

So far as registration is concerned, this being a mere administrative requirement in no way dependent upon the will of the parties, it is clear that want of consent on her part is immaterial. As to consent to the marriage, the trial judge has made no finding, but it is to be observed that although there was evidence that the parties knew that such a ceremony was invalid prior to the liberation of Austria, it is by no means clear that they were aware that after the liberation, which had taken place before the marriage, such a ceremony was still invalid. But in any event, in my opinion, it would be impossible

[1] [1940] Ch. 864; *post*, p. 227.

STARKOWSKI
v.
A.-G.
___
Lord
Tucker.

to hold that there is such an absence of consent as to vitiate the marriage where the parties have gone through a form of marriage in accordance with the rites of the Roman Catholic Church with the intention of creating a union binding on them in the eyes of the Church to which they belong.

I do not consider it necessary or desirable to express any opinion as to whether it follows from this decision that the result would necessarily be the same if the parties had acquired a domicile here and contracted a marriage valid by the law of this country before the passing of the foreign validating statute.

For the reasons stated above and those contained in the judgment of Barnard J. and the Court of Appeal, I would dismiss this appeal.

LORDS MORTON OF HENRYTON, REID, ASQUITH OF BISHOPSTONE, and COHEN delivered judgments to the same effect.

Appeal dismissed.

The validity of proxy marriages is a question of form, not a question of capacity to marry.

APT
v.
APT.

APT v. APT [1948] P. 83 (Court of Appeal)

Appeal from Lord Merriman P.[1]

On 15 January 1941, while the appellant was in this country, she being not only resident but domiciled here, a ceremony of marriage was celebrated at Buenos Aires between her and the respondent. She was represented by a person whom, by a power of attorney executed on 8 November 1940 in London, she had named as her representative to contract the marriage. The husband, as found by Lord Merriman P., was resident and domiciled in the Argentine at all material times. The wife gave evidence that she had at no material time any intention of revoking the power of attorney, that she was informed in due course of the performance of the ceremony, and that she was not merely ready and willing, but eager, to join her husband in Buenos Aires, but was prevented from doing so during the war. She further deposed that when, after the war, she renewed her efforts to join the husband, he took no steps to assist her and ignored her alternative suggestion of a meeting in the United States of America,

[1] [1947] P. 127.

and that it was this conduct on his part which decided her to present the petition in this matter.

A Dr. Palacios was called to give evidence as to the relevant Argentine law, and the result of his evidence, so far as material, may be summarized as follows: (1) Argentine law recognizes proxy marriages. Accordingly by that law the ceremony was valid and effectual, and the marriage would be recognized as a valid marriage by the law of the intended matrimonial domicile. (2) The intending spouse could revoke the power of attorney at any time before the ceremony, but if the power had been acted on before either the other spouse or the proxy had notice of the revocation the marriage would be valid. (3) If, however, the spouse giving the power of attorney had meanwhile lost the capacity to contract the marriage, for example, by an intervening marriage, or by becoming of unsound mind, although the marriage certificate would be prima facie evidence of the ceremony's having been performed, the court would declare the marriage null and void. The wife's petition for a decree of nullity having been dismissed, she now appealed.

The judgment of the court (Tucker, Bucknill, and Cohen L.JJ.) was delivered by

COHEN L.J.: On this evidence counsel for the wife contended that, in the circumstances above stated, it would be contrary to public policy for the English courts to recognise the validity of the marriage, and that, accordingly, his client was entitled to the decree which she sought. The petition was undefended, but, having regard to the importance of the matter, the President invoked the assistance of the King's Proctor, and the case was fully argued. The President in a considered judgment dismissed the petition. After a careful review of all the authorities, English and American, to which his attention had been called, he summarized his conclusions as follows: 'My conclusions therefore are: that the contract of marriage in this case was celebrated in Buenos Aires; that the ceremony was performed strictly in accordance with the law of that country; that the celebration of marriage by proxy is a matter of the form of the ceremony or proceeding, and not an essential of the marriage; that there is nothing abhorrent to Christian ideas in the adoption of that form; and that, in the absence of legislation to the contrary, there is no doctrine of public policy which entitles me to hold that the ceremony, valid where it was performed, is not effective in this country

63

APT
v.
APT.

Cohen L.J.

to constitute a valid marriage. For these reasons, whatever may be the petitioner's remedies as a wife, I am obliged to hold that this petition must be dismissed.'

With these conclusions and with the reasons which the President gives for them we so fully agree that it is only because of the importance of the matter, and out of respect to the arguments addressed to us by counsel on both sides, that we state shortly our reasons for rejecting the arguments addressed to us for the wife. These arguments may be summarised as follows: (1) It is contrary to the public policy of England to recognise any marriage by proxy; (2) it is not however necessary to reach a conclusion on the first point, since in any event it is contrary to the public policy of England to recognise a marriage by proxy if (a) the party giving the proxy is domiciled in England or (b) the power of attorney conferring authority on the proxy is executed in England or (c) the power of attorney authorises a marriage by proxy in a country where the law will recognise, as does Argentine law, the validity of a marriage contracted thereunder, notwithstanding the revocation of the proxy, if the revocation has not been communicated to the other spouse or the proxy before the ceremony takes place; and (3) the granting of a power of attorney in England is governed as to essential validity by English law, and it is contrary to English law to recognise powers of attorney given for the purpose of celebrating a marriage.

The first argument is, in our opinion, ill founded. Counsel was unable to suggest any statutory provision which was relevant to it. He referred us to s. 22 of the Marriage Act 1823, which prohibits marriages otherwise than in a church or without banns or licence, but he admitted that this section only applies to marriages within the English jurisdiction: see s. 33 of the Act. A proxy marriage, such as we are considering, is clearly a Christian marriage within the definition given by Lord Penzance in *Hyde* v. *Hyde*:[1] 'the voluntary union for life of one man and one woman, to the exclusion of all others.' A proxy marriage was recognised as valid by the canon law: see Swinburne's Treatise of Spousals or Matrimonial Contracts[2] where, as the President points out, the conditions of such a marriage are described. It is recognised as valid in a number of Christian countries beside the Argentine. The preponderance of the American authorities to which the President refers indicates that such a marriage is recognised as valid in many states of the United States of

---

[1] (1866) L.R. 1 P. & M. 136 ; *post*, p. 89.   [2] (1686), pp. 162, 163

America: see especially *Ex parte Suzanna*.[1] It was argued that *Reg.* v. *Millis*[2] precluded us from holding that such a marriage would be recognised in England, but that case concerned only marriages celebrated in England or Ireland; it did not expressly cover the point, and is in any event no authority for the general proposition that all proxy marriages, wherever celebrated, are void. See *Wolfenden* v. *Wolfenden*[3] where the President pointed out the limited operation of *Reg.* v. *Millis.*

Counsel for the wife invited us, none the less, to hold that proxy marriages were contrary to public policy since they would facilitate clandestine marriages, make easy the bestowal of British nationality on foreigners and the carrying on of the white-slave traffic, and make it possible for two minors to get married in, for example, Mexico, although they were both domiciled in England. So far as the argument is based on clandestine marriages, we have to bear in mind that the English courts have not regarded all such marriages as contrary to public policy; for example, Gretna Green marriages were held to be valid until they were prohibited by statute. Moreover, we have to bear in mind the frequent injunctions of the highest tribunal as to the danger of allowing judicial tribunals to roam unchecked in the field occupied by that unruly horse, public policy: see, for example, per Lord Atkin in *Fender* v. *Mildmay*.[4] In any event, a consideration of what is 'public policy' in a case where the matter is not governed by statute or by clearly established principle must necessarily involve balancing advantages against disadvantages. As against the considerations advanced by counsel must be weighed the following factors: (1) The unsatisfactory position that would arise in that, if Mr. Foster is right, the parties would be married in the Argentine, the place of the intended matrimonial domicile, but not married in England; (2) the fact that, if Mr. Foster is right, any children that might result from the marriage would be bastards in the eye of English law; and, above all, (3) we should in effect be holding that the law of the Argentine was contrary to essential justice and morality, a conclusion to which we should hesitate to come. . . .

In all the circumstances, we are satisfied that we cannot properly extend public policy to invalidate all proxy marriages. . . .

Finally, on this point we would repeat the citation from Lord Dunedin's speech in *Berthiaume* v. *Dastous*[5] which was quoted by

---

[1] (1924) 295 F. 713.   [2] (1844) 10 Cl. & F. 534.   [3] [1946] P. 61.
[4] [1938] A.C. 1, 10.   [5] [1930] A.C. 79 ; *ante*, p. 57.

the President. (His Lordship quoted the passage beginning 'If a marriage is good' and ending 'to need much quotation', and continued:) In our opinion, the method of giving consent as distinct from the fact of consent is essentially a matter for the lex loci celebrationis, and does not raise a question of capacity, or, as Mr. Foster preferred to call it, essential validity.

It will be convenient next to consider Mr. Foster's third point, since it seems to us to founder on the same rock as his first. Counsel was constrained to admit that there was no question of incapacity in the donor of the power, or of any statutory invalidity, and that, if the power had related to a commercial transaction, its validity could not be challenged, since the act to be performed under it was valid by the law of the intended place of performance: see *Chatenay* v. *Brazilian Submarine Telegraph Co. Ltd.*[1]. . . Counsel argued, however, that this power relates to a contract of marriage, and that this is not a mere matter of contract of marriage, but affects status. This is, if anything, an understatement, since the main element in the marriage contract is its effect on status; . . . but, as the status sought to be created by the proxy marriage now in question is, as we have already pointed out, that of a Christian marriage such as English law recognises and approves, the argument does not really assist counsel and he is driven to argue that the power of attorney is bad because proxy marriages are against the public policy of England, an argument which we have already given our reasons for rejecting.

We return to the second point. In our opinion, this also fails. As regards sub-division (*a*) thereof, we are unable to see any reason in public policy which would require the English courts, if they recognise the validity of proxy marriages celebrated outside the United Kingdom, to deny to a person domiciled in this country the right of so celebrating a marriage, provided, of course, that he or she has in other respects capacity to marry and does not infringe any provision of English law. (*b*) is really another way of stating the third argument presented for the wife. We think it impossible to hold that, in the absence of some statutory prohibition, it is contrary to public policy to execute in England a power of attorney which the same person could validly execute in the Argentine, the power of attorney being intended to authorise an act in the Argentine which is lawful by the law of that country. As regards (*c*), we agree with the President that this point does not arise. If a case occurs where the proxy is

[1] [1891] 1 Q.B. 79; *post*, p. 256.

66

revoked before the ceremony takes place but the other spouse and the proxy are unaware of the revocation, it may be that the courts of this country would hold that the purported marriage was void; but that would not be because of any general objection to proxy marriages, but because, on the facts of the particular case, the court was satisfied that the marriage was not a voluntary union.

Appeal dismissed.

APT
v.
APT.
Cohen L.J.

Section B: CAPACITY TO MARRY

Capacity to marry is governed (in general) by the lex domicilii of each party immediately before the marriage.

BROOK *v.* BROOK (1861) 9 H.L.C. 193 (House of Lords)

BROOK
v.
BROO

Appeal from a decision of Stuart V.-C.

William Charles Brook (hereinafter called the testator) married Charlotte Armitage in England in 1840. She died in 1847 and there were issue of that marriage one daughter and one son. In 1850 the testator married Emily Armitage, the sister of his deceased wife, in Holstein, Denmark. That marriage was valid by Danish law but void for consanguinity by English law. There were issue of that marriage one son and two daughters. The testator and Emily Armitage were British subjects domiciled in England and had merely gone over to Denmark on a temporary visit. In 1855 Emily Armitage died of cholera and two days later the testator died of the same complaint, leaving all five children him surviving.

By his will the testator gave all the residue of his property to his five children by name.

In 1856 Charles Armitage Brook, the son of the second marriage, died an infant and intestate. A bill was filed by his sisters and half-sister against his half-brother and the Attorney-General claiming that Charles Brook's share of the testator's real estate descended to his half-brother as heir at law and that his share of the testator's personal estate passed to his half-brother and the plaintiffs as next of kin. The Attorney-General alleged that the marriage of the testator and Emily Armitage was not valid, that Charles Brook therefore was a bastard without collateral relatives and that his share of the testator's property passed to the Crown.

67

Stuart V.-C. having consulted Cresswell J. held that the marriage was not valid and that the real and personal estate of Charles Brook had become vested in the Crown.

LORD CAMPBELL L.C.: My Lords, the question which your Lordships are called upon to consider in the present appeal is, whether the marriage celebrated on the 9th June 1850 in the duchy of Holstein, in the kingdom of Denmark, between William Leigh Brook, a widower, and Emily Armitage, the sister of his deceased wife, they being British subjects then domiciled in England, and contemplating England as their place of matrimonial residence, is to be considered valid in England, marriage between a widower and the sister of his deceased wife being permitted by the law of Denmark?

I am of opinion that this depends upon the question whether such a marriage would have been held illegal, and might have been set aside in a suit commenced in England in the lifetime of the parties before the passing of the Marriage Act 1835, commonly called Lord Lyndhurst's Act.

There can be no doubt that before Lord Lyndhurst's Act passed, a marriage between a widower and the sister of his deceased wife, if celebrated in England, was unlawful, and in the lifetime of the parties could have been annulled. Such a marriage was expressly prohibited by the legislature of this country, and was prohibited expressly on the ground that it was 'contrary to God's law'. Sitting here, judicially, we are not at liberty to consider whether such a marriage is or is not 'contrary to God's law', nor whether it is expedient or inexpedient.

Before the Reformation the degrees of relationship by consanguinity and affinity, within which marriage was forbidden, were almost indefinitely multiplied; but the prohibition might have been dispensed with by the Pope, or those who represented him. At the Reformation, the prohibited degrees were confined within the limits supposed to be expressly defined by Holy Scripture, and all dispensations were abolished. The prohibited degrees were those within which intercourse between the sexes was supposed to be forbidden as incestuous, and no distinction was made between relationship by blood or by affinity. The marriage of a man with a sister of his deceased wife is expressly within this category. *Hill* v. *Good*[1] and *Reg.* v. *Chadwick*[2] are solemn decisions that such a marriage was

---

[1] (1674) Vaugh. 302.   [2] (1847) 11 Q.B. 173, 205.

illegal; and if celebrated in England such a marriage unquestionably would now be void.

Indeed, this is not denied on the part of the appellants. They rest their case entirely upon the fact that the marriage was celebrated in a foreign country, where the marriage of a man with the sister of his deceased wife is permitted.

There can be no doubt of the general rule, that 'a foreign marriage, valid according to the law of a country where it is celebrated, is good everywhere'. But while the forms of entering into the contract of marriage are to be regulated by the lex loci contractus, the law of the country in which it is celebrated, the essentials of the contract depend upon the lex domicilii, the law of the country in which the parties are domiciled at the time of marriage, and in which the matrimonial residence is contemplated. Although the forms of celebrating the foreign marriage may be different from those required by the law of the country of domicile, the marriage may be good everywhere. But if the contract of marriage is such, in essentials, as to be contrary to the law of the country of domicile, and it is declared void by that law, it is to be regarded as void in the country of domicile, though not contrary to the law of the country in which it was celebrated.

This qualification upon the rule that 'a marriage valid where celebrated is good everywhere', is to be found in the writings of many eminent jurists who have discussed the subject.

Mr. Justice Story, in his valuable treatise on 'the Conflict of Laws', while he admits it to be the 'rule that a marriage valid where celebrated is good everywhere', says (s. 113*a*) there are exceptions; those of marriages involving polygamy and incest, those positively prohibited by the public law of a country from motives of policy, and those celebrated in foreign countries by subjects entitling themselves, under special circumstances, to the benefit of the laws of their own country, he adds (s. 114), 'in respect to the first exception, that of marriages involving polygamy and incest, Christianity is understood to prohibit polygamy and incest, and, therefore, no Christian country would recognise polygamy or incestuous marriages; but when we speak of incestuous marriages care must be taken to confine the doctrine to such cases as by the general consent of all Christendom are deemed incestuous.' The conclusion of this sentence was strongly relied upon by Sir FitzRoy Kelly, who alleged that many in England approve of marriage between a widower and the sister of his deceased wife; and

BROOK
v.
BROOK.

Lord
Campbell
L.C.

that such marriages are permitted in Protestant states on the Continent of Europe and in most of the States in America.

Sitting here as a judge to declare and enforce the law of England as fixed by Kings, Lords, and Commons, the supreme power of this realm, I do not feel myself at liberty to form any private opinion of my own on the subject, or to inquire into what may be the opinion of the majority of my fellow citizens at home, or to try to find out the opinion of all Christendom. I can as judge only look to what was the solemnly pronounced opinion of the legislature when the laws were passed which I am called upon to interpret. What means am I to resort to for the purpose of ascertaining the opinions of foreign nations? Is my interpretation of these laws to vary with the variation of opinion in foreign countries? Change of opinion on any great question, at home or abroad, may be a good reason for the legislature changing the law, but can be no reason for judges to vary their interpretation of the law.

Indeed, as Story allows marriages positively prohibited by the public law of a country, from motives of policy, to form an exception to the general rule as to the validity of marriage, he could hardly mean his qualification to apply to a country like England, in which the limits of marriages to be considered incestuous are exactly defined by public law.

That the Parliament of England in framing the prohibited degrees within which marriages were forbidden, believed and intimated the opinion, that all such marriages were incestuous and contrary to God's word, I cannot doubt. All the degrees prohibited are brought into one category, and although marriages within those degrees may be more or less revolting, they are placed on the same footing, and before English tribunals, till the law is altered, they are to be treated alike. . . .

It is quite obvious that no civilised state can allow its domiciled subjects or citizens, by making a temporary visit to a foreign country, to enter into a contract to be performed in the place of domicile, if the contract is forbidden by the law of the place of domicile as contrary to religion, or morality, or to any of its fundamental institutions.

A marriage between a man and the sister of his deceased wife, being Danish subjects domiciled in Denmark, may be good all over the world, and this might likewise be so, even if they were native born English subjects, who had abandoned their English domicile,

70

and were domiciled in Denmark. But I am by no means prepared to say that the marriage now in question ought to be, or would be, held valid in the Danish courts, proof being given that the parties were British subjects domiciled in England at the time of the marriage, that England was to be their matrimonial residence, and that by the law of England such a marriage is prohibited as being contrary to the law of God. The doctrine being established that the incidents of the contract of marriage celebrated in a foreign country are to be determined according to the law of the country in which the parties are domiciled and mean to reside, the consequence seems to follow that by this law must its validity or invalidity be determined.

Sir FitzRoy Kelly argued that we could not hold this marriage to be invalid without being prepared to nullify the marriages of Danish subjects who contracted such a marriage in Denmark while domiciled in their native country, if they should come to reside in England. But on the principles which I have laid down, such marriages, if examined, would be held valid in all English courts, as they are according to the law of the country in which the parties were domiciled when the marriages were celebrated.

I will now examine the authorities relied upon by the counsel for the appellants. They bring forward nothing from the writings of jurists except the general rule, that contracts are to be construed according to the lex loci contractus, and the saying of Story with regard to a marriage being contrary to the precepts of the Christian religion, upon which I have already commented.

But there are various decisions which they bring forward as con-clusive in their favour. They begin with *Compton* v. *Bearcroft*[1] and the class of cases in which it was held that Gretna Green marriages were valid in England, notwithstanding Lord Hardwicke's Marriage Act 1753. In observing upon them, I do not lay any stress on the proviso in this Act that it should not extend to marriages in Scotland or beyond the seas; this being only an intimation of what might otherwise have been inferred, that its direct operation should be con-fined to England, and that marriages in Scotland and beyond the seas should continue to be viewed according to the law of Scotland and countries beyond the seas, as if the Act had not been passed. But I do lay very great stress on the consideration that Lord Hardwicke's Act only regulated banns and licences, and the formalities by which the ceremony of marriage shall be celebrated. It does not touch the

BROOK
v.
BROOK.

Lord
Campbell
L.C.

[1] (1769) 2 Hagg. Cons. 444, n.

essentials of the contract or prohibit any marriage which was before lawful, or render any marriage lawful which was before prohibited. The formalities which it requires could only be observed in England, and the whole frame of it shows it was only territorial. The nullifying clauses about banns and licences can only apply to marriages celebrated in England. In this class of case the contested marriage could only be challenged for want of banns or licence in the prescribed form. These formalities being observed, the marriages would all have been unimpeachable. But the marriage we have to decide upon has been declared by the legislature to be 'contrary to God's law', and on that ground is absolutely prohibited.

The appellants' counsel next produced a new authority, the very learned and lucid judgment of Dr. Radcliff, in *Steele* v. *Braddell*.[1] The Irish statute, 9 Geo. 2, c. 11, enacts, 'that all marriages and matrimonial contracts, when either of the parties is under the age of twenty-one, had without the consent of the father or guardian, shall be absolutely null and void to all intents and purposes; and that it shall be lawful for the father or guardian to commence a suit in the proper Ecclesiastical Court in order to annul the marriage'. A young gentleman, a native of Ireland, and domiciled there, went while a minor into Scotland, and there married a Scottish young lady without the consent of his father or guardian. A suit was brought by his guardian in an Ecclesiastical Court in Ireland, in which Dr. Radcliff presided, to annul the marriage on the ground that this statute created a personal incapacity in minors, subjects of Ireland, to contract marriage, in whatever country, without the consent of father or guardian. But the learned judge said, 'I cannot find that any Act of Parliament such as this has ever been extended to cases not properly within it, on the principle that parties endeavoured to evade it.' And after an elaborate view of the authorities upon the subject, he decided that both parties being of the age of consent, and the marriage being valid by the law of Scotland, it could not be impeached in the courts of the country in which the husband was domiciled, and he dismissed the suit. But this was a marriage between parties who, with the consent of parents and guardians, might have contracted a valid marriage according to the law of the country of the husband's domicile, and the mode of celebrating the marriage was to be according to the law of the country in which it was celebrated. But if the union between these parties

[1] (1838) Milw. Ecc. Rep. (Ir.) 1.

had been prohibited by the law of Ireland as 'contrary to the word of God', undoubtedly the marriage would have been dissolved.

Another new case was brought forward, decided very recently by Sir Cresswell Cresswell, *Simonin* v. *Mallac*.[1] This was a petition by Valerie Simonin for a declaration of nullity of marriage. The petitioner alleged that a pretended ceremony of marriage was had between the petitioner and Leon Mallac of Paris, in the parish church of St. Martin's-in-the-Fields; that about two days afterwards the parties returned to Paris, but did not cohabit, and the marriage was never consummated; that the pretended marriage was in contradiction to and in evasion of the Code Napoléon; that the parties were natives of and domiciled in France, and that subsequently to their return to France the Civil Tribunal of the department of the Seine had declared the said pretended marriage to be null and void. Leon Mallac was served at Naples with a citation and a copy of the petition, but did not appear. Proof was given of the material allegations of the petition, and that the parties coming to London to avoid the French law, which required the consent of parents or guardians to their union, were married by licence in the parish church of St. Martin's-in-the-Fields. Sir Cresswell Cresswell, after the case had been learnedly argued, discharged the petition. But was there anything here inconsistent with the opinion which the same learned judge delivered as assessor to Stuart V.-C. in *Brook* v. *Brook*? Nothing whatever; for the objection to the validity of the marriage in England was merely that the forms prescribed by the Code Napoléon for the celebration of a marriage in France had not been observed. But there was no law of France, where the parties were domiciled, forbidding a conjugal union between them; and if the proper forms of celebration had been observed, this marriage by the law of France would have been unimpeachable. The case, therefore, comes into the same category as *Compton* v. *Bearcroft* and *Steele* v. *Braddell*. None of these cases can show the validity of a marriage which the law of the domicile of the parties condemns as incestuous, and which could not, by any forms or consents, have been rendered valid in the country in which the parties were domiciled. . . .

LORDS CRANWORTH, ST. LEONARDS, and WENSLEYDALE delivered judgments to the same effect.

Appeal dismissed.

BROOK
v.
BROOK.
—
Lord
Campbell
L.C.

[1] (1860) 2 Sw. & Tr. 67.

SOTTOMAYOR v. DE BARROS (No. 1) (1877) 3 P.D. 1 (Court of Appeal)

Woman's petition for nullity of marriage.

The petitioner Ignacia Clara Maxima Pacheco Pereira Pamplona da Cunha Sottomayor was born in Portugal in 1851. The respondent Gonzalo Lobo Pereira Caldos De Barros, who was the petitioner's first cousin, was born in Portugal in 1850. In 1858 the petitioner, her father and mother, and her uncle De Barros and his family, including the respondent, his eldest son, came to England, and the two families occupied a house jointly in Dorset Square, London. The petitioner's father came to this country for the benefit of his health, and De Barros for the education of his children and to superintend the sale of wine. On the 21st of June 1866 the petitioner, at that time of the age of $14\frac{1}{2}$ years, and the respondent, of the age of 16 years, were married at a registry office in London. No religious ceremony accompanied or followed the marriage, and although the parties lived together in the same house until the year 1872, they never slept together, and the marriage was never consummated. The petitioner stated that she went through the form of marriage contrary to her own inclination, by the persuasion of her uncle and mother, on the representation that it would be the means of preserving her father's Portuguese property from the consequences of the bankruptcy of the wine business. The petitioner returned to Portugal in 1873 and the respondent in 1874. By the law of Portugal first cousins are incapable of contracting marriage by reason of consanguinity, and any such marriage is held to be incestuous and therefore null and void, unless solemnized under the authority of a papal dispensation.

The petitioner applied for a decree of nullity on the ground that she and the respondent were under a personal incapacity to contract marriage. The suit was undefended and Phillimore J. ordered the papers to be sent to the Queen's Proctor, who filed an answer alleging (inter alia) that at the time of the marriage the petitioner and respondent were domiciled in England and not in Portugal; and that the petitioner and respondent intended at the time of the marriage to live together as man and wife in England, and did so live for six years, and that the validity of the marriage was to be determined by the law of England. By consent of the parties it was ordered that the question of law should be argued before the questions of fact.

Phillimore J. dismissed the petition.[1] The petitioner appealed.

[1] 2 P.D. 81.

The judgment of the court (James Baggallay and Cotton L.JJ.) was delivered by

COTTON L.J. (After stating the facts, and observing that the petitioner and respondent were domiciled in Portugal at all times, his Lordship continued:) Under these circumstances the petitioner, in November, 1874, presented her petition for the object above mentioned, and Sir R. Phillimore, before whom the case was heard, declined to declare the marriage invalid and dismissed the petition, but did so, as we understand, rather because he felt himself bound by the decision in the case of *Simonin* v. *Mallac*[1] than because he considered that on principle the marriage ought to be held good. If the parties had been subjects of Her Majesty domiciled in England, the marriage would undoubtedly have been valid. But it is a well-recognised principle of law that the question of personal capacity to enter into any contract is to be decided by the law of domicile. It is, however, urged that this does not apply to the contract of marriage, and that a marriage valid according to the law of the country where it is solemnised is valid everywhere. This, in our opinion, is not a correct statement of the law. The law of a country where a marriage is solemnised must alone decide all questions relating to the validity of the ceremony by which the marriage is alleged to have been constituted; but, as in other contracts, so in that of marriage, personal capacity must depend on the law of the domicile; and if the laws of any country prohibit its subjects within certain degrees of consanguinity from contracting marriage, and stamp a marriage between persons within the prohibited degrees as incestuous, this, in our opinion, imposes on the subjects of that country a personal incapacity, which continues to affect them so long as they are domiciled in the country where this law prevails, and renders invalid a marriage between persons both at the time of their marriage subjects of and domiciled in the country which imposes this restriction, wherever such marriage may have been solemnised.

But it is said that the impediment imposed by the law of Portugal can be removed by a Papal dispensation, and, therefore, that it cannot be said there is a personal incapacity of the petitioner and respondent to contract marriage. The evidence is clear that by the law of Portugal the impediment to the marriage between the parties is such that, in the absence of Papal dispensation, the marriage

[1] (1860) 2 Sw. & Tr. 67.

75

would be by the law of that country void as incestuous. The statutes of the English parliament contain a declaration that no Papal dispensation can sanction a marriage otherwise incestuous; but the law of Portugal does recognise the validity of such a dispensation, and it cannot in our opinion be held that such a dispensation is a matter of form affecting only the sufficiency of the ceremony by which the marriage is effected, or that the law of Portugal, which prohibits and declares incestuous, unless with such a dispensation, a marriage between the petitioner and respondent, does not impose on them a personal incapacity to contract marriage. It is proved that the courts of Portugal, where the petitioner and respondent are domiciled and resident, would hold the marriage void, as solemnised between parties incapable of marrying, and incestuous. How can the courts of this country hold the contrary, and, if appealed to, say the marriage is valid? It was pressed upon us in argument that a decision in favour of the petitioner would lead to many difficulties, if questions should arise as to the validity of a marriage between an English subject and a foreigner, in consequence of prohibitions imposed by the law of the domicile of the latter. Our opinion on this appeal is confined to the case where both the contracting parties are, at the time of their marriage, domiciled in a country the laws of which prohibit their marriage. All persons are legally bound to take notice of the laws of the country where they are domiciled. No country is bound to recognise the laws of a foreign state when they work injustice to its own subjects, and this principle would prevent the judgment in the present case being relied on as an authority for setting aside a marriage between a foreigner and an English subject domiciled in England, on the ground of any personal incapacity not recognised by the law of this country.

The counsel for the petitioner relied on the case of *Brook* v. *Brook*[1] as a decision in his favour. If, in our opinion, that case had been a decision on the question arising on this petition, we should have thought it sufficient without more to refer to that case as decisive. The judgment in that case, however, only decided that the English Courts must hold invalid a marriage between two English subjects domiciled in this country, who were prohibited from intermarrying by an English statute, even though the marriage was solemnised during a temporary sojourn in a foreign country. It is, therefore, not decisive of the present case; but the reasons given by the Lords who

---

[1] (1861) 9 H.L.C. 193 ; *ante*, p. 67.

delivered their opinions in that case strongly support the principle on which this judgment is based.

It only remains to consider the case of *Simonin* v. *Mallac*. The objection to the validity of the marriage in that case, which was solemnised in England, was the want of the consent of parents required by the law of France, but not under the circumstances by that of this country. In our opinion, this consent must be considered a part of the ceremony of marriage, and not a matter affecting the personal capacity of the parties to contract marriage; and the decision in *Simonin* v. *Mallac* does not, we think, govern the present case. We are of opinion that the judgment appealed from must be reversed, and a decree made declaring the marriage null and void.

Appeal allowed.

Note. The case was remitted to the Divorce Division in order that the questions of fact raised by the Queen's Proctor's pleas should be determined. On it appearing that the husband's domicile at the date of the marriage was not Portuguese but English, Sir James Hannen P. pronounced the marriage valid in reliance on the dictum of the Court of Appeal in *Sottomayor* v. *De Barros* (*No. 1*) (*ante*, p. 76) that 'our opinion on this appeal is confined to the case where both the contracting parties are, at the time of their marriage, domiciled in a country the laws of which prohibit their marriage'. But this dictum, and the subsequent decision in *Sottomayor* v. *De Barros* (*No. 2*) (1879) 5 P.D. 94, which was founded on it, are extremely difficult to reconcile with the reasoning in *Mette* v. *Mette* (1859) 1 Sw. & Tr. 416. In that case a ceremony of marriage took place in Frankfurt between a domiciled Englishman and his deceased wife's sister, who was domiciled in Frankfurt. The marriage was valid by the law of Frankfurt but void for consanguinity by English law. Sir Cresswell Cresswell following *Brook* v. *Brook* pronounced the marriage void on the ground that 'there could be no valid contract unless each was competent to contract with the other' (1 Sw. & Tr. 423). Falconbridge (pp. 711–14) discusses six different methods of reconciling *Mette* v. *Mette* and *Re Paine* [1940] P. 46 (*post*, p. 85) with *Sottomayor* v. *De Barros* (*No. 2*), all of which he rejects as untenable. The decision in the latter is based upon the grounds (1) that capacity to marry is governed by the law of the place of celebration, and (2) that an incapacity imposed by foreign law is less important than an incapacity imposed by English law and can therefore be disregarded. The former ground is clearly untenable since *Brook* v. *Brook* (*ante*, p. 67). The latter ground is 'unworthy of a place in a respectable system of the conflict of laws' (Falconbridge, p. 711).

OGDEN *v.* OGDEN [1908] P. 46 (Court of Appeal)

Appeal from a decision of Bargrave Deane J.

In September 1898 the appellant, an Englishwoman domiciled in England, married in England a man named Léon Philip, a Frenchman domiciled in France, then aged 19 years. The marriage took place without the knowledge either of his parents or of her parents.

After a short time Philip's father came to hear of the marriage. He took his son back to France (where he has ever since remained) and instituted proceedings in France to have the marriage annulled in accordance with the following provisions of the French Civil Code:

Article 148. The son who has not attained the full age of 25 years, the daughter who has not attained the full age of 21 years, cannot contract marriage without the consent of their father and mother.

Article 151. Where the children of a family have attained the majority fixed by article 148, they are required previously to contracting marriage to demand by a respectful and formal act the consent of their father and mother.

Article 152. From the majority fixed by article 148 until the age of 30 years completed for sons, and until the age of 25 years completed for daughters, the respectful act required by the preceding article, and on which consent to marriage shall not have been obtained, shall be twice more renewed from month to month; and one month after the third act it shall be lawful to proceed with the celebration of the marriage.

Article 170. A marriage contracted in a foreign country between natives of France and between a native of France and a foreigner shall be valid if celebrated according to the forms used in that country, provided that it has been preceded by the publications prescribed in article 63, under the title 'Of acts of the civil power', and that the Frenchman has not infringed the regulations contained in the preceding chapter.

Article 182. A marriage contracted without the consent of the father and mother in cases where such consent was necessary can be impeached only by those whose consent was necessary, or by such of the two married persons as stood in need of that consent.

In November 1901 a decree was pronounced by the Civil Tribunal of First Instance of the Seine annulling the marriage for lack of consent of parents in accordance with article 148. The appellant never went to France and did not appear personally in those proceedings.

After the decree Léon Philip married again in France, and in July 1903 the appellant instituted a suit in the High Court in England for a dissolution of her marriage on the ground of her husband's desertion and adultery. Her petition also asked for a declaration that her marriage was annulled. The petition was undefended, but was dismissed for want of jurisdiction, Léon Philip being domiciled in France.

In October 1904 the appellant went through a ceremony of marriage in England with the present petitioner, William Ogden. In July 1906 Ogden instituted the present suit against the appellant for a decree of nullity of marriage on the ground that at the time of the ceremony Léon Philip was still alive, and that the marriage of the appellant and Léon Philip had not been annulled or dissolved for any cause competent to the law of England.

The appellant by her answer denied that she was lawfully married to Léon Philip and pleaded that her marriage with him was annulled by the French decree.

Bargrave Deane J. pronounced a decree nisi, declaring the marriage between the petitioner and the appellant null and void on the ground that the appellant had a husband living at the time of her marriage with the petitioner. From this decision the present appeal was brought.

The judgment of the court (Cozens-Hardy M.R., Sir Gorell Barnes P., and Kennedy L.J.) was delivered by

SIR GORELL BARNES P.: . . . Two points were made for the appellant by her counsel, Sir Edward Clarke; the first, that her marriage with Léon Philip was not valid, inasmuch as, although the marriage was celebrated according to the forms required by the law of England, it was invalid both in this country and in France because Léon Philip was, by the law of France, being the law of his country and his domicile, incapable of contracting the marriage; the second, that the effect of the French decree was to annul the marriage, both in France and in this country. If both or either of these points were established in favour of the appellant, the contention on her part which followed as a matter of course was that at the time of the ceremony of marriage between herself and Mr. Ogden she was free to contract a marriage with him, and that, therefore, her marriage with him was valid, and his petition should be dismissed. . . .

(After discussing the provisions of the French Civil Code set out above, and observing that they rendered the marriage voidable, not void, his Lordship continued:) The simple question for determination in the present case upon the first point is whether or not a marriage taking place in England between an English person domiciled in England with a foreigner temporarily residing in this country, which it was not disputed would be held in England to be a valid marriage if celebrated between two inhabitants of this country,

OGDEN
v.
OGDEN.

Sir Gorell
Barnes P.

ought to be held invalid on the ground that the foreigner was by the statute law of his country subjected to the necessity of complying with certain formalities in order to be at liberty to enter into the marriage. It is desirable to state this limited proposition very clearly, because, with regard to questions which may be raised as to the validity of marriages in England between persons domiciled abroad, certain cases have been decided (to which reference will be made further on in this judgment) which do not necessarily involve the consideration of the particular point already indicated, or any decision thereupon; and it is desirable, therefore, to avoid the confusion which appears to have arisen sometimes between the consideration of the principles which have been laid down for determining the validity of a marriage where the ceremony alone was in question, and of those which have been considered, in determining whether it was lawful for the parties to intermarry at all.

Now, the argument for the appellant in the present case was that, although the marriage between her and Léon Philip was celebrated according to the forms required by the English law, it was invalid universally because Léon Philip was a minor in France, and under a disability by the law of France from contracting such marriage without the consent of his father, and without complying with the other formalities required by the law of France. In substance this contention amounted to this—that in regard to entering into a marriage in England with an inhabitant thereof, Léon Philip carried with him into this country an incapacity, which ought to be recognised by the law of England, to enter into matrimonial relationship with such inhabitant without complying with the provisions of the French code. It was urged that this principle had been recognised in this country, and cases were cited which it was said supported the contention. The cases cited, however, do not support it, and in truth the argument on behalf of the appellant appears to be based upon views which have been expressed by foreign jurists, but which have not been adopted in this country, where the English courts have not been very ready to admit a personal law of status and capacity dependent on domicile, and travelling with the person from country to country, although there has been, perhaps, less unwillingness in later years to give effect to the lex domicilii to some extent: see, for instance, *In re Goodman's Trusts*.[1]

It may be doubted whether there is much substantial difference of

[1] (1881) 17 Ch. D. 266; *post*, p. 222.

opinion between foreign and English jurists as to the general rule that between persons sui juris the validity of the marriage is to be decided by the law of the place where it is celebrated. There are certain exceptions, as, for instance, when the lex loci celebrationis violates the precepts of religion, or of public morals, as in the case of bigamy, or where the marriages are such as are generally recognised as incestuous. When, however, the competency of the parties to contract marriage is considered, there appears to be a diversity of opinion, not merely between foreign jurists and English jurists, but amongst the foreign jurists themselves, certain foreign jurists, but not all, maintaining that a person who is in his minority by the law of his native or acquired domicile is to be deemed everywhere in the same state or condition. This appears to be based upon the conception that the laws which have for their object the regulation of the capacity of persons are to be treated as personal laws and of absolute obligation everywhere when they have once attached upon the person by the law of his domicile. This conception would appear to result from the application of principles derived from sources of law different from those from which the English common law has been derived, and from considerations which have not had the same force in this country as abroad.

. . . We are concerned in this case only with the question of a disability imposed by foreign law upon one of the parties to the marriage in respect only of want of parental consent, and compliance with certain formalities required by such foreign law.

There appears to be no case in this country (certainly no case was cited to us in argument on this appeal) in which in such a case as last mentioned the view has been expressed that such a marriage would be held invalid in this country. We know of no principle recognised by English law which would justify the court in coming to the conclusion that such a marriage ought to be held invalid; for, although to a certain extent the lex domicilii is recognised in this country, for instance, in the familiar case where it is held that mobilia sequuntur personam, yet such recognition appears never to have been extended to the case of a matrimonial engagement entered into in this country between an inhabitant of another country and an inhabitant of this country. In such a case, where there are two different systems of law, one may well ask, which is to prevail? Why should it be recognised that a person who comes over to this country and validly enters into a marriage with one of its inhabitants according to English law should be held unable to do so here because of the regulations of a foreign system of jurisprudence which places upon him a personal incapacity to contract unless he complies with formalities required by the foreign law? It may be observed here that the 3rd section of article 1 of the French Civil Code ordains that the French laws relating to the conditions and privileges of persons are to govern Frenchmen although residing in a foreign country, so that it would seem from this provision that the French rule as to competency by reason of minority is not based upon domicile, but upon nationality, and therefore that even in the case of a Frenchman domiciled in England celebrating a marriage with a domiciled Englishwoman the French courts would be at liberty, if the question arose before them, to declare such a marriage null and void, on the ground that it was governed by the laws of France, although celebrated in this country; but it could hardly be contended in England, if both persons parties to a marriage were domiciled in this country, that our courts ought to hold such a marriage invalid because one of the parties by the laws of his or her nationality may not have adequate competency to enter into the contract. . . .

The case of *Brook* v. *Brook*[1] was much relied upon by the appellant's counsel. That case, however, so far from supporting the contention of the appellant, is, when carefully considered, a decision adverse to her. (His Lordship stated the facts and the decision in *Brook* v. *Brook*, and after observing that it had not met with approval in America, continued:) The reason why the case of *Brook* v. *Brook* may be considered to be adverse to the appellant is that the distinction is there drawn between the question of the validity of a marriage absolutely prohibited by the law of the domicile of both parties and the case in which a marriage, valid by the law of the place of celebration, if it took place between two inhabitants of that place, is called in question because one of the persons is domiciled abroad, and has not complied with certain forms and obtained certain consents required by the law of the place of his or her domicile. The Lord Chancellor (Lord Campbell) said: (His Lordship quoted the passage on p. 69, *ante*, beginning 'There can be no doubt of the general rule' and ending 'the law of the country in which it was celebrated'.) Again, in commenting on the case of *Simonin* v. *Mallac*,[2] next hereinafter referred to, Lord Campbell remarks: (His Lordship quoted the passage on p. 73, *ante*, beginning 'The objec-

---

[1] (1861) 9 H.L.C. 193 ; *ante*, p. 67.   [2] (1860) 2 Sw. & Tr. 67.

tion to the validity of the marriage' and ending 'in which the parties were domiciled'.)

It was contended that *Simonin* v. *Mallac* was wrongly decided, and therefore it is desirable to refer to it in some detail. (In that case a marriage celebrated in England between a man aged twenty-nine and a woman aged twenty-two, both of whom were domiciled in France, was held valid, although the parties had not obtained the consent of their parents as required by articles 151 and 152 of the French Civil Code, and although the marriage had been annulled in France on that ground. His Lordship stated the facts in *Simonin* v. *Mallac* and continued:) The argument was very much the same as that which was addressed to this Court, viz., that the law of the country of the domicile placed on the parties an incapacity to contract marriage without attending to the formalities prescribed, and that such incapacity travelled with them everywhere, and rendered them incapable of making a valid contract in any other country, especially where the intention was to evade the law of their own country. In the course of the judgment it was noted that according to the evidence the incapacity to contract was not absolute, but conditional only, and that the marriage, having been contracted between a man and woman of the respective ages of twenty-nine and twenty-two without attending to the formalities prescribed by the Code Napoléon, articles 151, 152, 153, and 154, might receive a different consideration from one absolutely prohibited by article 148 by parties respectively under those ages. The court, however, dealt with the case on the broad ground that by the decree of the French court, as evidenced by the law of France,[1] the marriage was void, and the question considered was whether the marriage was to be judged of here by the law of France or by the law of England. . . . That case is in accordance with the general views to be found expressed in the English decisions, and has met with approval in this court and in the House of Lords, or at least it may be said that where mentioned in those tribunals it has not been dissented from.

The case principally relied on by the appellant was the case of *Sottomayor* v. *De Barros*.[2] (His Lordship stated the facts in that case, read the passage beginning 'But it is a well-recognised principle of law' and ending 'wherever such marriage may have been solemnised',

OGDEN
v.
OGDEN.

Sir Gorell
Barnes P.

---

[1] *Sic* in the report : evidently a slip for 'by the law of France, as evidenced by the decree of the French court' (*Ed.*).

[2] (1877) 3 P.D. 1 ; *ante*, p. 74.

OGDEN
v.
OGDEN.

Sir Gorell
Barnes P.

ante, p. 75, and continued:) Now this court hearing this appeal is bound by the decision of the Court of Appeal in the case of *Sotto-mayor* v. *De Barros*. It is not necessary, even if we were at liberty to do so, to consider whether that case was rightly decided, but it is permissible to point out that the commencement of the paragraph above set out could scarcely be considered correct in stating that 'it is a well-recognised principle of law that the question of personal capacity to enter into any contract is to be decided by the law of domicile', for, if so, it would logically seem to follow that that part of the judgment which indicates that the opinion of the court was confined to cases where both the contracting parties were, at the time of their marriage, domiciled in a country, the laws of which prohibited their marriage, should not have expressed that limitation, and that the case of *Simonin* v. *Mallac* should have been overruled, and yet that case, according to our reading of the judgment, is approved. The probability is that that sentence should be read with the context and be confined to the case present to the minds of the court in relation to marriages which could not be contracted at all by the laws of the country of domicile. Even then it may be questioned whether that sentence is correct, and whether the question of capacity is really raised at all in such a case; that is to say, where both the parties are capable of entering into a marriage but may not marry each other because such a marriage would be illegal in their own country. That is rather a question of illegality than of capacity, and it may, perhaps, not be unreasonable for one country to refuse to recognise a marriage contracted in it between two persons by the laws of whose domicile a marriage between them is illegal, and yet it may be quite proper and reasonable for a country, in which a marriage takes place between persons domiciled in another country, to recognise it as a valid marriage when it would be legal in such other country if contracted after compliance with all formalities required in such other country, and, further, to protect its citizens in all cases of marriages where one of the contracting parties is domiciled in the country first referred to—that is to say, where the marriage takes place—and the other is domiciled in a foreign country, and there is a conflict between the laws of the two countries as to the validity of the marriage. The passage in the judgment expressly confining the decision to the case then before the court is as follows: (his Lordship read the passage beginning 'It was pressed upon us in argument' and ending 'not recognised by the law of this country', *ante*, p. 76,

and continued:) It was upon this passage that, when the case
subsequently came before Lord Hannen, he was able to decide in
favour of the marriage being valid notwithstanding the fact that one
of the parties was domiciled in Portugal.

The concluding passage in the judgment of the Court of Appeal is
as follows: (his Lordship read it). That may perhaps be considered
only a dictum by the learned Lords Justices, but it is really a very
strong statement that *Simonin* v. *Mallac* is clearly distinguishable
from the case before them, and we regard it as an approval of the
decision in that case, and, if so, it is an authority adverse to the contention of the appellant on the present appeal.

. . . After very careful consideration of the present case we have
come to the conclusion that the first point must be decided against
the appellant, and that the marriage between her and Léon Philip
must be declared valid in England.

(His Lordship proceeded (1) to hold that the French decree of
nullity was not entitled to recognition in England: but as to this, see
p. 207, *post*; (2) to suggest that the appellant's suit for divorce ought
not to have been dismissed for want of jurisdiction: but as to this,
see pp. 117–18, *post*.)

Appeal dismissed.

In re PAINE [1940] Ch. 46 (Chancery Division)

By her will dated in 1883 a testatrix gave £250 upon trust for her
daughter Ada Paine Toepfer for life and if she should leave any
child or children her surviving in trust for her absolutely, with a gift
over if she should not. The testatrix died in 1884.

In 1875 the testatrix's daughter married a domiciled German
named Franz Robert Toepfer of Frankfurt. That marriage was valid
by German law although the husband had previously married the
wife's sister, his first wife having died in 1872. The marriage was
void by English law.

Franz Toepfer and his second wife lived in England until their
respective deaths and had issue three children, of whom one only
survived her parents. Franz Toepfer died in 1919.

The trustee of the testatrix's will took out a summons for the
determination of the question whether the expression 'child or

children' included a child or children of the marriage of Ada Paine and Franz Toepfer.

BENNETT J. (after stating the facts, continued): I think that, on the evidence, I must hold that the husband never lost his domicile of origin, but it is plain that, at the time of the marriage, Mrs. Ada Paine Toepfer was a domiciled English woman. There were three children of the marriage, of whom one survived Ada Paine Toepfer, and the question to be determined is whether Ada Paine Toepfer had a child or children living at her decease, in which case the sum of £250 is to be held by the trustees of the testatrix's will for her absolutely, or whether she died without leaving any child or children her surviving, in which case the sum of £250 would devolve as under an intestacy.

The first question is whether the English law will regard the marriage between Ada Paine Toepfer and Franz Robert Toepfer as a valid marriage.

In my judgment, according to English law, the marriage was invalid, because by English law the lady had not the capacity to contract it. In my view that point is settled by the decision of Sir Cresswell Cresswell in *Mette* v. *Mette*.[1] That was a case in which the husband was domiciled in England and he was without the capacity to contract the marriage in question. The learned judge says in the course of his judgment: 'If Bernard Mette was incapacitated from contracting such a marriage, this latter distinction cannot have any effect. There could be no valid contract unless each was competent to contract with the other. The question rests upon the effect of domicile and naturalization.'

That statement of the law has been recognized by text book writers. In particular I refer to Dicey's Conflict of Laws[2] where the following statement appears: 'Rule 182. Subject to the exceptions hereinafter mentioned, a marriage is valid when (i) each of the parties has, according to the law of his or her respective domicile, the capacity to marry the other.'

In Westlake's Private International Law[3] this statement is to be found: 'A marriage is invalid . . . if either party is by his personal law under an incapacity to contract it, whether absolute, in respect of age, or relative, in respect of the prohibited degrees of consanguinity or affinity.'

---

[1] (1859) 1 Sw. & Tr. 416.   [2] (1931) 5th ed., p. 732.   [3] (1925) 7th ed., p. 57.

In Halsbury's Laws of England[1] it is stated: 'The marriage must be a good and legal marriage according to the law of the domicile of both contracting parties at the time of the marriage.'

In re
PAINE.
—
Bennett J.

On the authority of *Mette* v. *Mette*, supported as it seems to be by the text book writers, in view of the fact that the domicile of the lady was English, I come to the conclusion that her marriage, in the year 1875 to a domiciled German, at Frankfort on Main in Germany was invalid, because the husband had been the husband of the lady's deceased sister. The marriage was, therefore, a contract of marriage which, at that time, he was prohibited from making by English law.

It follows that the gift over takes effect. . . .

Note C: CAPACITY TO MARRY

THREE views have been suggested as to what law should govern capacity to marry.

(*a*) The law of the place of celebration. This was undoubtedly the rule of English law until *Brook* v. *Brook* (*ante*, p. 67), the earlier cases drawing no distinction between formality and capacity. The objection to it is that it provides insufficient safeguards against evasion of law. It is still apparently the prevailing rule in the United States (Goodrich, s. 113), but it is subject to exceptions so weighty (miscegenation, consanguinity, and lack of age) that in practice the American rule is not very different from the English.

(*b*) The law of the domicile of each party before the marriage. This is the orthodox English view.

(*c*) The law of the intended matrimonial home. This is Dr. Cheshire's view.

It is submitted that no unprejudiced person can read the English cases without concluding that, with two exceptions, they are consistent only with view (*b*). The authorities which Dr. Cheshire adduces in support of his view are (i) some inconclusive dicta of Lord Campbell in *Brook* v. *Brook* (*ante*, p. 67) which equally support view (*b*); (ii) an ex post facto rationalization of *Sottomayor* v. *De Barros* (*No. 2*) (*ante*, p. 77), which was certainly not the ratio of that case, and is inconsistent with the way that case was dealt with in *Chetti* v. *Chetti* [1909] P. 67; and (iii) a dictum of Lord Greene M.R. in *De Reneville* v. *De Reneville* [1948] P. 100 (*post*, p. 166), which was a case on jurisdiction and not on choice of law. Dr. Cheshire claims that his view is consistent with all the relevant decisions. It does not appear to be consistent with *Sottomayor* v. *De Barros* (*No. 1*) (*ante*, p. 74). The Queen's Proctor pleaded that since the parties intended to and did establish their matrimonial home in England, English law determined the validity of the marriage; but the Court of Appeal decided otherwise.

Under s. 1 of the Marriage (Enabling) Act 1960, marriages between a man and his deceased or divorced wife's sister or between a woman and her deceased or divorced husband's brother are now valid in English domestic

[1] 2nd ed., vol. 6, p. 286.

law. S. 1 (3) provides that the section does not validate a marriage if *either party* is at the time of the marriage domiciled in a country under whose law there cannot be a valid marriage between the parties. This is perhaps some indication that Parliament disapproved both of Dr. Cheshire's intended matrimonial home theory and of the anomalous decision in *Sottomayor* v. *De Barros (No. 2) (infra)*.

Capacity to marry includes the impediments of consanguinity, affinity, lack of age (*Pugh* v. *Pugh* [1951] P. 482), and possibly want of consent of parties (*Apt* v. *Apt, ante*, p. 62; *Way* v. *Way* [1950] P. 71, 78, 79; *H.* v. *H.* [1954] P. 258; see 3 I.C. L.Q. 454). If it also includes the impediment of bigamy (and there is high authority that it does, see *Shaw* v. *Gould* (1868) L.R. 3 H.L. 55 (*post*, p. 209), then we have a decision of the House of Lords which rejects view (*c*) in the clearest terms. In *Shaw* v. *Gould* a husband and wife were domiciled in England; the wife obtained a divorce in Scotland and went through a ceremony of marriage with a domiciled Scotsman; it was held that this second marriage was void because the divorce was void in England. Yet on view (*c*) the marriage should have been valid, because Scotland was the intended matrimonial home. Compare *Baindail* v. *Baindail* [1946] P. 122 (*post*, p. 95), where the second marriage was undoubtedly valid in India (the law of the matrimonial domicile), and yet it was held to be void. The question whether *De Reneville* v. *De Reneville* (*post*, p. 160) involves a modification of the orthodox view is discussed, *post*, p. 206.

The first exception referred to above is *Sottomayor* v. *De Barros (No. 2)* (*ante*, p. 77). Until that case is overruled it is necessary to make an exception to view (*b*), as to which, see Dicey, Rule 31 (2), Exception 3. Dr. Cheshire (p. 285) says that the necessity of formulating this exception 'makes nonsense of the dual domicile doctrine' (i.e. view (*b*)). This criticism seems unsound. The formulation of the exception is necessary because of a decision which ignored the doctrine of the dual domicile.

The second exception is *Ogden* v. *Ogden* (*ante*, p. 77). What was the ratio decidendi of that case? Was it (*a*) that capacity to marry is governed by the lex loci celebrationis? If so, how is the case to be reconciled with *Brook* v. *Brook* and *Sottomayor* v. *De Barros (No. 1)*? Was it (*b*) that a requirement of foreign law that a person cannot marry without the consent of his parents is a mere formality, no matter how stringently expressed, and therefore cannot invalidate a marriage celebrated in England? Was it (*c*) that a marriage celebrated in England between a person domiciled in England and a person domiciled abroad is not invalidated by any incapacity which, though existing under the foreign law, does not exist under English law? If so, the decision is on all fours with *Sottomayor* v. *De Barros (No. 2)*. Or was it (*d*) that capacity to marry is governed by the law of the intended matrimonial home, since the only home the parties ever had was in England? If so, one would expect Dr. Cheshire to approve the decision; yet at p. 50 he condemns it.

Poor Mrs. Ogden! It is easy to sympathize with her matrimonial misfortunes; and the decision has been described as 'grotesque from the social point of view' (Falconbridge, p. 74) because it left her married to a Frenchman who by French law was not only not her husband but was validly married to someone else, and with no means of escape from that position. There is no case in the English conflict of laws which has been subjected to more vigorous criticism. Yet the decision might not have seemed so grotesque if the Englishwoman, instead of remarrying, had sought maintenance from her French husband; or if the Frenchman had promised to marry her, and then sought to excuse himself on the ground that by French law he had no capacity to do so. There are obvious dangers in holding a marriage celebrated in England, and valid by English law, to be invalid under foreign law. There is no reported case which so decides. The nearest case is *Sottomayor* v. *De Barros (No. 1)*, where the Court of Appeal was prepared to treat the marriage as void, but stopped short of pronouncing a final decree.

Dr. Cheshire's theory that capacity to marry is governed by the law of the intended matrimonial home has (it is submitted) little to commend it on practical grounds. By making everything hinge on intention, it opens the door to evasion of law. It is not easy to see what is gained by substituting the imprecise word 'home' for 'domicile', which, however difficult it may sometimes be to ascertain, is at least a term of art. If the validity of the marriage is to remain in suspense while we wait and see (for an unspecified period) whether the parties have implemented their intention, serious administrative difficulties are likely to be encountered, especially where rights to property are involved. Moreover, Dr. Cheshire's theory seems to break down altogether if (as sometimes happens) the parties never establish a matrimonial home at all.

Has the lex loci celebrationis any effect on capacity to marry? It is believed that no marriage celebrated in England would be held valid by an English court if the parties were within the prohibited degree of English law or if either of them was under the age of sixteen, even if the marriage was valid by the law of their domicile. A more difficult question would be the validity of a marriage celebrated in a foreign country which the parties had capacity to contract by the law of their domicile, but not by the law of the place of celebration. The only reported English case which raises this question is *Breen* v. *Breen* [1964] P. 144, where Karminski J. was prepared to hold that the parties' incapacity to marry by the lex loci celebrationis was fatal to the validity of their marriage, even though this would have meant denying the validity of a decree of divorce pronounced by the High Court.

Section C: POLYGAMOUS MARRIAGES

Marriage is the voluntary union for life of one man and one woman to the exclusion of all others. The matrimonial machinery of the English court will not be applied to a marriage not within this definition.

HYDE *v.* HYDE (1866) L.R. 1 P. & M. 130 (Divorce Court)

HYDE
v.
HYDE.

This was a petition by a husband for a dissolution of marriage on the ground of adultery. There was no appearance by the respondent or the co-respondent.

The petitioner was an Englishman by birth, and in 1847, when he was about 16 years of age, he joined a congregation of Mormons in

London, and was soon afterwards ordained a priest of that faith. He made the acquaintance of the respondent, then Miss Hawkins, and her family, all of whom were Mormons, and they became engaged to each other. In 1850, Miss Hawkins and her mother went to the Salt Lake City, in the territory of Utah, in the United States; and in 1853 the petitioner, who had in the meantime been employed on a French mission, joined them at that place. The marriage took place at Salt Lake City in April 1853, and it was celebrated by Brigham Young, the president of the Mormon church, and the governor of the territory, according to the rites and ceremonies of the Mormons. They cohabited as man and wife at Salt Lake City until 1856, and had children. In 1856 the petitioner went on a mission to the Sandwich Islands, leaving the respondent in Utah. On his arrival at the Sandwich Islands, he renounced the Mormon faith and preached against it. A sentence of excommunication was pronounced against him in Utah in December 1856, and his wife was declared free to marry again. In 1857 a correspondence passed between the petitioner and his wife, who continued to live in Utah. In his letters he urged her to leave the Mormon territory, and abandon the Mormon faith, and to join him. In her letters she expressed the greatest affection for him, but refused to change her faith, or to follow him out of the Mormon territory. He did not return to Utah, and one of the witnesses was of opinion that he could not have done so after he had left the Mormon church without danger to his life. In 1857 he resumed his domicile in England, where he has ever since resided, and for several years he has been the minister of a dissenting chapel at Derby. In 1859 or 1860 the respondent contracted a marriage according to the Mormon form at Salt Lake City with the co-respondent, and she has since cohabited with him as his wife, and has had children by him.

At the time when the marriage between the petitioner and the respondent was celebrated, polygamy was a part of the Mormon doctrine, and was the common custom in Utah. The petitioner and the respondent were both single, and the petitioner had never taken a second wife. A counsellor of the Supreme Court of the United States proved that a marriage by Brigham Young in Utah, if valid in Utah, would be recognised as valid by the Supreme Court of the United States, provided that the parties were both unmarried at the time when it was contracted, and that they were both capable of contracting marriage. The Supreme Court, however, had no appellate jurisdiction over the courts of other States in matrimonial matters; and the matrimonial court of each State had exclusive jurisdiction within its own limits. Utah was a territory not within any State. There was a matrimonial court, having primary jurisdiction, in that territory, and the judge was nominated by the President of the United States, with the consent of the Senate. The judge was bound to recognize the laws which the people of Utah made for themselves, as long as they did not conflict with the laws of the United States. No evidence was given as to the law of that court respecting Mormon marriages.

THE JUDGE ORDINARY (Lord Penzance): The petitioner in this case claims a dissolution of his marriage on the ground of the adultery of his wife. Before the petitioner could obtain the relief he seeks, some matters would have to be made clear and others explained. The marriage, as it is called, would have to be established as binding by the lex loci, the divorce would have to be determined void, and the petitioner's conduct in wilfully separating himself from his wife would have to be accounted for. But I expressed at the hearing a strong doubt whether the union of man and woman as practised and adopted among the Mormons was really a marriage in the sense understood in this, the Matrimonial Court of England, and whether persons so united could be considered 'husband' and 'wife' in the sense in which these words must be interpreted in the Divorce Act. Further reflection has confirmed this doubt, and has satisfied me that this court cannot properly exercise any jurisdiction over such unions.

Marriage has been well said to be something more than a contract, either religious or civil—to be an institution. It creates mutual rights and obligations, as all contracts do, but beyond that it confers a status. The position or status of 'husband' and 'wife' is a recognised one throughout Christendom: the laws of all Christian nations throw about that status a variety of legal incidents during the lives of the parties, and induce definite rights upon their offspring. What, then, is the nature of this institution as understood in Christendom? Its incidents vary in different countries, but what are its essential elements and invariable features? If it be of common acceptance and existence, it must needs (however varied in different countries in its minor incidents) have some pervading identity and universal basis. I conceive that marriage, as understood in Christendom, may for

HYDE
v.
HYDE.
—
Lord
Penzance.

this purpose be defined as the voluntary union for life of one man and one woman, to the exclusion of all others.

There are no doubt countries peopled by a large section of the human race in which men and women do not live or cohabit together upon these terms—countries in which this institution and status are not known. In such parts the men take to themselves several women, whom they jealously guard from the rest of the world, and whose number is limited only by considerations of material means. But the status of these women in no way resembles that of the Christian 'wife'. In some parts they are slaves, in others perhaps not; in none do they stand, as in Christendom, upon the same level with the man under whose protection they live. There are, no doubt, in these countries laws adapted to this state of things —laws which regulate the duties and define the obligations of men and women standing to each other in these relations. It may be, and probably is, the case that the women there pass by some word or name which corresponds to our word 'wife'. But there is no magic in a name; and, if the relation there existing between men and women is not the relation which in Christendom we recognise and intend by the word 'husband' or 'wife', but another and altogether different relation, the use of a common term to express these two separate relations will not make them one and the same, though it may tend to confuse them to a superficial observer. . . .

Now, it is obvious that the matrimonial law of this country is adapted to the Christian marriage, and it is wholly inapplicable to polygamy. The matrimonial law is correspondent to the rights and obligations which the contract of marriage has, by the common understanding of the parties, created. Thus conjugal treatment may be enforced by a decree for restitution of conjugal rights. Adultery by either party gives a right to the other of judicial separation; that of the wife gives a right to a divorce; and that of the husband, if coupled with bigamy, is followed by the same penalty. Personal violence, open concubinage, or debauchery in face of the wife, her degradation in her home from social equality with the husband, and her displacement as the head of his household, are with us matrimonial offences, for they violate the vows of wedlock. A wife thus injured may claim a judicial separation and a permanent support from the husband under the name of alimony at the rate of about one-third of his income. If these and the like provisions and remedies were applied to polygamous unions, the court would be creating conjugal duties, not enforcing them, and furnishing remedies when there was no offence. For it would be quite unjust and almost absurd to visit a man who, among a polygamous community, had married two women, with divorce from the first woman, on the ground that, in our view of marriage, his conduct amounted to adultery coupled with bigamy. Nor would it be much more just or wise to attempt to enforce upon him that he should treat those with whom he had contracted marriages, in the polygamous sense of that term, with the consideration and according to the status which Christian marriage confers.

If, then, the provisions adapted to our matrimonial system are not applicable to such a union as the present, is there any other to which the court can resort? We have in England no law framed on the scale of polygamy, or adjusted to its requirements. And it may be well doubted whether it would become the tribunals of this country to enforce the duties (even if we knew them) which belong to a system so utterly at variance with the Christian conception of marriage, and so revolting to the ideas we entertain of the social position to be accorded to the weaker sex.

This is hardly denied in argument, but it is suggested that the matrimonial law of this country may be properly applied to the first of a series of polygamous unions; that this court will be justified in treating such first union as a Christian marriage, and all subsequent unions, if any, as void; the first woman taken to wife as a 'wife' in the sense intended by the Divorce Act, and all the rest as concubines. The inconsistencies that would flow from an attempt of this sort are startling enough. Under the provisions of the Divorce Act the duty of cohabitation is enforced on either party at the request of the other, in a suit for restitution of conjugal rights. But this duty is never enforced on one party if the other has committed adultery. A Mormon husband, therefore, who had married a second wife would be incapable of this remedy, and this court could in no way assist him towards procuring the society of his wife if she chose to withdraw from him. And yet, by the very terms of his marriage compact, this second marriage was a thing allowed to him, and no cause of complaint in her who had acquiesced in that compact. And as the power of enforcing the duties of marriage would thus be lost, so would the remedies for breach of marriage vows be unjust and unfit. For a prominent provision of the Divorce Act is that a woman whose husband commits adultery may obtain a judicial separation from

93

him. And so utterly at variance with Christian marriage is the notion of permitting the man to marry a second woman that the Divorce Act goes further, and declares that if the husband is guilty of bigamy as well as adultery, it shall be a ground of divorce to the wife. A Mormon, therefore, who had according to the laws of his sect, and in entire accordance with the contract and understanding made with the first woman, gone through the same ceremony with a second, might find himself in the predicament, under the application of English law, of having no wife at all; for the first woman might obtain divorce on the ground of his bigamy and adultery, and the second might claim a decree declaring the second ceremony void, as he had a wife living at the time of its celebration: and all this without any act done with which he would be expected to reproach himself, or of which either woman would have the slightest right to complain. These difficulties may be pursued further in the reflection that if a Morman had married fifty women in succession, this court might be obliged to pick out the fortieth as his only wife, and reject the rest. For it might well be that after the thirty-ninth marriage the first wife should die, and the fortieth union would then be the only valid one, the thirty-eight intervening ceremonies creating no matrimonial bond during the first wife's life.

Is the court, then, justified in thus departing from the compact made by the parties themselves? Offences necessarily presuppose duties. There are no conjugal duties, but those which are expressed or implied in the contract of marriage. And if the compact of a polygamous union does not carry with it those duties which it is the office of the marriage law in this country to assert and enforce, such unions are not within the reach of that law. So much for the reason of the thing.

In conformity with these views the court must reject the prayer of this petition, but I may take the occasion of here observing that this decision is confined to that object. This court does not profess to decide upon the rights of succession or legitimacy which it might be proper to accord to the issue of polygamous unions, nor upon the rights or obligations in relation to third persons which people living under the sanction of such unions may have created for themselves. All that is intended to be here decided is that as between each other they are not entitled to the remedies, the adjudication, or the relief of the matrimonial law of England.

Petition dismissed.

But a polygamous marriage will be recognized as valid in England for certain purposes. Thus it constitutes a bar to a subsequent monogamous marriage by one of the parties.

BAINDAIL v. BAINDAIL [1946] P. 122 (Court of Appeal)

In 1928 the respondent, a Hindu domiciled in India, married an Indian woman in India according to Hindu rites. This marriage was a polygamous marriage by the customs and laws of the Hindu race and was valid in India. In 1939, while his Indian wife was still living, the respondent went through a ceremony of marriage with the petitioner, an Englishwoman domiciled in England, at a registry office in London. In 1944 the petitioner, having discovered an invitation to the respondent's former Hindu marriage, presented a petition for nullity on the ground of bigamy. Barnard J. granted a decree. The respondent appealed.

LORD GREENE M.R.: The point raised by the appeal is a very short one. It was said that for the purposes of a claim to a decree of nullity the existence of the Hindu marriage must be disregarded by the courts of this country with the consequence that on May 5, 1939, the respondent was an unmarried man and was therefore not debarred by any existing union from marrying the petitioner. In support of that proposition a number of observations in decided cases have been cited. But it is to be observed that in no one of those cases was the question to which the court was addressing its observations in any way similar to the present question; it is not, in my opinion, legitimate to take those observations from their context and apply them to what is essentially a different question. I do not propose to go through all the cases cited to us but I will take what I think has been properly described as the high-water mark, the well-known decision of Lord Penzance in *Hyde* v. *Hyde*.[1] The headnote starts with this general proposition: 'Marriage as understood in Christendom is the voluntary union for life of one man and one woman, to the exclusion of all others.' But that, of course, does not enable any general answer to be given to the question: 'What is to be understood by "marriage" for the purpose of the various branches of English law in which the question of marriage is relevant?' For the purpose of enforcing the rights of marriage, or for the purpose of

BAINDAIL
v.
BAINDAIL.

[1] (1866) L.R. 1 P. & M. 130; *ante*, p. 89.

dissolving a marriage, it has always been accepted as the case, following Lord Penzance's decision, that the courts of this country exercising jurisdiction in matrimonial affairs do not and cannot give effect to, or dissolve, marriages which are not monogamous marriages. The word 'marriage' in the Matrimonial Causes Act, has to be construed for the purpose of ascertaining what the jurisdiction of the English courts is in these matters. The reasons are that the powers conferred on the courts for enforcing or dissolving a marriage tie are not adapted to any form of union between a man and a woman save a monogamous union. If a man by the law of his domicile is entitled to have four wives and then becomes domiciled in this country and wishes to be divorced here, nice questions would necessarily arise as to whether in consorting with the other wives he had been guilty of adultery and various questions of that kind. At any rate, rightly or wrongly, the courts have refused to regard a polygamous marriage as one which entitles the parties to come for matrimonial relief to the courts of this country. . . . Lord Penzance quite clearly saw how undesirable it would be to attempt to lay down any comprehensive rule as to the manner in which a polygamous marriage ought to be regarded by the courts of this country for purposes different from that with which he was immediately concerned. I do not feel myself bound by anything said in *Hyde* v. *Hyde* or any of the other cases on which reliance was placed in this connexion to hold that, for the purposes of the present petition, the court is bound, or ought, to disregard the existence of the Hindu marriage.

The problem, as it seems to me, requires to be approached de novo and from quite a different angle; that was the view which the learned judge took and, if I may respectfully say so, I entirely agree with the decision to which he came. The question as it presents itself to my mind is simply this: On May 5, 1939, when the respondent took the petitioner to the registry office, was he, or was he not, a married man so as to be incapable of entering into another legitimate union? The proposition I think would not be disputed that in general the status of a person depends on his personal law, which is the law of his domicile. By the law of the respondent's domicile at the time of his Hindu marriage he unquestionably acquired the status of a married man according to Hindu law; he was married for all the purposes of Hindu law, and he had imposed upon him the rights and obligations which that status confers under that law. That status he never lost.

Nothing that happened afterwards, save the dissolution of the marriage, if it be possible according to Hindu law, could deprive him of the status of a married man which he acquired under Hindu law at the time of his Hindu marriage; he was therefore a married man on May 5, 1939, according to Hindu law. Did that circumstance prevent him from entering into a valid marriage in this country? It is said that it did not because, whatever Hindu law may say and whatever his position may be in India, this country will not recognise the validity of the Hindu marriage. We are not considering in this case the question of construction of any words such as 'marriage', 'husband', 'wife', and so forth in the Divorce Acts. We are considering whether, according to what would have been the old ecclesiastical law, the existence of the Hindu marriage formed a bar. For the purpose of that consideration, what was his status on May 5, 1939? Unquestionably, as I have said, it was that of a married man. Will that status be recognised in this country? English law certainly does not refuse all recognition of that status. For many purposes, quite obviously, the status would have to be recognised. If a Hindu domiciled in India died intestate in England leaving personal property in this country, the succession to the personal property would be governed by the law of his domicile; and in applying the law of his domicile effect would have to be given to the rights of any children of the Hindu marriage and of his Hindu widow, and for that purpose the courts of this country would be bound to recognise the validity of a Hindu marriage so far as it bears on the title to personal property left by an intestate here; one can think of other cases.

Lord Maugham L.C., who delivered the leading opinion of the Committee of Privileges in *Lord Sinha's Case*[1] said this: 'On the other hand it cannot, I think, be doubted now, notwithstanding some earlier dicta by eminent judges, that a Hindu marriage between persons domiciled in India is recognised by our courts, that issue are regarded as legitimate and that such issue can succeed to property, with the possible exception to which I refer later'; that was the well-known exception of real estate. We have not been referred to the cases, if any, to which the learned Lord Chancellor was referring, and, in fact, I do not know of any English cases; there are cases no doubt in the Privy Council, but whether there are any purely English cases I do not know. But I do get assistance from that paragraph, quite apart from the question of authorities, as showing the way in

[1] (1939) 171 Lords' Journals 350; [1946] 1 All E.R. 348, n.

which these problems were striking a great master of the law, and one particularly familiar with problems of private international law. If he was not asserting that the law had been settled by decisions of the English courts, he was at least expressing his own opinion and to that I would pay the greatest respect. But quite apart from that, it seems to me that the matter rests in this way: the courts of this country do for some purposes give effect to the law of the domicile as affixing or imposing a particular status on a given person. It would be wrong to say that for all purposes the law of the domicile is necessarily conclusive as to capacity arising from status. There are some things which the courts of this country will not allow a person in this country to do whatever status with its consequential capacity or incapacity the law of his domicile may give him. The case of slavery, of course, is an obvious case. The status of slavery would not be recognised here, and a variety of other things involved in status will not be recognised here. In the case of infants where different countries have different laws, it certainly is the view of high authority here that capacity to enter in England into an ordinary commercial contract is determined not by the law of the domicile but by the lex loci. I refer to the illustrations in order to show that there cannot be any hard and fast rule relating to the application of the law of the domicile as determining status and capacity for the purpose of transactions in this country.

The practical question in this case appears to be: Will the courts of this country, in deciding upon the validity of this English marriage, give effect to the status possessed by the respondent? That question we have to decide with due regard to common sense and some attention to reasonable policy. We are not fettered by any concluded decision on the matter. The learned judge set out in a striking manner some of the consequences which would flow from disregarding the Hindu marriage for present purposes. I think it is certainly a matter to bear in mind that the prospect of an English court saying that it will not regard the status of marriage conferred by a Hindu ceremony would be a curious one when very little more than a mile away the Privy Council might be sitting and coming to a precisely opposite conclusion as to the validity of such a marriage on an Indian appeal. I do not think we can disregard that circumstance. We have to apply the law in a state of affairs in which this question of the validity of Hindu marriages is necessarily of very great practical importance in the everyday running of our Commonwealth and Empire.

If the marriage with the petitioner was a valid marriage it would have this consequence: that she is entitled to the consortium of her husband to the exclusion of any other woman, that he is entitled to the consortium of his wife, and that she is bound according to our notions of law to live with him provided he gives her a suitable home. If he decided to go back to India it would be her duty as a wife to follow him to the home that he would provide. Assume that this takes place. Directly they land in India by the law of India he is a man married to the Indian lady, and assuming as I think we are bound to assume that Hindu law would be the same in this respect as English law, that Hindu lady is his lawful wife in India and as such would be entitled to his consortium, he would be entitled to insist that she should live with him and she would be entitled to insist that he should provide a home for her. The position therefore would be that this English lady would find herself compelled in India either to leave her husband or to share him with his Indian wife. What the position would be with regard to divorce in India I do not know, but if he had an Indian domicile she apparently could not divorce him in England.[1] Whether or not she could divorce him in India because in India he was associating with a woman who under Indian law was his lawful wife I do not know and I do not stop to inquire. Is it right that the courts of this country should give effect to a ceremony of marriage, the result of which would be to put the petitioner into such a position? It seems to me that effect must be given to common sense and decency and that on a question which is not covered by authority considerations of that kind must carry very great weight. On principle it seems to me that the courts are for this purpose bound to recognise the Indian marriage as a valid marriage and an effective bar to any subsequent marriage in this country.

Those are the short grounds on which I think this appeal should be decided. If we have not thought it necessary to reserve judgment in order to study more fully the cases which have been cited it is not that we have failed to appreciate them, but because at any rate so far as I am concerned I do not find it necessary to examine them very closely. The opinion which I have formed relates and relates solely to the facts of the present case which are connected with the validity of the English marriage in the circumstances of this case. I must not be taken as suggesting that for every purpose and in every context

BAINDAIL
v.
BAINDAIL.

Lord
Greene
M.R.

[1] See now Matrimonial Causes Act 1965 s. 40 (1) (*b*), *post*, p. 116 (*Ed.*).

BAINDAIL
v.
BAINDAIL.

Lord
Greene
M.R.

an Indian marriage such as this would be regarded as a valid marriage in this country. Mr. Pritt in his reply drew an alarming picture of the effect of our decision on the law of bigamy if we were to decide against him. I think it right therefore to say that so far as I am concerned nothing that I have said must be taken as having the slightest bearing on the law of bigamy. On the question of whether a person is 'married' within the meaning of the statute (which is a criminal statute) when he has entered into a Hindu marriage in India I am not going to express any opinion whatever. It seems to me a different question in which other considerations may well come into play. I hope sincerely that nobody will endeavour to spell out of what I have said anything to cover such a question.

MORTON and BUCKNILL L.JJ. concurred.

Appeal dismissed.

A potentially polygamous marriage may become monogamous by reason of a change of religion, of domicile, or of law.

ALI
v.
ALI.

Cumming-
Bruce J.

ALI *v.* ALI [1966] 2 W.L.R. 620
(Probate Divorce and Admiralty Division)

Cross-petitions for **divorce.**

The parties were Mohammedans domiciled in India when they married there in 1958. The marriage was potentially polygamous by Mohammedan law. By the middle of 1961 the husband acquired a domicile of choice in England. In 1963 the husband petitioned for divorce on the ground of the wife's desertion since 1959. The wife cross-petitioned for divorce on the ground of the husband's cruelty before 1961 and of his adultery since that date.

CUMMING-BRUCE J. (having stated the facts and contentions of the parties): I now state the problems which in my opinion successively call for determination in connection with the effect of acquisition of domicile of choice upon a potentially polygamous marriage:

(1) What are the legal characteristics of the type of marriage over which the matrimonial courts exercise jurisdiction to pronounce a decree of divorce? The answer is accurately stated in Rule 38 of

Dicey's Conflict of Laws.[1] 'The matrimonial jurisdiction of the court is confined to marriages which are "the voluntary union for life of one man and one woman to the exclusion of all others"'. In *Brinkley* v. *Attorney-General*[2] Sir James Hannen, the President, considered the judgment of Lord Penzance in *Hyde* v. *Hyde*[3] and stated that the term 'Christian marriage' is used in matrimonial causes simply as a term of convenience to describe the concept of a voluntary union of the character described in Dicey's Rule. See also Lord Greene M.R. in *Baindail* v. *Baindail*.[4]

(2) If a marriage is at its inception potentially polygamous, can it subsequently be impressed with a monogamous character so as to found the jurisdiction of this court? Clearly the answer is affirmative: see *Cheni* v. *Cheni*.[5]

(3) Does acquisition of English domicile preclude this husband from marrying a second wife while his first wife is alive? . . . While he is thus domiciled and intends so to reside, he, being the husband of the respondent wife, cannot by marriage confer the status of wife upon any other woman. He has, by operation of the personal law which he has made his own, precluded himself from polygamous marriage to a second wife, although he has not changed his religion. If he purported to marry a second wife in England, or on a second temporary visit to India for that purpose, that marriage would not be recognised by English law as valid for any purpose whatsoever. This is because English law recognises the validity of his potentially polygamous marriage to the wife and denies him as a domiciled Englishman intending to reside in England the capacity to confer the status of wife on anyone else.

(4) Does the prohibition of his present personal law which prevents him taking the second, third or fourth wife previously permitted by his former personal law have the effect of impressing a monogamous character upon his potentially polygamous marriage with the wife? There is no authority upon this point and I express my opinion with diffidence. In *Cheni* v. *Cheni*, Sir Jocelyn Simon P. was considering the case of Sephardic Jews. The facts are sufficiently set out in the headnote to the report. He held that the potentially polygamous marriage had been converted by the birth of a child and the operation of Sephardic Jewish law into a monogamous marriage before the inception of the proceedings. The President

ALI
v.
ALI.

Cumming-
Bruce J.

---

[1] 7th ed. (1958), p. 288.   [2] (1890) 15 P.D. 76.
[3] (1866) L.R. 1 P. & M. 130; *ante*, p. 89.   [4] [1946] P. 122, 125; *ante*, p. 95.
[5] [1965] P. 85.

ALI
v.
ALI.

Cumming-
Bruce J.

said: 'Two spouses may contract a valid polygamous union and subsequently join a monogamous sect, or go through a second ceremony in a place where monogamy is the law. Again, a marriage in its inception potentially polygamous though in fact monogamous may be rendered monogamous for all time by legislative action proscribing polygamy: this, according to the evidence, has in fact happened in the State of Israel in relation to marriages of Sephardic Jews who are her nationals. Will the English court regard such marriages as monogamous or potentially polygamous for the purposes of exercising jurisdiction?' In his discussion of the decision of *Mehta* v. *Mehta*[1] he said, dealing with the circumstances in which monogamous marriages may change their character and become potentially polygamous: 'After all, there are no marriages which are not potentially polygamous, in the sense that they be rendered so by a change of domicile and religion on the part of the spouses. But, particularly in these days of widespread interpenetration of societies in different stages of development, it is not a reasonable presumption that spouses who marry polygamously will not by personal volition or act of state convert their marriages or have them converted into monogamous unions. An alternative way of putting the matter which commends itself to me is that of the editor of Dicey's Conflict of Laws,[2] that the marriage has, so to speak, the benefit of the doubt so far as jurisdiction is concerned, so that it is sufficient that it is either monogamous in its inception, or has become so by the time of the proceedings.' Part of this passage was cited with apparent approval in the advice of the Privy Council in *Attorney-General of Ceylon* v. *Reid*.[3]

Another example of conversion can be found in *Ohochuku* v. *Ohochuku*,[4] where the parties to a Nigerian potentially polygamous marriage were subsequently married in an English registry office. As by English law the parties were validly married, I find it a little difficult to see how the registrar succeeded in marrying them again. But the significance of the case is that it was recognised by Wrangham J. as a valid case of conversion of a potentially polygamous marriage into a monogamous marriage.

The chief difficulty I have felt is to determine whether the prohibition upon further marriage flowing from change of domicile does more than frustrate one of the features of the potentially poly-

---

[1] [1945] 2 All E.R. 690. [2] 7th ed. (1958), p. 272.
[3] [1965] A.C. 720. [4] [1960] 1 W.L.R. 183.

gamous union. There has indeed been no active assertion of monogamous intent. Indeed, on my finding of fact, the change of personal
law occurred after cohabitation ended and the husband made no
attempt to restore it. There is no reason to suppose that his acquisition of English domicile was intended to have any positive effect
upon the nature of the union, unless one element which played a
part (as to which there is no evidence) was to enable him to invoke
the jurisdiction of this court. It is clear that personal intention is
irrelevant to the legal consequences of a validly celebrated marriage,
but it seems at the very least curious that a union originally polygamous should change its legal character without any conscious act
on the part of either of the parties immediately directed to that end.
In my opinion, however, this anomaly is no more strange than many
other consequences of the English law which makes domicile the
test of personal law in matters of status. The husband in this case
carried into effect his intention of making England his country
of domicile. Thereby he subjected himself to monogamy as a
rule of his personal law and in my view this was as effective to
convert a potentially polygamous marriage to a monogamous marriage as specific legislation (having the same intendment) would
have been.

(5) If this view is right, why did not Lord Penzance adopt it in the
well-known case of *Hyde* v. *Hyde*? As far as I can tell from the facts,
the husband in the Mormon union was domiciled in England before the date of the wife's second marriage of which he complained
as an act of adultery. If it be the case that by taking up English
domicile his marriage was impressed with a monogamous character
by operation of law, the same effect in the eyes of English law
would be impressed upon the marriage of his wife. But Lord
Penzance rejected jurisdiction on the grounds that it was still a
potentially polygamous marriage. The answer to that problem is, I
think, rightly given by [counsel for the husband]. In 1866 the importance of domicile as affecting capacity to marry was still only
dimly appreciated and it has been during the succeeding century
that jurisprudence has developed the doctrine to the full degree
which it has now attained in English law. The point argued by
[counsel for the husband] was never argued before the judge
ordinary and in the circumstances, in spite of the great authority
which attaches to Lord Penzance's judgments, I take the view that
his silence and the fact that he decided that case differently from

ALI
v.
ALI.

Cumming-
Bruce J.

ALI
v.
ALI.

Cumming-
Bruce J.

the way in which it would have been decided had the rule of law that I have affirmed been applied, does not too much dismay me.

A similar problem arises in connection with the judgment of Lord Walker in the Scottish case of *Muhammad* v. *Suna.*[1] After considering *Hyde* v. *Hyde* and other authorities, Lord Walker used these words at the end of his judgment: 'It is perhaps not altogether satisfactory that a man who ventures into a polygamous union while domiciled abroad should, on acquiring a domicile in this country, be unable to sue in the court of his domicile for divorce (*Hyde*'s case) and yet be regarded by the court of his domicile as not free to marry (*Baindail*'s case). On the whole matter, however, I think that, illogical as the law may be in that respect, I must follow what guidance I can obtain from authority, which seems to me to point in no uncertain voice to the conclusion that in Scotland as well as in England the divorce court has no power to dissolve a polygamous union. I shall accordingly refuse a decree of divorce.' Two observations may be made upon that judgment. The first is the same observation as I have made in connection with Lord Penzance's judgment in *Hyde* v. *Hyde*, that the point argued before this court was never taken. The second point is that in *Muhammad* v. *Suna* the adultery complained of took place before the date of change of domicile, so that at the time of that alleged matrimonial offence the marriage was still a potentially polygamous union over which the court could exercise no jurisdiction.

(His Lordship proceeded to hold that he had no jurisdiction to pronounce a decree of divorce in respect of matrimonial offences which occurred before the marriage became monogamous in 1961.)

Decree nisi of divorce to wife in respect of husband's adultery since 1961.

NOTE D: POLYGAMOUS MARRIAGES

EVER since 1866 it has been settled that the matrimonial machinery of the English courts may not be applied to a polygamous marriage, even if it is only potentially polygamous. This applies (inter alia) to divorce (*Hyde* v. *Hyde, ante,* p. 89); nullity (*Risk* v. *Risk* [1950] P. 50); and applications for maintenance (*Sowa* v. *Sowa* [1961] P. 70). On the other hand, it has been clear since 1946 that such a marriage, if celebrated in a country where polygamy is permitted between persons there domiciled, may produce some of the usual consequences of marriage. For instance, it will be a bar to a subsequent monogamous marriage in England (*Baindail* v. *Baindail, ante,* p. 95);

[1] 1956 S.C. 366.

MARRIAGE

the children may be legitimate (*The Sinha Peerage Claim* [1946] 1 All E.R. 348, n.; *Bamgbose* v. *Daniel* [1955] A.C. 107); and the surviving spouse or spouses may be able to succeed to property on the husband's death intestate (*Coleman* v. *Shang* [1961] A.C. 481). The wife of a potentially polygamous marriage has been allowed to assert a contractual claim against the husband for 'deferred dower' under a marriage contract governed by Mohammedan law (*Shahnaz* v. *Rizwan* [1965] 1 Q.B. 390). On the other hand, a polygamous marriage is not a sufficient first marriage to support an indictment for bigamy (*R.* v. *Sarwan Singh* [1962] 3 All E.R. 612). Apart from the above matters, there is very little English authority as to how far our courts are prepared to recognize polygamous marriages as valid. But it is possible that English courts will do so for all purposes except (1) the application of the matrimonial machinery of the English courts; (2) the application of the criminal law of bigamy; (3) the capacity of the issue to succeed as heirs to real estate in England or to English peerages.

S. 113 (1) of the National Insurance Act 1965, s. 86 (5) of the National Insurance (Industrial Injuries) Act 1965, and s. 17 (9) of the Family Allowances Act 1965 (re-enacting s. 3 of the Family Allowances and National Insurance Act 1956) provide that a marriage performed outside the United Kingdom under a law which permits polygamy shall be treated as a valid marriage for any purpose of those Acts if the marriage has in fact at all times been monogamous.

To come within Lord Penzance's definition in *Hyde* v. *Hyde*, the marriage need not necessarily be a Christian marriage (*Brinkley* v. *A.-G.* (1890) 15 P.D. 76; *Penhas* v. *Tan Soo Eng* [1953] A.C. 304), and it is immaterial that it may be dissolved by mutual consent under the law of the parties' domicile (*Nachimson* v. *Nachimson* [1930] P. 217). On the other hand, if the husband's personal law does not permit him to take more than one wife, but does permit him to take concubines, the marriage is polygamous, at least if concubinage is a status recognized by that law (*Lee* v. *Lau* [1967] P. 14).

What law determines whether the marriage is monogamous or polygamous? Although this question has never been discussed by English judges, it seems that the only possible conclusion from the cases is that the matter is determined by the lex loci celebrationis and not by the law of the domicile. Thus, if a Mohammedan marries here in English form, his marriage is monogamous: *Chetti* v. *Chetti* [1909] P. 67; *R.* v. *Hammersmith Registrar* [1917] 1 K.B. 634; *Srini Vasan* v. *Srini Vasan* [1946] P. 67; *Baindail* v. *Baindail*, ante, p. 95; *Maher* v. *Maher* [1951] P. 342; *Ohochuku* v. *Ohochuku* [1960] 1 W.L.R. 183; *Russ* v. *Russ* [1964] P. 315, post, p. 145. Conversely, if a domiciled Englishman marries abroad according to polygamous rites, his marriage is polygamous: *Hyde* v. *Hyde*; *Re Bethell* (1887) 38 Ch. D. 220; *Risk* v. *Risk* [1950] P. 50. The potentially polygamous character of the marriage is the decisive factor, not the intention of the parties. If the lex loci celebrationis permits the husband to take more than one wife, the marriage is polygamous even if he does not do so and swears that he never meant to (*Hyde* v. *Hyde*), or even if he swears on the Bible that he will convert the potentially polygamous marriage into a monogamous one (*Sowa* v. *Sowa*).

Dr. Cheshire (pp. 266–70) contends that the law of the matrimonial domicile, and not the lex loci celebrationis, should determine whether a marriage is monogamous or polygamous. But this would mean that an English-

FAMILY LAW

woman who married a Mohammedan in England according to English formalities could obtain no matrimonial relief of any kind from English courts. As it is, she can obtain a decree for divorce (*Maher* v. *Maher*), nullity (*Baindail* v. *Baindail*), or judicial separation and maintenance (*Chetti* v. *Chetti*).

There is now clear authority for the proposition that a man or woman domiciled in England, or presumably in some other country where polygamy is forbidden, has no capacity to contract a polygamous marriage (*Ali* v. *Ali, ante*, p. 100). Although the matter is less clear, it seems that a marriage celebrated in England in accordance with polygamous forms and without civil ceremony as required by English law is invalid, whatever the domicile or religion of the parties may be.

A marriage which is monogamous in its inception is treated as a monogamous marriage, even though the husband could, by changing his religion without changing his domicile, have lawfully married another wife—at any rate if he does not do so (*Mehta* v. *Mehta* [1945] 2 All E.R. 690). On the other hand, a marriage which is potentially polygamous in its inception may become monogamous by reason of events occurring before proceedings are begun in England. This may happen, for instance, if the parties (being domiciled in an eastern country where the personal law is a religious law) change their religion from one which permits polygamy to one which does not (*The Sinha Peerage Claim*); if they change their domicile from a polygamous to a monogamous country (*Ali* v. *Ali, ante*, p. 100); if the law governing the marriage subsequently prohibits polygamy (*Parkasho* v. *Singh* [1967] 2 W.L.R. 946); or, under some systems of law, if a child is born (*Cheni* v. *Cheni* [1965] P. 85).

Until recently the rule in *Hyde* v. *Hyde* which denies matrimonial relief to either party to even a potentially polygamous marriage did not work as much hardship as might have been expected, largely because English judges mercifully held that a marriage celebrated in monogamous form in England is not a polygamous marriage within the rule, even though the personal law of one or both parties permits polygamy. Thus, an Englishwoman 'married' to a man whose personal law permits polygamy is denied matrimonial relief only if the ceremony of marriage was a polygamous form of ceremony, e.g. if it took place in the country of his domicile, or in a private house in England. But the situation has been transformed in the last fifteen years by the enormous influx of coloured immigrants into this country, many of whom come from countries where the law permits polygamy, and do not acquire an English domicile. To deny English matrimonial relief of any kind to such people seems a grave denial of justice; and it is submitted that the rule in *Hyde* v. *Hyde* is overdue for reconsideration by Parliament, possibly along the lines suggested by the National Insurance Act 1965, the National Insurance (Industrial Injuries) Act 1965, and the Family Allowances Act 1965 (see above). So far as maintenance is concerned, it is arguable that the English courts ought to be available even if the marriage is actually polygamous. A man who can afford to bring several wives to this country ought not to be allowed to leave them as a charge on public assistance.

Chapter 7

MATRIMONIAL CAUSES

Section A: DIVORCE

The English court has jurisdiction to pronounce a decree of divorce (apart from statute) only if the parties are domiciled in England at the time of the commencement of the proceedings.

NIBOYET *v.* NIBOYET (1878) 4 P.D. 1 (Court of Appeal)

BRETT L.J.: In this case the wife filed a petition praying for a dissolution of her marriage on the ground of alleged adultery and desertion by her husband. The petition in form prayed for a dissolution of the marriage. It contained also in the usual general terms an alternative prayer 'for such other and further relief in the premises as to the court may seem meet'. The material facts stated in the different pleadings, as the facts on which the parties relied, were that the parties in 1856 married at Gibraltar according to English form, that the wife was English by birth, the husband French by birth, that the husband had from 1862 to 1869 acted as French vice-consul at Sunderland, and from 1875 to 1876 and until he was cited to appear in this suit, as French consul at Newcastle. The adultery was committed in England. The wife was resident in England. The petition was served in England. The husband was residing in England. But the husband had never been domiciled in England. The husband appeared under protest and pleaded to the jurisdiction. No one appeared for the husband at the hearing, but the Queen's Proctor, by direction of the court, intervened and submitted for argument two propositions or questions: (1) Whether, it being admitted by the petitioner that the respondent has a French domicile, this court has any jurisdiction as a matter of general law? (2) If it has not jurisdiction as a matter of general law, whether the particular circumstances of this case give it jurisdiction? The arguments preferred in support of the appeal and in favour of the jurisdiction were: First, that the husband though not completely domiciled in England was bonâ fide and more than casually resident in England, and that such

107

residence made him liable to the jurisdiction of any court exercising jurisdiction in matrimonial causes in England; secondly, that his mere presence in England when charged with a matrimonial offence gave jurisdiction to the English court; thirdly, that the mere application to an English court of a person claiming its decree against another for an alleged matrimonial offence gives jurisdiction to the court. It was argued from these propositions that the mere fact of the statute constituting a court with power to grant divorce gave the court jurisdiction to entertain the prayer for divorce as against this respondent, if the case could be brought within any of these propositions. But it was further argued, fourthly, that upon the true construction of the terms of the statute it in terms enacts jurisdiction over all persons, English or foreign, and that an English court must obey the statute. The decision must in the end depend upon the construction of the statute, because before it no court in England had jurisdiction to grant divorce; but as preliminary to the decision it seems desirable to consider the matter according to some general principles. As has been frequently pointed out, a decree of dissolution of marriage cannot be the judicial declaration of a mere consequence agreed between the parties for the breach of a contract, as in ordinary cases of breach of contract, or a mere compensation or individual remedy for the breach of a private duty as in an action for damages, but can only be a judicial sentence of the law of the country in and for which the court is acting, by which such court assumes to alter not only the relation between the parties but the status of both. Marriage is the fulfilment of a contract satisfied by the solemnisation of the marriage, but marriage directly it exists creates by law a relation between the parties and what is called a status of each. The status of an individual, used as a legal term, means the legal position of the individual in or with regard to the rest of a community. That relation between the parties, and that status of each of them with regard to the community, which are constituted upon marriage are not imposed or defined by contract or agreement but by law. The limitations or conditions or effects of such relation and status are different in different countries. As that relation and status are imposed by law, the only law which can impose or define such a relation or status (i.e. relative position) so as to bind an individual, is the law to which such individual is subject. The power of a law which enacts restrictions on or grants relaxation of the personal condition of individuals is territorial, i.e. limited.

The meaning of that is, that it is only binding on the natural born subjects of the lawgiver or on those who have otherwise become his subjects. By the universal comity of nations foreigners do not by their mere sojourn in a country make themselves subject to its personal laws, other than its police or correctional law, or laws expressly enacted to bind all who are in fact within its territorial limits. By the universal independence of nations each binds by its personal laws its natural born subjects and all who may become its subjects. By the universal consent of nations every one who elects to become domiciled in a country is bound by the laws of that country, so long as he remains domiciled in it, as if he were a natural born subject of it. It follows then from the nature of the subject-matter, that laws which, for certain enacted or predicated causes, as distinguished from causes agreed upon between the parties, alter the personal relations of individuals to each other, or their relation to the community, can only bind the natural born subjects of the enacting country or foreigners who have become domiciled in it; but they may, consistently with principle and the universal consent of nations, bind both of these. The law then which enables a court to decree an alteration in the relation between husband and wife, or an alteration in the status of husband or wife as such, is as matter of principle the law of the country to which by birth or domicile they owe obedience. The only court which can decree by virtue of such law is a court of that country. Another mode of considering the subject, or another line of argument is this. A judgment or decree determining what is the status of an individual is a judgment or decree in rem. It is, therefore, if binding at all, not only a binding judgment as between the parties to the suit, but is to be recognised as binding in all suits and by all parties. Such a judgment, where the jurisdiction of the court which made it is recognised, is treated as binding and final, not only by all the courts of the same country but by the courts of all countries. The jurisdiction of the courts of a country in which people have elected to be and are in fact domiciled is in all countries admitted, and the judgment or decree in rem of the courts of a country in which people are domiciled is therefore treated as binding in all countries. But the jurisdiction of a country exercised, whether by legislation or by its courts, over the personal status of the subjects of another country who are merely present in it, or are merely sojourning in it, or are merely cited to it, is not admitted by the country of which such people are subjects or by other foreign

NIBOYET
v.
NIBOYET.

Brett L.J

countries. If, therefore, the courts of any country should assume, by a decree of divorce or any other decree determining the relation or the status of a married person, to alter that relation or status of a foreigner not domiciled, the decree would not be recognised as binding by the courts of any other country. Then the relation or status of a married person would be one in the country of the court making the decree, and another in all other countries. That is to say, a man or woman would be treated as married in one country and not so in another; or married people might be enjoined to live together in one country and to live apart in another. No court ought to assume or presume to place people in so deplorable a position, unless forced to do so by the express law of the country whose law it is administering. Another general consideration seems to be as follows. The status of marriage is the legal position of the married person as such in the community or in relation to the community. Which community is it which is interested in such relation? None other than the community of which he is a member, that is the community with which he is living as a part of it. But that in fact is the community in which he is living so as to be one of the families of it. That is the community in which he is living at home with intent that among or in it should be the home of his married life. But that is the place of his domicile. It follows that upon principle the only law which should assume to alter his status as a married man is the law of the country of his domicile; the only court which should assume to decree such alteration is a court administering the law of that country. The country or society of his birth is not interested in his marriage status so long as he is domiciled elsewhere.

From all these considerations it seems that the only court which on principle ought to entertain the question of altering the relation in any respect between parties admitted to be married, or the status of either of such parties arising from their being married, on account of some act which by law is treated as a matrimonial offence, is a court of the country in which they are domiciled at the time of the institution of the suit. If this be a correct proposition, it follows that the court must be a court of the country in which the husband is at the time domiciled; because it is incontestable that the domicile of the wife, so long as she is a wife, is the domicile which her husband selects for himself, and at the commencement of the suit she is ex hypothesi—still a wife. The case of an adulterous husband deserting his wife by leaving the country of his domicile and assuming to

domicile himself in another, might seem to raise an intolerable injustice; but we cannot help thinking that in such case, if sued by his
wife in the country in which he had left her, he could not be heard to
allege that that was not still the place of his married home, i.e., for
the purpose of that suit, of his domicile.[1] So much for the principle,
if there were no authorities. It is very right, however, to consider the
decisions of the courts of other countries, and very necessary to consider the decisions of the courts of our own country; the decisions in
our own country before the statute being, it should be observed,
necessarily decisions as to the extent to which English courts, or the
English legislature acting as if judicially, recognised the decisions of
foreign courts. Now the American authorities seem clear, and they
are of great importance, because the American courts have been
called upon oftener than any others to consider and deal with the
subject. . . . In America the only court which can decree any alteration in the relations between married people or in the status of either
of them as a married person, is the court of the country in which they
are domiciled at the time of the institution of the suit. It is equally
clear that the decisions in Scotland are to the contrary. The Scotch
courts will entertain a suit for divorce, and decree a divorce at the
instance of either party who has been resident for a certain period in
Scotland, though neither party is Scotch and neither is domiciled in
Scotland. This view of the courts of Scotland was, however, distinctly denied to be the law of England in *Rex* v. *Lolley*.[2] Lolley and
his wife were both English; the husband was domiciled in England;
the marriage was in England; the husband committed adultery in
England and Scotland; the wife instituted a suit against him in Scotland for a divorce; the Scotch court decreed a divorce; Lolley afterwards, and during the lifetime of the lady who had procured this
decree, married another woman in England. He was tried in England
for bigamy, and was convicted. The case was argued before all the
judges, and the conviction was confirmed, because they held that
the Scotch court had no jurisdiction recognised in England to grant
the first divorce, which was therefore to be treated in England as
null and void. This decision was treated by Lord Brougham in
McCarthy v. *De Caix*[3] as a decision that no sentence of a foreign
court can annul a marriage made in England. But it has since been
shewn that it only amounts to a decision that the Scotch court had,

NIBOYET
v.
NIBOYET.

Brett L.J.

[1] As to this, see Note E, *post*, p. 117.   [2] (1812) 2 Cl. & F. 567, n.
[3] (1831) 2 Cl. & F. 568, n.

in the view of the English law, no jurisdiction where the parties were not domiciled in Scotland, though they were for a time resident there. The elaborate judgment of Lord Brougham in *Warrender* v. *Warrender*[1] is a long criticism to shew that this was all that was necessary to be decided in *Lolley's Case*, that if it decided more it was wrong, and that the true and only condition of jurisdiction was domicile. In the case itself, Sir G. Warrender was married in England; the adultery charged against his wife was abroad; the husband was domiciled in Scotland at the institution of the suit; the wife was not in Scotland; it was held by the House of Lords that the Scotch court had jurisdiction, on account of the domicile of the husband and because the domicile of the husband was the domicile of the wife. . . .

On the grounds, then, of the nature of the subject-matter of the suit, of the nature of the judgment given in such suit, of the interest of the country in which the dispute arises, of the comity due to other nations, of the immense mischief of a judgment of such a nature being given under circumstances which will prevent it from being recognised everywhere, and of the preponderance of authority in England, I am of opinion that, unless the statute has otherwise enacted, the domicile of the husband in England at the institution of the suit is, according to the true construction of the statute, the fact which gives jurisdiction to the English Divorce Court to decree divorce; that with such a domicile the Court has jurisdiction over a foreigner as well as over an English subject; that without such domicile the court has no jurisdiction, though the party is an English subject. The same rule, I confess, seems to me to apply, for the same reason, to its power to grant any relief which alters in any way that relation between the parties which arises by law from their marriage. It applies, therefore, as it seems to me, to suits for judicial separation and to suits for the restitution of conjugal rights.[2] I do not think it does apply to suits for a declaration of nullity of marriage or in respect of jactitation of marriage.[3] I do not think that the statute binds the court to entertain and exercise a jurisdiction in

---

[1] (1835) 2 Cl. & F. 488.

[2] The English court has jurisdiction to grant decrees of restitution of conjugal rights or judicial separation on the basis of residence as well as on the basis of domicile: *Thornton* v. *Thornton* (1886), 11 P.D. 176; *Armytage* v. *Armytage* [1898] P. 178.

[3] This statement so far as it relates to nullity was disapproved by Lord Haldane in *Von Lorang* v. *Administrator of Austrian Property* [1927] A.C. 641, 654 (*post*, p. 188).

matters over which, according to the comity of nations, as inter-preted by English judges, and acted upon by the English Parliament
in its quasi judicial legislation, the English law ought not to assume
authority. It is true that the words of the statute are general; but
general words in a statute have never, so far as I am aware, been
interpreted so as to extend the action of the statute beyond the
territorial authority of the legislature. All criminal statutes are in
their terms general; but they apply only to offences committed
within the territory or by British subjects. When the legislature intends the statute to apply beyond the ordinary territorial authority
of the country, it so states expressly in the statute, as in the Merchant
Shipping Act, and in some of the Admiralty Acts. If the legislature
of England in express terms applies its legislation to matters beyond its legislatorial capacity, an English court must obey the
English legislature, however contrary to international comity such
legislation may be. But unless there be definite express terms to the
contrary, a statute is to be interpreted as applicable and as intended
to apply only to matters within the jurisdiction of the legislature by
which it is enacted. In this statute there are no such definite express
terms. It may be observed, moreover, that the preamble confines the
purview of the statute to English matrimonial causes. It does not say
to British causes, but to English causes. It thus limits the statute
and the action of the court to a part only of her Majesty's dominions
or subjects. It cannot be confined to matrimonial offences committed
in England, or it would not reach the case of a matrimonial offence
committed abroad by a domiciled English husband or wife. Yet it
is confined to an English matrimonial cause. It seems to me to follow
that it is confined to a matrimonial offence committed by persons
domiciled in England. I am of opinion that, upon principles of law,
irrespective of the terms used in the statute which are relied on, the
court had no jurisdiction, and that the statute did not by any terms
used in it give jurisdiction in this case. I am therefore of opinion
that the judgment should be affirmed.

NIBOYET
v.
NIBOYET.

Brett L.J.

Note. In this case Brett L.J. delivered a dissenting judgment, the majority
of the court (James and Cotton L.JJ.) deciding that it had jurisdiction to pronounce a decree of divorce though the respondent husband was domiciled
abroad.

LE MESURIER *v.* LE MESURIER [1895] A.C. 517 (Privy Council)

Appeal by the husband from a decree of the Supreme Court of Ceylon dismissing his petition for divorce on the ground of his wife's adultery.

The parties were married in England in 1883, the husband being domiciled in England and the wife before her marriage in France. From 1883 until the commencement of the suit the parties resided in Ceylon, the husband being a member of the Ceylon Civil Service; but he retained his English domicile of origin. The adultery was alleged to have taken place at Paris, Marseilles, and on board various steamships on voyages between England and Ceylon.

The judgment of their Lordships (Lords Herschell L.C., Watson, Hobhouse, Macnaghten, Morris, and Sir Richard Couch) was delivered by

LORD WATSON: . . . In order to sustain the competency of the present suit it is necessary for the appellant to shew that the jurisdiction assumed by the district judge of Matara was derived, either from some recognised principle of the general law of nations, or from some domestic rule of the Roman-Dutch law. If either of these points were established, the jurisdiction of the District Court would be placed beyond question; but the effect of its decree divorcing the spouses would not in each case be the same. When the jurisdiction of the court is exercised according to the rules of international law, as in the case where the parties have their domicile within its forum, its decree dissolving their marriage ought to be respected by the tribunals of every civilised country. The opinions expressed by the English common law judges in *Lolley's Case*[1] gave rise to a doubt whether that principle was in consistency with the law of England, which at that time did not allow a marriage to be judicially dissolved. That doubt has since been dispelled; and the law of England was, in their Lordships' opinion, correctly stated by Lord Westbury in *Shaw* v. *Gould*[2] in these terms: 'The position that the tribunal of a foreign country having jurisdiction to dissolve the marriages of its own subjects, is competent to pronounce a similar decree between English subjects who were married in England, but who before and at the time of the suit are permanently domiciled within the jurisdiction of such foreign tribunal, such decree being made in a bona fide suit without collusion or concert, is a position consistent with all the

---

[1] (1812) 2 Cl. & F. 567, n.   [2] (1868) L.R. 3 H.L. 55, 85 ; *post*, p. 209.

English decisions, although it may not be consistent with the resolution commonly cited as the resolution of the judges in *Lolley's Case.* On the other hand, a decree of divorce a vinculo, pronounced by a court whose jurisdiction is solely derived from some rule of municipal law peculiar to its forum, cannot, when it trenches upon the interests of any other country, to whose tribunals the spouses were amenable, claim extra-territorial authority. . . .

LE
MESURIER
v.
LE
MESURIER.
—
Lord
Watson.

(After considering the authorities down to and including *Niboyet* v. *Niboyet*[1] his Lordship continued:) The main reason assigned for their decision by the learned judges of the majority was that, before the Act of 1857 became law, the petitioner would have been entitled to sue her husband in the Bishop's Court, although he was not domiciled in England, and to ask either for restitution of conjugal rights, or for a divorce a mensâ et thoro, and in either case for proper alimony; and consequently that, after the Act of 1857 passed, jurisdiction in divorce might be exercised in the same circumstances. There appears to their Lordships to be an obvious fallacy in that reasoning. It is not doubtful that there may be residence without domicile sufficient to sustain a suit for restitution of conjugal rights, for separation, or for aliment; but it does not follow that such residence must also give jurisdiction to dissolve the marriage. Their Lordships cannot construe sect. 27 of the Act of 1857 as giving the English court divorce jurisdiction in all cases where any other matrimonial suit would previously have been entertained in the Bishop's Court. . . .

When carefully examined, neither the English nor the Scottish decisions are, in their Lordships' opinion, sufficient to establish the proposition that, in either of these countries, there exists a recognised rule of general law to the effect that a so-called matrimonial domicile gives jurisdiction to dissolve marriage. . . .

Bar says 'that in actions for divorce—unless there is some express enactment to the contrary—the judge of the domicile or nationality is the only competent judge'. And he adds: 'A decree of divorce, therefore, pronounced by any other judge than a judge of the domicile or nationality is to be regarded in all other countries as inoperative.'

Their Lordships have in these circumstances, and upon these considerations, come to the conclusion that, according to international law, the domicile for the time being of the married pair affords the

[1] (1878) 4 P.D. 1; *ante*, p. 107.

LE
MESURIER
v.
LE
MESURIER.
—
Lord
Watson.

only true test of jurisdiction to dissolve their marriage. They concur, without reservation, in the views expressed by Lord Penzance in *Wilson* v. *Wilson*,[1] which were obviously meant to refer, not to questions arising in regard to the mutual rights of married persons, but to jurisdiction in the matter of divorce: 'It is the strong inclination of my own opinion that the only fair and satisfactory rule to adopt on this matter of jurisdiction is to insist upon the parties in all cases referring their matrimonial differences to the courts of the country in which they are domiciled. Different communities have different views and laws respecting matrimonial obligations, and a different estimate of the causes which should justify divorce. It is both just and reasonable, therefore, that the differences of married people should be adjusted in accordance with the laws of the community to which they belong, and dealt with by the tribunals which alone can administer those laws. An honest adherence to this principle, moreover, will preclude the scandal which arises when a man and woman are held to be man and wife in one country and strangers in another.'

Appeal dismissed.

MATRIMONIAL CAUSES ACT 1965, s. 40

40. (1) Without prejudice to any jurisdiction exercisable by the court apart from this section, the court shall have jurisdiction to entertain proceedings by a wife, notwithstanding that the husband is not domiciled in England:

    (*a*) in the case of any proceedings under this Act (other than proceedings under section 14 or sections 23 to 28[2]), if:

        (i) the wife has been deserted by her husband, or

        (ii) the husband has been deported from the United Kingdom under any law for the time being in force relating to deportation, and the husband was immediately before the desertion or deportation domiciled in England;[3]

    (*b*) in the case of proceedings for divorce or nullity of marriage, if:

        (i) the wife is resident in England and has been ordinarily

---

[1] (1872) L.R. 2 P. & M. 435, 442.

[2] S. 14 deals with proceedings for presumption of death and dissolution of marriage. Ss. 23 to 28 deal with proceedings to vary maintenance agreements or to obtain maintenance from a deceased spouse's estate.

[3] This paragraph replaces s. 13 of the Matrimonial Causes Act 1937 and s. 18 (1) (*a*) of the Matrimonial Causes Act 1950, without change of substance.

resident there for a period of three years immediately preceding the commencement of the proceedings, and

(ii) the husband is not domiciled in any other part of the United Kingdom or in the Channel Islands or the Isle of Man.[1]

(2) In any proceedings in which the court has jurisdiction by virtue of the foregoing subsection the issues shall be determined in accordance with the law which would be applicable thereto if both parties were domiciled in England at the time of the proceedings.[2]

NOTE E: DIVORCE FOR THE DESERTED WIFE

AFTER a period of hesitation (*Niboyet* v. *Niboyet, ante*, p. 107) it was decided that English courts have jurisdiction to dissolve a marriage only if the spouses are domiciled in England at the date of the commencement of the proceedings (*Le Mesurier* v. *Le Mesurier, ante*, p. 114). Although the *Niboyet* case was a decision of the Court of Appeal and has never been overruled, and the *Le Mesurier* case was a decision of the Privy Council on appeal from Ceylon, English courts have ever since 1895 acted on the assumption that the *Niboyet* case is wrong and the *Le Mesurier* case is right.

This rule, combined with the rule that a married woman cannot acquire a domicile separate from her husband (*ante*, p. 51), produced serious hardship and injustice in the case of the deserted wife. For if the husband deserted his wife and acquired or resumed a foreign domicile, the wife was at best put to the expense of petitioning for divorce in the foreign country, and at worst was denied a remedy altogether, for example if the husband was domiciled in some country like the Republic of Ireland where there is no divorce, or if the wife could not discover where he was domiciled.

The hardship was so obvious that as early as 1878 suggestions were made obiter to the effect that the deserted wife might be allowed to petition for divorce in England although the husband was domiciled elsewhere (*Niboyet* v. *Niboyet, ante*, pp. 110–11). The suggestions became more pointed in 1908 when the Court of Appeal in *Ogden* v. *Ogden* (*ante*, p. 85) intimated that the wife's petition for divorce in that case ought not to have been dismissed for want of jurisdiction. Effect was given to these dicta in two undefended cases decided in 1913 (*Stathatos* v. *Stathatos* [1913] P. 46, and *De Montaigu* v. *De Montaigu* [1913] P. 154). In each of these cases the situation was that a domiciled Englishwoman had married a domiciled foreigner in England, and that the husband then deserted the wife and obtained a decree of nullity from the courts of his domicile on the ground that the marriage ceremony was

---

[1] This paragraph replaces s. 1 (1) and (2) of the Law Reform (Miscellaneous Provisions) Act 1949 and s. 18 (1) (*b*) of the Matrimonial Causes Act 1950, without change of substance.

[2] This subsection replaces s. 1 (4) of the Law Reform (Miscellaneous Provisions) Act 1949 and s. 18 (3) of the Matrimonial Causes Act 1950, without change of substance.

FAMILY LAW

formally invalid by the lex domicilii. In each case the wife was allowed to petition for divorce. At that time the foreign decree of nullity would not have been recognized in England (*Ogden* v. *Ogden, ante,* p. 85). But since *Von Lorang* v. *Administrator of Austrian Property* [1927] A.C. 641 (*post,* p. 185), it seems clear that the foreign decree would be recognized in similar circumstances: see *post,* p. 207.

After the rule that a married woman can in no circumstances acquire a separate domicile had been reasserted in *A.-G. for Alberta* v. *Cook* (1926) (*ante,* p. 48), it was held in two cases that if the husband, being domiciled in England, deserted his wife and acquired a foreign domicile, she could not petition for divorce: *H.* v. *H.* [1928] P. 206; *Herd* v. *Herd* [1936] P. 205.

This injustice has been met by s. 40 (1) (*a*) and (*b*) of the Matrimonial Causes Act 1965, re-enacting s. 18 (1) (*a*) and (*b*) of the Matrimonial Causes Act 1950, which in turn re-enacted respectively s. 13 of the Matrimonial Causes Act 1937, and s. 1 of the Law Reform (Miscellaneous Provisions) Act 1949. Section 40 (1) (*a*) applies to proceedings for divorce, nullity, judicial separation, restitution of conjugal rights, and applications to the High Court for maintenance under s. 22 of the Act; but not to petitions for a declaration as to status under R.S.C., Ord. 15, r. 16. On the other hand, it is of limited scope, because it only applies where the husband was domiciled in England immediately before the desertion or deportation, and not (for instance) where he never was domiciled in England at all.

Section 40 (1) (*b*) goes too far in the opposite direction and opens the doors of the English Divorce Court to any woman in the world who can establish a three years' residence in England, despite the fact that the decree may stand no chance of being recognized in the country of her domicile or nationality (see *Tursi* v. *Tursi* [1958] P. 54). On the other hand, it only applies to proceedings for divorce or nullity. It has been held that 'ordinary residence' can exist although the wife may have been temporarily absent from England on holiday or for business purposes, provided she does not sever all connexion with England (*Stransky* v. *Stransky* [1954] P. 428; *Lewis* v. *Lewis* [1956] I W.L.R. 200; contrast *Hopkins* v. *Hopkins* [1951] P. 116). The requirement that the husband must be domiciled in Scotland, Northern Ireland, the Channel Islands, or the Isle of Man was no doubt introduced to avoid any conflict of jurisdiction with the courts of those countries in cases where the hardship is, by reason of the short distances and of a substantial similarity in the grounds for divorce, not acute.

Both clauses are confined to proceedings by a wife and do not extend to cross-petitions by a respondent husband: *Levett* v. *Levett and Smith* [1957] P. 156; *Russell* v. *Russell and Roebuck* [1957] P. 375. Under both clauses, the court will apply English law, and not the law of the husband's domicile: s. 40 (2). Under both clauses, the courts of two countries may be simultaneously competent to dissolve the same marriage, the English court and the court of the husband's domicile. This had previously been stigmatized as one of the absurd consequences of holding that a wife could establish a separate domicile from her husband (see *A.-G. for Alberta* v. *Cook, ante,* pp. 49–50). Yet how much simpler the law would be if she had been allowed to do so. There would have been no need for s. 40 (1) (*a*) or (*b*), and we should never have heard of *Travers* v. *Holley* [1953] P. 246 (*post,* p. 119) or *Indyka* v. *Indyka* [1967] 3 W.L.R. 510 (*post,* p. 122). The court has jurisdiction to stay

118

MATRIMONIAL CAUSES

the wife's proceedings in England or the husband's proceedings in the
country of his domicile, but will only exercise it in a strong case (see *Orr-Lewis* v. *Orr-Lewis* [1949] P. 347; *Sealey* v. *Callan* [1953] P. 135).

*A foreign divorce will be recognized in England if it was
(1) granted or (2) recognized as valid by the courts of the country
where the parties were domiciled at the commencement of the proceedings, or (3) if it was obtained by the wife and the English court
would (mutatis mutandis) have had jurisdiction to grant her a
divorce under s. 40 (1) (a) or (b) of the Matrimonial Causes Act 1965,
or (4) there was a real and substantial connexion between the petitioner and the country where the divorce was granted.*

TRAVERS *v.* HOLLEY [1953] P. 246 (Court of Appeal)

A husband and wife were married in England in 1937, both parties
being domiciled in England. In November of that year they emi-
grated to New South Wales. In August 1940 the husband deserted
the wife (as she alleged). In 1941 he joined the Australian forces
and in 1943 obtained a transfer to the British forces. On 23 August
1943 the wife petitioned the New South Wales court for divorce on
the ground of the husband's desertion, and obtained a decree which
was made absolute on 13 November 1944.

After this divorce both parties remarried. The husband's second
marriage having proved unsatisfactory, he petitioned the High
Court for divorce from his first wife on the ground of her adultery
with her second husband. He contended that he had never acquired
a domicile of choice in New South Wales, and that even if he had,
he had resumed his English domicile of origin at some date prior to
23 August 1943.

Section 16 (a) of the New South Wales Matrimonial Causes Act
1899 provides as follows: 'Any wife who at the time of the institution
of the suit has been domiciled in New South Wales for three years
and upwards (provided she did not resort to New South Wales for
the purpose of such institution) may present a petition to the court
praying that her marriage may be dissolved on one or more of the
grounds following: (a) that her husband has without just cause or
excuse wilfully deserted the petitioner and without any such cause
or excuse left her continuously so deserted during three years and
upwards and no wife who was domiciled in New South Wales when
the desertion commenced shall be deemed to have lost her domicile

TRAVERS
v.
HOLLEY.

119

by reason only of her husband having thereafter acquired a foreign domicile.'

Mr. Commissioner Grazebrook Q.C. granted the husband a divorce. The wife appealed to the Court of Appeal. The majority of the Court of Appeal (Somervell and Hodson L.JJ., Jenkins L.J. dissenting) held that the husband had acquired a domicile of choice in New South Wales by August 1940, when the husband's alleged desertion began.

HODSON L.J., having stated the facts and referred at length to the evidence, said: Bearing in mind the circumstances surrounding the departure from England to a Commonwealth country, and the general probabilities of the case, particularly the letters which the husband wrote on reaching his destination—which the commissioner did not see—I would say that the evidence pointing to the acquisition of a domicile of choice in New South Wales ought to be accepted, and that the contrary indications do not counterbalance this evidence. . . . The husband has contended that even on such a finding of fact he is entitled to succeed because the New South Wales court would have no jurisdiction in the eyes of the courts of this country to dissolve the marriage, unless at the date of the institution of the proceedings in New South Wales both parties were there domiciled. . . . It is not, I think, necessary to form any conclusion as to when the husband abandoned his domicile of choice in Australia, since I think that even if he had done so at some time before the date of the institution of the New South Wales proceedings, and after the date of the desertion, the husband's contention fails.

The argument is that domicile of both spouses at the time of the proceedings is the sole test of jurisdiction in divorce: see *Le Mesurier* v. *Le Mesurier*,[1] which unequivocally established this test. Since the decision in that case the English courts have not recognized a decree of a foreign court unless the parties were at the time of the proceedings domiciled in the jurisdiction of the foreign court, or, if domiciled elsewhere, such decree would be recognized by the law of the domicile: *Armitage* v. *A.-G.*[2] For this purpose New South Wales is a foreign court, and, it is said, the husband not being domiciled in New South Wales in August 1943, the courts of this country will not recognize the decree of the court of that state.

---

[1] [1895] A.C. 517; *ante*, p. 114.   [2] [1906] P. 135.

I think that this argument is not valid at the present day. For many years after the decision in *Le Mesurier's* case the position was that the courts of this country only exercised jurisdiction in cases where both parties were domiciled here. Following certain dicta of Sir Gorell Barnes in *Ogden* v. *Ogden*,[1] there was thought to be an exception to this rule in the case of wives deserted by husbands who at the time of the desertion were domiciled in England. It was thought that they might obtain a decree in this country although this country was not the true domicile of the husband. In undefended cases these courts did not inquire what had happened to husbands after desertion in such circumstances, either because it was thought they were estopped from denying an English domicile or because the burden was upon them to show an abandonment and they had done nothing to discharge the burden.

When the question was raised in a defended case, however, the decision was against the view that there was any exception to the rule: *H.* v. *H.*[2] Indeed, the supposed exception had been adversely criticized in *A.-G. for Alberta* v. *Cook*.[3] The position has, however, been radically altered by statute. By the Matrimonial Causes Act 1937, s. 13,[4] it was provided that 'where a wife has been deserted by her husband . . . and the husband was immediately before the desertion . . . domiciled in England and Wales, the court shall have jurisdiction for the purpose of any proceedings' concerned with divorce. Since 1937 this exception has been largely extended, first by the Matrimonial Causes (War Marriages) Act 1944 (a temporary war measure), and later by the Matrimonial Causes Act 1950, s. 18. It is unnecessary to consider the effect of these later statutory provisions since, at the material time, when the New South Wales proceedings were instituted, the Act of 1937 was in force and section 13 of the Act corresponds in substance with the provision under which the New South Wales court claimed jurisdiction between the parties to this appeal.

It seems to me, therefore, that Parliament has cut the ground from the argument put forward on behalf of the husband. If English courts will only recognize foreign decrees of divorce where the parties are domiciled in the territory of the foreign court at the time of the institution of proceedings, because that is the jurisdiction which they

TRAVERS
v.
HOLLEY.
—
Hodson
L.J.

---

[1] [1908] P. 46 ; *ante*, p. 85.   [2] [1928] P. 206.
[3] [1926] A.C. 444 ; *ante*, p. 48.
[4] Now s. 40 (1) (*a*) of the Matrimonial Causes Act 1965 (*ante*, p. 116).

TRAVERS
v.
HOLLEY.
Hodson
L.J.

themselves claim, what is the situation when the courts of this country arrogate to themselves jurisdiction in the case of persons not domiciled here at the material date? It must surely be that what entitles an English court to assume jurisdiction must be equally effective in the case of a foreign court.

Lord Watson, in the *Le Mesurier* case, used the following language: 'A decree of divorce a vinculo, pronounced by a court whose jurisdiction is solely derived from some rule of municipal law peculiar to its forum, cannot, when it trenches upon the interests of any other country to whose tribunals the spouses were amenable, claim extra-territorial authority.' Conversely, it seems that where it is found that the municipal law is not peculiar to the forum of one country but corresponds with a law of a second country, such municipal law cannot be said to trench upon the interests of that country. I would say that where, as here, there is in substance reciprocity, it would be contrary to principle and inconsistent with comity if the courts of this country were to refuse to recognize a jurisdiction which mutatis mutandis they claim for themselves. The principle laid down and followed since the *Le Mesurier* case must, I think, be interpreted in the light of the legislation which has extended the power of the courts of this country in the case of persons not domiciled here. . . .

(His Lordship proceeded to discuss the question whether, in the event of the New South Wales decree not being recognized in England, the husband's remarriage on the strength of that decree amounted to conduct conducing to the wife's adultery which would constitute a discretionary bar to divorce.)

SOMERVELL L.J. delivered judgment to the same effect.

JENKINS L.J. dissented on the ground that, in his opinion, the husband never lost his English domicile of origin; but he agreed with the conclusion of the majority that, assuming that the husband had acquired a domicile in New South Wales by August 1940 and had abandoned it before August 1943, the New South Wales decree should be recognized in England.

Appeal allowed.

INDYKA
v.
INDYKA.

INDYKA *v.* INDYKA [1967] 3 W.L.R. 510 (House of Lords)

The husband married his first wife in Czecho-Slovakia in January 1938. Both parties were nationals of and domiciled in that country.

In September 1938 the husband joined the Czech army and later served with the Polish army. He was captured by the Russians and imprisoned in Siberia until he was released to serve again with the Polish army under General Sikorski. At the end of the war he came to England and became domiciled there in 1946. Throughout the war he was anxious but unable to communicate with his first wife. In January 1949 the first wife (who had continued to reside in Czecho-Slovakia) obtained a decree of divorce there on the ground of deep disruption of marital relations. Some time later the husband heard about this divorce. He believed that it was valid and that he was free to remarry. In 1959 he married his second wife, who was an Englishwoman domiciled in England. In 1964 the second wife petitioned for divorce on the ground of the husband's cruelty. The husband cross-petitioned for a decree of nullity on the ground of his bigamy, his first wife being alive in 1959.

INDYKA
v.
INDYKA.
Lord Reid.

Latey J. granted a decree of nullity.[1] He held that the Czecho-Slovak divorce could not be recognised in England under the doctrine of *Travers* v. *Holley*,[2] first because the husband did not desert his first wife and therefore the analogy of section 40 (1) (*a*) of the Matrimonial Causes Act 1965 was not applicable; and secondly because, although the first wife had been ordinarily resident in Czecho-Slovakia for three years immediately preceding the commencement of the proceedings, the divorce was granted eleven months before what is now section 40 (1) (*b*) of that Act was first enacted.

The Court of Appeal (Lord Denning M.R. and Diplock L.J.; Russell L.J. dissenting) reversed this decision on the ground that the date of the Czecho-Slovak divorce was irrelevant to the question of its recognition in England.[3]

The husband appealed.

LORD REID: This case raises the general question of the extent of the right or duty of the Courts of England to recognise a foreign decree of divorce which is valid in the country where it was pronounced. The essential facts are that when the wife began proceedings and obtained her decree both she and her husband were, according to our law, domiciled in England. But both were citizens of Czechoslovakia, their home was there after they married until he

---

[1] [1966] 2 W.L.R. 892.   [2] [1953] P. 246; *ante*, p. 119.
[3] [1966] 3 W.L.R. 603.

INDYKA
v.
INDYKA.

Lord Reid.

left it and the wife had resided in that country all her life. It is not clear from the evidence whether jurisdiction under Czech law depended on the nationality of the parties, or the residence of the wife or both, but clearly it had nothing to do with domicile in our sense. The question is whether your Lordships are precluded by English law from recognising this foreign decree by the mere fact that at the relevant time the parties were domiciled in England. I accept for the purposes of this case the present doctrine of English law that during the subsistence of a marriage the wife cannot have a domicile different from that of her husband. This rule may (or may not) be 'the last barbarous relic of a wife's servitude' (per Lord Denning M.R. in *Gray* v. *Formosa*),[1] but to alter it might have wide repercussions and I think that this matter had better be left to Parliament.

Inevitably the argument before Latey J. and the Court of Appeal turned on the application of the decision in *Travers* v. *Holley*.[2] In my opinion the decision in that case was right, but I think that it must be based on wider grounds than those adopted by the Court of Appeal—on grounds which the operation of the rule *stare decisis* would have prevented that Court from adopting. (His Lordship referred to *Travers* v. *Holley*, *Levett* v. *Levett*,[3] and *Robinson-Scott* v. *Robinson-Scott*[4] and continued:) The decision in *Travers* v. *Holley* was based on reciprocity and comity. Reciprocity appears to me to mean that we should say—if you will recognise that we have this jurisdiction we will recognise that you have a similar jurisdiction. I do not think that this was ever regarded as the test and it certainly could not be under the wider *Travers* v. *Holley* doctrine as stated in the passage which I have quoted from *Robinson-Scott* v. *Robinson-Scott*. Comity is a word of many meanings but for several reasons the meaning which it appears to have in *Travers* v. *Holley* does not appear to me to be a satisfactory basis for recognition. Comity has never been the basis on which we recognise or give effect to foreign judgments. This was made clear by Lord Blackburn in *Schibsby* v. *Westenholz*.[5] (His Lordship quoted the passage beginning 'We were much pressed with the argument' and ending 'which we have just laid down' and continued:) The *Travers* v. *Holley* doctrine would not lead to a rational development of the law. Too frequently when

---

[1] [1963] P. 259, 267.   [2] [1953] P. 246; *ante*, p. 119.
[3] [1957] P. 156.   [4] [1958] P. 71.
[5] (1870) L.R. 6 Q.B. 155; *post*, pp. 478–9.

Parliament is legislating to remove a particular injustice the provisions of the Bill are drafted as narrowly as possible to achieve that result so that they introduce an anomaly into the existing law rather than making any general reform. And the main reason for this is that such piecemeal changes can be enacted more speedily with less demands on the time of Parliament than a more general reform would require. Parliament only has in mind the particular circumstances in this country and it would be quite unrealistic to suppose that when Parliament entrusts a new jurisdiction to our Courts it has any intention to affect our rules for the recognition of foreign judgments. With rare exceptions Parliament has left the Courts free to develop those rules and I see no reason why, by adopting the doctrine of *Travers* v. *Holley*, we should tie that development to what Parliament has done with quite a different object in view.

To adopt this doctrine with regard to the 1949 Act would, in my view, lead to very undesirable consequences. The 1949 Act entitles any wife who has resided here for three years to sue for divorce. An Italian or a citizen of the Republic of Ireland may come to this country accompanied by his wife to take up a three or four years' appointment, there being no question of their acquiring an English domicile or even making their home here. If the husband commits a matrimonial offence the wife can petition for divorce as soon as she has resided here for three years. Probably Parliament never really intended such a result but it is the necessary result of the terms of the Act. This hardly accords with comity in any sense and it creates what has come to be known as a 'limping marriage' because such a decree of the English Court would rightly be refused recognition in the country of their nationality and domicile. It might have to be recognised in Scotland because the Courts of one part of the United Kingdom could hardly refuse to recognise something done in another part of the United Kingdom in the exercise of a power given by the Parliament of the United Kingdom. But other countries would be free to disregard it and probably many would refuse to recognise it. Then take the converse case. An Englishman accompanied by his wife takes a three years' appointment in one of the hundred odd countries of the United Nations where divorce is granted on some flimsy pretext or perhaps merely on request, but they have no intention of making their home there. If the wife, after residing there for three years, gets such a divorce are the English Courts really to be bound to recognise its validity? I can see no answer to that if we accept the *Travers* v. *Holley* doctrine as it is at present being applied. And the result would be the same if an English wife went to such a country, for the purpose of getting a divorce, resided there for three years, perhaps obtaining employment there, and then returned here with her decree. So I propose to consider whether there is not some more satisfactory basis for supporting the decision in *Travers* v. *Holley* and the cases which have followed on it.

The main obstacle is the ratio of *Le Mesurier's* case. But before dealing with that, it may be of assistance to look at the position before that case was decided. (His Lordship referred to *Shaw* v. *Gould*,[1] *Niboyet* v. *Niboyet*,[2] and *Le Mesurier* v. *Le Mesurier*.[3] He pointed out that the words 'or nationality' in the quotation from Bar, *ante*, p. 115, appeared to have escaped the notice of their Lordships. He repeated the quotation from Lord Penzance in *Wilson* v. *Wilson*,[4] *ante*, p. 116, and continued:) My first comment is that, although the English Courts honestly adhered to that principle until Parliament had to intervene, that did not in fact preclude the scandal of limping marriages. And the reason is not far to seek. From the wording of the judgment it seems to me that in laying down this test their Lordships must have thought that they were keeping in line with the practice in other civilised countries. But in fact they were not. Their view has been followed in the Commonwealth, but so far as I know nowhere else. So far as I have any knowledge of the matter the position appears to be (and to have been in 1895) that most European countries attach more importance to nationality or sometimes residence, and in the United States most if not all the states by permitting the wife to have a separate domicile for this purpose do not regard the Court of the husband's domicile as the only Court which has jurisdiction. But I would find it surprising if their Lordships really thought that they were keeping in line with other countries. It is just possible that they were actuated by the hope, common in Victorian times, that if England showed the way others would see the light and follow: if so any such hope has been grievously disappointed.

That this decision has had most unfortunate consequences can hardly be denied. Parliament has found it necessary to encroach on it on many occasions. (His Lordship referred to the Matrimonial

---

[1] (1868) L.R. 3 H.L. 55; *post*, p. 209.   [2] (1878) 4 P.D. 1; *ante*, p. 107.
[3] [1895] A.C. 517; *ante*, p. 114.   [4] (1872) L.R. 2 P. & M. 435, 442.

Causes (Dominion Troops) Act 1919; the Indian Divorces (Validity) Act 1921; the Indian and Colonial Divorce Jurisdiction Act 1926; the Matrimonial Causes Act 1937, s. 13; the Matrimonial Causes (War Marriages) Act 1944; and the Law Reform (Miscellaneous Provisions) Act 1949, s. 1, and continued:) There must surely be something wrong with a rule which has required such frequent remedial intervention by Parliament. But can we do anything about it? I think we can and should. It is true that it has frequently been approved in this House, and, but for these interventions by Parliament, I should have great doubt whether it would be proper for this House sitting judicially to depart from it. But I would draw a distinction between the rules which govern the jurisdiction of our Courts and the rules which determine the extent to which we should recognise foreign decrees. The former are statutory; although the original Act of 1857 does not mention domicile, the later Acts are all drafted on the assumption that domicile was the only ground of jurisdiction under it. Obviously we cannot revise an Act of Parliament: the most we can do is to suggest matters which might be borne in mind when an amending Bill is being drafted and passed. But Parliament has rarely intervened in the matter of recognition of foreign matrimonial decrees. The existing law is judge-made and I see no reason why that process should stop. I do not attach great importance to the fact that *Le Mesurier* was dealing with jurisdiction and not recognition, because I think that their Lordships must have intended their rule to apply to both, and I think that it has commonly been accepted as applying to both.

The essence of the rule in *Le Mesurier* is that there should be only one test, and only one Court with jurisdiction to apply it, and the purpose was to avoid limping marriages. That essence has been permanently destroyed by Parliament and that purpose was never achieved. There are now two general grounds of jurisdiction in this country—domicile and residence of the wife irrespective of any domicile which she has or ever had. So I see nothing to prevent our adding additional ground for recognition besides domicile. But the common law has not been built by judges making general pronouncements: it has been built by the rational expansion of what already exists in order to do justice in particular cases.

When we apply our test of domicile at present we neither recognise the validity of the ground on which the foreign Court had jurisdiction under its law, nor do we pay any heed to the ground on which

127

that Court granted decree of divorce. What we do is to make our own investigation into the facts to see whether, according to our law, the husband was domiciled within the jurisdiction of the foreign Court. If he was we recognise the decree no matter on what ground that Court claimed to have jurisdiction and no matter on what ground the decree was granted. If he was not, we refuse to recognise the decree. I would not in general depart from that method of approach. It would be most invidious if we were to say that we approve of some of the grounds on which foreign Courts claim jurisdiction but do not approve of others, or if we were to say that we approve of some of the grounds on which they decree divorce but do not approve of others. And I would certainly not be in favour of recognising as valid all the various grounds on which foreign countries claim jurisdiction, still less all the various grounds on which they grant divorces. Parliament has power to do that if ever it should desire to do so, but I would not think it proper for the Courts to do it.

I can see no difficulty in making one comparatively small change because some English authorities and present Scottish practice both point in that direction. I have already quoted the passage from the judgment of Brett M.R. in *Niboyet*[1] where he states his view that a husband who leaves his wife could not deprive her of her remedy by then acquiring another domicile. And it appears from what is said in *Herd's* case[2] that the English Courts were applying that rule until they were stopped by a too loyal adherence to the *ratio* in *Le Mesurier*. Moreover that rule is of ancient origin in Scotland. Two centuries ago Erskine wrote:[3] 'Action might perhaps be sustained at the suit of the innocent party against the deserter, though not residing in this Kingdom, upon evidence adduced that the desertion was wilful, and that the defender left the kingdom, and still remains abroad, from a deliberate purpose of abandoning the conjugal society, lest such wrong should be left without a remedy.' That view has been accepted and the existing law is stated in Walton, Husband and Wife:[4] 'It is a matter of daily practice that divorce for desertion is granted when the facts point to the husband having gone abroad animo manendi. There are dicta to the effect that the same rule applies when the husband has been guilty of adultery in Scotland and has afterwards abandoned his Scottish domicile.' *Le*

---

[1] *Ante*, p. 110–11.   [2] [1936] P. 205.   [3] Inst. I. 6. 44.
[4] 3rd ed. p. 384.

Mesurier's case has not been held in Scotland to prevent that practice from continuing and therefore it has not been thought necessary to enact for Scotland a counterpart of section 13 of the 1937 Act. So it would seem proper at least to hold that, where a husband leaves his wife in the matrimonial domicile and she has by the law of that country a right to obtain a divorce which accrued before he changed his domicile but only sues for and obtains her divorce thereafter, we ought to disregard that change of domicile and recognise the foreign decree.

But I think that we must go farther than that. First with regard to residence there are many references in English and Scots authorities to the matrimonial home, and matrimonial domicile, and the community with which the spouses are most closely connected, and with all respect to the Board in *Le Mesurier* I do not think that there would often be any real difficulty in determining where the spouses' matrimonial home was or with what community they were most closely associated. There may, of course, be cases where they have never settled down anywhere: even if intending to reside in a particular place for some considerable time they may abstain from associating themselves in any way with the community there and remain nomads. Everyone must have a domicile but not everyone has a real home. In such cases we would have to fall back on domicile. It would be quite wrong to exclude domicile as a test, but, once we get rid of the idea that there can only be one test and that there can never be jurisdiction in more than one Court, it seems to me to be very much in the public interest that there should be some other test besides that of domicile. If a man of English origin goes to another country and intends if possible to remain there for his working life it seems to me to be wrong that the question whether the English Court or the Court of that other country has jurisdiction to dissolve his marriage should depend upon the difficult question whether he does or does not intend to return to England when he retires. He may not know himself. And if proceedings are raised by his wife she may be still less able to supply the answer. Indeed if he has left her she may not know where he is, let alone whether he has acquired some new domicile. On the other hand, it does not seem right that if the spouses go to a country where divorce is easy, intending to stay there for only a few years and then to return home, either spouse should be entitled to take advantage of their short stay to obtain a divorce on trivial grounds.

I think that the need would best be met by reviving the old conception of the matrimonial home and to holding that if the Court where that home is grants decree of divorce we should recognise that decree. In this matter I can see no good reason for making any distinction between the husband and the wife. If we recognise a decree granted to the one we ought equally to recognise a decree granted to the other. But if the husband leaves the matrimonial home and the wife remains within the same jurisdiction I think that we should recognise a decree granted to her by the Court of that jurisdiction. I find much more difficulty in accepting the view that if a wife parts from her husband and goes to live by herself in a new jurisdiction, her residence there, whether for three years or any other period, must necessarily be accepted as sufficient to require us to recognise a decree granted to her. It would certainly be reasonable that, where such a wife is habitually resident within that jurisdiction and has no present intention of leaving it, we should recognise a decree granted to her there. But I do not wish to go farther than that without fuller consideration in an appropriate case.

There is one other matter which I should mention and which may require consideration by the legislature or by the Courts. In many countries jurisdiction depends on nationality, indeed one might almost say that in half the world domicile in one form or another prevails and in the other half nationality. If they are to live in peaceful co-existence it may be necessary to take note of this, and then it may be necessary to extend some protection to a wife who retains British nationality on marrying a foreigner and to foreigners who come under the protection of our law by establishing their home here. But on these questions I prefer to express no opinion.

Finally it is well recognised that we ought not to alter what is presently understood to be the law if that involves any real likelihood of injustice to people who have relied on the present position in arranging their affairs. But I have been unable to think of any case and counsel have been unable to suggest any case where such injustice would result from what I have invited your Lordships to accept.

I would dismiss this appeal on the grounds that the Czech decree dissolving the Appellant's first marriage ought to be recognised as valid because the first wife to whom it was granted had had her matrimonial home in Czechoslovakia and had continued to reside there after her husband left, and that the fact that he acquired a domicile of choice in England before the wife raised proceedings in her country does not prevent that recognition.

LORD MORRIS OF BORTH-Y-GEST: . . . Even if the decision in *Travers* v. *Holley* was new law I would consider that it was both reasonable and desirable. If a deserted wife may obtain a decree in England under the conditions laid down in 1937 (and now contained in section 40 (1) (*a*) of the Act of 1965) it seems to me to be reasonable to recognise a decree granted in another country in the exercise of a comparable jurisdiction. So also if jurisdiction is exercised in England on the basis of three years residence by a wife if the conditions of section 40 (1) (*b*) are satisfied, it seems to me to be reasonable to recognise a decree granted to a wife in another country that accepts jurisdiction in similar circumstances. These significant statutory exceptions to the rules which previously adhered so closely to domicile as the basis and the only basis for jurisdiction would seem to justify if not to require recognition of decrees of dissolution granted in another country in the exercise of a jurisdiction similar to or, I would say, substantially similar to that exercised by the court in England. I would, therefore, approve the decision in *Travers* v. *Holley*. Nor do I see any reason why after the passing of the Law Reform (Miscellaneous Provisions) Act 1949, our courts should not recognise the decree of the Czech court on the basis that though made before December, 1949, it was made by the court of a country in which the wife had been ordinarily resident for three years. The issue which the learned judge tried in the present case was whether the husband had been free to marry in March, 1959. In my view, he was free to marry because after December, 1949, our courts were entitled to treat the Czech decree of January, 1949, as having dissolved the husband's first marriage.

The years of conflict between 1939 and 1945 witnessed movements of combatants and others to and from different countries on a scale that would not have been expected in the calmer days of peace. In the present era the speed and ease of transport gives rise to conditions that differ widely from those obtaining in the latter part of the last century. All this means that if recognition of foreign decrees is closely circumscribed there will be increasing numbers of cases where a person is to be regarded in one country as married and in another country as not married. It can well be understood that when our courts were saying that domicile and nothing but domicile could be the basis for jurisdiction a decree in a country where there was no domicile was regarded as barren and valueless. But the changes made in 1937 and 1949 were far-reaching, and domicile thereafter no longer occupied its rôle of being essential. Before the time of those changes we recognised a foreign decree if the husband was domiciled in the country. Now that we assume jurisdiction if a wife has been ordinarily resident in England for three years I can see no reason why we should not recognise a decree made in some other country where the wife was resident for three years. But once the rigidity of insistence upon domicile has been displaced the question must be asked whether it is reasonable only to recognise decrees where the foreign jurisdiction is founded upon rules which mutatis mutandis are like ours. There is peril in assuming that only our rules are rational and justifiable. Looking back upon the course of judicial decisions it is readily seen that though doctrine evolved one way it might quite easily have evolved another way. This leads me to the view that no essential or funda-mental superiority of our basis for jurisdiction can be claimed over all others. While in the present case I would support recognition of the Czech decree on the basis adopted by the majority in the Court of Appeal I would also support it on a wider basis. The evidence was that the Czech court accepted jurisdiction on the ground that both the parties were and always had been Czechoslovakian citizens. The first wife at the time when she presented her petition in Czecho-slovakia undoubtedly had a real and substantial connection with that country. I see no reason why the decree of the Czech court should not in those circumstances be recognised.

LORD PEARCE: My Lords, we are here concerned with the prob-lem of 'limping marriages'. Perhaps 'unilateral marriages' is a better description since it brings home more clearly the harshness and absurdity of a situation where one spouse is held in the bonds of a marriage to which there is no other party, while the former partner is free and able to marry again. Of course, when there is such a re-marriage, the unilateral spouse may be able to take subsequent pro-ceedings based on adultery. But this may be fraught with difficulty and expense. From the view of public policy and common sense there is something wrong with any law to the extent to which it fosters such a situation. Yet it is not easy to see how the problem should be solved. It depends upon the interplay of jurisdiction and recognition of foreign decrees among the nations. It is a matter for each country to decide both in respect of what marriages or parties its courts will assume jurisdiction and also what decrees of divorce by foreign courts it will recognise. It may recognise all or none or take some intermediate position. In this it will be largely influenced by public policy. The boundaries which it sets for answering each of the problems need not necessarily coincide. But insofar as it confines its recognition more narrowly than its jurisdiction, it is adding to the sum of unilateral marriages. Thus the definition of jurisdiction should be closely related to that of recognition. And in *Le Mesurier* this fact was appreciated. . . .

We have to look at *Le Mesurier* afresh to see how much of it survives or should survive in a changed world. So far as jurisdiction is concerned, the alterations created by Parliament have been so many and so great that it must, I think, now be left to Parliament to deal with the matter. The Royal Commission on Marriage and Divorce, for the reasons there set out, made various recommendations on this subject, but these have not yet been adopted.

So far as recognition is concerned, Parliament has, apart from certain reciprocal arrangements within the Commonwealth under the Colonial and Other Territories Divorce Jurisdiction Acts 1926–50 and the Matrimonial Causes (War Marriages) Act 1944, refrained from intervening. And it is for the Courts to decide what decrees they will recognise, bearing in mind the policy of Parliament in extending jurisdiction and the social necessities that, in this country as in others, underlay that policy.

Up to the date of *Travers* v. *Holley* the broad general principle adopted by English and Scots' law had been that recognition should be given to divorce obtained in another country only if the husband and wife were domiciled in that country when the proceedings started. But to this rule there had been one sound and valuable exception laid down by *Armitage* v. *Attorney-General*,[1] namely, that a divorce obtained in a country other than that in which the parties were domiciled should receive recognition if it would be accepted as valid by the court of the country in which the parties were domiciled at the time of the proceedings. The English view being that the Court of domicil should be regarded as having the closest connection with the parties, the views of that court, as shown either by its own decree or by its acknowledgement of the decrees of

INDYKA
v.
INDYKA.
Lord Pearce.

[1] [1906] P. 135.

other countries, should on general principles decide the matter. . . .

To narrow the ground of recognition accorded by *Travers* v. *Holley* might cause grave difficulties in respect of those who may have remarried on the strength of it. But even more important it would create unnecessary hardship and difficulty in the future. Mr. Crispin, while attacking the decision, admitted frankly that common sense and practical benefit were all in its favour. It has worked well and it has removed much hardship. In my opinion it would be wrong to overrule or narrow it; one should rather broaden it, and regard our own jurisdiction as only an approximate test of recognition with a right in our Courts to go further when this is justified by special circumstances in the petitioner's connection with the country granting the decree. . . .

Thus recognition can no longer be confined to decrees of the Court of domicile, though that is the primary court to which one should look. Moreover, even at the time of *Le Mesurier* nationality could not properly be ignored. And in my opinion decrees of the court of nationality, when jurisdiction is taken on the ground of nationality, should be recognised. . . .

On the facts of the present case I accept the view of the majority of the Court of Appeal that the marriage in 1959 was good although the Czechoslovakian divorce was granted in 1949, a few months before this country extended its jurisdiction by allowing resident wives to obtain divorce in our Courts. The ground of recognition rests not on any exact measure of our own jurisdiction but on the wider ground of public policy in which our own jurisdiction is a most important element. The facts which made it right for our Courts to have wider jurisdiction and give wider recognition existed at the date of the Czech decree even though those facts did not until a few months later result in the statute by which this country took wider jurisdiction. When once the appreciation of these facts has been brought home to our Courts by Parliamentary extension of their jurisdiction, their recognition should be retrospective. And if our Courts were asked in 1959, at the date of the marriage, whether the husband was free to remarry, how could public policy tolerate the answer, 'No, because, although we have for ten years been ourselves taking similar jurisdiction in such a case as this, we did not start to do so until a few months after the date of the Czechoslovakian decree'? In my opinion the question whether a foreign decree should be recognised should be answered by the Court in the light of its present policy, regardless (within reason) of when the decree was granted.

There are further reasons which, in my opinion, compel the recognition of the decree. Both parties to the marriage were nationals of Czechoslovakia (and incidentally domiciled there as well until 1946), the matrimonial home was there, the petitioning wife resided there all her life, and their Courts took jurisdiction there on the ground of nationality. Undoubtedly the country of the nationality was the predominant country with regard to the parties to this marriage, and as such its decree ought to be recognised in this country.

LORD WILBERFORCE: . . . There can be no doubt that the crude facts speak strongly in favour of recognition. The divorce was granted by a court of the nationality of both spouses, and under Czech law, as an expert proved at the trial, nationality is the relevant connecting factor for purposes of divorce. Czechoslovakia is the country in which the spouses last lived together as man and wife: it is the country in which the wife continued to reside after cohabitation ceased. The reality of the connection between the law of Czechoslovakia and the marriage cannot be doubted, whether regarded in itself, or by comparison with the only alternative system of law, namely, English law.

What then, it may be asked, is the obstacle to recognition, or what reason is there for asserting that it is the courts of this country which alone should dissolve this marriage? The answer that is given is that England has, since 1946, become the domicile of the husband: that this necessarily involves attributing an English domicile to the wife, and that, since the law of this country admits domicile as the exclusive basis for jurisdiction in divorce, recognition must be refused to the Czech decree. This argument involves as its logical consequence that English law forces upon the wife the necessity of following her husband to whatever foreign country he may select as his domicile of choice, which she might or might not have means of identifying, and to which she might well find it impossible to go, and taking proceedings against him there under a—to her—foreign law. She would be obliged to do this because a foreign law, to which she has never submitted, into which it cannot in any sense be said that she married, substitutes for the law of her nationality, which is the connecting factor accepted by her country, a law based on domicile.

INDYKA
v.
INDYKA.
‾
Lord
Wilberforce.

It must be a powerful principle of law which compels these conclusions.

The principle in question is that of the exclusive authority, of the law of the domicile, meaning in relation to a married woman the domicile of her husband, a principle fastened upon English law by the case of *Le Mesurier* v. *Le Mesurier.* . . .

The jurisdiction of the English courts to dissolve marriages is not in issue here, and though this House may be free to review the matter, it would not be right to use the present as an occasion for reconsidering whether the accepted doctrine requires modification and, if so, in what direction. The issue which we have to face is narrower, namely, whether an English court can and ought to recognise a decree granted to a married woman by a court other than that of England, being the country in which her husband is domiciled. . . .

It must be accepted that a close relation exists between the domestic jurisdiction of English courts on the one hand and the principles of recognition of foreign decrees on the other. How close this should be is a matter to which I shall return when I come to consider *Travers* v. *Holley*, but there must be some relation. This is because a person's status, even when some foreign element is involved, ought so far as possible to depend upon one system, so as to avoid what Lord Penzance called the scandal of differing status in different countries.

Secondly, it is necessary at the present time (i.e., until the law is changed by Parliament or, so far as that is possible, by the judges) to start from the foundation that the jurisdiction of the English courts as regards dissolution of marriage rests, subject to specific statutory exceptions in favour of wives, upon domicile.

It is further necessary, in my opinion, for the purposes of this case to accept that in English law a married woman cannot acquire a domicile separate from that of her husband: to alter this rule would involve a number of consequences in relation to other matters than divorce which would be beyond what is appropriate for the decision of this case, and can probably be done only by Parliament.

Consistently with the first principle, the basic rule should be preserved that English courts should continue to recognise foreign decrees of divorce if, and only if, these are granted (or recognised—see *Armitage* v. *Attorney-General*) by the court of the husband's domicile.

There are two possible directions in which departure might be made from the strictness of these principles.

(1) Recognition might, in appropriate circumstances, be given to the factor of nationality whether of both parties, or conceivably of one party, to the marriage.

(2) Recognition might be given to decrees given on a residence basis, either generally, or in the particular case of wives living apart from their husbands where to subject them uniquely to the law of their husband's domicile would cause injustice, and where the jurisdiction of the court of the country of residence is appropriate.

As regards the first of these, the relevance of nationality as a connecting factor in certain cases may, in principle, be accepted. But in individual situations many factors are involved: nationality (and the complexities of 'British nationality'), sometimes double nationality, or statelessness, and especially as regards non-unitary states these may be combined in different ways with residence or with domicile. The present case is one in which, in combination with other factors, the nationality factor (of both spouses) appears to me to be relevant on the question of recognition. In other cases the nationality of one spouse may be similarly relevant at least in relation to the quality of residence, where jurisdiction is based on residence. Beyond this, at the present, I am unable to define the situations in which nationality may be taken into account.

As regards the second of these, although it may be possible without any general change in the law by Parliament for judicial decision to allow recognition generally to decrees based on the non-domiciliary residence of the spouses, to do so in the present context appears to me to go further than is justified by the considerations advanced before us.

On the other hand, it is my clear opinion that the particular departure from the rule, or tyranny, of the domicile which I have mentioned (above, (2)) is justified and is long overdue. . . .

How far should this relaxation go? In my opinion, it would be in accordance with the developments I have mentioned and with the trend of legislation—mainly our own but also that of other countries with similar social systems—to recognise divorces given to wives by the courts of their residence wherever a real and substantial connection is shown between the petitioner and the country, or territory, exercising jurisdiction. I use these expressions so as to enable the courts, who must decide each case, to consider both the length and quality of the residence and to take into account such other factors as nationality which may reinforce the connection.

INDYKA
v.
INDYKA.

Lord
Wilberforce.

137

Equally they would enable the courts (as they habitually do without difficulty) to reject residence of passage or residence, to use the descriptive expression of the older cases, resorted to by persons who properly should seek relief here for the purpose of obtaining relief which our courts would not give.

Applying the principle stated to the facts of this case, without recapitulation, the conclusion easily emerges that the Czechoslovakian divorce of 1949 should be recognised.

Finally, as to *Travers* v. *Holley*. I do not find it necessary to discuss either the case itself, or those which have followed it, in detail since I am in general agreement with what my noble and learned friend, Lord Reid, has said about it. The decision itself is clearly unexceptionable and it has provided a working rule which though not without some process of refinement has proved, if not its logic, at least its utility in the courts. It is only when it is invoked to lay down a cast iron rule that the courts' power and duty to recognise foreign decrees of divorce follows by implication from amendments to the domestic law as to divorce jurisdiction that I begin to find difficulties. For I am unwilling to accept either that the law as to recognition of foreign divorce (still less other) jurisdiction must be a mirror image of our own law or that the pace of recognition must be geared to the haphazard movement of our legislative process. There is no reason why this should be so, for the courts' decisions as regards recognition are shaped by considerations of policy which may differ from those which influence Parliament in changing the domestic law. Moreover, as a matter of history, it is the law as to recognition which has led and that as to domestic jurisdiction which has followed, and Parliament, by refraining from legislating as to recognition (as with minor exceptions it has done) must be taken to have approved this divergence. So I would not regard the *Travers* v. *Holley* rule as amounting to more than a general working principle that changes in domestic jurisdiction should be taken into account by the courts in decisions as to what foreign decrees they will recognise.

LORD PEARSON: My Lords, the former system of law, regulating the exercise of divorce jurisdiction by the English courts and their recognition of divorces granted in other countries as valid in England, was a compact and symmetrical system, and I think the main principles can be shortly stated as follows:

(1) Jurisdiction in divorce was based exclusively on domicile, so that—

   (a) an English court would not grant a divorce unless the parties were domiciled in England, and

   (b) a divorce granted by a court of another country would not be recognised as valid in England unless the parties were domiciled in that country or the divorce would be recognised in the country of their domicile.

(2) 'Domicile' had the meaning given to it in the English case-law, including *Winans'* case[1] and *Ramsay's* case.[2]

(3) The wife's domicile was always the same as that of her husband, so that

   (a) she could not have a separate qualification for suing for divorce in England, and

   (b) a divorce obtained by her in a court of some other country by virtue of a separate qualification would not be recognised as valid in England.

The domicile referred to is, of course, domicile at the relevant date, which is, I suppose, the date of the commencement of the proceedings but does not have to be defined for the purpose of the present appeal.

The former system was found to be, or became, unrealistic and disadvantageous in a number of respects. Many countries have taken nationality rather than domicile as the basis of divorce jurisdiction. Some of the countries which take domicile as the basis of divorce jurisdiction have a less exacting concept of domicile—more simply and directly related to the idea of a settled home or permanent residence—than the concept established by the English case-law. Some countries have allowed the wife in certain situations to have a separate qualification for suing for divorce. The discordance between the principles of the former system in this country and the actual practice of other countries was productive of 'limping' marriages: the parties might be still married according to the law of England though divorced according to the law of some other country or countries. There was conspicuous hardship in the case of a deserted wife living in England and having her husband domiciled in some other country.

Also there have been relevant changes in general conditions. There is greatly increased mobility. There have been transfers of

---

[1] [1904] A.C. 287.   [2] [1930] A.C. 588; *ante*, p. 45.

INDYKA
v.
INDYKA.

Lord
Pearson.

population and extensive displacements of persons as well as normal migration. There is more international trade and international travel. Divorces have become far more frequent, so that the stability of marriage has been diminished. Another new element is the prevalence of retirement pensions, which may render the application of the very exacting concept of domicile more difficult in relation at any rate to matrimonial jurisdiction, because it may quite often happen that a man intends to keep his home, earn his living and bring up his family over a period of many years in one country and yet to go to another country when he retires on pension.

The disadvantages of the former system, aggravated or at any rate made more manifest by changes in general conditions, have led to corrective legislation. The enactments dealing specially with wartime or post-war situations or with particular Commonwealth problems would not necessarily affect the validity of the general principles on which the former system was founded, because those principles might be still generally correct though needing some exceptions of a temporary or otherwise limited character. But there are two enactments having such generality and permanence that they must be regarded as affecting the general principles of the system. One of these enactments, relating primarily to the case of the deserted wife, began as section 13 of the Matrimonial Causes Act 1937 and was re-enacted as section 18 (1) (*a*) of the Act of 1950 and is now contained in section 40 (1) (*a*) of the Act of 1965. The other of these enactments, relating to a wife who has resided in England for three years, began as part of section 1 of the Law Reform (Miscellaneous Provisions) Act 1949 and was re-enacted as section 18 (1) (*b*) of the Matrimonial Causes Act 1950 and is now contained in section 40 (1) (*b*) of the Act of 1965.

These two enactments strike at the roots of the former system. An English court will now in some cases grant a divorce although the parties are not domiciled in England, and will now in some cases grant a divorce on the basis that the wife has, separately from her husband, a qualification of her own for suing for divorce.

These enactments, however, relate only to the exercise of jurisdiction by the English Courts. They contain no provision as to the recognition in England of the validity in England of divorces granted in other countries. In fact the law relating to such recognition is almost entirely judge-made law. But it does not follow that the law relating to such recognition must remain unaffected by the statutory changes in the basis of the exercise of divorce jurisdiction by the English Courts.

I think that as a minimum the principle of *Travers* v. *Holley* must be applied in this case. 'On principle it seems to me plain that our courts in this matter should recognise a jurisdiction which they themselves claim' (per Somervell L.J.) 'It would be contrary to principle and inconsistent with comity if the courts of this country refused to recognise a jurisdiction which mutatis mutandis they claim for themselves' (per Hodson L.J.).

No doubt the principle should be regarded as a general principle, not to be applied as a cast iron rule in every case without regard to the character of the relevant English legislation. But the jurisdiction exercised by the English courts under the two enactments to which I have referred (now contained in section 40 of the Matrimonial Causes Act 1965) is of a general and apparently permanent character —not related to special or transient conditions—and there is no evident reason for refusing recognition to divorces granted in other countries in cases where mutatis mutandis jurisdiction would be exercised by the English courts under either of those two enactments. The principle applies if the facts are such as would mutatis mutandis confer jurisdiction on the English courts, even though the court in the other country may have claimed jurisdiction on some other basis: *Robinson-Scott* v. *Robinson-Scott*.

In the present case the first wife when she obtained her divorce from the husband had been resident for more than three years, in fact all her life, in Czechoslovakia. But she obtained her divorce in February, 1949, some months before the passing of the Law Reform (Miscellaneous Provisions) Act 1949, which made three years' residence in England a qualification for a wife to sue for divorce in England. The husband married or purported to marry the second wife in 1959, about ten years later. On that sequence of dates can the *Travers* v. *Holley* principle be applied? There are arguments to the contrary as stated in the judgment of Latey J. at first instance and the minority judgment of Russell L.J. in the Court of Appeal, but on the whole I think an affirmative answer should be given for the reasons stated in the judgments of the Master of the Rolls and Diplock L.J. in the Court of Appeal and in the opinions of my noble and learned friends, Lord Morris of Borth-y-Gest and Lord Pearce.

Thus, my first ground for dismissing the appeal is that the first wife had been living in Czechoslovakia for more than three years and the *Travers* v. *Holley* principle applies, although the Czech court did not base their jurisdiction on residence and although the divorce in Czechoslovakia preceded by a few months the passing of the Act of 1949.

But I also think that wider considerations are involved in this appeal. So long as the former system prevailed, it was a symmetrical system: the domicile of the parties was the one and only basis on which any court anywhere could properly exercise divorce jurisdiction: therefore, the basis for recognising divorces granted in other countries was of necessity exactly coincident with the basis for exercising jurisdiction in this country. Now the former system is no longer maintainable. It has been undermined and discredited by its disadvantages and the changes in general conditions and the passing of the two enactments to which I have referred. It no longer stands in the way of a realistic and reasonable view being taken of the range of cases in which validity should be accorded in England to divorces granted in other countries.

At this stage I am conscious of the lack of the apparatus of law reform—issuing a questionnaire and awaiting considered replies to it, receiving memoranda, hearing oral evidence, collecting statistics and obtaining information as to the systems prevailing in other countries. But we have had valuable assistance from counsel, and there is a great deal of information set out in the Report of the Royal Commission on Marriage and Divorce, presented in 1956. The Royal Commission made recommendations for legislation on the subject of the recognition of divorces granted in other countries. Since then there has not been any legislation implementing those recommendations or otherwise providing for such recognition. In the meantime the courts have to operate. There is a practical need for some guidance to be given by your Lordships' House, even if it can only be given in rather general terms. I am not intending to say that there necessarily ought to be legislation, but only that in the absence of legislation it is appropriate that there should be some general guidance from this House.

There is the plain fact that divorce jurisdiction is exercised on different bases in different countries. It cannot be said that the English basis—of domicile according to English case law plus the two enactments in favour of wives—is the only reasonable basis. Domicile according to a less exacting definition would be a not unreasonable basis and would have some advantages. The basis of nationality would in a great many cases give the same result as any basis of domicile, and it has the advantage of simplicity, and it seems to have been in use in many countries for many years. Nationality, however, is not available as a basis for use by federal and other nations which contain states, provinces or countries having the same nationality but separate divorce jurisdictions. Such nations will naturally use domicile as their basis, or they might use some residential qualification falling short of domicile. Therefore, unless the nations now using nationality as their basis are willing to change it (which is not indicated), there must be in the international sphere at least two different bases of jurisdiction being used. The duality is in that sense inevitable, and in any case it exists, and it should not be ignored.

It seems to me that, subject to appropriate limitations, a divorce granted in another country on the basis of nationality or on the basis of domicile (whether according to English case law or according to a less exacting definition) should be recognised as valid in England. Also if the law of the other country concerned enables a wife living apart from her husband to retain or acquire a separate qualification of nationality or domicile for the purpose of suing for divorce, and the jurisdiction has been exercised on the basis of that qualification, that would not, normally at any rate, be a reason for refusing recognition.

One obvious limitation is that a decree obtained by fraud or involving grave injustice should not be recognised. In addition there is a limitation which can only be indicated in rather general terms and I will gratefully borrow some phrases. In the words of my noble and learned friend, Lord Wilberforce, there must be a real and substantial connection between the petitioner and the country or territory exercising jurisdiction. In the words of my noble and learned friend, Lord Pearce, the court must be not 'simply purveying divorce to foreigners who wish to buy it.' In the words of Mr. Commissioner Latey, the courts must not be used 'for the convenience of "birds of passage"' (*Arnold* v. *Arnold*[1]). An alleged domicile can be fictitious: the petitioner may have declared his intention to settle permanently in the country concerned, but the evidence may show that he was only resorting there temporarily in order to obtain a divorce. Similarly a nationality might be acquired tempo-

INDYKA
v.
INDYKA.
Lord
Pearson.

[1] [1957] P. 237, 253.

143

rarily for the purpose of obtaining a divorce. Also nationality might perhaps in some circumstances be regarded as insufficient to found jurisdiction, if there was no longer any real and substantial connection between the petitioner and the country of his or her nationality.

As to the validity in England of divorces granted in other countries on the basis of a merely residential qualification, I feel there is a difficulty. As a matter of general principle, I would have thought that mere residence, falling short of domicile according to the less exacting definition, ought not to be a sufficient qualification. The broad distinction is between a person who makes his home in a country and a person who is a mere sojourner there. A person may be appointed to some diplomatic or military or commercial post in a foreign country and serve there for three or more years without becoming either dissociated from the community of his home country or associated with the community of the foreign country. His wife may be in the same position. There is, however, the second of the enactments referred to above, the one now contained in section 40 (1) (*b*) of the Act of 1965, which enables a wife after three years' residence in England, to sue for divorce, whatever may be the nationality or domicile of her husband and herself or of either of them. The principle of *Travers* v. *Holley* then requires that a divorce obtained in a foreign country by a wife who has resided in that country for three years or more should be recognised as valid in England. On the facts of this case the question whether recognition should be extended to a divorce granted on the basis of any other residential qualification—for example a husband's residence for three years or more, or a wife's residence for some period less than three years—does not need to be decided and I prefer to express no opinion upon it except that there is a difficulty.

In my view, the divorce obtained by the first wife in Czechoslovakia in February, 1949, should be recognised as having been valid in England in 1959, so that the husband was free to marry and did validly marry the second wife in 1959. Such recognition should be given on two grounds. First, the *Travers* v. *Holley* principle should be applied as mentioned above. Secondly, the divorce was granted in Czechoslovakia on the basis of the first wife's proved Czechoslovakian nationality, and there was no lack of real and substantial connection with Czechoslovakia. The first wife had lived there all her life, and had been married there, and had her matrimonial home there and was left there by the husband. There is no suggestion that she had any intention or desire to go to any other country. The husband had originally Czechoslovakian domicile and presumably also nationality. There is a finding that he acquired an English domicile of choice in 1946, but there is no finding or evidence that he acquired any new nationality.

I would dismiss the appeal.

English courts will recognise extra-judicial divorces, provided they are valid by the law of the parties' domicile.

RUSS v. RUSS [1964] P. 315 (Court of Appeal)

In 1913 Esther May Rosser, an Englishwoman and a spinster, married at the Reading Register Office Hassan Darweesh, a Mohammedan domiciled in Egypt. Shortly after this ceremony they went through a Mohammedan ceremony of marriage in Egypt. Thereafter they lived in Egypt for nineteen years and had three children. In 1932 Hassan Darweesh, in the presence of witnesses and before an officer of the Sharia Court, said 'Talak' three times, thereby, according to the law of his religion and his domicile, divorcing his wife Esther, who was present at the ceremony. The divorce was recorded in the records of the court and was followed by further proceedings between the parties before the same court, as a result of which Esther obtained an order for maintenance against Darweesh.

In February 1936 Esther went through a Mohammedan ceremony of marriage with Abdul Ibrahim, a domiciled Egyptian. In July 1936 this marriage was terminated by a Talak divorce pronounced by Abdul Ibrahim in the presence of Esther, of witnesses, and of an officer of the court.

In 1942 Esther went through a ceremony of marriage with the appellant, Edwin Russ, at the church of St. Andrew in Cairo in accordance with the rites and ceremonies of the Church of Scotland. There had been no dissolution or annulment of this marriage when in 1945 the appellant went through a ceremony of marriage in Belgium with the intervener, Leonia Josephine De Waele. No proceedings for the dissolution or annulment of this marriage had been taken when the appellant went through a ceremony of marriage with the petitioner, Elizabeth Geffers, in 1950 at Westminster Register Office.

INDYKA
v.
INDYKA.
Lord
Pearson.

RUSS
v.
RUSS.

Russ
v.
Russ.

The petitioner sought a decree of nullity of her marriage to the appellant on the ground that in 1950 the marriage between the appellant and Esther was a valid and subsisting marriage, and further, and in the alternative, on the ground that the marriage between the appellant and the intervener was valid and subsisting. Scarman J. granted the petitioner a decree of nullity on the former ground.[1] The appellant appealed. The intervener resisted the appeal, contending that her purported marriage was void on the ground of the appellant's prior marriage to Esther. The petitioner took no part in the appeal.

At the trial evidence of Egyptian law was given by Dr. Jamal Nasir, an advocate in Mohammedan law who had practised in Mohammedan courts in Egypt. The effect of his evidence was thus summarised by Scarman J. in the course of his judgment: '(*a*) Egyptian law recognises and gives effect to Mohammedan religious law as the personal law of a Mohammedan domiciled in Egypt; (*b*) under Mohammedan law a man may have four wives: in other words, marriage is potentially polygamous; (*c*) under Mohammedan law a man may divorce his wife irrevocably by pronouncing "Talak" three times in the presence of witnesses: no judicial proceeding or investigation is required before a man exercises this right. The divorce is constituted by the unilateral declaration of the husband in the presence of at least two witnesses: the wife need not be present, nor be given notice of the intention to divorce. (*d*) Egyptian law recognises, and gives effect to, a Talak divorce pronounced by a Mohammedan domiciled in Egypt. The marriage is recognised by Egyptian law as dissolved with effect from the date of the declaration; and this is so wherever the marriage was solemnised. It gives effect to the dissolution in a number of ways: for instance, Talak may be and almost always is pronounced before an authorised officer of the Egyptian court concerned with questions of personal status, whose duty it is to record the divorce in the records of the court. The record then constitutes, as Dr. Nasir was at pains to point out, the solemn recognition by the courts of Egypt of the fact of divorce: and the parties to the dissolved marriage may have recourse to the appropriate Egyptian court in matters of the maintenance and support of the divorced wife'.

DONOVAN L.J.: When Edwin Russ married Esther Russ in Cairo on April 29, 1942, she was, according to the law of her Egyptian

[1] [1963] P. 87.

domicile, a single woman. The question now is whether she should, as at that time, be similarly regarded in English law. Edwin Russ, her ostensible husband, contends for a negative answer to this question, having married two other women since without bothering to divorce the predecessor of either. The ground of his contention is that in 1913 Esther was married in England, according to English law, to one Darweesh, a Mohammedan; and despite the fact that she thereby acquired his Egyptian domicile, nevertheless the Talak divorce from her which Darweesh effected in 1932, albeit valid in Egyptian law, will not be recognised by English law; and so by English law the lady was still a married woman when she purported to marry Edwin Russ in 1942. It is the case that after the 1932 Talak divorce, Esther in February 1936 married another Egyptian, and was divorced by him also by Talak in July 1936, but this feature of the story is not directly material.

The contention for Edwin Russ is based solely on the decision in *Rex* v. *Hammersmith Superintendent Registrar of Marriages, Ex parte Mir-Anwaruddin.*[1] In that case an Indian subject domiciled in India contracted a civil marriage in England according to English law, and his English wife deserted him after some six weeks. He returned to India to practise as an advocate, but came back to England some two years later, and while here pronounced a Talak divorce in his own favour in the presence of two witnesses, and embodied the pronouncement in a written document. He then applied to the registrar at Hammersmith for the necessary certificate and licence so that he might marry a Miss Ling here. The registrar refused, holding that the first marriage still subsisted and constituted a lawful impediment to the proposed second marriage. Proceedings by writ of mandamus followed.

According to the affidavit evidence filed by Dr. Anwaruddin, Talaknama was effective under the Mohammedan law of his domicile to dissolve marriage. The question which arose for decision was whether English law would recognise it as effective to dissolve the doctor's English marriage. Both the Divisional Court and the Court of Appeal held that it would not, and so refused the writ. Various reasons were given. . . . The reasons given in both courts for refusing relief to Dr. Anwaruddin may be summarised thus, using the term 'Christian marriage' to denote a marriage, whether in registry office or church, by which a woman is taken as a wife for life to the

Russ
v.
Russ.
—
Donovan
L.J.

[1] [1917] 1 K.B. 634.

147

exclusion of all others: (1) Talaknama would not apply in any event to a Christian marriage in England (Swinfen Eady L.J.). (2) There had been no judicial decree of divorce in the country of domicile (Lord Reading C.J.; Bray J.). (3) Talaknama was merely part of the law of the husband's religion which the wife did not take (Lord Reading C.J.). (I should comment here that, although this is true, Talaknama, being part of the law of the husband's religion, was also part of the law of his domicile.) (4) The wife had contractual rights under the Christian marriage which were governed by English law. Therefore Talaknama had no application (Darling J.). (5) The evidence of foreign law was defective, but in any event a mere agreement to separate without any judicial proceedings would not be enough (Bankes L.J.). (6) Talak divorce was contrary to natural justice (A. T. Lawrence J.).

One may, I hope, respectfully comment that this variety of reasons is perhaps a reflection of the difficulties which their authors felt between, on the one hand, their repugnance to the idea of divorce at will, and, on the other, their awareness of the rule that the law of the domicile should control the matter. Be that as it may, only Swinfen Eady L.J. went the length of holding that it was impossible in law for a Christian marriage contracted in England to be dissolved by Talaknama. This indeed had been the principal contention of the Solicitor-General, but no other judge in terms acceded to it. A. T. Lawrence J., in saying that a Talak divorce was contrary to natural justice, was clearly referring to the particular facts in the *Hammersmith* case, which included the fact that the wife had no prior notice of her husband's intention.

In these circumstances the decision ought not, in my opinion, to be regarded as laying down the universal rule for which [counsel for the appellant] here contends, namely, that a Christian marriage in England cannot, in the eye of English law, ever be dissolved by Talaknama, notwithstanding that the law of the parties' domicile permits it. Later decisions tend to support the opposite contention, though the relevant marriage was not celebrated in England; see, for example, *Har-Shefi* v. *Har-Shefi (No. 2)*,[1] *Baindail* v. *Baindail*,[2] *Sasson* v. *Sasson*.[3]

Turning to the other reasons given for the decision in the *Hammersmith* case, none of them have weight here. It is true that there does not appear to have been a decree of any court in the

[1] [1953] P. 220.   [2] [1946] P. 122; *ante*, p. 95.   [3] [1924] A.C. 1007.

present case, though why that should be treated as crucial is difficult to understand. Later decisions have shown that English law will recognise a foreign divorce in some cases where the decree of the foreign tribunal seems to have been a long way from our notions of a judicial proceeding; compare *Igra* v. *Igra*[1] and *Mountbatten* v. *Mountbatten*.[2] But it is, I think, sufficient to say in the present case (as did the judge) that there have been at least some judicial proceedings in Egypt. He said: 'Esther's divorce was in the presence of an authorised officer of the Egyptian court, was solemnly recorded in the records of the court, and has been the basis of legal proceedings in Egypt concerned with her right to support.' This is true. Again there was evidence in the present case, which there was not in the *Hammersmith* case, to the effect that the Talak divorce was effective in the country of the parties' domicile to dissolve the Christian marriage. And with regard to the requirements of natural justice, Esther had notice of what was proposed, for she was present at the ceremony, and afterwards approbated it by her conduct. Indeed, she married again on the footing that she had once more become single.

The reasoning of Darling J. to the effect that contractual rights were obtained by the wife in the *Hammersmith* case which were governed solely by English law, and that therefore a Talak divorce was ineffective, was adopted by no other judge. And indeed, if this were the true view, it would seem to follow that the general rule of English law whereby divorce is regulated according to the law of domicile would be almost wholly abrogated.

For the foregoing reasons I reach the conclusion that this court is not bound by the decision in the *Hammersmith* case to decide that the Talak divorce pronounced against Esther was ineffective in English law to dissolve her English marriage. It is, of course, tempting to say that what the courts here were considering in the *Hammersmith* case was the validity of a proposed second marriage in England, whereas we are now considering the effect of a Talak decree obtained in Egypt on an existing English marriage, and to distinguish the present case on that ground. But in my opinion to do so would be to avoid the issue. In terms of the relevant statute the question in the *Hammersmith* case was whether there was any lawful impediment to the proposed second marriage. The answer depended on whether Dr. Anwaruddin was married already, in other

RUSS
v.
RUSS.
—
Donovan
L.J.

[1] [1951] P. 404.   [2] [1959] P. 43.

words, on his status. In turn that depended on whether English law would recognise his Talak divorce. In the present case the issue is whether Edwin Russ was already married when he purported to marry Leonia De Waele in Belgium in 1945, and that depends on whether Esther was still a married woman when she earlier purported to marry Russ in 1942. In turn that depends on the efficacy of the Talak divorce to dissolve Esther's previous English marriage. So at bottom the question is really the same as in the *Hammersmith* case, and cannot be avoided by relying upon the distinctions in the surrounding facts.

In my opinion, the Talak divorce of 1932 was effective to dissolve Esther's English marriage to Hassan Darweesh of 1913. The reasons are these. After that marriage, both parties became domiciled in Egypt. It has been proved by competent evidence that the Talak divorce was effective in Egyptian law to dissolve the English marriage. The normal rule is that: 'When a marriage has been duly solemnised according to the law of the place of solemnisation, the parties become husband and wife. But when they become husband and wife what is the character which the wife assumes? She becomes the wife of the foreign husband in a case where the husband is a foreigner in the country in which the marriage is contracted. She no longer retains any other domicile than his, which she acquires. The marriage is contracted with a view to that matrimonial domicile which results from her placing herself by contract in the relation of wife to the husband whom she marries, knowing him to be a foreigner, domiciled and contemplating permanent and settled residence abroad. Therefore it must be within the meaning of such a contract, if we are to inquire into it, that she is to become subject to her husband's law, subject to it in respect of the consequences of the matrimonial relation and all other consequences depending upon the law of the husband's domicile': *per* Lord Selborne L.C. in *Harvey* v. *Farnie*.[1]

There is no reason in the present case to depart from that rule, though in special circumstances the courts here would do so: compare *In re Langley's Settlement Trusts*,[2] in which case this court, though not dealing with a question of divorce, held that while the status imposed by the law of a person's domicile ought generally to be recognised in England, nevertheless English courts retained a discretion as to giving operation to the results of such status.

[1] (1882) 8 App. Cas. 43, 50.   [2] [1962] Ch. 541.

I think that in contemplation of English law Esther Russ should be regarded as having been effectively divorced according to the custom of Talak before she married Edwin Russ in 1942; that Scarman J. came to the right conclusion, and that this appeal should be dismissed.

Russ
v.
Russ.
——
Donovan
L.J.

WILLMER and DAVIES L.JJ. delivered judgments to the same effect.

Appeal dismissed.

English courts are reluctant to allow foreign divorces to be challenged by third parties on grounds other than jurisdictional grounds.

PEMBERTON v. HUGHES [1899] 1 Ch. 781 (*post*, p. 497)

NOTE F: RECOGNITION OF FOREIGN DIVORCES

IT was settled by the decisions of the House of Lords in *Warrender* v. *Warrender* (1835) 2 Cl. & F. 488, *Shaw* v. *Gould* (1868) L.R. 3 H.L. 55 (*post*, p. 209) and *Harvey* v. *Farnie* (1882) 2 App. Cas. 43 and of the Privy Council in *Le Mesurier* v. *Le Mesurier* [1895] A.C. 517 (*ante*, p. 114) that English courts would recognize foreign divorces if the parties (i.e. the husband) were domiciled in the foreign country at the commencement of the proceedings. (It is immaterial that the husband abandons his domicile in the foreign country between the date of the commencement of the proceedings and the granting of the decree: *Mansell* v. *Mansell* [1967] 2 W.L.R. 328.) The *Le Mesurier* case was technically a decision on the jurisdiction of the Supreme Court of Ceylon, but their Lordships obviously intended their remarks to be of general application and to apply to recognition as well as to jurisdiction.

In *Armitage* v. *A.-G.* [1906] P. 135 it was held that English courts would also recognize divorces recognized as valid by the law of the country where the parties were domiciled at the date of the divorce.

In *Travers* v. *Holley* [1953] P. 246, *ante*, p. 119, it was held by the Court of Appeal that English courts would recognize a divorce obtained by a wife if the English court would (*mutatis mutandis*) have had jurisdiction to grant her a divorce under what are now s. 40 (1) (*a*) or (*b*) of the Matrimonial Causes Act 1965 (*ante*, p. 116). Thus if the husband was domiciled in the foreign country and then deserted his wife and changed his domicile, or if the wife was ordinarily resident in the foreign country for three years immediately preceding the commencement of the proceedings, a divorce obtained by her would be recognized in England. This decision has been followed in numerous reported cases, in all of which the husband was domiciled in England at the date of the divorce.

FAMILY LAW

In all these situations it was immaterial on what basis the foreign court assumed jurisdiction or on what grounds the divorce was granted: *Robinson-Scott* v. *Robinson-Scott* [1958] P. 71.

In *Indyka* v. *Indyka* [1967] 3 W.L.R. 510 (*ante*, p. 122) the whole subject was considered afresh by the House of Lords. It would be a hopeless task to extract one single ratio decidendi from the speeches in this case: the most that can be done is to collate the various views expressed.

The appeal was dismissed on three separate grounds:

(1) The divorce should be recognized under the doctrine of *Travers* v. *Holley* because the wife was ordinarily resident in Czecho-Slovakia for three years immediately preceding the commencement of the proceedings there, and it was immaterial that the decree was granted before what is now s. 40 (1) (*b*) of the Matrimonial Causes Act 1965 was first enacted: Lord Morris (p. 131); Lord Pearce (p. 134); Lord Pearson (pp. 141–2).

(2) The divorce should be recognized because there was a 'real and substantial connection' between the wife and Czecho-Slovakia since both parties were Czech nationals and the Czech court assumed jurisdiction on this ground: Lord Morris (p. 132); Lord Pearce (p. 135); Lord Wilberforce (p. 135); Lord Pearson (p. 144). All except Lord Morris added that the matrimonial home was in Czecho-Slovakia and the wife resided there all her life. Lord Pearce and Lord Pearson added that both parties were originally domiciled there. Lord Pearson added that the parties were married there; but this is not a significant factor: see *Peters* v. *Peters* [1967] 3 W.L.R. 1235.

(3) The divorce should be recognized because the parties' last matrimonial home was in Czecho-Slovakia and the wife continued to reside there after her husband left: Lord Reid (p. 130). Lord Reid was not troubled by the fact that the matrimonial home was abandoned ten years before the commencement of the proceedings.

When we come to enumerate the bases on which their Lordships thought that foreign divorces should be recognized in England, some differences of opinion are apparent, and no fewer than eight such bases can be identified in the speeches. They are as follows:

(1) *Domicile*. Their Lordships agreed (with varying degrees of emphasis) that domicile must remain the primary basis of recognition.

(2) *Armitage* v. *A.-G.* All of their Lordships except Lord Reid approved of the rule in this case.

(3) *Travers* v. *Holley*. All of their Lordships agreed that this case was rightly decided. But Lord Reid (with whom Lord Wilberforce agreed) was critical of the reasoning; and their Lordships differed as to how the principle should be applied in future. Lord Reid would only recognize divorces granted to wives whose husbands deserted them and then changed their domicile if the wife had grounds for divorce before the change of domicile (p. 129). (There is no corresponding limitation in s. 40 (1) (*a*) of the Matrimonial Causes Act 1965.) Lord Reid would not recognize divorces granted to wives after three years' ordinary residence in the foreign country unless the divorce was granted in the last matrimonial home, or unless the wife was 'habitually' resident in the foreign country and had no present intention of leaving it (pp. 125, 130). But Lord Morris (p. 131), Lord Pearce (p. 134) and Lord Pearson (p. 144) would recognize a divorce granted to a wife after three years' ordinary residence without qualification; and Lord Pearce even left

152

open the question whether less than three years' residence would suffice. He pointed out, what is undeniably true, that to narrow the ground of recognition accorded by *Travers* v. *Holley* might cause difficulties to those who had remarried in reliance on that decision (p. 134).

(4) *Nationality.* Only Lord Pearce (p. 134) and Lord Pearson (p. 143) came down squarely in favour of recognizing divorces on the basis of nationality alone, and then only (in Lord Pearce's view) if the foreign court assumed jurisdiction on this basis. Lord Wilberforce was more cautious: he said that recognition 'might in appropriate circumstances be given to the factor of nationality' (p. 137); but he pointed out some of the difficulties involved, as also did Lord Pearson.

(5) *Residence.* Apart from cases covered by the rule in *Travers* v. *Holley*, none of their Lordships was prepared to concede recognition on the basis of residence alone, and Lord Pearson was definitely opposed to doing so (p. 144). But Lord Reid would recognize it if the wife was 'habitually' resident in the foreign country and had no present intention of leaving it (p. 130); and Lord Wilberforce would recognize it if there was a 'real and substantial connection' between the wife petitioner and the divorce forum (p. 137).

(6) *'Domicile' according to a less exacting standard than that of English law.* Lord Pearson was prepared to recognize divorces granted on this basis (pp. 142–3).

(7) *Last matrimonial home.* Lord Reid would recognize divorces granted in the country where the parties last had a matrimonial home, at any rate if the petitioner continued to reside there; and he drew no distinction in this respect between husbands and wives (p. 130).

(8) *Real and substantial connection.* Lord Morris (p. 132), Lord Wilberforce (p. 137), and Lord Pearson (p. 143) would recognize a divorce if there was a 'real and substantial connection' between the petitioner and the country where the divorce was granted, e.g. because the last matrimonial home was there or the petitioner was a national of that country.

The attitude of their Lordships to the recognition of foreign divorces was liberal, realistic, and humane, but it is perhaps a pity that they canvassed so many different bases of recognition. The effect can only be to leave the law uncertain, especially in cases where the divorce was obtained by the husband. It will be seen that a majority can be found for (1), (2), (3), and (8) of the bases mentioned above. If English law had allowed a wife to establish a domicile separate from that of her husband, there would have been no difficulty about recognizing the Czech divorce on that basis. But, as Lord Reid (p. 124) and Lord Wilberforce (p. 136) pointed out, an alteration of the law in this matter would be better left to Parliament.

It is unlikely that the decision in *Indyka* v. *Indyka* will have any repercussions (except perhaps in Parliament) on the jurisdiction of the English court to grant divorce decrees, because Lord Reid (p. 127), Lord Morris, Lord Pearce (p. 133), and Lord Wilberforce (p. 136) emphasized that the question before the House was one of recognition, not one of jurisdiction; and that Parliament had on several occasions assumed that jurisdiction was founded on domicile alone.

Lord Pearce made a qualification which calls for some comment. He required the foreign divorce to be a 'genuine divorce' and would withhold recognition from decrees based on one day's residence and granted on the ground of incompatibility of temperament. He instanced *Mountbatten* v. *Mountbatten* [1959] P. 43, where the parties were domiciled in England, the wife had been ordinarily resident in New York for three years, and the wife obtained a divorce in Mexico with her husband's consent after a 24-hour visit to that country. Although there was evidence that the Mexican divorce would be recognized in New York, Arthian Davies J. refused to recognize it in England because he was unable to combine the principles of *Armitage* v. *A.-G.* and *Travers* v. *Holley*. Lord Pearce approved this result. But he did not seem to appreciate that if the parties had been domiciled instead of merely resident in New York, the Mexican divorce should have been recognized in England under the rule in *Armitage* v. *A.-G.*, which he had previously described as a 'sound and valuable exception' to the domicile principle. The recognition of extra judicial divorces (*Russ* v. *Russ* [1964] P. 315; *ante*, p. 145) is also difficult to reconcile with Lord Pearce's requirement that the divorce must be 'genuine'.

None of their Lordships attempted to answer the powerful reasoning of Latey J. in the court of first instance and of Russell L.J. in the Court of Appeal that the Czech divorce could not be recognized in England because it was granted before what is now s. 40 (1) (*b*) of the Matrimonial Causes Act 1965 was first enacted. As Latey J. and Russell L.J. pointed out, the divorce would certainly not have been recognized in England at least for eleven months after it was granted. To hold that it was retrospectively validated after the Law Reform (Miscellaneous Provisions) Act 1949 came into force in December 1949 raises some formidable difficulties. (*a*) Suppose that the husband had remarried before December 1949, and that his second wife had obtained a nullity decree in England before that date, and had then remarried. Would the Act have retrospectively validated the Czech divorce, invalidated the English nullity decree and invalidated the second wife's second marriage? (*b*) Suppose that the husband had died intestate before December 1949 without having remarried, and that his property in England had been handed over to his Czech wife as the surviving spouse: would she have had to return it when the 1949 Act retrospectively validated the Czech divorce?

In *Angelo* v. *Angelo* [1967] 3 All E.R. 314, the parties were married in London in 1960; the husband was domiciled in England; the wife was a German national who before her marriage was domiciled in Germany; the matrimonial home was in France. The wife left the husband, returned to Germany and obtained a divorce there in 1963 after six months' residence. The husband petitioned for a declaration that the German divorce was not recognized in England. The petition (which was undefended) came on for hearing a week after the decision in *Indyka* v. *Indyka*. Ormrod J. gave the husband leave to amend his petition so as to ask for the exact opposite of the declaration originally sought; and made a declaration that the divorce would be recognized in England on the basis that the wife was a German national and was habitually resident in Germany.

The Invalidity of Valid Foreign Divorces. A decree of divorce is analogous to a judgment in rem in that it binds third parties as well as the spouses. Consequently, to allow third parties to attack foreign divorces granted by courts having jurisdiction over the subject-matter would introduce the gravest uncertainty in family relationships, because the spouses may have remarried and had children in reliance on the foreign decree. English courts have therefore been reluctant to allow such divorces to be attacked on grounds other than jurisdictional grounds. They have recognized a German divorce obtained during the Nazi régime at the instance of the secret police on what were suspected to be racial grounds (*Igra* v. *Igra* [1951] P. 404). They have recognized a Florida divorce notwithstanding errors in applying its own procedure made by the Florida court (*Pemberton* v. *Hughes* [1899] 1 Ch. 781, *post*, p. 497). They have recognized divorces obtained by collusion (*Crowe* v. *Crowe* (1937) 157 L.T. 557), non-disclosure of material facts (*Vardy* v. *Smith* (1932) 48 T.L.R. 661, 49 T.L.R. 36), or the procuring of false testimony (*Perin* v. *Perin* 1950, S.L.T. 51). They have recognized divorces although the respondent received no notice of the proceedings until after they were over (*Boettcher* v. *Boettcher* [1949] W.N. 83; *Igra* v. *Igra* [1951] P. 404; *Arnold* v. *Arnold* [1957] P. 237; *Wood* v. *Wood* [1957] P. 254). But where the husband falsely told the foreign court that he did not know his wife's address, with the result that she was served only by advertisement in a local newspaper, the divorce was not recognized (*Macalpine* v. *Macalpine* [1958] P. 35). Question: if Mrs. Macalpine had wanted to remarry, could she have waived the want of notice?

Divisible Divorce. In *Wood* v. *Wood* [1957] P. 254 the Court of Appeal held that if a wife obtains a maintenance order from the English court, and is then validly divorced abroad, she can nevertheless enforce the maintenance order in England in the discretion of the court—at any rate if she had no opportunity of contesting the question of maintenance in the foreign court. A similar result had been reached by the Supreme Court of the United States in *Estin* v. *Estin* (1948) 334 U.S. 541. Hence, a foreign divorce may alter the status of the parties without terminating the husband's duty to support the wife. But his obligation to do so is at an end if it has not crystallized in a court order before the divorce. This is because the English statutes which confer jurisdiction on the courts to order a husband to pay maintenance to his wife presuppose that the parties are husband and wife or have been divorced in England (see Matrimonial Causes Act 1965, ss. 16, 22; Matrimonial Proceedings (Magistrates' Courts) Act 1960). However, in the United States the Supreme Court has reached an opposite result: *Vanderbilt* v. *Vanderbilt* (1957) 354 U.S. 416.

The Validity of Void Divorces. A foreign divorce granted without jurisdiction is not necessarily without effect in England. It may terminate the respondent's desertion, and thus prevent the petitioner from obtaining a divorce on that ground in England (*Joseph* v. *Joseph* [1953] 1 W.L.R. 1182). If a husband obtains, or encourages his wife to obtain, an invalid foreign divorce, and the wife then remarries, the husband may be held to have connived at her adultery and so be unable to obtain a divorce on that ground in England (*Lankester* v. *Lankester and Cooper* [1925] P. 114). Or the conduct of one spouse in not contesting an invalid foreign divorce may be held to have conduced to the adultery of the other (see *Clayton* v. *Clayton* v. *Sharman* [1932] P. 45; *Travers* v. *Holley*, ante, p. 122).

Suppose that a husband and wife are domiciled in England, and that the wife establishes a residence in Nevada for six weeks, obtains a divorce there, remarries in Nevada, and then claims a widow's share in the estate of her first husband on his death intestate. The divorce would certainly not be recognized in England, but would she be estopped from denying its invalidity? There is no English authority for this proposition, but there is American and Canadian authority: see Dicey, p. 329, n. 49.

Section B: NULLITY OF MARRIAGE

English courts have jurisdiction to annul a voidable marriage if both parties are either domiciled or resident in England at the commencement of the proceedings.

RAMSAY-FAIRFAX *v*. RAMSAY-FAIRFAX [1956] P. 115
(Court of Appeal)

Issue as to jurisdiction to hear a wife's petition for nullity on the ground of wilful refusal to consummate and impotence.

The parties were married in Egypt on 22 November 1947, according to the provisions of section 22 of the Foreign Marriage Act 1892, the husband being an officer serving in His Majesty's forces.

At the date of the presentation of the petition on 2 March 1954 the parties were domiciled in Scotland but resident in England. The husband had been so resident since 1951 and the wife since the spring of 1953. The husband, who had in December 1954 instituted nullity proceedings against the wife in Scotland raising similar allegations against her, appeared under protest and denied that the court had jurisdiction.

Willmer J. held that the court had jurisdiction to entertain the wife's suit. The husband appealed.

DENNING L.J.: The parties in this case went through a form of marriage on November 22, 1947, while the husband was a major in the Army and his wife was employed in Cairo; and they were married in Cairo by an Army chaplain under the provisions of section 22 of the Foreign Marriages Act 1892. It can therefore be treated in all respects as if it was a marriage made in the United Kingdom, in England, for instance, or in Scotland.

In 1954, while the parties were both living in this country, the wife filed a petition for nullity on the ground of incapacity or, alternatively wilful refusal to consummate the marriage. The important thing to notice is that the domicile of the husband is in Scotland. It follows that, unless and until the marriage is annulled, the domicile of the wife is also in Scotland, because she takes the domicile of her husband. It is suggested that because the domicile of the parties is in Scotland the courts of England have no jurisdiction to entertain this petition. The husband has, we are told, started proceedings in Scotland for nullity on like grounds, and wishes to proceed with his case there. The issue is whether the English courts have jurisdiction. It is a matter of practical importance, because in England the wife, after a decree for nullity, can get maintenance, whereas in Scotland she cannot get anything.

The jurisdiction in cases of nullity is, in my judgment, entirely different from the jurisdiction in cases of divorce. In cases of divorce, ever since *Le Mesurier* v. *Le Mesurier*,[1] the only courts which have had jurisdiction to decree a dissolution of a marriage are the courts of the domicile; but the jurisdiction of our courts in nullity cases is different, dating from 1857, when, by section 22 of the Matrimonial Causes Act 1857,[2] it was said: 'In all suits and proceedings, other than proceedings to dissolve any marriage, the said court shall proceed and act and give relief on principles and rules which in the opinion of the said court shall be as nearly as may be conformable to the principles and rules on which the ecclesiastical courts have heretofore acted and given relief.' That section shows plainly that the jurisdiction in nullity suits depends on the principles and rules which were observed in the ecclesiastical courts before 1857. It is true that the grounds of nullity have since been extended, but nevertheless, in my opinion, all suits for nullity, whether on the original grounds—for instance, for incapacity—or on the new grounds—for instance, for wilful refusal—are to be governed by the principles and rules which were observed in the old ecclesiastical courts.

It is quite clear that the ecclesiastical courts based their jurisdiction in cases of nullity on residence, not upon domicile. If the respondent, the defendant to a petition, was resident within the local jurisdiction of the court, then the court had jurisdiction to determine it. So in the present case. The husband and wife were, at the issuing of the petition, both resident in this country, and that is sufficient to give the court jurisdiction to decide the case. So much seems to me plain on the interpretation of the statutes. In addition, in *Baxter* v. *Baxter*[3] in the House of Lords, Viscount Jowitt L.C. said that

RAMSAY-
FAIRFAX
v.
RAMSAY-
FAIRFAX.

Denning
L.J.

---

[1] [1895] A.C. 517; *ante*, p. 114.
[2] Since repealed and re-enacted by section 32 of the Supreme Court of Judicature (Consolidation) Act 1925 which is, however, confined to procedure and practice.
[3] [1948] A.C. 274, 285.

RAMSAY-
FAIRFAX
v.
RAMSAY-
FAIRFAX.

section 22 manifestly applied to suits for nullity on the ground of incapacity. It must also apply to suits on the new ground of wilful refusal.

Denning
L.J.

That is a sufficient ground for the determination of this case, but, as there has been much difference of opinion on this matter, I must say a word about *Inverclyde* v. *Inverclyde*,[1] in which Bateson J. held that in a case of nullity on the ground of impotence the only court which had jurisdiction was the court of the domicile. The basis of his reasoning was that a case of nullity, whether for impotence or for wilful refusal,[2] was much more like a suit for divorce than anything else; and that it should be equated, so to speak, with a suit for dissolution and be governed solely by the law of the domicile, and that the only courts which should have jurisdiction should be the courts of the domicile. He said, in a sentence: 'To call it a suit for nullity does not alter its essential and real character of a suit for dissolution.'

I beg to differ from this view. Looking at the ground of wilful refusal from a legalistic standpoint, and treating marriage as a contract, the remedy of nullity does look like a remedy of divorce or dissolution, because it depends on events which occur subsequent to the marriage; but looking at it from a sensible standpoint, and having regard to the true ends of marriage, one of the principal aims of which is the procreation of children, it seems to me that the remedy falls more truly within the category of nullity. No one can call a marriage a real marriage when it has not been consummated; and this is the same, no matter whether the want of consummation is due to incapacity or to wilful refusal. Let the theologians dispute as they will, so far as the lawyers are concerned, Parliament has made it quite plain that wilful refusal and incapacity stand together as grounds of nullity and not for dissolution;[3] and being grounds of nullity, they fall within the old ecclesiastical practice, in which the jurisdiction of the courts is founded upon residence and not upon domicile.

Then [counsel for the husband] sought to draw a distinction between a marriage which was void and a marriage which was void-

[1] [1931] P. 29.

[2] *Sed quaere*: wilful refusal was not a ground for nullity in 1931 and is not mentioned in the judgment of Bateson J.

[3] In 1956 the Royal Commission on Marriage and Divorce recommended that wilful refusal should be a ground for divorce and not for nullity: Cmd. 9678, paras. 88, 89, 283.

able. He admitted that in marriages which were void, the courts where the parties resided had jurisdiction, but he said that in marriages that were voidable, it was only the courts of the domicile. However valid this distinction may be for some purposes, it is not valid for our present purposes. Take the case of impotence itself, which has always made a marriage voidable. The old ecclesiastical courts would certainly assume jurisdiction on the grounds of residence and not of domicile; and if they would assume jurisdiction, so should we also. Likewise with wilful refusal, which also makes a marriage voidable.

It is to be noticed that in 1944 there were two cases, *Easterbrook* v. *Easterbrook*[1] before Hodson J. and *Hutter* v. *Hutter*[2] before Pilcher J., in which it was held that the English courts have jurisdiction in nullity cases where both parties are resident here. In the first of those cases, a Canadian soldier married an English woman here, and it was held that although he was domiciled in some province in Canada, nevertheless the courts here had jurisdiction to determine his claim for nullity. Any other view would be most unfortunate. It would be absurd that a Canadian soldier married to an English woman should have to go to the courts of Canada to get his remedy (or, conversely, that she should) when they were both resident here. The next case was that of a United States soldier who married an English women here. Again it was held that the courts in this country had jurisdiction even though the soldier was domiciled in one of the States of America. It is far too late in the day to say that those two cases were wrongly decided, considering that many decrees must have been given on the self-same footing, and that many people have regulated their affairs on the basis of them. It would be very wrong to suggest now that those decisions were bad, and that the people who have acted on them have been guilty of bigamy. I am clearly of opinion that those two cases were rightly decided and should be upheld: but *Inverclyde* v. *Inverclyde* was wrongly decided and should be overruled.

One word more. It may be in these nullity cases that the courts of the domicile also have jurisdiction:[3] so may the courts of the place where the marriage was celebrated:[4] but the courts where both parties reside certainly have jurisdiction.

RAMSAY-
FAIRFAX
v.
RAMSAY-
FAIRFAX.

Denning
L.J.

---

[1] [1944] P. 10.   [2] [1944] P. 95.
[3] This is no longer doubted : see *De Reneville* v. *De Reneville, infra.*
[4] As to this, see *Ross Smith* v. *Ross Smith, post,* p. 170.

RAMSAY-
FAIRFAX
v.
RAMSAY-
FAIRFAX.
—
Denning
L.J.

I find myself in agreement with Willmer J. and would dismiss the appeal.

HODSON and MORRIS L.JJ. delivered judgments to the same effect.

Appeal dismissed.

English courts have (apart from statute) no jurisdiction to annul a voidable marriage if the respondent is neither domiciled nor resident in England.

The law of the husband's domicile at the date of the marriage determines whether the marriage is void or voidable.

DE RENEVILLE *v.* DE RENEVILLE [1948] P. 100 (Court of Appeal)

The wife petitioner, Comtesse Mary Margaret Motley de Reneville, was born in England of English parents, and was domiciled in England until her marriage. In 1935 she married the respondent, a domiciled Frenchman, in Paris, and lived with him there, at Brazzaville in the French Congo, and at Biskra in Algeria. In 1940 the petitioner left the respondent and returned to England, where she had since remained. She petitioned for nullity on the ground that the marriage had not been consummated owing to the incapacity or wilful refusal of the respondent. The respondent entered appearance under protest on the ground that the court had no jurisdiction to entertain the petition. He was at all material times resident as well as domiciled in France. An issue was directed to be tried between the respondent as plaintiff and the petitioner as defendant, to determine the question of jurisdiction. Jones J. held that there was no jurisdiction, and the petitioner appealed.

LORD GREENE M.R.: ... Before the argument before us had proceeded very far, it appeared that the procedure adopted of trying the question of jurisdiction on a preliminary issue, although no doubt a proper one, did in the special circumstances of the case lead to certain inconveniences. Two alternative matters of fact are alleged in the petition as grounds for a decree of nullity; neither of which was or could be proved or admitted on the trial of the issue. On one view of the law it appeared possible that our decision might be different according as the one or the other of these alternative allegations might be established. Thus, in so far as the answer to the issue as to jurisdiction might depend on domicile the question what was the domicile of the petitioner at the institution of the suit might, as it seemed to us, depend on whether the marriage was a void or voidable one, a question which, in its turn, might fall to be determined by the law of France on the ground either that the marriage was celebrated in that country, or that the matrimonial domicile contemplated by the parties was French. If under French law the marriage was void the result, as it then appeared to us, might well be that the domicile of the petitioner was English at the institution of the suit, a fact which, if established, would, according to some authority, give the English court jurisdiction to pronounce a decree of nullity. When these various possibilities and complications were adumbrated, the further difficulty emerged that so far as the trial of the issue was concerned no question of French law had been pleaded or raised in any way and that in so far as any question has to be decided by reference to French law, that law must on ordinary principles in the absence of proof to the contrary be assumed to be the same as English law. On this basis the question whether the marriage was void or voidable would ultimately have to be decided in accordance with provisions identical with those of English law.

As the result of some discussion, counsel on both sides were anxious, as was the court itself, to avoid the waste of money which would have been involved if the whole matter including the issue of jurisdiction had been sent back for trial. Accordingly, with the consent of counsel for both parties, we decided that the appeal should proceed on the basis that we would decide the question of jurisdiction on two alternative hypotheses, one that the marriage was void and the other that the marriage was voidable.

Various grounds have been suggested as forming foundations for the exercise of jurisdiction in nullity cases by the courts of this country. They may be listed as follows: (1) English domicile of both parties. (2) English domicile of the petitioner alone. (3) English residence of both parties. (4) English residence of the petitioner alone. (5) The fact that the marriage took place here. (6) Hardship. We are not concerned here to consider cases (3), (5) or (6). 'Whether there cannot be jurisdiction which is not that of the domicile in restricted instances to entertain a suit for nullity is a question we have not before us for determination', said Lord Haldane in *Von Lorang* v. *Administrator of Austrian Property*.[1] This doubtful question remains

DE RENE-
VILLE
v.
DE RENE-
VILLE.
—
Lord
Greene
M.R.

---

[1] [1927] A.C. 641 ; *post*, p. 185.

DE RENE-
VILLE
v.
DE RENE-
VILLE.

Lord
Greene
M.R.

to be answered by the House of Lords, and there is no need for us to attempt to answer it for the purposes of this appeal. I shall endeavour to confine myself to the questions actually raised.

The case presented on behalf of the petitioner was to the following effect. (A) It was said that in so far as the basis of jurisdiction is to be sought in domicile alone, the domicile of the petitioner is sufficient: that if the marriage was a void marriage, the petitioner had never lost or alternatively had resumed her English domicile of origin before the institution of the cause; that even if the marriage was only voidable, the effect of a decree of nullity would be to render it void ab initio, with the result that for the purposes of jurisdiction the petitioner ought to be regarded as already possessing the status of spinsterhood which, it was said, a decree would give her by its retroactive operation; and that accordingly, the fact that the respondent was domiciled in France is irrelevant on the question of jurisdiction.

(B) Alternatively, it was said that if the petitioner's case as to jurisdiction based on domicile cannot be supported, the court has jurisdiction by reason of the fact that at the inception of the suit she was resident in England and notwithstanding the fact that the respondent was then, as he still is, resident in France. I will deal with these two alternatives in the order in which I have stated them.

(A) That the courts of the country in which the parties are domiciled have jurisdiction to pronounce a decree of nullity whether the parties were or were not married in that country is set beyond doubt by the decision of the House of Lords in *Von Lorang* v. *Administrator of Austrian Property*. It will be noticed that I have said 'the parties' since in that case as in most other cases in which domicile as a basis of jurisdiction has been discussed the domicile of the parties was the same. In nullity cases the parties will have the same domicile at the date of the institution of the suit in one of two events, namely (1) if the marriage is by the proper law voidable and not void, in which case the wife will have acquired the same domicile as the husband by the mere fact of marriage and retains that domicile until the marriage is annulled. (2) If the marriage is void but nevertheless the wife on the facts acquired a domicile of choice in the country contemplated as that of the matrimonial domicile and has not subsequently changed that domicile. This occurred in the *Von Lorang* case, where the wife acquired in fact the husband's German domicile and therefore it was unnecessary to consider what the posi-

DE RENE-
VILLE
v.
DE RENE-
VILLE.

Lord
Greene
M.R.

tion would have been if the marriage had been a void marriage and the domiciles of the parties had been different. Throughout the opinions delivered in that case the word 'parties' in the plural is used and it is right to point out that Lord Phillimore said that as to matters of status 'the law which regulates or determines the personal status of the parties, if they are both subject to the same law, decides conclusively'. I do not, however, read this as an expression of opinion on a point which did not arise and was not for consideration, namely, has such a court jurisdiction where one only of the parties is subject to its law, that is, domiciled in its country. I will return to this later.

So far as English law is concerned there is a clear distinction between void and voidable marriages. 'Wilful refusal' is by s. 7 of the Matrimonial Causes Act 1937 a ground for treating the marriage as voidable, not for treating it as void. . . .

In what, for present purposes, does the distinction consist? It is argued that there is no real distinction by reason of the fact that in each case the form of the decree is the same and pronounces the marriage 'to have been and to be absolutely null and void to all intents and purposes in the law whatsoever'. It is perhaps unfortunate that a form of decree which was appropriate when a marriage was regarded as indissoluble and could only be got rid of by decreeing that it had never taken place is still used indiscriminately in the cases of both void and voidable marriages. It is particularly anomalous in the case of the new grounds of nullity laid down by the Act of 1937. In *Inverclyde* v. *Inverclyde*[1] Bateson J., rightly in my opinion, insisted on the necessity of looking behind the form and regarding the substance of the matter. The substance, in my view, may be thus expressed: a void marriage is one that will be regarded by every court in any case in which the existence of the marriage is in issue as never having taken place and can be so treated by both parties to it without the necessity of any decree annulling it: a voidable marriage is one that will be regarded by every court as a valid subsisting marriage until a decree annulling it has been pronounced by a court of competent jurisdiction. In England only the Divorce Court has this jurisdiction. The fact that in both cases the form of the decree is the same cannot alter the fact that the two cases are in this respect quite different. . . .

In the present case the question whether at the relevant date the

[1] [1931] P. 29.

De Rene-
ville
v.
De Rene-
ville.
—
Lord
Greene
M.R.

petitioner had an English domicile cannot, in my view, be answered until two other questions are answered, namely (a) was the marriage a void or voidable one, and (b) by reference to what law will the English court decide whether it was void or voidable?

The importance for present purposes of the distinction between 'void' and 'voidable' lies in this. If the marriage was voidable it must, in my opinion, be regarded as having had the effect of giving to the petitioner, as a matter of law, the French domicile of her husband and as precluding her from casting off that domicile before a decree of annulment is actually pronounced. It appears to me quite impossible to suggest that she is to be treated as having resumed, proleptically, so to speak, her English domicile, merely because she has presented a petition for a decree of nullity to which, in point of substance, she might or might not be able to establish her claim. To hold otherwise would be to allow oneself to be misled by the mere wording of a form of decree which was adopted in the past for reasons which are no longer appropriate. The fact that a domicile has been acquired by reason of a voidable marriage is a fact the existence of which cannot be undone by a declaration of nullity. Such a declaration sets the wife free to change her domicile in the future: it cannot in my opinion change it retrospectively in the manner here claimed.

If, however, the marriage is by its proper law a void marriage no decree of any court is required to avoid it. The petitioner in that case did not acquire the French domicile of the respondent by operation of law; she was free to acquire it or not as she chose and, if she acquired it, to abandon it or change it for a different domicile of choice. It is clear on the facts that if she was competent to do so she did abandon her French domicile (which I am assuming she had acquired) and that she thereby resumed her domicile of origin, which was English. Her domicile, therefore, on the hypothesis that the marriage was void, was English. This at once raises a question as to the jurisdiction of the English courts to entertain a petition for nullity by a supposed wife who is in a position to prove that her supposed marriage was void and that her domicile on that basis is English at the date of the presentation of the petition. This situation seems never to have arisen before the case of *White* v. *White*,[1] which was decided by my brother Bucknill when a judge of first instance. Before I examine that case I must point out that we are not on this

[1] [1937] P. 111

164

DE RENE-
VILLE
v.
DE RENE-
VILLE.
—
Lord
Greene
M.R.

hypothesis concerned to do what I have declined to do in the case of a voidable marriage, namely, to give to a decree of nullity which it is assumed will be obtained what I have called a proleptic operation in conferring on a wife a domicile, which, until she obtains the decree she is seeking, she is incapable in law of possessing. In the present case, if the marriage was void, the domicile of the petitioner is English: it would be held to be English by any court in the country before whom the relevant facts were established, for example, in matters of succession no decree of the Divorce Court would have to be produced in order to show that she had possessed that freedom in the choice of a domicile which the law denies to a woman so long as her status is that of a married woman. The fact that she has an English domicile can be established in the nullity proceedings themselves, as she attempted to establish it here, on a preliminary issue, whereas if all she could show was a voidable marriage, the trial of a preliminary issue could only result in a finding that at the date of the presentation of the petition she was domiciled in France.

In *White* v. *White* my brother Bucknill used words which (save as regards the reference to residence which was in my opinion unnecessary) I respectfully agree. He said: 'It seems to me just to the petitioner and also in the public interest that the petitioner, being domiciled and resident in this country, should have her status as a single or as a married woman judicially established by this court.' This view does, of course, theoretically at least, open up the possibility of conflicting judgments by the courts of the respective domiciles. But if it be not the right view, and if the only court with jurisdiction is a court in a country where both are domiciled, the problem of jurisdiction based on domicile in the case of a void marriage where the domiciles are different would appear to be insoluble. Bucknill J. attached importance to the fact that the respondent in *White* v. *White* had not objected to the jurisdiction. With great respect, I cannot agree with this. In the case before him the English domicile of the petitioner did, in my opinion, give the court jurisdiction whether or not the respondent objected. Moreover, I should have thought that on principle the exercise of jurisdiction in matrimonial causes affecting status could not depend on the submission of the respondent or his refusal to submit to the jurisdiction. In the present case, if the marriage was void and not merely voidable, the fact that the respondent has protested cannot, in my opinion, deprive the English court of jurisdiction to declare the status of a

De Rene-
ville
v.
De Rene-
ville.

Lord
Greene
M.R.

domiciled English woman. Conversely, if the marriage is voidable only, no such jurisdiction exists and could not be created by the fact, if fact it had been, that the respondent had not protested.

But the problem remains, by what law ought the question whether the marriage was void or merely voidable to be determined? If by English municipal law alone, the answer to the present appeal is, in my opinion, a clear one. Whichever of the grounds on which the petition is based is made good the marriage is a voidable marriage and the English court, as Jones J. rightly held, has no jurisdiction. That marriages governed by English law are, on the ground of incapacity, voidable and not void must now, I think, be accepted (see *Turner* v. *Thompson*,[1] *Inverclyde* v. *Inverclyde*, and *Adams* v. *Adams*[2]). Wilful refusal, as I have said, makes the marriage voidable only. Neither in the pleadings nor on the trial of the issue was any reference made to any law other than English law. If the true view be that the question into which class the marriage falls is for French law to decide, either because the marriage was celebrated in France or because the husband's (or the matrimonial) domicile was French, then the court has not been put into possession of what, in my view, would be a crucial matter of fact.

In my opinion, the question whether the marriage is void or merely voidable is for French law to answer. My reasons are as follows: The validity of a marriage so far as regards the observance of formalities is a matter for the lex loci celebrationis. But this is not a case of forms. It is a case of essential validity. By what law is that to be decided? In my opinion by the law of France, either because that is the law of the husband's domicile at the date of the marriage or (preferably, in my view) because at that date it was the law of the matrimonial domicile in reference to which the parties may have been supposed to enter into the bonds of marriage. In *Brook* v. *Brook*,[3] a case in which the marriage in Denmark (by the law of which country, assuming it applied, it was valid) of two persons domiciled in England was held to be void on the ground that although the lex loci governed the forms of marriage, its essential validity depended on the lex domicilii of the parties, Lord Campbell L.C. said this: 'But while the forms of entering into the contract of marriage are to be regulated by the lex loci contractus, the law of the country in which it is celebrated, the essentials of the contract

---

[1] (1887) 13 P.D. 37. [2] [1941] 1 K.B. 536, 542.
[3] (1861) 9 H.L.C. 193; *ante*, p. 69.

depend upon the lex domicilii, the law of the country in which the parties are domiciled at the time of the marriage, and in which the matrimonial residence is contemplated.' In the case of a void marriage, the matrimonial domicile contemplated will clearly be the same as that contemplated in the case of a voidable or non-voidable marriage, since the parties presumably intend to live together. In the present case, the matrimonial domicile was clearly French and it is, in my opinion, to French law that the question whether the marriage was void or voidable on the grounds alleged must be referred. In the *Von Lorang* case, the provision of French law by reference to which the German court had annulled the marriage was one which was regarded, apparently, as relating to form and not to substance. 'The validity of the marriage depended on French law, that being the law of the locus celebrationis', per Lord Dunedin.

I may summarize my conclusions on the question of jurisdiction as based on domicile in the following manner: (I) If (contrary to my view) English municipal law applies as such, or if that law is applicable on the basis that French law is or must be deemed to be the same as English law (a) the marriage was voidable only and not void whichever ground put forward for annulling the marriage be taken. (b) The domicile of the petitioner was French at the date when the suit was instituted. (c) The domicile of the petitioner cannot be notionally regarded as other than French: it remains French until a decree of nullity is pronounced by a court of competent jurisdiction. (d) The only competent courts are the courts of France.

(II) If, as in my opinion is the case, the question whether the marriage is void or voidable is to be determined by reference to French law then (a) if by that law (as theoretically, at least, is possible) it is void on both the grounds put forward, the English court has jurisdiction to pronounce a decree whichever of those grounds is established, (b) if by that law the marriage is void on one ground (for example, impotence) but voidable on the other (for example, wilful refusal) the English court has jurisdiction to pronounce a decree on the ground of impotence, but if that is not established, it has no jurisdiction to pronounce a decree on the ground of wilful refusal, (c) if by French law the marriage is in both cases voidable and not void the English court has no jurisdiction.

I have pointed out the difficulty which arises by reason of the applicability of French law and the omission to appreciate its applicability. But I think that in the circumstances the petitioner ought to

Note: Right margin annotations:
DE RENE-
VILLE
v.
DE RENE-
VILLE.

Lord
Greene
M.R.

De Rene-
ville
v.
De Rene-
ville.

Lord
Greene
M.R.

have an opportunity of submitting (if she be so advised) that the issue should be sent back to the judge to ascertain whether by French law the marriage is void or voidable for either and if so for which of the two reasons put forward in the petition. The decision of the judge on this question, should we consider that the petitioner ought to be allowed to raise it, would carry the consequences which I have indicated. We will hear argument on this matter when my brethren have delivered their judgments. I may add that it would be for the English court, after hearing evidence of French law, to decide whether in French law the marriage was void or voidable not merely in a verbal sense but in the sense of the words as understood in this country, that is, as indicating or not indicating as the case might be, that the marriage would be regarded in France as a nullity without the necessity of a decree annulling it.

So much for the question of domicile. I turn now to (B), the alternative ground of residence. I will assume that residence of both parties (a matter left open, as I think, by the House of Lords in the *Von Lorang* case) is sufficient to found jurisdiction. Is the residence of the petitioner alone sufficient? I agree with Jones J. that it is not.

Mr. Karminski, for the petitioner, placed in the forefront of his argument the decision of Jeune P. in the case of *Roberts* v. *Brennan*.[1] This was a case of bigamy and the wife was petitioning for a decree of nullity. The ceremony was performed in the Isle of Man. The domicile of the man was Irish; the woman was born in Wales. . . . I am quite unable to accept *Roberts* v. *Brennan* as an authority for the proposition that the mere residence of a petitioning wife in England is sufficient to give the court jurisdiction to entertain a nullity suit when the respondent husband is not resident here. If it be thought that *Roberts* v. *Brennan* does so decide, I am unable to agree with it.

On the question of residence as a basis for jurisdiction, reliance was also placed on *White* v. *White*. That again was a case of bigamy. The ceremony took place in Australia when the man had a wife alive. The petitioner was 'domiciled and resident' in England and the respondent was 'domiciled and resident' in Australia or Malta. These statements in the report I read as referring to the time of the Australian ceremony. The respondent did not appear. As the marriage was a void marriage, Bucknill J. had no difficulty in finding on the facts that the woman petitioner was domiciled in England at

[1] [1902] P. 143.

the date of the petition. This circumstance, in my opinion, as I have said, was sufficient to give to the English court jurisdiction to determine her status by a decree in a nullity suit, that court being the court of her domicile and thereby a court competent to determine her status. The judgment refers to the fact that the petitioner was both domiciled and resident here, but the reference to residence was, as I have said, in my view unnecessary for the decision. I cannot read this decision as meaning that residence of the petitioning wife alone is sufficient to found jurisdiction on the ground of residence even in the case of a void marriage.

DE RENE-
VILLE
v.
DE RENE-
VILLE.

Lord
Greene
M.R.

In *Hutter* v. *Hutter*[1] Pilcher J. had to deal with a petition by a husband for nullity of a marriage celebrated in England which had never been consummated owing to the wilful refusal of the wife. The husband was domiciled in the U.S.A. Wilful refusal was proved. Both parties were resident in England at the date of the petition. The actual decision was that the court had jurisdiction, the short ground being stated as follows: 'It would seem, therefore, that both in principle and on authority there is good ground for saying that in suits for nullity the mere residence of the parties in this country is sufficient to found the jurisdiction of the court.' This case is no authority for the view that residence of the petitioner alone is sufficient.

In *Robert* v. *Robert*[2] the parties were domiciled and the respondent husband was resident in Guernsey. The wife, who was petitioning for a decree on the ground of wilful refusal by her husband, was resident in England. Barnard J. held that the residence of the wife was sufficient to give him jurisdiction to entertain the suit. In so holding, Barnard J. was, in my respectful opinion, in error, and the case of *White* v. *White* which he relied on does not support his decision.

These are the only authorities which appear to touch upon the point of residence of the petitioner alone, and without expressing an opinion upon the question whether residence of both parties within the jurisdiction is sufficient, I am clearly of opinion that they cannot be accepted as establishing the proposition contended for. That a wife who is resident but, ex hypothesi, not domiciled here can compel her husband who is both domiciled and resident abroad to come to this country and submit the question of his status to the courts of this country appears to me to be contrary both to principle and to convenience.

[1] [1944] P. 95.   [2] [1947] P. 164.

DE RENE-
VILLE
v.
DE RENE-
VILLE.
—
Lord
Greene
M.R.

BUCKNILL L.J. delivered judgment to the same effect.

SOMERVELL L.J. concurred.

(Counsel then addressed the court on whether the case should be remitted to the court below to enable the petitioner to prove that by French law the marriage was void on either of the grounds alleged in the petition. The Court of Appeal refused to remit the case on the ground that the petitioner had relied throughout on English law.)

Appeal dismissed.

English courts have no jurisdiction to annul a voidable marriage merely because it was celebrated in England. Aliter if the marriage is alleged to be void.

Ross Smith v. Ross Smith [1963] A.C. 280 (House of Lords)

LORD REID: My Lords, the question in this case is whether the English court has jurisdiction to deal with a petition of the respondent, the wife, against the appellant for the annulment of their marriage on the ground of non-consummation owing to impotence or wilful refusal on the part of the appellant. The appellant is domiciled in Scotland and resident in the Middle East and his only connection with England is that he resided in Newcastle-upon-Tyne for a time while working there and during that time he was married to the respondent there on July 8, 1955. The wife resides in England, but the question of jurisdiction in this case depends solely on whether the fact that the marriage was celebrated in England is in itself sufficient to confer jurisdiction on the English courts. Karminski J. held that it was not, but his decision was reversed by the Court of Appeal.[1]

In *Simonin* v. *Mallac*[2] it was held for the first time that, by reason of the marriage having been celebrated in England, an English court had jurisdiction to entertain a petition for annulment of the marriage although the respondent was neither resident nor domiciled in England. In that case the allegation was that the marriage was void ab initio, but in the present case the allegation is that the marriage is voidable. The decision in *Simonin's* case has been followed in many cases both in England and in other jurisdictions within the Commonwealth, but in all the earlier cases the marriage was alleged to be void and not merely voidable. Karminski J. decided this case on the ground that there is a distinction between void and voidable

[1] [1961] P. 39.   [2] (1860) 2 Sw. & Tr. 67.

marriages in the matter of jurisdiction, but his decision was reversed by the Court of Appeal on the ground that there is no such distinction. Counsel for the appellant maintained that on this Karminski J. was right, but he also submitted a more far-reaching argument to the effect that *Simonin's* case was wrongly decided and that there is no jurisdiction at all to annul a marriage based on the place of its celebration, whether the allegation is that it is void or that it is voidable. Accordingly, it appears to me that the first question to be considered in this case is whether *Simonin* v. *Mallac* was or was not rightly decided. That case has stood for a century, but that is not in itself sufficient, in my view, to require that your Lordships should hold that it must now be followed. I shall have to deal further with the matter later, but it is proper to say at once that before holding that the decision should be overruled I must be convinced not only that the ratio decidendi is wrong, but that there is no other possible ground on which the decision can be supported. Accordingly, I propose first to deal with the reasons which were given for the decision and then to consider whether there is any other ground on which the decision can be supported.

In 1854 the parties, Valérie Simonin and Léon Mallac, were both French subjects over 21 years of age domiciled in France and resident in Paris. They wished to marry but were unable to obtain the consents required by the Code Napoléon. So they came to England and were married in London on June 21, 1854. They immediately returned to France but never cohabited and a plan to regularise the marriage by French law miscarried. The wife then raised an action in Paris for annulment of the marriage. The husband, though duly summoned, did not appear, and the French court on December 1, 1854, declared the marriage null and of no effect. It was not disputed that this judgment validly annulled the marriage according to the law of France, the parties' domicile.

In 1857 the wife came to reside in England and she may have acquired an English domicile. On December 23, 1858, she brought a petition in the English court for a decree of nullity of her English marriage. The argument which prevailed in this House in *Von Lorang* v. *Administrator of Austrian Property*[1] did not occur to anyone and it was not argued by Dr. Phillimore, Q.C., on her behalf that the English court was bound by the decision of the court of the parties' domicile. In the end the petition was dismissed, and the

ROSS SMITH
v.
ROSS SMITH.

Lord Reid.

---

[1] [1927] A.C. 641 ; *post*, p. 185.

Ross Smith
v.
Ross Smith.

Lord Reid.

Judge Ordinary, Sir C. Cresswell, giving the judgment of the court, which also included Channell B. and Keating J., said: 'It may be unfortunate for the petitioner that she should be held a wife in England and not so in France. If she had remained in her own country, she might have enjoyed there the freedom conferred upon her by a French tribunal; having elected England as her residence, she must be contented to take English law as she finds it, and to be treated as bound by the contract which she there made.'

But, before dealing with the merits, the court had to decide that they had jurisdiction. Dr. Phillimore argued that they had, and there was no argument to the contrary because there was no appearance for the husband on whom there had been personal service in Naples. The argument as reported was based on the contract having been entered into in England, the petitioner being now domiciled in this country, and the injustice of leaving her status to be determined on an indictment for bigamy or a question of legitimacy. Admitting that the lex loci contractus generally governs the validity of contracts, he founded on the parties' incapacity under the law of their domicile. Sir C. Cresswell did not proceed on England being now the petitioner's domicile, for 'that objection begs the main question in dispute, for if the marriage be valid it is not her domicile'.

In dealing with the question of jurisdiction Sir C. Cresswell first pointed out that section 42 of the Matrimonial Causes Act 1857 removed all objection on the ground of the citation having been served abroad, 'but in our opinion would not of itself suffice to give to the court authority to decide upon the rights of a party not otherwise subject to its jurisdiction'. Then follows what I think is the crucial sentence in the judgment: 'This question [that is, jurisdiction] therefore depends upon the first proposition, that the parties, by professing to enter into a contract in England, mutually gave to each other the right to have the force and effect of that contract determined by an English tribunal.' For that he cited as authority Huber and other civilians; and he referred to section 19 of the Common Law Procedure Act 1852, 'which allows a writ of summons to be issued against a person residing out of the jurisdiction' as appearing to have been founded on this principle. Then he continued: 'There is nothing contrary to natural justice in calling upon him to have the validity or invalidity of a supposed contract ascertained and determined by the tribunal of the country where it was entered into by him; for, according to Lord Stowell in *Dal-* Ross Smith
v.
Ross Smith. *rymple* v. *Dalrymple*,[1] it is an indisputable rule of law, as exercised in all civilised countries, that a man who contracts in a country Lord Reid. engages for a competent knowledge of the law of contracts in that country. If he rashly presumes to contract without such knowledge, he must take the inconveniences resulting from such ignorance upon himself, and not attempt to throw them upon the other party.'

Much of the rest of the judgment is occupied by an extensive citation of authority, English and foreign, to show that the validity of the marriage must be determined by the law of the place of celebration and that French law was not on this matter consistent with private international law. Finally Sir C. Cresswell summarises the matters which 'have led us to the conclusion that we ought not to found our judgment in this case on any other rule than the law of England as prevailing amongst English subjects'.

My Lords, the ratio decidendi contained in what I have called the crucial sentence cannot, in my judgment, now be held to be right, and it is the only ratio given for the decision on jurisdiction. The authorities which were cited deal, not with the proper court to determine the existence, force or effect of a contract, but with the proper law to be applied in determining these matters. Let me assume that they fully vouch the proposition that the proper law to be applied is the lex loci contractus, but it does not in the least follow that the courts of the place where the contract was made always have jurisdiction to entertain a suit involving these matters. It is almost obvious to us today that the mere fact that an ordinary contract has been made in a particular country does not confer jurisdiction on the courts of that country to entertain an action with regard to that contract against a defendant who is neither present, resident nor domiciled in that country when the action is commenced. But the principles of private international law (or conflict of laws) were developed surprisingly slowly, and that was by no means obvious in 1860. Indeed, so late as 1870 Blackburn J., speaking for himself and Mellor, Lush and Hannen JJ. in *Schibsby* v. *Westenholz*,[2] said that if a party to a contract made in a foreign country left it before a suit against him was instituted, they would be inclined to think that the laws of that country bound him, and the law was not finally settled contrary to that view until 1894.

(His Lordship referred to *Sirdar Gurdyal Singh* v. *Rajah of*

---

[1] (1811) 2 Hagg. Con. 54, 61.   [2] (1870) L.R. 6 Q.B. 155, 161; *post*, p. 480.

Ross Smith
v.
Ross Smith.

Lord Reid.

Faridkote[1] and continued:) So it is not surprising that at the time no one questioned the ground of judgment in *Simonin* v. *Mallac* and that this decision was accepted and followed in later cases. And after 1894 no one seems to have realised that this ground of judgment was no longer valid: perhaps this can be explained to some extent by the fact that even by that time rules as to jurisdiction had not been fully related to general principles and the rule in *Simonin* v. *Mallac* was simply accepted as a rule which had existed unchallenged for a generation. Indeed, it is only now that the rule has been seriously challenged. But now that the matter has been raised and fully argued I must hold that the ratio decidendi in *Simonin* v. *Mallac* is wrong. So, if the case is to be supported, it must either be by justifying the decision on some other ground or by holding that it is now too late to overrule it.

It is now argued that that decision can be supported by reference to the old jurisdiction of the ecclesiastical courts which Her Majesty's courts inherited by reason of the provisions of the Act of 1857. It is said that in some way an ecclesiastical court of a diocese had a larger or different jurisdiction in dealing with a marriage celebrated within the diocese from what it had in dealing with other marriages. So I am afraid I must detain your Lordships by considering in some detail the position before the Act of 1857 was passed.

It is not very easy to put oneself back a century but I can, I think, assume that the extensive citation and able exposition by counsel of the old cases and textbooks has put before your Lordships everything relevant that can now be discovered. Before going in detail it may make for clarity if I state my conclusions. There was a separate court for each diocese in England, and I am satisfied from an examination of all these authorities that each of these courts had full jurisdiction to deal with all cases arising out of marriage, wherever celebrated, subject only to one limitation: any person was entitled to object to the case against him being dealt with by any court other than the court of the diocese in which he resided. In that sense the jurisdiction of each court was founded on residence, but the respondent could if he chose waive any objection which he was entitled to take. That appears to have been in essence the effect of the Statute of Citations of Henry VIII which seems to have been, at least to a large extent, declaratory of the older law.

The importance of this is that there was no question of jurisdic-

[1] [1894] A.C. 670, 683.

tion being founded on anything having taken place in the diocese or in England, whether that be the celebration of the marriage or the matrimonial offence. I cannot find any trace of a principle or rule conferring any wider jurisdiction on an ecclesiastical court by reason of the locus celebrationis. In any case if the respondent was resident in the diocese the court could proceed: if he was not, it could not proceed effectively unless he chose to appear so as to waive objection. The only respect in which the place of celebration seems to have made any difference was in the question of what law should be applied in determining whether the celebration was valid. It took some time both in civil and ecclesiastical courts to evolve proper rules as to what matters a court should decide by applying foreign law, but it seems to have been settled by the latter part of the eighteenth century that at least the formal validity of the marriage must be determined by the lex loci celebrationis.

(His Lordship referred to *Scrimshire* v. *Scrimshire*,[1] *Harford* v. *Morris*,[2] *Sinclair* v. *Sinclair*,[3] *Dalrymple* v. *Dalrymple*[4] and *Donegal* v. *Donegal*[5] and continued:) It follows that, in my judgment, *Simonin* v. *Mallac* cannot now be supported either on the ground that it could be related to some jurisdiction previously possessed by the ecclesiastical courts or on the ground stated in the judgment. No other ground has been suggested in argument in this case or in any of the numerous cases which follow the decision in *Simonin's* case.[6] Should it, then, be overruled? That is, to my mind, a very difficult question. On the one hand, it has stood for a century virtually unchallenged and it has very frequently been followed. I do not think it necessary even to mention the numerous decisions which found on it. On this aspect the case could hardly be stronger. But, in my view, there is very little else to be said in favour of the decision. It would have been a compelling reason against overruling that decision if it could reasonably be supposed that anyone has regulated his affairs in reliance on its validity, but it would be fantastic to suppose that anyone has married, or indeed entered into any kind of transaction, on the faith of being able to obtain a decree of nullity in a particular jurisdiction. And no decree of nullity already pronounced could be affected.

---

[1] (1752) 2 Hagg. Con. 395.   [2] (1776) 2 Hagg. Con. 423.
[3] (1798) 1 Hagg. Con. 294.   [4] (1811) 2 Hagg. Con. 54.   [5] (1821) 3 Phillim. 597.
[6] But if, as Lord Reid says (*ante*, pp. 170, 171), the marriage was alleged to be void and the petitioner may have acquired an English domicile, might not the decision be justified on that ground? See *White* v. *White* [1937] P. 111 as explained in *De Reneville* v. *De Reneville*, ante, pp. 168–9 (*Ed.*).

Ross Smith
v.
Ross Smith.
Lord Reid.

From the strictly legal point of view it is in conflict with the principle finally settled in *Le Mesurier* v. *Le Mesurier*[1] and in *Von Lorang's* case[2] that the court of the parties' domicile is the proper court to determine status. But, it may be said, so is jurisdiction based on residence. That may be so, but that jurisdiction arises from the fact that by Act of Parliament, the Act of 1857, the whole previous jurisdiction of the ecclesiastical courts was expressly conferred on Her Majesty's courts. The English courts must therefore continue to exercise that jurisdiction whether or not it is in accord with the principles of private international law. So I think that *Inverclyde* v. *Inverclyde*[3] was clearly wrong in so far as it refused to recognise residence of the respondent as a ground of jurisdiction in a suit of a kind which could have been entertained by the ecclesiastical courts. And the same applies to the new jurisdiction based on residence created by recent legislation.[4] It is not for me to consider whether Parliament was right, but I may be permitted to say that I see much to commend these extensions of jurisdiction, in spite of the fact that they can create 'limping marriages'—marriages held invalid or dissolved in England though held valid by the law of the parties' domicile. But I see no such merits in the jurisdiction which we are now considering.

It is unnecessary, because there is jurisdiction on other grounds, where both parties are domiciled in England, and perhaps when only the petitioner is so domiciled. It is also unnecessary where the respondent is resident in England and when a petitioner so resident can take advantage of the recent legislation. What it does is to enable a foreigner who happens to have been married in England to come here and raise proceedings against a spouse who may never have had any other connection with England than the fact that the parties came here to be married: the respondent is then faced with the choice of incurring great expense and trouble in coming here to defend the case or allowing it to go by default.

Moreover, this jurisdiction cannot be exercised in every case. If the marriage sought to be annulled was between two foreigners who had the same domicile before marriage and the court of the domicile has already pronounced the marriage valid, then *Von Lorang's* case shows that the English court cannot question that.

---

[1] [1895] A.C. 517; *ante*, p. 114.   [2] [1927] A.C. 641; *post*, p. 185.
[3] [1931] P. 29.
[4] i.e., Matrimonial Causes Act 1965 s. 40; *ante*, p. 116.

But if the court of the domicile has not already pronounced, then this jurisdiction would enable the English court to entertain a petition for nullity, but a decree of the English court would not then prevent the court of the domicile from reaching a contrary decision, with the result that the English decree would not be recognised in other countries which follow our rule that the court of the domicile is paramount. I must return to this matter when considering the difference between void and voidable marriages, because it appears to me to be more important in the latter case.

On the whole, I would, in these circumstances, hold that *Simonin* v. *Mallac* should be overruled, but I shall not pursue that because I understand that your Lordships are equally divided on this matter. So I must now consider whether the same rule must also apply to voidable marriages.

The first point I would make is that I can see no logical reason why it should stop there. If the ratio decidendi given by Sir C. Cresswell were right, it could not stop there. That was that 'the parties, by professing to enter into a contract in England, mutually gave to each other the right to have *the force and effect* of that contract determined by an English tribunal'. But I need not elaborate this because this ratio decidendi was not seriously defended. But the same applies if the decision is supported as being in accord with the earlier law and practices of the ecclesiastical courts. It would seem that a suit for restitution of conjugal rights was frequently used for the purpose of establishing the validity of a marriage, and, indeed, that seems to have been its purpose in both *Scrimshire* and *Dalrymple*. It would indeed be strange if the jurisdiction of the ecclesiastical courts differed according to whether the suit was to have the validity of the marriage annulled by a petition for nullity or to have it affirmed by restitution of conjugal rights.

If *Simonin* v. *Mallac* is to be supported as an anomaly which is too deeply embedded in our law to be disturbed now, then logic does not enter into the matter and an extension of the doctrine to a new field must be justified in some other way. If, on the other hand, it is to be supported as a correct decision though based on the wrong grounds, then I can see no good reason for extending it only to cover voidable marriages; it ought at least to cover all cases, including restitution of conjugal rights, where the validity of the marriage is in issue. But it is a matter of express decision[1] that locus celebrationis

ROSS SMITH
v.
ROSS SMITH.
Lord Reid.

---

[1] *De Gasquet James* v. *Duke of Mecklenburg-Schwerin* [1914] P. 53.

Ross Smith *v.* Ross Smith. alone does not give jurisdiction in a petition for restitution of conjugal rights, so a logical solution seems to be ruled out in any event.

Lord Reid. I think it very important to see what practical differences there are in this connection between cases where the marriage is alleged to be void and cases where it is only alleged to be voidable. There are at least three. I accept the view that a wife alleging a void marriage can rely on her own domicile before marriage if there is nothing to show that it has been changed except the existence of the marriage. But in the case of a voidable marriage she cannot do that and must admit until the case has been decided that her domicile is that of her husband. That means that if the marriage is only voidable there is a court of a common domicile whose decision will be paramount. But if the marriage is alleged to be void there may be no such court and there is, therefore, at least something to be said for recognising the jurisdiction of the court of the locus celebrationis.

Secondly, a spouse who alleges a marriage to be void—and, indeed, anyone else with a proper interest—can allege and prove that fact in any court in any place if a decision on that matter is relevant to an issue properly before that court. So, if the validity of a marriage between foreigners can arise incidentally in a case in England, it is not so difficult to permit an English court to entertain a petition for a decree or declaration of nullity. But the question whether a marriage is voidable cannot be raised incidentally in other proceedings; it cannot be raised at all except by one of the spouses during the lifetime of the other, and so this reason for allowing the jurisdiction to the English courts only applies to void marriages.

And then a point is made in many of the decisions that the court of the locus celebrationis is the most fitting to determine the validity of the marriage. Lord MacDermott laid stress on this in *Addison* v. *Addison*.[1] That is true in most cases where the marriage is alleged to be void because generally the issue is one which has to be determined by the lex loci celebrationis. But it is not true where the marriage is alleged to be voidable. I have already pointed out that this jurisdiction is only necessary where the respondent is neither resident nor domiciled in England and the petitioner cannot take advantage of the recent legislation. In such cases I see no reason to suppose that the English court is the most fitting to determine the

[1] [1955] N.I. 1.

178

issue. Impotence is a question of fact and so is wilful refusal, and I see no reason why in the case of foreigners the evidence should be more readily available in England.

Finally, there is an important difference between cases where the lex loci celebrationis has to be applied to determine the issue and other cases. Broadly, the former are the cases where the marriage is alleged to be void and the latter the cases where it is alleged to be voidable. Let me suppose that the ground is wilful refusal. In some countries no relief is given on this ground, in others it may be regarded as desertion. Suppose a case where the law of the parties' domicile gives no relief on this ground. It seems to me quite contrary to principle that the wife should be able to come here and seek relief on that ground. If the husband goes to the court of the domicile the validity of the marriage will be affirmed. Indeed, it would seem that if the husband forestalls the wife and obtains such a decision from his court before proceedings are raised here, *Von Lorang's* case would prevent the English court from applying our rule. I do not deny the possibility of there being differing decisions in different countries where the question is whether the marriage is void, but the likelihood of that seems to me much greater where the marriage is only alleged to be voidable.

It would make this speech intolerably long if I dealt separately with even a fraction of the important cases cited in argument. I have paid particular attention to the judgment of Lord MacDermott in *Addison* both out of respect for his views and because his judgment was the first to deal at length with this matter, but for the reasons I have given I am unable to agree with it. In my judgment the rule in *Simonin* v. *Mallac* ought not to be extended to apply to voidable marriages and therefore this appeal should be allowed.

LORD MORTON OF HENRYTON and LORD GUEST agreed with LORD REID.

LORD COHEN and LORD MORRIS OF BORTH-Y-GEST held that it was too late to overrule *Simonin* v. *Mallac* but that it should be confined to marriages which are alleged to be void.

LORD HODSON and LORD MERRIMAN (who died shortly before judgment was delivered) held that *Simonin* v. *Mallac* was rightly decided and that it should not be so confined.

Appeal allowed.

ROSS SMITH
v.
ROSS SMITH.

Lord Reid.

English courts have jurisdiction to make a declaration as to status under Order 15, rule 16 of the Rules of the Supreme Court only if the petitioner is domiciled in England at the commencement of the proceedings.

GARTHWAITE v. GARTHWAITE [1964] P. 356 (Court of Appeal)

Preliminary issue of law.

The wife was born and brought up in England where she had lived all her life and where she had her home. On 1 December 1950 she married the husband, then a domiciled Englishman, in London. After the marriage the parties lived together in England and there was one child of the marriage. On 27 July 1956 the husband obtained a decree in Nevada, U.S.A., which purported to dissolve his marriage to the wife. The wife petitioned for a declaration that the marriage remained valid and subsisting. No other relief (apart from costs) was prayed for. A preliminary issue was directed to be tried as to whether the English court had jurisdiction to entertain the petition on the basis that the husband was domiciled in New York when the petition was filed. Ormrod J. held that the court had jurisdiction. The husband appealed.

DIPLOCK L.J.: It is clear law that if the wife is, as she asserts in her petition and seeks to establish in these proceedings, still married to the husband, she can have no independent domicile of her own but shares his domicile, both parties thus being domiciled in the state of New York: see *Harvey* v. *Farnie;*[1] *Lord Advocate* v. *Jaffrey.*[2] The question, therefore, is whether the English court has jurisdiction to make a declaration that a marriage, the parties to which are domiciled outside England, is a subsisting marriage.

(After tracing the history of the matrimonial courts and their jurisdiction in matrimonial causes, his Lordship continued:) In the result, the jurisdiction of the court to grant relief affecting the matrimonial status or conjugal rights of the parties to an issue of which the subject-matter is their matrimonial status is today restricted by reference to the persons between whom the issue is joined as follows: (1) In all cases which raise such an issue, the court has jurisdiction if the domicile of the parties is English. (2) In cases where the relief claimed is a decree of nullity of marriage, judicial separation, restitution of conjugal rights or jactitation of

[1] (1882) 8 App. Cas. 43, 50, 58.   [2] [1921] 1 A.C. 146.

marriage, the court also has jurisdiction if the respondent is, at the time of the commencement of the proceedings, resident in England. (3) In the cases specified in section 18 of the Matrimonial Causes Act 1950,[1] in proceedings brought by a wife petitioner, the court also has jurisdiction where the conditions prescribed by that section as to the domicile of the husband or the residence of the wife are fulfilled; and (4) anomalously, perpetuating early error in *Simonin* v. *Mallac*,[2] where nullity ab initio is alleged, the court also has jurisdiction if the marriage was celebrated in England (see *Ross Smith* v. *Ross Smith*).[3]

In the present appeal the husband was not, at the relevant time, resident in England; nullity ab initio is not alleged, nor is the case one of those specified in section 18 of the Matrimonial Causes Act 1950. We are, therefore, concerned here only with the jurisdiction of the court based upon the domicile of the parties. In such a case, where the issue is whether the parties are at the time of the commencement of the proceedings validly married or not, it may not be possible at the commencement of the proceedings to know whether they share the same domicile, as they must if they are validly married, or have different domiciles, as they may do if they are not validly married, for in such a case the woman may have retained or acquired a domicile other than that of the man the subsistence of her marriage to whom is in dispute. Up till now this problem has arisen only in proceedings for nullity of marriage. It has been resolved by limiting the court's jurisdiction to entertain such proceedings to cases where the domicile of the petitioner seeking from the court relief which will affect his or her matrimonial status or conjugal rights is English at the time at which the proceedings are commenced.

In such nullity proceedings, if the marriage is void, as distinct from voidable, the ostensible wife at the commencement of the suit may have a different domicile from that of the ostensible husband, and whether she has or has not cannot be determined until the decision whether the marriage was void or not. In the case of a wife's petition claiming that the marriage is void ab initio and asserting that she has an English domicile notwithstanding that her purported husband has not, the petition on its face alleges facts which, if correct, give the court jurisdiction to entertain it. It cannot

GARTH-
WAITE
v.
GARTH-
WAITE.

Diplock
L.J.

---

[1] Now s. 40 of the Matrimonial Causes Act 1965 ; *ante*, p. 116.
[2] (1860) 2 Sw. & Tr. 67.   [3] [1963] A.C. 280 ; *ante*, p. 170.

GARTH-
WAITE
v.
GARTH-
WAITE.

Diplock
L.J.

decline jurisdiction until it has ascertained whether or not the alleged facts upon which its jurisdiction is founded are true. When it has ascertained this, then if, but only if, such alleged facts are true, it has jurisdiction to adjudicate upon the claim to relief. If they are not true, it must decline to proceed further with the matter.

There is thus a preliminary issue which the court has to decide, namely, whether it has jurisdiction to adjudicate upon the claim for relief or not. This is no different from that which any court of limited jurisdiction has to do when proceedings are commenced before it alleging facts upon the truth of which its jurisdiction to hear and determine the proceedings depends. If, on the other hand, the petition on its face alleges facts which, if correct, deprive the court of jurisdiction to entertain it, there is no issue as to its jurisdiction to adjudicate upon the claim to relief, and the court must decline in limine to entertain the proceedings.

When the petition for nullity is brought by a woman in respect of a marriage alleged to be void ab initio, and the woman, apart from the purported marriage, would have an English domicile, the facts which establish jurisdiction may be the same as those which establish the right to relief, but this does not affect the fact that there are two stages involved, and different consequences flow according to whether the decision terminating the proceedings is reached at the first stage or at the second stage. If the court decides that it has no jurisdiction to entertain the proceedings, its decision to dismiss the petition on this ground does not create res judicata as respects the status of the parties or the petitioner's right to relief in a court of competent jurisdiction. If the court decides, correctly, that it has jurisdiction, and proceeds to adjudicate, this does create res judicata as respects the matrimonial status of the parties.

Where, however, the marriage sought to be annulled is not void ab initio but voidable—where, that is, it remains an effective marriage until annulled nunc pro tunc by decree of a court of competent jurisdiction—the wife retains the domicile of her husband until the decree is pronounced. In such a case, if the husband's domicile is not English, the wife petitioner is not of English domicile at the date of the petition and the High Court has no jurisdiction to entertain it notwithstanding that if it did entertain the petition and granted a decree of nullity, the wife's English domicile would be deemed to date back to before the date of presentation of the petition.

Thus the test whether the court is bound to decline jurisdiction in limine is whether the facts alleged in the petition would, if true, deprive the court of jurisdiction to hear and determine it (see *De Reneville* v. *De Reneville*;[1] *Casey* v. *Casey*[2]), and by parity of reasoning the same test applies where the issue is whether or not the matrimonial status has been validly terminated, as where the issue is whether or not it has been validly created. Lord Greene M.R. in *De Reneville* v. *De Reneville* referred to the test as a 'proleptic operation'. This esoteric phrase has, I think, misled Ormrod J. as to the simple basis upon which the High Court, which in exercising its jurisdiction in matrimonial causes acts in the same way as any other court of limited jurisdiction, declines jurisdiction in limine. He thought it unreasonable that the court should have jurisdiction to inquire into the matrimonial status of the wife if she were asserting that her former marriage to the husband had been validly dissolved so that she no longer shared the New York domicile of her husband, and had reverted to her English domicile of origin, and were seeking relief on that basis, but that the court should not have jurisdiction if she were asserting that her marriage was valid and subsisting, so that she did share the New York domicile of the husband.

If the suit was brought in the first-mentioned form, the court would be not only entitled but compelled to inquire into the validity of the Nevada divorce by the law of the husband's domicile at the date at which it was obtained in order to ascertain whether it had jurisdiction to adjudicate upon the wife's claim to relief; yet if the suit were brought in the second-mentioned form, it would not be entitled to embark upon such inquiry.

Ormrod J. sought to overcome this distinction which he regarded as unreasonable by relying upon the concept of a de facto domicile of the wife upon which he considered that the court could found jurisdiction so long as what he described as her de jure domicile was uncertain because it depended upon the result of the suit. With great respect to Ormrod J., the concept of a de facto domicile as distinct from de jure domicile is not possible in English law. Domicile is the legal consequence of a state of facts. The existence of the relevant facts determines a person's domicile; he or she must have a domicile at every moment while living; he or she can only have one domicile at any particular moment: see *Udny* v. *Udny*.[3] Since domi-

GARTH-
WAITE
v.
GARTH-
WAITE.
—
Diplock
L.J.

---

[1] [1948] P. 100 ; *ante*, p. 160.   [2] [1949] P. 420.
[3] (1869) L.R. 1 Sc. & Div. 441 ; *ante*, p. 39.

FAMILY LAW

GARTH-
WAITE
v.
GARTH-
WAITE.

Diplock
L.J.

cile is the inevitable legal consequence of a state of facts, de facto domicile must be identical with de jure domicile, and the facts alleged in the wife's petition, if correct, would entail her being domiciled in New York and so exclude the court's jurisdiction to entertain her petition.

[Counsel for the wife] has not sought on this appeal to support the ratio decidendi of Ormrod J. His contention that the High Court has jurisdiction in this case is based upon a much broader ground which he also argued before Ormrod J., but without avail. . . . [He] points out that the validity or continued subsistence of a marriage between persons domiciled outside England may incidentally come in question in proceedings in the High Court in which it has undoubted jurisdiction, for example, in connection with the administration of trusts or a claim under an insurance policy. In such a case, he contends, the Court of Chancery prior to 1873 and the High Court thereafter could make a declaration as to the validity of the marriage ancillary to the relief sought, and R.S.C., Ord. 15, r. 16, like its predecessor R.S.C., Ord. 25, r. 5. empowers it to make such a declaration where no other relief is sought. I agree that in a case such as that postulated the court may have to decide whether such a marriage is valid, or continues to subsist, in order to determine whether a party is entitled to the relief sought, but I do not accept that it has jurisdiction to make a declaration as to the validity of the marriage, at any rate if both spouses are parties to the suit. No authority has been cited in support of such a contention.

If the court had jurisdiction to make such a declaration, the declaration would create an estoppel per rem judicatam to prevent any party to the suit from asserting as against any other party the contrary of what was declared. The court, which ex hypothesi is not the court of the spouses' domicile, would thus by means of estoppel purport to affect their matrimonial status, and this it has no jurisdiction to do. On the other hand, a mere finding by the court incidental to other relief claimed that the marriage was valid or invalid, subsisting or not subsisting, would not operate as an 'issue estoppel' between the spouses as to their matrimonial status (see *Thoday* v. *Thoday*[1]) since the issue would be one which the court had no jurisdiction to determine in such a way as to affect their matrimonial status.

But the present case is much stronger than those postulated by

[1] [1964] 1 W.L.R. 371.

184

[counsel for the wife] as being analogous. In them, the court's findings as to the matrimonial status of foreign domiciled spouses would be merely incidental to the exercise of its jurisdiction in respect of a subject-matter with which it had jurisdiction to deal. In the present case the only subject-matter of the proceedings is the matrimonial status of a petitioner who asserts that her domicile is foreign, for the only relief that she asks is a declaration as to her status. In my view, the court has no jurisdiction to entertain a claim for this relief any more than it would, in the absence of its extended jurisdiction under section 18 of the Matrimonial Causes Act 1950, have jurisdiction to entertain a claim for dissolution of her marriage or for restitution of conjugal rights. . . .

WILLMER and DANCKWERTS L.JJ. delivered judgments allowing the appeal.

Appeal allowed.

GARTH-
WAITE
v.
GARTH-
WAITE.
—
Diplock
L.J.

A foreign decree of nullity of marriage pronounced by the courts of the country in which the parties were domiciled will be recognized in England.

VON LORANG *v.* ADMINISTRATOR OF AUSTRIAN PROPERTY [1927]
A.C. 641 (House of Lords)

VON
LORANG
v.
ADMINIS-
TRATOR OF
AUSTRIAN
PROPERTY.

Appeal from an interlocutor of the First Division of the Court of Session in Scotland recalling an interlocutor of the Lord Ordinary in an action of multiplepoinding.

In June 1897 the appellant, formerly Miss Salvesen, a British subject domiciled in Scotland, went through a form of marriage in Paris with Herr von Lorang, an Austrian subject. The parties thereafter settled in Wiesbaden, in Germany, where they lived together as man and wife, except during the period of the war, when Herr von Lorang served with the Austrian army and the appellant lived in Switzerland, until 1923. In that year the respondent claimed the movable property of the appellant in Scotland, which was then in the hands of her agents and bankers, under the Treaty of Peace (Austrian) Order, 1920, and an Amending Order of 1921, on the ground that she became an Austrian national by her marriage. The holders of the movable property brought an action of multiplepoinding to have it determined who was entitled to the property and to obtain their discharge. The property was claimed by the respondent

VON
LORANG
v.
ADMINIS-
TRATOR OF
AUSTRIAN
PROPERTY.

and by the appellant, who averred that she had recently discovered that her marriage in Paris was null and void because certain formalities required by the law of France had not been observed, and intimated that she intended to bring a suit of nullity of marriage in the civil Court of Wiesbaden, the court of the domicile of Herr von Lorang and herself, and the action of multiplepoinding was sisted for this purpose. The nullity suit was brought (the respondent not intervening), and the Court of Wiesbaden in 1924 declared the marriage null and void on the ground that it was formally invalid by French law. Herr von Lorang appeared and was represented by an advocate, but took no active part in the proceedings. Thereupon the respondent raised several objections to the validity of the decree of the German court, and in particular averred that the decree was obtained by collusion, and that it proceeded upon a mistaken view of the law of France; but the jurisdiction of the German court was admitted. The question for determination was whether the decree of the German court should be held binding on the Scottish courts for the purpose of excluding the respondent's averments from inquiry.

The Lord Ordinary (Lord Morison) repelled the respondent's claim for a proof, and preferred the appellant to the property.

The First Division, by a majority (the Lord President, Lord Blackburn and Lord Ashmore; Lord Sands dissenting), recalled the interlocutor of the Lord Ordinary and remitted the case to him to allow the parties a proof of their respective averments.

LORD HALDANE (having stated the facts, and having found that the appellant and Herr von Lorang were domiciled at Wiesbaden in 1923, continued): My Lords, I do not think that there are any materials before us on which exception can be taken to the judgment in Germany as having been obtained by what amounts in law to collusion. I will assume that both the husband and his wife had as their main motive to obtain that judgment in order, if possible, to avoid the application of the Austrian administrator's title to claim, but I think that, on the grounds assigned by the Lord Ordinary and Lord Sands, if they had the legal right to do this the motive for which they exercised it could make no difference in a case in which fraud practised on the German tribunal is not now alleged, and no collusion in any attempt to deceive that tribunal is established. The real question is simply whether the court of the domicile was competent to dispose conclusively and finally of the question before it.

VON
LORANG
v.
ADMINIS-
TRATOR OF
AUSTRIAN
PROPERTY.

Lord
Haldane.

If so it does not matter in law whether it had an exclusive jurisdiction. Had the question been one of divorce for adultery there could today have been no controversy as to the binding effect of the German decree. The status of married persons as dependent on divorce is a matter for which the court of their domicile is the appropriate court, and its decision is treated by our courts as not only being valid but as conclusive. The case before us is, however, not one of dissolving an existing marriage but of deciding that no valid marriage ever took place. The marriage was declared by the court of the domicile to have been void by reason of non-compliance with the formalities required by the law of France, where it was celebrated. If this was a judgment determining the status of the supposed husband and wife it may well be that it should be regarded as having been binding on third parties as having been a judgment in rem. For what does status mean in this connection? Something more than a mere contractual relation between the parties to the contract of marriage. Status may result from such a contractual relationship, but only when the contract has passed into something which private international law recognizes as having been superadded to it by the authority of the State, something which the jurisprudence of that State under its law imposes when within its boundaries the ceremony has taken place. This juridical result is more than any mere outcome of the agreement inter se to marry of the parties. It is due to a result which concerns the public generally, and which the State where the ceremony took place superadds; something which may or may not be capable of being got rid of subsequently by proceedings before a competent public authority, but which meantime carries with it rights and obligations as regards the general community until so got rid of. There is nothing unusual in this doctrine.

I cannot see how, for instance, a husband could plead as a good answer to a claim for necessaries supplied to his wife that the marriage which had been publicly celebrated was one which he was entitled if he took proceedings to have declared void for either impotency or for want of compliance with formalities which the public authority which had celebrated the marriage had assumed to have been complied with. For the marriage gives the husband and wife a new legal position from which flow both rights and obligations with regard to the rest of the public. The status so acquired may vary according to the laws of different communities. The disability

Von
LORANG
v.
ADMINIS-
TRATOR OF
AUSTRIAN
PROPERTY.
—
Lord
Haldane.

of monastic celibacy, for example, or that of a minor, or that of consanguinity, may be binding by the law of one country so as to invalidate the married status, while not binding by that of another. When, therefore, it is necessary to determine what married status implies and how far rights or acts are affected by it, it is necessary to determine the law by which they are fixed. It may be going too far to assert that these are all recognized in this country as referable only to the law of the domicile. But at least it is now established, since the decisions in *Le Mesurier* v. *Le Mesurier*;[1] *Lord Advocate* v. *Jaffrey*;[2] and *Attorney-General for Alberta* v. *Cook*,[3] that for a decree of dissolution of a marriage the court of the domicile is the true court of jurisdiction. That jurisdiction ought on principle to be regarded as exclusive. But for the purpose of the present case it is not necessary to refer to the point, for if the German court was competent to pronounce the judgment it did in the case before us the judgment, being that of the court of the domicile, was conclusive in our courts here, so far as competency is concerned, unless there is something in the decree of dissolution for nullity which distinguishes such a proceeding from one for divorce for adultery. In *Niboyet* v. *Niboyet*,[4] in which the judgment of the majority of the court is no longer law, Brett L.J., in the dissenting judgment which he delivered, observed that the court of the domicile was the only court that was entitled to alter the status of married people; but he went on to indicate that the principle, while it applies so as to include suits for judicial separation and for restitution of conjugal rights, did not apply to suits for a declaration of nullity. He gives no reasons for saying this. Whether there cannot be jurisdiction which is not that of the domicile in restricted instances to entertain a suit for nullity is a question we have not before us for determination. For, as I have pointed out, the only relevant issue is whether the German court was competent as against all other courts conclusively to declare the marriage in the present case void. I am unable as matter of principle to see how its competence as the court of the domicile can be successfully challenged, and if it was competent the decree brought the claim, even of the respondent who was not a party before it, to an end. For the decree did undoubtedly alter the status of the husband and wife. They ceased retrospectively to have been married people in the community of their country. For the purpose of the question

---

[1] [1895] A.C. 517; *ante*, p. 114.   [2] [1921] 1 A.C. 146.
[3] [1926] A.C. 444; *ante*, p. 48.   [4] (1878) 4 P.D. 1; *ante*, p. 114.

raised that status must be taken to have been a res and the judgment was therefore one in rem.

My Lords, if the status in question was a res within the meaning of the principle, the duty of our courts is clear. In *Castrique* v. *Imrie*[1] this House, adopting the language of Blackburn J., who was one of the judges who advised it, laid down that the inquiry is, first, whether the subject-matter was so situated as to be within the lawful control of the State under the authority of which the court sits; and, secondly, whether the sovereign authority of that State has conferred on the court jurisdiction to decide on the disposition of the thing, and the court has acted within its jurisdiction. . . .

There does not appear to be any reason why a judgment of nullity, even on such restricted grounds as the Lord President mentions, should not be regarded as disposing of the status of married persons. It does not do so the less because third parties may have it open to them to litigate elsewhere questions of validity in certain restricted instances before such questions have been disposed of in the court of the domicile. Such status is not dependent only on the contract of the parties to the marriage. Before Lord Lyndhurst's Act, for example, a man and woman in England standing in an affinity within the prohibited degrees might marry, and the marriage, though voidable, could only be got rid of by the sentence of an Ecclesiastical Court pronounced within the lifetime of the parties. But the status though voidable was not the less a status, a res with which the court could deal. That shows that though voidable and not void, it was that as to which the sentence of the appropriate court was essential for its dissolution.

My Lords, for these reasons I am unable to agree with the view of the Lord President that the foreign judgment in the case before us did not as soon as given establish conclusively against the respondent and every one else that the appellant, at the relevant date in the multiplepoinding proceedings, was not an Austrian national qua wife of an Austrian subject. If so, the claim of the administrator in the multiplepoinding became inept on March 28, 1924, the date of the decree of the Wiesbaden Court, which was made final on May 4 in that year. The interlocutor of the Lord Ordinary repelling the claim for the administrator was not pronounced until April 21, 1925, and ought accordingly to receive effect.

There were cited numerous authorities for the contention of the

VON
LORANG
v.
ADMINIS-
TRATOR OF
AUSTRIAN
PROPERTY.

Lord
Haldane

[1] (1870) L.R. 4 H.L. 414, 429.

189

VON
LORANG
v.
ADMINIS-
TRATOR OF
AUSTRIAN
PROPERTY.
___
Lord
Haldane.

respondent in the Court of Session. These I have examined, but they do not appear to me to modify the conclusion at which I have arrived as to the principle which must be applied. In considering them it should be borne in mind that some of the dicta in the older cases have been affected by the English Divorce Act of 1857, which for the first time enabled divorce a vinculo to be granted by a court of general law in England. Before that year it was the prevalent view that a marriage duly celebrated in England could not be got rid of (except by Act of Parliament) validly so far as England was concerned, even by a foreign decree, at least when the domicile at the time of the marriage was English. In the report of *Warrender* v. *Warrender*,[1] *Lolley's Case*,[2] which had been decided by eminent English judges, is explained, and it is yet more precisely explained by Lord Westbury in *Shaw* v. *Gould*[3] and by Lord Selborne in *Harvey* v. *Farnie*.[4] *Lolley's Case* appears in reality to have turned on domicile as much as on the indissoluble character of an 'English marriage'. After 1857 the indissoluble character of an English marriage disappeared, and the effect of this disappearance is noticeable in the later decisions. In the judgment in *Le Mesurier* v. *Le Mesurier* the modern doctrine of domicile as the true test prevails unrestrainedly. . . .

In considering the application of other authorities cited to us it is essential to bear in mind the limited scope of the only question before us. It is simply whether, when the court of the domicile of both the parties has pronounced their marriage to be invalid on the ground of nullity for want of formalities, a court here where they are not domiciled can review that decision. The reasons given by Lindley M.R. in *Pemberton* v. *Hughes*[5] are, in my opinion, conclusive against any attempt to reopen any such case on the footing of supposed irregularity of procedure. Our courts, as he says, never inquire whether a competent foreign court has exercised its jurisdiction improperly, provided that no substantial injustice according to our notions has been committed. In the present case the question was not divorce by way of dissolution for any offence but because of nullity for want of essentials required for the contract. It is said that this makes a difference, inasmuch as the marriage if a nullity could not change the domicile of the supposed wife. That is possibly true,

---

[1] (1835) 2 Cl. & F. 488.   [2] (1812) 2 Cl. & F. 567, n.
[3] (1868) L.R. 3 H.L. 55, 85.   [4] (1882) 8 App. Cas. 43, 54.
[5] [1899] 1 Ch. 781 ; *post*, p. 497.

on the grounds assigned by the then President of the Divorce Court, Sir Gorell Barnes, in his elaborate judgment in *Ogden* v. *Ogden*.[1] But it does not affect the litigation before us, in which the decree of nullity in the court of the husband's domicile was pronounced with retrospective effect before the claim of the Administrator of Austrian Property could be established. None of the cases cited to us seem to me to affect this simple point.

My Lords, for the reason that the judgment of the Wiesbaden Court was both competent and binding upon us, I think that we ought to recall the interlocutor of the First Division and to restore that of the Lord Ordinary. The appellant should have her costs in the Inner House and here. I move accordingly.

VISCOUNT DUNEDIN: My Lords, although I had made up my mind as to what, according to my opinion, the judgment of the House ought to be in this case, yet before I had penned a single sentence of the opinion which I should deliver, I had the advantage of reading the opinions of the noble Viscount on the Woolsack and of Lord Phillimore. Agreeing as I do with these opinions and also with every word of what I may without offence term the exceedingly able judgment of Lord Sands, if this were an ordinary case I should simply announce my concurrence. But the case is so important to the law that I need not apologize for adding some remarks of my own; only, as it would be useless to retrace the ground so thoroughly explored in the opinions mentioned, these remarks will be necessarily discursive, but I hope may serve some purpose.

First I would like to say that I thoroughly endorse the view of Lord Phillimore that the outlook of the English courts was necessarily different before and after 1857. I would like to add that I think there is another date of great moment, namely, the date of the decision of *Warrender* v. *Warrender* in this House, namely, 1835. Now I venture to say this: that before that judgment, without my considering whether it really was the law or not, any English lawyer would have said that the law of England is, that an English marriage is indissoluble by any court; it is something that cannot be broken, indissoluble in essence, and looking to *Lolley's Case*, who could say he was wrong? I think satisfactory proof of this may be found in the argument of Sir John Campbell A.-G., afterwards Lord Chancellor, in the *Warrender* case, wherein he says: 'It may be considered as

VON
LORANG
v.
ADMINIS-
TRATOR OF
AUSTRIAN
PROPERTY.
—
Lord
Haldane.

[1] [1908] P. 46; *ante*, p. 77.

191

VON
LORANG
v.
ADMINIS-
TRATOR OF
AUSTRIAN
PROPERTY.

Viscount
Dunedin.

absolutely certain that the bar of England could not have furnished a single counsel who would have set his name to the opinion, that judicial indissolubility was not a legal quality of every English marriage.' But when *Warrender's Case* was decided, that, as an abstract proposition, could no longer hold, though I doubt whether the majority of English lawyers appreciated it. They did not in those days pay much attention to Scotch cases. Besides, as a decision it did not necessarily say *Lolley's Case* was wrong, because Lolley was an Englishman and only went to Scotland for the purpose of obtaining a divorce, while Warrender was a Scotchman. In other words, if the law of *Le Mesurier* had then been fully known, Lolley's divorce in Scotland was no divorce at all. No one can read Lord Brougham's judgment without coming to the conclusion that he thought *Lolley's Case* was wrong in what it laid down, and when Lord Lyndhurst twitted him with having gone out of his way to approve *Lolley's Case* in *M'Carthy* v. *De Caix*,[1] when he was Chancellor, Lord Brougham retorted that he was then only sitting in Chancery, and was bound by *Lolley's Case*, but now he was in the House of Lords and was not. My Lords, I do not think it necessary to consider whether I should follow the iconoclastic tendencies of my fellow-countryman. All I want to point out is that I think all early English decisions, certainly up to 1835, and I think up to 1857, must be read in the light of the general opinion of the indissolubility of an English marriage.

The other point on which I want to say a few words is the question of what is a judgment in rem. All are agreed that a judgment of divorce is a judgment in rem, but the whole argument of the majority of the judges in the Court of Session turns on the distinction between divorce and nullity. The first remark to be made is that neither marriage nor the status of marriage is, in the strict sense of the word, a 'res', as that word is used when we speak of a judgment in rem. A res is a tangible thing within the jurisdiction of the court, such as a ship or other chattel. A metaphysical idea, which is what the status of marriage is, is not strictly a res, but it, to borrow a phrase, savours of a res, and has all along been treated as such. Now the learned judges make this distinction. They say that in an action of divorce you have to do with a res, to wit, the status of marriage, but that in an action of nullity there is no status of marriage to be dealt with, and therefore no res. Now it seems to me that celibacy is just as much a status as marriage. I notice that in the Oxford dictionary the

[1] (1831) 2 Cl. & F. 568, n.

word 'status' is defined (inter alia) as 'The legal standing or position of a person . . . condition in respect, e.g., of liberty or servitude, marriage or celibacy, infancy or majority.' The judgment in a nullity case decrees either a status of marriage or a status of celibacy.

The learned judges rest strongly on what was said on the subject in *Ogden* v. *Ogden*, but, first, I am not bound by *Ogden* v. *Ogden*, and so far as the dicta contradict what I have just said, I do not agree with them. And, further, a close perusal of the judgment in *Ogden* v. *Ogden* will show that it is very much wrapped up with the question of jurisdiction, and if the first marriage was null, there was no jurisdiction in the French court against the so-called wife defending.[1] But here the jurisdiction is undoubted. On this point I would cite the words of Sir James Hannen in the case of *Turner* v. *Thompson*:[2] 'A woman when she marries a man, not only by construction of law, but absolutely as a matter of fact, does acquire the domicile of her husband, if she lives with him in the country of his domicile. There is no ground here for contending that she did not take up that domicile. She had the intention of taking up her permanent abode with him, and of making his country her permanent home.' These words exactly fit this case. I am therefore of opinion that a decree of nullity savours of a res just as much as a decree of divorce. I accept the conditions laid down by Lord Lindley when he was Master of the Rolls in *Pemberton* v. *Hughes*. In order for a foreign decree to be immune from disturbance by an English court—and in my opinion Scottish may with perfect justice be substituted for English—it must be pronounced between persons subject to the foreign jurisdiction, and deal with a matter with which the court is competent to deal, and it must not offend against English ideas of substantial justice.

Although, as I said before, these remarks are discursive, and I do not wish to retrace traversed ground, yet I would put in the form of short propositions the points I hold proved, the proof of several of them being worked out, not by me, but by the opinions of my noble and learned friends.

1. The German court had jurisdiction over the parties, they being domiciled in Germany equally whether there was marriage or no marriage.

---

[1] See, however, Note B, *ante*, p. 52. The first marriage in *Ogden* v. *Ogden* was voidable, not void, and therefore the woman acquired the domicile of the man by operation of law: *De Reneville* v. *De Reneville*, *ante*, p. 160.

[2] (1888) 13 P.D. 37, 41.

Von
Lorang
v.
Adminis-
trator of
Austrian
Property.

Viscount
Dunedin.

Von
Lorang
v.
Adminis-
trator of
Austrian
Property.
—
Viscount
Dunedin.

2. This was a genuine action, and there was no collusion or fraud used to deceive the German court.

3. The validity of the marriage depended on French law, that being the law of the locus celebrationis.

4. The German court took proper steps to inform itself of the French law, and gave judgment according to the law proved before it.

5. That judgment is a judgment which is equivalent to a judgment in rem, and is therefore binding on the Scotch court without further inquiry.

It follows that I agree with the motion made from the Woolsack.

Lords Phillimore, Blanesburgh, and Warrington delivered judgments to the same effect.

Appeal allowed.

Lepre v. Lepre [1965] P. 52 (Probate Divorce and Admiralty Division)

The wife was born and lived most of her life in England. The husband was born and brought up in Malta and was a Roman Catholic. In April 1955 they went through a ceremony of marriage at the Portsmouth register office. That marriage was valid according to English law. The parties went to Malta in May 1955, but the wife returned to England with the child of the marriage in 1956, and in April 1957 obtained from the Portsmouth justices an order for maintenance for herself and the child. In order to enforce the order against the husband she started proceedings to secure its registration in Malta, but her application was adjourned by the Maltese court when the husband alleged the invalidity of the civil marriage ceremony by Maltese law. In December 1957 the husband issued a writ in the Civil Court of Malta praying for a decree of nullity on the ground that his marriage did not comply with canon law. In March 1960 the Maltese court pronounced a decree of nullity, holding that the husband was at all times domiciled in Malta and that by the law of his Maltese domicile he had an incapacity to contract a marriage otherwise than in accordance with canon law and that the marriage celebrated in the register office failed to comply with canon law because no Roman Catholic priest was present.

In December 1960 the wife filed a petition in the High Court seeking a declaration that the Maltese decree of nullity was invalid and of no effect in England and further praying that the marriage should be dissolved on the grounds of the husband's cruelty and desertion. The husband did not defend the petition and took no part in the proceedings.

SIR JOCELYN SIMON P.: I have to consider initially whether the decree of the Maltese court of March 28, 1960, should be recognised in England as annulling the marriage. That itself raises two questions: first, should such a decree in principle be recognised in the absence of fraud or of offence against our notions of justice; secondly, does the decree in this case in fact offend against our notions of justice?

On the first question differing views of great weight have been expressed. On the one side stand Willmer J. in *Chapelle* v. *Chapelle*[1] and Lord Denning M.R. and Donovan L.J. in *Gray* v. *Formosa*:[2] they would not recognise the decree as effective to annul the marriage. On the other side are Pearson L.J. in *Gray* v. *Formosa*, Herbstein J. in *De Bono* v. *De Bono*,[3] Reed J. in *Vassalo* v. *Vassalo*[4] and the distinguished academic figures who have commented on *Chapelle* v. *Chapelle*: they hold that the decree ought to be recognised. Those who take the first view argue in this way: the Maltese court can make a binding and conclusive decree annulling the marriage if both parties were domiciled in Malta at the commencement of the suit there (*Von Lorang* v. *Administrator of Austrian Property*);[5] the Maltese decree, however, declared the marriage void; the wife, therefore, never acquired the husband's Maltese domicile by operation of the law, but retained her English domicile throughout; it follows that the decree of the Maltese court was not a decree of the court of common domicile and was not binding and conclusive. Those who take the contrary view, that we should recognise the decree, retort that such a refusal to recognise the Maltese decree as effectively annulling the marriage involves that the parties remain married in the eye of English law; and the wife had thus, at the commencement of the Maltese proceedings, a domicile in law dependent on her husband's, which was then admittedly Maltese; both parties were therefore domiciled within the jurisdiction of the Maltese court,

---

[1] [1950] P. 134.　　[2] [1963] P. 259.　　[3] 1943 (2) S.A. 802.
[4] [1952] S.A.S.R. 129.　　[5] [1927] A.C. 641; *ante*, p. 185.

which in consequence had jurisdiction over their marriage. The views expressed by the Court of Appeal in *Gray* v. *Formosa* were obiter on this part of the case. I must therefore proceed to my own judgment guided but not governed by what has been said elsewhere.

The apparent dilemma is, in my view, to be resolved by, first, carefully isolating the legal system to which reference should be made in order to ascertain whether the Maltese court had a conclusive jurisdiction, and, secondly, bearing constantly in mind the crucial time for invoking such legal system. That time is unquestionably the commencement of the Maltese proceedings. The husband being then domiciled in Malta, where was the wife domiciled? This depends on whether the marriage was void or voidable or valid in the eye of the legal system which should be invoked: if valid or voidable, the wife remained married to the husband until the pronouncement of the decree of nullity, and therefore took his domicile until that event; if void, she had no legal tie with the husband and had her own domicile throughout: *De Reneville* v. *De Reneville*,[1] *per* Lord Greene M.R. In his judgment in that case, in which Somervell L.J. concurred, Lord Greene M.R. also indicated, first, the meaning of void and voidable in this connection and, secondly, what legal system should be invoked to determine whether the marriage was void or voidable. (His Lordship quoted the passage on p. 163, *ante*, beginning 'a void marriage is one' and ending 'court of competent jurisdiction'; the passage on p. 168, *ante*, beginning 'it would be for the English court' and ending 'without the necessity of a decree annulling it'; and the passage on p. 166, *ante*, beginning 'the question whether the marriage is void or merely voidable' and ending 'to enter into the bonds of marriage'). There is no question but that our law characterizes the marital defect alleged in the present case—that the ceremony did not take place in a Roman Catholic church in the presence of a priest—as a matter of formalities. Its legal result, says Lord Greene, must in these circumstances be referred to the lex loci celebrationis; that is, to English law. English law says without any doubt that the marriage was neither void nor voidable but valid. The wife and the husband were therefore married at the commencement of the Maltese proceedings; the wife had acquired and retained the husband's Maltese domicile; the decree was a judgment of the court of common domicile and should therefore be recognised here as binding and conclusive.

---

[1] [1948] P. 100; ante, p. 162.

De Reneville v. *De Reneville* was concerned with the jurisdiction of the English court to pronounce a decree of nullity. Where the jurisdiction of a foreign court is in question it may reasonably be argued that we should pay regard not solely to our own characterisation of the nature of the defect in question, but also as to how it is characterised by the foreign court. The same result, however, ensues. I had no expert evidence of Maltese law; but it is clear from the terms of the Maltese judgment that they characterised the defect not as one of formalities but as affecting the husband's capacity to marry and thus referable to the law of his Maltese domicile. I conclude, however, from the proceedings of the Maltese courts that in Maltese law the marriage was voidable and not void, in the senses indicated by Lord Greene. The wife's maintenance proceedings in Malta were not dismissed out of hand on the ground that she was not the wife of the husband; on the contrary, they were adjourned so that the husband could question the validity of the marriage in separate and appropriate proceedings: that, indeed, seems to be a common feature of these cases. The marriage being thus voidable and not void in Maltese law, the parties had a common domicile in Malta at the commencement of the Maltese proceedings, and the decree of nullity is binding and conclusive. In truth, there is no real difficulty in the present case: all the systems of law to which reference could conceivably be made—the lex loci contractus, the lex domicilii of the husband, the leges domicilii of the wife, the lex causae and the lex fori—concur at the time the Maltese proceedings started that the wife was married to the husband and domiciled with him in Malta. If that is so, then, whatever the words of the decree, it is inadmissible to relate it back so as to destroy the basis of the jurisdiction to make it. To cite again Lord Greene in *De Reneville* v. *De Reneville*: 'The fact that a domicile has been acquired by reason of a voidable marriage is a fact the existence of which cannot be undone by a declaration of nullity': a fortiori if the marriage is valid by our choice of law rule. To allow otherwise involves a circular argument from which there is no escape.

But even if this marriage were void ipso jure, so that the husband alone was domiciled in Malta at the start of the proceedings there, in my judgment we should still accord recognition to the Maltese decree. In the case of a marriage void ipso jure, such as a marriage alleged to be fundamentally defective as to formalities, the English court assumes jurisdiction in nullity if the petitioner alone is domiciled in England: *De Reneville* v. *De Reneville*, *Apt* v. *Apt*,[1] *Kenward* v. *Kenward*,[2] to cite only authorities in the Court of Appeal. Moreover, in such circumstances we purport to operate on the status not only of the petitioner who is domiciled within the jurisdiction but also of the respondent who is not; it is for this reason that we insist that he or she should be made a party to the proceedings, so as to be bound by our decree. If we ourselves claim a ground of jurisdiction we must concede a similar ground of jurisdiction to foreign courts: *Travers* v. *Holley*,[3] *Corbett* v. *Corbett*.[4] Therefore, even if the wife were, contrary to my view, domiciled in England at the start of the Maltese proceedings by reason of the nullity of the marriage, we should nonetheless concede recognition to the Maltese decree, because we would regard ourselves as competent to pronounce a decree of nullity of a marriage void ipso jure were the husband domiciled in England and the wife in Malta. In so far as *Ogden* v. *Ogden*[5] appears to be to the contrary, it is in my judgment in conflict with the reasoning of the later authorities in the Court of Appeal to which I have referred and must be taken to be confined to its particular facts—if, indeed, it can today stand at all in the light of the House of Lords decisions in *Von Lorang* v. *Administrator of Austrian Property* and *Ross Smith* v. *Ross Smith*.[6]

Furthermore, such assumption and concession of a binding jurisdiction in nullity based on the domicile of one party only seems to me to accord with principle. A judgment declaratory of the status of some subject-matter legally situated within the national and international jurisdiction of the court pronouncing the judgment constitutes a judgment in rem which is universally conclusive. The husband was legally situated within the jurisdiction of the Maltese court because he was domiciled in Malta. That court was, therefore, competent to declare his status by a decree of nullity; such a decree constitutes a judgment in rem, and should be regarded universally as conclusive as to his status, that is to say, that he is unmarried. [Counsel for the wife] conceded that for the purpose of criminal proceedings in this country we would be bound so to regard him; but not, he said, for the purpose of matrimonial proceedings, because the wife (on the present hypothesis) was not domiciled in Malta, so that her status was not within the competence of the Maltese court.

[1] [1947] P. 127; *ante*, p. 62.   [2] [1951] P. 124.
[3] [1953] P. 246; *ante*, p. 119.   [4] [1957] 1 W.L.R. 486.
[5] [1908] P. 46; *ante*, p. 77.   [6] [1963] A.C. 280; *ante*, p. 170.

The wife therefore, it is claimed, remains married to the husband, even though he is not married to her: the concept is no more difficult of acceptance than a finding that a respondent has committed adultery with a co-respondent, but not he with her. Such schizoid situations reflect little credit on the law, though the latter one is reasonably based on differential admissibility of evidence. But I cannot conceive how our courts could accept as conclusive the decree of a competent court of the husband's domicile that he is unmarried and, at the same time, purport to dissolve a marriage to which he is the other party. Moreover, there is high persuasive authority to suggest that this contention for the wife is not correct: see *Williams* v. *North Carolina*,[1] a decision of the Supreme Court of the United States, where comparable recognition problems arise after divorce owing to their rule that a wife retains during marriage a domicile independent of her husband's. Incidentally, further authority from the same eminent source indicates that recognition of the nullity decree of the court of the husband's domicile only might not necessarily exclude our courts from enforcing in favour of the wife in appropriate circumstances financial obligations arising out of the marriage—for example, under a prior maintenance order made in this country: see *Estin* v. *Estin*.[2]

Therefore, in my judgment, we should accept the Maltese decree as binding and conclusive—primarily as a decree of the court of the common domicile at the commencement of the proceedings there, though alternatively as a decree of the husband's domicile alone at that time—provided always that it is not vitiated by fraud or contrary to natural justice.

That brings me to the second main issue in this part of the case. I confess that I approach it with some misgiving. We are concerned here with the decree of a superior court of a Commonwealth country. Its procedure was manifestly solicitous of the forensic interests of the wife. The code of law applied was an ancient and honoured one. Moreover, limping marriages are themselves inherently liable to cause hardship and injustice: suppose, for example, the wife had remarried and had offspring in reliance on the Maltese decree—or, for that matter, the husband. The refusal to recognise an otherwise binding foreign judgment or rule of law on the ground that it is manifestly unjust is nowadays put as a matter of discretion. But as Lord Mansfield said in *Rex* v. *Wilkes*,[3] 'discretion when applied to

LEPRE
v.
LEPRE.

Sir Jocelyn
Simon P.

---

[1] (1942) 317 U.S. 287. [2] (1947) 334 U.S. 541. [3] (1770) 4 Burr. 2359.

a court of justice means sound discretion guided by law. It must be governed by rule, not by humour: it must not be arbitrary, vague, and fanciful; but legal and regular.' In short, there must be a reasonable consistency in its exercise. In *Corbett* v. *Corbett* Barnard J. recognised a foreign decree of nullity based on two grounds, one apparently identical with that which constituted the defect in the present case, the other—that a Jewess was incapable of marrying out of her faith—not easily distinguishable in principle: see also *Igra* v. *Igra*.[1] But in *Gray* v. *Formosa* the Court of Appeal, though not expressly adverting to *Corbett* v. *Corbett*, was unanimous that a decree pronounced by a Maltese court on a ground identical with that in the present case and in largely similar circumstances offended so grossly against our notions of justice that it should not be recognised. It is true that the present case differs in certain details from *Gray* v. *Formosa*. The husband here was not proved to have acquired an English domicile at the time of the marriage, and I am not satisfied that the child would be adversely affected by recognition of the decree. But to differentiate this case and *Corbett* v. *Corbett* from *Gray* v. *Formosa* on these grounds would be, in my opinion, to introduce idle distinctions into the law and throw it into confusion. Not least in matters relating to marriage is it incumbent on the law to speak with a clear, consistent and unequivocal voice. In truth, I do not believe that it was a mere cumulation of detail which impelled the Court of Appeal to their conclusion. I think the crux of their decision was that it was an intolerable injustice that a system of law should seek to impose extra-territorially, as a condition of the validity of a marriage, that it should take place according to the tenets of a particular faith. . . . Just as in *Chetti* v. *Chetti*[2] Sir Gorell Barnes P. refused to give effect to an incapacity to marry outside his caste or religion imposed extra-territorially on the husband by the law of his domicile, so, I think, the Court of Appeal discerned in *Gray* v. *Formosa* an attempt by Maltese law to impose an analogous incapacity based on creed: they would refuse to recognise the incapacity, so they refused to recognise the domiciliary decree founded upon it.

If that is so, the present case cannot be distinguished; and I am bound to hold that the Maltese decree of nullity, although on general jurisdictional grounds conclusive, should not be accorded recognition because it must be taken to offend intolerably against the

---

[1] [1951] P. 404.   [2] [1909] P. 67, 72.

concept of justice which prevails in our courts. It follows that the marriage is valid and subsisting.

(His Lordship then pronounced a decree nisi of divorce on the grounds of the husband's cruelty and desertion.)

Order accordingly.

A foreign decree of nullity of marriage pronounced by the courts of the country in which the parties were resident will be recognised in England.

MERKER *v.* MERKER [1963] P. 283 (Probate Divorce and Admiralty Division)

In April 1946 the parties went through a ceremony of marriage in Germany. At the time both parties were serving in the First Polish Armoured Division, which was stationed in Germany as part of the Allied Army of Occupation, and both were domiciled in Poland. The ceremony was performed in the local parish church, which was also used as a garrison chapel for the Polish forces, by a Polish Roman Catholic priest who was chaplain of the army unit to which the husband belonged. In 1947 a German court at Aurich pronounced the marriage null and void on the ground that there was no civil ceremony as required by German law. Later in 1947 the wife came to England, where she has since resided, and in 1960 she petitioned for a declaration that the marriage was null and void or alternatively that it had been annulled by the decree of the Aurich court.

SIR JOCELYN SIMON P. (having held that the marriage was a valid English common law marriage in accordance with the principles laid down by the Court of Appeal in *Taczanowska* v. *Taczanowski*[1]): A decree of nullity of marriage pronounced by a foreign court of competent jurisdiction will, in the absence of fraud or unless contrary to natural justice, be recognised as binding and conclusive by the courts of this country: *Von Lorang* v. *Administrator of Austrian Property*.[2] The first question to determine is therefore whether the decree of the Aurich court is in the international sense the judgment of a court of competent jurisdiction in the matter. In *Corbett* v. *Corbett*[3] the district court of Jerusalem had pronounced a decree of nullity on

---

[1] [1957] P. 301.   [2] [1927] A.C. 641 ; *ante*, p. 185.
[3] [1957] 1 W.L.R. 486.

MERKER
v.
MERKER.

Sir Jocelyn
Simon P.

the ground of the bride's incapacity to contract the marriage in question. The bridegroom was not domiciled in Palestine at the time of the proceedings; but Barnard J. recognised the decree as binding, since the court had jurisdiction as that of the place both of the celebration of the marriage and of the residence of the parties at the time of the proceedings. The decision has been criticised; but its authority as to jurisdiction seems now to have been placed beyond doubt by the combined effect of *Ross Smith* v. *Ross Smith*[1] and *Travers* v. *Holley*.[2] In the former case the House of Lords affirmed, in so far as it related to void marriages, the decision in *Simonin* v. *Mallac*,[3] that an English court has jurisdiction in nullity when the marriage has been celebrated in England, though refusing to extend the decision to voidable marriages. In *Travers* v. *Holley* the Court of Appeal laid down that where the courts of this country claim a ground of matrimonial jurisdiction it would be contrary to principle and inconsistent with comity to refuse to recognise the jurisdiction of a foreign court based on a similar ground. The Aurich court should therefore, in my view, be recognised as competent to annul the marriage in this case, on the ground that it was celebrated in Germany and was in German law properly void ipso jure. Even if regard were to be paid at this stage to the form of the Aurich judgment and the marriage were to be considered voidable in the conflict of laws sense (see *De Reneville* v. *De Reneville*[4]), the parties were both resident within the jurisdiction of the Aurich court at the time of the proceedings, and the English courts claim jurisdiction in such circumstances: *Ramsay-Fairfax* v. *Ramsay-Fairfax*;[5] *Ross Smith* v. *Ross Smith*. In *Mitford* v. *Mitford*[6] Sir Henry Duke P. recognised as binding a German decree annulling a voidable marriage; so far as recognition went ex loco celebrationis the decision cannot now stand, but it was also based on the court being that of the common residence. . . .

Declaration accordingly.

[1] [1963] A.C. 280; *ante*, p. 170.   [2] [1953] P. 246; *ante*, p. 119.
[3] (1860) 2 Sw. & Tr. 67.   [4] [1948] P. 100, 115; *ante*, p. 160.
[5] [1956] P. 115; *ante*, p. 156.   [6] [1923] P. 130.

NOTE G: JURISDICTION TO ANNUL A MARRIAGE

THIS is one of the most complicated subjects in the English conflict of laws, and only an outline can be presented here. It is convenient to treat the matter under three heads: (1) jurisdiction of the English court; (2) choice of law to be applied by the English court; (3) recognition of foreign decrees.

1. *Jurisdiction of the English court*

The battlefield presents a somewhat scarred appearance because of the undue insistence by some judges on the alleged doctrinal similarity between the annulment of a voidable marriage and the dissolution of a valid marriage (e.g. Bateson J. in *Inverclyde* v. *Inverclyde* [1931] P. 29, overruled in *Ramsay-Fairfax* v. *Ramsay-Fairfax* [1956] P. 115, *ante*, p. 156; Bucknill L.J. in *Casey* v. *Casey* [1949] P. 420); and the undue reliance by other judges on s. 22 of the Matrimonial Causes Act 1857 as determining the jurisdiction of the court, without paying sufficient attention to its repeal and replacement by s. 32 of the Supreme Court of Judicature (Consolidation) Act 1925, which is in terms confined to procedure and practice (e.g. Denning L.J. in *Ramsay-Fairfax* v. *Ramsay-Fairfax*, *ante*, p. 157).

The nature of the distinction between void and voidable marriages is clearly explained by Lord Greene M.R. in *De Reneville* v. *De Reneville*, *ante*, p. 163. In English domestic law a marriage is void for (*a*) lack of form, (*b*) lack of age, (*c*) the prohibited degrees of consanguinity or affinity, (*d*) bigamy, and (*e*) (perhaps) lack of consent of parties. A marriage is voidable if (*a*) one of the parties is incapable of consummating it, or (*b*) it has not been consummated owing to the wilful refusal of the respondent to consummate it, or (*c*) either party was at the time of the marriage of unsound mind or was suffering from mental disorder within the meaning of the Mental Health Act 1959, or (*d*) the respondent was at the time of the marriage suffering from venereal disease in a communicable form, or (*e*) the respondent was at the time of the marriage pregnant by some person other than the petitioner. The last four grounds are statutory: Matrimonial Causes Act 1965, s. 9.

Whether the marriage is void or voidable, the decree of nullity declares that the marriage never existed: it is retrospective. In the case of voidable marriages the retrospective nature of the decree is a historical anomaly which can no longer be justified. It is particularly anomalous in the case of wilful refusal, for this is, unlike every other ground of nullity, necessarily a post-matrimonial matter.

So far as jurisdiction is concerned, there are two respects in which the distinction between void and voidable marriages is important: (1) a voidable marriage confers the husband's domicile on the wife as a matter of law, while a void marriage does not have this effect. Thus the parties may have different domiciles if the marriage is alleged to be void, but not if it is alleged to be voidable. (2) The fact that the marriage was celebrated in England gives the court jurisdiction to annul it if it is alleged to be void, but not if it is alleged to be voidable for wilful refusal or impotence: *Ross Smith* v. *Ross Smith*, *ante*, p. 170.

There is authority of varying degrees of strength for the following propositions:

FAMILY LAW

(a) The court has jurisdiction to annul a marriage which is alleged to be voidable if
  (i) Both parties are domiciled in England at the date of the commencement of the proceedings: *De Reneville* v. *De Reneville*; *Parojcic* v. *Parojcic* [1958] 1 W.L.R. 356.
  (ii) Both parties are resident in England at the date of the commencement of the proceedings: *Ramsay-Fairfax* v. *Ramsay-Fairfax*, following *Easterbrook* v. *Easterbrook* [1944] P. 10 and *Hutter* v. *Hutter* [1944] P. 95 and overruling *Inverclyde* v. *Inverclyde*. (According to Diplock L.J. in *Garthwaite* v. *Garthwaite*, ante, p. 181, it is sufficient if the respondent is so resident.)
  (iii) The circumstances fall within s. 40 (1) (a) or (b) of the Matrimonial Causes Act 1965.
(b) The court has no jurisdiction to annul a marriage which is alleged to be voidable merely because
  (i) The petitioner is resident in England at the date of the commencement of the proceedings: *De Reneville* v. *De Reneville*.
  (ii) The marriage was celebrated in England: *Ross Smith* v. *Ross Smith*.
(c) The court has jurisdiction to annul a marriage which is alleged to be void if
  (i) The petitioner is domiciled in England at the date of the commencement of the proceedings: *White* v. *White* [1937] P. 111, as explained in *De Reneville* v. *De Reneville*, ante, pp. 168–9; *Mehta* v. *Mehta* [1945] 2 All E.R. 690; *Apt* v. *Apt*, ante, p. 62.
  (ii) Both parties are resident in England at the date of the commencement of the proceedings: *Mason* v. *Mason* [1944] N. Ir. 134; *Russ* v. *Russ* (1962) 106 S.J. 632. (According to Diplock L.J. in *Garthwaite* v. *Garthwaite*, ante, p. 181, it is sufficient if the respondent is so resident.)
  (iii) The marriage was celebrated in England: *Simonin* v. *Mallac* (1860) 2 Sw. & Tr. 67 (lack of parental consent); *Sottomayor* v. *De Barros*, ante, p. 74 (consanguinity); *Hussein* v. *Hussein* [1938] P. 159 (duress); *Linke* v. *Van Aerde* (1894) 10 T.L.R. 426 (bigamy). (In *Ross Smith* v. *Ross Smith* the House of Lords was equally divided on this question, so presumably the earlier authorities can still be relied upon. It was so held in *Padolecchia* v. *Padolecchia* [1967] 8 C.L. 497.)
  (iv) The circumstances fall within s. 40 (1) (a) or (b) of the Matrimonial Causes Act 1965.
(d) The court has no jurisdiction to annul a marriage which is alleged to be void merely because the petitioner is resident in England at the date of the commencement of the proceedings: *De Reneville* v. *De Reneville*, ante, p. 169.
(e) The court has no jurisdiction to annul a marriage, whether it is alleged to be void or voidable, merely because the respondent does not contest the jurisdiction of the court; *De Reneville* v. *De Reneville*, ante, p. 165.

If a woman alleges that her marriage is void and petitions for nullity on the basis that she is domiciled in England, and the man is domiciled abroad, there is an apparent difficulty in that her domicile depends on the very matter in controversy, namely, the validity of the marriage. If the marriage is

204

valid, she shares the foreign domicile of her husband; only if the marriage is void can she establish a separate domicile in England. The courts have cut this Gordian knot by regarding the invalidity of the marriage as a jurisdictional fact which must be proved like any other jurisdictional fact, even though the facts which establish jurisdiction are the same as those which establish the right to relief: see per Diplock L.J. in *Garthwaite* v. *Garthwaite*, *ante*, p. 182.

In that case Diplock L.J. also rejects the argument that there should be no restrictions on the jurisdiction of the English court to annul a marriage which is to be alleged to be void, since the validity of the marriage may have to be determined by any court before which the question may incidentally arise, e.g. the Court of Chancery when deciding questions of intestacy or of the validity of wills (see, e.g., *Brook* v. *Brook*, *ante*, p. 67); *In re Paine*, *ante*, p. 85). The reason is that such decisions only operate in personam, whereas a decree of nullity operates in rem. But for a cautiously-expressed opinion to the opposite effect, see per Lord Reid in *Ross Smith* v. *Ross Smith*, *ante*, p. 178.

2. *Choice of law*

In general, English courts apply the lex loci celebrationis to determine whether a marriage is invalid for want of form (*Berthiaume* v. *Dastous*, *ante*, p. 55), and the law of either party's antenuptial domicile to determine whether a marriage is invalid for want of capacity (*Brook* v. *Brook*, *ante*, p. 67; *Sottomayor* v. *De Barros* (*No. 1*), *ante*, p. 74) and (perhaps) for want of consent of parties (see *ante*, p. 88). Want of consent may possibly include the last three statutory grounds of voidability mentioned above, since in each of them it is provided that the court shall not grant a decree unless it is satisfied that the petitioner was at the time of the marriage ignorant of the facts alleged: Matrimonial Causes Act 1965, s. 9 (2) (*a*).

The question then arises, what law determines whether a marriage should be anulled for impotence or wilful refusal to consummate? Prior to 1947 it seems to have been assumed that English domestic law determined this question, regardless of the domicile of the parties. Thus, in *Easterbrook* v. *Easterbrook* [1944] P. 10 and *Hutter* v. *Hutter* [1944] P. 95, marriages were annulled for wilful refusal, although in each case the husband was domiciled abroad and there was no evidence that by the law of his domicile this was a ground for annulment. In neither case was foreign law pleaded. In *Robert* v. *Robert* [1947] P. 164, Barnard J. held that the question whether a marriage should be annulled for wilful refusal must be determined by the law of Guernsey, either because the marriage was celebrated there or because the parties were domiciled there at the date of the marriage. But the case is not of much authority, because no difference was shown to exist between the law of Guernsey and English law, and the decision was overruled in *De Reneville* v. *De Reneville* on the question of jurisdiction, though it was not expressly dissented from on the question of choice of law. In *Addison* v. *Addison* [1955] N. Ir. 1, 30, Lord MacDermott was inclined to think that impotence and wilful refusal were matters for the lex loci celebrationis. In *Ponticelli* v. *Ponticelli* [1958] P. 204, Sachs J. held that English law which was the lex fori and the law of the husband's domicile, and not Italian law which was the lex loci celebrationis and the law of the wife's antenuptial domicile, determined the question of wilful refusal. Had it been necessary to choose between the law of the husband's domicile and the lex fori, he would have preferred the former. On the other hand, in *Ross Smith* v. *Ross Smith* (*ante*, p. 179), Lord Reid and Lord Morris both gave as one of their reasons for declining jurisdiction the undesirability of granting relief on grounds unknown to the law of the parties' domicile. This could be taken to imply that, had jurisdiction been held to exist, English law as the lex fori would have been applied.

The remarks of Lord Greene M.R. in *De Reneville* v. *De Reneville* (*ante*, p. 166), to the effect that French law determined whether the marriage in that case was void or voidable, are open to at least three interpretations:

(1) Lord Greene may have intended to substitute a new rule on the law governing capacity to marry for the previously accepted one and to lay down that capacity to marry is governed, not by the law of each party's antenuptial domicile, but by the law of the husband's domicile at the date of the marriage. But it is incredible that he intended to overrule the orthodox view of the law governing capacity to marry without even mentioning it, even if he had power to do so.

(2) Lord Greene may have intended to lay down a new choice of law rule for questions of 'essential validity' other than capacity, e.g. impotence and wilful refusal. This would mean that *Easterbrook* v. *Easterbrook* and *Hutter* v. *Hutter* can only be supported on the basis that if foreign law is not pleaded English law is applied.

(3) Lord Greene may have intended to lay down that for the purpose of determining whether the court has jurisdiction (and for no other purpose) the question whether a marriage is void or voidable should be determined by the law of the husband's domicile at the date of the marriage. It is submitted that this is the best interpretation of his remarks and that if he intended them to have any wider application, they are to that extent obiter. This would mean that *De Reneville* v. *De Reneville* must be regarded as a decision on jurisdiction and not on choice of law.

If this third view is correct, it is an open question what law determines whether a marriage should be annulled for impotence or wilful refusal. The possibilities seem to be (*a*) English law as the lex fori; (*b*) the lex loci celebrationis; (*c*) the law of the husband's domicile at the date of the marriage. (*a*) is supported by *Easterbrook* v. *Easterbrook* and *Hutter* v. *Hutter*. (*b*) is supported by *Robert* v. *Robert* and *Addison* v. *Addison*. (*c*) is supported by *Robert* v. *Robert* and *Ponticelli* v. *Ponticelli*. It is submitted that (*a*) is the preferable view. There is no reported case in which foreign law has ever been applied to annul a marriage on the ground of impotence or wilful refusal, where it differed from English law.

S. 40 (2) of the Matrimonial Causes Act 1965 (*ante*, p. 117) appears to have no bearing on this question, for the law of the parties' domicile *at the date of the proceedings* can have no relevance in a nullity suit on any view.

3. *Recognition of foreign decrees*

The only propositions which can be laid down with certainty on this question are the following:

A foreign decree of nullity will be recognized in England if

(a) Both parties were resident in the foreign country at the commencement of the proceedings: *Mitford* v. *Mitford* [1923] P. 130; *Corbett* v. *Corbett* [1957] 1 W.L.R. 486; *Merker* v. *Merker, ante*, p. 201.

(b) Both parties were domiciled in the foreign country at the commencement of the proceedings: *Von Lorang* v. *Administrator of Austrian Property, ante*, p. 185.

(c) The decree would be recognized by the courts of the country where both parties were domiciled at the commencement of the proceedings: *Abate* v. *Abate* [1961] P. 29. Thus, the principle of *Armitage* v. *A.-G.* [1906] P. 135 applies to the recognition of foreign decrees of nullity just as it applies to the recognition of foreign decrees of divorce.

If only one party was domiciled in the foreign country at the commencement of the proceedings, conflicting views have been expressed as to whether the decree will be recognized in England. The view of Pearson L.J. in *Gray* v. *Formosa* [1963] P. 259 and of Sir Jocelyn Simon P. in *Lepre* v. *Lepre, ante*, p. 194, that such decrees will be recognized seems greatly preferable to the view of Willmer J. in *Chapelle* v. *Chapelle* [1950] P. 134 and of Lord Denning M.R. and Donovan L.J. in *Gray* v. *Formosa* that they will not, if only because English courts assume jurisdiction to annul a void marriage if the petitioner is domiciled in England, and therefore they should concede a jurisdiction which they themselves claim. Moreover, an argument can be propounded that this problem is really non-existent. (a) If the decree is pronounced in the country where the man is domiciled, the marriage must be either valid or invalid by the appropriate English choice of law rule. If it is valid (or voidable), the woman acquires the man's domicile by operation of law, and therefore the decree was pronounced in the common domicile of both parties and should be recognized in England under the principle of *Von Lorang's* case. If on the other hand the marriage is void by English law, it would be pointless for the English court to refuse to recognize a decree annulling it. (b) If the decree is pronounced in the country where the woman, but not the man, is alleged to be domiciled, again the marriage must be either valid or invalid by the appropriate English choice of law rule. If it is void, there is no need to rely on the foreign nullity decree in order to say so. If on the other hand the marriage is valid (or voidable) by English law, the woman acquires the man's domicile by operation of law, and therefore she was not domiciled in the country where the decree was pronounced and the decree cannot be recognized on the basis that she was.

In each of the cases in which a decree has been recognized because both parties were resident in the foreign country, the marriage was also celebrated there, and the earlier cases stress this fact as an additional basis of recognition. But it seems unsafe now to rely on this fact alone as a basis of recognition, for the reasons given by Sir Jocelyn Simon P. in *Merker* v. *Merker, ante*, p. 202.

The distinction between void and voidable marriages, so prominent in the jurisdictional rules of the English court, has not until quite recently been stressed when the recognition of foreign decrees has been in question; but it may require consideration in the future: see *Lepre* v. *Lepre, ante*, p. 197.

As has been seen (*ante*, p. 155) English courts are reluctant to allow third parties to attack foreign decrees of divorce on other than jurisdictional grounds, since that would introduce the gravest uncertainty into family relationships if, e.g., either party remarries on the strength of the decree. Precisely the same considerations apply to foreign decrees of nullity. Yet English courts appear to be more ready to allow foreign nullity decrees to be attacked than they are in the case of divorce. Thus in *Von Lorang's* case the House of Lords was careful to point out that the foreign decree was not obtained by fraud or collusion, and Lord Phillimore stated that if it had been, it would not have been recognized. In *Merker* v. *Merker* on the other hand, the German decree was recognized although it declared the marriage to be null and void, whereas by German law it should have declared the marriage to be non-existent. But in *Gray* v. *Formosa* and *Lepre* v. *Lepre* Maltese decrees were refused recognition on the ground that they were contrary to natural justice. Apparently it is not contrary to natural justice to recognize a foreign decree based on the ground that a Christian cannot marry a Jewess (*Corbett* v. *Corbett*) or on the ground that there was no civil ceremony (*Merker* v. *Merker*); but it is contrary to natural justice to recognize a decree based on the ground that there was no religious ceremony (*Lepre* v. *Lepre*).

Chapter 8

LEGITIMACY, LEGITIMATION, AND ADOPTION

Section A: LEGITIMACY

A child not born or conceived in lawful wedlock (that is, a marriage valid by English conflict of laws rules) is in general illegitimate in England.

BROOK *v.* BROOK (1861) 9 H.L.C. 193 (*ante*, p. 67)

SHAW *v.* GOULD (1868) L.R. 3 H.L. 55 (House of Lords)

APPEAL from a decision of Kindersley V.-C.[1]

John Wilson by his will dated the 27th of February 1832 bequeathed his personal estate upon certain trusts for the benefit of the child, children, or issue of his great-niece Elizabeth Hickson and devised his real estate to the first and other sons of the body of his said great-niece lawfully begotten. The testator died in 1835 domiciled in England.

On the 10th of June 1828 Elizabeth Hickson, being then about 16 years of age and domiciled in England, was induced by the fraud of a person named Buxton, also domiciled in England, to contract a marriage with him. The marriage was never consummated, and for his fraudful act Buxton was indicted, and convicted, and sentenced to three years' imprisonment. No formal dissolution of this fraudulently procured marriage ever took place in England.

In November 1844 Buxton was induced for a pecuniary consideration to go to Scotland so that Elizabeth Hickson, or Buxton, could divorce him. A suit was begun in the Court of Session in November 1845, and that court pronounced a decree of divorce in March 1846 on the ground of Buxton's adultery. Buxton thereupon returned to England.

---

[1] (1865) L.R. 1 Eq. 247.

209

In June 1846 Elizabeth Hickson went through a ceremony of marriage in Scotland with John Shaw, who was domiciled in Scotland. There were three children of that marriage, the present appellants. John Shaw died in 1852 (a few months after the death of Buxton). Mrs. Shaw died in 1863.

In 1865 the appellants petitioned for maintenance out of the trust funds, which had been paid into court under the Trustee Relief Act, 1859. The respondents, claiming to be interested in these funds in case the appellants should be declared not entitled to them, presented a cross-petition alleging that the appellants were not the children lawfully begotten of Elizabeth Hickson, because she still continued the wife of Buxton, the divorce from him having been obtained by collusion, and being in itself invalid for the purpose of dissolving an English marriage.

Kindersley V.-C. made an order refusing the petition of the appellants, and directing that the funds in court should be applied for the benefit of the respondents. That was the order appealed against.

LORD CRANWORTH: My Lords, the question to be decided in this case is one of a class which not unfrequently gives rise to great difficulties—the question, namely, how far the status of legitimacy or illegitimacy attaching on a subject of this country may or ought to be modified by the laws of another country. There is no dispute as to the facts material for the decision of this case:—[His Lordship stated them.]

If the law of Scotland on the subject of marriage and divorce was the same as that of England, the case would not have admitted of doubt. As Elizabeth Hickson was married to Thomas Buxton in 1828, and as she gave birth to three children during his lifetime, those children must, by the law of England, supposing that law alone to be in question, either be his children or be bastards. The former conclusion is that which in bygone days would possibly have been adopted, so reluctant were the Courts to receive any evidence of non-access by the husband while he was intra quatuor maria. Adopting, however, the more reasonable views on this subject by which the courts of this country are now guided, we may safely act on the hypothesis adopted by all parties in the argument of the case, that the children of Elizabeth are either her lawful children by John Shaw, or are illegitimate. That they are illegitimate, if we are to look only to the laws of England, is certain; for ex hypothesi they are not the children of **Buxton**, who was the husband of Elizabeth when they were born. This, therefore, brings us to consider whether, in order to help us in deciding this question, we are warranted in looking at any other law than that of England—whether we may to any extent be guided by the law of Scotland.

If the parties in this case had been Scotch, and not English, and if all which occurred had occurred not in England but in Scotland, there would, I presume, have been no question on the subject. If Thomas Buxton, being a domiciled Scotchman, had married in Edinburgh, Elizabeth Hickson, being a domiciled Scotchwoman, and afterwards, while their Scotch domicile continued, she had obtained a decree of divorce in the Court of Session, and then had married John Shaw, the issue of that marriage would certainly have been legitimate. The argument of the appellants is, that the consequence must be the same, though the parties were at the time of the first marriage domiciled in England, and were married there. The question, it is contended, is whether, when the second marriage was contracted, the parties to it had the capacity to contract marriage; in other words, whether the effect of the divorce was to enable them to enter into a valid contract of marriage, which, but for the divorce, they certainly could not have entered into. The whole, therefore, turns on the validity of the divorce. Now, the law of Scotland seems clear that a residence in Scotland for forty days makes that country the domicilium fori of any person so residing in the country, in which, for the purposes of litigation, he is to be treated as being domiciled. And it is assumed that this is true whatever be the nature of the litigation; that it holds equally in cases the decision in which may involve the personal status of those who may claim through the litigant parties; as also where it is a mere dispute between the litigant parties themselves. Taking this, however, to be the undoubted law of Scotland, the question is, whether that principle is one which this country is bound to recognize. I think it is not.

The facts of this case do not raise the question as to what would have been the status of these children if Buxton and Elizabeth Hickson, though married at Manchester, had always been Scotch persons, and had always lived in Scotland; or even what it would have been if, before the proceedings for the divorce, Buxton had actually bonâ fide quitted England permanently, and established himself in Scotland, so as to have acquired a Scotch domicile for all intents and purposes. It may be that in these circumstances the courts of this

211

SHAW
v.
GOULD.
—
Lord
Cranworth.

country would recognize the status of these children, so as to entitle them, after the death of their mother, to the fund given to her children; which, no doubt, must be construed as meaning her legitimate children. But on that point I express no opinion. The decision in *Doe* v. *Vardill*,[1] though the case did not turn on any question depending on the validity of a divorce, yet rests on principles hardly, to my mind, distinguishable from it; and it may certainly be assumed that these children could not, in any circumstances, claim real estate in England by descent.[2] But the opinions of the Judges in that case, and of the noble Lords who spoke in the House, left untouched the question of legitimacy, except so far as it was connected with succession to real estate. I think they inclined to the opinion that for purposes other than succession to real estate, for purposes unaffected by the Statute of Merton, the law of the domicile would decide the question of status. No such decision was come to, for no question arose except in relation to heirship to real estate. But the opinions given in the case seem to me to shew a strong bias towards the doctrine that the question of status must, for all purposes unaffected by the feudal law, as adopted and acted on in this country, be decided by the law of the domicile. Even, however, if that had been expressly so decided, it would not affect this case. The domicile to produce that result must be a bonâ fide domicile for all purposes, not, that which alone existed in this case, a mere residence of forty days, so as to give jurisdiction to the Scotch courts.

The important differences on the subject of marriage and divorce which exist in the different parts of the United Kingdom often give rise to perplexing difficulties, and exhibit a state of our law little creditable to us. But these difficulties make it more than usually incumbent on those who have to administer the law to take care that wherever a clear line has been drawn by judicial decision the course which it has marked out should be rigidly followed. Now, whatever be the difficulties in such cases as the present, I think the doctrine that no divorce in Scotland resting merely on a forum domicilii had, at all events before the passing of our English Divorce Act in 1857, any effect in England on the validity of an English marriage, is established on the highest authority.

It is impossible to have a stronger authority for this than the case

---

[1] (1840) 7 Cl. & F. 895.
[2] That is, as heirs under an intestacy: see Note H, *post*, p. 247.

of *Lolley*[1], for it was decided there by the twelve Judges that by the second marriage he was guilty of bigamy, though on general principles every leaning in a criminal case would be in favour of the party accused.

SHAW
v.
GOULD.
——
Lord
Cranworth.

That case was followed by Dr. Lushington in *Conway* v. *Beazley*.[2] There, as in the present case, the second marriage was had in Scotland, not, as in *Lolley's Case*, in England; and it was attempted on that ground to distinguish the two cases. But Dr. Lushington held that the principle was the same wherever the second marriage was solemnized, for that as neither of the parties to the first marriage had been, at any time, bonâ fide domiciled in Scotland the principle of *Lolley's Case* must prevail.

The same question arose in this House in *Dolphin* v. *Robins*.[3] The case was very fully considered, and the conclusion at which your Lordships arrived unanimously was, that the Scotch courts have no power to dissolve an English marriage where the parties are not really domiciled in Scotland, but have only gone there for such a time as, according to the doctrine of the Scotch courts, gives them jurisdiction in the matter.

These cases clearly decide the one now before the House, for if the first marriage here was not dissolved there could not have been a second marriage. Till the first was dissolved there was no capacity to contract a second. If after the second marriage Buxton and Elizabeth had again cohabited, and there had been an issue, that issue would certainly have been legitimate by the law of England, and it cannot be argued that the issue of both unions could share together.

The view which I take of this case relieves me from the necessity of considering whether the resort to Scotland for the purpose of the divorce, and the arrangements made among the parties for bringing about that object, were or were not of such a character as to taint the whole of the proceedings with fraud; I am not at all satisfied that they were, but I am glad to be relieved from the necessity of deciding on such a ground.

There is only one further observation which I desire to make; it is this: In saying that the Scotch courts have no power to dissolve an English marriage where the parties have only gone to Scotland for the purpose of obtaining there a domicilium fori, I do not mean to express any opinion as to what might be the effect of a divorce so

[1] (1812) 2 Cl. & F. 567, n.   [2] (1831) 3 Hogg. Ecc. 639.
[3] (1859) 7 H.L.C. 390.

213

SHAW
v.
GOULD.
—
Lord
Cranworth.

obtained considered merely as a Scotch question. In the anomalous state of our laws relating to marriage and divorce, it may be that such a proceeding may be valid to the north of the Tweed, but invalid to the south. And I am painfully sensible of the inconveniences which may result from such a state of the law. But it must be for the Legislature to set it right. The authorities seem to me to shew clearly that whatever may be the just decision of the Scotch courts in such a case as the present, on this subject of divorce according to Scotch law, it is one in which this country cannot admit any right in them to interfere with the inviolability of an English marriage, or with any of its incidents. To do so would be to allow a prejudice to English law to be created by the decisions of what, for this purpose, we must call a foreign law, thus going beyond what any country is called on to do.

On these short grounds I am of opinion that there was no foundation for this appeal, and I move your Lordships that it may be dismissed.

LORD CHELMSFORD: Whether the appellants answer the description respectively of 'sons lawfully begotten' and of 'children', depends upon whether their parents were lawfully married; and this again depends upon the effect of a divorce in Scotland dissolving the marriage of their mother with Thomas Buxton in England. (His Lordship proceeded to hold that the divorce was invalid in England, and therefore that the appellants were illegitimate and could not take under the will.)

LORDS WESTBURY and COLONSAY delivered judgment to the same effect.

Appeal dismissed.

In re PAINE [1940] Ch. 46 (*ante*, p. 85)

But a child may be legitimate in England if it is legitimate by the law of the domicile of each of its parents at the date of its birth.

In re
BISCHOFFS-
HEIM.

In re BISCHOFFSHEIM [1948] Ch. 79 (Chancery Division)

Henri Louis Bischoffsheim by his will, dated 26 August 1903, devised and bequeathed his residuary real and personal estate to his trustees on the usual trusts for sale, conversion, and investment. He directed his trustees to hold a share of his residuary estate (subject to certain prior interests) upon trust for his granddaughter Nesta Pamela Fitzgerald for life, with remainder to such her child or children as being male should attain the age of twenty-one years or being female should attain that age or marry.

In re
BISCHOFFS-
HEIM.

The testator died on 11 March 1908. On 30 April 1908 his grand-daughter, Nesta Pamela Fitzgerald, married Lord Richard Welles-ley. There were two children of that marriage, namely, the first and second defendants. On 29 October 1914 Lord Richard Wellesley was killed in action. On 12 March 1917 Nesta Pamela Wellesley married in New York, Lord George Wellesley, the brother of her first hus-band. There was one child of this marriage, namely, the third defendant, Richard Wellesley. Nesta Pamela Wellesley died on 21 February 1946.

The domicile of origin of Nesta Pamela Wellesley and of Lord George Wellesley was English. Accordingly, in 1917, a marriage be-tween them in this country would have been void under the Marriage Act 1835. It was their intention, however, prior to their marriage to acquire a domicile of choice in the State of New York, where their marriage would have been valid. It was questioned whether in fact they had succeeded in establishing such a domicile of choice at the date of the marriage but it was not disputed that they had established a domicile of choice in the State of New York in 1920, at the date when the third defendant, Richard Wellesley, was born.

This summons was taken out by the trustees of the testator's will for the determination of the question whether the defendant Richard Wellesley was entitled to share as a child of Nesta Pamela Wellesley in the share of the testator's residuary estate settled by his will on her for life, with remainder to her children.

ROMER J.: The domicile of origin both of Lord George Wellesley and his wife was English, and by the law of England a marriage between them would have been void under the Marriage Act 1835. Such a marriage was, on the other hand, unimpeachable by the law of New York, and the evidence plainly discloses that it was the definite aim both of Lord George and his bride to relinquish their domicile of origin and acquire an American domicile of choice be-fore the marriage was celebrated. Whether or not they succeeded in doing so was one of the subjects discussed before me. Whatever be the truth of that matter, however, it was fairly and rightly conceded by Mr. Gray, on behalf of the first two defendants, that Lord George and his wife had unquestionably acquired a domicile of choice in New York by the time that their son was born there in June 1920. From this fact sprang a different way of founding Mr. Richard Wellesley's claim to share in the testator's estate, and I propose to consider this aspect of the matter first.

The argument on his behalf was briefly as follows: Admitting that only a legitimate child could take under the gift to Nesta Pamela Fitzgerald's children, legitimacy is a question of status. That status is conferred or withheld, as the case may be, by the law of the domicile of origin, which is the law of the domicile of the parents at the time when the person whose legitimacy is in question was born. The status, once conferred, remains with the person concerned throughout his or her life and will be recognized and given effect to by our courts, save only in cases where that person claims to succeed to real estate in England. It is established by the evidence that Richard Wellesley received at birth the status of legitimacy by the law of New York and accordingly, it was contended, his claim, as a child of his parents, to a fund of English personalty will be recognised by the courts of this country.

There can be no doubt as to the general criterion of a person's legitimacy. 'In most cases', said Lord Brougham in *Fenton* v. *Livingstone*,[1] 'the legitimacy of a party is to be determined by the law of his birthplace and of his parents' domicile.' Richard Wellesley undoubtedly received at birth the status of legitimacy from the law of his domicile of origin, and such status is, in general, accorded international recognition. It is said, however, on behalf of the first and second defendants, that our courts will not accord universal recognition to a status of legitimacy conferred by a foreign domicile of origin. The acceptance by our law of the status so conferred is, it is contended, subject to exceptions: and the particular exception relied on in the present case is this: that an English court will not recognise as legitimate the child of a marriage which is incestuous, or which is otherwise contrary to religion or sound morality, notwithstanding that the child is legitimate according to the law of his domicile at birth. In such cases, it is said, our courts are not content to act merely on the fact that the status of legitimacy was bestowed by the law of the birthplace; they will, on the contrary, fasten their attention on the marriage of the parents and, finding that incestuous, treat

[1] (1859) 3 Macq. 497, 532.

the issue as bastards here, however full the measure of legitimacy that may be conferred upon them in the foreign land of their birth.

So far, at all events, as a court of first instance is concerned, I am of opinion that on the authorities, and especially having regard to the majority judgments in *In re Goodman's Trusts*,[1] the contentions which were advanced on behalf of Richard Wellesley, and which I have already summarized, must prevail.

(His Lordship discussed the cases of *In re Goodman's Trusts* and *In re Andros*,[2] and continued:) It is quite clear that in *In re Goodman's Trusts* both Cotton and James L.JJ. recognised only one exception to the general rule that the question of legitimacy or illegitimacy is to be decided exclusively by the law of the domicile of origin; and that exception relates to claims to succession to real estate (a term which would, of course, include titles of honour and dignity) in England. That, also, was the only exception referred to by Kay J. in *In re Andros*. I was referred to no authority which, in my judgment, compels me to entertain the further exception which was contended for in the present case. In *Fenton* v. *Livingstone* the House of Lords held that a person born of an English marriage between a man and his deceased wife's sister was not legitimate in Scotland as to the succession of real estate. Lord Brougham said 'Now it must be granted that the general rule is to determine the validity of a marriage by the law of the country where the parties were domiciled, and in most cases the legitimacy of a party is to be determined by the law of his birthplace and of his parents' domicile. But to this application of the lex loci contractus there are exceptions, from the nature of the case in which the question arises.' It is true that Lord Brougham there uses the word 'exceptions' in the plural. He proceeds, however: 'Thus, in deciding upon the title to real estate, the lex loci rei sitae must always prevail', and then discusses the principles on which that exception is founded. The noble Lord did not, however, in the course of his speech, refer to any other exception to the general rule apart from claims to real estate. The other speeches in *Fenton* v. *Livingstone* were consonant with the views expressed by Cotton and James L.JJ. in *In re Goodman's Trusts*, except that Lord Chelmsford did not wish to commit himself without further consideration. 'It seems to have been assumed', he said, 'throughout the argument before your Lordships, that if the claim in this case had been to movable property, the respondent would have succeeded;

In re
BISCHOFFS-
HEIM.
—
Romer J.

---

[1] (1881) 17 Ch. D. 266; *post*, p. 222.   [2] (1883) 24 Ch. D. 637.

but I am not disposed, without further consideration, to concede that if the marriage is regarded in Scotland as an incestuous marriage, and it had become necessary, in order to make out the title to be next of kin, to prove such a marriage, that result would have followed. It is, however, unnecessary to consider that question, as we are dealing with a different description of property.' At what conclusion Lord Chelmsford would have arrived on this question had he given it further consideration, I cannot, of course, say. But in *In re Goodman's Trusts* the matter was amply considered by the Court of Appeal, to whom *Fenton* v. *Livingstone* was cited. The case of *Brook* v. *Brook*[1] does not really bear on the point which I am now considering. The question before the House was (as stated by Lord Wensleydale) whether a marriage celebrated in 1850 in Denmark between a widower and the sister of his deceased wife, both being then, and subsequently, British subjects domiciled in England, and contemplating England as their future matrimonial residence, was valid in England, such a marriage being permitted by the law of Denmark. The right of the children of that marriage to succeed to property (apparently consisting of, or at least including, real estate in England (per Lord St. Leonards)), was in issue, but obviously their case could not be, nor was it, founded upon a status of legitimacy conferred upon them by a foreign domicile of origin, for their domicile at birth was English. Their right to succeed to property here, in the capacity of children of their parents, accordingly depended, and depended solely, on their being able to establish the validity of their parents' Danish marriage, and in this attempt they failed.

I should next, I think, refer to the much debated case of *Shaw* v. *Gould*.[2] (After stating the facts in that case his Lordship continued:) The case came before Kindersley V.-C.,[3] and he dismissed the children's claim. He held that at the time of the Scottish divorce (which was some eleven years prior to the passing of the Divorce Act 1857), the marriage between Buxton and Elizabeth Hickson was not only indissoluble by an English court but was indissoluble by any court at all; and that accordingly the Scottish decree was wholly inoperative to bring that marriage to an end. He also considered and rejected an alternative argument advanced on their behalf that they were entitled at all events to be treated under the law of Scotland as legiti-

---

[1] (1861) 9 H.L.C. 193 ; *ante*, p. 67.   [2] (1868) L.R. 3 H.L. 55 ; *ante*, p. 209.
[3] (1865) L.R. 1 Eq. 247.

mate children of a putative marriage. When the case came before the House of Lords on appeal, the main point which was argued and debated was as to the validity of the Scottish proceedings and decree. 'The whole', said Lord Cranworth,[1] 'turns on the validity of the divorce.' He held that it was invalid on the ground that Buxton was a domiciled Englishman at the time of the divorce, and that accordingly the Court of Session had no jurisdiction to grant it. Lord Chelmsford also addressed himself primarily (for he also considered the 'putative marriage' point, which is irrelevant for present purposes) to inquiring into the validity of the proceedings in Scotland.[2] 'Whether', he said, 'the appellants answer the descriptions respectively of "sons lawfully begotten", and of "children", depends upon whether their parents were lawfully married; and this again depends upon the effect of a divorce in Scotland dissolving the marriage of their mother with Thomas Buxton in England.' . . . Lord Colonsay, with some reluctance, accepted the view that the validity of the divorce was a relevant subject for inquiry, notwithstanding that the legitimacy of the appellants might be recognised in the land of their birth. The other noble Lords, however, expressed no views of their own on this aspect of the matter. They approached the case, as also had Kindersley V.-C., on the footing that the legitimacy of the appellants depended on the validity of their parents' marriage, which, in its turn, depended on the validity of the Scottish divorce. If the validity of the divorce was regarded as a legitimate subject for inquiry, and if it was invalid, as the Lords held it to be, it necessarily followed as a result of those considerations, when taken by themselves, that the appellants' domicile of origin was English, as their mother's domicile remained that of her lawful husband, Buxton. Accordingly, on the sequence of reasoning which was adopted by the House in their approach to the case as a whole, a claim founded on international acceptance of a status conferred by what was certainly the domicile of origin, if the validity of the divorce was disregarded as irrelevant, namely: by the law of Scotland, could not succeed or, indeed, arise; it was, so to speak, stillborn. It is not altogether surprising that, having regard to the very peculiar circumstances of the case, and to the fact that the important Divorce Act of 1857 had so recently been passed, the attention of the Lords (except, perhaps, Lord Colonsay) was attracted primarily to a consideration of the proceedings in Scotland. These proceedings were clearly

In re
BISCHOFFS-
HEIM.
‾‾
Romer J.

[1] *Ante*, p. 211.   [2] *Ante*, p. 214.

In re
BISCHOFFS-
HEIM.

Romer J.

relevant to the question whether John Shaw and Elizabeth were lawfully married, but this was not the question before the House; the point in issue was not as to the status of the parents but as to the status of the children, and that, as it seems to me, gave rise to different considerations. The relevance of the Scottish proceedings and of the decree which resulted therefrom appears to me to have been a matter rather of assumption by the House than one of direct decision. It is, however, to be noted that the claims under consideration were not confined to personal estate in England, for there was a claim to English real estate as well; and this may have had some effect on the line which was adopted both in the argument and in their Lordships' opinions.[1]

In view of the very special circumstances affecting *Shaw* v. *Gould*, I do not regard it as necessarily opposed to the majority view in *In re Goodman's Trusts*, nor did Cotton L.J. so regard it. I accordingly propose to follow the view which prevailed in *In re Goodman's Trusts*, namely, that where succession to personal property depends on the legitimacy of the claimant, the status of legitimacy conferred on him by his domicile of origin (i.e. the domicile of his parents at his birth) will be recognised by our courts; and that, if that legitimacy be established, the validity of his parents' marriage should not be entertained as a relevant subject for investigation. It is true that in *Shaw* v. *Gould* (as in the present case) the status in question was that of original legitimacy, whereas *In re Goodman's Trusts* and *In re Andros* were cases of legitimation (i.e., original bastardy converted into legitimacy through the subsequent marriage of the parents) but, in my judgment, there is no real distinction between the two classes of case. If in fact the status of legitimacy is conferred by the law of the domicile of origin the time of, as also the reason for, its conferment are surely immaterial.

The conclusion which I have formed and expressed on the legitimacy at birth of Richard Wellesley relieves me of the necessity of inquiring into the domicile of his parents at the time of their marriage in New York. The question is one which is not altogether easy of solution, and I will express no concluded opinion on it.

I will declare, in answer to question 1 of the summons, that upon the true construction of the will of the testator, and in the events

[1] *Sed quaere.* The rule in *Doe d. Birtwhistle* v. *Vardill* (1840) 7 Cl. & F. 895 (*post*, p. 247) 'relates only to the case of descent of land upon an intestacy, and does not affect the case of a devise in a will to children': *per* Stirling J. in *In re Grey's Trusts* [1892] 3 Ch. 88, 93.

which have happened, the defendant Richard Wellesley is entitled to share as a child of Nesta Pamela Wellesley in the share of the residuary estate of the testator settled by his will on his granddaughter, Nesta Pamela Wellesley, for her life with remainder to her children.

In re
BISCHOFFS-
HEIM.

Romer J.

LEGITIMACY ACT 1959

2.—(1) Subject to the provisions of this section, the child of a void marriage, whether born before or after the commencement of this Act, shall be treated as the legitimate child of his parents if at the time of the act of intercourse resulting in the birth (or at the time of the celebration of the marriage if later) both or either of the parties reasonably believed that the marriage was valid.

(2) This section applies, and applies only, where the father of the child was domiciled in England at the time of the birth or, if he died before the birth, was so domiciled immediately before his death.

(3) This section, so far as it affects the succession to a dignity or title of honour, or the devolution of property settled therewith, applies only to children born after the commencement of this Act.

(4) This section does not affect any rights under the intestacy of a person who died before the commencement of this Act, and does not (except so far as may be necessary to avoid the severance from a dignity or title of honour of property settled therewith) affect the operation or construction of any disposition coming into operation before the commencement of this Act.

(5) In this section the following expressions have the meanings hereby assigned to them, that is to say:

'void marriage' means a marriage, not being voidable only, in respect of which the High Court has or had jurisdiction to grant a decree of nullity, or would have or would have had such jurisdiction if the parties were domiciled in England;

'disposition' has the same meaning as in the Legitimacy Act 1926.

6.—(1) This Act shall not apply to Scotland or Northern Ireland.

(2) This Act may be cited as the Legitimacy Act 1959.

(3) This Act shall come into force on the expiration of three months beginning with the day on which it is passed.[1]

(4) It is hereby declared that nothing in this Act affects the Succession to the Throne.

---

[1] The Act received the royal assent on 29 July 1959 and therefore came into force on 29 October 1959.

Section B: LEGITIMATION

Legitimation by subsequent marriage is not recognized at common law unless the father is domiciled both at the date of the child's birth and at the date of the subsequent marriage in a country where the marriage legitimates the child.

In re GOODMAN'S TRUSTS (1881) 17 Ch. D. 266 (Court of Appeal)

This was an appeal by Hannah Pieret from a decision of Jessel M.R., disallowing her claim as one of the next of kin of Rachel Goodman.

Rachel Goodman died unmarried in 1878, domiciled in England, and a legacy given by her will having lapsed to her next of kin, was paid into Court under the Trustee Relief Act, and the question for decision was who were her next of kin at the time of her death.

It appeared that her sole next of kin were the children of her two deceased brothers. One of these brothers, Leyon Goodman, had three illegitimate children in England by Charlotte Smith, and in 1820 went to Holland with the intention of permanently residing there. While in Amsterdam he had another illegitimate child by Charlotte Smith, Hannah Pieret, the present appellant. In 1822, while still in Amsterdam, he married Charlotte Smith, and thereby the previously born children became legitimate according to the law of Holland. They afterwards had another child, Anne Denis, who claimed to be the only legitimate child according to the English law. The Master of the Rolls decided that Hannah Pieret was illegitimate according to English law, and she appealed from this decision.

JAMES L.J.: According to my view, the question as to what is the English law as to an English child is entirely irrelevant. There is, of course, no doubt as to what the English law as to an English child is. We have in this country from all time refused to recognise legitimation of issue by the subsequent marriage of the parents, and possibly our peculiarity in this respect may deserve all that was said in its favour by Professor, afterwards Mr. Justice, Blackstone, the somewhat indiscriminate eulogist of every peculiarity and anomaly in our system of laws. But the question is, What is the rule which the English law adopts and applies to a non-English child? This is a question of international comity and international law. According to that law as recognised, and that comity as practised, in all other civilized communities, the status of a person, his legitimacy or illegitimacy, is to be determined everywhere by the law of the country of his origin—the law under which he was born. It appears to me that it would require a great force of argument derived from legal principles, or great weight of authority clear and distinct, to justify us in holding that our country stands in this respect aloof in barbarous insularity from the rest of the civilized world. On principle, it appears to me that every consideration goes strongly to shew, at least, that we ought not so to stand. The family relation is at the foundation of all society, and it would appear almost an axiom that the family relation, once duly constituted by the law of any civilized country, should be respected and acknowledged by every other member of the great community of nations. England has been for centuries a country of hospitality and commerce. It has opened its shores to thousands of political refugees and religious exiles, fleeing from their enemies and persecutors. It has opened its ports to merchants of the whole world, and has by wise laws induced and encouraged them to settle in our marts. But would it not be shocking if such a man, seeking a home in this country, with his family of legitimated children, should find that the English hospitality was as bad as the worst form of the persecution from which he had escaped, by destroying his family ties, by declaring that the relation of father and child no longer existed, that his rights and duties and powers as a father had ceased, that the child of his parental affection and fond pride, whom he had taught to love, honour, and obey him, for whom he had toiled and saved, was to be thenceforth, in contemplation of the law of his new country, a fatherless bastard? Take the case of a foreigner resident abroad, with such a child. If that child were abducted from his guardianship and brought to this country, can any one doubt that the courts of this country would recognise his parental right and guardianship, and order the child to be delivered to any person authorized by him? But suppose, instead of sending, he were to come himself to this country in person, would it be possible to hold that he would lose his right to the guardianship of the child in this country because of the historical or mythical legend that the English barons and earls many centuries ago cried out in Latin, Nolumus leges Angliæ mutare? Can it be possible that a Dutch father, stepping on board a steamer at Rotterdam with his dear and lawful child, should on his arrival at the port of London

In re
GOODMAN'S
TRUSTS.

James L.J.

223

In re
GOODMAN'S
TRUSTS.

James L.J.

find that the child had become a stranger in blood and in law, and a bastard, filius nullius?[1]

It may be suggested that that would not apply to a mere transient visit or a temporary commorancy, during which the foreign character of the visitor and his family would be recognised, with all its incidents and consequences, but that it would only apply to a man electing to have a permanent English domicile. But what could, in that view, be more shocking than that a man, having such a family residing with him perhaps for years, in this country as his lawful family, recognised as such by every court in the kingdom, being minded at last to make this country his permanent domicile, should thereby bastardize his children; and that he could re-legitimate them by another change of domicile from London to Edinburgh? And why should we on principle think it right to lay down a rule leading to such results? I protest that I can see no principle, no reason, no ground for this, except an insular vanity, inducing us to think that our law is so good and right, and every other system of law is naught, that we should reject every recognition of it as an unclean thing.

But it is not merely on principle, but on authority, to my mind conclusive, that this question ought to be determined in favour of the appellant. I will not go through the roll of authorities which the Lord Justice Cotton has cited. But I content myself with the one case of *Doe* v. *Vardill*.[2] In that case we have the careful and elaborate judgment of the Judges summoned to advise the House of Lords. And in that judgment, or advice, there are two distinct propositions clearly and distinctly enunciated. The first was that the claimant was for all purposes and to all intents legitimate. The second was that such legitimacy did not necessarily, and did not in fact in that case, include heirship to English land. The first proposition was accepted by the law lords without any doubt or question; the second was questioned. After further reference to the Judges and further hearing, the case was at last determined in accordance with the second proposition. But the first proposition has never been really questioned. No doubt it may be said that the only decision was

---

[1] After this famous purple patch, 'it is almost with a sense of anticlimax that one discovers that the only question on which the court was asked to pronounce was whether a girl who had been legitimated by the subsequent marriage of her parents in Holland could succeed to certain property as "next of kin" on the intestacy of her English aunt' (Welsh, 63 L.Q.R. 65, 77).

[2] (1840) 7 Cl. & F. 895.

against the heirship in that case. But the weight of such an authority, particularly of advice tendered by the assembled Judges to the House of Lords, is not affected by that consideration. It is the ratio decidendi, the rules, maxims, and principles of law which are to be found there, by which we are to guide ourselves. In fact, as is well known, the House has frequently put hypothetical states of fact, and abstract questions of law, for the advice and opinion of the Judges, of which I recollect one notable instance in the *D'Este Case*.[1] What the assembled Judges said in *Doe* v. *Vardill*, and what the Lords held, was, that the case of heirship to English land was a peculiar exception to the rights incident to that character and status of legitimacy, which was admitted by both Judges and Lords to be the true character and status of the claimant. It was only an additional instance of the many anomalies which at that time affected the descent of land. Legitimate relationship in the first degree was of no avail if the claimant were an alien, or if he were of the half-blood, or in the direct ascending line, which, pace Professor Blackstone, were precious absurdities in the English law of real property. But in this particular case, the exception is, at all events, plausible. The English heirship, the descent of English land, required not only that the man should be legitimate, but as it were porphyro-genitus, born legitimate within the narrowest pale of English legitimacy. Heirship is an incident of land, depending on local law, the law of the country, the county, the manor, and even of the particular property itself, the forma doni. Kinship is an incident of the person, and universal. It appears to me that a statement of the law so given, and so accepted nearly fifty years ago, which has been adopted without question by jurists as a correct statement of English adhesion to the universal law and comity of nations, is not to be questioned at this time by any tribunal short of the House of Lords, and I should humbly think not by them. There is only one authority to the contrary, the case of *Boyes* v. *Bedale*,[2] on which I will say a few words. The decision there was on the ground that, in an Englishman's will, the children of a nephew must mean children who would be lawful children if they were English children. That seems to me a violent presumption. It was an accident in that case that the testator was an Englishman. But supposing it had been the will of a Frenchman, dying domiciled in England, and made in favour of his French relations and their children, or of his own children, there being children legitimate and

In re GOODMAN'S TRUSTS.

James L.J.

---

[1] *Sussex Peerage Case* (1844) 11 Cl. & F. 85.   [2] (1863) 1 H. & M. 798.

In re
GOODMAN'S
TRUSTS.

James L.J.

legitimated, what would have been said of such a presumption and such a construction? In that case, by way of obiter dictum, the learned Judge goes on to say that the same construction would be applied to kindred under the Statute of Distributions. This point was never argued and never considered, I believe, by counsel, and must, I think, have been hastily uttered by the Vice-Chancellor at the close of an oral judgment. It must be borne in mind that the Statute of Distributions is not a statute for Englishmen only, but for all persons, whether English or not, dying intestate and domiciled in England, and not for any Englishman dying domiciled abroad. And it was to provide for what was thought an equitable distribution of the assets, as to which a man had, through inadvertence, not expressed his testamentary intentions. And, as the law applies universally to persons of all countries, races, and religions whatsoever, the proper law to be applied in determining kindred is the universal law, the international law, adopted by the comity of states. The child of a man would be his child so ascertained and so determined, and, in the next degree, the lawful child of his brother or sister would be his nephew or niece.

The real importance of the case of *Dalrymple* v. *Dalrymple*[1] has not been sufficiently appreciated. There must have been hundreds of cases in which a Scotchman or a foreigner with legitimated children, or other kindred, elected to domicile himself for business, or health, or pleasure, in London or elsewhere in England. Can it be doubted that the English Court of Probate, of whose conception of the law the case of *Dalrymple* v. *Dalrymple* is an authoritative exponent, would, without question, have admitted the right of some child or next of kin to take out administration? And if such right had ever been questioned, would not the fact of such a question, viz., whether a man by changing his domicile had bastardized his child, have created a sensation which would have vibrated throughout the civilized world, wherever there was a writer on international law and comity? The fact that no such case is to be found shews the universal consensus of all persons conversant with the Court of Probate's administration (the appropriate court in that behalf) that no such question in fact existed.

That consensus goes back not only to the year in which the judgment in *Dalrymple* v. *Dalrymple* was pronounced, 1811, but to the furthest limit to which the knowledge and experience of the learned

[1] (1811) 2 Hagg. Cons. 54.

___-----

Judge who pronounced it extended. Moreover, if such a question had ever been raised in the distribution of assets by the Court of Chancery, the Chief Baron Alexander must, in his long experience in that court, have been aware of it, and would not have omitted to refer to it in the advice which, on behalf of the Judges, he tendered to the House of Lords.

In re GOODMAN'S TRUSTS.
James L.J.

COTTON L.J. delivered judgment to the same effect. LUSH L.J. dissented.

Appeal allowed.

The same rule applies at common law to other modes of legitimation, e.g. by recognition.

In re LUCK'S SETTLEMENT TRUSTS [1940] Ch. 864 (Court of Appeal)

In re LUCK'S SETTLEMENT TRUSTS

Appeal from Farwell J.

Under the marriage settlement and will of a testator domiciled at all material times in England, investments were held by trustees upon trust for Frederick Charles Luck for life and after his death for his children in equal shares, provided in the case of the marriage settlement that they were born within twenty-one years after the decease of the survivor of the testator and his wife. The settlement was made in 1867, the testator's wife died in 1892 and the testator died in 1896.

In 1893 Frederick Charles Luck, whose domicile of origin was English, married his first wife and had two children by her. In 1905 he left them and went to the United States of America. From 1905 till 1918 one Martha Croft lived with him as his wife and in 1906 she bore him a son in California, David Luck.

In 1922 Frederick Luck's first marriage was dissolved by a Californian court and he married Alma Hyam. There was no issue of this marriage. In 1925 he made a declaration in writing publicly acknowledging David Luck as his child. The effect of this was that by s. 230 of the Californian Civil Code, David Luck became the legitimate son of his father as from the date of his birth.

David Luck having claimed to be entitled to share in the trust funds settled by the marriage settlement and will, the trustees thereof took out a summons to determine whether he was so entitled.

Farwell J. found that Frederick Luck acquired a domicile of choice in California some time after 1906 (the date of David's birth)

FAMILY LAW

and before 1925 (the date of the declaration of recognition). The Court of Appeal agreed with this finding. There was no evidence as to the domicile of Martha Croft, but the Court of Appeal assumed that her domicile of origin was English and that she had acquired a domicile of choice in California some time between 1906 and 1925.

Farwell J. held that David Luck was legitimate and was entitled to share in the trust funds, although his father was not domiciled in California when David Luck was born. The two children of Frederick Charles Luck by his first marriage appealed.

LUXMOORE L.J. read the judgment of himself and LORD GREENE M.R. prepared by LORD GREENE: . . . Apart from the principles of private international law which form part of the law of England, that law did not recognise legitimation of a child born illegitimate until the passing of the Legitimacy Act 1926. In this respect the law of England differed from the civil and the canon law and from the law of Scotland and that of many continental countries all of which recognised one particular form—and so far as we know one form only—of legitimation, namely, legitimation by subsequent marriage of the parents. Under the law of France (and possibly in other countries) it appears that in addition to the marriage of the parents a formal recognition of the child by both of them was required: see *In re Wright's Trusts.*[1] But in the eye of English law in the narrower sense legitimation was impossible, except, of course, by Act of Parliament. A child born illegitimate remained illegitimate until his death with all the consequences which that status implied. These consequences affected not merely the child itself, but its mother and its natural father whose rights and duties towards the child were governed accordingly. This rigid rule of English municipal law has been qualified to meet the case of legitimation by subsequent marriage of the parents in cases where the law of the father's domicile at the time of the birth of the child and the law of the father's domicile at the time of the subsequent marriage recognises such legitimation. In these cases the English courts recognise the legitimation as effective: but where the father's domicile at either of the two times stated did not recognise such legitimation the marriage was regarded as inoperative to effect legitimation notwithstanding that the law of the father's domicile at the other of the two times recognised legitimation by subsequent marriage: see *In re Wright's Trusts*; *Udny* v.

[1] (1856) 2 K. & J. 595, 613.

228

Udny,[1] *In re Grove*.[2] The special case of heirship to land in England need not be considered.

An alteration of the law has been effected by s. 8 of the Legitimacy Act 1926, which enables legitimation to take place where the law of the father's domicile (not being English) at the date of the marriage recognises the marriage as effective to legitimate the child. In such cases legitimation takes place as from the date of the commencement of the Act or the date of the marriage, notwithstanding that the law of the country where the father was domiciled at the date of the birth did not recognise legitimation by subsequent marriage. It is to be noticed that legitimation under the section is not retrospective and in none of the cases which were decided before the Act did any question of retrospective legitimation arise.

It so happens that the only form of legitimation which has hitherto come up for consideration by the English courts has been legitimation per subsequens matrimonium. This was the method of legitimation commonly found in systems of law other than our own and it was in relation to this method that the rules adopted by the English courts came to be formulated.

So far as we are aware this is the first case which has arisen in the English courts where a different method of legitimation, namely, by adoption, has had to be considered. The next point which arises is whether the requirements with regard to the domicile of the father which exist in the case of legitimation per subsequens matrimonium must be complied with in such a case, or whether, as Farwell J. held, the matter falls to be decided by reference only to the law of the country in which the child was domiciled at the date when the legitimation is said to have taken place.

It is useful at the outset to consider certain consequences which flow from the view adopted by Farwell J. The law of California provides for legitimation per subsequens matrimonium as well as for legitimation by adoption by the natural father. Accordingly, if Frederick Charles Luck had on July 27, 1922, married Martha Anne Croft instead of Alma Hyam and had not in addition adopted David Luck, the English courts would not (apart from the operation of s. 8 of the Legitimacy Act 1926) have regarded David Luck as legitimate, since Frederick Charles Luck was domiciled in England at the date of the birth. If, however, in addition to marrying Martha Anne Croft, Frederick Charles Luck had adopted David Luck with her

In re
Luck's
Settle-
ment
Trusts.
—
Luxmoore
L.J.

[1] (1869) L.R. 1 Sc. & Div. 441 ; *ante*, p. 39.   [2] (1888) 40 Ch. D. 216.

229

In re
LUCK'S
SETTLE-
MENT
TRUSTS.

Luxmoore
L.J.

consent, the English courts would have recognised the legitimation. This result would, to say the least of it, be anomalous. A result even more anomalous would follow in a case where a man had two illegitimate children by two different women. If he subsequently married one of them but did not trouble to adopt her child and then adopted with her consent the child of the other woman, the former child would (apart always from the Legitimacy Act 1926) be regarded in this country as illegitimate, the latter as legitimated. These considerations in our view afford some reason for adopting, upon grounds of convenience, a uniform principle applicable to both cases. But this by itself is not sufficient and it becomes necessary to examine the authorities in which the rules applicable to cases of legitimation per subsequens matrimonium have been laid down.

(His Lordship referred to *Munro* v. *Munro*;[1] *In re Wright's Trusts*; *Udny* v. *Udny*; *In re Goodman's Trusts*;[2] and *In re Grove*, and continued:) In our judgment the principles laid down in the authorities which we have cited are not limited to the one case of legitimation per subsequens matrimonium. It is natural that references to that form of legitimation should have found a place in the statements of the law since that was the particular form that was relevant in those cases. But the language used is, we think, of wider import. In particular, Lord Hatherley in *In re Wright's Trusts* lays down the principle in quite general terms which clearly cover the present case. He regards the law of the father's domicile as 'fastening on' the child at its birth and as determining the nature of their relationship. If by the law of that domicile the relationship is immutably that of putative father and illegitimate child, nothing thereafter can change it. If, on the other hand, by the law of that domicile such relationship is not immutable but is capable of becoming that of father and legitimate child, that capacity when duly fulfilled is to be recognised by the courts of this country.

There appear to us to be sound reasons in principle why this should be the law. Legitimacy is not a unilateral matter affecting the child alone. If an illegitimate child is legitimated it is not only the status of the child which is affected: the status of the putative father is also changed since he becomes what he was not before, namely, the father of a legitimate child with all the consequential rights and duties which flow from that relationship. Moreover, the position of the child is changed as regards the father's relatives: for it acquires

---

[1] (1840) 7 Cl. & F. 842.   [2] (1881) 17 Ch. D. 266; *ante*, p. 222.

the capacity to succeed to their property as next of kin, while they similarly acquire a like right to succeed to his property. If the question of the effect of the adoption of David Luck upon his legitimacy is to be determined by the law of his domicile at the time, it would apparently follow that if he had been legitimated by a privilegium enacted by the legislature of California he would have been regarded as legitimate by the English courts, even if his father had been domiciled in England at the time. In other words, the English courts would recognise the jurisdiction of a foreign legislature to impose upon a domiciled Englishman the status of paternity which he did not acquire at the date of the child's birth and the potentiality of acquiring which he did not at the time possess. We cannot accept a view which would lead to that result.

When the question of legitimation per subsequens matrimonium first came up for examination in *In re Wright's Trusts* the law might have been laid down differently and it might have been held that the domicile of the father or of the child at the date of the marriage was the sole matter to be considered. Lord Hatherley's decision in that case was, we think, largely influenced by the Scotch law as laid down by the House of Lords in *Munro* v. *Munro*. It was natural that the English law on this matter should be founded upon the same principles as Scotch law which required the potentiality of legitimation to exist at the date of the birth. The result is that the English authorities have been based upon the principle that before subsequent legitimation can take place the status of illegitimacy as acquired at birth under the law of the domicile of the putative father must have as an integral part of itself the potentiality of subsequent legitimation. If it has not this potentiality, it is incapable of change since the capacity to be changed exists and exists only by virtue of the potentiality. It is in our opinion only within these narrow limits that the English law recognises an exception to the principle that bastardy is indelible, a principle which it always steadfastly maintained in opposition to the civil and the canon law save in so far as it was forced to recognise an exception in cases of persons not domiciled in England.

It was suggested that a logical distinction between the present case and the case of legitimation per subsequens matrimonium might be found in the circumstance that the act of adoption by the father was done deliberately for the purpose of legitimising the child, whereas marriage is contracted for its own sake and the consequential legitimation is, so to speak, only a collateral result. There appears to us to

In re
LUCK'S
SETTLE-
MENT
TRUSTS.
—
Luxmoore
L.J.

231

In re
LUCK'S
SETTLE-
MENT
TRUSTS.

——
Luxmoore
L.J.

be no substance in this distinction. Moreover, as we have already pointed out, it appears from *In re Wright's Trusts* that by French law an act of recognition was required in addition to the marriage and it was not suggested that this circumstance in any way affected the principles to be applied.

SCOTT L.J. dissented.

Appeal allowed.

LEGITIMACY ACT 1926

1.—(1) Subject to the provisions of this section, where the parents of an illegitimate person marry or have married one another, whether before or after the commencement of this Act, the marriage shall, if the father of the illegitimate person was or is at the date of the marriage domiciled in England or Wales, render that person, if living, legitimate from the commencement of this Act, or from the date of the marriage, whichever last happens.

(3) The legitimation of a person under this Act does not enable him or his spouse, children or remoter issue to take any interest in real or personal property save as is hereinafter in this Act expressly provided.

3.—(1) Subject to the provisions of this Act, a legitimated person and his spouse, children or more remote issue shall be entitled to take any interest—

(*a*) in the estate of an intestate dying after the date of legitimation;

(*b*) under any disposition coming into operation after the date of legitimation;

(*c*) by descent under an entailed interest created after the date of legitimation;

in like manner as if the legitimated person had been born legitimate.

(2) Where the right to any property, real or personal, depends on the relative seniority of the children of any person, and those children include one or more legitimated persons, the legitimated person or persons shall rank as if he or they had been born on the day when he or they became legitimated by virtue of this Act, and if more than one such legitimated person became legitimated at the same time, they shall rank as between themselves in order of seniority.

(3) Where property real or personal or any interest therein is limited in such a way that, if this Act had not been passed, it would

(subject or not to any preceding limitations or charges) have devolved (as nearly as the law permits) along with a dignity or title of honour then nothing in this Act shall operate to sever the property or any interest therein from such dignity, but the same shall go and devolve (without prejudice to the preceding limitations or charges aforesaid) in like manner as if this Act had not been passed. This subsection applies, whether or not there is any express reference to the dignity or title of honour and notwithstanding that in some events the property, or some interest therein, may become severed therefrom.

(4) This section applies only if and so far as a contrary intention is not expressed in the disposition, and shall have effect subject to the terms of the disposition and to the provisions therein contained.

8.—(1) Where the parents of an illegitimate person marry or have married one another, whether before or after the commencement of this Act, and the father of the illegitimate person was or is, at the time of the marriage, domiciled in a country, other than England or Wales, by the law of which the illegitimate person became legitimated by virtue of such subsequent marriage, that person, if living, shall in England and Wales be recognised as having been so legitimated from the commencement of this Act or from the date of the marriage, whichever last happens, notwithstanding that his father was not at the time of the birth of such person domiciled in a country in which legitimation by subsequent marriage was permitted by law.

(2) All the provisions of this Act relating to legitimated persons and to the taking of interests in property by or in succession to a legitimated person and the spouse, children and remoter issue of a legitimated person (including those relating to the rate of death duties) shall apply in the case of a person recognised as having been legitimated under this section, or who would, had he survived the marriage of his parents, have been so recognised; and, accordingly, this Act shall have effect as if references therein to a legitimated person included a person so recognised as having been legitimated.

(3) For the purposes of this section, the expression 'country' includes Scotland and any other part of His Majesty's Dominions, as well as a foreign country.

10.—(1) Nothing in this Act shall affect the succession to any dignity or title of honour or render any person capable of succeeding to or transmitting a right to succeed to any such dignity or title.

(2) Nothing in this Act shall affect the operation or construction of any disposition coming into operation before the commencement of this Act, or affect any rights under the intestacy of a person dying before the commencement of this Act.

12.—(1) This Act may be cited as the Legitimacy Act 1926.

(2) This Act shall come into operation on the first day of January, nineteen hundred and twenty-seven.

A child legitimated at common law can succeed to property under a disposition coming into operation before the date of his legitimation.

In re ASKEW [1930] 2 Ch. 259 (*ante*, p. 13)

In re HURLL [1952] Ch. 722 (Chancery Division)

In re
HURLL.

Adjourned summons.

Peter Hurll, by his will dated 24 March 1934, left one-third of his residuary estate on trust for his daughter Agnes during her life and after her death 'in trust for all the children or any the child of my said daughter who being male shall attain the age of 21 years or being female shall attain that age or previously marry and if more than one in equal shares absolutely'. There was nothing in the will to exclude the statutory power of advancement. The testator died on 6 October 1939.

The testator's daughter Agnes was married to an Italian in 1933, and at the date of the will she had acquired an Italian domicile. There were no children of that marriage, which was annulled in January 1943 by the Ecclesiastical Tribunal of the Sacred Rota and approved by the Royal Court of Appeal in Florence in April 1943.

In 1942 the daughter was interned in Italy in the town of Perugia, and during that time she formed an association with an Italian, one Giovanni Angelini; as a result of that association she gave birth to a child on 2 July 1943. The child was registered with the appropriate official in Perugia as being the child of Giovanni Angelini and the daughter. Giovanni Angelini was a bachelor at the time of the birth and of the conception of the child. The daughter was married to her first husband at the time of the conception, although the marriage had been annulled at the time of the birth.

On 14 October 1943 Giovanni Angelini and the daughter were

married in London. That marriage was annulled on 26 January1951, on the grounds of the wilful refusal of Giovanni Angelini to
consummate it. The parties had had only one child, who was the
infant plaintiff, Patrizio Giovanni Pietro Angelini. The daughter
had remarried, but there was no issue of that marriage.

The question on the summons was whether the plaintiff was
entitled to rank as the legitimate child of the daughter for the purpose of qualifying as the object of the statutory power of advancement applicable to her share under the father's will.

HARMAN J.: The question that I have to decide is whether the
infant plaintiff is entitled to a contingent interest in remainder in his
mother's settled share; and is an object of the power of advancement applicable by virtue of the statute.

It is admitted that if the Legitimacy Act 1926 had never been
passed the plaintiff would have been considered for this purpose as
the legitimate son of his parents. That is the result of the authorities
preceding the Act of 1926, and notably of *In re Grey's Trusts.*[1] In
that case the testator died in the year 1860. The marriage which
legitimated the boy in question was in 1880 and the boy was born
in 1877, that is to say, long after the testator's death. He became
legitimate in 1880 when the testator had been dead for 20 years. . . .
I cite the case to show that it does not matter that the child should
be born after the relevant instrument came into operation. . . .

The father of the plaintiff here was at all material times a domiciled Italian and was, therefore, at the date of the plaintiff's birth
and at the date of his marriage with the plaintiff's mother domiciled
in a country where legitimation by subsequent marriage is recognized in circumstances which exist here. Before 1927, therefore, the
plaintiff would have been an object of this power.

A person who would not have been an object of this power would
have been a person born out of wedlock whose father, though at the
time of his subsequent marriage with the mother he was domiciled
in a country which recognized legitimatio per subsequens matrimonium, was not in that position at the date of the birth of that person. It was always necessary under the common law for the father to
have been domiciled in such country at both dates.

With those circumstances in mind I must examine the Legitimacy
Act 1926, which, as is well known, makes legitimatio per subsequens

[1] [1892] 3 Ch. 88.

matrimonium for the first time part of the law of England in the case of persons of English domicile. (His Lordship read s. 1 (1) and (3) and continued:) Thus, legitimated persons can only take such interests in property as the Act expressly confers upon them; this is effected by section 3, which provides: 'Subject to the provisions of this Act, a legitimated person and his spouse, children or more remote issue shall be entitled to take any interest . . . (*b*) under any disposition coming into operation after the date of legitimation. . . .' A legitimated person is defined by section 11 as 'a person legitimated by this Act', and by subsection (2) of section 8 'this Act shall have effect as if reference therein to a legitimated person included a person . . . recognized as having been legitimated' under that section. For the purposes of this case section 8 is the important section, but before considering it I will refer to section 10 (2). (His Lordship read it.) If, therefore, the testator had died before January 1, 1927, this child would, admittedly, have continued to be entitled to the rights which the law would have given him before that date; but the will came into operation after the Act, so that that section does not save his rights if they are not saved otherwise.

The Act, so far as I have recited it, is confined to persons having a father domiciled in England at the date of the marriage, and it is obviously recognized that there might be another class of persons who, if special provision were not made for them, would be excluded from its benefits, namely, persons whom the Act did not legitimate by reason of the fact that the father, at the date of the birth of the child, was domiciled in some other country which did not recognize legitimatio per subsequens matrimonium. That class of persons would have been an obvious case of omission if the Act had not provided for them, and provision is made for them by section 8, which is in these terms. (His Lordship read section 8 (1) down to the words 'whichever last happens' and continued:) So far, all that seems to apply to the plaintiff, but the section continues: 'notwithstanding that his father was not at the time of the birth of such person domiciled in a country in which legitimation by subsequent marriage was permitted by law'.

If those last words cut down the category of people with whom the section is concerned, and limit it to persons whose father was not at the date of their birth domiciled in a country which recognized legitimatio per subsequens matrimonium, then it has no application to the plaintiff because his father was a domiciled Italian at all times. If, however, the section applies not only to that class but to the wider class of people whom the law recognized here, before the Act, as legitimate, then it may be said that the plaintiff, although he would have been regarded here as legitimate before 1927, must now rank with those who are legitimated (if at all) by the Act of 1926.

Prima facie I should have expected this Act to confer legitimacy on certain persons who were not legitimate before. It does so for persons whose father was domiciled in England and Wales without doubt, and also for a person whose father, though domiciled in England when the child was born, was domiciled elsewhere when he married. It is said that it also confers the kind of legitimacy provided by the Act on the further class of persons and, as it were, recognizes them again as legitimate. Mr. Pennycuick argued that it did not matter whether that was said per incuriam or not. His submission was that it was done in order that there should not be an anomalous class of people—better off, as it were, than those legitimated by the Act. Whether the legislature envisaged all possibilities, or whether, indeed, they have all been envisaged by anybody arguing this case, or by myself, I do not know. In this complicated legislation the only thing is to construe the actual language of the Act and to disregard the consequences unless they are patently clear.

It seems to me that the class of people to be affected by section 8 must be ascertained from a consideration of the whole of the section. One of the qualifications is that the father of the person was not at the date of that person's birth domiciled in a country which recognized legitimatio per subsequens matrimonium. That being so, the plaintiff does not come within the class affected by the section.

The other view is that 'notwithstanding' means whether his father was or was not so domiciled at the time of his birth. That seems to me to be a slight perversion of the meaning of the language used. That view also involves using the word 'recognized' in a very odd sense because, if a person is already recognized by law as legitimate, it is odd that you should find him recognized under the section. The difference, of course, is that if this child ought to be regarded as within the class legitimated by the Legitimacy Act, he would not be an object of the power, because the instrument came into force before his birth. But if he had rights before (as admittedly he had), and kept them, he is under no compulsion to have recourse to the enabling Act and can stand on what Dicey calls his common law rights.

Having been regarded by the common law as legitimate before

In re
HURLL.
—
Harman J.

1927, I do not think that section 8 of the Act has the effect of depriving him of those rights and including him in a new category having slightly less privilege than the old. It may be that that produces some anomaly, but that is immaterial, and I regard the language on the whole as having the narrower construction, which would leave out the plaintiff and those in his position as not being in need of the safeguard which the section was intended to bring to a narrowed class of persons who were not regarded as legitimate by the common law. I hold, therefore, that the plaintiff is entitled to be regarded as a child of the marriage of his parents, and entitled to share as a child of the defendant Agnes in the one-third share of the testator's residuary estate settled on her for life, with remainder to her children.

Declaration accordingly.

Section C: ADOPTION

ADOPTION ACT 1958

1.—(1) Subject to the provisions of this Act, the court may, upon an application made in the prescribed manner by a person domiciled in England or Scotland, make an order (in this Act referred to as an adoption order) authorizing the applicant to adopt an infant.

(5) An adoption order shall not be made in England unless the applicant and the infant reside in England and shall not be made in Scotland unless the applicant and the infant reside in Scotland, subject however to section twelve of this Act.

12.—(1) An adoption order may, notwithstanding anything in this Act, be made on the application of a person who is not ordinarily resident in Great Britain; and in relation to such an application subsection (5) of section one of this Act does not apply.

16.—(1) Where, at any time after the making of an adoption order, the adopter or the adopted person or any other person dies intestate in respect of any real or personal property (other than property subject to an entailed interest under a disposition to which subsection (2) of this section does not apply), that property shall devolve in all respects as if the adopted person were the child of the adopter born in lawful wedlock and were not the child of any other person.

(2) In any disposition of real or personal property made, whether by instrument inter vivos or by will (including codicil) after the date of an adoption order—

(*a*) any reference (whether express or implied) to the child or children of the adopter shall, unless the contrary intention appears, be construed as, or as including, a reference to the adopted person;

(*b*) any reference (whether express or implied) to the child or children of the adopted person's natural parents or either of them shall, unless the contrary intention appears, be construed as not being, or as not including, a reference to the adopted person; and

(*c*) any reference (whether express or implied) to a person related to the adopted person in any degree shall, unless the contrary intention appears, be construed as a reference to the person who would be related to him in that degree if he were the child of the adopter born in lawful wedlock and were not the child of any other person.

(4) The references in this section to an adoption order include references to an order authorizing an adoption made under the Adoption of Children Act (Northern Ireland) 1950 or any enactment of the Parliament of Northern Ireland for the time being in force.

17.—(2) For the purposes of subsection (2) of the last foregoing section, a disposition made by will or codicil shall be treated as made on the date of the death of the testator.

59.—(1) This Act has effect subject to the transitional provisions set out in the Fifth Schedule to this Act.

60. (1) This Act may be cited as the Adoption Act 1958.

(2) This Act does not extend to Northern Ireland.

(3) This Act comes into force on the first day of April, nineteen hundred and fifty-nine.

Fifth Schedule

Transitional Provisions

4.—(1) Subject to the following provisions of this paragraph, sections sixteen to eighteen of this Act apply in relation to an adoption order made under the Adoption Act 1950, or any enactment repealed by that Act, or the Adoption of Children Act (Northern Ireland) 1929, as they apply in relation to an adoption order within the meaning of those sections respectively.

(2) Nothing in sub-paragraph (1) of this paragraph affects the devolution of any property on the intestacy of a person who died

before the first day of January, nineteen hundred and fifty, or any disposition made before that date.

ADOPTION ACT 1964

1.—(1) Any provision (however expressed) in any enactment passed before the commencement of this Act under which a person adopted in pursuance of an adoption order is for any purpose treated as the child of the adopter, or any other relationship is deduced by reference to such an order, shall have effect, as respects anything done or any event occurring after the commencement of this Act,—

(a) if it extends only to adoptions in pursuance of orders made in the United Kingdom, as extending also to adoptions in pursuance of orders made, whether before or after the commencement of this Act, in the Isle of Man or in any of the Channel Islands;

(b) if it extends only to adoptions in pursuance of orders made in England or in Great Britain, as extending also to adoptions in pursuance of orders made, whether before or after the commencement of this Act, elsewhere in the United Kingdom or in the Isle of Man or in any of the Channel Islands.

4.—(1) This Act may be cited as the Adoption Act 1964.

(3) This Act shall be construed as one with the Adoption Act 1958.

An adoption made in any foreign country outside the United Kingdom, the Channel Islands, or the Isle of Man will be recognised as valid in England if at the time of the adoption the adopter was domiciled in such foreign country and the child resided there.

For the purposes of the succession to any property the succession to which is governed by English domestic law, a child validly adopted in any such foreign country will be treated as if he had been adopted in England under the Adoption Act 1958.

In re
VALENTINE'S
SETTLE-
MENT.

In re VALENTINE'S SETTLEMENT [1965] Ch. 831 (Court of Appeal)

Alastair Valentine was at all material times domiciled and resident in Southern Rhodesia. He was married and had one child, Simon, who was born in 1936. By orders of the Children's Court in Johannesburg, South Africa, Alastair and his wife adopted a girl

Carole in 1939 and a boy Timothy in 1944. It was assumed that both Carole and Timothy were resident and domiciled in South Africa at the times of the respective adoption orders.

In re VALENTINE'S SETTLE- MENT.

In 1946, by a settlement the proper law of which was English, Alastair's mother settled funds on trust for Alastair for life and then for his children at 21.

Alastair died in 1962 and the trustees of the settlement issued a summons to determine whether the settled funds devolved on Simon alone, or equally between Simon, Carole, and Timothy.

There was evidence that by South African law an adopted child was deemed to be the legitimate child of the adoptive parents, except that he did not become entitled to any property as a child of the adoptive parent under any instrument executed prior to the date of the adoption, nor could he inherit any property ab intestato from any relative of his adoptive parent. There was evidence that by the law of Southern Rhodesia an adoption order could not be made in favour of any applicant who was not domiciled and resident in the colony or in respect of any minor who was not so resident; and that the courts of Southern Rhodesia would not recognise as valid an adoption order granted by the courts of a country in which the adopter was not resident and domiciled.

Pennycuick J. held that the settled funds were held on trust for Simon alone. Timothy appealed.

LORD DENNING M.R.: In order to determine the case, we have to answer two questions. The first is whether the English courts will recognise the adoption orders so as to give the adopted children the status of children. If the answer is 'No', that will decide the case adversely to Carole and Timothy: for they will not be regarded as the children of Alastair in the eyes of English law at all: and Simon will take the whole because he is the only child recognised by English law. If the answer is 'Yes', so that the adopted children have the status of children, nevertheless the second question arises. It is whether the English courts will confer on these adopted children the rights and benefits given to 'children' by this settlement: for, whilst recognising their status, English law may not give them all the self-same rights and benefits as the natural-born child.

On both these points we have to consider the law as to adoption of South Africa, England and Southern Rhodesia. I will summarise the material provisions. [His Lordship did so, pointing out that by

In re
VALENTINE'S
SETTLE-
MENT.
—
Lord
Denning
M.R.

South African law Carole and Timothy would be regarded as entitled to succeed to the property under the settlement, but that by English and Southern Rhodesian domestic law they would not.]

Such being the various laws, I turn now to consider the first question, which is this: Do the courts of this country recognise the adoption orders made by the courts of South Africa so as to give these children the status of children?

I start with the proposition stated by James L.J. in *In re Goodman's Trusts*:[1] 'The family relation is at the foundation of all society, and it would appear almost an axiom that the family relation, once duly constituted by the law of any civilized country, should be respected and acknowledged by every other member of the great community of nations.' That was a legitimation case, but the like principle applies to adoption.

But when is the status of adoption duly constituted? Clearly it is so when it is constituted in another country in similar circumstances as we claim for ourselves. Our courts should recognise a jurisdiction which mutatis mutandis they claim for themselves: see *Travers* v. *Holley*.[2] We claim jurisdiction to make an adoption order when the adopting parents are domiciled in this country and the child is resident here. So also, out of the comity of nations, we should recognise an adoption order made by another country when the adopting parents are domiciled there and the child is resident there.

Apart from international comity, we reach the same result on principle. When a court of any country makes an adoption order for an infant child, it does two things: (1) it destroys the legal relationship theretofore existing between the child and its natural parents, be it legitimate or illegitimate; (2) it creates the legal relationship of parent and child between the child and its adopting parents, making it their legitimate child. It creates a new status in both, namely, the status of parent and child. Now it has long been settled that questions affecting status are determined by the law of the domicile. This new status of parent and child, in order to be recognised everywhere, must be validly created by the law of the domicile of the adopting parent. You do not look to the domicile of the child: for that has no separate domicile of its own. It takes its parents' domicile. You look to the parents' domicile only. If you find that a legitimate relationship of parent and child has been validly created by the law of the parents' domicile at the time the relation-

---

[1] (1881) 17 Ch. D. 266, 297; *ante*, p. 223. [2] [1953] P. 246, 257; *ante*, p. 122.

ship is created, then the status so created should be universally recognised throughout the civilised world, provided always that there is nothing contrary to public policy in so recognising it. That general principle finds expression in the judgment of Scott L.J. in *In re Luck's Settlement Trusts*.[1] I think it is correct, notwithstanding that the majority in that case created a dubious exception to it. But it is an essential feature of this principle that the parents should be domiciled in the country at the time: for no provision of the law of a foreign country will be regarded in the English courts as effective to create the status of a parent in a person not domiciled in that country at the time: see *In re Grove*[2] (legitimation by subsequent marriage); *In re Wilson*[3] (adoption). I ought to say, however, that in order for adoption to be recognised everywhere, it seems to me that, in addition to the adopting parents being domiciled in the country where the order is made, the child should be ordinarily resident there: for it is the courts of ordinary residence which have the pre-eminent jurisdiction over the child: see *In re P. (G.E.) (An Infant)*.[4] The child is under their protection and it would seem only right that those courts should be the courts to decide whether the child should be adopted or not.

In my opinion, therefore, the courts of this country will only recognise an adoption in another country if the adopting parents are domiciled there and the child is ordinarily resident there.

Now coming to this particular case, I fear that we in these courts cannot recognise these adoption orders as conferring the status of children on Carole and Timothy: for the simple reason that the adopting parents were not domiciled nor ordinarily resident in South Africa. So on the very first point Carole and Timothy fail.

I may, however, be wrong about this: because I recognise the force of the opinion which Salmon L.J. will express, namely, that the courts of this country should recognise an adoption in another country if it is effected by an order of the courts of that country, provided always that their courts apply the same safeguards as we do. If this be right, then we should recognise the adoption orders in South Africa as conferring the status of children on Carole and Timothy: for their courts have the same safeguards as we. There then arises the second question: What is the effect of this recognition? Does it give the adopted children the self-same rights and

[1] [1940] Ch. 864; *ante*, p. 227.   [2] (1888) 40 Ch. D. 216.   [3] [1954] Ch. 733.
[4] [1965] Ch. 568.

243

In re
VALENTINE'S
SETTLE-
MENT.
—
Lord
Denning
M.R.

benefits as natural-born children, especially in regard to succession to property? Or only the same rights and benefits as adopted children? I have shown above that, in none of the countries here under consideration, do adopted children have the same rights of succession as natural-born children. In South Africa they have no right to inherit on intestacy. In England they have no right to take under a disposition unless it was made after January 1, 1950. Similarly in Southern Rhodesia.

In my opinion, when English law recognises a foreign adoption order as conferring the status of a child, it does not give to the child all the self-same rights and benefits of succession as a natural-born child. It only gives the child the self-same rights and benefits as a child adopted in England by an English adoption order. I know that Barnard J. would not have given the foreign-adopted child even those rights. In *In re Wilby*[1] he would not allow the child (or in that case the parent) to succeed on an intestacy. But I think that case was wrongly decided. It may be suggested that the foreign-adopted child should have all the self-same rights of succession as that foreign country gives; and there are some passages in *In re Marshall*[2] which give colour to that view. But I am quite clear that we do not look to the law of succession of the foreign country. If we did, we might find that a foreign-adopted child had greater rights of succession in England than an English-adopted child. Which is absurd. The correct solution is this: the child is to be treated in English law just as if he had been adopted in England, no better and no worse.

Applying this principle here we have to treat Carole and Timothy just as if they had been adopted in England by parents domiciled in England. Would they then have taken anything under this settlement? Clearly not. This settlement was made on February 7, 1946, that is before January 1, 1950. According to our law, in that settlement the word 'children' does not include adopted children. In any settlement made before January 1, 1950, an English adopted child has all the rights and benefits of a natural-born child so far as custody, maintenance and education is concerned: but it has no right to succeed to property: and it is not regarded as a 'child' in a will or settlement. An English-adopted child would not take under this settlement. Nor should a South African-adopted child.

On this second point, too, I think that Carole and Timothy fail.

[1] [1956] P. 174.   [2] [1957] Ch. 263.

In my judgment the decision of Pennycuick J. was right and this appeal should be dismissed.

In re
VALENTINE'S
SETTLE-
MENT.
—
Lord
Denning
M.R.

DANCKWERTS L.J. delivered judgment to the same effect, except that he was 'not sure' that the child need be ordinarily resident in the country where he was adopted.

SALMON L.J. (dissenting): . . . There is clearly much to be said for the argument that, as adoption affects the status not only of the child but also of the father, our courts should not recognise the power of the South African court to make an adoption order altering Alastair's status since he was not domiciled within its jurisdiction. Our courts will not ordinarily recognise a decree of divorce unless the husband was domiciled in the country where the decree was granted: *Le Mesurier* v. *Le Mesurier.*[1] According to our law the wife takes the husband's domicile. There could, therefore, be no nexus between the foreign court and either of the parties to the divorce. The personal law of each would be alien to that of the court. Besides there are sound sociological reasons why such a divorce should not be recognised. In some countries the laws of divorce are far laxer than our own. If an Englishman could go abroad and obtain a divorce on almost any pretext and that divorce were to be recognised in England, the divorce rate might rise considerably. Such a weakening of the marriage tie is contrary to the interest of society. In the case of adoption, however, the position is very different when, as here, the foreign court certainly had jurisdiction over two of the parties concerned—the children and their natural parents. The evidence does not show whether or not the children were born legitimate. If they were legitimate, they, of course, took their father's domicile, and if illegitimate, their mother's. There is nothing in the evidence to suggest that the natural parent of either of them was domiciled or ordinarily resident anywhere other than in South Africa. Whilst it is, of course, a principle of English law that it will not recognise the right of a foreign court to impose a change of status upon anyone not domiciled within its jurisdiction, it is equally a principle of English law generally to recognise the right of a foreign court to make an order changing the status of anyone over whom it has jurisdiction. What happens, as here, when these two principles conflict? When the adopted child and its natural parents are domiciled within the jurisdiction of the

---

[1] [1895] A.C. 517; *ante*, p. 114. (But see *Indyka* v. *Indyka* [1971] 3 W.L.R. 510; *ante*, p. 122 [*Ed.*].)

foreign court and the adoptive father is not domiciled within its jurisdiction? There is no escape from the necessity of choosing between the two principles, for no compromise is possible. We could not regard the orders of the South African court as effective to sever the ties between the children and their natural parents and make them the children of Alastair and yet ineffective to make Alastair their father. The problem that confronts us has never yet arisen in this country. It has been suggested that according to the theory of our law no foreign adoption should be recognised unless, at the time it was made, both adopted child and adoptive parent were domiciled within the jurisdiction of the foreign country and that this appeal should be decided accordingly. Our law, however, develops in accordance with the changing needs of man. These have always been ascertained by experience rather than by the rigid application of abstract theory. Experience has shown that there are sound sociological reasons for recognising an adoption in circumstances such as these. Adoption—provided that there are proper safeguards —is greatly for the benefit of the adopted child and of the adoptive parents, and also, I think, of civilised society, since this is founded on the family relationship. It seems to me that we should be slow to refuse recognition to an adoption order made by a foreign court which applies the same safeguards as we do and which undoubtedly had jurisdiction over the adopted child and its natural parents.

The laws of adoption in South Africa are very nearly the same as our own. The principles underlying them are the same. The whole emphasis is upon the welfare of the child and elaborate precautions are laid down for assuring that the adoption order shall not be made unless it is for the benefit of the child; the consent of the natural parents is required. It is difficult to see why in these circumstances, unless compelled to do so, our courts should refuse to recognise these adoption orders made lawfully in South Africa which conferred nothing but benefits on all the parties concerned. . . .

Appeal dismissed.

NOTE H: LEGITIMACY, LEGITIMATION, AND ADOPTION

A DISTINCTION must be drawn between the question whether a child is legitimate or has been legitimated or adopted, and the question whether such a child can succeed to property under a gift to 'children' in a settlement or will or under an intestacy. The former is a question of status, governed (broadly speaking) by the law of the domicile of the child or its father (whose domicile, and at what date it is relevant, differing in the different cases). The latter is a question of construction, governed by the proper law of the settlement or the law of the domicile of the testator or intestate at the date of his death. The difference between the two questions is clearly stated by Lord Denning M.R. in *Re Valentine's Settlement* (*ante*, p. 241). They have not always been kept distinct, but there can be no doubt that they should be. For in some situations the child may succeed whether or not he is legitimate; in others, he may not succeed whether or not he has been legitimated or adopted. The law governing the succession, whether English or foreign, may accord different rights of succession to different classes of children. In English domestic law, legitimate children have greater rights of succession than children legitimated or recognized as having been legitimated under the Legitimacy Act 1926 or children adopted under the Adoption Act 1958. For under these statutes legitimated or adopted children can only succeed as 'children' if they were legitimated or adopted before the settlement was made or before the death of the testator or intestate (Legitimacy Act 1926 ss. 3 (1), 8 (2); Adoption Act 1958 ss. 16, 17). On the other hand, children recognized as having been legitimated at common law have succession rights equal to those of legitimate children (*Re Askew, ante*, p. 13; *Re Hurll, ante*, p. 247), except that they cannot succeed as heirs to real estate in England or to a peerage (*Doe d. Birtwhistle* v. *Vardill* (1840) 7 Cl. & F. 895). The importance of this exception is of course minimal after the abolition of descent to the heir for fee simple estates in 1925.

(A) *Legitimacy*

Some questions on *Re Bischoffsheim* (*ante*, p. 214):

(1) Was Romer J. justified in asserting that, according to the majority judgments in *Re Goodman's Trusts* (*ante*, p. 222), the question of legitimacy, whether original or acquired, is governed by the law of the child's domicile of origin? Suppose that before 1927 (*a*) a domiciled Englishman had an illegitimate child by a domiciled Dutch woman whom he subsequently married, or (*b*) a domiciled Dutchman had an illegitimate child by a domiciled English woman whom he subsequently married: (i) what would be the child's domicile of origin? (ii) would the child be legitimated by the subsequent marriage?

(2) Was Romer J. correct in assuming that a child's domicile of origin is the same as that of his parents at the date of his birth? What was the domicile of origin of the children in *Shaw* v. *Gould* (*ante*, p. 209) and *Re Paine* (*ante*, p. 85)?

(3) Can the decision be reconciled with *Shaw* v. *Gould* and *Re Paine*? If so, how? Would the decision in *Shaw* v. *Gould* have been different if Buxton had acquired a domicile in Scotland after the divorce but before the children were born? Would the decision in *Re Paine* have been different if the parties had settled in Germany immediately after the marriage?

(4) Could Richard Wellesley have succeeded to a peerage of the United Kingdom? In other words, was he 'porphyro-genitus, born legitimate within the narrowest pale of English legitimacy' within the meaning of James L.J.'s phrase in *Re Goodman's Trusts (ante,* p. 225)?

(5) Suppose that H and W, domiciled in Ruritania, are validly married there a month before their eldest child is born, but that by Ruritanian law the child is illegitimate because not conceived in lawful wedlock. Would he be illegitimate in England?

It is unfortunate that the scope of s. 2 of the Legitimacy Act 1959 *(ante,* p. 221) (which is retrospective as to status but not as to rights of succession) should have been so severely restricted by s. 2 (2), which says that the section 'applies and applies only' if the father is domiciled in England. In the face of these words, it is difficult to see how the cases of *Shaw* v. *Gould* and *Re Paine* could be differently decided today if the same facts were to recur.

(B) *Legitimation*

(1) *At common law* a child was recognized as having been legitimated if his father was domiciled at the date of his birth and at the date of the subsequent marriage in a country the law of which recognized legitimation by subsequent marriage: *Re Goodman's Trusts (ante,* p. 222). He was not so recognized if his father was domiciled at either date in some country (e.g. England) the law of which did not recognize legitimation by subsequent marriage: *Re Wright's Trusts* (1856), 2 K. &. J. 595 (date of birth); *Re Grove* (1888), 40 Ch. D. 216 (date of marriage).

The requirement that the father must be domiciled in a country recognizing legitimation at the date of the child's birth as well as at the date of the subsequent marriage or other legitimating event is anomalous, and it is perhaps unfortunate that the Court of Appeal in *Re Luck's Settlement Trusts (ante,* p. 227) did not overrule *Re Wright's Trusts.* There might be some point in looking to the law of the father's domicile at the date of the child's birth if it is necessary for the child to contend (as it was in *Re Luck*) that he was legitimated as from the date of his birth. There can be no point in doing so if it is not so necessary, or if the legitimation has no retrospective operation under the foreign law.

Assuming that the Court of Appeal were not prepared to overrule *Re Wright's Trusts,* the decision in *Re Luck* seems correct in principle, because David Luck was not entitled to share in the trust funds under either of the rules that might have been selected as analogies: not under the common law rule, because his father was domiciled in England when he was born; nor under the Legitimacy Act 1926, because *(a)* his father was married to a third person when David was born (s. 1 (2)); *(b)* the marriage settlement and will came into operation before the date of his legitimation (s. 3 (1) *(b)*) and before the commencement of the Act (s. 10 (2)). On the other hand, if *Re Wright's Trusts* had been overruled or distinguished, as Scott L.J. proposed, there would have been a difficulty in allowing David to share in the trust funds settled by the marriage settlement (as opposed to the will), because the perpetuity period expired in 1917, twenty-one years after the dropping of the lives in being.

(2) *The Legitimacy Act 1926* introduced legitimation by subsequent marriage into English domestic law for the first time (s. 1 (1)); laid down a new conflict rule for the recognition of foreign legitimations, whereunder the

LEGITIMACY, LEGITIMATION, AND ADOPTION

father's domicile at the date of the marriage is alone relevant (s. 8); and regulated the succession rights of children legitimated by s. 1 (1) or recognized as having been legitimated under s. 8 (ss. 1 (3), 3, and 10 (2)). However, the Act has not abolished the old common law rule, and it may still be necessary to have recourse to it, for one of four reasons:

(a) A child is only recognized as having been legitimated under s. 8 from 1 January 1927, or from the date of the marriage, whichever last happens.

(b) The Act only applies to legitimation by subsequent marriage, not to other modes of legitimation.

(c) The Act was not available if the child's father or mother was married to a third person when the child was born: s. 1 (2). But this restriction (which did not apply to legitimation at common law) has been repealed by s. 1 of the Legitimacy Act 1959 as from 29 October 1959.

(d) A child legitimated or recognized as having been legitimated under the Act can only succeed to property if the intestate died or the disposition came into operation *after* the date of his legitimation (s. 3 (1)) and also *after* 1 January 1927 (s. 10 (2)). But a child legitimated under the common law rule can succeed to property whenever the intestate died or the disposition came into operation: *Re Askew*; *Re Hurll* (*ante*, p. 234). A will comes into operation when the testator dies and not when some benefit under the will becomes vested or payable. Hence, if the testator gives property to A for life and then to A's children, a child of A who is legitimated after the testator's death cannot succeed under the Act: *Re Hepworth* [1936] Ch. 750; though he can do so if he was also legitimated at common law: *Re Hurll*. Similarly, an appointment under a special power comes into operation when the power is created, and not when it is exercised. Hence, a child legitimated between these two dates is not an object of the power: *Re Hoff* [1942] Ch. 298. (This was an additional reason, not noticed in the judgment, why Margarete Askew was not an object of the power by virtue of the Act.) But he is an object of the power if he was also legitimated at common law: *Re Askew*.

Suppose that a testator domiciled in England dies after 1927 having by his will given one moiety of his residue to A for life and then to A's children, and the other moiety to B for life and then to B's children. A and B each had a child who was legitimated by subsequent marriage after the testator's death. A was domiciled throughout in England and B in Holland. Could it be contended that the child of A should succeed because England is now a country which recognizes legitimation by subsequent marriage and therefore he was legitimated at common law? If so, it means that s. 3 of the Act is a dead letter. If not, it means that foreign-legitimated children have greater rights under English wills than English-legitimated children.

(C) *Adoption*

(1) *Jurisdiction of the English court.* English courts have jurisdiction to make an adoption order if (a) the applicant is domiciled in England or Scotland, and (b) the applicant and the infant reside in England: Adoption Act 1958, s. 1 (5). Exceptionally, the High Court or a county court (but not a magistrates' court) may make an order although the applicant is not ordinarily resident in England: s. 12 (1). But the infant must normally be so resident, because under s. 3 (1) he must have been continuously in the care and possession of the applicant for at least three months immediately preceding the date of the order; and unless he is over the upper limit of

school age, this care and possession must be in England: *Re W. (Spinster) (An Infant)* [1962] Ch. 918, 925.

The Act does not mention the domicile of the infant as a jurisdictional requirement. This is no doubt because it would unduly hamper adoptions if proof of domicile were required in the case of infants who are waifs or strays or whose natural parents cannot be traced. Very many adopted children are illegitimate and the domicile of the mother may be quite uncertain. Cheshire (pp. 381–2) and Graveson (pp. 327–8) suggests that if the infant is domiciled abroad, the court would, or at any rate should, refuse to make an order unless satisfied that the adoption would be in accordance with the law of the infant's domicile. This seems quite impracticable. It would introduce by the back door an inquiry into the infant's domicile, a factor which the Act deliberately treats as immaterial for jurisdictional purposes, for very good reasons. Many adoptions are made in magistrates' courts, which are quite unsuited to investigating complicated questions of foreign law and the conflict of laws. The only possible justification for invoking the law of the infant's domicile would be to safeguard the interests of the natural parents. But their interests seem to be adequately safeguarded by the requirement that they must consent to the making of the order (s. 4 (1) (a)), unless the court dispenses with their consent on certain narrowly-defined grounds (s. 5).

(2) *Recognition of foreign adoptions.* The Adoption Act 1958 applies to Scotland as well as to England, and therefore there can be no doubt that adoptions made in Scotland will be recognized in England. In general, the Act does not apply to Northern Ireland; but it contains several sections (e.g. s. 16 (4)) providing that references to adoption orders include references to adoption orders made in Northern Ireland. S. 1 of the Adoption Act 1964 provides in more general terms for the recognition in England and Scotland of adoption orders made not only in Northern Ireland but also in the Channel Islands and the Isle of Man.

The Adoption Acts 1958–64 contain no provision for recognizing adoptions effected in other foreign countries. According to the majority of the Court of Appeal in *Re Valentine's Settlement, ante,* p. 240, they will be recognized if (a) the adopter was domiciled in such foreign country, and (b) the child was resident there (though Danckwerts L.J. was 'not sure' about this second requirement). The dissenting opinion of Salmon L.J. in that case seems attractive at first sight. But it is not easy to see how the question whether the foreign court applied the same safeguards as we do can be relevant when the question whether to recognize the foreign adoption arises a quarter of a century later, when the children are grown up, as happened in *Re Valentine's Settlement.* Moreover, since the English safeguards are probably the strictest in the world, not many foreign adoptions would be recognized if this is to be the test.

Lord Denning M.R. enters one caveat: the foreign adoption should not be recognized if recognition would be contrary to English public policy. It is more than usually necessary to keep this factor in mind when deciding whether to recognize a foreign adoption, because the laws of some foreign countries differ so widely from English law as to the objects and effects of adoption. Hence, if the adoption was made for some ulterior object other than the welfare of the child, some at least of its effects might have to be denied recognition in England. But a mere difference between the foreign law and English domestic law should not be sufficient for the withholding of recognition on this ground. In particular, the fact that the child was over the age of 21, or that the adoption was not made by court order, should not prevent recognition. A system of law which is prepared to recognize polygamous marriages (*ante*, p. 95) or extra-judicial divorces (*Russ* v. *Russ, ante*, p. 145) should not be too squeamish about recognizing foreign adoptions.

(3) *Succession by adopted children.* A child adopted in England, Scotland or Northern Ireland can succeed to property under English wills, settlements or intestacies as if he were a child of the adopter born in lawful wedlock, provided the testator or intestate died or the settlement was executed after the date of the adoption order and also after 1 January 1950: Adoption Act 1958, ss. 16, 17 (2) and Fifth Schedule, para. 4. A child adopted in the Channel Islands or the Isle of Man can succeed to property under English wills, settlements, or intestacies as if he were a child of the adopter born in lawful wedlock, provided the testator or intestate died or the settlement was executed after the date of the adoption order and also after 16 July 1964: Adoption Act 1958, ss. 16, 17 (2); Adoption Act 1964, s. 1 (1). The Adoption Acts 1958–64 do not in terms apply to the succession by children adopted in other foreign countries. Assuming that the adoption is one which the English court can recognize, no less than four views about this matter have been expressed in the cases.

(*a*) According to one view, the court should deny all rights of succession to such adopted children because ss. 16 and 17 of the Adoption Act 1958 (as extended by s. 1 (1) of the Act of 1964) only apply to adoption orders made in the British Islands. This was the view of Barnard J. in *Re Wilby* [1956] P. 174. But each member of the Court of Appeal in *Re Valentine's Settlement* expressed disapproval of *Re Wilby*, so this view is now quite untenable.

(*b*) According to a second view, the court should go to the opposite extreme and allow the adopted child to succeed as if he were the legitimate natural-born child of the adopter. This was the view of Salmon L.J. in *Re Valentine's Settlement.* But it leads to the surprising result that foreign-adopted children would have greater rights of succession than English-adopted children under English settlements, wills, and intestacies, which (as Lord Denning tersely put it) 'is absurd'.

(*c*) According to a third view, the court should allow the law governing the adoption to determine the question, and permit the adopted child to succeed if that law would permit him to do so, but not otherwise. This was the view of the Court of Appeal in *Re Marshall* [1957] Ch. 507, for while they preferred not to express any concluded opinion on the 'difficult question' whether in any circumstances a foreign-adopted child can take as a 'child' of his adoptive parents (at pp. 519–20), they indicated that he could only do so if the law governing the adoption placed adopted children in a position substantially equivalent to that of natural children of the adopter, both as regards property rights and status (at p. 523). But this view might lead to the same surprising result as view (*b*) if the law governing the adoption happened to be more generous than English law in the matter of rights of succession, and was for this reason rejected by Lord Denning and Danckwerts L.J. in *Re Valentine's Settlement* (*ante*, p. 244). Moreover, it is contrary to principle, because the law of the testator's domicile, not that of the beneficiary's domicile, governs the construction of a will. Rights of succession do not crystallize when a child is adopted, any more than they do when a child is born or legitimated or when a woman marries. Why should different results be reached in the case of adoption?

(d) According to a fourth view, the court should treat the foreign-adopted child as though he had been adopted in England (notionally shifting the place, but not the date, of the adoption) and give him the same rights of succession, no more and no less, as a child adopted in England would have had. This was the view of Lord Denning in *Re Valentine's Settlement*, and it is submitted that it is the best view. It is consistent with the decision (but not with the reasoning) of the Court of Appeal in *Re Marshall*, because if the child in that case had been adopted in England, he would not have been entitled to succeed, because the testator died before 1 January 1950.

If the succession is governed by foreign law, an 'incidental question' may be presented: see *ante*, p. 22.

PART III

LAW OF OBLIGATIONS

Chapter 9

CONTRACTS

Section A: **DOCTRINE OF THE PROPER LAW**

The essential validity of a contract is governed by its proper law, i.e. the law of the country with which the contract has the most real connexion.

The proper law may be the lex loci contractus.

PENINSULAR AND ORIENTAL STEAM NAVIGATION COMPANY *v.* SHAND (1865) 3 Moo. P.C. (N.S.) 272. (Privy Council)

Appeal from the Supreme Court of Mauritius.

The plaintiff, the Chief Justice of the court below, took a ticket in England for his passage from Southampton to Alexandria and from Suez to Mauritius on board the defendants' steamships, for which he paid one entire sum of £315. One of the conditions of carriage was that the defendants did not hold themselves liable for damage to or loss of passengers' baggage.

The voyage from Southampton to Alexandria was on board the Ceylon and from Suez to Mauritius on board the Norna. At Suez the Norna lay a little distance out at sea in consequence of the shallowness of the water; the passengers were conveyed to her in a small steamboat, the baggage in another vessel. It was on board this small vessel that the plaintiff's baggage (consisting of cloaks, an overcoat and plaids) was last seen. It was missed by the plaintiff when on board the Norna, and on arrival at Mauritius it was not forthcoming.

253

P. & O.
STEAM
NAVIGATION
COMPANY
v.
SHAND.
—
Turner L.J.

The Supreme Court of Mauritius held that the contract was governed by French law (which prevailed generally at Mauritius) and that by that law the defendants were liable in spite of the exemption clause.

The defendants appealed.

THE judgment of their Lordships (Knight Bruce and Turner L.JJ. and Coleridge J.) was delivered by

TURNER L.J. (after stating the facts his Lordship continued): The general rule is, that the law of the country where a contract is made governs as to the nature, the obligation, and the interpretation of it. The parties to a contract are either the subjects of the Power there ruling or as temporary residents owe it a temporary allegiance: in either case equally they must be understood to submit to the law there prevailing, and to agree to its actions upon their contract. It is, of course, immaterial that such agreement is not expressed in terms; it is equally an agreement in fact, presumed de jure, and a foreign court interpreting or enforcing it on any contrary rule defeats the intention of the parties, as well as neglects to observe the recognized comity of nations. Their Lordships are speaking of the general rule; there are, no doubt, exceptions and limitations on its applicability, but the present case is not affected by these, and seems perfectly clear as to the actual intention of the contracting parties.

This is a contract made between British subjects in England, substantially for safe carriage from Southampton to Mauritius. The performance is to commence in an English vessel, in an English port; to be continued in vessels which for this purpose carry their country with them; to be fully completed in Mauritius; but liable to breach, partial or entire, in several other countries in which the vessels might be in the course of the voyage. Into this contract, which the appellants frame and issue, they have introduced for their own protection a stipulation, professing in its terms to limit the liability which, according to the English law, the contract would otherwise have cast upon them. When they tendered this contract to the respondent, and required his signature to it, what must it be presumed that he understood to be their intention as to this stipulation? What would any reasonable man have understood that they intended? Was it to secure to themselves some real protection against responsibility for accidental losses of luggage and for damage to it; or to stipulate for something to which, however clearly expressed, the law would allow no validity? This question leaves untouched, it will be observed, the extent of the contemplated protection; it asks, in effect, was it intended that the stipulation in case of an alleged breach of contract should be construed by the rules of the English law, which would give some effect to it? or by those of the French or any other law, according to which it would have none, but be treated as a merely fruitless attempt to evade a responsibility inseparably fixed upon the appellants as carriers? The question appears to their Lordships to admit of one answer only; but if they take the respondent so to have understood the intention of the appellants, they must take him to have adopted the same intention; it would be to impute want of good faith on his part to suppose that with that knowledge he yet intended to enter into a contract wholly different on so important an article; he could not have done this if the intention had been expressed, and there is no difference as to effect between that which is expressed in terms and that which is implied and clearly understood.

P. & O.
STEAM
NAVIGATION
COMPANY
v.
SHAND.
—
Turner L.J.

The actual intention of the parties, therefore, must be taken clearly to have been to treat this as an English contract, to be interpreted according to the rules of English law; and as there is no rule of general law or policy setting up a contrary presumption, their Lordships will hold that the court below was wrong in not governing itself according to those rules.

It is a satisfaction to their Lordships to find that in the year 1864 the Cour de Cassation in France pronounced a judgment to the same effect in a case under precisely the same circumstances, which arose between the appellants and a French officer who was returning with his baggage from Hong Kong in one of their ships, the Alma, and who lost his baggage in the wreck of that vessel in the Red Sea. The same question arose as here on the effect to be given to the stipulation in the ticket; two inferior courts, those of Marseilles and Aix, decided it in favour of the plaintiff on the provisions of the French law; the Supreme Court reversed these decisions, and held that the contract having been made at Hong Kong, an English possession, and with an English Company, was to receive its interpretation and effect according to English law.

(His Lordship proceeded to hold that by English law the clause in the contract exempted the appellants from liability.)

Appeal allowed.

Or the proper law may be the lex loci solutionis.

CHATENAY *v.* BRAZILIAN SUBMARINE TELEGRAPH CO., LTD. [1891]
1 Q.B. 79 (Court of Appeal)

Appeal from a judgment of Day J. on a preliminary issue.

In 1880 the plaintiff, who was a Brazilian subject and resident in Brazil, executed, in favour of one Broe, a stockbroker carrying on business in the City of London, a power of attorney to purchase and sell shares in public companies and public funds. The power of attorney was in the Portuguese language, and was executed by the plaintiff in Brazil with the formalities required by the Brazilian law. Broe, purporting to act under the power of attorney, disposed of certain shares in the defendant company which were the property of the plaintiff and registered in his name. Broe did not account to the plaintiff for the proceeds of the sale of these shares, the purchasers of which were registered as owners in the books of the company. The plaintiff issued an originating summons asking for the rectification of the register by inserting therein his name as holder of the shares, and an issue was directed to be tried by a jury in London to determine whether the plaintiff was entitled to have the register so rectified. Before this issue came on for trial an order was made that the question whether Brazilian or English law was to govern the construction of the power of attorney should be tried by a judge without a jury. The matter came on before Day J., who decided that English law was to govern the construction of the power of attorney, and a certificate to that effect was accordingly made out.

The defendants appealed.

LORD ESHER M.R.: In this case a person resident in Brazil and carrying on business there wrote down that which he intended to be an authority to an agent, if that agent would accept the delegation. The person whom he desired to be his delegate did afterwards accept that delegation. The question raised is, what is the meaning of that document? Now, I agree that it has one meaning, and no more; and the question is, what was the meaning of the plaintiff when he wrote that document? The court has to ascertain that meaning from a consideration of what it is that was written under the circumstances in which it was written; that is, in other words, having regard to the words used, and to the surrounding circumstances at the time they were used.

Now, this writing was a business document, written in Brazil in the Brazilian language, and with the formalities necessary according to the Brazilian law and custom, by a man of business carrying on business in Brazil. An English court has to construe it, and the first thing, therefore, that the English court has to do is to get a translation of the language used in the document. Making a translation is not a mere question of trying to find out in a dictionary the words which are given as the equivalent of the words of the document; a true translation is the putting into English that which is the exact effect of the language used under the circumstances. To get at this in the present case you must get the words in English which in business have the equivalent meaning of the words in Brazilian, as used in Brazil, under the circumstances. Therefore you would want a competent translator, competent to translate in that way, and, if the words in Brazil had in business a particular meaning different from their ordinary meaning, you would want an expert to say what is that meaning. Amongst those experts you might want a Brazilian lawyer—and a Brazilian lawyer for that purpose would be an expert. That is the first thing the court has to do. Then, when the court has got a correct translation into English, it has to do what it always has to do in the case of any such document—either a contract, or such an authority as this—that is to say, determine what is to be taken to be the meaning of the party at the time he wrote it, and what is to be inferred from the language which he has used. There are certain inferences which are adopted in ascertaining the meaning of the language used, unless in the particular instance the contrary intention appears. One inference which has been always adopted is this: if a contract is made in a country to be executed in that country, unless there appears something to the contrary, you take it that the parties must have intended that that contract, as to its construction, and as to its effect, and the mode of carrying it out (which really are the result of its construction), is to be construed according to the law of the country where it was made. But the business sense of all business men has come to this conclusion, that if a contract is made in one country to be carried out between the parties in another country, either in whole or in part, unless there appears something to the contrary, it is to be concluded that the parties must have intended that it should be carried out according to

CHATENAY
v.
BRAZILIAN
SUBMARINE
TELEGRAPH
COMPANY.
—
Lord
Esher M.R.

CHATENAY
v.
BRAZILIAN
SUBMARINE
TELEGRAPH
COMPANY.
—
Lord
Esher M.R.

the law of that other country. Otherwise a very strange state of things would arise, for it is hardly conceivable that persons should enter into a contract to be carried out in a country contrary to the laws of that country. That is not to be taken to be the meaning of the parties, unless they take very particular care to enunciate such a strange conclusion. Therefore the law has said, that if the contract is to be carried out in whole in another country, it is to be carried out wholly according to the law of that country, and that must have been the meaning of the parties. But if it is to be carried out partly in another country than that in which it is made, that part of it which is to be carried out in that other country, unless something appears to the contrary, is taken to have been intended to be carried out according to the laws of that country.

Now, applying those rules to the present case, the first thing to be done is to get at the true construction of the language used in the authority. When the plaintiff used the Brazilian language in this document he must have used it in the business sense given to it in Brazil. Therefore, that has to be ascertained; and then having got that, the equivalent in the English language must be found. Having got in English the equivalent of the Brazilian words, we have to see what the meaning of the language so used is. If it appears that the contract is to be performed in Brazil wholly—that is to say, that the contract shall be performed according to Brazilian law—that is the construction of it, and that is the meaning of the parties; but if it appears that it was to be wholly carried out in England, we should infer that the meaning of the parties and the true construction of the contract were that it was to be carried out according to English law. If we find that the authority might be carried out in England, or in France, or in any other country, we come to the conclusion that it must have been intended that in any country where in fact it was to be carried out, that part of it which was to be carried out in that country was to be carried out according to the law of that country. That would be putting one construction only on the document, and not putting a different construction on it in different countries. The one meaning that he had was, 'I give an authority which if carried out in England is to be carried out according to the law of England; if in France, according to the law of France.' That is one meaning, though this authority is to be applied in a different way in different places.

If that is so, then the way to express that in the present case is this.

This authority was given in Brazil, and the meaning is to be established by ascertaining what the plaintiff meant when he wrote it in Brazil. The authority being given in Brazil, and being written in the Portuguese language, the intention of the writer is to be ascertained by evidence of competent translators and experts, including if necessary Brazilian lawyers, as to the meaning of the language used; and if according to such evidence the intention appears to be that the authority shall be acted upon in foreign countries, it follows that the extent of the authority in any country in which the authority is to be acted upon is to be taken to be according to the law of the particular country where it is acted upon.

Now, that I consider to be a mere expansion of the judgment of Day J. It is the same judgment, but it is in an expanded form. His judgment, therefore, is not altered, but is held to be a correct judgment, although we express it in an expanded form. It follows that the appeal fails, and must be dismissed.

LINDLEY and LOPES L.JJ. delivered judgment to the same effect.

Appeal dismissed.

Or the proper law may be the law of the country to which a ship belongs.

LLOYD v. GUIBERT (1865) L.R. 1 Q.B. 115 (Exchequer Chamber)

WILLES J.: The facts disclosed by the record are as follows: The plaintiff below, a British subject, at St. Thomas, a Danish West India Island, chartered the ship Olivier, belonging to the defendants, who are Frenchmen, for a voyage from St. Marc, in Hayti, to Havre, London, or Liverpool, at the charterer's option. The plaintiff must have known that the ship was French. The charter-party was entered into by the master in pursuance of his general authority as master, and not under any special authority from the owner. The plaintiff shipped a cargo at St. Marc for Liverpool, with which the vessel sailed. On her voyage, she sustained damage from a storm, which compelled her to put into Fayal, a Portuguese port, for repair. There the master properly borrowed money upon bottomry of the ship, freight, and cargo, and repaired the ship, which proceeded with the cargo, and arrived in safety at Liverpool. The bondholder proceeded in the Court of Admiralty against the ship, freight, and cargo. The ship and freight were insufficient to satisfy the bond; the deficiency

CHATENAY
v.
BRAZILIAN
SUBMARINE
TELEGRAPH
COMPANY.
—
Lord
Esher M.R.

and costs fell upon the plaintiff as owner of the cargo, and in respect thereof he seeks to be indemnified by the defendants as shipowners.

The defendants abandoned the ship and freight; and it must be taken as fact (because it is alleged and not denied) that, by the law of France, they abandoned in time, and in such manner and under such circumstances as are required by the French law, and that according to such law, abandonment, by which we understand a giving up of the ship and freight to the shippers, absolved them from liability. This law, if applicable, is one which furnishes an absolute bar to the plaintiff's claim by way of satisfaction or discharge, and affected the validity of the claim, and not merely the mode of proceeding to enforce it.

By the English law, a shipowner, under such circumstances, is liable personally, and not merely to the value of the ship and freight. And it is alleged, and not denied, that the Danish Portuguese and Haytian laws agree in this respect with our own. The law of Hayti was not however relied upon in argument.

Upon these facts, it was insisted for the plaintiff that the decision ought to proceed upon either what was called the 'general maritime law', as regulating all maritime transactions between persons of different nationalities at sea; the Danish law, as that of the place where the contract was made (lex loci contractus); the Portuguese law, because the bottomry bond, which in one sense caused the question to arise, was given in a Portuguese port, and the rule that the place governs the act (locus regit actum) was supposed, therefore, to furnish a solution; or the English law, as being that of the place of the final act of performance by the delivery of the cargo (quasi lex loci solutionis), in either of which alternatives the liability of the defendants was established. And it was argued, that, the charterparty having been entered into bonâ fide in the ordinary course of business by the master, within the scope of his ostensible authority to contract for the employment of the vessel, which the owner, by appointing a master and sending him abroad in command, allows him to assume, the right of the charterer could no more be narrowed by a provision of foreign law unknown to him than by secret instructions from the owners, which would clearly be inoperative—a proposition which needs no authority in our law.

For the defendants, it was answered, that by the French law they are absolved; and that that law, as being that of the ship, governs the case, either because of the character of the transaction itself, showing that the plaintiff impliedly submitted his goods to the operation of the law of the ship, or because the master, who entered into the contract (although his doing so was within the scope of the authority which he was allowed by the owners to assume), was disabled by the French law from binding his owners, otherwise than with the exception expressed or implied of exemption from liability by abandonment, and that of such disability, or lack of authority, his flag was sufficient notice.

Upon this latter ground, the Court of Queen's Bench gave judgment for the defendants, not expressing any opinion upon the former; whereupon the plaintiff brought error, and the case was well argued at the sittings after Trinity Term last, before Erle C.J., Pollock C.B., Martin B., Keating J., Pigott B., and myself, when we took time to consider.

In determining a question between contracting parties, recourse must first be had to the language of the contract itself, and (force, fraud, and mistake apart) the true construction of the language of the contract (lex contractus) is the touchstone of legal right. It often happens, however, that disputes arise, not as to the terms of the contract, but as to their application to unforeseen questions, which arise incidentally or accidentally in the course of performance, and which the contract does not answer in terms, yet which are within the sphere of the relation established thereby, and cannot be decided as between strangers.

In such cases it is necessary to consider by what general law the parties intended that the transaction should be governed, or rather to what general law it is just to presume that they have submitted themselves in the matter. . . .

In the diversity or conflict of laws, which ought to prevail, is a question that has called forth an amazing amount of ingenuity, and many differences of opinion. It is, however, generally agreed that the law of the place where the contract is made, is primâ facie that which the parties intended, or ought to be presumed to have adopted as the footing upon which they dealt, and that such law ought therefore to prevail in the absence of circumstances indicating a different intention, as for instance, that the contract is to be entirely performed elsewhere, or that the subject-matter is immovable property situate in another country, and so forth; which latter, though sometimes treated as distinct rules, appear more properly to be classed as exceptions to the more general one, by reason of the circumstances

LAW OF OBLIGATIONS

LLOYD
v.
GUIBERT.

Willes J.

indicating an intention to be bound by a law different from that of the place where the contract is made; which intention is inferred from the subject-matter and from the surrounding circumstances, so far as they are relevant to construe and determine the character of the contract.

The present question does not appear to have ever been decided in this country, and in America it has received opposite decisions, equally entitled to respect. We must therefore deal with it as a new question, and endeavour to be guided in its solution by a steady application of the general principle already stated, viz., that the rights of the parties to a contract are to be judged of by that law by which they intended, or rather by which they may justly be presumed to have bound themselves.

We must apply this test successively to the various laws which have been suggested as applicable; and first to the alleged general maritime law.

(His Lordship held that there was no general rule in maritime law upon the subject, and continued:) In one other point of view the general maritime law, as administered in England, or (to avoid periphrasis) the law of England, viz. as the law of the contemplated place of final performance, or port of discharge, remains to be considered. It is manifest, however, that what was to be done at Liverpool (besides that, it might at the charterer's option have been done at Havre) was but a small portion of the entire service to be rendered, and that the character of the contract cannot be determined thereby. . . . It is unnecessary, however, to discuss this point further, because we have been anticipated and the question set at rest, in an instructive judgment of the Judicial Committee, delivered by the Lord Justice Turner, since the argument of the present case, in that of *Peninsular and Oriental Company* v. *Shand*.[1]

Next, as to the law of Portugal: the only semblance of authority for resorting to that law, as being the law of the place where the bottomry bond was given, is *Cammell* v. *Sewell*;[2] and we consider that the judgment in that case, if applicable at all, as to which we say nothing, could only affect the validity of the bottomry, and not the duties imposed upon the shipowner towards the merchant by the fact of the bottomry, which duties must be traced to the contract of affreightment and the bailment founded thereupon.

---

[1] (1865) 3 Moo. P.C. (N.S.) 272 ; *ante*, p. 253.
[2] (1860) 5 H. & N. 728 ; *post*, p. 353.

262

The law of Hayti was not mentioned nor relied upon in argument; and there remain only to be considered the laws of Denmark and of France, between which we must choose.

In favour of the law of Denmark, there is the cardinal fact that the contract was made within Danish territory; and, further, that the first act done towards performance was weighing anchor in a Danish port.

For the law of France, on the other hand, many practical considerations may be suggested; and, first, the subject-matter of the contract, the employment of a sea-going vessel for a service, the greater and more onerous part of which was to be rendered upon the high seas, where, for all purposes of jurisdiction, criminal or civil, with respect to all persons, things, and transactions, on board, she was, as it were, a floating island, over which France had as absolute, and for all purposes of peace as exclusive, a sovereignty as over her dominions by land, and which, even whilst in a foreign port, was never completely removed from French jurisdiction.

Further, it must be remembered that, although bills of lading are ordinarily given at the port of loading, charter-parties are often made elsewhere; and it seems strange and unlikely to have been within the contemplation of the parties that their rights or liabilities in respect of the identical voyage should vary, first, according as the vessel was taken up at the port of loading or not; and secondly, if she were taken up elsewhere, according to the law of the place where the charter-party was made, or even ratified. If a Frenchman had chartered the Olivier upon the same terms as the plaintiffs did, it would seem strange if he could appeal to Danish law against his own countryman because of the charter-party being made or ratified in a Danish port, though for a service to be rendered elsewhere, by a transient visitor, for the most part within French jurisdiction.

Moreover, there are many ports which have few or no seagoing vessels of their own, and no fixed maritime jurisprudence, and which yet supply valuable cargoes to the ships of other countries. Take Alexandria, for instance, with her mixed population and her maritime commerce almost in the hands of strangers. Is every vessel that leaves Alexandria with grain under a charter-party or bill of lading made there, and every passenger vessel leaving Alexandria or Suez, be she English, Austrian, or French, subject to Egyptian law? As to not a few half-savage places in Africa and Asia, with neither seagoing ships nor maritime laws, a similar question—what is the law

LLOYD
v.
GUIBERT.

Willes J.

in such cases, or is there none except that of the court within whose jurisdiction the litigation first arises?

Again, it may be asked, does a ship which visits many ports in one voyage, whilst she undoubtedly retains the criminal law of her own country, put on a new sort of civil liability, at each new country she visits, in respect of cargo there taken on board? An English steamer, for instance, starts from Southampton for Gibraltar, calling at Vigo, Lisbon, and Cadiz. A Portuguese going in her from Southampton to Vigo would naturally expect to sail subject in all respects to English law, that being the law of the place and the ship. But if the locality of the contract is to govern throughout, an Englishman going from Vigo to Lisbon on the same voyage would be under English law as to crimes and all obligations not connected with the contract of carriage, but under Spanish law as to the contract of carriage; and a Spaniard going from Lisbon to Cadiz during the same voyage would enjoy Portuguese law as to his carriage, and be subject to English law in other respects.

The cases which we have thus put are not extreme nor exceptional; on the contrary, they are such as would ordinarily give rise to the question, which law is to prevail. The inconvenience and even absurdities which would follow from adopting the law of the place of contract in preference to that of the vessel, are strong to prove that the latter ought to be resorted to.

No inconvenience comparable to that which would attend an opposite decision has been suggested. The ignorance of French law on the part of the charterer is no more than many Englishmen contracting in England with respect to English matters might plead as to their own law, in case of an unforeseen accident.

Nor can we allow any weight to the argument, that this is an impolitic law, as tending to interfere with commerce, especially in making merchants cautious how they engage foreign vessels. That is a matter for the consideration of foreigners themselves, and nothing short of a violation of natural justice, or of our own laws, could justify us in holding a foreign law void because of being impolitic. No doubt the French law was intended to encourage shipping, by limiting the liability of shipowners, and in this respect it goes somewhat further than our own; but whether wisely or not is matter within the competence and for the consideration of the French legislature, and upon which, sitting here, we ought to pronounce no opinion.

Exceptional cases, should they arise, must be dealt with upon their own merits. In laying down a rule of law, regard ought rather to be had to the majority of cases upon which doubt and litigation are more likely to arise; and the general rule, that where the contract of affreightment does not provide otherwise, there, as between the parties to such contract, in respect of sea damage and its incidents, the law of the ship should govern, seems to be not only in accordance with the probable intention of the parties, but also most consistent and intelligible, and therefore most convenient to those engaged in commerce.

For these reasons we have arrived at the same conclusion as the Court of Queen's Bench; and without examining the grounds upon which the court proceeded, we are of opinion that the judgment was right, and ought to be affirmed.

Judgment affirmed.

Or the proper law may be the lex situs of land which is the subject-matter of the contract.

MOUNT ALBERT BOROUGH COUNCIL *v.* AUSTRALASIAN ETC. LIFE INSURANCE SOCIETY LTD. [1938] A.C. 224 (Privy Council)

Appeal from the New Zealand Court of Appeal.

In 1926 the appellants, a New Zealand borough council, and a local body within the New Zealand Local Bodies' Loans Act 1926, borrowed money for public works from the respondents, a company incorporated in Victoria, Australia, and carrying on business in Australia and New Zealand. As security for the loan the appellants issued in New Zealand debentures totalling £130,000 repayable in Melbourne, Victoria, and bearing interest payable in Melbourne half-yearly. The debentures were issued under the Local Bodies' Loans Act 1913, of New Zealand, and the loan and interest were secured on a special rate of 3*d.* in the £ on the rateable value of all rateable property in the borough of Mount Albert, i.e. they were charged on land in the borough.

The respondents claimed that the interest due on 1 March 1935 was £3,696. 17*s.* 6*d.* The appellants, however, paid £3,250, alleging that as the interest was payable at Melbourne, the payment was governed by the Financial Emergency Act 1931 of Victoria, which provided for a reduction in the rate of interest on mortgages and other securities.

LLOYD
v.
GUIBERT.

Willes J.

MOUNT
ALBERT
BOROUGH
COUNCIL
v.
AUSTRAL-
ASIAN ETC.
LIFE
INSURANCE
SOCIETY
LTD.

MOUNT
ALBERT
BOROUGH
COUNCIL
v.
AUSTRAL-
ASIAN ETC.
LIFE
INSURANCE
SOCIETY
LTD.
—
Lord
Wright.

In the action the respondents claimed £446. 17*s.* 6*d.* as being the balance of interest alleged to be due to them. The New Zealand Court of Appeal gave judgment for the respondents (plaintiffs). The Mount Albert Borough Council now appealed.

The judgment of their Lordships (Lords Atkin, Macmillan, Wright, and Maugham) was delivered by

LORD WRIGHT: . . . The debentures and the interest coupons in so far as they give a security on real property, namely, a portion of the local rate in New Zealand, are beyond question governed by the New Zealand law. The security can be enforced only in the Courts of New Zealand and in the manner provided by the Loans Act. It is not disputed that these rights are governed by New Zealand law. But in their Lordships' judgment it is equally true that the personal obligation to pay is a New Zealand contract, governed by New Zealand law. It seems impossible to sever this personal covenant from the mortgage provisions which secure it. Indeed, the whole tenor of the transaction is only consistent with its being governed by New Zealand law. The loan was agreed in New Zealand, the money under the loan was paid by the respondents to the appellants there. The appellants were a statutory body in New Zealand which in borrowing were acting under the statutory powers contained in the Loans Act as set out above. The respondents carried on business in New Zealand as well as in Australia. It is true that the place of re-payment of the loan, and of payment of interest from time to time, was to be Melbourne, in Australia. But even that was fixed in accordance with s. 32 of the Loans Act of 1913, which required payment of the debt to be at the place within or out of New Zealand named in the debenture, so that the obligation to pay has statutory sanction. Mr. O'Shea, in his able and exhaustive argument, has contended that the payment is governed by Victorian law because Victoria is the place of performance, and that Victorian law for this purpose includes s. 19, sub-s. 1, of the Financial Emergency Act. He further contends that s. 19, sub-s. 1, applies to the debt because it is a specialty debt and the coupon, which is the document of title, must necessarily be presented at the place of payment in Melbourne when payment is due and demanded, and thus at the relevant moment the lex situs applies so as to introduce the statutory reduction of interest. Their Lordships are not prepared to accept either contention. While they think that the lex situs applies to the security

266

in New Zealand, they do not think that the lex situs of the actual coupon can be applied to the instrument, whether or not the personal obligation to pay is properly regarded as a specialty debt. Nor can they accept the view that the obligation to pay is here governed by the place where it is stipulated that payment is to be made, in the sense that the amount of the debt, as expressed in the instrument creating it, can lawfully be varied by the Victorian Financial Emergency Act so as to bind a foreign jurisdiction, or indeed at all. So to hold would be, in their Lordships' judgment, to confuse two distinct conceptions, that is, to confuse the obligation with the performance of the obligation. It is well established in the law of England and of New Zealand, which in this respect follows it, that the proper law of a contract has to be first ascertained where a question of conflict of laws arises.

The proper law of the contract means that law which the English or other court is to apply in determining the obligations under the contract. English law in deciding these matters has refused to treat as conclusive, rigid or arbitrary criteria such as lex loci contractus or lex loci solutionis, and has treated the matter as depending on the intention of the parties to be ascertained in each case on a considera-tion of the terms of the contract, the situation of the parties, and generally on all the surrounding facts. It may be that the parties have in terms in their agreement expressed what law they intend to govern, and in that case prima facie their intention will be effectuated by the court. But in most cases they do not do so. The parties may not have thought of the matter at all. Then the court has to impute an inten-tion, or to determine for the parties what is the proper law which, as just and reasonable persons, they ought or would have intended if they had thought about the question when they made the contract. No doubt there are certain prima facie rules to which a court in deciding on any particular contract may turn for assistance, but they are not conclusive. In this branch of law the particular rules can only be stated as prima facie presumptions. It is not necessary to cite authorities for these general principles. Sometimes their application involves difficulty; but not in this case. It has been already pointed out that there are, in their Lordships' opinion, such circumstances as lead to the inference that in the present case the proper law of the contract is the law of New Zealand, and accordingly that law should prima facie govern the rights and obligations to be enforced under the contract by a court before which the matter comes, a fortiori a

(margin note:) MOUNT ALBERT BOROUGH COUNCIL *v.* AUSTRAL-ASIAN ETC. LIFE INSURANCE SOCIETY LTD. — Lord Wright.

MOUNT
ALBERT
BOROUGH
COUNCIL
v.
AUSTRAL-
ASIAN ETC.
LIFE
INSURANCE
SOCIETY
LTD.

Lord
Wright.

New Zealand court. It is true that, when stating this general rule, there are qualifications to be borne in mind, as for instance, that the law of the place of performance will prima facie govern the incidents or mode of performance, that is, performance as contrasted with obligation. Thus in the present case it is not contested that the word 'pound' in the debenture and coupon is to be construed with reference to the place of payment, and as referring to the 'pound' in Victorian currency.[1] Again, different considerations may arise in particular cases, as, for instance, where the stipulated performance is illegal by the law of the place of performance. But there is no question of illegality here, since the Victorian statute is not prohibitory. . . .

Appeal dismissed.

Or the proper law may be the law intended by the parties.

VITA FOOD
PRODUCTS
INC.
v.
UNUS
SHIPPING
CO.

VITA FOOD PRODUCTS INC. *v.* UNUS SHIPPING CO. [1939] A.C. 277
(Privy Council)

Appeal from the Supreme Court of Nova Scotia.

The appellant was a body corporate incorporated under the laws of the State of New York; the respondent was a body corporate incorporated under the laws of the Province of Nova Scotia. The respondent owned a motor vessel called the Hurry On which was registered at Halifax, Nova Scotia. In January 1935 the respondent agreed to carry a cargo of herrings from Middle Arm, Newfoundland, for delivery to the appellant in New York, and accordingly bills of lading were signed in Newfoundland by the agents of the parties.

The Newfoundland Carriage of Goods by Sea Act 1932 provided in s. 1 that 'subject to the provisions of this Act' the Rules set out in the Schedule thereto should 'have effect in relation to and in connection with the carriage of goods by sea in ships carrying goods from any port in this Dominion to any other port whether in or outside this Dominion'. Section 3 provided that 'Every bill of lading or similar document of title issued in this Dominion which contains or is evidence of any contract to which the Rules apply shall contain an express statement that it is to have effect subject to the provisions

---

[1] Such matters have since been held to be part of the substance of the obligation: *Bonython* v. *Commonwealth of Australia* [1951] A.C. 201 (*post*, p. 289).

of the said Rules as expressed in this Act.' Sections 4, 5, and 6 contained certain provisions to which the Rules were subject.

The Rules scheduled to the Act were identical with those scheduled to the United Kingdom Carriage of Goods by Sea Act 1924. They are commonly called the Hague Rules and were settled by an International Conference on Maritime Law held at Brussels in 1922 and 1923. Article III, rule 8, provided that any clause, covenant, or agreement lessening the carrier's liability under the Rules should be null and void and of no effect. Article IV, rule 2, provided that 'neither the carrier nor the ship shall be responsible for loss or damage arising or resulting from (*a*) act, neglect, or default of the master, mariners, pilot or the servants of the carrier in the navigation or in the management of the ship; . . . (*c*) perils, dangers and accidents of the sea or other navigable waters'.

Owing to the inadvertence of the parties in using obsolete forms the bills of lading did not contain the statement required by section 3 of the Newfoundland Act. The bills of lading conferred on the carrier a number of immunities, some of which were wider and some narrower than those contained in the Rules. Clause 7 of the bills provided that the carrier should not be liable for any loss or injury arising from any act or omission, negligence, default or error in judgment of the pilots, masters, mariners, engineers, stevedores, workmen or other men in the service of the carrier. They also contained a statement that 'this contract shall be governed by English law', and a provision that the United States Harter Act 1893 should apply to shipments from the United States and that save as so provided the bills of lading were subject to the terms and provisions of, and exemptions from liability contained in, the Canadian Water Carriage of Goods Act 1910 (which, however, only applied to shipments of goods from any port in Canada).

The Hurry On sailed from Middle Arm on 16 January 1935, bound for New York with the herrings on board. Two days later she ran into bad weather and ice off the coast of Nova Scotia. The captain decided to make for a port of refuge, but in an attempt to do so ran ashore on the coast of Nova Scotia in a gale of wind owing (as was ultimately admitted) to his negligence. The herrings were unloaded, reconditioned, and forwarded by another ship to New York, where the appellant took delivery of them in a damaged condition and paid freight.

The appellant brought an action against the respondent in Nova

Vita Food
Products
Inc.
v.
Unus
Shipping
Co.

Scotia claiming damages for the failure of the respondent to deliver the cargo in New York in like condition as received on board. The appellant claimed that the respondent operated the Hurry On as a common carrier and that as such it was an insurer of the safety of the cargo. The respondent pleaded that the bills of lading or, alternatively, the Rules exempted it from liability, even if the damage was caused by the captain's negligence; and that the contract was governed by the law of Newfoundland. The appellant admitted that the contract was governed by the law of Newfoundland, but alleged in reply that the bills of lading were illegal, null and void under Newfoundland law in that, contrary to section 3 of the Act of 1932, they did not contain an express statement that they were to have effect subject to the Rules; and that therefore the respondent could not take advantage of any of the exemptions from liability provided by the Rules or by the bills of lading.

Chisholm C.J. and the Supreme Court of Nova Scotia rejected the appellant's contention, and the Supreme Court also held that, if the bills of lading were illegal, the parties were in pari delicto and the action must fail. The appellant appealed.

The judgment of their Lordships (Lords Atkin, Russell of Killowen, Macmillan, Wright, and Porter) was delivered by

LORD WRIGHT: ... The first question to determine is the true construction of ss. 1 and 3 of the Act. Sect. 1 provides for the application of the rules to every bill of lading for the carriage of goods by sea in ships from any port in Newfoundland to any other port, whether in or outside that Dominion. The appellant contended that since s. 1 only provided that the rules should have effect 'subject to the provisions of this Act,' the rules could not apply to a bill of lading unless the terms of s. 3 were complied with. Their Lordships do not so construe the section. In their opinion the words 'subject to the provisions of this Act' merely mean in this connection that the rules are to apply but subject to the modifications contained in ss. 2, 4, 5 and 6 sub-s. 3 of the Act. To read these words as meaning that the rules are only to have effect if the requirements of s. 3 are complied with, would be to put an unnecessarily wide interpretation upon them instead of the narrower meaning, which is more natural and obvious. In their Lordships' judgment s. 1 is the dominant section. Sect. 3 merely requires the bill of lading to contain an express statement of the effect of s. 1. This view of the relative effect of the sections raises the question whether the mandatory provision of s. 3, which cannot change the effect of s. 1, is under Newfoundland law directory or imperative, and, if imperative, whether a failure to comply with it renders the contract void, either in Newfoundland, or in courts outside that Dominion.

It will be convenient at this point to determine what is the proper law of the contract. In their Lordships' opinion the express words of the bill of lading must receive effect, with the result that the contract is governed by English law. It is now well settled that by English law (and the law of Nova Scotia is the same) the proper law of the contract 'is the law which the parties intended to apply'. That intention is objectively ascertained, and, if not expressed, will be presumed from the terms of the contract and the relevant surrounding circumstances. But as Lord Atkin, dealing with cases where the intention of the parties is expressed, said in *Rex* v. *International Trustee for, etc., Bondholders A/G*[1] (a case which contains the latest enunciation of this principle), 'Their intention will be ascertained by the intention expressed in the contract if any, which will be conclusive'. It is objected that this is too broadly stated and that some qualifications are necessary. It is true that in questions relating to the conflict of laws rules cannot generally be stated in absolute terms but rather as prima facie presumptions. But where the English rule that intention is the test applies, and where there is an express statement by the parties of their intention to select the law of the contract, it is difficult to see what qualifications are possible, provided the intention expressed is bona fide and legal, and provided there is no reason for avoiding the choice on the ground of public policy. In the present case, however, it might be said that the choice of English law is not valid for two reasons. It might be said that the transaction, which is one relating to the carriage on a Nova Scotian ship of goods from Newfoundland to New York between residents in these countries, contains nothing to connect it in any way with English law, and therefore that choice could not be seriously taken. Their Lordships reject this argument both on grounds of principle and on the facts. Connection with English law is not as a matter of principle essential. The provision in a contract (e.g., of sale) for English arbitration imports English law as the law governing the transaction, and those familiar with international business are aware how frequent such a provision is even where the parties are not English and the trans-

[1] [1937] A.C. 500, 529.

Vita Food
Products
Inc.
v.
Unus
Shipping
Co.

Lord
Wright.

actions are carried on completely outside England. Moreover in the present case the Hurry On, though on a Canadian register, is subject to the Imperial statute, the Merchant Shipping Act 1894, under which the vessel is registered, and the underwriters are likely to be English. In any case parties may reasonably desire that the familiar principles of English commercial law should apply. The other ground urged is that the choice of English law is inconsistent with the provisions of the bill of lading, that in respect of certain goods the Harter Act or the Canadian Water Carriage of Goods Act of 1910 (now repealed, but in force at the date of the bill of lading) was to apply. It has been explained that the incorporation of these Acts may have only contractual effect, but in any case, though the proper law of the contract is English, English law may incorporate the provisions of the law of another country or other countries as part of the terms of the contract, and apart from such incorporation other laws may have to be regarded in giving effect to the contract. The proper law of the contract does indeed fix the interpretation and construction of its express terms and supply the relevant background of statutory or implied terms. But that part of the English law which is commonly called the conflict of laws requires, where proper, the application of foreign law; e.g., English law will not enforce a performance contrary to the law of the place of performance in circumstances like those existing in *Ralli Bros.* v. *Compania Naviera Sota y Aznar,*[1] and the law of the place of performance, though it will not be effective to affect the construction of the contract in regard to its substance (which must be ascertained according to the rule of the proper law, as was held in *Jacobs, Marcus & Co.* v. *Crédit Lyonnais*[2] will still regulate what were called in that case the incidents and mode of performance in that place. English law will in these and sometimes in other respects import a foreign law, but the contract is still governed by its proper law. The reference to the United States and the Canadian Acts does not on any view supersede English law which is to govern the contract, nor does Newfoundland law, though Newfoundland was the place where the contract was made, apply to oust English law from being the law of the contract, and as such from being the law which defines its nature, obligation and interpretation, though Newfoundland law might apply to the incidents of performance to be done in Newfoundland. There is, in their Lordships' opinion, no ground for refusing to give effect to the express

[1] [1920] 2 K.B. 287; *post*, p. 292. [2] (1884) 12 Q.B.D. 589; *post*, p. 284.

272

CONTRACTS

selection of English law as the proper law in the bills of lading. Hence English rules relating to the conflict of laws must be applied to determine how the bills of lading are affected by the failure to comply with s. 3 of the Act.

If, however, by reason of this failure to obey the Act the bills of lading were illegal in Newfoundland, it would not follow as a necessary consequence that a Nova Scotian court, applying the proper law of the contract, would in its own forum treat them as illegal, though the position of a court in Newfoundland might be different, if it held them illegal by Newfoundland law. A court in Newfoundland would be bound to apply the law enacted by its own Legislature, if it applied, and thus might treat the bills as illegal, just as the Supreme Court in the United States treated as void an exemption of negligence in a bill of lading issued in the United States, though in relation to the carriage of goods to England in an English ship; *Liverpool and Great Western Steam Co. v. Phenix Insurance Co.*[1] Such a clause, it was held, was against public policy and void by the law of the United States, which was not only the law of the forum but was also held to be the proper law of the contract. This decision may be contrasted with *In re Missouri Steamship Co.*[2] where in similar circumstances the Court of Appeal, holding the proper law of the bill of lading to be English, held that English law did not apply the American rule of public policy, though the shipment took place in America and the bill of lading was issued there, and that the clause, being valid in English law, must receive effect.

With these considerations in mind it is necessary first to consider if the bills of lading are illegal by Newfoundland law. If they are not, the question of illegality cannot arise in the courts of another jurisdiction, e.g., those of Nova Scotia. Illegality is a concept of so many varying and diverse applications, that in each case it is necessary to scrutinize the particular circumstances with precision in order to determine if there is illegality and if so what is its effect. . . . Each case has to be considered on its merits. Nor must it be forgotten that the rule by which contracts not expressly forbidden by statute or declared to be void are in proper cases nullified for disobedience to a statute is a rule of public policy only, and public policy understood in a wider sense may at times be better served by refusing to nullify a bargain save on serious and sufficient grounds.

Are there such grounds for holding that the Newfoundland law

VITA FOOD PRODUCTS INC. v. UNUS SHIPPING CO.

Lord Wright.

[1] (1889) 129 U.S. 397.   [2] (1888) 42 Ch. D. 321.

VITA FOOD
PRODUCTS
INC.
v.
UNUS
SHIPPING
CO.

Lord
Wright.

does in Newfoundland nullify bills of lading such as those in question? In their Lordships' opinion there are not. . . . It would be a grave matter if business men when dealing with a bill of lading had in a case like the present to inquire into the foreign law ruling at the port of shipment. The omission of what is called the clause paramount does not make the bills of lading illegal documents, in whole or in part, either within Newfoundland or outside it. Sect. 3 is in their Lordships' judgment directory. It is not obligatory, nor does failure to comply with its terms nullify the contract contained in the bill of lading. This, in their Lordships' judgment, is the true construction of the statute, having regard to its scope and its purpose and to the inconvenience which would follow from any other conclusion. If that is so, the bills of lading are binding according to their terms and consequently the respondent is entitled to succeed in its defence.

But on the basis that the bills of lading were illegal in Newfoundland in that their issue without the clause paramount was prohibited by the law of that country it was argued that no court in any country would enforce their terms and exemptions, and the carriage would therefore be upon the terms implied where goods are taken for carriage by a common carrier, i.e., subject only to the exception of the Act of God and the King's Enemies. No further terms, it was said, could be implied nor could any reliance be put upon the provisions of the Hague Rules, since they had not been incorporated in the bills of lading by the insertion of the clause paramount. The appellant contended that, unless the clause was inserted, no contract between carrier and shipper which included the provisions of the Hague Rules was entered into. Nor could the Act be said to have incorporated them even in Newfoundland itself, since s. 1 only provided that the rules should have effect 'subject to the provisions of this Act', a phrase which the appellant maintained meant (inter alia) that the rules were not incorporated unless the provisions of s. 3 were complied with. For reasons already explained their Lordships do not so construe the section.

But whatever view a Newfoundland court might take, whether they would hold that the contracts contained in the bills of lading must be taken to have incorporated the Hague Rules or whether they would hold them to have been illegal, the result would be the same in the present case, where the action was brought not in a Newfoundland but in a Nova Scotian court. It may be that, if suit were brought on these bills of lading in a Newfoundland court, and the court held they were illegal, the court would refuse to give effect to them, on the basis that a court is bound to obey the laws of its own legislature or its own common law, as indeed the United States Supreme Court did in *Liverpool and Great Western Steam Co.* v. *Phenix Insurance Co.* But it does not follow that any other court could properly act in the same way. If it has before it a contract good by its own law or by the proper law of the contract, it will in proper cases give effect to the contract and ignore the foreign law. This was done in the *Missouri* case, both by Chitty J. and by the Court of Appeal. Lord Halsbury, having stated that the contrary view would mean that no country would enforce a contract made in another country unless their laws were the same, said 'that there may be stipulations which one country may enforce and which another country may not enforce, and that to determine whether they are enforceable or not you must have regard to the law of the contract, by which I mean the law which the contract itself imports to be the law governing the contract.' Having held that the law of the contract was English, he went on to hold that the exception of negligence, even if of no validity in the place where made, must receive effect in English law, although the exception of negligence was invalid in the United States as being against the public policy of that country, and although to do an act contrary to public policy is one type of illegal action. The same attitude is illustrated in *Dobell* v. *Steamship Rossmore Co.*,[1] where the Harter Act, which declares certain stipulations to be unlawful and imposes penalties on shipowners inserting them in bills of lading, was not considered as affecting the English contract as a part of the contract where its provisions were infringed, save so far as it was expressly incorporated. Foreign law was also disregarded in *Trinidad Shipping Co.* v. *G. R. Alston & Co.*,[2] where the contract was an English contract and payment of certain rebates on freight were rendered illegal by the law of the United States, where the freight was payable. From the rule which he states Lord Halsbury in the *Missouri* case puts aside 'questions in which the positive law of the country [sc. the foreign country] forbids contracts to be made. Where a contract is void on the ground of immorality, or is contrary to such positive law as would prohibit the making of such a contract at all, then the contract would be void all over the world, and no civilised country would be called on to

Vita Food
Products
Inc.
v.
Unus
Shipping
Co.
—
Lord
Wright.

---

[1] [1895] 2 Q.B. 408.   [2] [1920] A.C. 888.

LAW OF OBLIGATIONS

VITA FOOD
PRODUCTS
INC.
v.
UNUS
SHIPPING
CO.
—
Lord
Wright.

enforce it.' In this passage Lord Halsbury would seem to be referring
to matters of foreign law of such a character that it would be against
the comity of nations for an English court to give effect to the transaction, just as an English court may refuse in proper cases to enforce performance of an English contract in a foreign country where
the performance has been expressly prohibited by the public law
of that country. The exact scope of Lord Halsbury's proviso has not
been defined. There may also be questions in some cases as to the
effect of non-performance of conditions which by the foreign law
of the place where a contract was entered into are essential to its
formation, though even in that case the validity of the contract may
depend on its proper law. But whatever the precise ambit of that
saving expression, it is clear that it does not apply to such a statutory enactment as s. 3, even if disobedience to it were regarded as
rendering the bill of lading in some sense illegal. . . .

(His Lordship proceeded to express disapproval of *The Torni*,[1]
and refused to distinguish it either on the ground that the bills of
lading in that case provided that they were to be 'construed in
accordance with' (not 'governed by') English law; or on the ground
that s. 4 of the Palestine Carriage of Goods by Sea Ordinance, which
was otherwise identical with s. 3 of the Newfoundland Act of 1932,
contained the additional words 'and shall be deemed to have effect
subject thereto, notwithstanding the omission of such express statement'.)

Appeal dismissed.

*Or the proper law may be the system of law with which the con-
tract has its closest and most real connexion.*

BONYTHON *v.* COMMONWEALTH OF AUSTRALIA [1951] A.C. 201;
post, p. 289.

THE ASSUN-
ZIONE.

THE ASSUNZIONE [1954] P. 150 (Court of Appeal)

In pursuance of a charterparty signed in Paris after negotiations
between brokers resident in France on behalf of French shippers,
and brokers resident in Italy on behalf of Italian shipowners, the
Italian steamship Assunzione, commanded by an Italian master,
loaded a cargo of wheat at Dunkirk for delivery at Venice. During
the voyage the cargo was damaged and the charterers sued the

[1] [1932] P. 78.

276

shipowners for short delivery and damage to the cargo. The charter-party was in the English language and used the printed form of Uniform General Charter of the Documentary Council of the Baltic and White Sea Conference ('Gencon'). It contained additional clauses in the French language. It provided that freight and demurrage should be paid in Italian lire in Naples. Bills of lading in the French language were signed by the master at Dunkirk and indorsed by the Italian consignees. The wheat was shipped under an exchange agreement made between the French and Italian Governments, but the shipowners did not know this.

THE ASSUN-ZIONE.

Willmer J. on a preliminary point of law held that Italian and not French law should be applied to the contract of affreightment. The charterers appealed.

SINGLETON L.J. (having stated the facts): We have had a considerable number of authorities cited to us upon the question of what law should be applied. The parties did not state their desire, or their intention, upon the subject. It has been said that when that happens one must endeavour to find what the intention of the parties was on the matter. That does not appear to me to be very helpful, for in most cases neither party has given it a thought, and neither has formed any intention upon it; still less can it be said that they have any common intention. I am not sure how far it is necessary to consider all the authorities which have been cited to us, and which go back to the year 1865, but I must refer to some of them. Sir Robert Aske, on behalf of the plaintiffs, relies on what he described as the general rule; that is, that the law to be applied should be the law of the country in which the contract was made.

(His Lordship referred to *P. & O. Steam Navigation Co. Ltd.* v. *Shand*,[1] *Lloyd* v. *Guibert*,[2] *Chartered Bank of India* v. *Netherlands India Steam Navigation Co. Ltd.*,[3] *In re Missouri Steamship Co. Ltd.*,[4] *The Industrie*,[5] *Mount Albert Borough Council* v. *Australasian Life Insurance Society Ltd.*[6] and *R.* v. *International Trustee for the Protection of Bondholders A/G*[7] and continued): Upon the authorities Sir Robert Aske submitted that it was not possible to spell out of the cases any rule other than that of the place where the contract was made. Mr. Mocatta (counsel for the defendants)

---

[1] (1865) 3 Moo. P.C. (N.S.) 272 ; *ante*, p. 253.
[2] (1865) L.R. 1 Q.B. 115 ; *ante*, p. 259. [3] (1883) 10 Q.B.D. 521.
[4] (1889) 42 Ch. D. 321. [5] [1894] P. 58. [6] [1938] A.C. 224 ; *ante*, p. 265.
[7] [1939] A.C. 500.

claimed that no stronger inference could be drawn from the place where the contract was made than from the flag of the country under which the ship sailed; indeed, he submitted that one ought, in the circumstances of this case, to have regard first to the flag which the ship wore, and he relied on the decision in *Lloyd* v. *Guibert*. His main contention was that this was not a case of an inference to be drawn one way or the other; it was a case, he submitted, in which the facts should be weighed, and that if they were weighed, those pointing towards the application of the Italian law weighed down any which could be found pointing the other way.

Without doubt there are features in this case which appear to point one way, and others which appear to point in another direction. When there are a number of circumstances which have to be considered in deciding which system of law applies, a presumption or inference arising from one alone becomes of less importance. In such a case an inference which might be properly drawn may cancel another inference which would be drawn if it stood by itself. When such a position arises all the relevant circumstances must be borne in mind, and the tribunal must find, if it can, how a just and reasonable person would have regarded the problem. No good purpose is served by saying that the French charterers would never have agreed to the application of Italian law, or by saying that the Italian shipowners would never have agreed to the application of French law, for that would have meant that there would have been no contract; and there is a contract.

I can summarise the facts relied upon fairly shortly. The charterers, who were also shippers under the bills of lading, were a French organisation; the contract was entered into by a charterparty which was made in France, after discussions to which I have referred, and the bills of lading were issued in France. The language of the charterparty is English, but no one contends that English law is to be applied. Some support is given to the argument of counsel for the plaintiffs by the bills of lading which are in French, and which contain the particular terms which I have mentioned. Sir Robert relies, too, upon the exchange agreement; upon the fact that in making arrangements for the carriage of the wheat from Dunkirk to an Italian port the charterers were acting in pursuance of what had been agreed between two Government departments. I do not see, in the circumstances of this case, that great help is given by that fact, if it be a fact. . . .

CONTRACTS

With regard to the circumstances which support the defendants' THE ASSUN-ZIONE.

contention that Italian law should be applied, I mention these: The
ship was an Italian ship owned by two Italians in partnership, and a Singleton L.J.
ship wearing the Italian flag; the owners were Italians; the master
was an Italian; the contract was for carriage from a French port to
an Italian port; the cargo was to be delivered at an Italian port. It is
right to say that loading was at a French port and discharging at an
Italian port, and one may appear to cancel the other, but there are
further considerations; the charterparty provided that freight and
demurrage should be paid in Italian currency. . . . Although I believe it to be impossible to state any rule of general application, I
feel that matters of very considerable importance are the form of,
and place of, payment. In this case payment has to be made in
Italian lire, and in Italy. In the circumstances of this case I regard it
as a very important feature, coupled as it is with the facts that the
ship was an Italian ship and that the destination was an Italian
port. . . .

One must look at all the circumstances and seek to find what
just and reasonable persons ought to have intended if they had
thought about the matter at the time when they made the contract.
If they had thought that they were likely to have a dispute, I hope it
may be said that just and reasonable persons would like the dispute
determined in the most convenient way and in accordance with
business efficacy.

Applying the rule which I have stated, and weighing all the facts
to which attention was directed, I am satisfied that the scale comes
down in favour of the application of Italian law, and that the decision of Willmer J. was right. In my opinion, the appeal should be
dismissed.

BIRKETT and HODSON L.JJ. delivered judgments to the same
effect.

Appeal dismissed.

NOTE J: THE PROPER LAW OF A CONTRACT

(1) In spite of what was said in *Vita Food Products Inc.* v. *Unus Shipping
Co.*, *ante*, p. 268, it now seems clear that the proper law of a contract should
be defined not as the law intended by the parties, but as the 'system of law by
reference to which the contract was made or that with which the transaction
has its closest and most real connexion': *per* Lord Simonds in *Bonython* v.
Commonwealth of Australia, *post*, p. 290. This formulation was approved
by the House of Lords in *Tomkinson* v. *First Pennsylvania Banking and*

Trust Co. [1961] A.C. 1007 and by McNair J. in *Rossano* v. *Manufacturers Life Insurance Co. Ltd.* [1963] 2 Q.B. 352, when he pointed out that the correct formulation is the 'system of law' and not the 'country' with which the transaction has its closest and most real connexion. In that case the country with which the contract was most closely connected was Egypt, but the system of law with which it was most closely connected was that of Ontario, and it was rightly held that Ontario law was the proper law.

The difference in formulation between the law intended by the parties and the law with which the contract has its closest and most real connexion becomes important in cases where the parties have made an express selection of the proper law, for if they have not, the court is likely to reach the same result whether it inquires what is the law which the parties ought or would have intended if they had thought about the question when they made the contract, or whether it inquires with what system of law was the contract most closely connected. The crucial question is, therefore, can the parties select the law of a country with which their contract has no substantial connexion? In *Re Helbert Wagg & Co. Ltd.'s Claim* [1956] Ch. 323, 341, Up-john J. said: 'This court will not necessarily regard' the parties' choice of law 'as being the governing consideration where a system of law is chosen which has no real or substantial connexion with the contract looked on as a whole.'

There is no reported case in which a contract, void in its entirety by the law most closely connected with it, has been upheld by reason of the parties' choice of another legal system under which the contract was valid. All the reported cases refer to the validity of particular clauses such as arbitration or exemption clauses. With the exception of the cases on arbitration clauses, there is no reported case in which a different result would have been reached if the court had applied the objective test.

If the contract contains a clause referring disputes to arbitration in a particular country, there is an almost irrebuttable presumption that the law of that country is the proper law of the contract as a whole: *Hamlyn* v. *Talisker Distillery Co.* [1894] A.C. 202; *Spurrier* v. *La Cloche* [1902] A.C. 446. The reason for this rule is no doubt that arbitrators are, more often than not, tradesmen and not lawyers, and it would lead to much inconvenience if they had to concern themselves with intricate questions of the conflict of laws or to apply a foreign system of law. A striking illustration is afforded by *Suisse Atlantique Société d'Armement Maritime S.A.* v. *N.V. Rotterdamsche Kolen Centrale* [1967] 1 A.C. 361, where a contract between Swiss shipowners and Dutch charterers for the carriage of coal from the United States to ports in Belgium, Holland and Germany had no connexion of any kind with England except that it contained a clause providing for arbitration in London. Yet nobody argued that any other law than English law should be applied to the dispute between the parties.

(2) Some questions on *P. & O. S.S. Co.* v. *Shand, ante,* p. 253:

Would the decision have been different if (*a*) the plaintiff had taken his ticket and boarded the ship in Mauritius for a voyage in the opposite direction, or (*b*) if the plaintiff had been a Frenchman who took his ticket and boarded the ship at Marseilles? If not, should not the case be cited as an example of the lex loci solutionis, not the lex loci contractus?

CONTRACTS

(3) Some questions on *Vita Food Products Inc.* v. *Unus Shipping Co., ante,* p. 268:

(*a*) Was the defendant exempted from liability by the bills of lading or by the Hague Rules? What would have been decided if, in the event which happened, the defendant was exempt from liability under the bills but not under the Rules, or vice versa?

(*b*) Was the statement that English law was the proper law of the contract ratio decidendi or obiter dictum? Would it have made any difference if the law of Newfoundland had been held to be the proper law? Did the court say 'The proper law of the contract is English law, therefore it doesn't matter whether failure to comply with s. 3 of the Newfoundland Carriage of Goods by Sea Act, 1932, makes the contract illegal by the law of Newfoundland'? Or did the court say 'Failure to comply with s. 3 of the Newfoundland Act does not make the contract illegal by the law of Newfoundland, therefore it doesn't matter what is the proper law of the contract'? Or what did it say?

(*c*) Was it an advance towards a decision of the case to say (*ante,* p. 273) 'English law is the proper law of the contract. Hence English rules *of the conflict of laws* must be applied to determine how the bills of lading are affected by the failure to comply with s. 3 of the Act'? Or was this just a lapsus calami on Lord Wright's part? It has since been laid down by the Court of Appeal that 'the principle of renvoi finds no place in the field of contract': *Re United Railways of the Havana and Regla Warehouses Ltd.* [1960] Ch. 52, 96–97, 115.

(*d*) If both parties pleaded that the contract was governed by the law of Newfoundland, was it open to the court to decide otherwise?

The case is discussed by Morris and Cheshire in 56 L.Q.R. 320 (1940).

Section D: CAPACITY

Capacity to contract is governed by the proper law of the contract.

CHARRON *v.* MONTREAL TRUST CO. (1958) 15 D.L.R. (2d) 240
(Ontario Court of Appeal)

CHARRON
v.
MONTREAL
TRUST CO.

Peter Charron was domiciled in Quebec. In 1906 he came to Ontario and joined the Royal Canadian Mounted Police. In 1908 he married the plaintiff in Ontario and lived with her there until they separated in 1920. They entered into a separation agreement in Ontario form in 1920. Peter Charron then resigned from the Mounted Police and returned to Quebec, where he died in 1953 having by his will appointed the defendant his executor. The plaintiff sued to recover arrears of payments due under the separation agreement. One of the defences was that by Quebec law spouses have no capacity to enter into a separation agreement. McRuer C.J. gave judgment for the plaintiff. The defendant appealed.

The judgment of the court (Aylesworth, Gibson, and Morden JJ.A.) was delivered by

MORDEN J.A. (having stated the facts): I will assume for the purpose of this appeal that the husband and therefore his wife, the plaintiff, lacked the capacity by the law of their domicile to make this agreement.

Apart from marriage and marriage settlements in which situations capacity is regulated, broadly speaking, by the lex domicilii, there is no clear decision whether capacity to contract is to be tested by the lex loci contractus or the lex domicilii. Examples could be given in particular instances of the unfairness and unreality of applying one law or the other. To vary the facts of the instant case, let us assume the spouses had been both domiciled and resident in Quebec and had come to Ontario for a short visit during which the agreement under consideration was made; upon such assumption, in my opinion, it would be against common sense to decide the parties' capacity by Ontario law. In the present case, the marriage had taken place in Ontario and for many years thereafter and until the date of this agreement the parties had cohabited in Ontario. It would be unrealistic in the circumstances here to apply Quebec law in deciding the parties' capacity. The solution to this problem, in my opinion, is that adopted by the learned writers on private international law and to decide that a party's capacity to enter into a contract is to be governed by the proper law of the particular contract, that is, the law of the country with which the contract is most substantially connected.[1] In this case there is no doubt that the proper law of the agreement was the law of Ontario, and by that law neither party to the agreement lacked the necessary capacity. Therefore, I agree with the learned Chief Justice's statement that 'the contract is a good enforceable contract under the laws of Ontario'.

Appeal dismissed.

[1] Cheshire, Private International Law, 5th ed., pp. 221–4; Dicey's Conflict of Laws, 7th ed., pp. 769–74; Falconbridge, Conflict of Laws, 2nd ed., pp. 383–5.

CONTRACTS

Note K: CAPACITY TO CONTRACT

THERE is an extraordinary lack of modern English authority on this subject, and neither judicial dicta nor the views of text-writers are in agreement. Some of the conflicting dicta are referred to by Scrutton L.J. in *Republica de Guatemala* v. *Nunez* [1927] 1 K.B. 669, *post*, pp. 364–5. The problem is usually expressed in terms of a choice between the law of the domicile and the law of the place of contracting. An illustration will make the nature of the problem clear. Suppose that a man aged 24, domiciled in Ruritania, buys goods on credit in an English shop: could he refuse to pay for them on the ground that by Ruritanian law infancy ends at the age of 25? Most students coming fresh to this subject would say no, and that commercial convenience requires that the lex loci contractus should govern. In many situations, this is undoubtedly true. But if we assume that the customer never left Ruritania, the contract being concluded by correspondence, and that the shopkeeper knew the customer was a Ruritanian and also knew that by Ruritanian law infancy ends at 25, then the answer is not nearly so obvious. And it seems absurd to make the validity of the contract depend on whether the letter of acceptance was posted in England or in Ruritania. Moreover, it is clear that an application of the lex loci contractus will not necessarily mean that the contract is valid, for example in the converse situation of an Englishman aged 24 buying goods on credit in Ruritania. In that situation, it could be argued that English law has no interest in protecting the defendant because he is over 21, and that Ruritanian law has no interest in protecting him because he is not a Ruritanian, and that therefore the contract should be valid.

The following solutions of the problem have been suggested:

(1) *The law of the domicile.* The majority of continental jurists assert that capacity to contract is governed by the personal law (which for Anglo-American courts means the law of the domicile). At least one decision of the United States Supreme Court supports this view: *Union Trust Co.* v. *Grosman* (1918) 245 U.S. 412. But continental courts (France) and legislatures (Germany) have abandoned this principle when its application would lead to injustice to their own subjects; and most American courts prefer the lex loci contractus: *Milliken* v. *Pratt* (1878) 4 Mass. 374, Restatement, s. 333. The objection to the law of the domicile is that it hinders commerce by enabling a party to carry an incapacity about with him wherever he goes.

(2) *The law of the place of contracting.* In many situations, this law has strong claims. But the place of contracting may sometimes be fortuitous. It is unreasonable that the capacity not only of the offeree but also of the offeror should be governed by Spanish law merely because the letter of acceptance happened to be posted in Madrid.

(3) *The law intended by the parties.* Whatever plausibility this law may have for essential validity (*ante*, p. 253), it is almost universally agreed that it cannot apply to capacity: for otherwise a party could confer capacity on himself by choosing the law of some country with which the contract had no substantial connexion. As Lord Macnaghten said in *Cooper* v. *Cooper* (1888) 13 App. Cas. 88, 99: 'It is difficult to suppose that Mrs. Cooper could confer capacity on herself by contemplating a different country as the place where the contract was to be fulfilled.'

(4) *The law most favourable to the contract.* This view is adopted by

283

Wolff, who says the contract will be valid if the parties have capacity by either the lex domicilii or the lex loci contractus (s. 262). But this seems to carry the principle in favorem negotii much too far. The conflict of laws is not a science for upholding whenever possible the validity of a contract, a marriage, or a will; it is a science for determining what law should govern the validity of these matters.

(5) *The law with which the contract has the most substantial connexion.* This is the view of Dicey (pp. 744–9) and of Dr. Cheshire (pp. 201–2) and it has much to commend it. It would furnish the necessary flexibility and would allow the necessary weight to be given to all the relevant factors. It would enable the courts to discriminate between the usual type of case where commercial convenience requires the contract to be upheld if the parties had capacity by the law of the place of contracting, and the exceptional type of case where the stringent policy of the law of the domicile requires an opposite result (e.g. *Union Trust Co.* v. *Grosman*). It would not necessarily follow that the proper law governing capacity should be the same as the proper law governing essential validity, nor that the proper law governing the capacity of one party should be the same as the proper law governing the capacity of the other: though in normal cases such splitting of the contract should be avoided.

In *Charron* v. *Montreal Trust Co.* (*ante*, p. 281) the court applied the proper law of the contract. On the facts of the case this coincided with the lex loci contractus. Particular significance therefore attaches to the statement that the decision would have been different if the parties had been resident as well as domiciled in Quebec, and had made the contract during a temporary visit to Ontario.

Section C: DISCHARGE

The proper law of the contract, and not the law of the place of performance as such, determines what are excuses for non-performance.

JACOBS
v.
CRÉDIT
LYONNAIS.

JACOBS v. CRÉDIT LYONNAIS (1884), 12 Q.B.D. 589 (Court of Appeal)

Appeal from a Divisional Court (Denman and Manisty JJ.).

The judgment of the Court of Appeal (Brett M.R. and Bowen L.J.) was read by

BOWEN L.J.: The plaintiffs in this case are esparto merchants carrying on business in the city of London, and the defendants are a banking firm also carrying on business in the City.

By a contract made in London on the 6th of October 1880, the defendants agreed to sell to the plaintiffs 20,000 tons of Algerian esparto, to be shipped from Algeria during the year 1881 by monthly deliveries on board ships or steamers to be provided by the plaintiffs, payment to be made by cash on arrival of the ship or steamer at her port of destination. The defendants delivered a portion of the esparto under the contract, but failed to deliver the remainder; and this action was brought by the plaintiffs for its non-delivery. The defendants in their statement of defence admitted the non-delivery complained of, but alleged that the insurrection in Algeria and the military operations connected with it had rendered the performance of the contract impossible; and that by the French Civil Code, which prevails throughout Algeria, 'force majeure' is an excuse for non-performance. The plaintiffs demurred to this defence on the ground that the contracts were governed by English law and not by the law of Algeria. . . . The Queen's Bench Division having given judgment upon [the demurrers] for the plaintiffs, the case now came before us upon appeal.

The first matter we have to determine is, whether this contract is to be construed according to English law or according to French. To decide this point we must turn to the contract itself, for it is open in all cases for parties to make such agreement as they please as to incorporating the provisions of any foreign law with their contracts. What is to be the law by which a contract, or any part of it, is to be governed or applied, must be always a matter of construction of the contract itself as read by the light of the subject-matter and of the surrounding circumstances. Certain presumptions or rules in this respect have been laid down by juridical writers of different countries and accepted by the courts, based upon common sense, upon business convenience, and upon the comity of nations; but these are only presumptions of prima facie rules that are capable of being displaced, wherever the clear intention of the parties can be gathered from the document itself and from the nature of the transaction. The broad rule is that the law of a country where a contract is made presumably governs the nature, the obligation and the interpretation of it, unless the contrary appears to be the express intention of the parties. 'The general rule', says Lord Mansfield, 'established ex comitate et jure gentium is that the place where the contract is made, and not where the action is brought, is to be considered in expounding and enforcing the contract. But this rule admits of an exception where the parties at the time of making the contract had a view to a different kingdom': *Robinson* v. *Bland*[1] (see *P. & O. Steam Navigation Co.* v. *Shand*).[2] This principle was explained by the Exchequer Chamber in the case of *Lloyd* v. *Guibert*[3] as follows.

---

[1] (1760) 2 Burr. 1077.   [2] (1865) 3 Moo. P.C. (N.S.) 272 ; *ante*, p. 253.
[3] (1865) L.R. 1 Q.B. 115 ; *ante*, p. 259.

LAW OF OBLIGATIONS

JACOBS
v.
CRÉDIT
LYONNAIS.
—
Bowen L.J.

(His Lordship read the passage beginning 'It is, however, generally agreed' and ending 'the character of the contract', *ante*, pp. 261–2, and continued:) It is obvious, however, that the subject-matter of each contract must be looked at as well as the residence of the contracting parties or the place where the contract is made. The place of performance is necessarily in many cases the place where the obligations of the contract will have to be enforced, and hence, as well as for other reasons, has been introduced another canon of construction, to the effect that the law of the place of fulfilment of a contract determines its obligations. But this maxim, as well as the former, must of course give way to any inference that can legitimately be drawn from the character of the contract and the nature of the transaction. In most cases no doubt where a contract has to be wholly performed abroad, the reasonable presumption may be that it is intended to be a foreign contract determined by foreign law; but this prima facie view is in its turn capable of being rebutted by the expressed or implied intention of the parties as deduced from other circumstances. Again, it may be that the contract is partly to be performed in one place and partly in another. In such a case the only certain guide is to be found in applying sound ideas of business, convenience, and sense to the language of the contract itself, with a view to discovering from it the true intention of the parties. Even in respect of any performance that is to take place abroad, the parties may still have desired that their liabilities and obligations shall be governed by English law; or it may be that they have intended to incorporate the foreign law to regulate the method and manner of performance abroad, without altering any of the incidents which attach to the contract according to English law. Stereotyped rules laid down by juridical writers cannot, therefore, be accepted as infallible canons of interpretation in these days, when commercial transactions have altered in character and increased in complexity: and there can be no hard-and-fast rule by which to construe the multiform commercial agreements with which in modern times we have to deal. In the present case the contract was made in London between merchants carrying on their business in the city of London, and payment was to be made in London. Presumably, therefore, we should infer that this was an English contract and intended to be governed by English law; but it still remains to be considered whether anything in the contract itself or the nature of its stipulations displaces this prima facie view either wholly or in part. Now

it cannot be contended that the parties have in express terms provided that any portion of this contract is to be construed or applied
otherwise than according to English law; but it was suggested by the
appellants that such an intention ought to be inferred from certain
provisions as to the collection of the esparto in Algeria and as to its
shipment thence. The esparto was to be shipped by the Compagnie
Franco-Algerienne, or their agents, from Arzew, or any other port
with safe anchorage, by sailing ships or steamers during the year
1881. The quality of the esparto was to be finally approved by the
plaintiff's representatives at the works of the Compagnie Franco-
Algerienne, at Ain-el-Hadjar, in Algeria, before being baled, and no
claim respecting quality was to be allowed after the delivery of the
bales at Arzew. The necessary ships or steamers were to be supplied
by the plaintiffs, otherwise the esparto was to be warehoused by
the Compagnie Franco-Algerienne at the plaintiffs' peril and risk.
Insurance was to be effected by the defendants for the invoice
amount at selling price, and 2 per cent. over in the United Kingdom
on the usual conditions. Payment to be made by cash on arrival of
the ship or steamer at port of destination. Finally, the contract contained an arbitration clause, with a provision that it should be made
a rule of the High Court of Judicature on the application of either of
the contracting parties.

There is absolutely nothing in any part of this contract, as it
appears to us, which can amount to an indication that it is in any
way or in any part of it to be treated as anything except an English
contract, unless it be the mere fact that the esparto is to be collected
in Algeria, approved at the works of a French company in Algeria
before shipment, and to be delivered on board ships of the plaintiffs
at an Algerian port, after which it is to be at plaintiffs' risk. To hold
that on this ground only the ordinary presumption is to be displaced,
and that the parties must have meant some law other than the
English to govern the construction of any portion of the contract as
regards the liabilities of the contracting parties, would be to introduce a serious element of uncertainty into mercantile contracts.
The mere fact that a contract of this description,—made in England
between English resident houses, and under which payment is to be
made in England upon delivery of goods from up country in an
Algerian port,—is partly to be performed in Algeria, does not put
an end to the inference that the contract remains an English contract between English merchants, to be construed according to

English law, and with all the incidents which English law attaches to the non-performance of such contracts.

Now one of the incidents which the English law attaches to a contract is that (except in certain excepted cases as that of common carriers and bailees, of which this is not one,) a person who expressly contracts absolutely to do a thing not naturally impossible, is not excused for non-performance because of being prevented by vis major.

'The rule laid down in the case of *Paradine* v. *Jane*[1] has often', says Lord Ellenborough, 'been recognized in courts of law as a sound one; that when a party by his own contract creates a duty or charge upon himself, he is bound to make it good, if he may, notwithstanding any accident by inevitable necessity; because he might have provided against it by his contract': *Atkinson* v. *Ritchie*.[2] If inevitable necessity occurring in this country would not excuse non-performance, why should non-performance be excused on account of the inevitable necessity arising abroad? So to hold would be to alter the liability which English law attaches to contracts, and would, in the absence of an expressed or implied intention to that effect, be contrary to authority as well as principle. The Solicitor-General, in his argument, admitted that he was driven to contend that the law of the place of fulfilment not merely governed the mode of performance of this particular contract, but governed also the obligations in respect of performance, and the liabilities in respect of non-performance of it. It seems to us, however, that the true principles of construction to be applied do not admit of this interpretation of this contract. To what extent foreign law is to be incorporated in any contract must be, as we have said, a question of construction of the contract itself read by the light of the surrounding circumstances. If a contract made in England by English subjects or residents, and upon which payment is to be made in England, has to be performed in part abroad, it might be unreasonable to assume that the mode in which any part of it has to be performed abroad was intended to be in accordance with the law of the foreign country, and to construe the contract as incorporating silently to that extent all provisions of a foreign law which would regulate the method of performance, and which were not inconsistent with the English contract. But it cannot be gathered from such a contract as the present that the parties desired to go further and to discharge

[1] (1647) Aleyn 27.   [2] (1809) 10 East 530.

the defendants from performance whenever circumstances arose which would, according to foreign law, excuse them. The contract has absolutely provided that delivery of the esparto shall be duly made, not that the bargain as to such delivery need only be observed when the foreign law would insist upon such observance. The contract being an English contract, only such portions of the French Civil Code can be applied to its provisions as to performance in Algeria as are not inconsistent with the express language of the contract as interpreted according to English law. If the parties had wished, in addition to this, to incorporate a provision of French law which in the event of vis major would operate to excuse the contracting parties for non-performance, and thus to vary the natural construction of the instrument according to English law, they should have done so in express terms. Read by English law the contract is not susceptible of such an interpretation, and there is nothing to show that in this respect the parties desired the contract to be governed by the French.

For these reasons we are of opinion that the judgment of the court below was right and must be affirmed with costs.

Judgment affirmed.

The proper law of the contract, and not the law of the place of performance as such, determines the substance of the obligation.

MOUNT ALBERT BOROUGH COUNCIL *v.* AUSTRALASIAN ETC. LIFE INSURANCE SOCIETY LTD. [1938] A.C. 224 (Privy Council)
(*ante,* p. 265)

BONYTHON *v.* COMMONWEALTH OF AUSTRALIA [1951] A.C. 201 (Privy Council)

Appeal from the High Court of Australia.

In 1895 the Government of Queensland issued debentures of varying amounts to secure a loan of £2,000,000 of which £1,250,000 was raised in England and the balance in Australia. The debentures entitled the holders to repayment in 'pounds sterling' in 1945 (together with interest in the meantime) either in Brisbane, Sydney, Melbourne, or London at the holder's option. In 1931 the Australian pound was devalued in relation to the English pound by 25 per cent. In 1932 the public debt of Queensland was taken over by the

JACOBS
v.
CRÉDIT
LYONNAIS.
—
Bowen L.J.

BONYTHON
v.
COMMON-
WEALTH OF
AUSTRALIA.

Commonwealth of Australia which issued consolidated inscribed stock maturing in 1945 in lieu of the debentures to the holders thereof.

The plaintiffs, who were holders of some of the inscribed stock, exercised their option for repayment in London and claimed to be entitled to be paid in London the face value of their stock in English currency or, alternatively, to be paid in Australia the equivalent in Australian currency of such value in English currency. The High Court of Australia by a majority rejected their claim. The plaintiffs appealed.

The judgment of their Lordships (Viscount Simon, Lords Simonds, Morton of Henryton, MacDermott, and Reid) was delivered by

LORD SIMONDS: ... The conclusion to which, as a matter of construction, their Lordships come, that the substantial obligation under the debenture is the same whatever the place of payment, clears the way to a solution of the whole problem. It has been urged that, if London is chosen as the place of payment, then English law as the lex loci solutionis governs the contract and determines the measure of the obligation. But this contention cannot be accepted. The mode of performance of the obligation may, and probably will, be determined by English law; the substance of the obligation must be determined by the proper law of the contract, i.e. the system of law by reference to which the contract was made or that with which the transaction has its closest and most real connection. In the consideration of the latter question, what is the proper law of the contract, and therefore what is the substance of the obligation created by it, it is a factor, and sometimes a decisive one, that a particular place is chosen for performance. ...

In the present case it is clear that, if it had been provided that payment would be made in London only, that would have been an important factor in determining the substance of the obligation, though other factors could not be ignored. But payment in London was only one of four alternative modes of performance, and the fact that London might be chosen as the place of payment becomes a factor of little or no weight. If the substance of the obligation is in every case the same, how can it affect the rights of one debenture-holder who elects to be paid in Melbourne that another has elected to be paid in London?

The question, then, is what is the proper law of the contract, or, to relate the general question to the particular problem, within the framework of what monetary or financial system should the instrument be construed. On the assumption that express reference is made to none, the question becomes a matter of implication to be derived from all the circumstances of the transaction. Applying this test to the present case, their Lordships find in the circumstances overwhelming evidence that it was to the law of Queensland that the parties looked for the determination of their rights. The debentures were issued on the authority of a Queensland Act which empowered the Governor-in-Council to raise by way of loan not more than £2,000,000 for the public service of the Colony. By the same Act the loan was secured on the public revenues of the Colony, and was made repayable on January 1, 1945. These circumstances must be of great, if not decisive, weight in determining what is the proper law of the contract: see *Rex* v. *International Trustee for the Protection of Bondholders A/G*[1] and compare *Mount Albert Borough Council* v. *Australasian etc. Life Insurance Society Ltd.*[2] It is not inconceivable that the legislature of a self-governing colony should authorize the raising of a loan in terms of a currency other than its own, but where it uses terms which are apt to describe its own lawful money, it must require the strongest evidence to the contrary to suppose that it intended some other money. Here there are no countervailing features except (*a*) that the lender was given a choice of payment in London, and (*b*) that the larger part of the authorized loan of £2,000,000 was in fact raised in London. The weight of the first factor has already been discussed: the second is more difficult to assess. As has been pointed out by Dixon J., no details of this transaction have been given and the history and fate of the debentures issued in London were not revealed. The safer course is to examine the contract as between the present appellants or their predecessors in title and the Government of Queensland and to disregard what must be a matter of mere speculation, whether the fact that similar debentures had been, or were to be, issued in London was a circumstance from which an intention could fairly or reasonably be implied that the debentures issued to them in Queensland were to be repaid in anything but the lawful money of Queensland. ....

The Government of a self-governing country, using the terms appropriate to its own monetary system, must be presumed to refer

BONYTHON
v.
COMMON-
WEALTH OF
AUSTRALIA.
—
Lord
Simonds.

[1] [1937] A.C. 500. [2] [1938] A.C. 224 ; *ante*, p. 265.

BONYTHON
v.
COMMON-
WEALTH OF
AUSTRALIA.

Lord
Simonds.

to that system whether or not those terms are apt to refer to another system also. It may be possible to displace that presumption,[1] but, unless it is displaced, it prevails, and, if it prevails, then it follows that the obligation to pay will be satisfied by payment of whatever currency is by the law of Queensland valid tender for the discharge of the nominal amount of the debt. It becomes an irrelevant consideration whether the parties ever thought that the money of account of Queensland and England might at a future date, though still bearing the same name, become disparate in value or whether in fact that divergence took place. The law of Queensland governs the contract and that law determines the meaning of the word 'pound'. . . .

Their Lordships will humbly advise His Majesty that this appeal should be dismissed.

Appeal dismissed.

Section *D*: ILLEGALITY

An English court will not enforce a contract which is valid by its proper law but the performance of which is illegal by the law of the place of performance: at any rate if (a) the proper law is English, or (b) the place of performance is in England.

RALLI
BROTHERS
v.
COMPANIA
NAVIERA
SOTA Y
AZNAR.

RALLI BROTHERS *v.* COMPANIA NAVIERA SOTA Y AZNAR [1920]
2 K.B. 287 (Court of Appeal)

In July 1918 an English firm chartered a Spanish steamship from the owners, a Spanish firm, to carry a cargo of jute from Calcutta to Barcelona at a freight of £50 per ton, one half to be paid to the owners in London on the vessel sailing from Calcutta, and the other half to be paid at Barcelona, after the arrival of the ship. The charter-party was made in London in the English language and form and the Court of Appeal held (what had not been disputed) that English law was its proper law. The steamship arrived at Barcelona in December 1918. Meanwhile in September 1918 there came into force in Spain a decree having the force of law which fixed the maximum freight on jute imported into Spain at 875 pesetas per ton, and imposed penalties upon persons infringing it. The freight reserved by the charter-party was largely in excess of 875

[1] This presumption was displaced in *National Mutual Life Association of Australasia Ltd.* v. *A.-G. for New Zealand* [1956] A. C. 369.

CONTRACTS

pesetas per ton. The receivers of the cargo at Barcelona tendered the balance of the freight at this rate but refused to pay the balance at the rate reserved by the charter party. The Spanish shipowners then claimed to recover the balance of the freight from the charterers in England, notwithstanding that it exceeded the freight limited by Spanish law. The matter came before Bailhache J. in the form of a special case stated by a commercial umpire. The learned judge decided in favour of the charterers. The shipowners appealed.

RALLI BROTHERS *v.* COMPANIA NAVIERA SOTA Y AZNAR.

Scrutton L.J.

SCRUTTON L.J. (after stating the facts, continued): I accept the contention of the shipowners that the charterers remain liable for the freight, in spite of the provision that half of it is to be paid by the receivers. But I think they remain liable to pay it in Spanish currency at the Spanish port of discharge to a Spanish company resident in Spain. To pay freight in Spain to a Spaniard for goods to be discharged in Spain at a rate in excess of the maximum freight fixed by Spanish law for the carriage of such goods is illegal by the law of Spain. What then is the effect on the contract of illegality by the law of the place where it is to be performed, such law not being British law?

In my opinion the law is correctly stated by Professor Dicey in Conflict of Laws, 2nd ed., p. 553, where he says: 'A contract . . . is, in general, invalid in so far as . . . the performance of it is unlawful by the law of the country where the contract is to be performed'—and I reserve liberty to consider whether it is any longer an exception to this proposition that this country will not consider the fact that the contract is obnoxious only to the revenue laws of the foreign country where it is to be performed as an obstacle to enforcing it in the English courts. The early authorities on this point require reconsideration in view of the obligations of international comity as now understood.

The argument addressed to us was that illegality by foreign law was only impossibility in fact, which the parties might have provided against by their contract, and for which they must be liable, if they had not expressly relieved themselves from liability. This is the old doctrine of *Paradine* v. *Jane*:[1] 'When the party by his own contract creates a duty or charge upon himself, he is bound to make it good, if he may, notwithstanding any accident by inevitable necessity, because he might have provided against it by his contract.' It was

[1] (1647) Aleyn 26, 27.

293

RALLI
BROTHERS
v.
COMPANIA
NAVIERA
SOTA Y
AZNAR.

Scrutton
L.J.

emphasized by Lord Ellenborough in *Atkinson* v. *Ritchie*,[1] where he said: 'No exception (of a private nature at least) which is not contained in the contract itself, can be engrafted upon it by implication, as an excuse for its non-performance.' And Lord Bowen as late as 1884 in the case of *Jacobs* v. *Crédit Lyonnais*,[2] cited Lord Ellenborough's approval of *Paradine* v. *Jane* with approval. But the numerous cases, of which *Metropolitan Water Board* v. *Dick, Kerr & Co.*[3] is a recent example, most of which are cited in McCardie J.'s exhaustive judgment in *Blackburn Bobbin Co.* v. *Allen & Sons*,[4] have made a serious breach in the ancient proposition. It is now quite common for exceptions, or exemptions from liability, to be grafted by implication on contracts, if the parties by necessary implication must have treated the continued existence of a specified state of things as essential to liability on the express terms of the contract. If I am asked whether the true intent of the parties is that one has undertaken to do an act though it is illegal by the law of the place in which the act is to be done, and though that law is the law of his own country; or whether their true intent was that the doing of that act is subject to the implied condition that it shall be legal for him to do the act in the place where it has to be done, I have no hesitation in choosing the second alternative. 'I will do it provided I can legally do so' seems to me infinitely preferable to and more likely than 'I will do it, though it is illegal'.

. . . Where a contract requires an act to be done in a foreign country, it is, in the absence of very special circumstances, an implied term of the continuing validity of such a provision that the act to be done in the foreign country shall not be illegal by the law of that country. This country should not in my opinion assist or sanction the breach of the laws of other independent States.

LORD STERNDALE M.R. and WARRINGTON L.J. delivered judgments to the same effect.

Appeal dismissed.

But an English court will enforce a contract which is valid by its proper law but illegal by the law of the place of contracting.

VITA FOOD PRODUCTS INC. *v.* UNUS SHIPPING CO. [1939] A.C. 277
(*ante*, p. 268)

---

[1] (1809) 10 East 530, 533.   [2] (1884) 12 Q.B.D. 589; *ante*, p. 288.
[3] [1919] A.C. 119.   [4] [1918] 1 K.B. 540, 546.

Chapter 10

TORTS

Actions in England upon torts committed abroad will succeed only if (a) the act would have been actionable if committed in England, and (b) the act was not justifiable by the law of the place where it was committed.

(a) Actionable in England

THE HALLEY (1868) L.R. 2 P.C. 193 (Privy Council)

APPEAL from the High Court of Admiralty.[1]

The plaintiffs, as owners of a Norwegian barque called the Napoleon, brought an action against the defendants, as owners of a British steamship called the Halley, for damages in respect of a collision which occurred in January 1867 in Flushing roads between the Napoleon and the Halley. The defendants pleaded that the collision was caused by the sole negligence of the pilot whom they were compelled by Belgian or Dutch law to have on board the Halley. The plaintiffs replied that by Belgian or Dutch law the owners of a ship were liable for the negligence of a compulsory pilot. Phillimore J. held that the action succeeded. The defendants appealed.

The judgment of their Lordships (Sir William Erle, Lord Justice Wood, Lord Justice Selwyn, Sir James Colville, and Sir Edward Vaughan Williams) was delivered by

LORD JUSTICE SELWYN: The claim of the respondents is stated by the learned Judge to be founded upon a tort committed by the defendants in the territory of a foreign state, and we are not called upon to pronounce any opinion as to the rights which the respondents might have obtained, either against the appellants as the owners of the Halley, or as against that ship, if the respondents had instituted proceedings and obtained a judgment in the foreign court. For this cause is a cause for damage instituted by petition in the High Court of Admiralty in England; and it is admitted by the counsel for the respondents that the question before us must be decided

[1] L.R. 2 A. & E. 3.

upon the same principles as would be applicable to an action for damages for the collision in question if commenced in the Court of Queen's Bench or Common Pleas. But it is contended on their part, and has been held by the learned Judge in the court below, that the respondents are entitled to plead that the law of Belgium, within whose territorial jurisdiction the collision took place, renders the owners of the Halley, although compelled to take a pilot on board, liable to make reparation for the injury which she has done.

Their Lordships agree with the learned Judge in his statement of the common law of England, with respect to the liability of the owner of a vessel for injuries occasioned by the unskilful navigation of his vessel, while under the control of a pilot, whom the owner was compelled to take on board, and in whose selection he had no voice. This exemption of the owner from liability when the ship is under the control of what has been termed a 'compulsory pilot' has also been declared by express statutory enactments (vide Merchant Shipping Act 1854 s. 388).[1] Their Lordships think that the tort upon which this cause is founded is one which would not be recognized by the law of England as creating any liability in, or cause of action against, the appellants.

It follows, therefore, that the liability of the appellants, and the right of the respondents to recover damages from them, as the owners of the Halley, if such liability or right exists in the present case, must be the creature of the Belgian law; and the question is, whether an English Court of Justice is bound to apply and enforce that law in a case when, according to its own principles, no wrong has been committed by the defendants, and no right of action against them exists.

The counsel for the respondents, when challenged to produce any instance in which such a course has been taken by any English Court of Justice, admitted his inability to do so, and the absence of any such precedent is the more important, since the right of all persons, whether British subjects or aliens, to sue in the English courts for damages in respect of torts committed in foreign countries has long since been established; and, as is observed in the note to *Mostyn* v. *Fabrigas*,[2] there seems to be no reason why aliens should not sue in England for personal injuries done to them by other aliens abroad, when such injuries are actionable both by the law of England and also by that of the country where they are committed, and the

---

[1] Repealed by the Pilotage Act 1913 (*Ed.*). [2] (1774) 1 Cowp. 161.

impression which had prevailed to the contrary seems to be erroneous. . . .

It is true that in many cases the courts of England inquire into and act upon the law of foreign countries, as in the case of a contract entered into in a foreign country, where, by express reference, or by necessary implication, the foreign law is incorporated with the contract, and proof and consideration of the foreign law therefore become necessary to the construction of the contract itself. And as in the case of a collision on an ordinary road in a foreign country, where the rule of the road in force at the place of collision may be a necessary ingredient in the determination of the question by whose fault or negligence the alleged tort was committed. But in these and similar cases the English court admits the proof of the foreign law as part of the circumstances attending the execution of the contract, or as one of the facts upon which the existence of the tort, or the right to damages, may depend, and it then applies and enforces its own law so far as it is applicable to the case thus established; but it is, in their Lordships' opinion, alike contrary to principle and to authority to hold, that an English Court of Justice will enforce a foreign municipal law, and will give a remedy in the shape of damages in respect of an act which, according to its own principles, imposes no liability on the person from whom the damages are claimed. . . .

Appeal allowed.

(b) Not justifiable by the lex loci delicti commissi

PHILLIPS *v.* EYRE (1870) L.R. 6 Q.B. 1 (Exchequer Chamber)

Error from the judgment of the Court of Queen's Bench in favour of the defendant.[1]

The judgment of the Court (Kelly C.B., Martin, Channell, Pigott, and Cleasby BB, Willes and Brett JJ.) was delivered by

WILLES J.: This is an action complaining of false imprisonment and other injuries to the plaintiff by the defendant in the island of Jamaica. The plea states in effect that the defendant was governor of the island; that a rebellion broke out there which the governor and others acting under his authority had arrested by force of arms;

---

[1] L.R. 4 Q.B. 225.

PHILLIPS
v.
EYRE.

Willes J.

that an Act was afterwards duly passed by the legislature of the island, and received the royal assent, by which it was enacted by the governor, legislative council, and assembly of the island, amongst other things that the defendant and all officers and other persons who had acted under his authority, was thereby indemnified in respect of all acts, matters, and things done in order to put an end to the rebellion, and all such acts were 'thereby made and declared lawful, and were confirmed'. The plea further states that the grievances complained of in this action were measures used in the suppression of the rebellion, and were reasonably and in good faith considered by the defendant to be proper for the purpose of putting an end to, and bonâ fide done in order to put an end to, the rebellion, and so were included in the indemnity. To this plea the plaintiff demurred, and also replied that the defendant as governor was, by the law of Jamaica, a necessary party to the making of the Act. The defendant demurred to that replication, and issues in law were raised upon the validity of the plea and replication, upon which issues the Court of Queen's Bench gave judgment for the defendant, whereupon the plaintiff has assigned error.

It was agreed at the bar that, for the purpose of this argument, the decision ought to turn upon the colonial Act, and numerous objections were urged against its validity and effect. . . .

(After considering the nature and effect of an Act of Indemnity, and disposing of objections (1) that the Crown had no power to create a legislative assembly in a settled colony; (2) that the Act in question was contrary to English statute law and was therefore void; (3) that the defendant was as governor a necessary party to the passing of the Act and so could take no benefit thereunder; (4) that the Act was retrospective in character and therefore contrary to natural justice, his Lordship continued:)

The last objection to the plea of the colonial Act was of a more technical character; that assuming the colonial Act to be valid in Jamaica and a defence there, it could not have the extra-territorial effect of taking away the right of action in an English court. This objection is founded upon a misconception of the true character of a civil or legal obligation and the corresponding right of action. The obligation is the principal to which a right of action in whatever court is only an accessory, and such accessory, according to the maxim of law, follows the principal, and must stand or fall therewith. 'Quæ accessorium locum obtinent extinguuntur cum principales res peremptæ sunt.' A right of action, whether it arise from contract governed by the law of the place or wrong, is equally the creature of the law of the place and subordinate thereto. The terms of the contract or the character of the subject-matter may shew that the parties intended their bargain to be governed by some other law; but, primâ facie, it falls under the law of the place where it was made. And in like manner the civil liability arising out of a wrong derives its birth from the law of the place, and its character is determined by that law. Therefore, an act committed abroad, if valid and unquestionable by the law of the place, cannot, so far as civil liability is concerned, be drawn in question elsewhere unless by force of some distinct exceptional legislation, superadding a liability other than and besides that incident to the act itself. In this respect no sound distinction can be suggested between the civil liability in respect of a contract governed by the law of the place and a wrong.

Our courts are said to be more open to admit actions founded upon foreign transactions than those of any other European country; but there are restrictions in respect of locality which exclude some foreign causes of action altogether, namely, those which would be local if they arose in England, such as trespass to land: *Doulson* v. *Matthews*,[1] and even with respect to those not falling within that description our courts do not undertake universal jurisdiction. As a general rule, in order to found a suit in England for a wrong alleged to have been committed abroad, two conditions must be fulfilled. First, the wrong must be of such a character that it would have been actionable if committed in England; therefore, in *The Halley*,[2] the Judicial Committee pronounced against a suit in the Admiralty founded upon a liability by the law of Belgium for collision caused by the act of a pilot whom the shipowner was compelled by that law to employ, and for whom, therefore, as not being his agent, he was not responsible by English law. Secondly, the act must not have been justifiable by the law of the place where it was done. Therefore in *Blad's Case*,[3] and *Blad* v. *Bamfield*,[4] Lord Nottingham held that a seizure in Iceland, authorized by the Danish Government and valid by the law of the place, could not be questioned by civil action in England, although the plaintiff, an Englishman, insisted that the seizure was in violation of a treaty between this country and Denmark—a matter proper for remonstrance, not litigation. And in

PHILLIPS
v.
EYRE.

Willes J.

[1] (1792) 4 T.R. 503. [2] (1868) L.R. 2 P.C. 193 ; *ante*, p. 295.
[3] (1673) 3 Swanst. 603. [4] (1674) 3 Swanst. 604.

PHILLIPS
v.
EYRE.
Willes J.

Dobree v. *Napier*,[1] Admiral Napier having, when in the service of the Queen of Portugal, captured in Portuguese water an English ship breaking blockade, was held by the Court of Common Pleas to be justified, by the law of Portugal and of nations, though his serving under a foreign Prince was contrary to English law, and subjected him to penalties under the Foreign Enlistment Act. And in *Reg.* v. *Lesley*,[2] an imprisonment in Chile on board a British ship lawful there, was held by Erle C.J., and the Court for Crown Cases Reserved, to be no ground for an indictment here, there being no independent law of this country making the act wrongful or criminal. As to foreign laws affecting the liability of parties in respect of bygone transactions, the law is clear that, if the foreign law touches only the remedy or procedure for enforcing the obligation, as in the case of an ordinary statute of limitations, such law is no bar to an action in this country; but if the foreign law extinguishes the right it is a bar in this country equally as if the extinguishment had been by a release of the party, or an act of our own legislature. This distinction is well illustrated on the one hand by *Huber* v. *Steiner*,[3] where the French law of five years' prescription was held by the Court of Common Pleas to be no answer in this country to an action upon a French promissory note, because that law dealt only with procedure, and the time and manner of suit (tempus et modum actionis instituendæ), and did not affect to destroy the obligation of the contract (valorem contractus); and on the other hand by *Potter* v. *Brown*,[4] where the drawer of a bill at Baltimore upon England was held discharged from his liability for the non-acceptance of the bill here by a certificate in bankruptcy, under the law of the United States of America, the Court of Queen's Bench adopting the general rule laid down by Lord Mansfield in *Ballantine* v. *Golding*,[5] and ever since recognized, that 'what is a discharge of a debt in the country where it is contracted is a discharge of it everywhere'. So that where an obligation by contract to pay a debt or damages is discharged and avoided by the law of the place where it was made, the accessory right of action in every court open to the creditor unquestionably falls to the ground. And by strict parity of reasoning, where an obligation, ex delicto, to pay damages is discharged and avoided by the law of the country where it was made, the accessory

---

[1] (1836) 2 Bing. N.C. 781.   [2] (1860) Bell C.C. 220.
[3] (1835) 2 Bing. N.C. 202; *post*, p. 522.   [4] (1804) 5 East 124.
[5] (1784) Cooke's Bankrupt Law 487.

right of action is in like manner discharged and avoided. Cases may possibly arise in which distinct and independent rights or liabilities or defences are created by positive and specific laws of this country in respect of foreign transactions: but there is no such law (unless it be the Governor's Act already discussed and disposed of) applicable to the present case.

It may be proper to remark, before quitting this part of the subject, that the colonial Act could not be overruled upon either of these two latter grounds of objection without laying down that no foreign legislation could avail to take away civil liability here in respect of acts done abroad; so that, for instance, if a foreign country after a rebellion or civil war were to pass a general Act of oblivion and indemnity, burying in one grave all legal memory alike of the hostilities, and even the private retaliations which are the sure results of anarchy and violence, it would, if the argument for the plaintiff prevailed, be competent for a municipal court of any other country to condemn and disregard, as naturally unjust or technically ineffectual, the law of a sovereign state, disposing, upon the same constitutional principles as have actuated our own legislature, of matters arising within its territory—a course which to adopt would be an unprecedented and mischievous violation of the comity of nations.

The judgment of the Court of Queen's Bench for the defendant was right, and is affirmed.

Judgment affirmed.

PHILLIPS
v.
EYRE.

Willes J.

MACHADO *v.* FONTES [1897] 2 Q.B. 231 (Court of Appeal)

MACHADO
v.
FONTES.

Appeal from Kennedy J. at chambers.

The plaintiff brought this action to recover damages from the defendant for an alleged libel upon the plaintiff contained in a pamphlet in the Portuguese language alleged to have been published by the defendant in Brazil.

The defendant delivered a statement of defence (in which, amongst other defences, he denied the alleged libel), and he afterwards took out a summons for leave to amend his defence by adding the following plea: 'Further the defendant will contend that if (contrary to the defendant's contention) the said pamphlet has been published in Brazil, by the Brazilian law the publication of the said pamphlet in Brazil cannot be the ground of legal proceedings against the defendant in Brazil in which damages can be recovered, or (alternatively) cannot be the ground of legal proceedings against the defendant in Brazil in which the plaintiff can recover general damages for any injury to his credit, character, or feelings.'

The summons came before Kennedy J. in chambers, who allowed the plea to be added, but expressed some doubt as to the propriety of so doing, and gave leave to the plaintiff to bring the present appeal.

LOPES L.J.: I am of opinion that this appeal ought to be allowed. [The Lord Justice then referred to the facts, and, after reading the plea, continued:—]

Now that plea, as it stands, appears to me merely to go to the remedy. It says, in effect, that in this case no action in which damages could be recovered would lie in Brazil, and, assuming that any damages could be recovered in Brazil, they would be special damages only. Mr. Walton contends that that is not the meaning of the plea: that the plea is intended to raise a larger question than that, and to say that libel cannot be made the subject of any civil proceedings at all in Brazil, but it is only the subject-matter of criminal proceedings; and, for the purposes of what I am about to say, I will assume that to be so.

Now the principle applicable in the present case appears to me to be this: where the words have been published outside the jurisdiction, then, in order to maintain an action here on the ground of a tort committed outside the jurisdiction, the act complained of must be wrongful—I use the word 'wrongful' deliberately—both by the law of this country, and also by the law of the country where it was committed; and the first thing we have to consider is whether those conditions are complied with.

In the case of *Phillips* v. *Eyre*[1] Willes J. lays down very distinctly what the requisites are in order to found such an action. He says this: 'As a general rule, in order to found a suit in England for a wrong alleged to have been committed abroad, two conditions must be fulfilled: First, the wrong must be of such a character that it would have been actionable if committed in England. . . . Secondly, the act must not have been justifiable by the law of the place where it was done'. Then in *The Mary Moxham*[2] James L.J., in the course of his judgment, uses these words: 'It is settled that if by the law of

---

[1] (1870) L.R. 6 Q.B. 1; *ante*, p. 299. [2] (1876) 1 P.D. 107.

the foreign country the act is lawful or is excusable, or even if it has been legitimized by a subsequent act of the Legislature, then this court will take into consideration that state of the law—that is to say, if by the law of the foreign country a particular person is justified, or is excused, or has been justified or excused for the thing done, he will not be answerable here.'

Both those cases seem to me to go this length: that, in order to constitute a good defence to an action brought in this country in respect of an act done in a foreign country, the act relied on must be one which is innocent in the country where it was committed. In the present case there can be no doubt that the action lies, for it complies with both of the requirements which are laid down by Willes J. The act was committed abroad, and was actionable here, and not justifiable by the law of the place where it was committed. Both those conditions are complied with; and, therefore, the publication in Brazil is actionable here.

It then follows, directly the right of action is established in this country, that the ordinary incidents of that action and the appropriate remedies ensue. Therefore, in this case, in my opinion, damages would flow from the wrong committed just as they would in any action brought in respect of a libel published in this country.

It is contended that it would be much better that this question should not be decided at the present time, but that a commission should go to Brazil, and that the Brazilian law should be inquired into. If our view is correct, it seems to me that that would be a great waste of time and money, because, having regard to the authorities I have mentioned, this plea is absolutely bad, and ought to be struck out.

RIGBY L.J.: I am of the same opinion. I do not propose to decide this case on any technical consideration as to what may be the precise meaning of the allegation that is proposed to be introduced into the defence; I give it the widest possible construction it can reasonably bear; and I will assume it to involve that no action for damages, or even no civil action at all, can be maintained in Brazil in respect of a libel published there. But it does not follow from that that the libel is not actionable in this country under the present conditions, and having regard to the fact that the plaintiff and defendant are here.

Willes J., in *Phillips* v. *Eyre*, was laying down a rule which he expressed without the slightest modification, and without the

MACHADO
v.
FONTES.
Lopes L.J.

MACHADO
v.
FONTES.

Rigby L.J.

slightest doubt as to its correctness; and when you consider the care with which the learned judge prepared the propositions that he was about to enunciate, I cannot doubt that the change from 'actionable' in the first branch of the rule to 'justifiable' in the second branch of it was deliberate. The first requisite is that the wrong must be of such a character that it would be actionable in England. It was long ago settled that an action will lie by a plaintiff here against a defendant here, upon a transaction in a place outside this country. But though such action may be brought here, it does not follow that it will succeed here, for, when it is committed in a foreign country, it may turn out to be a perfectly innocent act according to the law of that country; and if the act is shewn by the law of that country to be an innocent act, we pay such respect to the law of other countries that we will not allow an action to be brought upon it here. The innocency of the act in the foreign country is an answer to the action. That is what is meant when it is said that the act must be 'justifiable' by the law of the place where it was done.

It is not really a matter of any importance what the nature of the remedy for a wrong in a foreign country may be.

The remedy must be according to the law of the country which entertains the action. Of course, the plea means that no action can be brought in this country in respect of the libel (if any) in Brazil. But I think the rule is clear. It was very carefully laid down by Willes J. in *Phillips* v. *Eyre*; and in the case of *The Mary Moxham* all the learned judges of the Court of Appeal in their judgments laid down the law without hesitation and in a uniform manner; and first one judge and then another gave, in different language but exactly to the same purport and effect, the rule enunciated by Willes J. So that if authority were wanting there is a decision clearly binding upon us, although I think the principle is sufficient to decide the case.

I think there is no doubt at all that an action for a libel published abroad is maintainable here, unless it can be shewn to be justified or excused in the country where it was published. James L.J. states in *The Mary Moxham* what the settled law is. Mellish L.J. is quite as clear upon the point as James L.J. in laying down the general rule; and Baggallay L.J. also takes the same view. We start, then, from this: that the act in question is primâ facie actionable here, and the only thing we have to do is to see whether there is any peremptory bar to our jurisdiction arising from the fact that the act we are dealing with is authorized, or innocent or excusable, in the country

where it was committed. If we cannot see that, we must act according to our own rules in the damages (if any) which we may choose to
give. Here we cannot see it, and this appeal must be allowed with
costs.

Appeal allowed.

KOOP *v.* BEBB (1951) 84 Com. L.R. 629 (High Court of Australia)

The infant plaintiffs brought an action in the Supreme Court of
Victoria against the defendant for damages for the death of their
father, who was a passenger in a motor truck being driven by the
defendant and who was killed as a result of the defendant's negligence. The accident occurred in New South Wales and the father
died in hospital in Victoria.

Section 15 of the Wrongs Act 1928 (Victoria) provides that when
the death of a person is caused by a wrongful act, neglect, or default
and the act, neglect, or default is such as would (if death had not
ensued) have entitled the party injured to maintain an action and
recover damages in respect thereof, then the person who would have
been liable if death had not ensued shall be liable to an action for
damages notwithstanding the death of the person injured. Section 16 provides that every such action shall be for the benefit of
the wife, husband, parent, and child of the person whose death has
been so caused. Section 17 provides that where there is no executor
or administrator of the person deceased, the action may be brought
by any of the persons for whose benefit such action would have
been.

Dean J. held that the action failed because the Victorian Parliament has power to make laws 'in and for Victoria' only and therefore the words 'within Victoria' must be inserted in s. 15 immediately
after the words 'wrongful act neglect or default'. The plaintiffs
appealed.

The judgment of DIXON, WILLIAMS, FULLAGAR, and KITTO JJ. was
as follows:

... Section 15 should be considered as enacting a rule of the law of
Victoria, to be applied in the Victorian courts, and to be applied as
it stands, without textual emendation. Its effect in relation to a case
which includes an extra-Victorian element depends upon the application of the rules of private international law which form part of
the law in Victoria. ...

It is necessary to ascertain the rule of private international law which defines the conditions of civil liability in Victoria for an act done in New South Wales. In the present state of authority it must be accepted that an action of tort will lie in one State for a wrong alleged to have been committed in another State, if two conditions are fulfilled: first, the wrong must be of such a character that it would have been actionable if it had been committed in the State in which the action is brought; and secondly, it must not have been justifiable by the law of the State where it was done: *Walpole* v. *Canadian Northern Railway*;[1] *McMillan* v. *Canadian Northern Railway*.[2]

The language in which these conditions are expressed is that of Willes J. in *Phillips* v. *Eyre*.[3] For his statement of the first condition, his Lordship relied upon the decision in *The Halley*,[4] although (it may be remarked) in that case the Privy Council decided that the defendant was not liable in England for an act done abroad by another person, not because of the character of the act according to English law, but because the person who did it was not one for whose defaults the defendant was responsible according to English law. At least the first condition is free from ambiguity. The second is not. It was interpreted by a Court of Appeal consisting of Lopes and Rigby L.JJ. in *Machado* v. *Fontes*[5] as meaning that the act complained of must not have been 'innocent' in the country where it was done. Their Lordships held that if the act was contrary in any respect to the law of that country, then, although it gave rise to no civil liability there, it was not 'justifiable' there, and the second condition was therefore fulfilled. No previous decision had gone so far. The statement that the act must not have been justifiable by the law of the place where it was done was framed by Willes J. for the purposes of a judgment directed to the effect to be conceded in an action in England to a statute of indemnity, which had been passed in the country where the act was committed and which had the effect of curing retrospectively the wrongfulness of the act in that country. The statement of the condition does not in terms deny that the act complained of must be of a character which attracts civil liability in the country where it was done; and it would be difficult to reconcile such a denial with the principle which Willes J. had previously

---

[1] [1923] A.C. 113, 119.   [2] [1923] A.C. 120, 123–4.
[3] (1870) L.R. 6 Q.B. 1 ; *ante*, p. 299.   [4] (1868) L.R. 2 P.C. 193 ; *ante*, p. 295.
[5] [1897] 2 Q.B. 231 ; *ante*, p. 301.

stated, that 'the civil liability arising out of a wrong derives its birth from the law of the place, and its character is determined by that law'.[1] The learned Lords Justices in *Machado* v. *Fontes* relied also upon the judgments in *The Mary Moxham*[2] which was the converse of *The Halley*, in the sense that the question was whether liability for an act of negligence in another country could be imposed in England upon a person who, according to the law of that other country, was not responsible for the fault of the person who did the act, and it was decided that it could not. The judgments fall short of supporting the doctrine of *Machado* v. *Fontes*. That case has been dissented from in *Naftalin* v. *L.M.S. Railway*[3] and has been much criticized by text writers. (See further, *M'Elroy* v. *M'Allister*.[4]) Its correctness was questioned and left undecided by the Privy Council in *Canadian Pacific Railway* v. *Parent*.[5] In the judgment of Cussen J. in *Varawa* v. *Howard Smith Co. Ltd.* (*No. 2*)[6] will be found a critical analysis of the case and of the authorities which it purported to apply. It seems clear that the last word has not been said on the subject, and it may be the true view that an act done in another country should be held to be an actionable wrong in Victoria if, first, it was of such a character that it would have been actionable if it had been committed in Victoria, and, secondly, it was such as to give rise to a civil liability by the law of the place where it was done. Such a rule would appear to be consonant with all the English decisions before *Machado* v. *Fontes* and with the later Privy Council decisions. It may be added that, however the rule should be stated, courts applying the English rules of private international law do not accept the theory propounded by Holmes J. in *Slater* v. *Mexican National Railroad Co.*[7] (see also *New York Central Railroad Co.* v. *Chisholm*[8]) when he said: 'The theory of the foreign suit is that although the act complained of was subject to no law having force in the forum, it gave rise to an obligation, an obligatio, which, like other obligations, follows the person, and may be enforced wherever the person may be found. . . . But as the only source of this obligation is the law of the place of the act, it follows that that law determines not merely the existence of the obligation, but equally determines its extent.' English law as the lex fori enforces an obligation of its own creation in respect of an act done in another country which

KOOP
v.
BEBB.

---

[1] *Ante*, p. 299. [2] (1876) 1 P.D. 107. [3] 1933 S.C. 259, 274–5.
[4] 1949 S.C. 110. [5] [1917] A.C. 195, 205. [6] [1910] V.L.R. 509.
[7] (1904) 194 U.S. 120. [8] (1925) 268 U.S. 29.

KOOP
v.
BEBB. would be a tort if done in England, but refrains from doing so unless the act has a particular character according to the lex loci actus.
Uncertainty exists only as to what that character must be.

There is no necessity to express a concluded opinion upon the controversy which surrounds *Machado* v. *Fontes*. It is enough that, on
any view, an act, which would have been actionable in Victoria if
committed there, is actionable in Victoria though committed in New
South Wales if it is actionable in New South Wales. If the defendant
in this case is guilty of the negligence alleged against him, his negligence was, when the action was commenced, actionable in New
South Wales at the suit of the plaintiffs, and would have been actionable in New South Wales at the suit of their father if he had survived.
This is so because the law of New South Wales includes both the
Compensation to Relatives Act 1897–1946, which enacts provisions
not differing in any relevant respect from those of Part III of the
Victorian Wrongs Act, and also the rules of the common law with
respect to liability for negligence. The plaintiffs are therefore entitled
to maintain their present action, either because the co-existence of
Part III of the Wrongs Act and the Compensation to Relatives Act
(N.S.W.) gives them under the rule of private international law
above discussed a right of action against the defendant for causing
the death of their father by negligence in New South Wales, or because Part III of the Wrongs Act applies to this case of its own force,
the condition that their father would have been entitled to sue the
defendant in Victoria for injuring him by negligence in New South
Wales being satisfied by the application of the same rule of private
international law. . . .

MCTIERNAN J. delivered a judgment allowing the appeal.
Appeal allowed.

*In the United States the traditional rule is that tort liability is
governed by the lex loci delicti: but not every aspect of tort liability
is governed by that law.*

BABCOCK
v.
JACKSON.

Fuld J. BABCOCK v. JACKSON (1963) 12 N.Y. 2d. 473, 191 N.E. 2d. 279
(New York Court of Appeals)

FULD J. On Friday September 16 1960 Miss Georgia Babcock
and her friends, Mr. and Mrs. William Jackson, all residents of
Rochester, N.Y., left that city in Mr. Jackson's automobile, Miss

Babcock as guest, for a week-end trip to Canada. Some hours later,

as Mr. Jackson was driving in the Province of Ontario, he apparently lost control of the car; it went off the highway into an adjacent stone wall, and Miss Babcock was seriously injured. Upon her return to this State, she brought the present action against William Jackson, alleging negligence on his part in operating his automobile.

At the time of the accident, there was in force in Ontario a statute providing that 'the owner or driver of a motor vehicle, other than a vehicle operated in the business of carrying passengers for compensation, is not liable for any loss or damage resulting from bodily injury to, or the death of, any person being carried in . . . the motor vehicle'.[1] Even though no such bar is recognized under this State's substantive law of torts, the defendant moved to dismiss the complaint on the ground that the law of the place where the accident occurred governs and that Ontario's guest statute bars recovery. The court at Special Term, agreeing with the defendant, granted the motion and the Appellate Division, over a strong dissent by Halpern J., affirmed the judgment of dismissal without opinion.

The question presented is simply drawn. Shall the law of the place of the tort[2] *invariably* govern the availability of relief for the tort or shall the applicable choice of law rule also reflect a consideration of other factors which are relevant to the purposes served by the enforcement or denial of the remedy?

The traditional choice of law rule, embodied in the original Restatement of Conflict of Laws and until recently unquestioningly followed in this court, has been that the substantive rights and liabilities arising out of a tortious occurrence are determinable by the law of the place of the tort. It had its conceptual foundation in the vested rights doctrine, namely, that a right to recover for a foreign tort owes its creation to the law of the jurisdiction where the injury occurred and depends for its existence and extent solely on such law. Although espoused by such great figures as Holmes J.[3] and Professor Beale,[4] the vested rights doctrine has long since been discredited because it fails to take account of underlying policy con-

[1] R.S.O. 1960 c. 172 s. 105 (2). (All the footnotes to this case form part of Fuld J.'s opinion. Many footnotes have had to be omitted. *Ed.*)
[2] In this case, as in nearly all such cases, the conduct causing injury and the injury itself occurred in the same jurisdiction. The phrase 'place of the tort', as distinguished from 'place of wrong' and 'place of injury', is used herein to designate the place where both the wrong and the injury took place.
[3] See *Slater* v. *Mexican National Railroad Co.* (1904) 194 U.S. 120.
[4] Conflict of Laws, Vol. II, pp. 1286–92.

siderations in evaluating the significance to be ascribed to the circumstance that an act had a foreign situs in determining the rights and liabilities which arise out of that act. 'The vice of the vested rights theory', it has been aptly stated, 'is that it affects to decide concrete cases upon generalities which do not state the practical considerations involved.'[1] More particularly, as applied to torts, the theory ignores the interest which jurisdictions other than that where the tort occurred may have in the resolution of particular issues. It is for this very reason that, despite the advantages of certainty, ease of application and predictability which it affords, there has in recent years been increasing criticism of the traditional rule by commentators[2] and a judicial trend towards its abandonment or modification. . . .

The 'center of gravity' or 'grouping of contacts' doctrine adopted by this court in conflicts cases involving contracts impresses us as likewise affording the appropriate approach for accommodating the competing interests in tort cases with multi-State contacts. Justice, fairness and 'the best practical result' may best be achieved by giving controlling effect to the law of the jurisdiction which, because of its relationship or contact with the occurrence or the parties, has the greatest concern with the specific issue raised in the litigation. The merit of such a rule is that 'it gives to the place having the most interest in the problem paramount control over the legal issues arising out of a particular factual context' and thereby allows the forum to apply 'the policy of the jurisdiction most intimately concerned with the outcome of the particular litigation'.[3]. . .

Comparison of the relative 'contacts' and 'interests' of New York and Ontario in this litigation, *vis-à-vis* the issue here presented, makes it clear that the concern of New York is unquestionably the greater and more direct and that the interest of Ontario is at best minimal. The present action involves injuries sustained by a New York guest as the result of the negligence of a New York host in the operation of an automobile, garaged, licensed and undoubtedly insured in New York, in the course of a week-end journey which began and was to end there. In sharp contrast, Ontario's sole rela-

---

[1] Yntema, 37 Yale L.J. 468, 482–3.

[2] See Dicey, Conflict of Laws, 7th ed., pp. 937 *et seq.*; Leflar, The Law of Conflict of Laws, pp. 217 *et seq.*; Stumberg, Principles of Conflict of Laws, 2nd ed., pp. 201 *et seq.*; Morris, The Proper Law of a Tort, 64 Harv. L. Rev. 881; Ehrenzweig, 69 Yale L.J. 595; Currie, 10 Stan. L. Rev. 205.

[3] *Auten* v. *Auten* (1954) 308 N.Y. 155, 124 N.E. 2d 99, 102.

tionship with the occurrence is the purely adventitious circumstance that the accident occurred there.

New York's policy of requiring a tortfeasor to compensate his guest for injuries caused by his negligence cannot be doubted—as attested by the fact that the Legislature of this State has repeatedly refused to enact a statute denying or limiting recovery in such cases; and our courts have neither reason nor warrant for departing from that policy simply because the accident, solely affecting New York residents and arising out of the operation of a New York based automobile, happened beyond its borders. Per contra, Ontario has no conceivable interest in denying a remedy to a New York guest against his New York host for injuries suffered in Ontario by reason of conduct which was tortious under Ontario law. The object of Ontario's guest statute, it has been said, is 'to prevent the fraudulent assertion of claims by passengers, in collusion with the drivers, against insurance companies',[1] and quite obviously the fraudulent claims intended to be prevented by the statute are those asserted against Ontario defendants and their insurance carriers, not New York defendants and their insurance carriers. Whether New York defendants are imposed upon or their insurers defrauded by a New York plaintiff is scarcely a valid legislative concern of Ontario simply because the accident occurred there, any more so than if the accident had happened in some other jurisdiction.

It is hardly necessary to say that Ontario's interest is quite different from what it would have been had the issue related to the manner in which the defendant had been driving his car at the time of the accident. Where the defendant's exercise of due care in the operation of his automobile is in issue, the jurisdiction in which the allegedly wrongful conduct occurred will usually have a predominant, if not exclusive, concern. In such a case, it is appropriate to look to the law of the place of the tort so as to give effect to that jurisdiction's interest in regulating conduct within its borders, and it would be almost unthinkable to seek the applicable rule in the law of some other place.

The issue here, however, is not whether the defendant offended against a rule of the road prescribed by Ontario for motorists generally or whether he violated some standard of conduct imposed by that jurisdiction, but rather whether the plaintiff, because she was a guest in the defendant's automobile, is barred from recovering

---

[1] Survey of Canadian Legislation, 1 U. of Toronto L.J. 358, 366.

BABCOCK
v.
JACKSON.

Fuld J.

damages for a wrong concededly committed. As to that issue, it is New York, the place where the parties resided, where their guest-host relationship arose and where the trip began and was to end, rather than Ontario, the place of the fortuitous occurrence of the accident, which has the dominant contacts and the superior claim for application of its law. Although the rightness or wrongness of defendant's conduct may depend upon the law of the particular jurisdiction through which the automobile passes, the rights and liabilities of the parties which stem from their guest-host relationship should remain constant and not vary and shift as the automobile proceeds from place to place. Indeed, such a result, we note, accords with 'the interests of the host in procuring liability insurance adequate under the applicable law, and the interests of his insurer in reasonable calculation of the premium'.

Although the traditional rule has in the past been applied by this court in giving controlling effect to the guest statute of the foreign jurisdiction in which the accident occurred, it is not amiss to point out that the question here posed was neither raised nor considered in those cases and that the question has never been presented in so stark a manner as in the case before us with a statute so unique as Ontario's.[1] Be that as it may, however, reconsideration of the inflexible traditional rule persuades us, as already indicated, that, in failing to take into account essential policy considerations and objectives, its application may lead to unjust and anomalous results. This being so, the rule, formulated as it was by the courts, should be discarded.

In conclusion, then, there is no reason why all issues arising out of a tort claim must be resolved by reference to the law of the same jurisdiction. Where the issue involves standards of conduct, it is more than likely that it is the law of the place of the tort which will be controlling but the disposition of other issues must turn, as does the issue of the standard of conduct itself, on the law of the jurisdiction which has the strongest interest in the resolution of the particular issue presented.

[1] We note that the Supreme Court of Canada has upheld the refusal of the Quebec courts to apply the Ontario guest statute to an accident affecting Quebec residents which occurred in Ontario. (See *McLean* v. *Pettigrew* [1945] 2 D.L.R. 65.) This decision was dictated by the court's resort to the English choice of law rule, whereby the foreign tort is deemed actionable if actionable by the law of the forum and not justifiable by the law of the place of the tort. (See *Phillips* v. *Eyre* (1870) L.R. 6 Q.B. 1.) However that may be, it would seem incongruous for this court to apply Ontario's unique statute in circumstances under which its own sister Provinces would not.

The judgment appealed from should be reversed, with costs, and the motion to dismiss the complaint denied.

DESMOND C.J. and DYE, BURKE and FOSTER JJ. concurred with FULD J.

VAN HOORHIS and SCILEPPI JJ. dissented.

Appeal allowed.

NOTE L: TORTS

BOTH branches of the English conflict rule for tort liability have been subjected to severe criticism. By insisting that the tortious act must be actionable in England as well as not justifiable by the law of the place where it was committed, English law 'manifests an illiberal attitude which does not obtain elsewhere except in China and Japan' (Lorenzen, p. 376). 'One would look far to find a more striking example of "mechanical jurisprudence", blind adherence to a verbal formula without regard to policies or consequences' (Hancock, *Torts in the Conflict of Laws*, p. 89). A plaintiff can sue in England on a foreign contract valid by its proper law although it is not a valid contract by English domestic law (*Re Bonacina* [1912] 2 Ch. 394). Why should it be different in the law of torts? Under modern conditions the law of tort, like the law of contract, serves the purpose of adjusting economic and other interests, i.e. it is an instrument of distributive rather than of retributive justice, and wholly different from the law of crime. The only English authority for the requirement that the act must be actionable in England is *The Halley* (*ante*, p. 295). That case has been followed in Scotland (*M'Elroy* v. *M'Allister* 1949 S.C. 110), Canada (*O'Connor* v. *Wray* [1930] 2 D.L.R. 899) and Australia (*Anderson* v. *Eric Anderson Radio and T.V. Pty. Ltd.* (1965) 114 C.L.R. 20). The requirement may work serious hardship and injustice when there is a fatal accident in Scotland on which action is brought in England, or vice versa, because the plaintiff can often recover no more than trivial damages for funeral expenses, that being the only point at which Scottish and English law coincide; see *M'Elroy* v. *M'Allister, supra*. For criticisms of *The Halley*, see Dicey, pp. 913–14, 920–2; Cheshire, pp. 243–5.

The controversial case of *Machado* v. *Fontes* (*ante*, p. 301), which has been followed in England (*Boys* v. *Chaplin* [1967] 3 W.L.R. 266), Canada (*McLean* v. *Pettigrew* [1945] 2 D.L.R. 65) but not in Scotland (*Naftalin* v. *L.M.S.R.* 1933 S.C. 259; *M'Elroy* v. *M'Allister, supra*), has been criticized by the High Court of Australia (*Koop* v. *Bebb, ante*, p. 305), and by Dicey, pp. 923–6; Cheshire, pp. 246–8; Falconbridge, pp. 815–20; Hancock, *Torts in the Conflict of Laws*, pp. 15–18; Robertson, 4 Mod. L.R. 27 (1940); but defended by Lorenzen (47 L.Q.R. 483); and Gutteridge (6 Camb. L.J. 20). It is clear that in Scots law the act must be actionable by the law of the place where it was done.

In 1949 the present writer suggested that the proper law of the tort, and not the lex loci delicti as such, should govern tort liability in the conflict of laws: 12 M.L.R. 248; cf. 64 Harv. L. Rev. 881 (1951); Dicey, pp. 914–18. There are as many different kinds of torts as there are different kinds of contracts, and as many different kinds of question that can arise in tort cases as there are in contract cases: is it likely that a single mechanical formula will produce satisfactory results when applied to all kinds of torts and all kinds of questions? This of course does not mean (as has sometimes been erroneously suggested) that standards of conduct should be governed by any law other than the lex loci delicti.

The traditional rule for tort liability in the United States is (or until recently was) that the lex loci delicti governs, subject only to the public policy of the forum. This qualification has been narrowly construed, at any rate as between sister states, ever since the celebrated decision of the New York Court of Appeals in *Loucks* v. *Standard Oil Co.* (1918) 120 N.E. 198, where Cardozo J. said: 'We are not so provincial as to say that every solution of a problem is wrong because we deal with it otherwise at home.' However, in recent years American courts, dissatisfied with the results which a mechanical application of the place of tort formula would have produced, have escaped from it by recharacterizing the issue as a matter of contract law, governed by the proper law of the contract (for an early and grotesque example, see *Levy* v. *Daniels U-Drive Auto Renting Co.* (1928) 143 Atl. 163), or of administration of estates, governed by the law of the deceased's domicile (see *Grant* v. *McAuliffe* (1953) 264 P. 2d. 944), or of domestic relations, governed by the law of the spouses' domicile (see *Haumschild* v. *Continental Casualty Co.* (1959) 195 N.W. 2d. 814), or of procedure, governed by the lex fori (see *Kilberg* v. *Northeast Airlines* (1961) 172 N.E. 2d. 526. But these exercises in characterization have their dangers. They may produce acceptable results in the instant case, but they will not do so if the facts are slightly varied.

In the famous case of *Babcock* v. *Jackson* (*ante*, p. 308) the New York Court of Appeals discarded the traditional place of tort rule, 'despite the advantages of certainty, ease of application and predictability which it affords', in favour of a rule giving controlling effect to the law of the country 'which, because of its relationship or contact with the occurrence or the parties, has the greatest concern with the specific issue raised in the litigation' (*ante*, p. 310). This of course is closely akin to the proper law of the tort rule advocated by the present writer. For the court used as an analogy the proper law of the contract theory which it had recently announced as governing liability for breach of contract (*Auten* v. *Auten* (1954) 124 N.E. 2d. 99). The court proceeded to demonstrate that in the case before it there was no real conflict between the laws of Ontario and of New York, because the interest of Ontario in having its law applied was 'at best minimal'. Of course, if the facts had been reversed, that is to say if the host and guest had been domiciled and resident in Ontario, the trip had started there, the car had been insured there, and the accident had happened in New York, there would have been a real conflict between the interest of Ontario in protecting its insurance companies against collusive claims, and the interest of New York in inducing careful driving on its highways by the sanction of money damages. See comments on *Babcock* v. *Jackson* in 63 Col. L. Rev. 1212 (1963). It by no means follows that in such a case the result should be different, because a New York court could well conclude that the interest of New York was greater than the interest of Ontario; and a New York court did reach that result on precisely those facts in *Kell* v. *Henderson* (1966) 270 N.Y.S. 2d. 552.

One very important point which emerges from *Babcock* v. *Jackson* is that a rational choice between two laws cannot be made unless their content is known. The law to be applied is the law of the country with the strongest interest, and the strength of its interest may well depend on the content, purpose, and scope of its law. This of course does not mean that the forum should choose either the law which it thinks is the better law or the law which gives the result it likes best.

In 1967 a committee of the Canadian Conference of Commissioners on Uniformity of Legislation produced a tentative draft of a model statute on tort liability in the conflict of laws, which might well be enacted in England with appropriate modifications. It runs as follows:

1. When deciding the rights and liabilities of the parties to an action in tort the court shall apply the local law of the state which has the most substantial connection with the occurrence and with the parties regardless of whether or not the wrong is of such a character that it would have been actionable if committed in this Province.

2. When determining whether a particular state has a substantial connection with the occurrence and the parties the court shall consider the following important contacts:

   (*a*) the place where the injury occurred;
   (*b*) the place where the conduct occurred;
   (*c*) the domicile and place of business of the parties; and
   (*d*) the place where the relationship, if any, between the parties is centred.

3. When deciding which state, among the states having any contacts within section 2, has the most substantial connection with the occurrence and the parties, the court shall consider chiefly the purpose and policy of each of the rules of local law that is proposed to be applied.

PART IV

LAW OF PROPERTY

Chapter 11

IMMOVABLES

Section A: **DISTINCTION BETWEEN MOVABLES AND IMMOVABLES**

The primary division of property according to the English conflict of laws is into movables and immovables, not into realty and personalty. Leaseholds in England are interests in immovables.

FREKE *v*. CARBERY (1873) L.R. 16 Eq. 461 (Court of Chancery)

THE testator was a domiciled Irishman who died in 1845. He was entitled to stocks and funds in England and to a leasehold house in Belgrave Square, London. By his will he gave his personal property to trustees on trusts for accumulation extending beyond any of the periods allowed by the Accumulations Act 1800, which did not apply to Ireland. The validity of the trusts for accumulation was not disputed so far as these related to the testator's stocks and funds; but the question was raised whether these trusts were valid as to the proceeds of sale of the house in Belgrave Square.

LORD SELBORNE L.C.: The only remaining question which has been argued is as to the leasehold estate. Now I confess that is a point upon which I need no authority. The territory and soil of England, by the law of nature and of nations, which is recognized also as part of the law of England, is governed by all statutes which are in force in England. The leasehold property in Belgrave Square is part of the territory and soil of England, and the fact that the testator had a chattel interest in it, and not a freehold interest, makes it in no way whatever less so. An Act of Parliament, limiting the period for which accumulations are permitted, has as much force in

Belgrave Square, as it has in any other part of England: and, for that purpose, it appears to me to be totally immaterial what is the quantity of interest dealt with by the will. All the general doctrines and maxims which are to be found in any of the books of authority really go the same way. The passage which Mr. Fry quoted from Story, in which the words of Lord Loughborough[1] were cited with approbation, is simply a translation into the phraseology of the English law of the maxim of the general law, mobilia sequuntur personam, and is certainly not meant to apply arbitrarily in a new sense, because Lord Loughborough used the word 'personal' instead of 'movable'. The doctrine depends upon a principle which is expressed in the Latin words; and that is the only principle of the whole of our law as to domicile when applicable to the succession of what we call personal estate. It is so, not by any special law of England, but by the deference which, for the sake of international comity, the law of England pays to the law of the civilised world generally. Domicile is allowed in this country to have the same influence as in other countries in determining the succession of movable estate; but the maxim of the law of the civilised world is mobilia sequuntur personam, and is founded on the nature of things. When 'mobilia' are in places other than that of the person to whom they belong their accidental situs is disregarded, and they are held to go with the person. But land, whether held for a chattel interest or held for a freehold interest, is in nature, as a matter of fact, immovable and not movable. The doctrine is inapplicable to it. . . .

I hold, therefore, that as to the proceeds of the house in Belgrave Square, they must necessarily follow the law applicable to the house itself, and are in no degree brought under a different law by the direction in the will; and that as to the house and the proceeds of the house the Thellusson Act does apply.

The lex situs determines whether an interest in a thing is an interest in a movable or in an immovable.
Mortgages on freehold land are interests in immovables.

In re HOYLES [1911] 1 Ch. 179 (Court of Appeal)

A testator who died in February 1888, domiciled in England, gave one-third of his real and personal property after the death of his

---

[1] In *Sill* v. *Worswick* (1791) 1 H. Bl. 665, 690.

wife to charity. His property included $16,340 invested on legal mortgages of freehold land in the city of Toronto, in the province of Ontario, Canada. A summons was taken out to determine whether the charitable gift was void to any and what extent under the Mortmain Act 1736, which was in force at the date of the testator's death. It was proved that the Mortmain Act 1736 was in force in Ontario and that by the law of that province mortgages were impure personalty, and that bequests thereof to charity by persons domiciled in Ontario were void.

Swinfen Eady J. held that the bequest of mortgages to charity was void.

FARWELL L.J.: I am of opinion that Swinfen Eady J.'s judgment is quite right.

At the date of the death of the testator the laws of England and of Ontario were the same, and the Statute of Mortmain of George II applied in Ontario as it then did in England. If a testator domiciled in England had devised to a charity a mortgage of real estate in England, it would have been void under the statute, and if a testator domiciled in Ontario had devised to a charity a mortgage of real estate in Ontario, that devise also would have been void under the statute. But it is argued that if a testator domiciled in England devises to a charity a mortgage on land in Ontario, or a testator domiciled in Ontario devises to a charity a mortgage on land in England, the statute has no application in either case. It is sought to establish this amazing proposition by an argument founded on the division of property in certain cases into movable and immovable. But this division is no part of the law either of England or of Ontario; in both England and Ontario the division is into real and personal property. The division into movable and immovable is only called into operation here when the English courts have to determine rights between domiciled Englishmen and persons domiciled in countries which do not adopt our division into real and personal property. In such cases, out of international comity and in order to arrive at a common basis on which to determine questions between the inhabitants of two countries living under different systems of jurisprudence, our courts recognise and act on a division otherwise unknown to our law into movable and immovable. But when there is no such difficulty there is no ground for attempting any such division. In this case the law is the same in both countries; the mortgaged property savours of the realty in both countries; the Statute of Mortmain applies in both countries; and any argument founded on what would be the case if the law of Ontario required us to consider movables and immovables is merely hypothetical and has no application to the present case. There is no necessity for ascertaining which law is applicable because the law in both countries is the same.

But even if this were not so, and the case were that put by Mr. Sargant of a domiciled Frenchman, I should come to the same conclusion. International law is a matter of international comity. No country can be expected to allow questions affecting its own land, or the extent and nature of the interests in its own land which should be regarded as immovable, to be determined otherwise than by its own courts in accordance with its own interests.

. . . It is true that a mortgage is as between mortgagor and mortgagee regarded as personal estate for many purposes; but the fact that it is so for certain purposes in questions between our fellow subjects here has no bearing on the question whether such a mortgage should be regarded as movable or not in questions of international law. The mortgage undoubtedly affects the land directly; the mortgagee can enter and take possession at any time after his estate has become absolute at law; he can by foreclosure acquire the full title to the land in fee, and the legislature has forbidden any devises of land for any estate or interest whatsoever in any way charged or incumbered by any person or persons whatsoever in trust or for the benefit of any charitable use whatsoever and has made them void: Mortmain Act 1736, ss. 1 and 2. And the reason is stated in the preamble: 'Whereas gifts or alienations of lands, tenements or hereditaments, in mortmain, are prohibited or restrained by Magna Charta, and divers other wholesome laws, as prejudicial to and against the common utility; nevertheless this public mischief has of late greatly increased by many large and improvident alienations or dispositions made by languishing or dying persons, or by other persons, to uses called charitable uses, to take place after their deaths, to the disherison of their lawful heirs.' It is for this court to determine whether mortgages on land are movables or immovables, and in order to come to a conclusion we are bound to consider the result of our decision on the general welfare of this country as shown by our laws, and if a decision in one way will involve results which our law considers prejudicial to the public interest, or immoral, or the like, it is our duty to decide the other way. Mr. Sargant invites

IMMOVABLES

us to leave the Mortmain Act out of sight and decide as a preliminary abstract question whether mortgages on land are movable or immovable. But we should fail in our duty if we did not consider that Act and the effect of our decision upon devises within it. We must have regard to the fact that such gifts have been regarded as prejudicial to and against the public utility and a public mischief, and we must accordingly come to such conclusion as will avoid these evils.

Cozens-Hardy M.R. delivered judgment to the same effect.

Fletcher Moulton L.J. doubted but did not dissent.

Appeal dismissed.

An interest in the proceeds of sale of English freeholds which are subject to a trust for sale but not yet sold is an interest in an immovable.

In re Berchtold [1923] 1 Ch. 192 (Chancery Division)

Originating Summons.

On 2 April 1906 Count Richard Berchtold died, being a person of Hungarian nationality and domicile. He left a will in English form dealing with his estate in England. By that will he devised all his freehold estate in Birmingham to English trustees upon trust for sale and conversion with power to postpone such sale and conversion for so long as they should think fit. The proceeds of sale and the investments for the time being representing the same and the rents and profits of such part of the estate as should for the time being remain unsold were directed to be held in trust for his son Count Nicholas subject to the payment of an annual sum to the testator's wife during her life. Count Richard left him surviving his wife (who died in 1913), his only son Count Nicholas, and an only daughter, the defendant Countess Szokolyi.

Count Nicholas died intestate on 9 July 1911. He was of Hungarian nationality and domicile. He left him surviving his widow the plaintiff and one child only, Count Antoine, who was killed in action on 23 October 1915, under the age of 21 years. He was of Hungarian nationality and domicile. He died intestate leaving his mother, the plaintiff, his sole next of kin. The estate of Count Nicholas in this country consisted of his beneficial interest in the Birmingham freeholds under the will of Count Richard. No part of the Birmingham freeholds had been sold before the date of the summons.

In re
Hoyles.
—
Farwell
L.J.

In re
Berchtold.

The summons asked 'Whether the persons or person beneficially entitled to the proceeds of sale of the said real estate (if sold) and to the rents and profits thereof (until sale) are the persons or person who would be entitled according to English law or the persons or person who would be entitled according to the law of Hungary.'

RUSSELL J.: It is conceded that when a conflict of laws arises on the death of an intestate, the devolution of his immovables is governed by the lex situs; the devolution of his movables is governed by the lex domicilii. It is further conceded that whether particular property is a movable or an immovable is decided according to the lex situs.

The questions which arise in the present case, arise in regard to (1) the interest owned by Count Nicholas at his death in respect of the Birmingham freeholds which were subject to a trust for sale, and the other provisions contained in Count Richard's will; and (2) the interest owned by Count Antoine at his death in respect of the same freeholds. If these respective interests are immovable property according to the lex situs (i.e., the law of England) the law applicable to their devolution will be the law of England, and being, according to English law, personal estate, they will devolve upon the persons entitled by English law to the intestate's personal estate. The result of this solution would be that the plaintiff would take one-third on the intestacy of Count Nicholas as his widow, and the remaining two-thirds on the intestacy of Count Antoine as his mother and sole next of kin. On the other hand, if these respective interests are movable property according to the lex situs, the law applicable to their devolution will be the lex domicilii or law of Hungary. The result of this solution would be that, subject to a usufruct in favour of the plaintiff as the widow of Count Nicholas (as to the extent of which usufruct there is a question) the whole devolves upon and belongs to the Countess Szokolyi as the only sister of Count Nicholas, Count Antoine having died intestate and without leaving him surviving any issue, or any brother and sister, or any issue of a deceased brother or sister, or a father, or any brother of his deceased father. It will thus be seen that the primary question for decision can thus be framed. Were the interests taken by Count Nicholas and Count Antoine under or by virtue of the will of Count Richard, so far as regards the Birmingham freeholds thereby devised upon trust for sale, immovable property or movable property according to English law? The distinction between real estate and personal estate under English law has nothing to do with the question. The alternatives and the only alternatives for consideration are immovable property or movable property. It is said that there is no decision of the English courts directly upon the point. There is a decision on the exact point in the Irish courts, which though entitled to the highest respect, is not binding on me. I will first consider the matter apart from that decision.

Different classes of property have come under the consideration of the courts of this country and have been held to be immovables. Leaseholds are immovables: *Freke* v. *Lord Carbery*[1] and *Duncan* v. *Lawson*.[2] A testatrix's share of a rent-charge issuing out of lands during the lives of herself and two others and the life of the longest liver was held to be an estate pur autre vie applicable by law as personal estate and chargeable with duty as personal estate under the Legacy Duty Act 1796; and was held not to be exempt from duty by reason of the foreign domicile of the testatrix because the property was as much land as if land to the annual value of the rent-charge had been given, and was accordingly immovable property: *Chatfield* v. *Berchtoldt*.[3] Scotch heritable bonds are immovables: *In re Fitzgerald*.[4] A mortgage debt secured by land is immovable property: *In re Hoyles*.[5] Numerous authorities were cited for the purpose of showing that an interest in the proceeds of sale of real estate subject to a trust for sale was under different statutes treated as an interest in land. I will refer to a few. (After referring to *Briggs* v. *Chamberlain*,[6] *Brook* v. *Badley*,[7] *Bowyer* v. *Woodman*,[8] and *In re Thomas*,[9] his Lordship continued:) These authorities are only decisions that the property in question in each case fell within the wording of the relevant statute, but they certainly show that an interest in property such as I have to consider in the present case is aptly described as being 'an interest in land', or 'a sum of money payable out of land'.

Let me now consider what rights existed in Count Nicholas during his lifetime and at his death in regard to the Birmingham freeholds by virtue of the dispositions contained in the will of Count Richard. Subject to his mother's £500 a year, he was absolutely entitled to the proceeds of sale if and when the sale took place. No sale in fact

---

[1] (1873) L.R. 16 Eq. 461 ; *ante*, p. 317. [2] (1889) 41 Ch. D. 394.
[3] (1872) L.R. 7 Ch. App. 192. [4] [1904] 1 Ch. 573.
[5] [1911] 1 Ch. 179 ; *ante*, p. 318. [6] (1853) 11 Hare 69.
[7] (1868) L.R. 3 Ch. App. 672. [8] (1867) L.R. 3 Eq. 313. [9] (1886) 34 Ch. D. 166.

took place; the property continued to be land, immovable property. Subject to his mother's interest, Count Nicholas was entitled down to his death to the rents and profits of that immovable. . . . Further, subject to the interest of the mother of Count Nicholas, the land was his in equity. As to Count Antoine, his position was the same as regards so much of the benefit taken by Count Nicholas under Count Richard's will as passed to Count Antoine upon the intestacy of Count Nicholas, except that at the time of Count Antoine's death, the £500 a year had ceased to be payable owing to the previous death of Count Nicholas' mother. The rights and interests of Count Nicholas and Count Antoine, under or by virtue of the will of Count Richard in relation to the Birmingham freeholds and the proceeds of sale thereof being such as I have described, are those rights and interests more properly to be classified as immovable property, or as movable property? In my opinion, they should be classified as immovable property equally with the freehold land out of which the money is eventually to be paid. That is the conclusion to which I have come independently of the Irish decision to which I will now refer. (His Lordship referred to *Murray* v. *Champernowne*,[1] and continued:) That decision seems to me to cover the exact point and is in my opinion right. . . .

On behalf of the Countess Szokolyi it was argued that according to English law land directed to be sold and turned into money must be considered to be money; and that on the principle that equity considers done what should be done, the Birmingham freeholds are, in the eye of the law, money. This argument, to be effective, must add the words 'for all purposes'. That the Birmingham freeholds are to be treated as money for some purposes, no one doubts. Thus the interest of the taker is personal estate. But this equitable doctrine of conversion only arises and comes into play where the question for consideration arises as between real estate and personal estate. It has no relation to the question whether property is movable or immovable. The doctrine of conversion is that real estate is treated as personal estate, or personal estate is treated as real estate; not that immovables are turned into movables, or movables into immovables. As Farwell L.J. pointed out in *In re Hoyles*, the fact that a mortgage is regarded as personal estate for certain purposes in questions between our fellow subjects here has no bearing on the question whether such a mortgage

[1] [1901] 2 I.R. 232.

should be regarded as a movable or not in questions of international law. . . .

I answer the second question in the summons by declaring that the persons or person beneficially entitled to the proceeds of sale of the Birmingham freeholds and to the rents and profits thereof until sale are the persons or person who would be entitled thereto according to the law of England.

In re
BERCHTOLD.
—
Russell J.

NOTE M: MOVABLES AND IMMOVABLES

IN English domestic law, the leading distinction between proprietary interests in things is the historical and technical distinction between realty and personalty. In the English conflict of laws, however, the leading distinction between things is the more universal and natural distinction between movables and immovables. This distinction is capable of application to the different systems of law in the world, which the distinction between realty and personalty is not. The suggestion of Farwell L.J. in *Re Hoyles* (*ante*, p. 319) that our courts only adopt the distinction between movables and immovables when the conflict is between English law and the law of some civil law country, and not when the conflict is between English law and another common law country, looks plausible, but is (it is submitted) unsound. At any rate it has not been followed: *Macdonald* v. *Macdonald*, 1932 S.C. 79 (H.L.); *Re Cutcliffe* [1940] Ch. 565.

The importance of the distinction between movables and immovables is most apparent in the field of succession, because succession to movables is (in general) governed by the law of the testator's domicile, while succession to immovables is (in general) governed by the lex situs.

If there is a conflict between the lex situs and the lex fori as to whether a particular thing is movable or immovable, the lex situs is decisive: *Re Hoyles*.

Leasehold interests in land in England (*Freke* v. *Carbery, ante*, p. 317; *Duncan* v. *Lawson* (1889) 41 Ch. D. 394); mortgages on land in England (*Re Hoyles*); and interests in land in England held on trust for sale but not yet sold (*Re Berchtold, ante*, p. 321) are all interests in immovables, though they are personal estate for the purposes of English domestic law. The decision in *Re Hoyles*, that mortgages are interests in immovables, has been followed in Canada (*Re Landry and Steinhoff* [1941] 1 D.L.R. 699; *Re Ritchie* [1942] 3 D.L.R. 330) but not followed in New Zealand (*Re O'Neill* [1922] N.Z.L.R. 468) or Australia (*Re Young* [1942] V.L.R. 4; *Re Williams* [1945] V.L.R. 213; *Haque* v. *Haque* (*No. 2*) (1965) 114 C.L.R. 98).

Section 75 (5) of the Settled Land Act 1925, re-enacting section 22 (5) of the Settled Land Act 1882, provides that capital money arising under the Act while remaining uninvested and unapplied, and securities on which an investment of any such capital money is made, shall for all purposes of disposition, transmission, and devolution be treated as land. Under this section, Morton J. held in *Re Cutcliffe* [1940] Ch. 565 that stock in England which represented the reinvestment of the proceeds of sale of English settled land was immovable. This decision has not escaped criticism, but would appear to be perfectly correct. The gist of the criticism is that 'the doctrine of conversion is a characteristic doctrine of domestic English law arising from the distinction between realty and personalty, and whether it is a judge-made rule, as in the *Berchtold* case, or has been expressed in statutory form, as in the *Cutcliffe* case, in either event the doctrine can have no application to a particular situation unless it has first been decided in accordance with the conflict rules of the forum that the proper law is domestic English law, or some other law that distinguishes between realty and personalty and includes the doctrine of conversion' (Falconbridge, p. 589). The answer would appear to be that in the *Berchtold* case the doctrine of conversion said that realty was to be treated as personalty, while in the *Cutcliffe* case the statute said that capital money and securities were to be treated as land. In other words in the *Berchtold* case the doctrine of conversion that had to be considered was formulated in terms appropriate only to domestic English law, while in the *Cutcliffe* case the statute that had to be considered was expressed in terms appropriate also to the conflict of laws. The stock was in England; English law (lex situs) therefore had to decide whether it was movable or immovable; and English law said it was immovable. How could the decision have been otherwise?

Section B: JURISDICTION

English courts have no jurisdiction to adjudicate upon the right of property in or the right of possession to foreign immovables, or to give damages for trespass thereto, unless the case falls within one of the three exceptions mentioned below.

BRITISH SOUTH AFRICA COMPANY *v.* COMPANHIA DE MOÇAMBIQUE
[1893] A.C. 602 (House of Lords)

British South Africa Company v. Companhia de Moçambique.

By their statement of claim the plaintiffs, a Portuguese company, alleged that they were in possession of large tracts of land and mines and mining rights in South Africa; and that the defendant company by its agents wrongfully broke and entered and took possession of the said lands, mines, and mining rights, and ejected the plaintiff company, its servants, agents, and tenants therefrom. The plaintiffs claimed (1) a declaration that the plaintiff company were lawfully in possession and occupation of the lands, mines, and mining rights; (2) an injunction restraining the defendant company from continuing to occupy or from asserting any title to the said lands, mines, and mining rights; (3) £250,000 damages for trespass.

The defence alleged that the lands in question were in South Africa, out of the jurisdiction of the High Court, and that the statement of claim disclosed no cause of action.

By an order of Collins J. in chambers the questions of law raised by the pleadings were set down for hearing before a Divisional Court.

The Divisional Court (Lawrance and Wright JJ.) made an order that judgment be entered for the defendants dismissing the action for want of jurisdiction.

In the Court of Appeal the plaintiffs formally abandoned their claim for a declaration of title and an injunction, and that court by a majority (Fry and Lopes L.JJ.; Lord Esher M.R. dissenting) declared that the High Court had jurisdiction to entertain the claim for damages for trespass. In the course of his judgment Fry L.J. said:[1] 'In a case like the present, where, according to the allegations of the plaintiffs, there are no courts of adequate jurisdiction in the locus rei sitae, it is obvious that to repel the jurisdiction is to produce a total failure of justice. If neither Africa nor England afford a forum the plaintiff is remediless.

'. . . Suppose that in a foreign country A enters upon a close, of which B claims to be in possession, and each assaults the other, and both A and B come to this country. A could sue B here for the personal injury, although B's defence might be the possession of the close; it would be strange if B could not also sue A for entry on the close. Or, again, suppose in a foreign land A enters upon the house of B, and injures the house, the furniture, and the person of B, and both A and B come hither. It would be strange if B could sue A for the injuries to his furniture and his person, but not to his house.'

The defendants appealed to the House of Lords.

LORD HERSCHELL: My Lords, the principal question raised by this appeal is whether the Supreme Court of Judicature has jurisdiction to try an action to recover damages for a trespass to lands situate in a foreign country.

It is not in controversy that prior to the Judicature Acts no such jurisdiction could have been exercised; but it is asserted on behalf of the respondents that the only barrier to its exercise was the technical one, that the venue in such a case must be local, and that the rules made under the Judicature Acts which have abolished local venues have removed the sole impediment which prevented the courts entertaining and adjudicating on cases of this description.

The nature of the controversy between the parties renders it necessary to consider the origin of the distinction between local and transitory actions, and the development of the law which determined the venue or place of trial of issues of fact.

BRITISH
SOUTH
AFRICA
COMPANY
v.
COMPANHIA
DE
MOÇAM-
BIQUE.

[1] [1892] 2 Q.B. 413–14.

BRITISH
SOUTH
AFRICA
COMPANY
v.
COMPANHIA
DE
MOÇAM-
BIQUE.

Lord
Herschell.

It was necessary originally to state truly the venue—that is, the place in which it arose—of every fact in issue, whether those on which the plaintiff relied, or any matter stated by way of defence; and if the places were different, each issue would be tried by a jury summoned from the place in which the facts in dispute were stated to have arisen. After the statute 17 Car. 2, c. 8, which provided that 'after verdict judgment should not be stayed or reversed for that there was no right venue, so as the cause were tried by a jury of the proper county or place where the action was laid', the practice arose, which ultimately became regular and uniform, of trying all the issues by a jury of the venue laid in the action, even though some of the facts were laid elsewhere. When juries ceased to be drawn from the particular town, parish, or hamlet where the fact took place, that is, from amongst those who were supposed to be cognisant of the circumstances, and came to be drawn from the body of the county generally, and to be bound to determine the issues judicially after hearing witnesses, the law began to discriminate between cases in which the truth of the venue was material and those in which it was not so. This gave rise to the distinction between transitory and local actions, that is, between those in which the facts relied on as the foundation of the plaintiff's case have no necessary connection with a particular locality and those in which there is such a connection. In the latter class of actions the plaintiff was bound to lay the venue truly; in the former he might lay it in any county he pleased. It was, however, still necessary to lay every local fact with its true venue on peril of a variance if it should be brought in issue. Where a local matter occurred out of the realm, a difficulty arose, inasmuch as it was supposed that the issue could not be tried, as no jury could be summoned from the place, and it was by the general rule essential that a jury should be summoned from the venue laid to the fact in issue. It was, however, early decided that, notwithstanding the general rule, such matters might be tried by a jury from the venue in the action, and thus the difficulty was removed and the form was introduced of adding after the statement of the foreign place the words, 'To wit at Westminster in the county of Middlesex', or whatever else might happen to be the venue in the action. . . .

It is, I think, important to observe that the distinction between local and transitory actions depended on the nature of the matters involved and not on the place at which the trial had to take place. It was not called a local action because the venue was local, or a transi-

tory action because the venue might be laid in any county, but the
venue was local or transitory according as the action was local or
transitory. It will be seen that this distinction is material when the
Judicature Rule upon which so much turns comes to be examined.

My Lords, I cannot but lay great stress upon the fact that whilst
lawyers made an exception from the ordinary rule in the case of
a local[1] matter occurring outside the realm for which there was no
proper place of trial in this country, and invented a fiction which
enabled the courts to exercise jurisdiction, they did not make an
exception where the cause of action was a local matter arising
abroad, and did not extend the fiction to such cases. The rule that in
local actions the venue must be local did not, where the cause of
action arose in this country, touch the jurisdiction in the courts, but
only determined the particular manner in which the jurisdiction
should be exercised; but where the matter complained of was local
and arose outside the realm, the refusal to adjudicate upon it was in
fact a refusal to exercise jurisdiction, and I cannot think that the
courts would have failed to find a remedy if they had regarded the
matter as one within their jurisdiction, and which it was proper for
them to adjudicate upon.

The earliest authority of importance is *Skinner* v. *East India Company*.[2] The House of Lords in that case referred it to the judges to
report whether relief could be obtained in respect of the matters
mentioned in the petition, either at law or in equity, and if so in
what manner. The judges answered, 'that the matters touching the
taking away of the petitioner's ship and goods and assaulting of his
person, notwithstanding the same were done beyond the seas, might
be determined upon by His Majesty's ordinary Courts at Westminster. And as to the dispossessing him of his house and island,
that he was not relievable in any ordinary Court of Law.'

Notwithstanding the opinion thus expressed, Lord Mansfield
entertained and acted on the view that where damages only were
sought in respect of a trespass committed abroad, an action might
be maintained in this country, although it was one which would here
be a local action (see *Mostyn* v. *Fabrigas*[3]). . . .

The view acted on by Lord Mansfield in the two cases referred to
has not been followed. It came before the Court of Queen's Bench
for consideration in *Doulson* v. *Matthews*,[4] which was an action of

BRITISH
SOUTH
AFRICA
COMPANY
v.
COMPANHIA
DE
MOÇAM-
BIQUE.

Lord
Herschell.

---

[1] *Sic* in the report; evidently 'transitory' was meant (*Ed.*).
[2] (1665) 6 St. Tr. 710, 719.   [3] (1774) 1 Cowp. 161, 180.   [4] (1792) 4 T.R. 503.

BRITISH
SOUTH
AFRICA
COMPANY
v.
COMPANHIA
DE
MOÇAM-
BIQUE.
—
Lord
Herschell.

trespass for entering the plaintiff's house in Canada and expelling him therefrom. The decisions of Lord Mansfield were relied on by the plaintiff, but the action was held not to lie. Buller J. in delivering judgment said: 'It is now too late for us to inquire whether it were wise or politic to make a distinction between transitory and local actions: it is sufficient for the courts that the law has settled the distinction, and that an action quare clausum fregit is local. We may try actions here which are in their nature transitory, though arising out of a transaction abroad; but not such as are in their nature local.'

In saying that we may not try actions here arising out of transactions abroad which are in their nature local, I do not think that the learned judge was referring to the mere technical difficulty of there being no venue in this country in which these transactions could be laid, but to the fact that our courts did not exercise jurisdiction in matters arising abroad 'which were in their nature local'. The case of *Doulson* v. *Matthews* has ever since been regarded as law, and I do not think it has been considered as founded merely on the technical difficulty that in this country a local venue was requisite in a local action. . . .

The question what jurisdiction can be exercised by the courts of any country according to its municipal law cannot, I think, be conclusively determined by a reference to principles of international law. No nation can execute its judgments, whether against persons or movables or real property, in the country of another. On the other hand, if the courts of a country were to claim, as against a person resident there, jurisdiction to adjudicate upon the title to land in a foreign country, and to enforce its adjudication in personam, it is by no means certain that any rule of international law would be violated. But in considering what jurisdiction our courts possess, and have claimed to exercise in relation to matters arising out of the country, the principles which have found general acceptance amongst civilised nations as defining the limits of jurisdiction are of great weight.

It was admitted in the present case, on behalf of the respondents, that the court could not make a declaration of title, or grant an injunction to restrain trespasses, the respondents having in relation to these matters abandoned their appeal in the court below. But it is said that the court may inquire into the title, and, if the plaintiffs and not the defendants are found to have the better title, may award damages for the trespass committed. My Lords, I find it difficult to

BRITISH
SOUTH
AFRICA
COMPANY
v.
COMPANHIA
DE
MOÇAM-
BIQUE.

Lord
Herschell.

see why this distinction should be drawn. It is said, because the courts have no power to enforce their judgment by any dealing with the land itself, where it is outside their territorial jurisdiction. But if they can determine the title to it and compel the payment of damages founded upon such determination, why should not they equally proceed in personam against a person who, in spite of that determination, insists on disturbing one who has been found by the court to be the owner of the property?

It is argued that if an action of trespass cannot be maintained in this country where the land is situate abroad a wrong-doer by coming to this country might leave the person wronged without any remedy. It might be a sufficient answer to this argument to say that this is a state of things which has undoubtedly existed for centuries without any evidence of serious mischief or any intervention of the legislature; for even if the Judicature Rules have the effect contended for, I do not think it can be denied that this was a result neither foreseen nor intended. But there appear to me, I confess, to be solid reasons why the courts of this country should, in common with those of most other nations, have refused to adjudicate upon claims of title to foreign land in proceedings founded on an alleged invasion of the proprietary rights attached to it, and to award damages founded on that adjudication.

The inconveniences which might arise from such a course are obvious, and it is by no means clear to my mind that if the courts were to exercise jurisdiction in such cases the ends of justice would in the long run, and looking at the matter broadly, be promoted. Supposing a foreigner to sue in this country for trespass to his lands situate abroad, and for taking possession of and expelling him from them, what is to be the measure of damages? There being no legal process here by which he could obtain possession of the lands, the plaintiff might, I suppose, in certain circumstances, obtain damages equal in amount to their value. But what would there be to prevent his leaving this country after obtaining these damages and repossessing himself of the lands? What remedy would the defendant have in such a case where the lands are in an unsettled country, with no laws or regular system of government, but where, to use a familiar expression, the only right is might? Such an occurrence is not an impossible or even an improbable hypothesis. It is quite true that in the exercise of the undoubted jurisdiction of the courts it may become necessary incidentally to investigate and determine the title

BRITISH
SOUTH
AFRICA
COMPANY
v.
COMPANHIA
DE
MOÇAM-
BIQUE.

Lord
Herschell.

to foreign lands; but it does not seem to me to follow that because such a question may incidentally arise and fall to be adjudicated upon, the courts possess, or that it is expedient that they should exercise, jurisdiction to try an action founded on a disputed claim of title to foreign lands.

Reliance was placed on the decisions of Courts of Equity, as showing that our courts were ready, when no technical difficulty of venue stood in the way, to adjudicate on the title to lands situate abroad. If the refusal of the Common Law Courts to exercise jurisdiction in cases of the nature now under consideration had been regarded as the result of a mere technical difficulty, I cannot help thinking that the Courts of Equity, which were, in early days, at all events, keen to supplement the deficiencies of the Common Law, when the requirements of justice were impeded by technical difficulties, would have found some means of affording a remedy. Lord Mansfield, in his judgment in *Mostyn* v. *Fabrigas*, refers to a case of an injury in the East Indies similar to that with which he had to deal in the case of Captain Gambier, in which Lord Hardwicke in a Court of Equity had directed satisfaction to be made in damages. But in this exercise of jurisdiction he has not been followed by any judge of the Court of Chancery.

Whilst Courts of Equity have never claimed to act directly upon land situate abroad, they have purported to act upon the conscience of persons living here. (His Lordship referred to *Lord Cranstown* v. *Johnston*,[1] and continued:) My Lords, the decisions of the Courts of Equity do not, to my mind, afford any substantial support to the view that the ground upon which the Courts of Common Law abstained from exercising jurisdiction in relation to trespasses to real property abroad was only the technical difficulty of venue. . . .

The terms of rule 1 of Order 36, which are relied on by the plaintiffs, are as follows: 'There shall be no local venue for the trial of any action except where otherwise provided by statute.' The language used appears to me important. The rule does not purport to touch the distinction between local and transitory actions—between matters which have no necessary local connection, and those which are local in their nature. It deals only with the place of trial, and enables actions, whatever their nature, to be tried in any county. But it is, in my opinion, a mere rule of procedure, and applies only to those cases in which the courts at that time exercised jurisdiction.

[1] (1796) 3 Ves. 170.

It has been more than once held that the rules under the Judicature Acts are rules of procedure only, and were not intended to affect, and did not affect, the rights of parties. . . .

According to the contention of the respondents in this case the rule under consideration had the effect of conferring upon them a right of action in this country which they would not otherwise have possessed. As I have already pointed out, a person whose lands, situate in this country, were trespassed upon always had a right of action in respect of the trespass. The rules relating to venue did no more than regulate the manner in which the right was to be enforced. But in respect of a trespass to land situate abroad there was no right of action, for an alleged right which the courts would neither recognise nor enforce did not constitute any right at all in point of law.

My Lords, I have come to the conclusion that the grounds upon which the courts have hitherto refused to exercise jurisdiction in actions of trespass to lands situate abroad were substantial and not technical, and that the rule of procedure under the Judicature Acts have not conferred a jurisdiction which did not exist before. If this conclusion be well founded, I do not think that the allegation contained in paragraph 16 of the statement of claim, 'that the defendant company did and committed the acts above mentioned and complained of with intent to injure and destroy the trade of the plaintiff company, and to deprive it of its aforesaid lands, territories, mines, minerals and mining rights and property', disclosed a cause of action cognisable by our courts any more than the paragraph complaining of trespass. . . .

LORD HALSBURY delivered judgment to the same effect.

LORDS MACNAGHTEN and MORRIS concurred.

Appeal allowed: judgment of Divisional Court restored.

BRITISH SOUTH AFRICA COMPANY v. COMPANHIA DE MOÇAMBIQUE.
— Lord Herschell.

Exception 1: English courts have jurisdiction to adjudicate upon rights in foreign immovables, if the defendant is affected by some personal obligation arising out of contract or implied contract, fiduciary relationship or fraud, or other conduct which in the view of a Court of Equity would be unconscionable.

DESCHAMPS *v.* MILLER [1908] 1 Ch. 856 (Chancery Division)

On 6 October 1831 a contract of marriage in French form was made in France in consideration of the then contemplated marriage of Jean Deschamps and Marie Taris, who were both then domiciled and residing in France. The agreement provided that the marriage should be governed by the régime dotal with community of acquired property under the French law. The plaintiff, Thomas Deschamps, the son of the marriage, alleged that by the law of France his mother, Marie Taris, became entitled, by virtue of the contract and marriage, to one-half of the after-acquired property of Jean Deschamps (with some unimportant exceptions), and also to a life interest, on his death, in the other half of the property.

About the year 1836 Jean Deschamps went to India, and there, in 1839, in the lifetime of his wife, Marie Deschamps, he went through a form of marriage in Madras with Cecilia Taylor.

By an indenture date 14 February 1865, Jean Deschamps, in consideration of his natural love and affection for his so-called 'wife Cecilia Deschamps' and of a share in her father's estate which he had received, conveyed and assigned his business premises at Madras to a trustee, upon trust for Jean Deschamps for his life without impeachment of waste, and after his death upon trust to sell the same, and to hold the net proceeds of sale on trusts for the benefit of Cecilia Taylor and her children, if any, by Jean Deschamps, and in default of children for certain relations of Cecilia Taylor.

By deeds executed by him in 1866 and 1869 Jean Deschamps conveyed other real estate at Madras to be held upon the trusts of the settlement of 1865.

According to the plaintiff, all these properties were after-acquired property of Jean Deschamps settled without the knowledge of Marie Deschamps, and in breach of trust, and with intent to defraud her and deprive her of her rights in the property subject to the marriage contract of 1831; there was no good or valuable consideration for

334

the settlement; by French law the husband could dispose of after-acquired property during the coverture, but only for 'good consideration', which meant full consideration in money or money's worth.

Jean Deschamps died on 14 December 1885, and his wife died intestate in France on 14 March 1890, and the plaintiff claimed that by the law of France he was entitled to all her rights under the marriage contract of 1831.

The defendants took the preliminary objection that the court had no jurisdiction.

PARKER J.: ... It is said that the action relates to the title and possession of real estate out of the jurisdiction of the court, and therefore that it ought not to be entertained by the court, even though all parties to the action are resident within the jurisdiction. ...

The question is whether under these circumstances the court ought to entertain jurisdiction. In my opinion the general rule is that the court will not adjudicate on questions relating to the title to or the right to the possession of immovable property out of the jurisdiction. There are, no doubt, exceptions to the rule, but, without attempting to give an exhaustive statement of those exceptions, I think it will be found that they all depend on the existence between the parties to the suit of some personal obligation arising out of contract or implied contract, fiduciary relationship or fraud, or other conduct which, in the view of a Court of Equity in this country, would be unconscionable, and do not depend for their existence on the law of the locus of the immovable property. Thus, in cases of trusts, specific performance of contracts, foreclosure, or redemption of mortgages, or in the case of land obtained by the defendant by fraud, or other such unconscionable conduct as I have referred to, the court may very well assume jurisdiction. But where there is no contract, no fiduciary relationship, and no fraud or other unconscionable conduct giving rise to a personal obligation between the parties, and the whole question is whether or not according to the law of the locus the claim of title set up by one party, whether a legal or equitable claim in the sense of those words as used in English law, would be preferred to the claim of another party, I do not think the court ought to entertain jurisdiction to decide the matter.

In the present case there is, in my opinion, no such personal obligation as above mentioned, and I do not think I could assume jurisdiction in this case without acting contrary to the decision in

Norris v. *Chambres*.[1] In that case there was a contract for sale of immovables abroad, and a deposit was paid. The vendor refused to complete, and the purchaser claimed a lien for the deposit on the property agreed to be sold; but he claimed that lien, not as against the vendor with whom he had contracted, but against a third party who had purchased subsequently with notice of the prior contract and of the claim to the lien for the deposit. There was no personal obligation based on contract, fiduciary relationship, fraud, or other unconscionable conduct between the parties, and the right, if there was a right, to succeed in the action depended, therefore, solely on whether the law of the locus of the immovable property would recognize any lien as arising out of the contract for sale coupled with the payment of a deposit, and, if so, what was the position, with regard to such lien, of a purchaser with notice. The court refused to entertain the action. In a similar way here, the question depends on whether the Indian law will recognize the French contract as having created an interest in the wife, and, if so, what is the position with regard to such interest of the defendants, who in their pleadings claim to have purchased for value without notice. There is no obligation on the part of the defendants to the plaintiff based on any contract, fiduciary relationship, fraud, or other unconscionable conduct. Such obligation, if any, as exists depends, in my opinion, on the Indian law relating to immovables, and on that alone. It was suggested that the defendants have since action, or shortly before action, sold some of the property in dispute, and that this at any rate gives the court jurisdiction. I do not think, however, that I could so decide without acting contrary to the decision of Kay J. in *In re Hawthorne*.[2] In my opinion, therefore, the preliminary objection which I have been discussing succeeds.

Exception 2: Where an English court has jurisdiction to administer an estate or a trust, and the property includes movables or immovables situated in England and immovables situated abroad, the court has jurisdiction to determine questions of title to the foreign immovables for the purposes of the administration.

In re HOYLES [1911] 1 Ch. 179 (*ante*, p. 318)

In re ROSS [1930] 1 Ch. 377 (*ante*, p. 10)

---

[1] (1861) 29 Beav. 246 ; affd. 3 D.F. & J. 583.   [2] (1883) 23 Ch. D. 743.

IMMOVABLES

Exception 3: English courts have jurisdiction to entertain an action in rem against a ship to enforce a maritime lien on the ship for damage done to foreign immovables.

THE TOLTEN [1946] P. 135 (Court of Appeal)

By their statement of claim the plaintiffs alleged that they were the owners and occupiers of a wharf at Lagos, Nigeria, and that damage was caused thereto by the negligent navigation of the defendant ship. They brought an action in rem against the ship seeking to enforce a maritime lien on the ship for the damage caused. The defendants objected that the court had no jurisdiction to adjudicate in an action in rem for damage done by a ship to foreign land.

Bucknill J. decided in favour of the plaintiffs on the ground that the Judicature Act 1925, s. 22 (1) (*a*) (re-enacting the Admiralty Court Act 1861), provided that the High Court should have jurisdiction over 'any claim for damage done by a ship'.

The defendants appealed.

SOMERVELL L.J.: Mr. Devlin for the defendants submitted that the *Moçambique* case[1] laid down a general principle as summarized in the first sentence of the headnote:—'The Supreme Court of Judicature has no jurisdiction to entertain an action to recover damages for a trespass to land situate abroad'; and that the general words of the Judicature Act must be read subject to this rule, as they must be read subject to the rule against impleading a foreign sovereign, as applied to the arrest of a State ship in *The Parlement Belge.*[2] I think there is force in this last point, and feel unable to give as much weight to the part of the argument based on the general words of the Judicature Act as was given, I think, by the learned trial judge, with whose conclusion I agree.

Mr. Bateson for the plaintiffs submitted in the first place that the rule in the *Moçambique* case ought to be confined to cases in which the issue raised by the claim involved, as in that case, a conflict as to title between plaintiff and defendant. He submitted that the rule was in the main based on the ineffectiveness of orders of the courts of one country purporting to decide questions of title regarding foreign land. He submitted that in actions such as this, where the trespass complained of is clearly not based on the assertion of a title adverse

---

[1] [1893] A.C. 602; *ante*, p. 326.   [2] (1880) 5 P.D. 197.

to the plaintiff, neither the principle of ineffectiveness nor any principle of international comity, also referred to in the *Moçambique* case, apply.

In my opinion, the House of Lords laid down the rule generally so far as common law actions in personam are concerned. Lord Herschell refers to two cases in which Lord Mansfield entertained and acted on the view that where damages only were sought in respect of a trespass committed abroad an action might be maintained in this country. These cases are referred to by Lord Mansfield in *Mostyn* v. *Fabrigas*.[1] Lord Mansfield's decisions were clearly on the basis that no question of title would arise. Lord Herschell says: 'The view acted on by Lord Mansfield in the two cases referred to has not been followed' and he regarded them as overruled by the Court of King's Bench in *Doulson* v. *Matthews*.[2] This may not have been necessary to the decision, as there was a clear conflict of title between the two parties to the *Moçambique* case, but I think that this court should apply the rule as laid down and, in my opinion, this is fatal to Mr. Bateson's first submission.

As the other two points raised by Mr. Bateson to some extent overlap it is convenient to consider them together. The first is that the rule should not be applied to admiralty jurisdiction which has always been wider than the common law jurisdiction, the second that the rule should in any event not apply to claims where there is a maritime lien and that there is a maritime lien in this case. In putting forward these submissions Mr. Bateson, as a basis for his argument, drew attention to the admitted exception to the rule. This exception is based on decisions of the Court of Equity 'showing that our courts were ready, when no technical difficulty of venue stood in the way, to adjudicate on the title to lands situate abroad'. This quotation is from Lord Herschell's speech in the *Moçambique* case (*ante*, p. 332), and it is, to my mind, clear that he accepts the validity of the exception.

In Dicey's Conflict of Laws,[3] the first sentence of the 'Comment' dealing with this Exception to the rule reads as follows: 'The principle on which this exception, originally derived from the practice of the Court of Chancery, rests is that, though the court has no jurisdiction to determine rights over foreign land, yet, where the court has jurisdiction over a person *from his presence in England,* or now

---

[1] (1774) 1 Cowp. 161, 180.   [2] (1792) 4 T.R. 503.
[3] 5th ed. (1931), p. 207.

from the court having jurisdiction to serve him with a writ or notice thereof, though he is out of England, the court has jurisdiction to and will, in a fit case and in the exercise of its discretion, compel him to dispose of or otherwise deal with his interest in foreign land so as to give effect to obligations which he has incurred with regard to the land.'

It is unnecessary to consider the precise limits of the exception. Mr. Devlin submitted that it was not really an exception as the rule applies only to real or mixed actions, and that proceedings in equity at any rate are not within those categories. The importance, to my mind, is that the existence of the exception negatives any suggestion that the courts have recognised a general principle that no decisions will be given which may determine or affect rights in or over foreign land. If there were any such principle it would be an end of this case. The plaintiffs have alleged they are the owners and occupiers of the wharf, and that must be taken to be a relevant fact on which the court would pronounce in giving its decision. It does not, however, follow that, because there is one exception, there should be another. . . .

The ultimate issue in this case is whether a claim in rem in respect of which a maritime lien is exercisable in which the plaintiff claims for damage to foreign land should be treated as barred by the rule in the *Moçambique* case. That rule is said in part to be based on principles of international comity. Speaking broadly, I should have thought that it was in the interests of nations inter se that where damage is done which gives rise to a maritime lien, that lien should be enforceable in the courts of any country to which the ship may proceed. I have assumed, and think I am entitled to assume, that the law of other countries or, at any rate, most other countries is the same as ours on the matter in question here. Does the fact that the plaintiff asserts and, if it is disputed, will have to prove his ownership and occupation of the foreign land which has been damaged, compel one to make an exception to what is as between nations desirable?

In the *Moçambique* case there was a conflict as to title between plaintiff and defendant. Although, as I have stated, I think the rule as laid down by the House of Lords covers cases where there is no such conflict, it is undoubtedly the dispute as to title between plaintiff and defendant which is the origin of the rule. Here we are dealing with a special procedure, namely, the enforcement of maritime liens by proceedings in rem under admiralty jurisdiction. We are dealing

THE
TOLTEN.
—
Somervell
L.J.

with a class of claim in which any issue as to title is very unlikely, and a dispute as to title, in which the defendant owners of the colliding vessel are themselves claiming the title as against the plaintiff, is so improbable that, in my view, its theoretical possibility can be disregarded. I do not think the conflicting dicta in *The Mary Moxham*[1] can be regarded as authority either way. All I wish to say about that case is that if the claim fell under the rule as subsequently laid down in the *Moçambique* case, I doubt whether a mere consent would have entitled the court to entertain the claim. That, however, does not arise here. I do not think that what was said in the *Moçambique* case is to be read as covering or being intended to cover an admiralty claim such as the present. The point therefore being uncovered by authority I think that the nature of a maritime lien and the unlikelihood of any dispute as to title arising, lead to the conclusion that the present claim should be allowed to proceed and that the point taken by the defendants is bad in law. . . .

It is unnecessary in this case to consider whether claims enforceable in rem against a ship but which do not give rise to a maritime lien should, if they concern foreign land in the same way as the claim here, be entertained. It may be that such a claim is difficult to imagine. All I need say is that, by relying as I do on the existence of the maritime lien, I do not intend to imply that the class of claim referred to in this paragraph, if it should arise, would necessarily be outside admiralty jurisdiction.

I think the appeal should be dismissed, with costs.

Scott and Cohen L.JJ. delivered judgments to the same effect.

Appeal dismissed.

Note N: JURISDICTION OVER FOREIGN LAND

Although Lord Herschell in the *Moçambique* case (*ante*, p. 333) says that 'the grounds upon which the courts have hitherto refused to exercise jurisdiction in actions of trespass to lands situate abroad were substantial and not technical', it may be doubted whether he explains convincingly what those grounds were, or whether he rebuts the powerful arguments adduced by Fry L.J. in the court below (*ante*, p. 327).

Three views are tenable as the precise scope of the *Moçambique* rule:

(*a*) English courts have no jurisdiction to adjudicate upon the title to foreign immovables. Scott L.J. in *The Tolten* expressed the view that the House of Lords (but not the Court of Appeal) might hereafter restrict the scope of the *Moçambique* rule to this narrow proposition, and might grant damages for trespass to foreign land. 'I recognise', he said, 'that in a case

[1] (1876) 1 P.D. 43, 107.

where the action is brought by a party in possession of land and structures, suing merely for damages for negligence, or even, it may be, for trespass quare clausum fregit, and the plaintiff relies solely on his possession as the foundation for his action, the House of Lords might hereafter distinguish the *Moçambique* case.' But this observation was obiter and was not concurred in by the other Lords Justices; moreover, Scott L.J. went on to say: 'I do not think, however, that it would be right for this court to attempt that distinction, as I am satisfied that, in regard to common law actions, no such distinction was then in the mind of the House.'

(*b*) English courts have no jurisdiction to adjudicate upon the title to foreign immovables, or to grant damages for trespass thereto. This view seems to be adopted in Cheshire (p. 505).

(*c*) English courts have no jurisdiction to adjudicate upon the title to foreign immovables, or to grant damages for trespass or other torts thereto (e.g. nuisance, negligence or liability under the rule in *Rylands* v. *Fletcher* (1868) L.R. 3 H.L. 330). There is no English case which carries the *Moçambique* rule as far as this, though there are Canadian cases (*Brereton* v. *Canadian Pacific Railway Co.* (1894) 29 O.R. 57; *Albert* v. *Fraser Companies* [1937] 1 D.L.R. 39). It is, however, a legitimate deduction from *The Tolten* that the rule does so extend, for if it did not, it would have been easy to say so, the case being one of negligence.

Unless the scope of the *Moçambique* rule is restricted by the House of Lords in the manner suggested by Scott L.J. above, it is apparent that the rule may produce at worst a total denial of justice and at best some glaring anomalies. 'Suppose', said Scott L.J. in *The Tolten*, 'ship A, by one and the same act of negligent navigation at Lagos, to have caused injury to (1) the plaintiffs' wharf, (2) merchandise on the wharf, (3) people on the wharf, (4) ship B lying near the wharf. On those assumed facts, the injured parties numbers 2, 3, and 4 can conduct a suit in rem in the admiralty court, but if the *Moçambique* rule is applied, number 1 is barred. Can anything more contrary to common sense be imagined?' It will be seen that this is the same argument as that adduced by Fry L.J. in the Court of Appeal in the *Moçambique* case (*ante*, p. 327). The Court of Appeal in *The Tolten* were able to avoid so inequitable and absurd a result by creating a third exception to the *Moçambique* rule. But one has only to vary the illustration so as to take it out of this exception to see that serious anomalies remain. Suppose that an English motorist, negligently driving his car while on a temporary visit to France, causes damage to (1) a Frenchman sitting in his garden having tea, (2) a valuable tea service, (3) a greenhouse fixed to the land. If the *Moçambique* rule is applied, the Frenchman can recover damages for (1) and (2) but not for (3).

The question whether the parties can by agreement waive the *Moçambique* rule and confer jurisdiction on the court which it would not otherwise possess, does not appear to be satisfactorily settled. If the rule is founded on considerations of policy, on principle one would conclude that waiver ought not to be allowed: and this is the view of Cheshire (p. 506), Dicey (p. 150), Beale (p. 1655), Graveson (p. 124, n. 86), and Somervell L.J. in *The Tolten* (*ante*, p. 340). However, *The Mary Moxham* (1876) 1 P.D. 107, and *Re Duke of Wellington* [1948] Ch. 118, the Court of Appeal seems to have assumed that waiver is permissible.

Of the three exceptions to the *Moçambique* rule, the first two are derived from the practice of the Court of Chancery and the third from the practice of the Court of Admiralty. This fact is significant; it suggests that the rule was a common law rule only and as such ought not to have been allowed to survive the Judicature Act 1873. The scope of each of the exceptions is very ill defined.

The first exception is the oldest. It can be traced back to the case of *Arglasse* v. *Muschamp*, 1 Vern. 75, decided in 1682, though *Penn* v. *Baltimore* (1750) 1 Ves. Sen. 444, is usually regarded as the leading case. In the early cases in which the equitable jurisdiction was invoked, the land was situated within British territory, and the exercise of jurisdiction could be justified on the ground that, if there were any courts in the countries then being colonized by Englishmen, the decisions of those courts could not command the same respect as those of the courts in England. In modern times the jurisdiction is much less easy to justify. A modern judge could hadly say, as Shadwell V.-C. said in *Bent* v. *Young* (1838) 9 Sim. 180, 191, 'I consider that in the contemplation of the Court of Chancery every foreign court is an inferior court.' The equitable jurisdiction is 'open to the strong objection that the court is doing indirectly what it dare not do directly', per Lord Esher in the *Moçambique* case [1892] 2 Q.B. 404–5. The exercise of jurisdiction may easily lead to embarrassing conflicts with the courts of the country where the land is situated—for in the last resort only those courts can control the land and the rights of the parties thereto. This aspect of the matter becomes obvious when we consider the converse situation: what effect would an English court give to a foreign decree in personam purporting to affect land in England? This question seems never to have arisen in England, but it has arisen in Canada. In *Duke* v. *Andler* [1932] 4 D.L.R. 529, A agreed with B in California to sell to B land situated in British Columbia. A and B were both residents of California. The land was conveyed to B in accordance with British Columbia law and B was registered as the proprietor thereof. Subsequently A sued B in California to have the conveyance set aside because of B's fraud. The Californian court ordered B to reconvey the land to A and, on his refusal to do so, the clerk of the court purported to reconvey it in B's name. A sued B in Canada for a declaration that he was entitled to be registered as the proprietor of the land. The Supreme Court of Canada held that he was entitled to no such declaration.

The second exception is supported by the decisions in *Nelson* v. *Bridport* (1846) 8 Beav. 547; *Re Piercy* [1895] 1 Ch. 83; *Re Moses* [1908] 2 Ch. 235; *Re Stirling* [1908] 2 Ch. 344; *Re Pearse's Settlement* [1909] 1 Ch. 305; and *Re Duke of Wellington* [1948] Ch. 118, as well as by those in *Re Hoyles (ante,* p. 318) and *Re Ross (ante,* p. 10). It has never been formulated by English judges, though it was specifically approved by the Court of Session in *Jubert* v. *Church Commissioners for England,* 1952 S.C. 160, 162; and its existence is recognized by Dicey (p. 155), Cheshire (pp. 506–7), and Graveson (pp. 124–5). In all the cases cited above the court decided a naked question of title to foreign land, in the absence of any contract, fiduciary relationship, or equity between the parties. Even if the *Moçambique* rule can be waived, that cannot be the explanation of all the cases, because in some of them infants were parties. The scope of the exception is naturally somewhat vague. It may perhaps be justified on the ground that the court can make its adjudication effective through its control of the trustees or of the other assets situated in England.

As to the scope of the third exception, the actual decision in *The Tolten* is confined to the enforcement by actions in rem of maritime liens against a ship for damage done to foreign land. Scott L.J. thought that the court had jurisdiction to entertain any Admiralty action in respect of foreign land, whether in rem or in personam. Somervell L.J. was inclined to agree (*ante*, p. 340); but Cohen L.J. expressed no opinion on this point, which therefore remains doubtful.

Section C: CHOICE OF LAW

In general, the lex situs determines all questions as to the essential validity of conveyances and wills of immovables and who are entitled thereto on intestacy.

FREKE v. CARBERY (1873) L.R. 16 Eq. 461 (*ante*, p. 317)

In re HOYLES [1911] 1 Ch. 179 (*ante*, p. 318)

In re BERCHTOLD [1923] 1 Ch. 192 (*ante*, p. 321)

In re ROSS [1930] 1 Ch. 377 (*ante*, p. 10)

The question whether a beneficiary is put to his election is governed by the law of the testator's domicile at the date of his death.

In re OGILVIE [1918] 1 Ch. 492 (Chancery Division)

Administration action.

Margaret Ogilvie died on 2 April 1908, a widow, domiciled in England, possessed of real and personal estate in England and Scotland, and, as absolute owner in equity, of a tramway undertaking at Asuncion, in Paraguay, the property of which consisted of (inter alia) land. She had eight children, of whom four sons (Glencairn, Fergus, Gordon, Campbell) and one daughter were living at her death; of the three who had died in her lifetime, two left issue who were living and sui juris, and one had died an infant and bachelor. By her will and codicils she gave benefits to her surviving daughter, to her sons Glencairn, Fergus, and Campbell, and to certain of her grandchildren, including the children of her two deceased children who had died leaving issue. She made no provision for her son

343

In re
OGILVIE.

Gordon. She did not dispose of the residue of the personal estate in England and Scotland. She gave to her sons Glencairn and Fergus and her grandson Gerald all her Paraguayan property upon trust for sale and to apply the proceeds for such charitable purposes as they should think fit. The tramway undertaking had been sold and the purchase-money paid into court. The case now came before the court on a summons to proceed with an inquiry which had been directed on further consideration, and for the purpose of enabling the court to ascertain the effect of Paraguayan law on the disposition of the Paraguayan property all parties agreed to be bound by an opinion of a Paraguayan jurist, which, shortly, was as follows: (1) By the law of Paraguay the testamentary dispositions of Mrs. Ogilvie, in so far as the property situate in that republic is concerned, whether movable or immovable, real or personal, are governed by the law of Paraguay. . . . (3) They are not valid by the law of Paraguay, inasmuch as they infringe upon the legal portions, under that law, of the obligatory heirs, and the bequest in favour of charity must, accordingly, be reduced until these portions are provided for. (4) These portions are not to be affected in amount by reason of the obligatory heirs or some of them having, by the will, been given benefits out of property of the testatrix situate in other countries. The transmission of property locally situate is, by the law of Paraguay, considered as completely independent of any disposition of property situate outside the republic. (5) The legal portion of the lawful descendants is four-fifths of all the properties existing at the death: the children inherit per capita; the grandchildren, children of deceased children, inherit per stirpes. (6) One-fifth only of the Paraguayan property has by the will, according to the law of Paraguay, been effectually given for charitable purposes.

YOUNGER J.: It seems clear, in the first place, that the testatrix's son Gordon, as one of the Paraguayan obligatory heirs for whom no other provision is made by the will, is left free by the law of this country to take what the law of Paraguay gives him. Accordingly, one-seventh of four-fifths of the undisposed-of proceeds of the undertaking falls to him. The real question is whether those of the obligatory heirs who take other benefits under the will can be allowed at the same time to gain by the partial invalidity in Paraguay of Mrs. Ogilvie's disposition of the tramway undertaking, or whether they must be put to their election either to treat the whole

344

will as valid or, in case they find it to their interest in any instance to take advantage of its invalidity in Paraguay, to submit to make compensation, out of the other benefits given them by the will, to the charities ultimately disappointed by their refusal to allow the provision made for charity to have full effect.

In re
OGILVIE.
—
Younger J.

In the main the authorities on this subject are clear. The testatrix here very plainly intended to deal by her will with her Paraguayan property as well as with her English movable and immovable estate. She purported to dispose of her Paraguayan property by express words of gift. There is, therefore, no room here for the difficulty which, although ultimately solved in the same sense, arose in the case of *Orrell* v. *Orrell*.[1] Again, in these cases of election the court has always shown a special tenderness to the heir-at-law of English real estate as contrasted with the customary heir or the person compendiously described—pace Joyce J. in *In re de Virte*[2]—as the 'foreign heir'. The principle is well established that, where a testator who dies domiciled in England makes a will which purports to dispose of, but is, in fact, inoperative to pass English real estate, his heir-at-law, as contrasted with the customary heir or the foreign heir in the corresponding case, is not put to his election between that realty and other benefits given him by the will—*Hearle* v. *Greenbank*[3]—unless there be contained in the will itself some such express condition, as, for instance, was found in *Boughton* v. *Boughton*,[4] that if any who receive benefit by the will shall dispute any part of it they shall forfeit all claim under it.

This distinction between the English heir-at-law and any other heir is not very satisfactory, but, although frequently severely criticized, it was too well established, even in the time of Sir William Grant, to remain open to effective discussion. In *Brodie* v. *Barry*,[5] Sir William Grant deals with the point. He says: 'If it were now necessary to discuss the principles, upon which the doctrine of election depends, it might be difficult to reconcile to those principles, or to each other, some of the decisions, which have taken place on this subject. . . . This is, or is not, a case of election according as the English will is, or is not, to be read against the Scotch heir. Where land and personal property are situated in different countries, governed by different laws, and a question arises upon the combined effect of

---

[1] (1871) L.R. 6 Ch. App. 302.   [2] [1915] 1 Ch. 920, 926.
[3] (1749) 1 Ves. Sen. 298.   [4] (1750) 2 Ves. Sen. 12.
[5] (1813) 2 V. & B. 127, 129, 133.

those laws, it is often very difficult to determine, what portion of each law is to enter into the decision of the question. It is not easy to say, how much is to be considered as depending on the law of real property; which must be taken from the country where the land lies; and how much upon the law of personal property; which must be taken from the country of the domicile; and to blend both together; so as to form a rule, applicable to the mixed question, which neither law separately furnishes sufficient materials to decide.' Then, after a discussion as to whether the law of England or the law of Scotland ought to determine the question in the case before him, and finding it unnecessary in that case to decide it, the result being the same under both, he proceeds: 'As to the law of England'—and this is the point —'a will of land in Scotland must be held analogous to that of copyhold estate in England; and the will is equally to be read against the heir.' And it is now, I think, clearly established that this is by the law of England always so if the realty in question is situate not in England, but, say, in Paraguay or in any other foreign country, and it is by the law of Paraguay or that country, and not by the law of England, that the devise of it fails to have effect. In such a case the Paraguayan or other foreign heir, to whom, say, a pecuniary legacy is given by the will, is put to his election here in England, whether the will does or does not contain any such express condition as that found in *Boughton* v. *Boughton.*

Further, it has since Sir William Grant's time become, I think, well settled, in accordance with what was plainly his own view, that the question whether in any particular case, like *Brodie* v. *Barry* or like the present, a case of election is or is not raised depends upon the domicile of the testator at death—for it is the law of that domicile which governs it. The reasons for this are given by Lord Brougham in his judgment in *Dundas* v. *Dundas.*[1] In that case a testator domiciled in Scotland had, by a will inoperative under the Statute of Frauds, purported to devise his English real estate to a stranger and had, by his same will, given benefits to his English heir-at-law. The Court of Session held that the heir-at-law was put to his election. The House of Lords affirmed that decision. And although the House of Lords in dealing with a Scotch appeal applies to it the principles of Scotch law applicable, *Orrell* v. *Orrell*, to cite no other case, shows that in this respect the principles of the law of England are the same.

[1] (1830) 2 Dow. & Cl. 349.

The result at first sight may seem strange. It would appear remarkable that the question whether the English heir of a Scottish testator resident in England at his death is or is not put to his election under his will may, in fact, turn upon the question whether the testator had or had not then lost his domicile of origin—a question which many testators in that situation might themselves find it difficult to answer. But the point is one of substance, and I am inclined to think that it discloses the clue by which the difficulty in the present case may be solved. If by the law of the domicile the gift of the tramway be, irrespective of its locality, to any extent invalid, there is no case of election; if it is only by the law of lex rei sitae that the gift is inoperative, then the foreign heirs are put to their election.

And the foreign heirs, in argument, ultimately accepted that position. But they said that by the law of England a foreign heir would not be put to his election in a case like the present, where the invalidity of the gift by the law of Paraguay was not due to any such formal matter as, for instance, a defect in signature or attestation, but was due to its being contrary to a cardinal principle of public policy adopted in Paraguay, the country where the property is situated. Cases like *Orrell* v. *Orrell*, *Brodie* v. *Barry*, and *Dundas* v. *Dundas*, where the foreign heir was put to his election, were all of them, they pointed out, cases in which the devise of the foreign realty might have been effectively made if it had been made in due form; here, on the other hand, the devise of the tramway undertaking to charity could not to the extent of four-fifths of the property be by the law of Paraguay, made valid by any means whatever. To such a case, so it was said, this court must apply the principles of *In re Oliver's Settlement*,[1] and *In re Beales' Settlement*,[2] approved by the Court of Appeal in *In re Nash*,[3] and refuse to assist indirectly, by an application of the doctrine of election, a breach or evasion of positive rules of foreign law, just as in these cases it refused to, shall I say, encourage, by applying the doctrine, a breach of the rule against perpetuities. The argument is plausible, but, in my opinion, it is not sound. It is not open to me to consider the correctness of the principle as applied to the rule against perpetuities upon which *In re Oliver's Settlement* and the cases following it proceed. That principle has been accepted by the Court of Appeal and is binding upon me. Some day it may come under the notice of the House of Lords,

---

[1] [1905] 1 Ch. 191.   [2] [1905] 1 Ch. 256.
[3] [1910] 1 Ch. 1.

and then the powerful reasoning of Mr. Theobald in the preface to the 7th edition of his Law of Wills and the views of the learned editors of Jarman on Wills, 6th ed. p. 851, may meet with more consideration than they have hitherto received, and even *In re Bradshaw*[1] may, as a decision, at the last come to its own, and the question may be asked whether any advantage is gained by driving testators, if they would attain the same end, to resort in that matter to the use of an express condition, the necessity for which, in cases then already established, was so deplored by Sir William Grant in *Brodie* v. *Barry*. Accepting, however, as I must, the principle to the full, it does not, I think, apply here.

This court does not, in these cases of election, against a foreign heir, presume to sit in judgment upon the wisdom or the reverse according to its own notions of the municipal law of any foreign country. If it finds that an English testator has by his will manifested an intention to dispose of foreign heritage away from the foreign heir, and has, in fact, so far as words are concerned effectually so disposed of it, this court merely says that it is against conscience that that foreign heir, given a legacy by the same will, and to that extent an object of mere bounty on the part of the testator, shall take and keep, under the protection of the foreign law, the land by the will destined for another, without making to that other out of his English legacy, so far as it will go, compensation for his disappointment, thus effectuating the testator's whole intentions. That object, as I take it, is, in the eye of this court, always the paramount object of attainment. But in so attaining it the court violates no foreign law; it leaves that law, as it must, untouched. If the heir can obtain under the protection of the foreign law property which the testator destined for others, he will, so far as this court is concerned, be at perfect liberty to take it and keep it; it is the legacy subject to its own jurisdiction that the court alone will touch and administer and, if necessary, impound for the purpose of effectuating the testator's intention, and so doing justice as it sees it. And, in my opinion, the court will always take this course upon the conditions presupposed, unless the heir's legacy would, if applied in compensating the disappointed devisees of the foreign land, be applied in a way or for purposes for which the testator himself could not, by English law, validly by his will have directed that legacy to be so applied. It is with the English law only that the court at this stage is concerned. If, in the result, no

[1] [1902] 1 Ch. 436.

principle of that law is violated, the hand of the court will not be stayed. The foreign heir will be put to his election; and compensation, partial or complete, will, if necessary, be provided for the disappointed devisee. From this point of view the question what precise principle or provision of the foreign law, as such, has been left unobserved by the testator becomes quite immaterial in this court, and I cannot doubt that it is for this reason that no such distinction as that suggested in argument here has, so far as I can find, ever before been taken.

In re
OGILVIE.
—
Younger J.

In my opinion these Paraguayan heirs are in this case put to their election.

NOTE O: IMMOVABLES AND THE LEX SITUS

IT is usually said that generally speaking all questions relating to immovables are governed by the lex situs. There is much to be said for such a rule on grounds of practical convenience. It is obvious that in the long run the choice of any other law will be ineffective, because only officials appointed by the courts of the situs can lawfully control the land. If this is so, it follows that if the lex situs is a foreign law—that is, if the land is situated abroad—the lex situs should mean not the domestic rule of the lex situs, but whatever system of domestic law the lex situs would apply. Most modern writers are therefore agreed that the question of title to land is an exceptional case justifying the application of the total renvoi doctrine (*ante*, pp. 23–24): Dicey, pp. 63–64, 520; Cheshire, pp. 71, 502; Restatement, s. 8; Cook, pp. 264, 279–80; Falconbridge, pp. 217–20. An example will perhaps make the reasoning clear. Suppose that a British subject domiciled in England dies intestate leaving land in Spain. Suppose that by Spanish domestic law (lex situs) X is entitled to the land, but that Spanish courts would apply English domestic law, according to which Y is entitled. The argument is that it is useless for the English court to decide in favour of X, if Spanish officials will not lift a finger to help him recover the land from Y.

Now if the lex situs means, for an English court dealing with foreign land, that system of domestic law which the lex situs would apply, it follows that there is nothing in the nature of the legal universe which compels an English court dealing with land in England to apply English domestic law. There is no logical or practical reason why a court sitting at the situs of the land should not apply some other law, e.g. the law of the domicile, at any rate in relation to capacity and matrimonial property: two matters in which the case for applying the law of the domicile seems strong. In practice, however, most English courts have applied the lex situs when dealing with land in England.

It is now necessary to consider separately (1) Formalities, (2) Essential validity, (3) Capacity, (4) Matrimonial Property, (5) Contracts, (6) Construction of Wills, and (7) Election. It will be assumed that for an English court dealing with land in England, the lex situs means domestic English law, and that for an English court dealing with land abroad, the lex situs means whatever system of domestic law the lex situs would apply.

(1) *Formalities*. It has been decided that a written instrument leasing land in Scotland need not be under seal since a seal is not required by Scots law: *Adams* v. *Clutterbuck* (1883), 10 Q.B.D. 403. Under s. 2 (1) (*b*) of the Wills Act 1963 (*post*, p. 458) a will dealing with land is to be treated as properly executed if its execution conformed to the internal law in force in the country where the land is situated. But compliance with the formalities of the lex situs is no longer obligatory as it was at common law, because the Act introduces a number of other possible forms for wills of immovables as well as movables. These are considered in a later chapter.

(2) *Essential validity*. The lex situs determines all questions of essential validity, e.g. what estates can be created: *Nelson* v. *Bridport* (1846) 8 Beav. 547; what are the incidents of those estates: *Re Miller* [1914] 1 Ch. 511; whether the limitations infringe the rule against perpetuities or accumulations: *Freke* v. *Carbery* (*ante*, p. 317); whether gifts to charities are valid: *Duncan* v. *Lawson* (1889) 41 Ch. D. 394; *Re Hoyles* (*ante*, p. 318); whether the testator must leave a fixed part of his estate to his wife or children: *Re Ross* (*ante*, p. 10); who is entitled on an intestacy: *Duncan* v. *Lawson* (*supra*); *Re Berchtold* (*ante*, p. 321).

(3) *Capacity*. There appears to be no English case in which an English court has had to consider the question of capacity to transfer land at home. The question was considered in the American case of *Proctor* v. *Frost* (1938), 89 N.H. 304, where the law of the domicile and not the lex situs was applied. A married woman domiciled with her husband in Massachusetts in that state became surety for her husband, and as security gave a mortgage on her New Hampshire land. The mortgagee brought a bill in equity in New Hampshire for foreclosure. The defence was that by a New Hampshire statute a married woman could not become surety for her husband. The New Hampshire court rejected this defence on the ground that 'the primary purpose of the statute . . . was not to regulate the transfer of New Hampshire real estate, but to protect married women [sc. domiciled] in New Hampshire from the consequences of their efforts, presumably ill-advised, to reinforce the credit of embarrassed husbands'.

The question what law governs capacity to transfer land abroad came before the Court of Appeal in *Bank of Africa* v. *Cohen* [1909] 2 Ch. 129, where the lex situs was applied. The reasoning is, however, most unsatisfactory. A married woman, domiciled and resident with her husband in England, executed a deed in England whereby she agreed to mortgage land in Johannesburg to a bank as security for past and future advances made and to be made by the bank to her husband. The bank sued for specific performance of the deed. The defence was that by the Roman-Dutch law in force in the Transvaal, a married woman was incapable of becoming surety for her husband unless (*a*) she obtained a pecuniary benefit from the contract, or (*b*) she was engaged in trade, or (*c*) she clearly and specifically renounced the benefits of the Sc. Velleianum or the Authentica si qua mulier. None of these exceptions applied, but the trial Judge found as a fact that the defendant knew quite well what she was doing. The Court of Appeal held that the defendant's capacity to make the contract was governed by Roman-Dutch law and the contract was therefore void.

This decision is incomprehensible. The bank was left without security for advances made on the faith of the defendant's promise, and the defendant was allowed to break that promise with impunity although she knew quite well what she was doing. More specifically:

(a) The court made no attempt to ascertain the policy of the Transvaal law, or whether a Transvaal court would have applied Transvaal domestic law to this very case. Had it done so, it might well have discovered that the Transvaal law laid down a policy not for Transvaal land but for Transvaal married women, and that the Transvaal court would have applied English domestic law to this case because the defendant was domiciled and resident in England.

(b) The court was not dealing with a mortgage but with a contract to make a mortgage. As we shall see, contracts affecting land are not governed by the lex situs as such but by their proper law, which need not necessarily be the lex situs. The court made no attempt to ascertain the proper law of the contract, but baldly asserted that the defendant's capacity was governed by the lex situs, and mechanically applied its domestic law.

(4) *Matrimonial property.* If the court is dealing with foreign land, it should apply whatever system of domestic law the lex situs would apply. The scanty English authority is consistent with this view. Thus, in *Re Pearse's Settlement* [1909] 1 Ch. 305, by an English marriage settlement the intended wife, who was domiciled before and after the marriage in England, covenanted to settle after-acquired property. She became entitled to land in Jersey. By the law of Jersey no trusts of land were permitted and all transfers thereof had to be for value. Eve J. held that the land was not caught by the covenant. This decision is obviously correct. The Jersey law laid down a policy for Jersey land and not for people domiciled in Jersey.

If the court is dealing with land in England, it has been held that the law of the domicile at the date of the marriage, and not the lex situs, applies. Thus in *Re De Nicols (No. 2)* [1900] 2 Ch. 410, a husband and wife, both domiciled in France, married there without an antenuptial contract, with the result that the French system of community of goods applied to their present and after-acquired property. The husband subsequently purchased land in England. On his death it was held by Kekewich J. that his widow's rights in the land were governed by French law. This decision has been criticized, but it appears to be in accordance with the best modern ideas; it has never been overruled; and moreover it does not stand alone. In *Chiwell v. Carlyon* (1897) 14 S.C. 61 (Cape of Good Hope), the facts were exactly the same, except that the spouses were domiciled at the Cape. Stirling J. sent a case for the opinion of the Supreme Court of Cape Colony. In other words, he decided that the matter was one for Cape law. The opinion of the Cape court was that the English land was held in community. The case is unfortunately not reported in England, but the record shows that Stirling J. gave judgment in accordance with this opinion. Of course it is a question of fact whether the foreign system of law extends its matrimonial property régime to land in England: *Callwood v. Callwood* [1960] A.C. 659.

(5) *Contracts.* Contracts relating to land are governed, not by the lex situs as such, but by their proper law, which is usually but not necessarily the lex situs: *British South Africa Co. v. De Beers Consolidated Mines Ltd.* [1910] 2 Ch. 502. The proper law governs essential validity; interpretation; effect: *Re Anchor Line Ltd.* [1937] Ch. 483; and formalities: *Re Smith* [1916] 2 Ch. 206. On principle, it should also govern capacity to contract. But this is doubtful in view of *Bank of Africa v. Cohen, supra.*

LAW OF PROPERTY

(6) *Construction of wills.* The construction of a will of land is governed, not by the lex situs as such, but by the law intended by the testator, which is presumed to be the law of his domicile at the time of making the will: *Studd* v. *Cook* (1883) 8 App. Cas. 577. Thus in *Re Voet* [1949] N.Z.L.R. 742, a testator domiciled in South Africa specifically devised land in New Zealand which was subject to a mortgage. By New Zealand law the mortgage debt was payable primarily out of the mortgaged property; by South African law it was payable out of the testator's general assets. It was held that South African law governed. But the incidents of the estate created must be determined by the lex situs, because this is a matter not of construction but of essential validity: *Re Miller* [1914] 1 Ch. 511.

(7) *Election.* In *Re Ogilvie, ante,* p. 346, Younger J. lays down that the question whether a legatee of movables under a will must elect between benefits under the will and foreign land coming to him outside the will is governed by the law of the testator's domicile, and this view is consistent with all the previous cases on the subject. In *Re Allen's Estate* (1945) 114 L.J. Ch. 298, however (where *Re Ogilvie* was not cited), Cohen J. held that a beneficiary under the will of a testator domiciled in South Africa was put to her election, although it was 'common ground' that by South African law no case for election arose. The decision is perhaps right in the result, because in the circumstances the beneficiary was bound to elect by South African as well as by English law. But the reasoning is criticized in detail in 10 Conveyancer 102 and 24 Can. Bar Rev. 528, and Cheshire (p. 520, n. 1) and Dicey (p. 611) treat the case as wrongly decided. It was disapproved and not followed in *Re Mengel* [1962] Ch. 791, 800.

Chapter 12

TRANSFER OF TANGIBLE MOVABLES

If movable property is disposed of in a manner binding according to the law of the country where it is, that disposition is binding everywhere.

CAMMELL v. SEWELL (1860) 5 H. & N. 728 (Exchequer Chamber)

ERROR from the Court of Exchequer.[1]

The plaintiffs were underwriters in Hull; the defendants merchants in London. The action was brought to recover part of a cargo of deals shipped on board the Prussian ship Augusta Bertha at Onega, in Russia, by the Onega Wood Company, for Messrs. Simpson & Whaplate of Hull, and by them insured with the plaintiffs.

On the 17th of September 1852 the Augusta Bertha, having put into Haroe Roads in consequence of the shifting of her deck cargo, drove from her anchorage on the rocks at Smaage, about three miles from Molde in Norway. On the 19th the captain began discharging the cargo, which was ultimately stacked on two small islands. The cargo was not materially damaged. Witnesses, however, stated that as it stood it was exposed to injury from the weather and sea water: that possibly some of it might be washed away in storms; and that it would require to be watched. The wreck lay out of the track of shipping. There was no harbour; the anchorage at Smaage was bad, and ships could not have been readily obtained for the purpose of forwarding the cargo to its destination. There was a conflict of testimony as to whether or not a prudent owner, if uninsured, would have sold the cargo on the spot.

On the 23rd of September the captain notified the consignees of the wreck. The consignees gave notice of abandonment to the plaintiffs who paid as for a total loss.

The captain instructed surveyors to survey the vessel and cargo, and on the 27th of September they reported that a sale of the cargo by public auction was best for all parties. On the 15th of October the sale was held, Mr. Jervell, the representative of the plaintiffs,

[1] 3 H. & N. 617.

353

CAMMELL
v.
SEWELL.

protesting against the sale. The cargo was bought by Mr. Clausen, the British Vice-Consul.

Mr. Jervell then instituted a suit before the superior diocesan Court of Trondhjem to set aside the sale, making the captain and his agent and Mr. Clausen defendants: but on the 25th of November 1853[1] the court confirmed the sale.

The cargo remained in Norway throughout the winter, and in the spring it was shipped to London by a vessel called the Mindet under a bill of lading indorsed by Clausen to the defendants, who had made advances on the cargo. The Mindet arrived in the Thames in April 1853, when the plaintiffs immediately caused a notice to be served on the defendants requiring them to deliver up the deals. The cargo was afterwards sold by auction, and the net proceeds received by the defendants on the 9th of December 1853 were £1,470. 4s. 2d. The plaintiffs claimed this sum. By Norwegian law the sale conferred a good title on Clausen.

The Court of Exchequer (Pollock C.B., Martin B., and Channell B.) gave judgment for the defendants on the ground that the Norwegian judgment was in the nature of a judgment in rem and as such conclusively determined the title to the deals. The plaintiffs appealed.

CROMPTON J.: In this case the majority of the court (Cockburn C.J., Wightman, Williams, Crompton, and Keating JJ.) are of opinion that the judgment of the Court of Exchequer should be affirmed. At the same time we are by no means prepared to agree with the Court of Exchequer in thinking the judgment of the Diocesan Court in Norway conclusive as a judgment in rem, nor are we satisfied that the defendants in the present action were estopped by the judgment of that court or what was relied on as a judicial proceeding at the auction. It is not, however, necessary for us to express any decided opinion on these questions, as we think that the case should be determined on the real merits as to the passing of the property.

If we are to recognise the Norwegian law, and if according to that law the property passed by the sale in Norway to Clausen as an innocent purchaser, we do not think that the subsequent bringing the property to England can alter the position of the parties. The difficulty which we have felt in the case principally arises from the mode in which the evidence is laid before us in the mass of papers and depositions contained in the appendix.

[1] *Sic* in the report. It is thought that this is a misprint for 1852 (*Ed.*).

We do not see evidence in the case sufficient to enable us to treat the transaction as fraudulent on the part of Clausen, although there are circumstances which would have made it better for him not to have become the purchaser. Treating him, therefore, as an innocent purchaser, it appears to us that the questions are—did the property by the law of Norway vest in him as an innocent purchaser? and are we to recognise that law? That question of what is the foreign law is one of fact, and here again there is great difficulty in finding out from the mass of documents what is the exact state of the law. The conclusion which we draw from the evidence is, that by the law of Norway the captain, under circumstances such as existed in this case, could not, as between himself and his owners, or the owners of the cargo, justify the sale, but that he remained liable and responsible to them for a sale not justified under the circumstances; whilst, on the other hand, an innocent purchaser would have a good title to the property brought by him from the agent of the owners.

It does not appear to us that there is anything so barbarous or monstrous in this state of the law as that we can say that it should not be recognised by us. Our own law as to market overt is analogous; and though it is said that much mischief would be done by upholding sales of this nature, not justified by the necessities of the case, it may well be that the mischief would be greater if the vendee were only to have a title in cases where the master was strictly justified in selling as between himself and the owners. If that were so, purchasers, who seldom can know the facts of the case, would not be inclined to give the value, and on proper and lawful sales by the master the property would be in great danger of being sacrificed.

There appears nothing barbarous in saying that the agent of the owners, who is the person to sell, if the circumstances justify the sale, and who must, in point of fact, be the party to exercise his judgment as to whether there should be a sale or not, should have the power of giving a good title to the innocent purchaser, and that the latter should not be bound to look to the title of the seller. It appears in the present case that the one purchaser bought the whole cargo; but suppose the farmers and persons in the neighbourhood at such a sale buy several portions of the goods, it would seem extremely inconvenient if they were liable to actions at the suit of the owners, on the ground that there was no necessity for the sale. Could such a purchaser coming to England be sued in our courts for a conversion, and can it alter the case if he re-sell, and the property comes to this country?

CAMMELL
v.
SEWELL.

Crompton
J.

355

CAMMELL
v.
SEWELL.

Crompton
J.

Many cases were mentioned in the course of the argument, and more might be collected, in which it might seem hard that the goods of foreigners should be dealt with according to the laws of our own or of other countries. Amongst others our law as to the seizure of a foreigner's goods for rent due from a tenant, or as to the title gained in them, if stolen, by a sale in market overt, might appear harsh. But we cannot think that the goods of foreigners would be protected against such laws, or that if the property once passed by virtue of them it would again be changed by being taken by the new owner into the foreigner's own country. We think that the law on this subject was correctly stated by the Lord Chief Baron in the course of the argument in the court below, where he says 'if personal property is disposed of in a manner binding according to the law of the country where it is, that disposition is binding everywhere'. And we do not think that it makes any difference that the goods were wrecked, and not intended to be sent to the country where they were sold. We do not think that the goods which were wrecked here would on that account be the less liable to our laws as to market overt, or as to the landlord's right of distress, because the owner did not foresee that they would come to England. . . .

In the present case, which is not like the case of *Freeman* v. *The East India Company*,[1] the case of an English subject purchasing in an English colony property which he was taken to know that the vendor had no authority to sell, we do not think that we can assume on the evidence that the purchase was made with the knowledge that the sellers had no authority, or under such circumstances as to bring the case within any exception to the foreign law, which seems to treat the master as having sufficient authority to sell, so as to protect the innocent purchaser where there is no representative of the real owner. It should be remarked also, that Lord Stowell, in the passage, cited in the case of *Freeman* v. *The East India Company*, from his judgment in the case of *The Gratitudine*,[2] states that if the master acts unwisely in his decision as to selling still the foreign purchaser will be safe under his acts. The doctrine of Lord Stowell agrees much more with the principles on which our judgment proceeds than with those reported to have been approved of in the case of *The Eliza Cornish*,[3] as, on the evidence before us, we cannot treat Clausen otherwise than as an innocent purchaser, and as the law of Norway

---

[1] (1822) 5 B. & Ald. 617.   [2] (1801) 3 C. Rob. 240.
[3] (1853) 1 Sp. Ecc. & Adm. 36.

appears to us, on the evidence, to give a title to an innocent pur- CAMMELL
chaser, we think that the property vested in him, and in the defen- SEWELL.
dants as subpurchasers from him, and that, having once so vested, it Crompton
did not become divested by its being subsequently brought to this J.
country, and, therefore, that the judgment of the Court of Exchequer
should be affirmed.

BYLES J. dissented on the grounds (1) that the law of Norway
allowing indiscriminate sales of cargo by the masters of all ships
wrecked on the Norwegian coast was so inconvenient and dangerous
that effect could not be given to it in England; (2) that he could not
concur in the universality of the proposition that a disposition of
movable property, effectual by the law of the country where that
property might at the time be locally situated, was necessarily binding without exception in any country to which it might afterwards
come.

Judgment affirmed.

*A title to goods acquired in accordance with the lex situs will be
recognized as valid in England if the goods are removed from the
country where they were situated when such title was acquired, until
such title is displaced by a new title acquired in accordance with the
law of the country to which they are removed.*

CENTURY CREDIT CORPORATION *v.* RICHARD (1962) 34 D.L.R. (2d) CENTURY
291 (Ontario Court of Appeal)   CREDIT
                                                          CORPORA-
                                                            TION
                                                             v.
                                                          RICHARD.

Moses sold a car to Foldes under a conditional sales contract
which reserved the title in Moses until the price was fully paid. At
the time of the sale the car was situated and both parties resided in
Montreal in the Province of Quebec. On the same day Moses
assigned the contract for value to the plaintiff respondent.

Subsequently Foldes, without the knowledge of the respondent,
brought the car into Ontario where it was sold in a damaged condition to Hamilton Car Refinishers and resold to the defendant
appellant, who bought it without notice of the respondent's title.

The respondent sued the appellant claiming possession of the car
and damages for its wrongful detention. Under the law of Quebec,
the conditional sales contract was sufficient to reserve the title in
the unpaid vendor until payment in full of the purchase price without the necessity for any registration of the contract. If the sale had

CENTURY
CREDIT
CORPORA-
TION
v.
RICHARD.
—
Kelly J.A.

taken place in Ontario, the vendor's reservation of title would have been invalid as against purchasers from Foldes unless the contract had been registered in Ontario.

The trial judge gave judgment for the plaintiff. The defendant appealed. The judgment of the court (Laidlaw, MacKay, and Kelly JJ.A.) was delivered by

KELLY J.A.: The point at issue in this appeal can be stated as follows: Does a sale in Ontario to a purchaser in Ontario by a person who has agreed in Quebec to buy a vehicle from a resident of Quebec under a contract by which the title and ownership are reserved to the seller and who has obtained possession of the vehicle with the consent of the seller to him, transfer title to the purchaser in Ontario notwithstanding that the original seller's right to the title and ownership would have been enforceable in Ontario against the original buyer who signed the conditional sales contract?

In considering the respective rights of the parties the respondent as assignee of Moses, the original seller, stands in no higher position than its assignor, and for the purpose of this judgment I will refer to the rights of the respondent as those of an unpaid seller.

At the outset consideration must be given to the conflicts of law problem presented by the facts. The applicable principles are stated in Dicey's Conflict of Laws, 7th ed., in Rules 86 and 88. Rule 87 is inapplicable due to the particular facts of this case.

Rule 86.—(1) A transfer of a tangible movable which is valid and effective by the proper law of the transfer and by the law of the place where the movable is at the time of the transfer (lex situs) is valid and effective in England.

(2) A transfer of a tangible movable which is invalid or ineffective by the proper law of the transfer and by the lex situs of the movable at the time of the transfer is invalid or ineffective in England.

Rule 88.—A title to goods acquired or reserved in accordance with Rules 86 or 87 will be recognised as valid in England if the goods are removed out of the country where they were situated at the time when such title was acquired, until such title is displaced by a new title acquired in accordance with the law of the country to which they are removed.

Applying these rules to the present facts the absence of registration in Ontario is not a circumstance invalidating the contract in Ontario and the title reserved by the respondent will remain valid in

Ontario unless and until it is superseded by a valid title acquired in accordance with the laws of Ontario.

If the laws of Ontario were to seek to invalidate the respondent's title by refusing to recognise that the transaction which took place in Quebec had the effect of continuing the title in the respondent, this attempt of Ontario law to invalidate a transaction taking place in Quebec would be bad because the validity of a Quebec transaction must be decided according to the laws of Quebec, the lex situs: to the extent that s. 12 of the Conditional Sales Act of Ontario seeks to make subject to that Act a contract made out of Ontario with respect to goods not then in Ontario but subsequently brought into Ontario, it is an attempt to legislate with respect to such a transaction, the effects of which are to be decided according to the law of Quebec and for this reason offends against the above-quoted Rule 86. However, if the laws of Ontario provide that a later transaction which takes place wholly within Ontario has the effect of overriding prior titles, then since Ontario does not seek to give its laws any extraterritorial effect the laws of Ontario prevail and the title created under the laws of Ontario displaces the title reserved in the Quebec transaction.

The sale by Foldes to Hamilton Car Refinishers took place in Ontario and its effect must be decided according to Ontario law. The applicable statutory provisions appear to be s. 25 (2) of the Sale of Goods Act and s. 2 (1) of the Factors Act:

25 (2). Where a person having bought or agreed to buy goods obtains, with the consent of the seller, possession of the goods or the documents of title to the goods, the delivery or transfer by that person, or by a mercantile agent acting for him, of the goods or documents of title, under a sale, pledge or other disposition thereof to a person receiving the same in good faith and without notice of any lien or other right of the original seller in respect of the goods, has the same effect as if the person making the delivery or transfer were a mercantile agent in possession of the goods or documents of title with the consent of the owner.

2 (1). Where a mercantile agent is, with the consent of the owner, in possession of goods or of the documents of title to goods, a sale, pledge or other disposition of the goods made by him when acting in the ordinary course of business of a mercantile agent, is, subject to this Act, as valid as if he were expressly authorized by the owner of the goods to make the disposition, if the person taking under it

CENTURY
CREDIT
CORPORA-
TION
v.
RICHARD.
—
Kelly J.A.

acts in good faith and has not at the time thereof notice that the person making it has not authority to make it.

The sale by Foldes in Ontario to a purchaser who received the vehicle in good faith and without notice of any lien or other right of the original seller, by reason of s. 25 of the Sale of Goods Act, has the same effect as if Foldes in making the delivery and transfer were a mercantile agent in possession of the goods with the consent of the owner. Applying s. 2 (1) of the Factors Act, this sale by Foldes is as valid as if it were expressly authorized by the owner and the title acquired by the purchaser by virtue of this sale is absolute. As I have said before the respondent can stand in no higher position than the original seller in Quebec and therefore respondent's title is displaced by the valid sale in Ontario. . . .

Appeal allowed.

NOTE P: THE TRANSFER OF TANGIBLE MOVABLES

(1) Modern writers are agreed that the validity of a transfer of tangible movables is governed either by the lex situs or by the proper law of the transfer. Hence, if these two laws coincide, e.g. if goods in France are sold by a contract the proper law of which is French, it is clear that the validity and effect of the transfer are governed by French law.

(2) Disagreement begins when the two laws do not coincide, e.g. if goods in Germany are transferred by a contract the proper law of which is English, the title passing by English law at the date of the contract, by German law not until delivery. In this situation, most writers think that the lex situs governs; but Dr. Cheshire (pp. 409–12) prefers the proper law of the transfer, at any rate when the question arises between the original parties thereto. Of course the proper law of the contract determines all contractual questions that may arise, e.g. whether the contract includes these goods, or whether the seller is liable for defects in their quality. And of course the seller may be contractually liable to deliver the goods to the buyer and so to make him owner. But we are concerned not with the law of contract, but with the law of property. It is no use saying that the seller is contractually liable to deliver the goods to the owner if, e.g., he has fraudulently sold and delivered the goods to a third party, or has become insolvent, or if the transaction is by way of gift, so that there is no contract at all. Accordingly, it is submitted that the lex situs, and not the proper law of the transfer, governs the proprietary as opposed to the contractual effects of the transfer. *Inglis* v. *Robertson* [1898] A.C. 616 is a clear decision in this sense: whisky stored in a bonded warehouse in Glasgow was hypothecated in England by one English merchant to another; the proper law of the transfer was therefore English law; but Scots law was held to govern, because the whisky was in Scotland. The lex situs is also supported by dicta of Maugham J. in *Re Anziani* [1930] 1 Ch. 407, 420 ('I do not think that anyone can doubt that, with regard to the

transfer of goods, the law applicable must be the lex situs. Business could not be carried on if that were not so'); and of Devlin J. in *Bank voor Handel en Scheepvart* v. *Slatford*, *post*, p. 382 ('There is little doubt that it is the lex situs which, as a general rule, governs the transfer of movables when effected contractually'). On the other hand, there is no authority whatsoever for Dr. Cheshire's view: and the authors of the two most recent monographs on the subject reject it (Lalive, *The Transfer of Chattels in the Conflict of Laws*, pp. 74–83 (1955); Zaphiriou, *The Transfer of Chattels in Private International Law*, pp. 31–38 (1955)).

(3) The claims of the lex situs are less strong when the goods are in transit and the parties do not know precisely where they are: in such circumstances, no doubt a transfer which was valid and effective by its proper law would be upheld.

(4) More complicated questions arise if a title to goods is validly acquired in one country (X) and then the goods are taken to another country (Y). Even if the circumstances are such that the title acquired under the law of X would not have been acquired under the law of Y, it is clear that the title acquired in X will be upheld, for the goods were in X at the material time. 'If according to [Norwegian] law the property passed by the sale in Norway to Clausen as an innocent purchaser, we do not think that the subsequent bringing the property to England can alter the position of the parties': *Cammell* v. *Sewell*, *ante*, p. 354. It follows that if there is a transaction in X (e.g. a hire-purchase contract) whereby the possession of goods passes to B, but the title is validly retained by A in accordance with the law of X but not in accordance with the law of Y, and B takes the goods to Y and sells them there to a third party C, the title of A will prevail, unless the sale in Y has the effect by the law of Y of overriding prior titles: for the general principle is nemo dat quod non habet.

(5) If, however, B, having no title to goods in X by the law of X, brings the goods to Y and sells them there to a third party C in circumstances which by the law of Y override all prior titles (e.g. a sale in England in market overt), then the title of C will prevail, for the goods were in Y at the material time: *Cammell* v. *Sewell*; *Century Credit Co.* v. *Richard*, *ante*, p. 357. It makes no difference that the original owner of the goods did not consent to their being brought to Y: 'We do not think that goods which were wrecked here would on that account be the less liable to our laws as to market overt, or as to the landlord's right of distress, because the owner did not foresee that they would come to England': *Cammell* v. *Sewell*, *ante*, p. 356.

Chapter 13

ASSIGNMENT OF INTANGIBLE MOVABLES

The validity or invalidity of an assignment of a chose in action on the ground of lack of form or lack of capacity is governed by the proper law of the assignment.

REPUBLICA DE GUATEMALA *v.* NUNEZ [1927] 1 K.B. 669 (Court of Appeal)

APPEAL from a judgment of Greer J.[1]

In 1906 Manuel Estrada Cabrera, the then president of the republic of Guatemala, deposited with Messrs. Lazard Bros., bankers of London, a sum of money which with interest amounted by the end of the year 1920 to £21,533. In April 1920 Cabrera was deposed and imprisoned by his political opponents. Subsequently the money so deposited with Lazard Bros. was claimed on behalf of the republic of Guatemala. Lazard Bros. refused to pay it over, as they had received notice that it was also claimed by one Nunez, an illegitimate son of Cabrera. In October 1921 an action was commenced on behalf of the republic of Guatemala against Lazard Bros. to recover the money, whereupon the defendants took out an interpleader summons. They were ordered to pay the money into court, and were dismissed from the action, Nunez being substituted in their place as defendant.

The action then proceeded as between the republic of Guatemala as plaintiffs and Nunez as defendant. The plaintiffs alleged that the money was the money of the republic misappropriated by Cabrera and that Cabrera had transferred it to the republic as public funds by letters dated 12 July and 11 October 1921.

The defendant Nunez claimed the money as the assignee of his father Cabrera. In support of his claim a letter was produced on behalf of the defendant Nunez, dated 24 July 1919, signed by Cabrera, and addressed to Messrs. Lazard Bros. in New York, in which Cabrera requested them to transfer the balance of his account with their London house to Nunez. This letter Greer J. held to be a genuine document signed before July 1921, and intended to operate

[1] 95 L.J. K.B. 955.

as an assignment of the funds in question by Cabrera to his son Nunez. On 20 July 1921 the defendant Nunez and his solicitor gave oral notice of this assignment to Messrs. Lazard Bros. of New York, and on 22 July wrote to Messrs. Lazard Bros., London, giving them written notice of the assignment, which notice was received in London on 4 August and acknowledged on that date.

Evidence was given that by Guatemalan law an assignment of money exceeding $100 in amount if without consideration was void, unless made by a written contract before a notary, duly stamped, and unless the assignee signed before the notary to signify his acceptance. These formalities had not been complied with in the present case. Further, by Guatemalan law a minor could not accept a voluntary assignment; it had to be made to and accepted by a tutor or legal representative appointed by a judge to act on his behalf. At the time of the assignment in question Nunez was a minor, and no legal representative had been appointed to act for him.

Greer J. held that, the assignment having been executed in Guatemala, its validity must be determined by the law of that country, and by that law it was bad. He therefore dismissed the defendant's claim. He dismissed the plaintiff's claim also on the ground that the two documents on which they relied had been extorted by duress from Cabrera while he was in prison and that apart from those two documents there was no evidence that the money had been wrongfully appropriated by Cabrera.

The defendant appealed. The plaintiffs also appealed, and their appeal was dismissed, but it is not reported.

SCRUTTON L.J.: This appeal raises a question of some difficulty. Freed from the picturesque facts, which do not assist the court to determine the dry question of law, the problem which emerges is this. (His Lordship stated the facts and continued:) It will be seen, therefore, that if Guatemalan law, being both the law of the domicile of both parties and the lex loci actus, is to be applied, the document was a nullity. If English law, as the law of the situs of the debt assigned, or the lex loci solutionis of the contract to pay, is to be followed, the document was effective. It is to be assumed, however, that in any case it is English law which the English courts enforce; the question is whether English law directs them to ascertain the validity of the assignment by the law of Guatemala, or by the law of England applicable to such documents.

REPUBLICA
DE
GUATE-
MALA
v.
NUNEZ.
—
Scrutton
L.J.

On the question of the law applicable to an assignment of personal property invalid by the law of the country where the transaction takes place, or by the lex domicilii of the parties to the transaction, but valid by the law of the country where the property is, or is deemed to be, situate, the English authorities are scanty and unsatisfactory. Channel J. in *Dulaney* v. *Merry*[1] 'had not found any clear case of a transfer, good according to the law of the domicile of the owner, and made there, but held bad for not conforming to the law of the country where the goods are situate'. Mr. Dicey has not found any clear case in reference to individual assignments by gift or sale as to the validity of an assignment good by the lex domicilii of the owner, but bad in the country where the goods are situate. Conversely, I have not been able to find, nor could counsel refer me to, any clear statement of the principles governing the question whether a transaction in personal property, as distinct from land, invalid by the law of the country where the transaction takes place, may be valid by the law of the place where the property is situate. Mr. Foote[2] points out that in most of the judgments where general statements are made the transaction took place in the country where the property was, and a conflict between the lex loci actus and the lex loci rei sitæ was not dealt with.

There seem to me, however, in this case to be two clear matters which help to a conclusion. First, in cases of personal property, the capacity of the parties to a transaction has always been determined either by the lex domicilii or the law of the place of the transaction; and where, as here, the two laws are the same it is not necessary to decide between them. In *Lee* v. *Abdy*[3] an assignment was made in Cape Colony by a man there domiciled to his wife of a policy issued by an English company, and it was assumed for the purposes of the case that such an assignment was invalid by the law of the Colony, husband and wife not being capable of entering into such a transaction. A Divisional Court, composed of Day and Wills JJ. held that, on that assumption, the assignment, though valid by the law of England, could not be enforced against the company in England. Neither judge draws a distinction between the lex domicilii or the lex loci actus. The Court of Appeal, in *Sottomayor* v. *de Barros*,[4] a case of marriage, laid down in general terms: 'It is a well-recognized principle of law that the question of personal capacity to enter into

---

[1] [1901] 1 Q.B. 536.   [2] Private International Law, 5th ed., p. 293.
[3] (1886) 17 Q.B.D. 309.   [4] (1877) 3 P.D. 1 ; *ante*, p. 75.

any contract is to be decided by the law of domicile'; and Lord Halsbury says, in *Cooper* v. *Cooper*,[1] that 'incapacity to contract by reason of minority . . . is regulated by the law of domicile'. Lord Macnaghten, in the same case, is more doubtful, treating the question as not finally settled, but with a preponderance of opinion in favour of the lex domicilii. 'But,' he says, 'when the contract is made in the place where the person whose capacity is in question is domiciled there can be no room for dispute. It is difficult to suppose that Mrs. Cooper (the infant) could confer capacity on herself by contemplating a different country as the place where the contract was to be fulfilled.' Lord Watson declines to decide the point, as the two laws are the same. The opinion of the Court of Appeal, in *Sottomayor* v. *de Barros*, in favour of the lex domicilii, was criticized by the same court in *Ogden* v. *Ogden*[2] and by Sir James Hannen in the later *Sottomayor* case.[3] But most of the authorities seem to agree that capacity to contract depends either on the lex domicilii or the lex loci actus, and here they are the same: see also per Lord Eldon in *Male* v. *Roberts*[4] as to infancy. It seems to me, therefore, that Nunez, being a minor incapable by the law of his domicile or the law of the place where the transaction takes place, of receiving a valid donation, so that a gift to him, without the intervention of a next friend judicially appointed to receive it, would be void and a nullity in Guatemala, cannot claim that he has received a good title to the deposit by such an invalid donation.

This view would support the judgment of Greer J., but is not the express ground on which he puts his decision, which is, I think, that a contract void in the place where it is made, by reason of the omission of formalities required by the law of that place, is void elsewhere; the case of void contracts being distinguished from that of contracts merely inadmissible in evidence by reason of the absence of formalities, such as the requirements of stamp laws, not invalidating the contract itself. This seems to me a second point on which the authorities are fairly clear—namely, that where a transaction is invalid or a nullity by the law of the place where the transaction takes place owing to the omission of formalities or stamp, it will not be recognized in England. In *Bristow* v. *Sequeville*,[5] Rolfe B. agrees 'that if for want of a stamp a contract made in a foreign country is void, it cannot be enforced here', distinguishing it from a case where

---

[1] (1888) 13 App. Cas. 88, 99.   [2] [1908] P. 46; *ante*, p. 84.
[3] (1879) 5 P.D. 94.   [4] (1800) 3 Esp. 163.   [5] (1850) 5 Exch. 275, 279.

REPUBLICA
DE
GUATE-
MALA
v.
NUNEZ.
—
Scrutton
L.J.

the contract is not void but only not admissible in evidence. . . . The negotiable instrument cases of *Alcock* v. *Smith*[1] and *Embiricos* v. *Anglo-Austrian Bank*[2] appear to proceed on the same principle. In each case a bill of exchange, accepted and payable in England and therefore representing an English debt, was dealt with in another country; in *Alcock's* case by execution in Norway; in *Embiricos'* case by purchase for valuable consideration in Vienna after theft and forgery of indorsement. In each case the foreign transaction would not have legal effect in England, but in each case it was held that, being valid by the *lex loci actus*, the English law would give effect to it. I cannot think that the suggested difference between the piece of paper and the chose in action represented by it is satisfactory. I refer to the judgments of Romer J. and of Kay L.J. in the former case. In the present case the private unstamped donation made in Guatemala from one Guatemalan subject to another was a nullity by the law of Guatemala. I think it was therefore a nullity by the law of England.

Reliance was, however, placed on the opinion of Mr. Dicey as stated in rule 153[3] of his work on the Conflict of Laws, to which great weight is, of course, added by the opinion of Cozens-Hardy J. in *In re Maudslay, Sons and Field*[4] that it is right. It is to be observed, however, firstly, that in this case the question was whether the English courts would give effect to seizure in France of a French debt as against English debenture-holders administering an English company's affairs; that is to say, the *lex loci actus* and, if debts have a situs, the *lex loci rei sitæ* were the same; and the learned judge's opinion was therefore not necessary for the decision, Secondly, while Cozens-Hardy J. thinks the opinion of Mr. Dicey right, he also thinks the authorities cited by the author for that opinion do not support it; and Greer J., after consideration, has come to the same conclusion. . . .

We were also referred to *Kelly* v. *Selwyn*,[5] where, in the administration in England of the English estate of an English testator, priority was given to an English assignment, later in date but prior in notice, over an earlier New York assignment for which the law of New York did not require notice. Priorities have been said to be questions for the *lex fori* (*The Colorado*[6]), and I think this is the

---

[1] [1892] 1 Ch. 238. [2] [1905] 1 K.B. 677; *post*, p. 388.
[3] See now rule 84 in the eighth edition. [4] [1900] 1 Ch. 602.
[5] [1905] 2 Ch. 117; *post*, p. 367. [6] [1923] P. 102.

ground of the decision. It seems to me, therefore, that the authorities cited by Mr. Dicey do not support the proposition that a transaction as to an English debt, void by the law of the country where it takes place and by the law of the domicile of the parties to it, will be treated as valid in the country where the debt is deemed to be situated. In my opinion, both the capacity of the parties to enter into such a transaction and the validity and effect of such a transaction in form and results must be determined by one or other of those laws; and in this case they are the same.

For these reasons, I think the judgment of Greer J. dismissing the claim of Nunez should be affirmed on the grounds (1) that Nunez, as an infant, was not, by the law of Guatemala, capable of himself receiving a valid donation; and (2) that the transaction, apart from infancy, was void as not carried out in the way required by the law of Guatemala.

The result is that both claims on the fund in court fail. The court has notice that the trustee in bankruptcy of Cabrera claims the fund, and the fund must remain in court till that and any other claim made to the court is disposed of.

BANKES L.J. agreed that the assignment to Nunez was invalid, on the ground that Cabrera and Nunez were domiciled in Guatemala.

LAWRENCE L.J. held (1) that the validity of the assignment as regards form was governed by the lex situs (English law); (2) that the validity of the assignment as regards capacity was governed by the law of Guatemala.

Appeal dismissed.

Where there are two or more competing assignments of a chose in action, each valid by its own proper law, questions of priority are determined by the proper law of the original contract.

KELLY v. SELWYN [1905] 2 Ch. 117 (Chancery Division)

Under the will of his father A. H. Solomon, who died in March 1888, Arthur Hammond Selwyn was entitled to a protected life interest in a legacy of £20,000, and was also contingently entitled in reversion to certain other legacies bequeathed to various members of the testator's family. The will contained a trust for sale, under which, at the time of the events hereinafter mentioned, all the real

367

KELLY
v.
SELWYN.
estate had been converted, and the whole estate was invested in English trust securities.

By an indenture of 8 June 1891, A. H. Selwyn, being then domiciled in the State of New York, assigned to his wife, an American lady, all his share and interest of what nature or kind soever which he then had or might thereafter have in the estate of his late father A. H. Solomon under or by virtue of his said will or otherwise (except his life interest in the £20,000 legacy), whether in possession, reversion, remainder, or expectancy, for her sole and separate use absolutely. According to the law of the State of New York, notice to the trustees of the will was not necessary to complete an assignment of a chose in action or reversionary interest in personalty, and no notice of the deed of 8 June 1891 was sent to the English trustees.

By an indenture of 10 August 1894, A. H. Selwyn, being then in England, assigned all his share and interest in the estate of his late father, whether under his said will or otherwise, or whether in remainder, reversion, or expectancy (except his life interest in the £20,000 legacy), to the plaintiff Thomas Kelly by way of mortgage to secure £400 and interest. Notice of this assignment was forthwith given by the plaintiff to the trustees of A. H. Solomon's will.

In September 1903 notice of the assignment of 8 June 1891 was given to the trustees of the will on behalf of Mrs. Selwyn.

A reversionary interest in A. H. Solomon's estate having recently fallen in, a portion of which would have been payable to A. H. Selwyn or persons claiming under him, the plaintiff commenced the present action against the trustees of the will and Mrs. Selwyn, claiming a declaration that he was entitled by virtue of his security of 10 August 1894 to a first charge on A. H. Selwyn's interest in his father's estate in priority to any right or claim of Mrs. Selwyn under the assignment in her favour of 8 June 1891.

WARRINGTON J.: The important question in this case has resolved itself into one of law upon which there does not seem to be any direct authority, though the case, I think, comes within certain well-known principles. [Having stated the facts, his Lordship continued:]

Under these circumstances the question I have to determine is which of these two assignments is to have priority. But for one circumstance, which I will mention directly, there can be no doubt, in the case of an English trust fund created by an English testator with trustees in England, that by the law of England, if that is the proper law to apply to this case, the mortgagee who first gave to the trustees notice of his security would take priority over the secret assignment (as I may call it) in favour of the wife, who did not give notice of it till later. But it is said on behalf of the wife (and this is the circumstance I referred to just now) that owing to the accident of the assignment in favour of the wife having been executed in the State of New York, where the English doctrines of notice are not recognised or are not in force, the law which I ought to regard myself as administering is not the law of England, but the law of New York, at any rate as far as that assignment is concerned.

A number of cases have been cited to me, none of which are actually in point; in fact, I do not think they were at all in point on the actual question which I have to determine. The first case, *In re Queensland Mercantile and Agency Co.*,[1] merely decided that where there is a chose in action owing from persons residing in a particular country (in that case in Scotland), an assignment in that case by process of law of those choses in action, valid according to the law of Scotland, would be valid elsewhere. I do not think that case decided anything more. If it is of any value in assisting me in the present case (I do not think it is) it is rather in favour of the defendant Mrs. Selwyn than in favour of the plaintiff; but I do not think that is the point which I have to decide. The assignment in New York is valid, but what I have to determine in administering an English trust fund, constituted by an English testator who may be taken to have made his will with the English law in his mind, is, in what order am I to treat the several claimants who come here with charges on the trust fund? The doctrine of notice, as I understand it, is that till notice is given, the assignee of a share in a trust fund is not completely constituted a cestui que trust, and that the order in which the fund is to be administered is the order in which the several claimants claiming to be assignees completely constituted themselves cestuis que trust. That is the point which I have to determine.

Another case that was cited and a good deal relied on is *Lee v. Abdy*,[2] which seems to me like *In re Queensland Mercantile and Agency Co.*, and merely decided this: that if a question arises whether an assignment of a chose in action is valid according to the law where it is executed, that question will be determined by the law of the place where it is executed. The question in *Lee v. Abdy*

---

[1] [1891] 1 Ch. 536 ; [1892] 1 Ch. 219.   [2] (1886) 17 Q.B.D. 309.

was whether an assignment made by a husband to his wife, which according to the law of Cape Colony was for that reason void, was to be treated as a good assignment of an English policy of assurance.

I have listened to the citations from Foote, Dicey, and Westlake, but I do not think there is anything in those passages that actually guides me in what I have to decide in this case. The ground on which I decide it is that, the fund here being an English trust fund and this being the court which the testator may have contemplated as the court which would have administered that trust fund, the order in which the parties are to be held entitled to the trust fund must be regulated by the law of the court which is administering that fund. On that footing it seems to me that the assignment to the plaintiff of August 1894 is entitled to priority over the assignment to Mrs. Selwyn of June 1891 by reason of the notice given by the plaintiff to the trustees of the will, and I must make a declaration to that effect.

NOTE Q: THE ASSIGNMENT OF INTANGIBLE MOVABLES

VARIOUS views have been suggested as to the law which should govern the assignment of intangible movables. The view of Story and Phillimore, that the law of the creditor's domicile is the test, is a relic of the outworn maxim 'mobilia sequuntur personam', and need not be taken seriously today. Westlake (s. 152) and Dicey (3rd ed., rule 153) thought that the lex situs of the debt is the test. This view has been overruled by the majority of the Court of Appeal (*Republica de Guatemala* v. *Nunez, ante*, p. 362) and by Maugham J. in *Re Anziani* [1930] 1 Ch. 407, at any rate so far as voluntary assignments are concerned. The objection to it is that though a debt may be regarded as situated in the place where it is properly recoverable (*New York Life Insurance Co.* v. *Public Trustee* [1924] 2 Ch. 101), that is presumably where the debtor resides and may be sued, the debtor may reside in more places than one. Cheshire (pp. 422–4), Wolff (ss. 512, 516), and Falconbridge (pp. 494–8) think that the proper law of the debt is the test. This view avoids problems of priorities between competing assignments, and also avoids the necessity for distinguishing between questions arising between debtor and creditor and questions arising between assignor and assignee. In most cases, however, the proper law of the debt coincides with the lex situs of the debt, and hence this view is inconsistent with the most recent authorities.

It is submitted that the key to the problem lies in distinguishing between (1) questions of assignability, governed by the proper law of the debt; (2) questions of the intrinsic validity of the assignment, governed by the proper law of the assignment; (3) questions of priorities, governed by the proper law of the debt; and (4) questions of attachment or garnishment (involuntary assignment), governed by the lex situs of the debt. All the cases are consistent with this view. It is now accepted by Dr. Cheshire (pp. 424–32).

ASSIGNMENT OF INTANGIBLE MOVABLES

(1) *Assignability*. The proper law of the debt determines whether the debt is assignable, and if so under what conditions (so far as they affect the debtor). English authority for this proposition is scanty, but it is clearly reasonable in principle, and is neatly illustrated by two American cases. In *Northwestern Mutual Life Insurance Co.* v. *Adams* (1914) 155 Wis. 335, it was held that a policy of life insurance made in Wisconsin was validly assigned in Minnesota, although by Minnesota law life insurance policies could not be assigned. Conversely, in *Coleman* v. *American Sheet and Tinplate Co.* (1936) 285 Ill. App. 542, it was held that an assignment in Illinois of future wages due under a contract of employment governed by Indiana law was invalid, since by Indiana law such assignments are prohibited. The proper law of the debt also determines whether the assignee takes subject to equities and whether notice of the assignment must be given to the debtor (*Kelly* v. *Selwyn, ante*, p. 367). The question whether the assignee can sue in his own name or whether he must join the assignor is probably a question of substance, governed by the proper law of the debt, and not a question of procedure, governed by the lex fori.

(2) *Intrinsic validity of assignment*. The intrinsic validity of an assignment is governed by the proper law of the assignment. Thus, that law determines whether the assignment must be in writing (formalities), whether an assignment to an infant or to the wife of the assignor is valid (capacity), and whether consideration is necessary (essential validity). These propositions are supported, not by the dicta, but by the decisions in *Lee* v. *Abdy* (1886) 17 Q.B.D. 309, *Republica de Guatemala* v. *Nunez* (*ante*, p. 362), and *Re Anziani* [1930] 1 Ch. 407. It is true that the judges speak of the law of the domicile of the assignor and assignee and of the law of the place where the assignment was made. But it is submitted that this language must be interpreted broadly as meaning the proper law of the assignment. It can scarcely be doubted that Cape law, Guatemalan law, and Italian law respectively were the proper laws of the three assignments in question. There are many dicta in older cases asserting that the validity of a contract is governed by the law of the place where it is made. But these dicta have not prevented judges in later cases from establishing the more reasonable principle that the validity of a contract is governed by its proper law.

There is no reason to doubt that an assignment, like a contract, which complied with the formalities prescribed by either the proper law of the assignment or the law of the place where the assignment was made would be formally valid in England.

(3) *Priorities*. The priorities of competing assignments are governed by the proper law of the debt: *Kelly* v. *Selwyn, ante*, p. 367. Questions of priorities arise if there are two or more competing assignments, each intrinsically valid by its proper law, of a debt capable of assignment by its proper law. This was not the case in *Republica de Guatemala* v. *Nunez*, because each of the assignments was, for different reasons, invalid, and the money went to President Cabrera's creditors. It was the case in *Kelly* v. *Selwyn*, but there is some doubt as to the ratio of that case. Scrutton L.J. in the *Guatemala* case (*ante*, pp. 366–7) thought that the ratio was that priorities are governed by the lex fori; but Warrington J. applied 'the law of the court which is administering the fund', which is at least equally consistent with the proper law of the debt. In *Le Feuvre* v. *Sullivan* (1855) 10 Moo.

P.C. 1, an English policy of insurance on the life of an assured domiciled in Jersey was assigned first in England to a creditor of the assured and then in Jersey to the wife of the assured. It was held that priorities were governed by English law, because the policy was 'in every sense an English instrument forming or evidencing an English contract'—i.e. clearly because English law was the proper law of the debt. In this case Jersey law was the lex fori, and therefore it is inconsistent with Scrutton L.J.'s explanation of *Kelly* v. *Selwyn*.

(4) *Attachment and garnishment.* The validity and effect of an attachment or garnishment of a debt are governed by the lex situs of the debt: *Re Queensland Mercantile Agency Co.* [1891] 1 Ch. 536; [1892] 1 Ch. 219; *Rossano* v. *Manufacturers Life Insurance Co. Ltd.* [1963] 2 Q.B. 352.

Chapter 14

GOVERNMENTAL SEIZURE OF PROPERTY

English courts will recognize a foreign decree affecting property situated within the territory of the foreign country at the time of the decree, even if it is later brought to England.

LUTHER *v.* SAGOR [1921] 3 K.B. 532 (Court of Appeal)

THE plaintiffs were a Russian company incorporated in Russia in 1898. They had a factory or mill at Staraja Russa in Russia where in 1919 they had a large stock of manufactured boards. On 20 June 1918 a confiscatory decree was signed by Lenin in the presence of the Council of People's Commissars purporting to vest in the Russian State the capital and assets of all mechanical sawmills and all woodworking establishments belonging to private or limited companies. In January 1919 officials armed with authority from the Soviet Government took possession of the plaintiff's factory or mill at Staraja Russa and of the manufactured goods lying there. In August 1920 a contract was made in London between one Krassin, the representative of the Russian Commercial Delegation in London, and the defendants, an American firm carrying on business in London, whereby Krassin sold to the defendants a quantity of plywood including the boards seized by the officials as above stated. Under this contract the defendants obtained possession of the plywood boards and imported them into England.

Roche J. found that His Majesty's Government had not recognized the Russian Soviet Government as the government of a sovereign state; he therefore gave judgment for the plaintiffs. The defendants appealed. Before the hearing of the appeal the Foreign Office informed the defendants' solicitors that His Majesty's Government recognized the Soviet Government as the de facto Government of Russia.

BANKES L.J. (having held that the de facto recognition of the Soviet Government related back to the seizure of the plaintiffs' goods, continued:) It is necessary now to deal with the point made

LUTHER
v.
SAGOR.

Bankes
L.J.

by the respondents, that the decree of confiscation of June 1918, even if made by the Government which is now recognized by His Majesty's Government as the de facto Government of Russia, is in its nature so immoral, and so contrary to the principles of justice as recognized by this country, that the courts of this country ought not to pay any attention to it. This is a bold proposition. The question before the court is not one in which the assistance of the court is asked to enforce the law of some foreign country to which legitimate objection might be taken, as in *Hope* v. *Hope*[1] and *Kaufman* v. *Gerson*.[2] The question before the court is as to the title to goods lying in a foreign country which a subject of that country, being the owner of them by the law of that country, has sold under an f.o.b. contract for export to this country. The court is asked to ignore the law of the foreign country under which the vendor acquired his title, and to lend its assistance to prevent the purchaser dealing with the goods. I do not think that any authority can be produced to support the contention. Authority appears to negative it. (After quoting from *Santos* v. *Illidge*,[3] his Lordship continued:) The respondents' position is rendered all the more difficult from the fact that the vendor in the present case is a duly recognized sovereign state whose law conferred the title which is challenged. Even if it was open to the courts of this country to consider the morality or justice of the decree of June 1918, I do not see how the courts could treat this particular decree otherwise than as the expression by the de facto government of a civilized country of a policy which it considered to be in the best interest of that country. It must be quite immaterial for present purposes that the same views are not entertained by the Government of this country, are repudiated by the vast majority of its citizens, and are not recognized by our laws. Taking the view I do of the point I do not consider it necessary to discuss the authorities to which our attention has been called. . . .

WARRINGTON L.J.: . . . Some reliance was placed by the respondents upon the principle enunciated in such cases as *Kaufman* v. *Gerson* that the courts of this country will not enforce a contract invalid by our law as being in contravention of some essential principle of justice or morality, notwithstanding that by the law of the country where it was made no such objection could be raised to it. In my opinion this principle has no application. The appellants are

[1] (1857) 8 D.M. & G. 731. [2] [1904] 1 K.B. 591.
[3] (1860) 8 C.B. N.S. 861, 876.

374

not seeking to enforce such a contract. They are resisting an endeavour on the part of the respondents to induce the court to ignore and override legislative and executive acts of the Government of Russia and its agents affecting the title to property in that country; it is that which, in my opinion, we are not at liberty to do. . . .

SCRUTTON L.J.: . . . It remains to consider the argument that the English courts should refuse to recognize the Soviet legislation and titles derived under it as confiscatory and unjust. This was based on the general principle stated by Mr. Dicey in his work on the Conflict of Laws[1] that 'English courts will not enforce a right otherwise duly acquired under the law of a foreign country . . . (B) where the enforcement of such right is inconsistent with the policy of English law, or with the moral rules upheld by English law, or with the maintenance of English political institutions'. When this is expanded later in the same work, the only head applicable to this case is (Inconsistency with) 'Morality', i.e. as supported by English courts. There are very few instances in which this principle has been applied. Rights derived from a contract for the sale of slaves made in a country where such a sale is legal have been enforced by English courts: Santos v. Illidge. Gaming debts incurred abroad where gaming is legal have been enforced here: Quarrier v. Colston;[2] though securities payable in England for gaming debts of the same character have not been enforced: Moulis v. Owen.[3] Two cases in particular in which English courts have ignored foreign law of which they disapproved, Simpson v. Fogo and Kaufman v. Gerson, have been the subject of considerable adverse comment. The former can perhaps be treated as a retaliation by English courts on foreign states whose tribunals refuse to recognize rights acquired by English law. The latter decision, in which English courts refused to recognize a contract validly made in France on the ground that it was contrary to English principles of morality, is adversely criticized by Mr. Dicey,[5] who treats it as a mistaken application of the sound principle that English courts will not enforce foreign contracts, valid where made, where the court deems the contract to be in contravention of some essential principle of justice and morality. But it appears a serious breach of international comity, if a state is recognized as a sovereign independent state, to postulate that its legislation is 'contrary to

LUTHER
v.
SAGOR.
Warrington
L.J.

[1] 2nd ed. (1908) p. 33.   [2] (1842) 1 Ph. 147.
[3] [1907] 1 K.B. 746.   [4] (1863) 1 H. & M. 195.
[5] Conflict of Laws, 2nd ed., Appendix 3, p. 727.

375

essential principles of justice and morality'. Such an allegation might well with a susceptible foreign government become a casus belli; and should in my view be the action of the Sovereign through his ministers, and not of the judges in reference to a state which their Sovereign has recognized. The English courts act on the rule 'that an intention to take away the property of a subject without giving to him a legal right to compensation for the loss of it is not to be imputed to the Legislature unless that intention is expressed in unequivocal terms': *Central Control Board* v. *Cannon Brewery Co.*[1] If it were they must give effect to it, and can hardly be more rigid in their dealings with foreign legislation. Individuals must contribute to the welfare of the State, and at present British citizens who may contribute to the State more than half their income in income tax and super tax, and a large proportion of their capital in death duties, can hardly declare a foreign state immoral which considers (though we may think wrongly) that to vest individual property in the State as representing all the citizens is the best form of proprietary right. I do not feel able to come to the conclusion that the legislation of a state recognized by my Sovereign as an independent sovereign state is so contrary to moral principle that the judges ought not to recognize it. The responsibility for recognition or non-recognition, with the consequences of each, rests on the political advisers of the Sovereign and not on the judges.

Appeal allowed.

It is immaterial that the property belongs to persons who are not nationals of the foreign State and that no compensation is payable, unless the decree is penal (i.e. discriminatory).

In re
HELBERT
WAGG
& CO.
LTD.'S
CLAIM.

In re HELBERT WAGG & CO. LTD.'S CLAIM [1956] Ch. 323
(Chancery Division)

By a loan agreement made in 1924 between a German company ('the company') and Helbert Wagg & Co. Ltd. ('the claimant'), the claimant agreed to lend the company £350,000 at $7\frac{1}{2}$ per cent. interest. The loan was redeemable in 1945. The proper law of the contract was German. In June 1933 a German moratorium law provided that a Konversionskasse for foreign debts should be created, that debts payable in foreign currencies must be converted into

---

[1] [1919] A.C. 744, 752.

Reichsmarks and paid into the Konversionkasse, and that the debtor's liability should thereby be discharged. The company duly paid Reichsmarks into the Konversionkasse at the appropriate rate of exchange, and continued to do so after the outbreak of war in 1939. By 1945 the company had paid the full equivalent in Reichsmarks of the whole loan outstanding and interest thereon. On 3 September 1939 there was outstanding under the loan agreement £174,142 in respect of capital, and the claimant claimed, under the Distribution of German Enemy Property Act 1949, to rank as creditor in respect of that amount and interest thereon. The Administrator of German Property rejected the claim. The claimant appealed to the High Court.

In re
HELBERT
WAGG
& CO.
LTD.'S
CLAIM.

UPJOHN J.: The first question that I must determine is whether the applicability of the Moratorium Law is to be tested by reference to the local situation of the debt or by the proper law of the contract. I am concerned with the effect of a law passed in 1933 upon a series of debts which, though accrued, only became payable on or after September 3, 1939. In my judgment, the question whether a liability to pay a debt payable on a future date has become modified or annulled by legislation must depend upon the question whether such legislation affects the contractual obligation, for the matter still rests in contract. Indeed, it does not seem appropriate to speak of a debt having a local situation until it is payable and can be recovered by suit, for its situs primarily depends upon the residence of the debtor when it is recoverable. . . . The power of legislation to affect a contract by modifying or annulling some term thereof is a question of discharge of the contract which, in general, is governed by the proper law (see *Kahler* v. *Midland Bank*[1]).

(After holding that the proper law of the contract was German, his Lordship continued:) For the reasons I have already given, I do not think that the situs of the debt is the relevant consideration, but as the matter has been very fully argued before me . . . I think I ought to express my views thereon. (After holding that the situs of the debt was in Germany, his Lordship continued:) I start with the elementary proposition that it is part of the law of England, and of most nations, that in general every civilized State must be recognized as having power to legislate in respect of movables situate within that State and in respect of contracts governed by the law of

[1] [1950] A.C. 24.

In re
HELBERT
WAGG
& CO.
LTD.'S
CLAIM.
—
Upjohn J.

that State, and that such legislation must be recognized by other States as valid and effectual to alter title to such movables and to sustain, modify or dissolve such contracts. The substantial question I have to determine is what limit is to be imposed upon that proposition when the effect of such legislation comes to be debated in the courts of other States. I may note in passing that the modern tendency is to deny extraterritorial validity to legislation, for example, upon movables situate outside the State at the time of the legislation: *Bank voor Handel en Scheepvart N.V.* v. *Slatford*.[1]

To this general principle of recognition in foreign courts of territorial validity of legislation there are undoubted limitations or exceptions as the following examples show: (1) No State will enforce the fiscal laws, however proper, of another State, nor penal statutes, using that phrase in the strict sense of meaning statutes imposing penalties recoverable by the State for infringement of some law. 'The penal laws of foreign countries are strictly local and affect nothing more than they can reach and seize by virtue of their authority', *per* Lord Loughborough in *Folliott* v. *Ogden*.[2] (2) English law will not recognize the validity of foreign legislation intended to discriminate against nationals of this country in time of war by legislation which purports to confiscate wholly or in part movable property situated in the foreign State. As long ago as 1817 such confiscation was described by Lord Ellenborough C.J. in *Wolff* v. *Oxholm*[3] as 'not conformable to the usage of nations'. . . . (3) English courts will not recognize the validity of foreign legislation aimed at confiscating the property of particular individuals or classes of individuals: *Banco de Vizcaya* v. *Don Alfonso de Borbon y Austria*,[4] which treated the Spanish laws purporting to expropriate the ex-King of Spain's property as examples of penal legislation; and see *Anglo-Iranian Oil Co.* v. *Jaffrate* (*The Rose Mary*),[5] where Campbell J., sitting in the Supreme Court of Aden, held certain laws of the State of Persia which he found to be passed to nationalize the plaintiff company only without compensation were confiscatory and ineffectual to pass title. . . .

I do not challenge the correctness of the decision in the *Rose Mary* case upon the facts of that case, but Campbell J. came to the conclusion that the authorities both of this and other countries justified the

---

[1] [1953] 1 Q.B. 248; *post*, p. 381.   [2] (1789) 1 H. Bl. 123, 135.
[3] (1817) 6 M. & S. 92.   [4] [1935] 1 K.B. 140.
[5] [1953] 1 W.L.R. 246.

formulation of a more general principle, namely: (1) all legislation that expropriates without compensation is contrary to international law; and (2) that such law is incorporated in the domestic law of Aden and accordingly such legislation will not be recognized as valid in the courts of Aden. Unless the law of England takes a different view of international law from the law of Aden, the judge's conclusions can only be correct if his interpretation of *Luther* v. *Sagor*[1] and *Princess Paley Olga* v. *Weisz*[2] is correct. Those cases, both in the Court of Appeal, were concerned with the effect of Russian legislation introduced shortly after the Russian Revolution of 1917 which in fact expropriated certain types of private property situate in Russia without any compensation. They established the principle that this court will not inquire into the legality of acts done by a foreign government in respect of property situate in its own territory. Campbell J. considered that principle to be valid only where the property confiscated belongs (as in both those cases) to subjects of the confiscating State. However, all three judgments in *Luther* v. *Sagor* laid down the principle in perfectly general terms and it was in no way limited, at any rate in express terms, to a recognition of the validity of such legislation in relation only to nationals of the confiscating State. . . .

In equally general terms were the judgments of two members of the court in *Princess Paley Olga* v. *Weisz*. It seems clear the Scrutton L.J. drew no distinction between the operation of legislation upon the property of a national of the confiscating State and a foreigner who had movables in that State. . . . It is true that Russell L.J., in that case, said: 'This court will not inquire into the legality of acts done by a foreign government against its own subjects in respect of property situate in its own territory', but it was sufficient for the decision of the case before him, and he dealt with the point very briefly.

Maugham J. in *Re Russian Bank for Foreign Trade*,[3] also stated the principle in the same limited way but his remarks were obiter.

On the other hand, in *Perry* v. *Equitable Life Assurance Society of the United States of America*,[4] the plaintiff, a British subject residing in Russia, took out a policy of life assurance with the defendants, the proper law of the contract being Russian. It was held that certain confiscatory decrees of the Russian Government

In re
HELBERT
WAGG
& CO.
LTD.'S
CLAIM.
—
Upjohn J.

---

[1] [1921] 3 K.B. 532 ; *ante*, p. 373.   [2] [1929] 1 K.B. 718.
[3] [1933] Ch. 745.   [4] (1929) 45 T.L.R. 468.

In re
HELBERT
WAGG
& CO.
LTD.'S
CLAIM.
—
Upjohn J.

were effective to annul the contract, though it is true that no point was taken that such decrees could be valid only against Russian nationals. This case was quoted without disapproval by Lord Radcliffe in *Kahler* v. *Midland Bank*.[1]

In *Re Banque des Marchands de Moscou, Royal Exchange Assurance* v. *The Liquidator*[2] (which does not appear to have been cited to Campbell J.), Vaisey J. expressed the view that the general principle was not limited to nationals of the confiscating State. I respectfully agree with him, for it seems to me that on this question nationality must be irrelevant. If the principle be true in respect of a State in relation to its own nationals, it must surely be conceded in relation to those persons who, though not subjects of the State, nevertheless bring their movables within its jurisdiction for business or private reasons or for the like reasons enter into contracts governed by the law of the State, and in general enjoy the same benefits and protection and are subject to the same disadvantages and disabilities as subjects of the State.

With all respect to Campbell J. I think that *Luther* v. *Sagor* and *Princess Paley Olga* v. *Weisz* laid down principles of general application not limited to nationals of the confiscating State.

In my judgment the true limits of the principle that the courts of this country will afford recognition to legislation of foreign States in so far as it affects title to movables in that State at the time of the legislation or contracts governed by the law of that State rest in considerations of international law, or in the scarcely less difficult considerations of public policy as understood by these courts. Ultimately I believe the latter is the governing consideration. But, whatever be the true view, the authorities I have reviewed do show that these courts have not on either ground recognized any principle that confiscation without adequate compensation is per se a ground for refusing recognition to foreign legislation. That view is further supported by the authorities on exchange control legislation which I must now consider. . . .

Appeal dismissed.

[1] [1950] A.C. 24, 56.   [2] [1952] 1 T.L.R. 739.

GOVERNMENTAL SEIZURE OF PROPERTY

But English courts will not recognize a foreign decree purporting to affect property situated outside the territory of the foreign State.

BANK VOOR HANDEL EN SCHEEPVART N.V. *v.* SLATFORD [1953] 1 Q.B. 248 (Queen's Bench Division)

BANK VOOR
HANDEL EN
SCHEEP-
VART
N.V.
v.
SLATFORD.

Before the war of 1939–45 the plaintiff, a Dutch bank, in the ordinary course of business deposited gold bars to the value of two million pounds with the City Safe Deposit in London. In May 1940 the Netherlands were invaded and became enemy territory. The plaintiff bank retained its commercial domicile in the Netherlands, and thus at once acquired enemy character on that ground. The Royal Netherlands Government thereafter, with the approval of the British Government, exercised their sovereign powers from London. On 24 May 1940 they issued a decree (called the A. 1 decree), with the object of preventing property belonging to persons resident in occupied Holland from being used in a manner incompatible with the interests of the Netherlands. This decree purported to transfer such property (including the gold bars) to the State for so long as might be necessary. On 3 July 1940 the Board of Trade, under the Trading with the Enemy Act 1939, made a vesting order transferring the gold to the custodian. On 24 July the custodian sold the gold and retained the proceeds as enemy property. On 19 May 1950 the Netherlands Government made an order returning the property in the gold to the bank. The bank claimed against the custodian in conversion the present value of the gold bars, on the ground that the order of July 1940 was invalid since the property in the gold was then in the Netherlands Government by virtue of the A. 1 decree.

DEVLIN J.: The custodian submits that the English courts will not enforce it [the A. 1 decree] since they will treat it as having no extra-territorial effect. The plaintiff's submission is that the general rule is to the contrary, and that the legislation of a foreign State affecting the title of its nationals to movables in England will be applied by the English courts unless, first, the legislation is contrary to public policy—as, for instance, confiscatory or penal legislation—or, secondly, its application would infringe English legislation. Alternatively, the plaintiffs submit that, if it be the general rule that foreign legislation is not enforceable, then the decree falls within an exceptional category.

381

BANK VOOR
HANDEL EN
SCHEEP-
VART
N.V.
v.
SLATFORD.

Devlin J.

I think it is convenient to begin by considering what is the general principle of our law with regard to foreign legislation affecting property within our territory. There is little doubt that it is the lex situs which as a general rule governs the transfer of movables when effected contractually. The maxim mobilia sequuntur personam is the exception rather than the rule, and is probably to be confined to certain special classes of general assignments such as marriage settlements and devolutions on death and bankruptcy. Upon this basis the A. 1 decree, not being a part of English law, would not transfer the property in this case. But decrees of this character have received in the authorities rather different treatment. Although there is not, as far as I am aware, any authority which distinguishes general legislation, such as part of a civil code, from ad hoc decrees, the effectiveness of such decrees does not appear on the authorities to be determined exclusively by the application of the lex situs. Apart from two recent cases on which the plaintiffs greatly rely, there has been no case in which such a decree has been enforced in this country, but the grounds for refusing effect to them have been variously put. Sometimes it is said that the decree is confiscatory. In the textbooks it is said sometimes that as a matter of public international law no State ought to seek to exercise sovereignty over property outside its own territory, and therefore the principle of comity is against enforcement; and sometimes it is said that the principle of effectiveness is against enforcement, since no State can expect to make its laws effective in the territory of another State. Dicey[1] states: 'A State's authority, in the eyes of other States and the courts that represent them, is, speaking very generally, coincident with, and limited by, its power. It is territorial. It may legislate for, and give judgments affecting, things and persons within its territory. It has no authority to legislate for, or adjudicate upon, things or persons not within its territory.'

The Solicitor-General has argued on principle that no foreign legislation, whether confiscatory or not, can be allowed to affect property in this country. It is beyond dispute that confiscatory legislation will not be allowed to do so, and the Solicitor-General contends that the distinction between confiscatory and non-confiscatory is not a satisfactory one. In *A/S Tallinna Laevauhisus* v. *Estonian State S.S. Line*,[2] legislation which provided for compensation amounting to 25 per cent. of the value was held to be confiscatory. Pre-

---

[1] Conflict of Laws, 6th ed. (1949) p. 13.   [2] (1946) 80 Ll. L. Rep. 99.

GOVERNMENTAL SEIZURE OF PROPERTY

sumably any decree which did not provide for full compensation would be held to be confiscatory. Now that decrees involving State acquisition and requisition are comparatively common, it may not be easy to ascertain whether full compensation is provided for or not. The Compensation (Defence) Act 1939 places certain limits on the amount of compensation: for example, no account is to be taken of any appreciation in value due to the war. While that is doubtless a healthy rule for British nationals, it might well result in a neutral getting less than the full value of his goods. If a decree, such as the A. 1 decree, contemplates that the property taken is to be preserved for the benefit of its owners and to be returned to them at the conclusion of the war, but contains no legal obligation to that effect, is the hope and expectation that the subject will get his property returned to him sufficient to save it from being confiscatory?

There are other considerations of principle which can be advanced in support of the defendants' argument. First, in the construction of our own statutory legislation we accept the principle that, unless the contrary is made clear, an Act of Parliament is not intended to have extraterritorial effect. Secondly, the principle as submitted by the defendants is in harmony with the principle which favours the lex situs generally. Thirdly, if extraterritorial effect is given to foreign property legislation, it can only be at the expense of English law affecting the same subject-matter. . . .

There are three comparatively recent authorities in point. In *Lorentzen* v. *Lydden & Co. Ltd.*,[1] Atkinson J. decided that a decree of the Royal Norwegian Government acquiring, in return for compensation, property of its subjects in England was effective to transfer such property to the Norwegian Government. In *O/Y Wasa Steamship Co. Ltd.* v. *Newspaper Pulp and Wood Export Ltd*,[2] Morris J. followed this decision and applied it to the decree A. 1 which I have to consider in this case. In both these cases the property concerned was a claim for damages for breach of a charterparty. The latter case involved a great number of points, and I am told by counsel concerned in this case that the principle in *Lorentzen* v. *Lydden & Co. Ltd.* was not much debated. The main authority on which the plaintiffs rely is therefore *Lorentzen* v. *Lydden & Co. Ltd.* I think that that case is directly in point; I am unable to distinguish it upon the ground suggested—namely, that the point that the decree was in conflict with the Trading with the Enemy legislation

[1] [1942] 2 K.B. 202.   [2] (1949) 82 Ll. L. Rep. 936.

383

BANK VOOR
HANDEL EN
SCHEEP-
VART
N.V.
v.
SLATFORD.

Devlin J. was not expressly taken in argument. The defendants rely mainly on *Government of the Republic of Spain* v. *National Bank of Scotland (The El Condado)*,[1] a decision of the Inner House of the Court of Session and therefore of high persuasive authority. The court was considering a claim by the Spanish consul to the possession of a Spanish ship which he had sought to requisition while she was at Glasgow in accordance with powers granted by a Spanish decree. It does not appear from those parts of the decree set out in the report whether it provided for compensation or not, but it is clear that it was not treated by the court as confiscatory. The Scottish court refused to enforce the decree. The plaintiffs are unable to distinguish this case from *Lorentzen* v. *Lydden & Co. Ltd.* or from the present case except by saying that different considerations of public policy are involved.

In *Lorentzen* v. *Lydden & Co. Ltd.* Atkinson J. surveyed the earlier authorities in order to arrive at his conclusion that there was no general rule preventing him from enforcing the Norwegian decree. I do not find it entirely clear whether he held that all foreign property legislation was enforceable unless contrary to public policy, or that the general rule excluded all such legislation, subject to certain exceptional categories, within one of which the Norwegian decree fell. I shall examine the cases to see if any general rule can be extracted from them.

(After considering *Lecouturier* v. *Rey*,[2] *Sedgwick Collins & Co.* v. *Rossia Insurance Co.*,[3] *The Jupiter (No. 3)*,[4] and *Re Russian Bank for Foreign Trade*,[5] his Lordship continued:) While it is true that in all these cases there was confiscatory legislation, I think it would be surprising if, with so many masters of the law all intending to restrict the statement of the principle to confiscatory legislation, no one of them had used in his statement of the principle some words of limitation. This consideration disposes me to think that the view of these dicta taken by the Court of Session in *The El Condado* is the right one. The Lord Justice Clerk, having stated that the principle clearly applies to confiscatory or penal laws, inquires whether it equally applies to legislation which is not confiscatory or penal in the full sense. He treats *The Jupiter (No. 3)* as being an authority in point, and concludes that the decree cannot apply to movable property

---

[1] 1939 S.C. 413.   [2] [1910] A.C. 262, 265, 273.
[3] [1926] 1 K.B. 1, 15.   [4] [1927] P. 122, 145.
[5] [1933] Ch. 745, 767.

outwith the territory and jurisdiction of the foreign sovereign State. Lord Mackay says that he finds in the cases 'a most emphatic train of eminent English judges in favour of the view that such "decrees" of a foreign country as purport to have extraterritorial effect, and to attach property in a subject situated, and at a time when it is situated, in this country or its territorial waters, will not be recognized by our laws and courts'. Lord Wark reviews all the English authorities and concludes by adopting the passage in Dicey which I have cited.

My recollection of the argument in *Lorentzen* v. *Lydden & Co. Ltd.* is that Atkinson J. was referred to *The El Condado*; but he does not distinguish it in his judgment. I recognize the force of the point that, if the principle were as wide as the custodian says it is, there would be no need for any case to have been decided on the basis that the legislation was confiscatory. But the dicta in the English cases seem to me to be sufficient to support the conclusion in *The El Condado*; and for the reasons that I have given I think that the rule there laid down is a sound one. If Atkinson J. is to be taken as deciding that the general rule was otherwise, I respectfully prefer the decision in *The El Condado*.

The question next arises whether the A. 1 decree belongs to a special category which should form an exception to this general rule. The real ground stated by Atkinson J. in *Lorentzen* v. *Lydden & Co. Ltd.* for regarding the Norwegian decree as exceptional is that, England and Norway being engaged together in a desperate war for their existence, public policy required that effect should be given to the decree. This reasoning at once gives rise to three comments. The first is that it amounts to the formulation of a new head of public policy, and that is not a matter to be lightly undertaken. The second is that it is using public policy, not in accordance with precedent, as a restriction upon acts which are thought to be harmful to the community, but in a novel way as a positive force to give to an act validity which it would otherwise lack. The third is that it would appear to cast on the court the duty of considering to some extent the political merits of the decree itself.

The plaintiffs in their argument before me accept that it is not possible for the courts to judge of the expediency of any particular decree; and I think that they admit also that it would be beyond the wit of man to devise a principle which would admit the politically desirable decrees and exclude the undesirable. They therefore put

BANK VOOR
HANDEL EN
SCHEEP-
VART
N.V.
v.
SLATFORD.

Devlin J.

Bank voor
Handel en
Scheep-
vart
N.V.
v.
Slatford.

Devlin J.
their submission on this point in a form which seeks a middle way between these two extremities. They submit that the exceptional category consists of decrees of an allied Power in respect of the property of its nationals made in this country with the approval, or at least with the acquiescence, of His Majesty's Government with a view to keeping property out of the hands of a common enemy. . . . No doubt one could formulate a broad rule of policy that allied governments should be assisted in time of war. But the extent to which a particular decree serves that end seems to me to be entirely a matter for political decision by the Government of the day, which would have to consider whether all its provisions or some or none of them fitted in with their war policy. A power at war is not bound to regard everything that its allies do as politically desirable. . . .

In my judgment it would be unwise, in the light of these considerations and of the authorities, to propound as a new rule of public policy the principle for which the plaintiffs contend. I need hardly say that it is only after much thought that I have rejected the guidance given by the decision of Atkinson J. in *Lorentzen* v. *Lydden & Co. Ltd.*; and I have done so only because upon reflection I think that it cannot be made to conform with the authorities which regulate the use of public policy. In this respect I may say that I have had from the Solicitor-General the benefit of a much fuller and more able presentation of the relevant considerations than Atkinson J. had in the unsuccessful argument before him.[1]

I have been dealing with public policy as a force which has to be invoked by the plaintiffs in order to succeed. Many of these considerations would also apply on the first part of the argument. If foreign legislation is as a general rule to be admitted, it would have to be excluded when politically harmful; and the difficulty of formulating any satisfactory principle of exclusion is in my view a formidable argument against the validity of the rule.

In my judgment the claim against the custodian fails.

Action dismissed.

[1] This argument was presented by Mr. Devlin as he then was (*Ed.*).

Chapter 15

TRANSFER OF NEGOTIABLE INSTRUMENTS

72. Where a bill drawn in one country is negotiated, accepted, or payable in another, the rights, duties, and liabilities of the parties thereto are determined as follows:—

(1) The validity of a bill as regards requisites in form is determined by the law of the place of issue, and the validity as regards requisites in form of the supervening contracts, such as acceptance, or indorsement, or acceptance suprà protest, is determined by the law of the place where such contract was made.
Provided that—

   (a) Where a bill is issued out of the United Kingdom it is not invalid by reason only that it is not stamped in accordance with the law of the place of issue;

   (b) Where a bill, issued out of the United Kingdom, conforms, as regards requisites in form, to the law of the United Kingdom, it may, for the purpose of enforcing payment thereof, be treated as valid as between all persons who negotiate, hold, or become parties to it in the United Kingdom.

(2) Subject to the provisions of this Act, the interpretation of the drawing, indorsement, acceptance, or acceptance suprà protest of a bill, is determined by the law of the place where such contract is made.
Provided that where an inland bill is indorsed in a foreign country the indorsement shall as regards the payer be interpreted according to the law of the United Kingdom.

(3) The duties of the holder with respect to presentment for acceptance or payment and the necessity for or sufficiency of a protest or notice of dishonour, or otherwise, are determined by the law of the place where the act is done or the bill is dishonoured.

(4) Where a bill is drawn out of but payable in the United Kingdom and the sum payable is not expressed in the currency of the United Kingdom, the amount shall, in the absence of

387

some express stipulation, be calculated according to the rate of exchange for sight drafts at the place of payment on the day the bill is payable.

(5) Where a bill is drawn in one country and is payable in another, the due date thereof is determined according to the law of the place where it is payable.

EMBIRICOS v. ANGLO-AUSTRIAN BANK [1905] 1 K.B. 677 (Court of Appeal)

Appeal from a judgment of Walton J.[1]

The action was brought by Messrs. L. & M. Embiricos against the Anglo-Austrian Bank to recover damages for the wrongful conversion of a cheque. On 6 March 1903 a Roumanian bank drew a cheque at Braila, in Roumania, on a London bank payable to the plaintiffs or order. The same day the plaintiffs at Braila specially indorsed the cheque to G. Embiricos & Co., a London firm, and wrote to them a letter which, with the cheque, the plaintiffs placed in an envelope addressed to G. Embiricos & Co. in London. The cheque was stolen from the envelope by a clerk of the plaintiffs. On 9 March 1903 the cheque was presented at the bank of Messrs. Schelhammer & Schatterer, in Vienna, by a person who desired that it might be cashed. It then bore the indorsement G. Embiricos & Co., in addition to the special indorsement to that firm by the plaintiffs. The indorsements were apparently regular and in order, but that of G. Embiricos & Co. was in fact a forgery, though Messrs. Schelhammer & Schatterer were ignorant of the forgery. They telegraphed to the Roumanian bank, and, having ascertained from them that the cheque was in order, they cashed it, and on the same day they indorsed it to the defendants and posted it to them in London, where the defendants cashed it at the bank on which it was drawn.

According to an affidavit made as to the Austrian law by a doctor of law of the University of Vienna, 'the holder of a cheque which he has bought bonâ fide without gross negligence and for value is identified as the proprietor of the cheque, and entitled to the proceeds thereof against all the world, notwithstanding that the cheque has been previously stolen, and notwithstanding that the indorsement has been forged'.

Walton J. gave judgment for the defendants. He held, upon the

1 [1904] 2 K.B. 870.

authority of *Alcock* v. *Smith*,[1] that the transfer of the cheque in Vienna was governed by Austrian law, and gave the Vienna bank a good title to the cheque, which title they transferred to the defendants.

The plaintiffs appealed.

VAUGHAN WILLIAMS L.J.: Walton J. decided the case in favour of the defendants on the ground that, by the transfer of the cheque to the Vienna bank, a good title to the cheque, which the English court was bound to recognise, passed to the Vienna bank, and that that bank gave an equally good title to the defendants who, when they presented the cheque for payment to the bank on which it was drawn, were dealing with their own property and not with the plaintiffs' property. He pointed out that the only question in this action is between the original payees and the subsequent holders of the cheque, who derived their title to the cheque through an indorsement which had been forged. And that, inasmuch as under the English law no title could be made under a forged indorsement, but under the Austrian law the bonâ fide holder of a cheque, for which he has given value in ignorance of any flaw in the title of the transferor, is entitled to the cheque, although it has been previously stolen and the indorsements upon it have been forged, it became necessary to decide whether the validity of the transfer of this cheque ought to be governed by Austrian or by English law. Walton J. held that the question of the validity of the transfer ought to be governed by Austrian law, first, because it was decided by Romer J., and on appeal by the Court of Appeal in *Alcock* v. *Smith*, that the ordinary rule as to the transfer of chattels which is thus stated in rule 140[2] of Dicey's Conflict of Laws, that 'Assignment of a movable which can be touched (goods) giving a good title according to the law of the country where the movable is situate at the time of the assignment (lex situs) is valid', applies to a bill of exchange, and, I suppose, to any negotiable instrument; and Walton J. also seemed to be of opinion that his judgment could be justified by the words of s. 72 of the Bills of Exchange Act, 1882. For the learned judge said that if the 'interpretation' of the indorsement means the legal effect of the transfer by indorsement, it would cover this case.

I think that the view taken by Walton J. of the effect of the decision in *Alcock* v. *Smith*, that the rule that the validity of the transfer

EMBIRICOS
v.
ANGLO-
AUSTRIAN
BANK.

[1] [1892] 1 Ch. 238.   [2] See now rule 81.

EMBIRICOS
v.
ANGLO-
AUSTRIAN
BANK.
—
Vaughan
Williams
L.J.

of chattels must be governed by the law of the country in which the transfer takes place, applies to a bill or a cheque, and applies to the transfer of bills or cheques in cases where the transfer is by indorsement, is right; although in the case of *Alcock* v. *Smith* the transfer was not by indorsement, but by process of law in the shape of a judicial arrestment. This conclusion seems sufficient to negative the cause of action in the present case, which is an action by the payee against an indorsee, who claims under a forged indorsement giving him a good title in the country where the indorsement was made.

But it would manifestly be an unsatisfactory state of the law if the legal result is that the indorsement is effective to give the indorsee of a bill a good title as against the payee, but not effective according to English law to give that indorsee a good title against the drawer or the acceptor. And it would be convenient, as well from a legal as from a commercial point of view, that it should be established that the title by such an indorsement is good as against the original parties to a negotiable instrument, having regard to the contractual liability incurred by them thereby. I do not think that *Alcock* v. *Smith* decides this question; on the contrary, it seems to me that the judgments of Romer J. and the Court of Appeal both disclaim so doing; and, further, it seems to me that the law as laid down by Pearson J. in *In re Marseilles, &c., Land Co.*[1] and by Lush J. in *Lebel* v. *Tucker*[2] is, in effect, authority to the contrary. At all events, it has never been decided that the liability of an acceptor in England of a bill drawn abroad or of the drawer of a cheque payable in England amounts to a contract to pay on a forged indorsement valid by the foreign law, but invalid by the law of England. It may, however, be that the contract of the drawer or acceptor is to pay on any indorsement recognised by the law of England, even though that indorsement be invalid according to what I will call for convenience the local law of England. I am disposed to think that this is the true contract. If the contract of the drawer of a cheque or acceptor of a bill were limited to payment on indorsements valid by the English local law an argument might be raised that, even though the indorsement abroad was valid to legalize the possession by the indorsee claiming under the foreign indorsement, yet he would be guilty of a conversion if he used a negotiable instrument to the possession of which he was entitled for the purpose of obtaining and did obtain payment from an original party to the negotiable instrument from

[1] (1885) 30 Ch. D. 598.   [2] (1867) L.R. 3 Q.B. 77, 83.

whom he could not have recovered by process of law. User of a chattel by a person entitled to possession in such a manner would perhaps give a right of action for money had and received.

I, however, have come to the conclusion that as between the payees and these indorsees there is no cause of action for conversion, and that the judgment of Walton J. must be affirmed.

It is to be observed that our decision in the present case does not increase the liability of the bank upon which the cheque was drawn and which paid the cheque. I wish to add that I am not satisfied that, having regard to the terms of s. 72 (2) of the Bills of Exchange Act 1882, that section is conclusive of the present case, and I do not think that s. 24 governs the case of an indorsement abroad.

ROMER and STIRLING L.JJ. delivered judgments to the same effect.

Appeal dismissed.

KOECHLIN *v.* KESTENBAUM [1927] 1 K.B. 616, 889 (Court of Appeal)

Appeal from a decision of Rowlatt J.

A bill of exchange was drawn in France by E. Vigderhaus upon the defendants in London to the order of M. Vigderhaus. It was sent to London, accepted there by the defendants payable at a London bank, returned to Paris, indorsed there by E. Vigderhaus, and discounted by the plaintiffs. On presentation for payment the defendants refused to meet it on the ground that it did not bear the indorsement of M. Vigderhaus as required by s. 32 (1) of the Bills of Exchange Act 1882, but merely the indorsement of E. Vigderhaus in his own name.

Evidence was given that M. Vigderhaus had given authority to his son E. Vigderhaus to sign and indorse all cheques, bills, or commercial documents in his own name for account of M. Vigderhaus, and that by French law a duly authorized agent may indorse a bill in his own name and need not add the words 'per pro'.

Rowlatt J. gave judgment for the defendants. The plaintiff appealed.

SARGANT L.J.: As regards the first question, it seems to me that the judge had ample material upon which he was entitled to come to the conclusion that French law was as contended for by the appellants. It is quite clear, according to the evidence of the French expert, who is also a member of the English bar and who knew what he was talking about, that by French law an indorsement may be in the form employed in this case. That view is strengthened by the evidence of the constant practice of M. Vigderhaus and in similar concerns, as given by the bank manager and by M. Vigderhaus.

The second point, I think, is really concluded by the decision in *Bradlaugh* v. *De Rin*,[1] adopted, as I think it is, by s. 72 of the Bills of Exchange Act 1882. That decision, so far as the point of law is concerned, was not affected by the reversal of the decision in the Exchequer Chamber,[2] where the question was entirely one of fact. The decision of the Court of Common Pleas drew a marked distinction between a foreign bill, such as was there in question, and an inland bill, such as was being dealt with in *Lebel* v. *Tucker*,[3] and it seems to me that the Legislature in 1882 adopted that view, and drew the marked distinction which had been thus recognized by the Court of Common Pleas in *Bradlaugh* v. *De Rin*. The result was that any one dealing with a foreign bill of exchange was in a less certain position than a person dealing with an inland bill, because in the case of an indorsement abroad on a foreign bill he might find substituted for the person to whom he was originally liable as acceptor not merely a person to whom the transfer would have been good if made in England, but a person to whom the transfer by indorsement would be good if made according to the law of the country in which it was made. That is rendered perfectly clear by s. 72 (1) and (2) of the Act. The matter was carried probably further than was contemplated by the actual language of the sub-sections by the decision in *Embiricos* v. *Anglo-Austrian Bank*.[4] Here we have a case which does not go nearly as far as that. In my judgment the question whether this bill could properly be indorsed in the name of the payee M. Vigderhaus only or could rightly be indorsed by the son, E. Vigderhaus, in his own name if he had authority in fact to do so is purely a question of form, and is therefore covered in terms by s. 72 (1); but if it is not covered by that sub-section it is covered by s. 72 (2), in view of the very wide effect of the decision in *Embiricos* v. *Anglo-Austrian Bank*. It is said on behalf of the respondents that the contract of acceptance itself was merely to pay the original payee or some person to whom a transfer had been made by him personally. In my view that is to deal with the matter as if we were concerned with an inland bill and to neglect entirely the provisions of s. 72 with reference to foreign bills. If the indorsement in fact made is, accord-

[1] (1868) L.R. 3 C.P. 538.   [2] (1870) L.R. 5 C.P. 473.
[3] (1867) L.R. 3 Q.B. 77.   [4] [1905] 1 K.B. 677; *ante*, p. 388.

ing to the law of the place where it is made, sufficient to give a title to the indorsee, it appears to me that by the express terms of the Act the indorsee is entitled to sue. The effect is not to increase the liabilities of the acceptor, but merely to enlarge the methods by which the right to enforce those liabilities can be transferred from the person originally entitled to them to some subsequent indorsee. In conclusion I wish to say that the decision of Rowlatt J. practically amounted to this, that, in order that there may be an effectual transfer entitling the indorsee to sue, it was necessary to have an indorsement which should be good both by the law of the place where it was made and by the law of England construed in the narrow sense of the municipal law of England. In my judgment that is unsound, and would in many cases introduce insuperable difficulties. The solution is to be found in this, that it is only requisite that the transfer should be made in accordance with the total law of England, which includes not only the municipal law but the law of the foreign country which is by the law of England and by the very terms of s. 72 recognized as being a law which the law of England will itself recognize.

KOECHLIN
v.
KESTEN-
BAUM.
—
Sargant
L.J.

BANKES L.J. and AVORY J. delivered judgments to the same effect.

Appeal allowed.

NOTE R: NEGOTIABLE INSTRUMENTS

(i) Sub-ss. (1) and (2) of s. 72 of the Bills of Exchange Act 1882 lay down the general principle that the validity of a bill of exchange and of each supervening contract associated with it depends on the lex loci contractus. Sub-s. (1) relates to form and sub-s. (2) to interpretation. The Act does not deal in express terms with matters such as capacity of parties or essential validity, nor with the proprietary as opposed to the contractual aspects of bills, notes, and cheques. In *Alcock* v. *Smith* [1892] 1 Ch. 238, 256, Romer J. held that 'interpretation' in sub-s. (2) is wide enough to cover legal effect, but this opinion was not adopted by the Court of Appeal in that case or (semble) in *Embiricos* v. *Anglo-Austrian Bank* (*ante*, p. 388). However, in *Koechlin* v. *Kestenbaum* (*ante*, p. 391) a wider effect was given to the sub-section. It is still arguable, however, that the transfer of a bill is governed not by s. 72 (2) of the statute, but by the general principles of the conflict of laws relating to tangible movables, i.e. the lex situs, which in the case of a negotiable instrument must necessarily coincide with the lex loci actus. The question whether the transfer is governed by s. 72 (2) or by the general rule of the lex situs would assume practical importance in cases where the proviso to the sub-section might apply: if the question in *Alcock* v. *Smith* had arisen 'as regards the payer' and not (as it did) as between indorsees, the court would have had to apply English law if it had regarded s. 72 (2), and not the lex situs, as applicable. Whatever justification there may have been in *Koechlin* v. *Kestenbaum* for treating the question as one of interpretation, it is hard to see how that term can be stretched to cover the effect of a forged indorsement (*Embiricos* v. *Anglo-Austrian Bank*) or of the transfer of an overdue bill (*Alcock* v. *Smith*).

Sub-ss. (1) and (2) have undoubtedly altered the principle underlying the cases decided before the Act, under which the validity of indorsements of negotiable instruments was tested by the proper law of the original contract made by the acceptor of the bill or the maker of the note, i.e. the law of the place where the bill was drawn or the note was made. Thus in *Trimbey* v. *Vignier* (1834) 1 Bing. N.C. 151, the validity of an indorsement in France of a note made in France was governed by French law quâ the law of the place where the note was made; in *Lebel* v. *Tucker* (1867) L.R. 3 Q.B. 77, the validity of an indorsement in France of a bill of exchange drawn, accepted, and payable in England was governed by English law; and in *Bradlaugh* v. *De Rin* (1868) L.R. 3 C.P. 538, reversed on a point of fact, L.R. 5 C.P. 473, the validity of an indorsement in France of a bill of exchange drawn in France and accepted in England was governed by French law quâ the law of the place of drawing. There can be little doubt that if the converse case to *Lebel* v. *Tucker* had arisen before 1882 (i.e. a bill drawn, accepted, and payable in France, indorsed in England), the validity of the indorsement would have been tested by French law. But if such a case were to arise now the validity of the indorsement would be held to depend on English law, because the proviso to sub-s. (2), which states what the draftsman conceived to be the effect of *Lebel* v. *Tucker*, is limited to inland bills, i.e. to bills which are drawn within the British Islands and either payable therein or drawn upon some person resident therein (Bills of Exchange Act 1882, s. 4). The result is that the law loses the harmony which it hitherto possessed by reason of the fact that analogous principles were held to apply to inland bills and foreign bills. It seems clear that the draftsman of the section misinterpreted the effect of the older cases, especially *Lebel* v. *Tucker*.

(ii) The provisos to sub-ss. (1) and (2) are exceptions to the main principles enunciated therein.

Proviso (*a*) to sub-s. (1) illustrates the refusal of English private international law to enforce the revenue laws of foreign countries.

Proviso (*b*) to sub-s. (1) may be illustrated thus: A bill issued in France does not express the value received as required by French law. The bill is sent to A in England who indorses it to B. B can sue A on the bill but cannot sue any of those who became parties to it in France.

The proviso to sub-s. (2) is an attempt to state the effect of *Lebel* v. *Tucker*, and still further narrows its ratio by introducing a new limitation to questions arising 'as regards the payer'. The effect was considered in *Alcock* v. *Smith*: if the question arises between two indorsees and the liability of the acceptor is not in question, the proviso is inoperative and the case falls within sub-s. (2).

(iii) The words 'subject to the provisions of this Act' at the beginning of sub-s. (2) refer to sub-ss. (3), (4), and (5).

(iv) The obscurity of the language used in sub-s. (3) has often been noticed: see e.g. Westlake, s. 231; Dicey, p. 836; Cheshire, p. 237.

(v) Sub-s. (5) may be illustrated thus: French law does not allow days of grace, as English law does. Consequently a bill drawn in Paris on London is entitled to three days of grace, while a bill drawn in London on Paris is not entitled to any.

For a full discussion (highly critical of the drafting of the Act) see Falconbridge, pp. 316–57; Dicey, pp. 817–40.

Chapter 16

WINDING UP OF COMPANIES

The English court has jurisdiction to wind up a company incorporated outside the United Kingdom, even if it has been dissolved under the law of its place of incorporation, and even if it never carried on business in England, provided there are assets of the company situated in England.

In re AZOFF-DON COMMERCIAL BANK [1954] Ch. 315 (Chancery Division)

PETITION

On 17 November 1953 a petition was presented by certain Norwegian banks for the compulsory winding up of the Azoff-Don Commercial Bank. That bank was established in 1871 under the laws of the Empire of Russia and the evidence showed that it had by 1922 been dissolved under the laws of the Union of Soviet Socialist Republics. Its head office had been at Petrograd; it had never had an office or place of business in England and particulars of it were not registered under the Companies Acts. But it provided mercantile credits and banking facilities in England and had substantial assets in England. In particular it was for many years a customer of Hambros Bank, London, and had a current and other accounts at that bank.

The petitioners were creditors of the company for nearly six million kroner (nearly £300,000), and the petition was opposed by the Crown and by another person who, the court held, had no locus standi in the proceedings.

Section 399 (5) (*a*) of the Companies Act 1948, re-enacting s. 338 (1) (*d*) (i) of the Companies Act 1929, which in turn re-enacted earlier legislation, provides that an unregistered company may be wound up under that Act 'if the company is dissolved, or has ceased to carry on business, or is carrying on business only for the purpose of winding up its affairs'.

WYNN PARRY J.: This is a petition for the compulsory winding up of Azoff-Don Commercial Bank, to which I shall refer as the

WINDING UP OF COMPANIES

company. . . . The Crown opposes the petition on three grounds,
which can be shortly stated. First, it is said that, on the company
becoming dissolved in Russia by the year 1922 at the latest, the
assets became vested in the Crown as bona vacantia; that therefore
the court has no jurisdiction to wind up the company unless the
Crown consents; the Crown does not consent and therefore the court
cannot make a winding up order. Secondly, the Crown contends that
to ground jurisdiction in the court to wind up a foreign company
which has been dissolved by the law of the country of its incorporation it is necessary to show that the company has carried on business
in this country. The presence of assets, however valuable, is not
sufficient. The company never carried on business in this country
and therefore I cannot make the winding up order. Thirdly, the
Crown contends that even if there is jurisdiction to do so I should
not make a winding up order at the suit of foreign creditors in
respect of debts payable in Norway in Norwegian kroner, but that I
should leave the Crown to get in the English assets with a view to the
Crown being in a position to make ex gratia payments among
English creditors in respect of rouble debts, which of course will be
irrecoverable. I may observe that there is no evidence of the existence
of any English creditors.

(His Lordship held that the Crown's prerogative right to bona
vacantia was capable of being cut down by provisions of the Companies Act 1948, and continued:) The position of such a company as
this was exhaustively considered by the House of Lords in *Russian
and English Bank* v. *Baring Brothers Ltd.*[1] The conflict between the
views of the members of the House who heard the appeal consisted
in this, that the minority, Lord Russell and Lord Maugham, considered that it was the affairs of the dissolved company which were
to be wound up, while the majority, Lord Blanesburgh, Lord Atkin
and Lord Macmillan, considered that it was the company which was
to be wound up, the company being deemed for the limited purposes
of the liquidation not to have ceased to exist.

I quote from the speeches of the majority. . . . In the course of his
speech Lord Atkin said:[2] 'The liquidator deals with the company's
property in right of the company or usually in the name of the company, possessing the powers of the directors and the special statutory powers given to him by the Act. On the assumption adopted by
the judgments under appeal not only is there no property of the

In re
AZOFF-DON
COMMER-
CIAL BANK.
—
Wynn
Parry J.

[1] [1936] A.C. 405.   [2] At p. 426.

In re
AZOFF-DON
COMMER-
CIAL BANK.
—
Wynn
Parry J.

company in existence, with the result that none of the statutory powers of the liquidator in respect of property comes into existence, but there is the further difficulty that all that which had been the movable property of the company has become vested in the Crown as bona vacantia. For some reason which I cannot appreciate some of the learned judges in the courts below seem to have thought that this obvious difficulty might be cured by obtaining a vesting order under section 190. But when that section is looked at the power of the court is found to be to "direct that all or any part of the property of whatsoever description belonging to the company . . . shall vest in the liquidator by his official name". The initial futility remains. 1. There is no property belonging to the company. 2. What has been the property of the company now belongs to a third person, the Crown, and there is no power to vest the property of a third person in the liquidator. The result is that if the company for the purposes of winding up is to be treated as dissolved there never can be any assets over which the liquidator can exercise any powers of any kind. On the assumption I prefer to adopt the Crown acquired a defeasible title defeated upon the making of a winding up order.'

Finally, Lord Macmillan said:[1] 'Be that as it may, it is manifest that the legislature has not been deterred by the fact that a company has ceased to exist from authorizing it to be wound up. Now the purpose of pronouncing a winding up order is to secure the collection and distribution of the assets of the company to which it relates. The logical inquirer may ask how a company which has ceased to exist can have any assets. But when the legislature authorized the making of a winding up order in the case of a dissolved company it must be presumed to have intended such order to be effective and to result in the collection and distribution of assets. To hold that the legislature has authorized the collection of the assets of a dissolved company, but has withheld the power of recovering these assets, would be to attribute a singular ineptitude to Parliament.'

The burden of these passages is, I think, that it must never be forgotten that the statutory provision of the application of the winding up provisions of the Companies Act to a foreign corporation which has been dissolved under the law of the country of its incorporation is made with a view to something effective being achieved, namely, the collection of its assets and their distribution among the creditors, and it is no doubt for this reason that it appears to be accepted, as I

---

[1] At p. 437.

shall show later in this judgment, that the court will not exercise its jurisdiction to wind up such a company if it has no assets within the jurisdiction. If the contention of the Crown were correct it must follow that a most far-reaching limitation must be placed on the plain language of sections 399 and 400 of the Companies Act 1948, for the justification of which the whole Act can be searched in vain. The result must be that the two sections are to be regarded as a dead letter except on such occasions as the Crown allows them to have any force, a curious form of legislation.

In re
AZOFF-DON
COMMER-
CIAL BANK.
—
Wynn
Parry J.

The truth is that if the Crown's contention is correct the Act does not work, whereas if that contention is rejected it does work; a complete system of administration is applied to the company's affairs and at the end of the administration any surplus goes to the Crown as bona vacantia under section 354, where and where only the Crown's right to property as bona vacantia is mentioned. In my judgment, therefore, the highest title which the Crown can claim to the property of the company in this country is a defeasible title liable, as Lord Atkin said, to be defeated by the winding up order. It is a title liable to be defeated without its consent and even against its wish in every case where the conditions prescribed by the Act as interpreted by the relevant authorities exist.

I turn now to the second ground on which the Crown opposes the petition, namely, that in the case of a foreign dissolved corporation it is a condition for grounding jurisdiction in the court to wind it up that it should be shown that the corporation had at some time before its dissolution carried on business in this country, and that it has not been shown that the company did so. I think that this point is covered by the decision of the Court of Appeal in the recent case of *Banque des Marchands de Moscou* v. *Kindersley.*[1] Three points were decided. The first dealt with the ground on which Harman J. had dismissed the summons. This point has no materiality for my present purpose. The second point decided was that if proof of conduct of business entered into by the bank was necessary to the existence of jurisdiction in the English courts to wind up the bank under the Companies Act 1929 s. 338 (1) (*d*) (i), that condition was satisfied on the evidence. The third point decided was (I read from the headnote): 'That in the case of a foreign corporation (such as the bank) which had been dissolved and extinguished in the country in which it was established, it was not necessary as a statutory condition of

[1] [1951] Ch. 112.

In re
AZOFF-DON
COMMER-
CIAL BANK.
—
Wynn
Parry J.

jurisdiction in the English courts to wind them up to prove that they had, before their dissolution, established at some place in England a branch or other business place, and that that business had ceased: it was sufficient that there were assets of the bank in this country, and persons here claiming as creditors of the bank or said to be indebted to it, as being indicia of a business in some sense formerly conducted here.'

Having dealt with the first point, Evershed M.R., whose judgment was the judgment of the court, said this: 'But I agree with Harman J. that in the case of a foreign corporation, such as the bank, which has, ex hypothesi, been dissolved and extinguished in the country where it was established, it is not necessary, as a statutory condition of jurisdiction in the English courts to wind it up, to prove that it had, before its dissolution, established at some place in England a branch or other business and that business had ceased.'

Evershed M.R. then proceeded to consider the scope of and jurisdiction conferred by section 338 (1) (*d*) (i) of the Companies Act 1929, without regard to the effect of subsection (2). He said: 'Subsection (1) (*d*) (i) of section 338 of the Act of 1929 provided as follows: "The circumstances in which an unregistered company may be wound up are as follows: (i) if the company is dissolved, or has ceased to carry on business, or is carrying on business only for the purpose of winding up its affairs." This form of words is substantially identical with that which has consistently appeared in all the relevant legislation since the Act of 1848. As a matter of language, it is plain that the three conditions named are independent and not cumulative. Assuming, therefore, in the case of a foreign corporation which has by its local law been extinguished, that it is covered by the words "is dissolved"—which words must, as it is conceded, be taken to mean "has been dissolved"—it would appear from the language used that no other condition has to be fulfilled in order to confer upon the English court jurisdiction to wind it up. As a matter of general principle, our courts would not assume, and Parliament should not be taken to have intended to confer, jurisdiction over matters which naturally and properly lie within the competence of the courts of other countries. There must be assets here to administer and persons subject, or at least submitting, to the jurisdiction who are concerned or interested in the proper distribution of the assets. And when these conditions are present the exercise of the jurisdiction remains discretionary.'

Pausing there, it is, I think, clear that it is the considered view of the Court of Appeal that for the purpose of grounding jurisdiction in the court under section 338 (1) (*d*) (i) of the Companies Act 1929, it is not necessary to show that the dissolved corporation has carried on a business in this country. The Master of the Rolls then proceeded to discuss the circumstances in which the court will exercise its discretionary jurisdiction. He continued: 'Prima facie if the local law of the dissolved foreign corporation provided for the due administration of all the property and assets of the corporation wherever situate among the persons properly entitled to participate therein, the case would not be one for interference by the machinery of the English courts. In the present case there are substantial assets standing in the name of the bank or its liquidator, and there are persons within the jurisdiction having claims to participate in the distribution of those assets. At the same time, by reason of the total extinction in Russia of the bank and the absence of any machinery under Russian law for the due distribution of the assets among the persons regarded as properly having claims upon them, there would be, unless the machinery of winding up under the Companies Act is available, no means of any kind existing for the administration of the English assets. The existence of assets here, the presence here of persons claiming as creditors of the bank or said to be indebted to them, seem to constitute at least the indicia of a business in some sense formerly conducted here. Where, therefore, the circumstances exist which, upon the general principle above referred to, would make the case appropriate for the exercise by our court of its winding up jurisdiction, it would appear that the question whether the foreign corporation carried on business in this country would generally be academic, unless it is also necessary to show that that business was carried on directly and from some established or specified place or places in this country.'

That passage indicates that in order to justify the exercise by the court of its discretionary jurisdiction it is enough to show the existence of assets here and the presence here of persons claiming as creditors of the bank or said to be indebted to them; those circumstances being treated as constituting 'at least indicia of some business formerly conducted here', subject to the proviso: 'unless it is also necessary to show that that business was carried on directly and from some established . . . place or places in this country'. His

In re
AZOFF-DON
COMMER-
CIAL BANK.
—
Wynn
Parry J.

In re
AZOFF-DON
COMMER-
CIAL BANK.
—
Wynn
Parry J.

Lordship then proceeded to deal with the relevant authorities and his conclusion was that it was not necessary so to show. . . .

Finally, he stated what I take to be his general conclusion on this point: 'I think that, in circumstances such as exist in the present case, it is unnecessary as a foundation for a winding up order to prove that the bank had any branch or office in England or carried on their business operations in England from some established or specific or identifiable place of business. . . .'

In my view, therefore, that case is authority for the proposition that I have jurisdiction to make a winding up order and that, further, I should be justified in exercising that jurisdiction if I can find on the evidence some commercial subject-matter on which a winding up order can operate. In view of the evidence at paragraphs 5, 6 and 7 of the petition I am satisfied that that condition is fulfilled.

As regards the third point taken by the Crown, which was described as relating to the merits, I can see no merit in the suggestion that I should refuse to make a winding up order which will benefit the petitioners as foreign creditors, but that I should leave it to the Crown to make ex gratia payments to English creditors for rouble debts—as to the existence of which creditors there is, as I have said, no evidence—to the exclusion no doubt of the petitioners as mere foreign creditors notwithstanding that their debts are clearly established; a somewhat surprising proposition. The object of a winding up order is to ensure distribution of the assets among the whole body of creditors. No other basis of distribution would be fair. As Pearson J. said in *In re Klœbe*:[1] '. . . but whatever the law in France or India may be, the law of England has always been that you must enforce claims in this country according to the practice and rules of our courts, and according to them a creditor, whether from the furthest north or the furthest south, is entitled to be paid equally with other creditors in the same class. I must refuse to alter that which has always been the law of this country, and which I must say, for the sake of honesty, I hope will always be the law of this country.' I therefore make the usual compulsory order.

[1] (1884) 28 Ch. D. 175 ; *post*, p. 443.

In the English winding up of a dissolved foreign corporation the dissolution of the corporation is disregarded for all the purposes of the winding up.

In re RUSSIAN COMMERCIAL AND INDUSTRIAL BANK [1955] Ch. 148
(Chancery Division)

In re
RUSSIAN
COMMER-
CIAL AND
INDUSTRIAL
BANK.

Adjourned summons.

The summons was taken out in the compulsory liquidation of Russian Commercial and Industrial Bank (hereinafter called the bank) by the applicant as a creditor of the bank asking that the decision of the official receiver as liquidator rejecting the applicant's proof might be reversed.

The bank was incorporated in Russia in 1890 with a view to carrying on the business of bankers in Russia and elsewhere. The bank did in fact carry on such business in Russia until December 1917, when the Bolsheviks took possession of the bank's head office and branch offices in Russia and confiscated all its assets. It was common ground between the parties that the bank was dissolved under the laws of the Union of Soviet Socialist Republics in December 1917 or January 1918, the exact date being immaterial.

In 1911 the bank established a place of business in England and filed the particulars required to be filed by s. 274 of the Companies (Consolidation) Act 1908. Banking business was conducted at the English branch from 1911 until long after the dissolution of the bank in Russia. In February 1922 a petition for the compulsory winding up of the bank was presented to the court, and in October 1922 an order was made on that petition for its compulsory winding up.

The applicant was the executor of one Ronaasen, who died in 1935, and who for many years prior to the winding up order had a current account with the bank at the London branch. This account showed a credit balance due to Mr. Ronaasen of 36,430 roubles on 1 July 1921. At the date of the dissolution of the bank in Russia the rate of exchange between the rouble and the pound was 360 roubles to £1 sterling. At the date of the presentation of the winding up petition in England the rate was 400,000 roubles to £1 sterling. If the former date was applicable the debt amounted to over £100. If the latter date was applicable the debt amounted to two shillings only.

In re
RUSSIAN
COMMER-
CIAL AND
INDUSTRIAL
BANK.
—
Wynn
Parry J.
WYNN PARRY J. (after holding that the date for converting the rouble debt into sterling was the date when it became due, and that it became due on the termination of the relationship of banker and customer, his Lordship continued:) In this case the bank was dissolved in December 1917 or January 1918, it matters not which. In my view the effect of that dissolution was to terminate the relationship of banker and customer. The persona juridica having ceased to exist, it appears to me impossible to say that the previous relationship of banker and customer continued.

In October 1922 came the order for compulsory winding up. The effect of such an order in relation to a foreign dissolved company has been authoritatively stated by Lord Atkin in *Russian and English Bank* v. *Baring Brothers Ltd.*[1] In the course of his speech he said: 'My Lords, I think that we are entitled to imply, indeed I think it is a necessary implication, that the dissolved foreign company is to be wound up as though it had not been dissolved, and therefore continued in existence. This seems to me with respect the necessary result of saying that it shall be wound up in accordance with the provisions of the Act. There is nothing abnormal in such a provision. The municipal law of this country, as of other countries, accepts the principle of international law that countries ordinarily accept the existence of juristic persons brought into being or recognized as existing in their country of origin. Similarly they accept the destruction or cessation of such a juristic personality under the law of its country of origin. But if the municipal law chooses it may in defined conditions refuse to accept or may accept only under conditions either the creation or destruction of a foreign juristic person: whether it has done so is for the municipal courts to decide, but if it has, then the municipal court must accept the situation. I see nothing incongruous in the legislature saying in effect, we accept the existence of a foreign corporation coming to trade in this country; we shall only impose a condition of registration. But if the corporation does trade here, acquires assets here and incurs debts here, we shall not accept its dissolution abroad without a stipulation that if desirable it may be wound up here so that its assets here shall be distributed among its creditors (I do not stay to consider whether its English creditors or creditors generally) and for the purpose of the winding up it shall be deemed not to have been dissolved; for that event would defeat our municipal provisions for winding up a corpora-

[1] [1936] A.C. 405, 427.

tion. This does not appear to me to be recreating or reconstituting a new corporation; it is for particular and limited purposes refusing to recognize the dissolution of the old.'

It is to be observed that Lord Atkin was careful to say that the refusal to recognize the dissolution was for particular and limited purposes and not for all purposes. The particular and limited purposes are as he states 'so that its assets here shall be distributed among its creditors' and 'for the purposes of the winding up it shall be deemed not to have been dissolved'.

The interesting question then presents itself: What is the scope of the phrase 'for the purposes of the winding up it shall be deemed not to have been dissolved'? If a foreign company is dissolved according to the law of the country of its incorporation, and is subsequently wound up here, can any recognition be given, for the purposes of the winding up, to the fact of dissolution? The question is a very real one in the case of a company such as the bank, because the evidence shows that for a considerable time after its dissolution in Russia business was carried on at the London branch and transactions in the normal course of banking business were entered into as if the dissolution had not occurred. It is surely clear that in the winding up of the bank and similar companies, regard must be had to those post-dissolution transactions. The difficulty of doing otherwise is recognized by Lord Atkin in *Russian and English Bank* v. *Baring Brothers Ltd.* He said: 'Nor is it any easier to confine the distribution to assets existing at the date of the dissolution amongst creditors in existence at the same date.'

Again, in the earlier case of *Russian and English Bank* v. *Baring Brothers Ltd.*,[1] Eve J. said: 'But I cannot help thinking that these difficulties can be mitigated, and the acts of those who have intermeddled with the affairs and assets of the branch, after the destruction of the parent company, be regularized by adoption and ratification by a liquidator in a winding up constituted under section 338 of Part X of the Companies Act 1929.'

For myself I can see no other logical conclusion than that for all purposes of the liquidation concerning the distribution of assets among the creditors the dissolution of the bank is to be ignored. A customer of the bank to whom money is owing on current account at the date of the dissolution can only obtain payment (either in whole or in part) by proving in the winding up; but if he proves in the

In re
RUSSIAN
COMMER-
CIAL AND
INDUSTRIAL
BANK.
—
Wynn
Parry J.

---

[1] [1932] 1 Ch. 435, 444.

In re
RUSSIAN
COMMER-
CIAL AND
INDUSTRIAL
BANK.
—
Wynn
Parry J.

winding up he must accept that the dissolution which, looked at out-side the winding up, was effective to determine the relation of banker and customer, is to be treated by the liquidator who examines his claim, and the court which may have to pronounce on it, as not having taken place. In other words, he can rely on the dissolution as having terminated the relation of banker and customer, if he stays outside the winding up, in which case he will be without remedy; or, on the other hand, he can prove in the liquidation, in which case he must accept the non-recognition by the liquidator and the court of the event which in fact caused the termination of the relationship of banker and customer between the bank and him-self. In the liquidation, therefore, the relationship must be deemed to have continued. On this basis the commencement of the liquida-tion is the earliest date when that relationship came to an end; and that is the date when the debt became due.

The summons must therefore be dismissed.

Judgment for the liquidator.

NOTE S: THE WINDING UP OF FOREIGN COMPANIES

(1) English law recognizes the existence of corporations duly created in a foreign country and allows them to sue and be sued here in their corporate capacity, although if they establish a place of business here they must file with the Registrar of Companies the name and address of a person resident in Great Britain who is authorized to accept service of process on their behalf: Companies Act 1948, ss. 406–15.

(2) Similarly, English law recognizes the dissolution of a foreign corpora-tion under the law of its place of incorporation (*Lazard Brothers* v. *Midland Bank, ante*, p. 36) or its amalgamation with another foreign company, and in the latter case will enforce the obligations of the old company against the new to the extent provided by the law of their place of incorporation (*National Bank of Greece and Athens S.A.* v. *Metliss* [1958] A.C. 509; *Adams* v. *National Bank of Greece and Athens S.A.* [1961] A.C. 255).

(3) A foreign corporation may have a branch in England, or may carry on business in England through agents, or may otherwise acquire assets and incur liabilities in England. Difficulties arise if the corporation is dissolved under the foreign law, particularly if the English branch continues to carry on business in ignorance of the dissolution or of its precise legal effect. The position has been elaborately worked out in a series of cases dealing with the dissolution of Russian banking and other companies during the Bolshevik Revolution of 1917–18. At first it was held that the Soviet decrees declaring banking and other key industries to be state monopolies did not have the effect of dissolving the Russian companies engaged in those activities

(*Russian Commercial and Industrial Bank* v. *Comptoir d'Escompte de Mulhouse* [1925] A.C. 112; *Banque Internationale de Commerce de Petrograd* v. *Goukassow* [1925] A.C. 150). But from 1932 onwards it has been consistently held, in the light of more precise evidence as to the effect of the decrees in Soviet law, that the Russian banks were in fact dissolved in or about December 1917 or January 1918 (*Lazard Brothers* v. *Midland Bank*, ante, p. 36). As will be seen, the difficulties in the position at common law have been largely removed by the winding up provisions of the Companies Acts 1929 and 1948, and their interpretation by the courts.

(4) At common law, neither a dissolved foreign corporation nor its unincorporated English branch can sue (*Russian and English Bank* v. *Baring Brothers* [1932] 1 Ch. 435) or be sued (*Lazard Brothers* v. *Midland Bank*) in English courts. Its English assets vest in the Crown as bona vacantia, even though the decree of dissolution purports to vest them in the foreign State, for foreign governmental decrees cannot affect property in England (*Bank voor Handel en Scheepvart* v. *Slatford*, ante, p. 381). Hence the English branch of a dissolved Russian bank and those who meddle in its affairs are in an unenviable position: it has been described as 'a submerged wreck floating on the ocean of commerce', with 'neither compass nor officers nor crew: no one who could direct its movements' (*Re Russian Bank for Foreign Trade* [1933] Ch. 745, 764, *per* Maugham J.).

(5) But it is now clearly established that the High Court has jurisdiction in its discretion to wind up a foreign corporation as an 'unregistered company' under s. 399 (5) (*a*) of the Companies Act 1948, and its predecessors, on the ground that it 'is' (i.e. 'has been') 'dissolved', provided only that it has assets in England (*Re Russian and English Bank* [1932] 1 Ch. 663; *Re Russian Bank for Foreign Trade* [1933] Ch. 745; *Banque des Marchands de Moscou* v. *Kindersley* [1951] Ch. 112; *Re Azoff-Don Commercial Bank*, ante, p. 396). The difficulty that the corporation has no assets because they have already vested in the Crown as bona vacantia is met by treating the Crown's title as defeasible upon the making of a winding up order.

(6) In the Companies Act 1928 there appeared for the first time what is now s. 400 of the Act of 1948, which provides that 'where a company incorporated outside Great Britain which has been carrying on business in Great Britain ceases to carry on business in Great Britain, it may be wound up as an unregistered company under this part of this Act, notwithstanding that it has been dissolved or otherwise ceased to exist as a company under or by virtue of the laws of the country under which it was incorporated'. This section was presumably designed to enable the dissolved Russian companies to be wound up in England, but it has remained a dead letter because in *Re Russian and English Bank* [1932] 1 Ch. 663 it was held not to be retrospective; and although this view has been challenged (by Lord Blanesburgh in *Russian and English Bank* v. *Baring Brothers* [1936] A.C. 405, 416) it has never been over-ruled. The importance of the section is, however, that it has helped to familiarize English judges with the phenomenon of the English winding up of a non-existent foreign company: see the remarks of Lord Macmillan in *Russian and English Bank* v. *Baring Brothers* [1936] A.C. 405, 437, cited ante, p. 398.

(7) Section 245 (1) of the Companies Act 1948 (re-enacting s. 191 (1) of the Act of 1929) provides that 'the liquidator in a winding up by the court shall

have power, with the sanction either of the court or of the committee of inspection, (a) to bring . . . any action . . . in the name of the company and on behalf of the company'. It was held by a bare majority of the House of Lords in *Russian and English Bank* v. *Baring Brothers* [1936] A.C. 405, reversing both the courts below, that under this section the liquidator could bring an action to recover the assets of the dissolved Russian bank, even though it did not exist under the law of its place of incorporation, and even though an action by the bank claiming precisely similar relief, but brought before the winding up order, had been stayed (*Russian and English Bank* v. *Baring Brothers* [1932] 1 Ch. 435). Thus the dissolved foreign company is wound up as though it had not been dissolved: it is revivified by the English winding up order. This does not mean that English law calls a new corporation into existence on the ashes of the old. It means that English law only recognizes the dissolution of a foreign corporation until a subsequent winding up order is made in England. Thus the remarkable result follows that a corporation owing its existence to foreign law can be dissolved under foreign law, with the result that all its English assets pass to the Crown as bona vacantia: yet on the making of a winding up order it rises from the grave, perhaps twenty or thirty years later, and can sue to recover property which for all that time has been at least notionally the property of the Crown.

(8) It is now well settled that pre-dissolution assets may be wound up, pre-dissolution debtors sued, and pre-dissolution creditors paid. But what if the corporation's English branch or agents carried on business in England during the interregnum between its dissolution under foreign law and the making of a winding up order? Is the effect of such an order to revivify the corporation retrospectively, or only with effect from its date? In *Re Russian Commercial and Industrial Bank* (*ante*, p. 403), Wynn Parry J. held that the corporation could operate a banking account during the interregnum. But his attention was not called to an earlier inconsistent decision of Vaisey J. in *Re Banque des Marchands de Moscou, Wilenkin* v. *The Liquidator* [1952] 1 T.L.R. 739, where it was held that an agent employed by the corporation during the interregnum could not prove for his commission in the subsequent winding up. Vaisey J. said: 'These metaphysical conceptions seem to me to be extremely difficult, and when there is a hypothesis on a hypothesis, such as one has when it is said that the non-existent bank was none the less deemed to be employing a non-appointed agent to conduct its non-existent affairs, one gets into a maze of metaphysics from which there is really no logical escape.' Nevertheless, the view of Wynn Parry J. seems preferable. It was clearly Lord Atkin's view in *Russian and English Bank* v. *Baring Brothers* [1936] A.C. 405 (see *ante*, p. 405).

(9) Although the English winding up order affects only that portion of the company's property which is situated in the United Kingdom, the liquidation is a liquidation of the company and not merely of its English affairs. Accordingly foreign creditors are entitled to be paid pari passu with English creditors (*Re Azoff-Don Commercial Bank*, *ante*, p. 396). The Statute of Limitations does not apply during the time between the foreign dissolution and the making of a winding up order, because during the interval there was no one who could have been sued (*Re Russo-Asiatic Bank* [1934] Ch. 720, 738). But a creditor will be unable to prove for his debt if it has been ex-

tinguished under its proper law or if the liability to repay has been transferred to a third party under the lex situs: *Re Banque des Marchands de Moscou, Royal Exchange Assurance* v. *The Liquidator* [1952] 1 T.L.R. 739; *Re Banque des Marchands de Moscou (No. 2)* [1954] 1 W.L.R. 1108; *Re United Railways of the Havana and Regla Warehouses Ltd.* [1960] Ch. 52.

(10) If a foreign company is being wound up in England and also in its place of incorporation, and there are surplus assets in the hands of the English liquidator after all creditors have been paid, he would normally hand them over to the foreign liquidator, because the English liquidation is regarded as ancillary to that which takes place in the country of incorporation (*Re Commercial Bank of South Australia* (1886) 33 Ch. D. 174, 178; *Re Vocalion (Foreign) Ltd.* [1932] 2 Ch. 196, 207). However, this course is impracticable if, as in the Russian bank cases, there is no liquidation taking place in the country of incorporation and no machinery there for the payment of creditors or disposal of the assets. It was held by Roxburgh J. in *Re Banque des Marchands de Moscou* [1958] Ch. 182 that in such a case the surplus assets were divisible among the former shareholders in such proportions as their shares bore to the total issued capital of the bank at the date of dissolution, and did not pass to the Crown as bona vacantia. His Lordship considered that the reasoning of Wynn Parry J. in *Re Azoff-Don Commercial Bank* (*ante,* p. 396) postponing the title of the Crown to the claims of creditors was equally applicable to the claims of beneficiaries. His conclusion was based on the uncontradicted evidence of a single expert witness who asserted that under Soviet law any surplus assets not caught by the Soviet confiscatory decrees would belong to the shareholders. When confronted with clause 2 of the Soviet Decree of 26 January 1918, which provides that 'all bank shares are declared null and void and payment of dividends of any kind whatsoever is unconditionally stopped', the witness replied that the Decree did not mean what it said, because in September 1917 Lenin had made a speech saying: 'Do not be afraid of our project of nationalizing the banks. No one will suffer the slightest injury. Anyone who had shares will after the nationalization retain his money again in shares as before. Everyone who had a deposit will retain his deposit.' The witness was positive that in Russia 'you have to construe statutes in the light of speeches made by politicians, otherwise you get lost'. Similar evidence by the same witness as to the effect of the same decree had been rejected with incredulity by Maugham J. in *Re Russian Bank for Foreign Trade* [1933] Ch. 745, 759–60.

For further details, the reader is referred to a valuable series of articles by Dr. Michael Mann in 15 M.L.R. 479, 18 M.L.R. 8, 180, 4 I.C.L.Q. 226, and 7 I.C.L.Q. 610, on which the above account is largely based.

Chapter 17

EFFECT OF MARRIAGE ON MOVABLES

In the absence of a marriage contract the rights of husband and wife to each other's movables, whether possessed at the time of the marriage or acquired afterwards, are governed by the law of the matrimonial domicile.

The matrimonial domicile means (in the absence of special circumstances) the husband's domicile at the time of the marriage.

In re EGERTON'S WILL TRUSTS.

In re EGERTON'S WILL TRUSTS [1956] Ch. 593 (Chancery Division)

IN May 1932 the testator, who was then domiciled in England, married a Frenchwoman domiciled in France. In 1934 they settled in France and acquired a domicile there in accordance with their antenuptial intention. In 1951 the testator died having by his will made provision for his wife which she regarded as unsatisfactory. She claimed to be entitled to share in his estate in accordance with the French doctrine of community of property.

ROXBURGH J.: . . . Mr. Wilberforce [counsel for the widow] has propounded an argument which might almost be said to set the professors by the ears. To start on a safe foundation, I will first read rule 171 in Dicey's Conflict of Laws, 6th ed. p. 795, which says: 'Where there is no marriage contract or settlement, and where no subsequent change of domicile on the part of the parties to the marriage has taken place, the rights of the husband and wife to each other's movables, whether possessed at the time of the marriage or acquired afterwards, are governed by the law of the matrimonial domicile, without reference to the law of the country where the marriage is celebrated or where the wife is domiciled before marriage.' That is indisputable law. So that, prima facie, the law applicable to the present case, on the finding of fact which I have just made, is English law. I have deliberately used the phrase 'prima facie'. I can disregard the words of the rule 'where no subsequent change of domicile on the part of the parties to the marriage has taken place'. In truth there was a subsequent change in the domicile in the present case. But I need not pursue that question further because, for reasons connected with French law, which I need not elaborate but which Mr. Wilberforce found quite compelling, he did not base any argument on the subsequent change of domicile.

What Mr. Wilberforce did was to explore the problem which has been the subject of debate between Dr. Morris, the author of the note that I am going to read, and Dr. Cheshire. The particular note refers to a somewhat different position, namely, where there is a marriage contract, but for the present purpose that is not important because it is really a discussion of the phrase 'matrimonial domicile'. The passage in the text of Dicey (at p. 541) is as follows: 'The marriage contract, or settlement, will be construed with reference to the proper law of the contract, i.e., in the absence of reason to the contrary, by the law of the husband's actual domicile at the time of the marriage. The husband's actual domicile at the time of the marriage is hereinafter termed the "matrimonial domicile".' I have read that passage in order to explain the note, because it is the note and not the passage which really raises the issue. Dr. Morris says this: 'Whether in this Exception and in the rest of this Digest the term "matrimonial domicile" ought to be extended, so as to mean the intended domicile of the husband, when, as occasionally happens, he, though domiciled in one country, intends, to the knowledge of both parties to the marriage, to become immediately domiciled in another country (e.g., France)',—and I stress at once the word 'immediately'—'is a question on which there is no decisive English authority. On the theory, however, of a tacit or express contract between the parties about to marry, that their mutual property rights shall be determined by the law of their matrimonial domicile, the extension of that term so as to include the country in which they intend to become, and do become, domiciled immediately after the marriage'—and I again stress that word—'seems to some authorities reasonable. For instance, if H, domiciled in England, marries in England W, domiciled in South Africa, and H and W sail to South Africa immediately after the ceremony'—and again I stress the word 'immediately'—'intending to make it their permanent home, it would seem reasonable at first sight to hold that South Africa, and not England, was their matrimonial domicile. The difficulty is, however, that there is no conclusive English authority in favour of this view, and there are practical difficulties in its application. What if H and W do not sail to South Africa until a month—or a year—after the ceremony? Where is the line to be drawn? Are the rights of the spouses to be

411

in suspense until they actually acquire a new domicile in pursuance of their pre-matrimonial intention? It is submitted that the safer rule to adopt is that the matrimonial domicile means the husband's domicile at the time of the marriage. In a clear case where the parties change their domicile very shortly after the marriage'—and I do again stress the words 'in a clear case'—'in pursuance of a pre-matrimonial intention to that effect, the change of domicile might well be a "reason to the contrary" within the meaning of the Exception. This way of looking at the matter has the advantage of avoiding the use of a term of ambiguous meaning which suggests either that a change of domicile can be effected by mere intention, or that "matrimonial domicile" means something different from "domicile" simpliciter.'

Different, however, is the approach of Dr. Cheshire in Private International Law. The passage is too long for me to read in extenso, and I am only going to read extracts. It begins with these words (4th ed. p. 491): 'Although there is no clear-cut and decisive authority, the prevalent view is that the determining domicile is that which the husband possesses *at the time of the marriage.* On the whole it is an unobjectionable view, for in the vast majority of cases the parties retain the husband's domicile immediately after the marriage. Nevertheless, a rule better calculated to function more justly and more conveniently in every case is one which selects the country of the intended matrimonial home. This is equivalent in the normal case to the domicile at the time of the marriage, but its merit is that it meets the not unusual case where the parties intend to settle immediately after marriage in another country.' After leaving something out, I read again (at p. 492): 'It is respectfully submitted, however, that the just and reasonable view to take'—on the facts, which he had just mentioned—'is that the law of the country in which the parties intended to settle immediately, in which in fact they did settle, and in which so far as they could foresee they would remain for the rest of their married lives, should be allowed to govern their mutual proprietary rights. The reasonable inference from the circumstances is that they intended to submit themselves in toto to the matrimonial régime, proprietary as well as personal, obtaining in their future home.' Then he says (on p. 493): 'The view that the matter should be governed by the law of the intended matrimonial home lacks neither doctrinal analogy nor juristic support.' Then he says later: 'It is undeniable, of course, that the practical application of the doctrine of the intended matrimonial home may in some cases encounter considerable difficulties. . . . How quickly must the intention to settle in the specified country be implemented? What if there is unforeseen delay or some accident which frustrates the design? Will effect be given to the alleged intention if it remains a secret locked in the breasts of the parties? These difficulties are no more insuperable than those which often attend the ascertainment of intention in a disputed case of domicile. Everything hinges on intention, but the dominion of the lex domicilii of the husband at the time of the marriage is not displaced unless the intention to acquire a new home is established by irrefragable evidence. In fact, the suggested rule goes no further than this: There is a strong presumption that the lex domicilii of the husband at the time of the marriage governs the mutual proprietary rights of the spouses. This presumption is rebutted if it is proved that they intended before the marriage to establish their home in some country other than the husband's domicile and that they have in fact carried this intention out. The presumption may be rebutted, though not lightly, if the question falls to be considered before the intention has been carried out.' If that suggested rule is in fact a rule of English law, then I think there is no doubt that Mr. Wilberforce's client would succeed in the present case, because the [widow] has deposed to the following statement in an affidavit, she has not been cross-examined on it, and it is a statement which I accept. She says this: 'Neither before nor at the time of my marriage to the testator, nor at any time afterwards, was there any discussion or express agreement between us as to community or separation of property. It was however agreed between us before marriage that as soon as possible we would settle in France and establish our permanent and only home there. We carried this intention into effect, and neither of us ever had a permanent home outside France after the date of our marriage.'

I have, therefore, to approach this controversy between Dr. Morris and Dr. Cheshire with that caution and respect which they both deserve. I think a good starting point is a passage in the judgment of Vaughan Williams L.J. in the Court of Appeal in *In re Martin*,[1] where he says this: 'In my opinion, the effect of the husband's domicile on the matrimonial property is based on the presumption that you must read the law of the husband's domicile into the marriage contract as a term of it, unless there is an express agreement to the

In re
EGERTON'S
Will
TRUSTS.
—
Roxburgh J.

---

[1] [1900] P. 211 ; *post*, p. 456.

contrary.' I must respectfully differ from those last words 'unless there is an express agreement to the contrary', because I see no reason why, if the facts warrant it, an agreement which is sometimes erroneously called 'a tacit agreement' might not be as effective as an express agreement. . . . For my part, I see no reason why an appropriate agreement excluding the presumption could not be inferred from the conduct of the parties if the circumstances of the case justify such an inference, and it is, I think, something of that kind which Dicey must have contemplated when he used the somewhat wide phrase 'in the absence of reason to the contrary'.

There is one point which I must consider which I do not remember meeting before, and on which no authority has been cited to me, and which is very material in this case. Mr. Wilberforce has submitted that in deciding whether or not an agreement is to be inferred from conduct, the only conduct which can be considered is conduct earlier than or contemporaneous with the date on which the alleged contract was made. I see no reason for such a limitation, which I should have thought would have put the court into blinkers and preclude it from doing palpable justice in some cases. I will give an example, though perhaps a fanciful one. Supposing that it might be relevant to determine whether there was to be inferred from the conduct of two parties an intention to make a voyage to South Africa, and supposing that the evidence before the date of the journey was that they had consulted tourist offices, obtained particulars of fares, possibly even booked some accommodation, had written to friends and said that they were coming, and supposing that it was quite uncertain at that date whether there was any reason to go to South Africa other than what was to be inferred. Then when the departure comes, they go to New Zealand. It would be ridiculous to exclude from the circumstances from which the inference had to be drawn the circumstance that in the end, at any rate, they went to New Zealand. That is perhaps an extreme case. But I certainly take the view that if it is a question of inferring something from conduct, the court must look at the conduct as a whole and not stop its investigation at any particular date. That approach, as I think, gets rid of all the difficulties.

I would, first of all, like to consider—though it is obiter in this case—the case where the parties agreed before the marriage to change their domicile immediately. I can well conceive that in certain circumstances that mere fact might be enough to lead the court to infer that the parties intended their proprietary rights to be regulated by the law of the new domicile from the moment of their marriage. Take, for example, the case of two comparatively poor persons, one, the woman, having a few National Savings Certificates, and the man being a weekly wage earner. They both decide to emigrate to Australia. I can well believe that the court might think that that was enough in those circumstances to lead to the inference that they intended their proprietary rights (which at that stage were nugatory, but which might thereafter become of great value) to be regulated from the beginning of their married life by the law of Australia. I can well believe that the court might in those circumstances draw some such inference. However, take the case of an elderly widower who was a director of half a dozen companies in England and held shares and debentures and exchequer bonds and various things in England. He marries a young wife, and being ill and in need of a warm climate, agrees to leave immediately to take up his home in South Africa. I cannot imagine that any court would ever draw the inference from the mere fact that they had decided immediately to leave for South Africa to make it their permanent home, and did so, that he intended that all his proprietary rights should, as from the date of their marriage, be governed by the law of South Africa. I have only given those illustrations to show that what inference the court might or might not draw from the circumstances of an immediate change of domicile would depend on all the circumstances of the case. There does not seem to me to be any particular difficulty. Indeed, I think that I am, roughly speaking, adopting the solution which Dr. Morris has suggested, though in place of the somewhat vague phrase 'reason to the contrary' I should prefer to put it that an inference was to be drawn from all the circumstances of the case that the law of the new domicile was intended to apply as from the date of the marriage.

But I am not really concerned with that case, because the evidence of the [widow] is 'We would settle in France as soon as possible'. That very phrase, in my view, connotes that circumstances might not make it possible to settle there immediately, and indeed there were circumstances which did stand in the way of an immediate departure. There were certain circumstances connected with the testator's release from the army, and there may have been—though there is no evidence of that—financial and business reasons. The evidence is singularly meagre in this case. I think that the difficulties of inferring

In re
EGERTON'S
WILL
TRUSTS.
—
Roxburgh J.

anything of that sort are very much greater because, if it is once conceded that the parties contemplated that a period of time is to elapse before they change their domicile, it is most improbable that they intend the new law, or rather, the law of the new domicile, to apply before they actually change their domicile. If, therefore, any inference of this nature is to be drawn, a dichotomy of property rights appears to result, so that they would have some property subject to the law of the matrimonial domicile, that is to say, the husband's domicile at the time of the marriage, and some property subject to the law of the State in which they had a newly acquired domicile. Such an agreement could be made—I see no juristic difficulty—but it seems to me an improbable arrangement and, therefore, strong evidence would be required to justify any such inference merely from conduct and without any express agreement, written or oral.

In the present case there is no evidence of any intention to substitute the new law, that is to say, the law of the changed domicile, for the law of England. All the matters on which Mr. Wilberforce relies are equivocal and could not possibly be said to be evidence which would justify any such inference. I have deliberately said that, because, even if I am wrong in thinking that I am entitled to have regard to the declarations in the three documents to which I have referred, I should still hold that there was not enough evidence to justify the inference which Mr. Wilberforce asks me to make. But if, as I think, I am entitled to look at those documents, then there is strong evidence that no agreement between these parties is to be inferred from their conduct that the law of France was to apply as soon as they took up their residence in France. I myself should have thought that if any kind of change of that sort was in contemplation the testator would, at some stage, have been bound to have discussed it with [his wife], and her evidence is that he never did. In my opinion, in the circumstances of this case, it would be quite fantastic to infer from what is merely the change of domicile that it was arranged at the time of the marriage, tacitly or by conduct, that French law should apply to their property rights as soon as they settled in France, and I decline to draw any such inference.

If that be the right basis in law, that is, of course, the end of the matter. If, however, Professor Cheshire's view is to be adopted, then I think that Mr. Wilberforce would succeed, but I can find no foundation in the authorities for Professor Cheshire's view. In my judgment, it is reasonably plain that there is a presumption that the law of the husband's domicile applies to a marriage, and that the presumption can be rebutted. It can certainly be rebutted by express contract, and, in my judgment, it could also be rebutted by what is loosely called a tacit contract, if the circumstances warrant the inference of such a tacit contract. Therefore, in substance, I adhere to the view expressed by Dr. Morris. The widow is not entitled to have the estate administered under the régime of community of property in accordance with French law.

Declaration accordingly.

In re
EGERTON'S
WILL
TRUSTS.
—
Roxburgh J.

FRANKEL'S ESTATE *v.* THE MASTER 1950 (1) S.A. 220 (Appellate Division of the Supreme Court of South Africa)

FRANKEL'S
ESTATE
v.
THE
MASTER.

A husband and wife were married in 1933 in Czechoslovakia, the husband being then domiciled in Germany (which was his domicile of origin) and the wife, immediately before the marriage, in Czechoslovakia. At the time of the marriage they intended and had determined and agreed to leave Germany and to establish their permanent home in Johannesburg where the husband had been promised employment. They arrived in Johannesburg about four months later, the husband entering upon the promised employment and both of them having the intention of settling there permanently. In 1937 the husband was appointed a director of a Durban company controlled by his employers, and in consequence he and his wife moved to Durban with the intention of settling there permanently. In 1938 the husband was naturalized as a British subject. The husband and wife lived in Durban until 1948 when the husband died. There was no antenuptial contract. The law of Germany in 1933 was that a marriage without antenuptial contract was a marriage out of community.

The widow applied for a declaration that the parties were married in community of property according to the laws of the Union of South Africa. The substantial respondent was the Commissioner for Inland Revenue. The Natal Provincial Division dismissed the application. The widow appealed.

SCHREINER J.A.: The question in this appeal is whether, where a man and woman at the time of their marriage intend to settle in a country other than that of the man's domicile, that country's law, and not the law of the man's domicile, governs the proprietary rights

FRANKEL'S
ESTATE
v.
THE
MASTER.

Schreiner
J.A.

of the spouses. It is not in dispute that where no question of intention to settle in some other country is involved the law of the man's domicile at the time of the marriage governs those rights, unless before the marriage the parties have expressly agreed otherwise; but it is contended for the appellants that where there is such an intention to settle in another country this intention has in law the same effect as if the parties had expressly agreed that their proprietary rights should be governed by the law of the country of proposed settlement.

The appellants support their case by reference to several lines of authority. Some writers advance as a reason for the adoption of the rule that the law of the man's domicile governs the proprietary rights of the spouses the fact that they will generally be going to live in that domicile; and this reason is claimed by the appellants to be the true general principle, of which the predominance of the law of the man's domicile is only the most important application. The practice of seeking a wider, underlying, principle behind a recognized specific rule is a valuable means of improving the form of the law, by making it more logical and harmonious, but the practice may, if pursued incautiously, have unsatisfactory effects on the law's substance. If some reason for a rule of law has appealed to the fertile brain of an early writer and has been accepted, possibly without re-examination, by later writers, it may take the place of the rule itself, although it was not in fact the reason or the only or most important reason for the adoption of the rule into the customary or statutory law. If the result is a better, fairer, clearer rule it may be of no importance that the modification rested on a weak foundation. But unless the result is good it is difficult to see why the rule should be changed because a writer or writers conceived a plausible but possibly erroneous reason for its introduction. The certainty of a generally accepted rule should not, without good cause, be weakened by doubts as to the reasons that may have led to its establishment. In the present case, whatever may have been written on the subject, I am not convinced that the domicile of the man was chosen, by whoever chose it, because that was where the parties were most likely to have their home after the marriage. It may be so but it may not. At least equally plausible seems to me to be the proposition that the law treated the husband as generally the dominant partner and when the need for fixing a law to govern the proprietary rights of the spouses was in question it was his law, that is under our system the law of his domicile, that was made to govern. At all events the possibility that the inaugurators of the generally accepted rule that the man's domicile provides the law of the marriage had in mind the fact that the parties would probably be living there seems to furnish no sufficient reason for doubting the full applicability of the rule.

The appellants rely upon another line of authorities who make the statement, sometimes with a confusing introduction of the place of celebration of the marriage as a factor, that the law of the woman's domicile will govern the proprietary rights of the spouses if the man intends to settle at that domicile after the marriage. But these statements are fairly explainable on the basis that the man may change his domicile when he comes to get married at the woman's home with the intention of going on living there.

The appellants, however, do have in their favour certain opinions expressed by jurists of importance in favour of the view for which they contend. So far as Pothier and Story are concerned there is no doubt that they did support the proposition that where at the time of the marriage the parties intend to make a particular country their home their proprietary rights should be governed by the law of that country and not by the law of the man's domicile at the date of the marriage. And some modern textbook writers have adopted the same view. But the considerations against this view seem to me to be preponderant. In the first place it may be remarked that Story's reasoning does not appear to have found favour in the United States of America.[1] Then, if one looks at the matter from the logical point of view, there seems to be a decided jump in inferring from a decision to settle in a particular country a tacit agreement that the law of that country is to govern the spouses' proprietary rights. It would depend on what assumption regarding the very question in issue is to be attributed to the parties. If they assume that the law of the man's domicile will govern, the fact that they intend to settle in another country becomes irrelevant. The analogy of ordinary contracts, which are generally governed in regard to their performance by the law of the place of performance, seems to be a false one, for in regard to such contracts the law of the domicile of the parties to the contract is irrelevant. Where parties in marrying make no express contract as to the law that is to govern their proprietary rights the natural inference is that they intend those rights to be governed by

FRANKEL'S
ESTATE
v.
THE
MASTER.
—
Schreiner
J.A.

---

[1] See notes in 43 Harv. L. Rev. 1286 and 44 Harv. L. Rev. 523, citing Conflict of Laws Restatement, s. 18.

FRANKEL'S
ESTATE
v.
THE
MASTER.
—
Schreiner
J.A.

whatever law is applicable, according to the law of the place where the issue arises. There seems to be no greater justification for attributing to them an assumption that their proprietary rights will be governed by the law of their proposed place of settlement, no matter what the law of the man's domicile is, than for attributing to them an assumption that the law of the man's domicile will apply, no matter where they make their home.

When one turns to considerations of convenience the appellants' contention is seriously weakened. In a matter of this sort it is of the greatest importance that there should, as far as possible, be certainty not only as to what the law is but as to its application. Now it is clear that, if the mere intention of the spouses regarding their future home is to decide what law is to govern their proprietary rights, a world of uncertainty is introduced into the problem. How firm or definite must their intention be? Must their resolve be fixed to remain in the new country permanently, whatever the conditions may prove to be? How soon must it be their intention to move thither? Answers of some kind to these and similar questions might no doubt be given if the facts could be established or if use were made of the burden of proof, but the result could only be to leave it in serious doubt what law would govern the rights of any married couple who at the time of their marriage considered migrating to another country. They themselves could not be certain of their position, especially if one spouse had somewhat different views from the other as to the advisability or urgency of moving to the new country. So far as other persons, like creditors, are concerned, they would be entirely unable to ascertain or prove the law governing the rights of the spouses. No doubt questions of considerable difficulty can arise as to where any particular person is domiciled but, by comparison, such questions, answerable as they are by external facts such as circumstances of birth and conduct, would appear to be simple.

These considerations lead me to the conclusion that the appeal must be dismissed with costs.

WATERMEYER C.J., CENTLIVRES J.A., GREENBERG J.A., and VAN DEN HEEVER J.A. delivered judgments to the same effect.

Appeal dismissed.

EFFECT OF MARRIAGE ON MOVABLES

Where there is a marriage contract or settlement, it governs the rights of husband and wife over all movables comprised within its terms which are then possessed or afterwards during the coverture acquired, even if there is a change of domicile, and even if the contract is implied by law.

DE NICOLS *v.* CURLIER [1900] A.C. 21 (House of Lords)

In 1854 Nicolas Daniel Thevenon, a Frenchman, married a Frenchwoman in Paris. In accordance with French law and custom the municipal officer who performed the ceremony formally called upon the parties to declare whether they had executed any contract of marriage, to which they both replied in the negative, when their answers were duly recorded on the usual 'Minute'; and it appeared from the evidence in the present case that no contract of marriage was executed.

At the date of the marriage the husband was a man of no means whatever, being a working coachmaker in Paris at wages. The wife was an assistant in a linen business, and had a little property of her own amounting altogether to about £120. In October 1863 they came over to England, and with a sum of about £400, which represented their sole property, set up in London a small restaurant, called the 'Café Royal', in Glasshouse Street, Regent Street. Ultimately under their joint management this restaurant expanded into a large establishment of the same name in Regent Street. Shortly after their arrival in England the husband changed his name to 'Daniel Nicolas de Nicols', and in 1865 took out letters of naturalization as a British subject under that name. He and his wife remained in England until his death, she actively assisting him in the management of the café. Out of that business, and from an interest in a valuable building site in London, the husband amassed a large fortune. On 28 February 1897 he died, having made a will dated 22 March 1895, in the English form, in which, after appointing three persons his executors and trustees and bequeathing various legacies, he devised and bequeathed to them his residuary real and personal estate in trust for sale, and to hold the proceeds upon trust for his wife for life, and after her death upon trust for his daughter (the only child of the marriage), her husband and children. The testator was at his death possessed of property of the total value of about

£600,000, comprising considerable freehold and leasehold properties, besides investments in numerous stocks and shares. It was said
that he also had £100,000 worth of wine in France. There was only
one child of his marriage, a daughter, who was married and had
several children, of whom one, a daughter, was now the wife of the
Marquis de Bruille.

This was an originating summons taken out by Madame de Nicols,
the testator's widow, against the executors and trustees of his will,
his daughter and her children, to ascertain (amongst other things)
what were the rights and interests of the plaintiff in the real and
personal estate of her late husband, the testator, by reason of their
having married without any marriage contract or settlement, the
parties being at the time domiciled in France. Subsequently the
question for decision was formulated in chambers as follows: 'Did
the change of domicile alter the legal position of the parties to the
marriage in reference to property?' The summons was then adjourned into court for argument on this question, and now came on
for hearing. Upon the summons being opened it was arranged that
the argument should, for the present, be confined to the effect of the
change of domicile on the testator's 'movable goods' only.

Kekewich J. decided in favour of the widow.[1] His decision was
reversed by the Court of Appeal.[2] The widow appealed.

LORD MACNAGHTEN: The question for your Lordships' consideration is whether Mr. and Mrs. De Nicols continued subject to the
system of community of goods after they became domiciled in England. On the one hand it is contended that the change of domicile
from French to English destroyed the community altogether, and,
therefore, that the testator's will operated upon the whole of the
property vested in him which, but for that change, would have been
common. On the other hand it is said that the community continued
notwithstanding the change of domicile, and that Mr. De Nicols
remained bound by the article of the Code Civil, which provides that
a testamentary donation by the husband cannot exceed his share of
the community.

If the case were not embarrassed by the judgment of this House in
Lashley v. *Hog*,[3] which was discussed so fully at the bar, it would
not, I think, present much difficulty.

[1] [1898] 1 Ch. 403.   [2] [1898] 2 Ch. 60.
[3] (1804) 4 Paton, 581.

Putting aside *Lashley* v. *Hog* for the moment, the only question would seem to be what was the effect according to French law of the marriage of Mr. and Mrs. De Nicols without a marriage contract? Upon that point there cannot, I think, be any room for doubt. It is proved by the evidence of M. Lax, the expert in French law called on behalf of the appellant, that, according to the law of France, a husband and wife intermarrying without having entered into an ante-nuptial contract in writing are placed and stand by the sole fact of the marriage precisely in the same position in all respects as if previously to their marriage they had in due form executed a written contract, and thereby adopted as special and express covenants all and every one of the provisions contained in arts. 1401 to 1496 in Title V of the Code Civil, headed 'Of Marriage Contracts and the respective rights of spouses'. . . .

The expert who was called on behalf of the executors does not attempt to contravene this conclusion of law. He endeavours to minimize its effect by treating it as a self-evident proposition—as in fact being nothing more than what the Code declares. He adds, however, that in his opinion the effect of a change of domicile or nationality upon the community system was never considered by the framers of the Code. That may be so. But if there is a valid compact between spouses as to their property, whether it be constituted by the law of the land or by convention between the parties, it is difficult to see how that compact can be nullified or blotted out merely by a change of domicile. Why should the obligations of the marriage law, under which the parties contracted matrimony, equivalent according to the law of the country where the marriage was celebrated to an express contract, lose their force and effect when the parties become domiciled in another country? As M. Lax points out, change of domicile and naturalization in a foreign country are not among the events specified in the Code as having the effect of dissolving or determining the community. Let us suppose a case the converse of the present one. Suppose an Englishman and an Englishwoman, having married in England without a settlement, go to France and become domiciled there. Suppose that at the time of the acquisition of the French domicile the husband has £10,000 of his own. Why should his ownership of that sum be impaired or qualified because he settles in France? There is nothing to be found in French law, nothing in the Code Civil, to effect this alteration in his rights. Community of goods in France is constituted by a marriage

423

De Nicols
v.
Curlier.

Lord Mac-
naghten.

in France according to French law, not by married people coming to France and settling there. And the community must commence from the day of the marriage. It cannot commence from any other time. It appears to me, therefore, that the proposition for which the executors contend cannot be supported on principle. That, I think, was the view of the Court of Appeal. But they considered that the judgment of Lord Eldon in *Lashley* v. *Hog* compelled them to decide in favour of the executors. Mr. and Mrs. Roger Hog, an Englishman by domicile and an Englishwoman, intermarried in England without a settlement. Mr. Hog made a fortune in England, settled in Scotland and became domiciled there. After this change of domicile the wife died in the lifetime of the husband. Some years later the husband died a domiciled Scotsman. There was a good deal of litigation as to the administration of Mr. Hog's estate, and there were appeals to this House. In one of these appeals, among other things, this House determined that Mrs. Lashley, who was one of the children of the marriage, had 'a claim in right of her mother the wife of the said Mr. Roger Hog, who at the time of her death had his domicile in Scotland, to a share of the movable estate of her father at the time of her mother's death'.

No doubt if the law had not been altered by the Intestate Movable Succession (Scotland) Act 1855, s. 6, that decision would be binding upon this House in a similar case. But when you are asked to apply the decision to a case where the circumstances are different, it seems to me that the proper course is to ascertain, if you can, the principle of the decision, and then to see if that principle is applicable to the circumstances of the case under consideration. This is the case of a French marriage with a settlement prescribed and constituted by the law of the land and followed by naturalization in a foreign country. *Lashley* v. *Hog* was the case of an English marriage without a settlement and a change of residence to another part of the United Kingdom.

Now, what was the principle on which Lord Eldon proceeded? After a long discussion Lord Eldon comes to the point by asking this question: 'Why should it be thought an unreasonable thing that where there is no express contract the implied contract should be taken that the wife is to look to the law of the country where the husband dies for the right she is to enjoy, in case the husband thinks proper to die intestate?' Then his Lordship goes on to say: 'This has been the principle, which it seems to me has been adopted, as far as we can collect what has been the principle adopted, in cases in those parts of the island with which we are best acquainted, and not being aware that there has been any decision which will countervail this; thinking that it squares infinitely better with those principles upon which your Lordships have already decided in this case, it does appear to me attending to the different sentiments to be found in the text-writers upon the subject that it is more consonant to our own laws, and more consonant to the general principle, to say that the implied contract is that the rights of the wife shall shift with the change of residence of the wife, that change of residence being accomplished by the will of the husband whom by the marriage contract in this instance she is bound to obey.'

I may observe in passing that in that passage Lord Eldon was referring to the difference of practice in the administration of intestates' effects then prevailing in the different provinces of York and Canterbury, and also to a previous decision in the case of *Lashley* v. *Hog* on the question of legitim. It is not, I think, very easy to see how the principle which Lord Eldon selects as the ground of his decision could in the case of an English marriage and the subsequent acquisition of a Scotch domicile be legitimately extended so as to deprive the husband of his own property, and transfer it in his lifetime to the next of kin of his wife. It seems to me that the result can only be reached by one or other of two alternatives. Either it must be held that the implied contract on the part of the husband is that in case of a change of domicile the wife shall enjoy all the rights of a woman married in the country where the new domicile is established, and that he will surrender in her favour so much of his rights as may be inconsistent therewith; or else it must be assumed that marriage in Scotland is not required to create communion of goods, but that communion of goods is incidental to the status of married persons in Scotland; or, as Lord Eldon puts it, 'the law of Scotland "recognises" communion of goods "in the married state".'

Now, if that assumption be necessary in order to support Lord Eldon's conclusion in *Lashley* v. *Hog*, it is obvious that there is so wide a divergence between the law of Scotland, or what is assumed to be the law of Scotland, and the law of France as to make the decision inapplicable to the present case. If, on the other hand, Lord Eldon's conclusion is a legitimate extension or development of the principle on which his argument is founded, it seems to me that there is no room for the application of the principle in the circumstances

DE NICOLS
v.
CURLIER.

Lord Mac-
naghten.

425

DE NICOLS
v.
CURLIER.

Lord Mac-
naghten.

of the present case. The principle, as Lord Eldon explains, is founded on the notion that upon an English marriage without an express settlement there is an implied contract that the expectations of the wife are to depend upon the domicile of the husband. Lord Eldon admits, and it was conceded at the bar, that, if there had been a written contract dealing with the whole property of the spouses present and future, the principle of *Lashley* v. *Hog* could not apply. Now the effect of what took place on the occasion of the French marriage, so far as it amounted to a compact in respect of property, must, I think, be determined by French law; and it has been proved by the evidence in this case that what did take place was to all intents and purposes, according to the law of France, equivalent to a written contract.

It appears to me, therefore, that the case is not governed by the decision in *Lashley* v. *Hog*, and I think the appeal ought to be allowed.

LORDS HALSBURY, MORRIS, SHAND, and BRAMPTON delivered judgment to the same effect.

Appeal allowed.

The essential validity of a marriage settlement or contract is governed by its proper law. The proper law is presumed to be (but is not necessarily) the law of the matrimonial domicile.

DUKE OF
MARL-
BOROUGH
v.
A.-G.

DUKE OF MARLBOROUGH *v.* ATTORNEY-GENERAL [1945] Ch. 78
(Court of Appeal)

Appeal from Vaisey J.

This originating summons taken out by the tenth Duke of Marlborough raised the question whether, on the true construction of a settlement, dated 6 November 1895, and executed in New York on the occasion of the marriage between the ninth duke and Miss Consuelo Vanderbilt (now Madame Balsan) and in the events which happened, estate duty became payable on or in respect of the funds therein comprised by reason of the death of the ninth duke on 30 June 1934. Miss Vanderbilt was the daughter of Mr. W. K. Vanderbilt, a citizen of the United States domiciled in New York. At the time of her marriage she was a minor. The settlement comprised a fund of two and a half million dollars in the stock of an American railway, and no English property at all. There was also a covenant by Mr. Vanderbilt to settle an annual sum of $100,000 for the wife's separate use without power of anticipation during the joint lives of himself and the wife, and a covenant for the payment by his executors on his death of a further $2,500,000. There was a covenant for the settlement of the wife's after-acquired property 'with a minimum of £10,000'. The trustees were Mr. Vanderbilt and the Hon. Ivor Churchill Guest (afterwards Lord Wimborne). The investment clause provided a wide range of British and American securities in which the trustees might invest. In fact, the funds had always been invested in American securities, and the administration of the trust had taken place in America, but it was the intention of the parties that Miss Vanderbilt should marry a domiciled Englishman and that the matrimonial domicile of the parties should be English. The settlement contained a covenant that the husband and wife would as soon as possible take all necessary steps to procure the approval of the Chancery Division of the English High Court of Justice under the Infant Settlements Act 1855. Provision was made for the case of the court refusing to approve, and for the possibility of the wife repudiating the settlement. On 27 January 1896 Chitty J. in chambers sanctioned the settlement. On the death of the duke the question arose whether for the purpose of succession duty (and therefore of estate duty) the settlement was to be treated as an American or an English settlement. Vaisey J. held that it was an English settlement, and that both succession duty and estate duty became payable thereon on the death of the ninth duke. The tenth duke appealed.

The judgment of the court (Lord Greene M.R., Finlay and Morton L.JJ.) was delivered by

LORD GREENE M.R.: . . . Counsel for the duke and for the Crown were in agreement in submitting that in the case of a marriage settlement the question whether succession duty is payable under s. 2 of the Succession Duty Act 1853 is to be answered by reference to the law governing the settlement—in other words, the proper law of the settlement. They agreed that duty attaches if, and only if, the proper law of the settlement is English (or Scottish as the case may be). . . .

It may well be the case that the proper law of a settlement can be changed by subsequent events, but we do not see how this can happen without the concurrence of the beneficiaries agreeing to a

DUKE OF MARL-BOROUGH
v.
A.-G.

DUKE OF
MARL-
BOROUGH
v.
A.-G.

Lord
Greene
M.R.

change in the proper law and thereby, in effect, making a new settlement. It cannot, we think, be effected by a change in trusteeship. . . .
In determining what is the proper law of the settlement the nature
and situation of the property settled is, no doubt, a matter to be
taken into consideration, but the relevant date for this purpose can
only be the date of the settlement itself since we do not see how a
change, for example, from foreign investments to English investments can turn what was originally a foreign settlement into an
English settlement. As in the case of trustees, so in the case of investments a change may be quite fortuitous and cannot affect the question what law governs the settlement. . . . We do not ourselves think
that in the case of a marriage settlement what we may call the
notional character or location of settled property (which, as we have
said, is a relevant consideration) is to be ascertained by reference to
the rule 'mobilia sequuntur personam'. That character and location
is, we think, a relevant consideration for what it is in fact, not for
what (for some purposes) it notionally is by virtue of a conventional
rule of law. In the case of a wife who acquires the domicile of her
husband on marriage it does not appear to us to be right to attribute
to personal property which she settles a character and location by
reference to her antenuptial domicile which ex hypothesi is going to
be changed immediately after the marriage takes place. Moreover,
in the case of both spouses, the matrimonial domicile is the one
which must be taken to be in their contemplation when they execute
the settlement. For these reasons, although, as we have said, the
character and location of the settled property are relevant matters to
be taken into consideration in deciding what is the proper law of the
settlement they are not, in our opinion, to be ascertained by reference
to anything but the true facts relating to the property. . . .

We have come to the conclusion that in the case of a marriage
settlement succession duty is exigible only where the proper law of
the settlement is English (or Scottish) law. The question, therefore,
in the present case is whether that law is the law of England or the
law of the State of New York. On what principle is it to be answered?
On the same principle, as it seems to us, as a similar question arising
in the case of any other personal contract. For this we cannot do
better than quote the words of Lord Watson in *Hamlyn & Co.* v.
Talisker Distillery.[1] 'When two parties living under different systems
of law enter into a personal contract, which of these systems must be

[1] [1894] A.C. 202, 212.

applied to its construction depends upon their mutual intention, either as expressed in their contract, or as derivable by fair implication from its terms. In the absence of any other clear expression of their intention it is necessary and legitimate to take into account the circumstances attendant upon the making of the contract and the course of performing its stipulations contemplated by the parties.' At the outset of the inquiry in the present case lies a question as to the admissibility of certain direct evidence as to the actual intention of the parties, particularly the intention of Mr. W. K. Vanderbilt himself. We cannot see on what principle evidence of this character is admissible and counsel for the duke was unable to refer to any case in which it was admitted for the purpose of determining the proper law of a contract. The language of Lord Watson appears to us quite clearly to imply that such evidence is inadmissible. The question what law the parties to a contract contemplate as governing its meaning and operation is, we venture to think, a question of construction the answer to which depends, as Lord Watson says, on 'their mutual intention, either as expressed in their contract or as derivable by fair implication from its terms'. For this purpose, all such evidence of the circumstances as is generally admissible for the purpose of construing a written contract is admissible to ascertain its proper law. Direct evidence of intention is, in our opinion, clearly inadmissible for that purpose.

When we turn to the settlement in this case and such circumstances as are admissible, we find the following matters to be considered. Miss Vanderbilt, the settlor of the railway stock, was at the date of the settlement domiciled in the State of New York but the matrimonial domicile of the parties was clearly to be English. The securities which she settled were American securities, but the terms of the settlement permitted their sale and the re-investment of the proceeds in English securities. Mr. W. K. Vanderbilt himself was domiciled in the State of New York. Of the two trustees, one was Mr. W. K. Vanderbilt, the other was Mr. Ivor Guest, a domiciled Englishman resident in England, so that, presumably, both the courts of the State of New York and the English court would have been competent to enforce the trusts of the settlement. The settlement was executed in New York in triplicate, one part being handed to the English trustee, who brought it to England. For some reason he did not have it stamped, but this can have no bearing on the question what is the proper law of the settlement. The settlement

DUKE OF MARL-BOROUGH v. A.-G.

Lord Greene M.R.

DUKE OF
MARL-
BOROUGH
v.
A.-G.
Lord
Greene
M.R.

itself was drafted in English form. Taking into account these considerations alone and attaching particular weight to the fact of the matrimonial domicile being English, we should have had little hesitation in deciding that the proper law of the settlement was English, but there are certain provisions in the settlement which appear to us to place this beyond all possible doubt. The first is the reference to 'the statutory power of appointing a new trustee', a phrase which would be quite meaningless if the law of the State of New York were contemplated. The next provision is the special indemnity given to the trustees 'in addition to the indemnity given by law to trustees'. The law referred to can only be the law of England since the evidence shows that the law of the State of New York, although it recognises the validity of a contractual indemnity to trustees, does not of itself provide for any indemnity. The last provision is that for the making of an application to the English courts under the Infant Settlements Act with a view to making Miss Vanderbilt's settlement binding on her by English law. It is true that this only affects her own part of the settlement. It points, however, quite clearly to English law as being the proper law of the settlement so far as her part in it was concerned, and we can see no reason for thinking that Mr. W. K. Vanderbilt's part of the settlement was intended to be governed by a different law to that which was to govern the settlement of her property by his daughter. . . .

Appeal dismissed.

In re
BANKES.

In re BANKES [1902] 2 Ch. 333 (Chancery Division)

In 1877 Kate Gruinard Anderton, a widow, domiciled in England, became engaged to be married to Angelo Favaroni, an officer in the Italian army. At that time she was possessed of £4,000, and, in order to meet the requirements of the Italian Government with reference to the marriage of officers, she deposited £1,000 with the military authorities in that country. On 28 March 1878 she and Favaroni executed in Italy a marriage settlement in English common form, whereby it was agreed that the trustee should hold the remaining sum of £3,000 in trust after the marriage, to permit it to remain in its then state of investment or call in and invest it, and pay the income during the joint lives of herself and Favaroni to her for her separate use without power of anticipation; and after the death of either of them to the survivor, and then for the children of the marriage; and subject thereto, if Mrs. Favaroni survived her husband, upon trust after his death for her, her executors, administrators, and assigns; but if he survived her, then after his death as she should by will or codicil appoint; and in default of appointment, in trust for such person or persons as under the statutes for the distribution of the effects of intestates would have become entitled thereto at the decease of Mrs. Favaroni had she died possessed thereof intestate and without having been married.

The settlement contained a covenant by Mrs. Favaroni to settle her after-acquired property.

The marriage took place on 28 July 1878 at Florence, and Mr. and Mrs. Favaroni lived in Italy continuously after that time, and were domiciled there. There were no children of the marriage. By a decree dated the 8th and registered on the 28th of March, 1898, of the Civil and Criminal Court of Florence, the court approved of the official report, declared by the President of the Court, of the legal voluntary separation which had taken place between Mr. and Mrs. Favaroni, subject to certain conditions, and ordered the execution of the report. Since the date of the decree Mr. and Mrs. Favaroni had lived apart from one another.

On the death of her mother in 1899 Mrs. Favaroni became entitled to certain legacies bequeathed by the wills of her father and mother. Questions arose whether these legacies were caught by the agreement to settle after-acquired property contained in the settlement, or could be paid and transferred to Mrs. Favaroni on her separate receipt.

The trustee of the settlement commenced an action to determine these questions, and claimed a declaration that the £1,000 legacy was subject to the covenant, and ought to be paid to him; and that the property bequeathed by Mr. Bankes was also subject to the clause. There was evidence that according to Italian law the settlement was void because it was not executed before a notary, and because it altered the order of succession under that law; that after marriage the husband and wife remained entitled to their respective fortunes as before; that this position could not be affected by a settlement unless it was attested by a notary; that the separation had no effect upon the individual rights of property; and that the marriage continued after the separation.

431

BUCKLEY J.: The question I now have to determine is whether to this settlement, which was executed on 28 March 1878, the English law or the Italian law is to be applied.

The relevant facts are these: the document is in the English form; it contains this covenant to settle after-acquired property, which would be wholly inoperative if Italian law were applicable to the case. Beyond that the instrument as a whole would, according to the Italian law, have been perfectly invalid, for the evidence is that, inasmuch as it openly violates the legal order of succession established by Italian law, it can have no effect at all in Italy. The further fact is that the wife's domicile was English, and this document provides that the settled fund, which was an English mortgage, if realized and reinvested, should be reinvested in English investments. This is therefore an instrument dealing with the property of a lady who was English, dealing with property which was English, providing that in case that particular property changed its form the new form which it assumed should be English, the whole contained in a document which is in the common English form, with the further fact that unless the English law is to be applied the whole thing was invalid, and might have been put behind the fire the moment it was executed, because in Italian law it had no effect at all. It seems to me that upon those facts I ought to arrive at the conclusion that the parties intended to contract according to the English law. The general proposition, as stated in Dicey's Conflict of Laws, at p. 653, is this: 'A marriage contract or settlement will, in the absence of reason to the contrary, be construed with reference to the law of the matrimonial domicile.' The matrimonial domicile here was Italian, no doubt, so that primâ facie this ought to be construed with reference to the law of the matrimonial domicile. But is there reason to the contrary? It seems to me, on the facts I have mentioned, there is reason to the contrary. I therefore think the English law, and not the Italian law, ought to be applied.

Then this is further argued—that although according to the English law the lady covenanted that she would at a future time so dispose of her after-acquired property as that it would come within the settlement, yet when she married an Italian she acquired an Italian domicile, and according to the Italian law such a covenant is invalid, and that therefore, upon the doctrine of *Viditz* v. *O'Hagan*,[1] she could not when the covenant fell to be performed be called upon to

---

[1] [1900] 2 Ch. 87; *post*, p. 433.

perform it. It seems to me that is not so. In *Viditz* v. *O'Hagan* the point was that the settlement was executed by an infant who could not bind herself, and the question was whether, by acts done after attaining majority, and after a foreign domicile had been acquired, there had been such an affirmation of the settlement as that it became binding; in other words, the settlement when executed was nothing, and, unless the English law as to affirmation and confirmation applied, it never became binding. Now, here, if I am right, the settlement at the outset was binding because it was executed by a person competent to bind herself. Then, if I am entitled to treat the English law as being applicable to it, she could according to our law bind herself in respect of her after-acquired property, and although it took the form of a covenant and not of an assignment, that would make no difference. On that ground it seems to me the covenant was effectual. I therefore hold that this matter is throughout to be governed by English law.

In re
BANKES.
—
Buckley J.

Capacity to make a marriage settlement contract is governed by its proper law.

VIDITZ *v.* O'HAGAN [1900] 2 Ch. 87 (Court of Appeal)

Appeal against the decision of Cozens-Hardy J.

In November 1864 the Honourable Frances Netterville, then aged 18, the only child of Viscount Netterville, an Irish peer, was married at Berne in Switzerland to Mr. Viditz, an Austrian. By marriage articles under seal in English form dated 24 November 1864, and executed before the marriage at the British Legation at Berne, and made between Mr. Viditz of the first part, the Honourable Frances Netterville of the second part, trustees of the third part, and Viscount Netterville of the fourth part, it was declared and agreed that all personal property to which the wife was then entitled or to which she might become entitled during the joint lives of the husband and the wife should be vested in the trustees upon the usual trusts for the benefit of the wife for life, and after her death upon trusts for the issue of the marriage, with an ultimate trust for Viscount Netterville absolutely.

The husband was domiciled in Austria before and after the marriage and it was contemplated that the parties should live in Austria, as in fact they did. Mrs. Viditz attained 21 on 5 November 1867.

VIDITZ
v.
O'HAGAN.

Subsequently she became entitled to various sums of money and executed various documents appointing new trustees of the settlement of 1864 and, under a power in the settlement, appointing one fourth of the trust funds to one of her daughters.

In 1893 she and her husband executed in Austria and in accordance with Austrian law a notarial act by which they purported to revoke the deed of 1864 and to vest in Mrs. Viditz the unrestricted administration of all her property.

In 1896 Mr. and Mrs. Viditz and their four children commenced this action against the trustees of the settlement claiming a declaration that by virtue of the notarial act of November 1893 the deed of 1864 was revoked and was void by Austrian law.

Expert evidence was given to the effect that by Austrian law the marriage articles of 1864 were void, not having been executed as notarial acts; that children do not acquire vested interests under the marriage contracts of their parents, but only an expectancy; that a husband and wife have a right to revoke their marriage contract, notwithstanding the birth of issue and acts of ratification, and that this right of revocation cannot be waived and is not lost by lapse of time.

Cozens-Hardy J. held that the marriage articles were valid and were governed by English law, and that the wife, not having repudiated them within a reasonable time after she had attained twenty-one, was absolutely bound by them.

The plaintiffs appealed.

LINDLEY M.R.: Two questions arise. The first is, whether, upon the true construction of the marriage articles of November 1864 (assuming that they are binding on the wife), the sum of £5,000, which is payable to her under the compromise of the probate action, is or is not comprised in the articles. (Having held that it was not, his Lordship continued:) This brings me to the second point, which is a much more difficult one, namely, whether the settlement has or has not become binding on the wife. She was an Irish lady, and was under twenty-one when she executed the marriage articles. They were executed in contemplation of her marriage with an Austrian gentleman, and it was contemplated that after their marriage they should (as they in fact did) live in Austria; in other words, that the wife should become domiciled in Austria, which was the domicile of the husband.

Now, according to English law, this settlement by her was a

434

voidable contract in the sense explained by the House of Lords in *Edwards* v. *Carter*.[1] After the marriage she lived with her husband in Austria, and in 1867 she became of age. By the Austrian law she was unable to ratify or confirm this contract; she could always repudiate it, but could never ratify it, i.e., deprive herself of the right to repudiate it. This was the case in *Cooper* v. *Cooper*,[2] but it was not so in *Edwards* v. *Carter*. We have to consider what is the consequence of that. In the course of her married life she executed some documents which, if they are to be governed by English law, clearly amounted to a ratification of the settlement. By the Austrian law these documents were invalid in so far as they purported to be irrevocable ratifications.

The position is a simple one. This lady never had, either before or after her marriage, power to make an irrevocable settlement. Can we in those circumstances hold that the settlement has become irrevocable? That is the paradox put to us. Cozens-Hardy J. has taken this view of it. He says, first, that, upon the authority of *Van Grutten* v. *Digby*,[3] this was an English settlement to be governed by an English law, and that by the English law as expounded by the House of Lords in *Edwards* v. *Carter* (which affirmed a decision of this court) a covenant in a marriage settlement by an infant or a settlement made on his marriage by an infant is voidable, and it is binding on him unless it is repudiated within a reasonable time after he attains twenty-one. It is said that this lady always had at all events power to repudiate the settlement—she could do that by Austrian law—and that, inasmuch as she did not repudiate it within a reasonable time after she attained twenty-one, the contract has become irrevocable. Is that reasoning sound? I think it is not, and for this reason. In the first place, as regards *Van Grutten* v. *Digby*, the point which we have now to consider did not arise for determination. There was no question there about incapacity to contract. There was a settlement made by persons of mature age and binding upon them when it was made. Romilly M.R. was clearly right in saying that that contract must be governed by the law of England, regardless of any change of the domicile of the parties afterwards. But in the present case the difficulty arises from the incapacity to contract, and that difficulty, as it seems to me, is not touched and still less governed by *Van Grutten* v. *Digby*.

VIDITZ
v.
O'HAGAN.

Lindley
M.R.

---

[1] [1893] A.C. 360. [2] (1888) 13 App. Cas. 88.
[3] (1862) 31 Beav. 561.

435

Now, what is the effect of the English law as expounded by the House of Lords in *Edwards* v. *Carter*? What is the theory of it? The theory is, I apprehend, this—that there are some contracts of infants which by English law are absolutely void. There are a few (not a great many) contracts which in the view of English law cannot possibly be for the benefit of the infant—take a bond with penalties as an illustration—and they are void. An infant cannot so contract. The great bulk of infants' contracts are only voidable. What does that mean? It means that when the infant comes of age he can elect either to affirm or to disaffirm the contract. If he does nothing within a reasonable time after he attains twenty-one, the presumption is that he has affirmed the contract. The contract is binding and has been binding on him ever since he attained twenty-one, unless he proves the contrary by repudiating it within a reasonable time. But I think it would be an entire mistake to apply that part of English law which relates to repudiation within a reasonable time if you shut out the other part which relates to the ability to ratify.

Now, by the alteration of the wife's domicile in this case her ability to ratify her contract was lost. Ought we then to apply what I may call the mutilated English doctrine relating to infants, and to say that this contract has become irrevocable because it was not repudiated within a reasonable time? It seems to me that this would be contrary to good sense, and it would land us in the paradox which I have already mentioned, namely, that the contract had become irrevocable, although the lady never had, either before or after she was married, the capacity to enter into an irrevocable contract.

As to the authorities, the nearest case to the present which has been cited, and the nearest which I know, is *Cooper* v. *Cooper*, in which a very similar difficulty had to be met by the House of Lords, but the question of reasonable time did not receive attention. In that case a lady did succeed in repudiating a marriage settlement made when she was an infant after the lapse of much more than a reasonable time, if you shut out of consideration the change of her domicile between the execution of the settlement and the repudiation. The question of reasonable time was not discussed there, but so far as it goes the case is in favour of the present appellants.

In my opinion, the effect of the change of domicile was that the English doctrine of reasonable time became inapplicable by reason of the impossibility after that change of the wife's effectually ratifying her contract. An alternative view of the case (perhaps it is only the same view in another shape) is that the effect of the change of domicile was to enlarge the reasonable time for repudiation. This may not perhaps be quite so satisfactory a way of putting it; but I confess I do not see how it can be said that a reasonable time for repudiation had expired when there was no possibility of her doing anything else but repudiate. However, I think the former is the truer view, and any other view would be difficult to reconcile with *Cooper* v. *Cooper*.

I may refer to the observations of Lord Watson in that case. He said: 'Being of opinion that the capacity of the appellant to bind herself by the marriage contract must be determined by the law of England, I agree with your Lordships that the discharge which she seeks to set aside cannot stand in the way of her claiming her legal rights as a Scotch widow. The rule seems to be clear that an infant cannot, during minority, effectually subject herself to any contractual obligation which cannot be shewn to have been for her benefit. She may ratify the contract, after attaining majority, and so become liable to implement it, but, in the circumstances of the present case, any such ratification of the contract would, according to the law of Scotland, have been revocable by her as a donation inter virum et uxorem.' That, so far as it goes, although it does not quite touch the point, appears to me an authority in favour of the conclusion at which I have arrived.

I think, therefore, that the appeal must be allowed, and a declaration made in accordance with the plaintiff's claim.

RIGBY and COLLINS L.JJ. concurred.

Appeal allowed.

VIDITZ
v.
O'HAGAN.
Lindley
M.R.

NOTE T: THE EFFECT OF MARRIAGE ON MOVABLES

THE effect of marriage on the movable property of the spouses differs in accordance with whether there is, or is not, a marriage contract or settlement.

1. *When there is no contract or settlement*

The governing principle here is that the effect of marriage on the rights of the husband and wife to each other's movables, whether possessed at the time of the marriage or subsequently acquired, is determined by the law of the matrimonial domicile, i.e. the law of the husband's domicile at the moment of the marriage: *Re Martin* [1900] P. 211, *post*, p. 453; *Re Egerton's Will Trusts*, *ante*, p. 410; *Frankel's Estate* v. *The Master*, *ante*, p. 417. This

LAW OF PROPERTY

case is printed here because it was very fully argued and because the South African courts have had more experience of dealing with this type of question perhaps than any others.

What happens if the domicile changes during the marriage? It used to be thought that the law changes too. But this view rested on the unsatisfactory Scots case of *Lashley* v. *Hog* (1804) 4 Paton 581, which was adversely criticized in *De Nicols* v. *Curlier* (*ante*, p. 421). It is now generally agreed that a change of domicile does not necessarily affect the rights of the parties. Whether it does so or not depends on whether the effect of marriage according to the law of the matrimonial domicile is to confer vested rights (e.g. the old rule of English common law) or merely inchoate rights (e.g. a spes successionis). In the former case a change of domicile is irrelevant: rights have vested, and ought not to be divested by an act which one party (the husband) can effect without the consent of the other. But new acquisitions made since the change of domicile will be subject to the law of the new domicile, since there can be no vested rights in hypothetical future acquisitions. If, however, the effect of marriage according to the law of the matrimonial domicile is to confer a mere spes successionis, the rights of the spouses will depend on the law of the domicile at death of the one who dies first: it is really a question of succession (*Re Groos* [1915] 1 Ch. 572). The distinction between vested and inchoate rights is accepted by Dr. Cheshire, but *Chiwell* v. *Carlyon* (1897) 14 S.C. 61, the case on which he relies, is scarcely an impressive authority, because it dealt with land. See Cheshire, pp. 460–4; Dicey, pp. 640–3.

Problems. (1) H and W, domiciled in Hungary, marry. They subsequently acquire a domicile in England. H wins a prize in a football pool. Are W's rights (if any) in the prize money governed by English or Hungarian law?

(2) H and W, domiciled in England, marry. They subsequently acquire a domicile in France. H wins a prize in a French lottery. Are H's rights in the prize money affected by the French system of community of goods?

2. Where there is a contract or settlement

Here the terms of the contract (assuming it to be valid) govern the rights of husband and wife to all movables within its terms which are then possessed or subsequently acquired, notwithstanding any change of domicile. This is logical, because the contract creates vested rights. The rule applies even if the contract is implied by law: *De Nicols* v. *Curlier* (*ante*, p. 421). Whether it is so implied is a question of foreign law and therefore a question of fact.

The essential validity of the contract is governed by its proper law, which is presumed to be (but is not necessarily) the law of the matrimonial domicile. Circumstances which, singly or together, have been held to rebut this presumption (in cases where the husband and wife were domiciled in different countries before their marriage) are the fact that the settled property belonged to the wife or her family; the language and legal style of the settlement; the fact that its provisions are invalid by the law of the matrimonial domicile; the place of management of the trust; the place of residence of the trustees; the place of investment of the securities. The relevant time for giving effect to the last two factors is the date of the settlement: subsequent changes are disregarded, *Duke of Marlborough* v. *A.-G.* (*ante*, p. 426) illustrates the application of the presumption in favour of the law of the matrimonial domicile; *Re Bankes* (*ante*, p. 430) illustrates its rebuttal. The former case is very near the line: see 61 L.Q.R. 223.

Formal validity. The settlement will be formally valid in England if it complies with the formalities prescribed by either the law of the place of contracting (*Guépratte* v. *Young* (1851) 4 De G. & Sm. 217) or the proper law (*Van Grutten* v. *Digby* (1862) 31 Beav. 561).

Capacity. On principle, capacity to make a marriage settlement contract should be governed by its proper law: Dicey, pp. 632–4; Cheshire, pp. 465–8. That is the law which governs capacity to make a commercial contract, and there is no reason why a different principle should apply here. It is some-times said, however, that capacity to make a marriage settlement is governed, not by the proper law (which is presumed to be the law of the matrimonial domicile), but by the law of the domicile of the party alleged to be incapable. According to this view, the capacity of an English girl under 21 to make an antenuptial settlement prior to her marriage with a domiciled foreigner would be governed by English law. It must be admitted that very strong dicta favouring this view are to be found in *Cooper* v. *Cooper* (1888) 13 App. Cas. 88, where the widow of a domiciled Scotsman was allowed to repudiate a marriage contract on the ground that when she executed it she was an infant by the law of her domicile. But it is impossible to take the statements of the House of Lords in that case at their face value. The law of the woman's domicile at the date when she executed the contract was Irish law, which throughout the case was treated as the same as English law. Lord Halsbury said that by the law of England the contracts of an infant are void; Lord Macnaghten said that Mrs. Cooper's contract was voidable in the sense that it was binding on her until she repudiated it, which she had elected to do.

Yet in *Edwards* v. *Carter* [1893] A.C. 360, the House of Lords held that an infant's marriage settlement contract was neither void, nor voidable when-ever the infant chose to repudiate it, but voidable only within a reasonable time after the infant had attained his majority. The House further held that it was too late for the infant to repudiate at the age of 26, and yet Mrs. Cooper had been allowed to repudiate her contract 33 years after she attained 21. It is plain that there is a direct inconsistency between *Cooper* v. *Cooper* and *Edwards* v. *Carter* which cannot be resolved unless we assume that Scots law as the law of the matrimonial domicile as well as Irish law as the lex domicilii at the date of the contract exerted an influence on the decision in the former case. The true position would appear to be that by Irish law the contract was voidable for a short time only, but by Scots law it was voidable for ever, because any ratification by Mrs. Cooper would have been revocable as a donation inter virum et uxorem: see *per* Lord Watson in the passage cited in *Viditz* v. *O'Hagan, ante,* p. 437.

In *Viditz* v. *O'Hagan* the Court of Appeal expressly adopted this view of *Cooper* v. *Cooper*. It is hard to see how the Court of Appeal could have arrived at their decision unless they were able to distinguish *Cooper* v. *Cooper* on the ground that Scots law as well as Irish law played its part in the decision. Two passages from Lord Lindley's judgment make this point clear. Speaking of the case before him, he said: 'By the Austrian law she was unable to ratify or confirm this contract; she could always repudiate it, but could never ratify it, i.e. deprive herself of the right to repudiate it. *This was the case in Cooper* v. *Cooper, but it was not so in Edwards* v. *Carter*' (*ante*, p. 435). And speaking of *Cooper* v. *Cooper* he said: 'In that case a lady did succeed in repudiating a marriage settlement made when she was an infant after the lapse of much more than a reasonable time, *if you shut out of consideration the change of her domicile between the execution of the settlement and the repudiation*' (*ante*, p. 436). The clear inference from the concluding words in this passage is that in Lord Lindley's view the House of Lords in *Cooper* v. *Cooper* did not shut out of consideration the law of Scotland. If so, *Cooper* v. *Cooper* is no authority for the proposition that capacity to make a marriage settlement contract depends upon the lex domicilii at the date of the contract.

The cases are fully discussed in an article in 54 L.Q.R. 78 (1938)

Chapter 18

ADMINISTRATION AND SUCCESSION TO MOVABLES

Section *A*: ADMINISTRATION OF ESTATES

In the administration of the English estate of a deceased person who died domiciled abroad, foreign creditors are entitled to dividends pari passu with English creditors.

In re KLŒBE (1884) 28 Ch. D. 175 (Chancery Division)

THIS was an action for the administration of the estate in England of Charles Jules Alexander Klœbe, a domiciled Greek, who died at Syra on the 15th of February 1882, intestate and insolvent. The deceased carried on business in England in partnership under the style of Charles Klœbe & Co., and was possessed of property in England. It did not appear whether there were any foreign assets. The Chief Clerk had certified that the assets consisted of a sum of £1,710. 19s. 2d., the balance of the administrator's account in court, and a sum of £1,837. 11s. 9d. Consols also in court. That there was one separate debt of £50. 7s. due to a foreign creditor, and that the partnership debts amounted to £3,432. 4s. 7d. due to English creditors, and £8,456. 18s. 3d. due to foreign creditors. The action now came on on further consideration.

PEARSON J.: At the end of the argument I stated I had no doubt what my decision should be, but in consequence of my being told that there were decisions of learned Judges to whom I am bound to pay, and do pay, the greatest respect, who had supported a contrary contention, I thought it better to look at those judgments to see if they really supported that contention, and I am glad to find that they do not. It appeared to me, if that contention had anything in it, it must have been the practice of the court to inquire in actions for the administration of deceased persons domiciled abroad as to the nationality of creditors, and I can find no case in which the court in distributing assets has made an inquiry as to the nationality of

441

different creditors, or ordered that English creditors should be paid in priority to others. There is not a fragment of authority for such a practice. I think Mr. Westlake in a passage cited lays down the law perfectly correctly. In sect. 102 of the last edition of his work on Private International Law, he says: 'Every administrator, principal or ancillary, must apply the assets reduced into possession under his grant in paying all the debts of the deceased, whether contracted in the jurisdiction from which the grant issued or out of it, and whether owing to creditors domiciled or resident in that jurisdiction or out of it, in that order of priority which according to the nature of the debts or of the assets is prescribed by the laws of the jurisdiction from which the grant issued.' All that is there said, and no doubt correctly, is that although mobilia sequuntur personam, in the collection, the lex fori must be observed: so also is it to be observed in the administration of those assets when collected. Therefore, if a man dies domiciled in England, possessing assets in France, the French assets must be collected in France, and distributed according to the law of France. If the French creditors are entitled according to that law to be paid in priority, that rule must be observed, because it is the lex fori, and for no other reason. But if it should happen that a man died domiciled in France, leaving assets in England, those assets can only be collected under an English grant of administration, and being so collected must be distributed according to the law of England. No doubt in a case in which French assets were distributed so as to give French creditors, as such, priority, in distributing the English assets the court would be astute to equalize the payments, and take care that no French creditors should come in and receive anything till the English creditors had been paid a proportionate amount. But subject to that, which is for the purpose of doing what is equal and just to all the creditors, I know of no law under which the English creditors are to be preferred to foreigners. On the other hand the rule is they are all to be treated equally, subject to what priorities the law may give them, from whatever part of the world they come, and in the case cited by Mr. Cookson of *De La Vega* v. *Vianna*,[1] Lord Tenterden says: 'A person suing in this country must take the law as he finds it; he cannot, by virtue of any regulation in his own country, enjoy greater advantages than other suitors here, and he ought not therefore to be deprived of any superior advantage which the law of this country may confer. He is to have the same rights

[1] (1830) 1 B. & Ad. 284.

which all the subjects of this kingdom are entitled to.' And that has been the rule in this country, as far as I know, from the earliest time. . . .

The law of England has always been that you must enforce claims in this country according to the practice and rules of our courts, and according to them a creditor, whether from the furthest north or the furthest south, is entitled to be paid equally with other creditors in the same class. I must refuse to alter that which has always been the law of this country, and which I must say, for the sake of honesty, I hope will always be the law of this country.

If in the administration of the English estate of a deceased person who died domiciled abroad there remain surplus assets in the hands of the administrator after all debts recoverable by English law have been duly paid, the surplus assets must be beneficially distributed in accordance with the law of the deceased's domicile, and not paid to the domiciliary administrator for the benefit of creditors whose claims are statute-barred by English law, but not by the law of the domicile.

In re LORILLARD [1922] 2 Ch. 638 (Court of Appeal)

Appeal from a decision of Eve J.

LORD STERNDALE M.R.: This is an unusual question arising in certain administration proceedings in this country and in the United States of America. It seems to me to be entirely a matter of discretion, and I do not see my way to differ from the decision of Eve J. The testator, who was domiciled in America, died in this country. Administration proceedings are going on both in America and in England. In England there are no debts. There are debts in America which according to English law are statute barred, but not so according to the law of New York. If claims in respect of these debts had been made here they would rightly have been rejected. The English administrator asked for the directions of the court as to what course he ought to pursue. For the beneficiaries in England it was contended that the American creditors were completely barred, the debts being over twenty years old. For the creditors in New York it was contended that as the testator was at the time of his death domiciled there the American administration was the principal proceeding to which the English administration was merely ancillary, and that

In re
KLŒBE.
—
Pearson J.

In re
LORILLARD.
—
Lord
Sterndale
M.R.

In re
LORILLARD.
—
Lord
Sterndale
M.R.

accordingly the applicant as administrator in New York was entitled to receive the surplus assets in England remaining after the satisfaction of the testator's debts in order that they might be applied in paying the debts of bona fide creditors in any part of the world and for this purpose they ought to be transferred to America. The authorities do not throw much light upon the question as to the duty of the English administrator. It would seem to be his duty to see that the debts are paid—i.e., debts which are due according to English law. Eve J. has made an order giving the American creditors a period of two months within which to bring in their claims in this country, and intimating that if they did not do so the surplus assets would be distributed among the beneficiaries. The American creditors, however, did not present their claims, presumably knowing that if they did so they would be rejected. It is argued that it is still the duty of the English administrator to transfer the moneys in his hands to the American administrator. I cannot see any principle under which it is necessary for the English court in such circumstances to order the administrator here to hand over the surplus assets to the American administrator. No authority has been cited in favour of such a course, and I cannot say that Eve J. has wrongly exercised his discretion in the matter. The appeal must therefore be dismissed.

WARRINGTON and YOUNGER L.JJ. delivered judgments to the same effect.

Appeal dismissed.

Section *B*: INTESTATE SUCCESSION

Intestate succession to movables is governed by the law of the deceased's domicile at the date of his death.

If the deceased died intestate and without next of kin and domiciled abroad, the State of his domicile is entitled to his movables in England as against the Crown's right to bona vacantia if the foreign State claims as ultimus heres, but not if it claims under a jus regale.

In re
MAL-
DONADO.

In re MALDONADO [1954] P. 223 (Court of Appeal)

Appeal from Barnard J.

Eloisa Hernandez Maldonado died at Santander, Spain, on 11 October 1924, a widow and intestate, with no ascendant, descendant, or collateral relative entitled to succeed to her estate under Spanish law. The deceased was a Spanish subject and at the time of her death was domiciled in Spain. Her English estate consisted of securities in the custody of Hambros Bank Ltd., London, which at the time of her death were valued at £13,515, but which now amounted to over £26,000.

In re MAL-DONADO.

The State of Spain brought proceedings in the Probate, Divorce, and Admiralty Division claiming that letters of administration to the estate of the intestate in England should issue to the duly constituted attorney of the Spanish State as the sole and universal heir to her estate by Spanish law. The defendant, the Treasury Solicitor, claimed that the deceased's estate in England passed to the Crown as bona vacantia.

Article 956 of the Spanish Civil Code provides that when a person dies intestate leaving no issue, parents or grandparents, surviving spouse or collaterals within the sixth degree, the State inherits as being the ultimus heres, the assets being devoted to charitable institutions as therein mentioned.

There was a conflict of evidence among the Spanish lawyers, the witnesses for the plaintiff asserting that under article 956 the Spanish State took the property of a deceased intestate as heir, and the witnesses for the defendant asserting that it took the property by virtue of a jus regale. Barnard J. preferred the witnesses for the plaintiff on this point; he said: '1 am satisfied on the evidence before me that the State of Spain is a true heir just as any individual heir according to Spanish law.' That finding was not challenged in the Court of Appeal.

Barnard J. decided in favour of the Spanish State. The Treasury Solicitor appealed.

JENKINS L.J.: The general rule to be applied in a case such as this is summed up in the maxim mobilia sequuntur personam, and is thus stated in Dicey's Conflict of Laws, 6th ed., at p. 814: 'Rule 177. The distribution of the distributable residue of the movables of the deceased is (in general) governed by the law of the deceased's domicile (lex domicilii) at the time of his death.' Thus, in the present case the personalty in question should, prima facie, devolve in accordance with Spanish law, and, therefore, go to the State of Spain for application in accordance with the provisions of article 956.

There is, however, an admitted exception to the general rule to the effect that if, according to the law of the foreign State in which the deceased is domiciled, there is no one entitled to succeed to the movable property of the deceased owing, for example, to the bastardy of the deceased, or to the failure of kin near enough in degree to qualify for succession under the law of the domicile, and, by the law of the foreign State, the State itself is, in such circumstances, entitled to appropriate the property of the deceased as ownerless property by virtue of some jus regale corresponding to our law of bona vacantia, English law will not recognize the claim of the foreign State as part of the law of succession of the domicile, but will treat it merely as being the assertion by the foreign State of a prerogative right which has no extra-territorial validity and one which must yield to the corresponding prerogative right of the Crown. That appears from Dicey at p. 818 in the passage to which Evershed M.R. has already referred: 'Where a person dies, e.g., intestate and a bastard, and under the law of the country where he is domiciled there is no succession to his movables, but they are bona vacantia, and leaves movables situate in a country, e.g. England, in which he is not domiciled, the title to such movables is governed by the lex situs, i.e., under English law the movables being situate in England, the Crown is entitled thereto. In such a case the foreign Treasury claims not by way of succession but because there is no succession.'

The law of the relevant foreign State, however, may be such as to constitute the State itself the successor to the deceased in the absence of any individual with a prior right of succession under that law, and the question then arises whether the claim of the foreign State should be recognized under the general rule as being the claim of a person entitled to succeed according to the law of the domicile, or whether it should be treated as falling within the exception, on the ground that the claim of the foreign State, as self-constituted successor, does not differ in substance, or in principle, from a claim by a foreign State by virtue of its paramount right to ownerless property within its dominions as bona vacantia or the equivalent.

Accordingly, two questions were debated below: first, whether under the Spanish Civil Code the State takes as a true heir or successor in the eye of Spanish law, or takes by virtue of a jus regale; and secondly, if it takes in the former capacity, whether English law will recognize the State of Spain as a true heir or successor for the purpose of the maxim mobilia sequuntur personam. Barnard J., having heard evidence on both sides in regard to the Spanish law, answered the first question in the former sense, and the second question in the affirmative, holding in effect that the answer to the second followed from the answer to the first. Barnard J.'s decision on the first question has not been challenged by the Crown in this court. The sole issue before us, therefore, is whether the State of Spain, being admittedly according to its own law the true heir of, or successor to, the intestate, should be recognized as such by English law in its application of the general rule that is expressed in the maxim mobilia sequuntur personam.

This question has not been the subject of any direct decision, but the distinction between a sovereign state claiming 'jure regali' and claiming as true heir or successor was recognized in *In re Barnett's Trusts*,[1] and *In re Musurus*.[2] Inasmuch as the foreign law in each of those cases was held to give the foreign State concerned a jus regale, as distinct from a true right of succession, there was no actual decision on the present question; but the distinction was recognized. Indeed, as it was pointed out, both those cases would have been susceptible of a short and simple answer if the view then taken of the law had been that in no circumstances could a foreign State claim the assets of a deceased intestate situated in this country, whether the claim was founded on jus regale or on a true right of succession.

The question has also been discussed in various textbooks on this branch of the law. In Dicey, at p. 818, the passage cited above continues: 'It does not follow that the decision would be the same if the law of the domicile was such that the foreign Treasury claimed as ultimus heres. That would be a true case of succession and would, it is submitted, be governed by the law of the domicile.' There are also the passages in the works on Private International Law by Wolff (2nd ed. p. 579), Bar (2nd ed. p. 843) and Cheshire (4th ed. p. 59), to which Evershed M.R. has referred. I treat those passages as incorporated in this judgment. The conclusion of Barnard J., therefore, has the support of no inconsiderable weight of learned opinion, and although, for my part, I find it difficult to embrace with enthusiasm either side of this highly technical question, his conclusion also commends itself to me on the ground of consistency.

In cases such as the present, English law professes to apply the law of the domicile to the devolution of the intestate's movables situated

In re
MAL-
DONADO.

Jenkins L.J.

---

[1] [1902] 1 Ch. 847.   [2] [1936] 2 All E.R. 1666.

in this country. If the law of the domicile is that of a foreign State under whose law of intestacy the State itself is the successor, why should English law not give effect to that provision as part of the law of succession which it professes to apply?

The reasons why it is claimed that English law does not do so are expressed in a variety of ways. First, the distinction between succession by a sovereign State and the appropriation of bona vacantia by a foreign State is said to be a mere matter of words. This argument is not without persuasive force, but I do not think that the question can truly be said to be one of distinction without difference. The foreign State can only succeed under its own law of succession where the succession is governed by that law. On the other hand, where the case is not one of succession, but of appropriation of ownerless property, the right applies to any ownerless property which may be reached by the law of the foreign State concerned, irrespective of the law by which its devolution is governed, provided only that by the relevant law it is in fact ownerless.

Second, it is said that the foreign State, being omnipotent so far as its own law of succession is concerned, can constitute itself successor in circumstances in which it could equally well rely on a claim based on jus regale. But in accepting the foreign State's law of succession, English law recognizes the foreign State as being the arbiter of what the succession is to be. The foreign State could, for instance, enact that older relatives should be preferred to younger, or that male relatives should be preferred to female, or vice versa, or even that fair-haired relatives should be preferred to dark-haired; and to such distinctions, unreasonable as they might seem, English law would, as I understand the matter, have no objection. Why, then, should English law stop short of recognizing the foreign State itself as the successor where, according to its own law, it is indeed such? The answer that English law recognizes it to be the function of the relevant foreign law to regulate succession as between individual subjects or citizens, but declines to recognize rights conferred by the foreign State on itself in exercise of that function, does not commend itself to me. It involves distinctions at least as arbitrary and artificial as those discerned by the Crown in the distinction between jus regale and true inheritance by the State. For example, it was, I think, conceded in argument that if the Spanish law of succession provided that in circumstances such as those of the present case the estate of the intestate was to go to some person, or body,

or corporation, other than the State itself for application to charitable purposes such as those stated in article 956 of the civil code,
there would be no reason why the English courts, in applying the
general rule to the inheritance, should not recognize and allow
effect to be given to that provision. Why, then, should not the same
result ensue where, as here, the estate goes by Spanish law to the
Spanish State itself for application to those same charitable
purposes?

Third, it is said that private international law is concerned only
with the rights of individuals and not with the competing rights of
sovereign States. That may well be so. But it is clear that English law
recognizes the legitimate proprietary rights of foreign sovereign
States, and I see no reason why a right of succession to an intestate's
estate should not be held to answer that description.

Fourth, it is said that English law should not recognize as 'heir'
or 'successor' any person not bound by some personal nexus with
the deceased. I cannot follow this submission. The heir or successor
is surely the person, whether related to the deceased or not, who
under the relevant law is entitled to inherit or to succeed.

Fifth, it is said that there is no reciprocity, because Spanish law
would not give effect to a claim by the Crown in respect of bona
vacantia. But non constat that Spanish law would not recognize a
right to succession belonging to the Crown if any such right existed,
and it could easily be made to exist by Act of Parliament if that
were thought expedient.

There might be a case where a so-called right of succession
claimed by a foreign State could be shown to be in truth no more
than a claim to bona vacantia. If so, it would, no doubt, be right to
apply the recognized exception to the general rule; but this has not
been shown to be such a case. On the contrary, it has been found
(and the Crown has accepted the finding) that the State of Spain is,
in the eye of Spanish law, the true heir; and I would add that, to
my mind, notwithstanding what the President said in *In re Musurus*,
the conclusion that this is a case of genuine succession is reinforced
by the circumstance that the State of Spain is by article 956 of the
Spanish Civil Code enjoined to apply the property of the intestate
to the charitable purposes therein mentioned.

Accordingly, for the reasons given by Evershed M.R. and such
additional reasons as I have been able to offer, I agree that this
appeal fails and should be dismissed.

EVERSHED M.R. and MORRIS L.J. delivered judgments to the same effect.

Appeal dismissed.

Section C: WILLS OF MOVABLES

In general, succession to movables is governed by the law of the testator's domicile at the date of his death.

In re COHN [1945] Ch. 5 (*ante*, p. 1)

In re ANNESLEY [1926] Ch. 692 (*ante*, p. 7)

In re ROSS [1930] 1 Ch. 377 (*ante*, p. 10)

The question whether a will is revoked by the subsequent marriage of the testator is governed by the law of his domicile at the date of the marriage.

In re MARTIN [1900] P. 211 (Court of Appeal)

In 1870 the testatrix, an unmarried Frenchwoman then in England in the domestic service of an English family, made a holograph will in one of the forms recognized as valid by French law which was not attested as required by the Wills Act, 1837. By that will she gave the residue of her property to the plaintiff, her sister.

In 1874 the testatrix left domestic service, established a laundry business in London, and married a French refugee named Louis Guillard, known in London as Martin, who was then fifty-one years old.

Prior to 1868 Guillard, then a Professor of French in France, fled to Belgium to escape prosecution for an offence alleged to have been committed by him in connection with his professorship. In his absence he was convicted and sentenced by a French court to ten years' imprisonment, and in 1868 or 1869, after the date of his conviction, he came over from Belgium to England.

After the marriage the husband joined his wife in carrying on the laundry business. In 1890, the period of prescription of twenty years under French criminal law having expired, he separated from his wife and returned to France, where he remained and where he was still living at the date of the action.

In 1895 the testatrix, who had continued to carry on the laundry in London, died in a fire which occurred at the business premises.

Her next of kin were her sister, the plaintiff, and her brother, the defendant. As it was believed that she had died intestate, the brother took out letters of administration in England to her estate, the husband renouncing. Subsequently the sister propounded the will of 1870, claiming a grant of administration with the will annexed, and asking that the letters of administration granted to the brother should be revoked. There was evidence that by French law marriage does not revoke a will.

All the Judges held that at the date of the testatrix's death the domicile of the husband, and therefore of the testatrix, was French; but there was a difference of opinion as to the domicile of the husband at the date of the marriage, Sir F. H. Jeune P. and Lindley M.R. holding that it was French, and Rigby and Vaughan Williams L.JJ. that it was English.

Sir F. H. Jeune P. held that the husband and wife, though domiciled in France, intended to marry in accordance with English matrimonial law, but that s. 18 of the Wills Act 1837 (by which a will is revoked by the subsequent marriage of the testator), is part of the testamentary law of England and not part of the matrimonial law. He therefore held that the will was not revoked. The defendant appealed.

LINDLEY M.R.: The will which is in question in this case was made in this country by a Frenchwoman before her marriage, and was not attested as required by English law. By English law, by which I mean English law irrespective of all foreign law, the will is therefore clearly invalid. But foreign law must be taken into account. Those principles of private international law which are recognised in this country are part of the law of England; and on those principles the validity of the will, so far as it affects movable property, depends on the law of the domicile of the testatrix when she died. The domicile of the testatrix must be determined by the English Court of Probate according to those legal principles applicable to domicile which are recognised in this country and are part of its law. Until the question of the domicile of the testatrix at the time of her death is determined, the Court of Probate cannot tell what law of what country has to be applied. The testatrix was a Frenchwoman,

In re
MARTIN.

451

but it would be contrary to sound principle to determine her domicile at her death by the evidence of French legal experts. The preliminary question, by what law is the will to be governed, must depend in an English court on the view that court takes of the domicile of the testatrix when she died. If authority for these statements is wanted, it will be found in *Bremer* v. *Freeman*;[1] *Doglioni* v. *Crispin*,[2] and *In re Trufort*.[3] In each of the last two cases a foreign court had determined the domicile and the English court had also to determine it, and did determine it to be the same as that determined by the foreign court. But, as I understand those cases, the English court satisfied itself as to the domicile in the English sense of the term, and did not simply adopt the foreign decisions. The course universally followed when domicile has to be decided by the courts of this country proceeds upon the principles to which I have alluded.

But, further, the validity of a will of movables made by a person domiciled in a foreign country at the time of such person's death not only may, but must, depend on the view its courts take of the validity of the will when made and on its subsequent revocation if that question arises. These questions may or may not turn on the domicile of the testator as understood in this country. For example, in this case it is agreed on all hands that by the law of France the will in question, being a holograph will made by a French subject, was valid when made, whatever her domicile may have been when she made it. It is also agreed on all hands that by French law marriage does not revoke the prior wills of the spouses. But the testatrix married a Frenchman in this country after she made her will, and the question whether her will was thereby revoked as to her movables is the real question on which this case turns.

By whatever court this question is to be decided, the English law of marriage, which in such a case involves and, indeed, turns on English views of domicile, must be considered. If this view be ignored, the effect of the marriage will be inadequately and, indeed, erroneously ascertained. If the domicile of the testatrix is to be treated as English, when she became a married woman her will was revoked by her marriage, for such is the law of England whatever the intentions of the parties may be: 1 Jarman on Wills, c. 7; but if her domicile was French, her will would not be revoked by English law, and still less by French law. Both laws are alike in regarding her

---

[1] (1857) 10 Moo. P.C. 306, 359 *et seq.*   [2] (1866) L.R. 1 H.L. 301.
[3] (1887) 36 Ch. D. 600.

domicile as that of her husband as soon as she married him. The effect of her marriage must, therefore, depend on the English view of his domicile. It would be useless, and, indeed, entirely misleading, to ask a French expert what effect the French law would give to an English marriage, without explaining the English law to him, and no explanation of that law would be adequate or correct if it excluded the English view of the domicile of the parties.

In re MARTIN.
—
Lindley M.R.

Having thus stated the principles which, in my opinion, ought to be applied to the case, I proceed to consider the facts and the evidence of the experts called at the trial.

(His Lordship referred to the facts and continued:) Upon the question of domicile (in the English sense) my own conclusions are that the domicile of the testatrix was French when she made her will; French up to the time she married; French by her marriage; and French when she died. Her domicile was French by and after marriage because, in my opinion, her husband's domicile was French.

The domicile of the testatrix being French when she made her will and when she died, it became necessary to ascertain the effect of her will on her movable property according to French law. The husband being, in my opinion, domiciled in France when she married, it became necessary to ascertain the effect of such marriage by French law upon her will; and if, in order to ascertain this, it became necessary for the French experts to be told what the English law was, they should have been told that it depended on the view which an English court would take of the domicile, in the English sense, of the husband; and if I am right in my view of his domicile, the experts should have been told that by English law the marriage in this case did not revoke the wife's will. It was not necessary or, indeed, proper on this occasion to pursue the inquiry further and to see what matrimonial régime the parties intended to adopt. It is not necessary to cite authorities to show that it is now settled that, according to international law as understood and administered in England, the effect of marriage on the movable property of spouses depends (in the absence of any contract) on the domicile of the husband in the English sense. This being clear the will was not revoked; and if not revoked it was clearly valid as regards the wife's movable property. Sect. 18 of the Wills Act does not apply to the wills of foreigners who die domiciled abroad, and the effect of the marriage was not to vest the wife's property in the husband. French law did not so vest it, neither did international law as understood and administered in this country. The English law applicable to English people, and according to which a woman's personal property formerly vested in her husband on marriage, and according to which her will was revoked by marriage even before the Wills Act, could not, on principle, apply to French spouses married in England, but (according to English views) domiciled in France when they married.

In my opinion the will has been properly admitted to probate; but it will not apply to leasehold property, for that is not regarded as movable property, to which the lex domicilii is applicable. . . .

VAUGHAN WILLIAMS L.J.: I agree in the conclusion of Sir F. Jeune that the husband and wife intended to keep up an establishment in England, and that they intended to marry under English law, and to adopt it as their matrimonial law; but I base this conclusion on the fact, which Sir F. Jeune does not accept, that at the date of the marriage the husband had an English domicile, for I find no other evidence of an agreement embodying that intention, unless it be as an inference from the actual domicile at the date of the marriage. . . .

(His Lordship referred to the facts and continued:) This, in my judgment, is sufficient to show that his actual domicile at the time of the marriage was, according both to English and French law, English.

I gather, however, from the judgment of Sir F. Jeune that his view is that England became the matrimonial domicile by the agreement of the husband and wife at the time of the marriage; but I do not quite understand where he finds such an agreement unless it is to be inferred from a change of the husband's domicile. There is no express agreement, and I know of no English decision in which such an agreement has been inferred inconsistently with the fact of domicile. Husband and wife cannot by mere tacit agreement choose a matrimonial domicile.

Mr. Westlake, in Private International Law, 3rd ed., p. 68, says: 'By the matrimonial domicile is to be understood that of the husband at the date of the marriage, with a possible exception in favour of any other which may have been acquired immediately after the marriage, in pursuance of an agreement to that effect made before it.'

If this exception can be supported, for which there is no English authority, no doubt there is evidence from which one may infer that the actual English domicile after marriage was in pursuance of an ante-nuptial agreement.

I doubt, however, if domicile can be directly affected by the marriage contract. Such an agreement as to the intended matrimonial place of residence may no doubt be evidence, and cogent evidence, of adoption of a new domicile as from a date anterior to the marriage; or it may be evidence of an agreement as to the law which shall govern the movable property of the parties marrying; but I can find no case in which an inferred agreement, as distinguished from an express agreement, has been allowed to outweigh the prima facie inference that the law of the country of the husband's domicile is to govern the movable property of the married couple.

If my conclusion is right, and if one ought to come to the conclusion—from the evidence of the husband's conduct in making his home in England for an indefinite time and going into such a business as by French law put an end to his French domicile and gave him an English domicile—that he adopted an English domicile at the time of his marriage, then at that time his wife's movables became his property; and I think that, his wife's property in the movables having thereby ceased, it follows, quite independently of the 18th section of the Wills Act, that this loss of the power of disposition put an end to her will while it was still ambulatory, and rendered it of no effect, and that nothing but republication could revive it.

If, however, the French domicile of the husband continued at and after the marriage and down to the wife's death, then it would follow that the French law, by which alone this will can be supported (for it is not in the form required by the English Wills Act), must govern the testamentary validity of this will, and also the rights of property of the husband and wife, unless there can be found some binding marriage contract determining the relative rights of the property of the husband and wife.

Sir F. Jeune has found, as I understand, that there is such an agreement or contract. Assuming that there is, I differ from his conclusion in law on this assumption, for I think that the rule of the English law which makes a woman's will null and void on her marriage is part of the matrimonial law, and not of the testamentary law, and that probate of this will ought not to be granted; but as I am not sure that we ought to infer that there was at the time of the marriage an agreement that the English law should govern the matrimonial property, I prefer to ground my judgment on the change of the husband's domicile at the time of marriage; and I think that, if he did change it from a French to an English domicile, then his subsequent reversion to a French domicile will not prevent English law continuing to govern the matrimonial property.

In my opinion, the effect of the husband's domicile on the matrimonial property is based on the presumption that you must read the law of the husband's domicile into the marriage contract as a term of it, unless there is an express agreement to the contrary.

I think, therefore, that the decision of the Court below ought to be reversed, and the grant of letters of administration with the will annexed revoked.

RIGBY L.J. delivered a judgment concurring with the conclusions of Vaughan Williams L.J.

Appeal allowed.

NOTE U: SOME PROBLEMS ON WILLS

(1) T, a testator domiciled in Germany, makes a will in notarial form at the age of 17. He acquires an English domicile and dies. By German law persons over the age of 16 can make valid wills in notarial form. Is the will valid? See Cheshire, p. 482, Dicey, p. 595, Illustration 4.

(2) T, domiciled in France, makes a will when aged 19. She dies domiciled in France at the age of 29. By French law persons over 16 and under 21 can dispose by will of one-half of the property they could have disposed of if over 21. To what extent (if any) is the will valid? See *Re Lewal's Settlement* [1918] 2 Ch. 391, *post*, p. 466.

(3) T is domiciled in a country where the age of majority is 25 and a minor cannot make a will. He makes a will at the age of 22. He dies domiciled in England without having confirmed his will. Is the will valid? See Dicey, p. 596, Illustration 5.

(4) T, domiciled in the Republic of Ireland, by his will gives movables in England to English trustees on trust for A for life and then for such of A's children as shall attain 25. If Irish law applies, the gift to A's children is void for remoteness. If English law applies, it is validated by ss. 3 (1) and 4 (1) of the Perpetuities and Accumulations Act 1964. Is the gift valid? See Cheshire, pp. 491–510 and Dicey, pp. 602–3 and 604, Illustration 6.

(5) T, a British subject domiciled in France, makes a will in English language and legal style in which she gives a number of specific legacies and annuities to friends and gives her residue to another friend. Under French law, she can only dispose of one-third of her property because she leaves two children surviving her. There are indications in the will that T intended it to be governed by English law. What law determines (*a*) whether T had power to dispose of all her property or whether the legacies, annuities, and residuary gift must abate so as to leave two-thirds of the property available for the children; (*b*) in what order the various bequests are to abate? See Dicey, p. 606; *Re Annesley, ante*, p. 7.

(6) T, domiciled in England, gives movables to A for life and then to the children of X. After A's death, X, who is domiciled in Germany, marries Y, a German woman, a week before their eldest child is born. Y had several children by her previous marriage, some of whom predecease A and some of whom survive him. What law determines (a) whether on the context of the will the gift includes illegitimate children and stepchildren; (b) whether X's eldest child is legitimate; (c) when the class of children is to be ascertained? See Dicey, pp. 606–7 and 609, Illustration 3.

(7) T, a British subject domiciled in France, makes a will in English language and legal style in which he gives the residue of his property to be equally divided between ten named legatees, most of whom are British subjects resident in England. Two of these legatees die before T. By English law, lapsed shares of residue are undisposed of and pass to the testator's next of kin: by French law, they are divided among the surviving legatees. Who is entitled to the lapsed shares? See Dicey, p. 608, Illustration 1; *Re Cunnington* [1924] 1 Ch. 68.

(8) T, a French citizen domiciled in England, gives a legacy of 'one million francs' to X, who resides in Switzerland. Is X entitled to one million French or Swiss francs? See Dicey, pp. 607–8.

(9) T, while domiciled in Italy, writes to his solicitor instructing him to destroy his will. By Italian law this amounts to a revocation of the will whether or not the solicitor complies with the direction. By English law it does not. T dies domiciled in England. Is the will revoked? See Cheshire, pp. 498–9, Dicey, pp. 611–12 and 613, Illustration 2.

(10) T, while domiciled in England, writes to his solicitor instructing him to destroy his will. T dies domiciled in Italy. Is the will revoked? See F. A. Mann, 31 B.Y.I.L. 231; Dicey, pp. 612 and 614, Illustration 3.

(11) T, a lady domiciled in France, makes a will, marries a domiciled Englishman, and dies domiciled in France. By English law, marriage revokes a will; by French law it does not. Is the will revoked? See *Re Martin, ante,* p. 450.

(12) T, a lady domiciled in England, makes a will, marries a domiciled Frenchman, and dies domiciled in England. Is the will revoked?

WILLS ACT 1963

1. A will shall be treated as properly executed if its execution conformed to the internal law in force in the territory where it was executed, or in the territory where, at the time of its execution or of the testator's death, he was domiciled or had his habitual residence, or in a state of which, at either of those times, he was a national.

2.—(1) Without prejudice to the preceding section, the following shall be treated as properly executed—

(a) a will executed on board a vessel or aircraft of any description, if the execution of the will conformed to the internal law in force in the territory with which, having regard to its registration (if any) and other relevant circumstances, the vessel or aircraft may be taken to have been most closely connected;

(*b*) a will so far as it disposes of immovable property, if its execution conformed to the internal law in force in the territory where the property was situated;

(*c*) a will so far as it revokes a will which under this Act would be treated as properly executed or revokes a provision which under this Act would be treated as comprised in a properly executed will, if the execution of the later will conformed to any law by reference to which the revoked will or provision would be so treated;

(*d*) a will so far as it exercises a power of appointment, if the execution of the will conformed to the law governing the essential validity of the power.

(2) A will so far as it exercises a power of appointment shall not be treated as improperly executed by reason only that its execution was not in accordance with any formal requirements contained in the instrument creating the power.

3. Where (whether in pursuance of this Act or not) a law in force outside the United Kingdom falls to be applied in relation to a will, any requirement of that law whereby special formalities are to be observed by testators answering a particular description, or witnesses to the execution of a will are to possess certain qualifications, shall be treated, notwithstanding any rule of that law to the contrary, to be a formal requirement only.

4. The construction of a will shall not be altered by reason of any change in the testator's domicile after the execution of the will.

5. (*Repealed.*)

6.—(1) In this Act—

'internal law' in relation to any territory or state means the law which would apply in a case where no question of the law in force in any other territory or state arose;

'state' means a territory or group of territories having its own law of nationality;

'will' includes any testamentary instrument or act, and 'testator' shall be construed accordingly.

(2) Where under this Act the internal law in force in any territory or state is to be applied in the case of a will, but there are in force in that territory or state two or more systems of internal law relating to the formal validity of wills, the system to be applied shall be ascertained as follows—

(*a*) if there is in force throughout the territory or state a rule indicating which of those systems can properly be applied in the case in question, that rule shall be followed; or

(*b*) if there is no such rule, the system shall be that with which the testator was most closely connected at the relevant time, and for this purpose the relevant time is the time of the testator's death where the matter is to be determined by reference to circumstances prevailing at his death, and the time of execution of the will in any other case.

(3) In determining for the purposes of this Act whether or not the execution of a will conformed to a particular law, regard shall be had to the formal requirements of that law at the time of execution, but this shall not prevent account being taken of an alteration of law affecting wills executed at that time if the alteration enables the will to be treated as properly executed.

7.—(1) This Act may be cited as the Wills Act 1963.

(2) This Act shall come into operation on 1st January 1964.

(3) The Wills Act 1861 is hereby repealed.

(4) This Act shall not apply to a will of a testator who died before the time of the commencement of this Act and shall apply to a will of a testator who dies after that time whether the will was executed before or after that time, but so that the repeal of the Wills Act 1861 shall not invalidate a will executed before that time.

(5) It is hereby declared that this Act extends to Northern Ireland, and for the purposes of section 6 of the Government of Ireland Act 1920 this Act shall be deemed to be an Act passed before the appointed day within the meaning of that section.

NOTE V: THE WILLS ACT, 1963

AT common law, a will of movables had to comply with the formalities prescribed by the law of the testator's last domicile: *Bremer* v. *Freeman* (1857) 10 Moo. P.C. 306. This rule led to much inconvenience and hardship when, e.g., the testator changed his domicile after executing his will, or became mortally ill in a country other than that of his domicile. So the courts tried to inject some flexibility into the rigid rule of common law by admitting to probate wills which complied with either the domestic law of the testator's last domicile, or the domestic rules of any system of law referred to by the conflict rules of that law: *Collier* v. *Rivaz* (1841) 2 Curt. 855. Thus the doctrine of renvoi obtained a foothold in English law, obviously as an escape device. The Wills Act 1861 (Lord Kingsdown's Act) allowed other forms as alternatives: but it was confined to the wills of British subjects and to wills of personal estate, and it was notoriously badly drafted.

After plaguing law students and others for just over a century it was re-pealed and replaced by the Wills Act 1963, which gives effect to the Fourth Report of the Private International Law Committee (Cmnd. 491 (1958)) and to a Draft Convention on the Formal Validity of Wills made at The Hague in 1961.

Apart from s. 2 (1) (*b*) the Act applies equally to wills of movables and wills of immovables. The reference is always to the internal law of the foreign country in question. Thus, renvoi is excluded.

Under s. 1, if a testator is domiciled in one country, habitually resident in a second and a national of a third, and changes all three between the execution of his will and the date of his death, he has a choice of no less than seven systems of domestic law, which should be enough to save most wills from formal invalidity so far as the conflict of laws is concerned. There is no requirement in the Act that all the testamentary instruments executed by a testator must conform to the same system of law. Hence, a will and six codicils could each derive its formal validity from a different system.

'Habitual residence' is a favourite expression of the Hague Conferences on Private International Law. Though it has been used before in English statutes, there is as yet no authoritative exposition of what it means. One may hazard the guess that it will be held to mean much the same thing as domicile, minus the artificial elements in that concept (e.g. the revival of the domicile of origin, and the rule that a married woman's domicile is the same as that of her husband), and minus the stress now placed on the ele-ment of intention in domicile. Of course, these are very large deductions.

The reference to the law of the testator's nationality is an even greater innovation than the reference to the law of his habitual residence. If the testator is a national of a composite state like the Commonwealth or the United States of America, or a citizen of, e.g., the United Kingdom and Colonies, there is an obvious difficulty in ascertaining his nationality for the purposes of the Act. S. 6 (2) attempts to solve this problem. It deserves close attention because it is repeated almost verbatim in other Hague Con-ventions on Private International Law, e.g., that on Adoption. One has to think of a testator who is a citizen of, e.g., the United Kingdom and Colonies or of the United States of America and who is domiciled and habitually resident elsewhere and who makes his will elsewhere, the will being formally invalid by the law of the place where it was made and of the testator's domicile and habitual residence, so that it is necessary to invoke the law of his nationality in order to admit it to probate. It is not easy to imagine how s. 6 (2) (*a*) can help in circumstances like these, because it is doubtful if there is a composite state in the world which has a uniform conflicts rule, but different rules of domestic law, for the formal validity of wills: certainly the United Kingdom and the United States have no such uniform conflicts rule. And as for s. 6 (2) (*b*), how can we determine whether our hypothetical testator is 'most closely connected' with, e.g., England or Scot-land, or New York or California, when ex hypothesi he is domiciled and habitually resident outside the United Kingdom or the United States? The only possible answer seems to be, look and see where he keeps his property. But in that case it might have been more sensible to make the formalities of the lex situs available for wills of movables, as they are for wills of immovables under s. 2 (1) (*b*). At best it can be said that the alternative

460

of nationality, though it will not work for citizens of the United Kingdom or of the United States, will do no obvious harm in that connection, and will be beneficial in the case of most other countries. But it is a pity that the provisions for determining the 'relevant time' at which the testator must be 'most closely connected' with a system of law are so frighteningly obscure.

The law of the country where the will was executed is given an extended meaning in the case of wills made on board a vessel or aircraft 'of any description'. In addition to the law of the place where the vessel or aircraft happens to be, s. 2 (1) (a) allows as an alternative the law in force in the territory with which the vessel or aircraft is 'most closely connected' (again the magic phrase, which is supposed to solve all difficulties, but which probably does no more than paper over the cracks of disagreement between various delegations at the Hague Conference). This law will normally be the law of the flag or, in the case of ships wearing flags like the Red Ensign or the Stars and Stripes, the law in force at the port of registration. The cautious drafting is presumably designed to allow for exceptions in the case of flags of convenience. There is no requirement that the vessel or aircraft should have been in motion when the will was made. Hence a will formally valid by French law would be admissible to probate if executed on board a French ship in Southampton Docks, or on board a French aircraft grounded at London Airport.

Under s. 2 (1) (c) a later will, in so far as it revokes an earlier will or any provision therein, will be treated as properly executed if it complies with any of the forms allowed for the earlier or the later will. Hence, if the testator is domiciled in one country, habitually resident in another and a national of a third, and changes all three between the execution of the earlier and the later will, and again between the execution of the later will and the date of his death, there may be a choice of nine systems of law for the revoking (as opposed to the disposing) provisions of the later will, or eleven if the wills are made in different countries.

Under s. 6 (3), retrospective alterations in the law are relevant if they validate, but irrelevant if they invalidate, the will.

S. 3 resolves a celebrated problem of characterization which has long troubled continental European courts and writers, namely, the precise effect of enactments like article 992 of the Dutch Civil Code, which provides that Dutch nationals cannot make wills even outside Holland except in the 'authentic form' prescribed by Dutch law. Does this enactment relate to form or to capacity? The answer is that it relates to form, whatever Dutch law may say. Hence if a Dutch testator makes a holograph will in France which is valid by French law, the will must be admitted to probate in England, even though it might be void under Dutch law. See also Dicey, p. 601, Illustrations 2–4.

S. 4 replaces a highly ambiguous section of the Wills Act 1861. It is probably only declaratory of the common law, because at common law a will is presumably (but not necessarily) construed in accordance with the law of the testator's domicile at the time of executing the will. 'If a question arises as to the interpretation of the will and it should appear that the testator has changed his domicile between making his will and his death, his will may fall to be construed accordingly to the law of his domicile at the time he made it': *per* Lord Denning in *Philipson-Stow* v. *I.R.C.* [1961] A.C. 727, 761.

Section D: POWERS OF APPOINTMENT

A will made in exercise of a power of appointment will be treated as properly executed if its execution conformed to (a) any system of law applicable under section 1 of the Wills Act 1963, or (b) the law governing the essential validity of the power.

In re PRICE [1900] 1 Ch. 442 (Chancery Division)

Dame Elizabeth Price, by her will, dated 28 March 1876, bequeathed a sum of £2,000 to trustees upon trust for investment and payment of the income to 'Maria the wife of Monsieur Adolphe Gay' during her life. The will then proceeded: 'And from and after her decease to pay and transfer the last-mentioned sum of £2,000 in such manner as she the said Maria Gay shall by her last will appoint, and, in default of such appointment, then to such person or persons as would at the time of her decease be the next of kin of the said Maria Gay in case she had died intestate and without being married.'

Lady Price died on 18 March 1878.

At the date of the will Maria Gay was the wife of Adolphe Gay, a French subject domiciled in France. Monsieur Gay died on 12 October 1882; and in October 1886 Madame Gay married Monsieur Auguste Dié Forfillier, also a French subject domiciled in France.

On 2 June 1887 Madame Forfillier made a holograph will in the French language, of which the following is a translation:

'I the undersigned declare that I bequeath to my dear husband Auguste Dié Forfillier, everything which I possess at the present moment, and which I hereafter may possess. . . . And I declare that this will annuls all the others, as I have informed Mr. Archibald Willett, solicitor, Bromley, Kent, and that it shall thus be considered in England the same as in France, and I repeat that I leave everything which I possess at the present moment and which I may come to possess afterwards to my dear husband.'

The will was unattested.

On 16 February 1898 Madame Forfillier died, and on 30 October 1898 letters of administration with the will annexed were granted by the Probate Division to the defendant Edward Latter as the attorney of Monsieur Forfillier. At the date of her death Madame Forfillier had no interest in any property in England except the property subject to the power of appointment.

462

This summons was taken out by the trustees of the will of Lady Price to have it determined who was entitled to the fund of £2,000.

Madame Forfillier was at the time of her death a French subject by virtue of the Naturalization Act 1870, s. 10, sub-s. 1. She was also domiciled in France. The law of France was stated in the evidence to be that the will of Madame Forfillier was a complete testamentary disposition of the whole of the property which the testatrix might have at her death or which she might by law dispose of; that the mode of disposition by appointment was not practised in France; and that if a French court had to consider the effect of the will in this respect it would inquire into and apply the English law bearing on this point; and would also take cognizance of and give effect to the fact that the testatrix had no interest in any property in England except that which was subject to the power of appointment.

STIRLING J.: Under the will of Lady Price the fund is to be paid and transferred in such manner as Madame Forfillier 'shall by her last will appoint.' The first question arises as to the word 'will' which there occurs—whether it means any instrument recognised by the law of England as a will or a will executed in accordance with the law of England. I shall first consider the three authorities which have been cited to me as bearing on this subject. The first is the case of *D'Huart* v. *Harkness.*[1] There, under the will of an English lady, a sum of Consols was held upon trust for her daughter for her separate use for life, and after her decease upon trust for such persons as her said daughter 'by her last will and testament in writing duly executed' should direct or appoint. The daughter was an English-woman by birth, but she married a domiciled Frenchman and re-sided in France till her death; she made a will, which was not attested, whereby she bequeathed the sum of Consols to her husband. This will was valid by the law of France and had been admitted to probate in this country. It was held by Lord Romilly that the will was a valid execution of the power. It will be observed that, as regards the facts, that case is as near to the present case as one case can be to another. The material portion of the judgment is this: 'A sum of money is given simply, to such person as the Baroness shall by her last will duly executed appoint. What does that mean? It means a will so executed as to be good according to the English

---

[1] (1865) 34 Beav. 324.

law. Here it is admitted to probate, and that is conclusive that it is good according to the English law. The English law admits two classes of wills to probate, first, those which follow the forms required by the Wills Act 1837, s. 9, and secondly, those executed by a person domiciled in a foreign country, according to the law of that country, which latter are perfectly valid in this country. Accordingly, where a person domiciled in France executes a will in the mode required by the law of that country, it is admitted to proof in England, though the English formalities have not been observed. When a person simply directs that a sum of money shall be held subject to a power of appointment by will, he does not mean any one particular form of will recognised by the law of this country, but any will which is entitled to probate here. A power to appoint by will, simply, may be executed by any will which according to the law of this country is valid, though it does not follow the forms of the statute.'

(His Lordship referred to *Re Kirwan's Trusts*[1] and *Hummel* v. *Hummel*[2] and continued:) I am of opinion that I ought to follow *D'Huart* v. *Harkness* and not *In re Kirwan's Trusts*. But I go further. I think that on principle *D'Huart* v. *Harkness* was well decided. The general rule on the subject is, as stated by Mr. Dicey[3] that 'Any will of movables which is valid according to the law of the testator's domicile at the time of his death is valid' in England. It follows that the provisions of an English statute prescribing formalities with reference to wills do not apply to the wills of persons not domiciled in England.

In *Bremer* v. *Freeman*[4] it appears to have been contended that the provisions of s. 20 of the Wills Act as to the revocation of wills applied to the wills of persons domiciled abroad. Lord Wensleydale in delivering the judgment of the court said that for reasons referred to by him it was unnecessary to consider the point, but added: 'Their Lordships, however, do not wish to intimate any doubt that the law of the domicile at the time of the death is the governing law (see Story, Conflict of Laws, § 473), nor any that the Wills Act 1837 applies only to wills of those persons who continue to have an English domicile, and are consequently regulated by the English law.'

Section 9 of the Wills Act prescribes that 'no will shall be valid

[1] (1883) 25 Ch. D. 373. [2] [1898] 1 Ch. 642.
[3] Conflict of Laws, 1st ed. (1896) p. 684. [4] (1857) 10 Moo. P.C. 306.

unless it shall be in writing and executed in manner hereinafter mentioned'. Notwithstanding this language, it is the practice of the Probate Division, on the principle just stated, to admit to probate or otherwise recognise as valid the wills of persons domiciled abroad, although not executed as prescribed by the Act. The present case affords an instance of this being done. I fail to see why the provisions of s. 10 of the Wills Act should apply to the will of Madame Forfillier any more than those of s. 9.

There is, however, a series of cases referred to in the argument which seems to establish that a will purporting to be made in execution of a power is valid if it satisfies the requirements of the instrument creating the power, although it would be invalid according to the law of the domicile of the testator at the time of his death: see *In the Goods of Alexander*;[1] *In the Goods of Hallyburton*;[2] *In the Goods of Huber*.[3] These cases, however, do not lay down that a power to appoint by will (without special formalities) conferred on a person domiciled abroad cannot be executed by a will valid by the law of the domicile of the donee of the power at the time of his death, and consequently do not appear to me to affect the decision of the present case. . . .

In my opinion, therefore, it was competent for Madame Forfillier to exercise the power conferred on her by Lady Price's will by such a will as has been recognised by the Probate Division. It remains to be considered whether she has done so. This question is one of construction.

In general a will is to be construed according to the law of the domicile of the testator: 'but this is a mere canon of interpretation, which should not be adhered to when there is any reason, from the nature of the will, or otherwise, to suppose that the testator wrote it with reference to the law of some other country': Dicey, Conflict of Laws, p. 695. Considering first the law of France, according to which prima facie the will is to be construed, the evidence shews that the will of Madame Forfillier is a complete disposition of all the property which she could dispose of; but it also appears that the mode of disposition by appointment is not practised in France, and that if a French court had to consider the effect of the will in this respect it would apply the English law. It is contended with regard to the law of England that the provisions of the Wills Act, including s. 27, are

In re
PRICE.
—
Stirling J.

---

[1] (1860) 29 L.J. (P.M. & A.) 93.   [2] (1866) L.R. 1 P. & M. 90.
[3] [1896] P. 209.

inapplicable, and that consequently the law of England applicable is the law as it existed before that Act, and that, there being no reference in the will either to the power or to the property, it is not a good execution of the power. If I am to apply the law as it existed before the Wills Act, questions of difficulty might arise; but it appears to me that I can decide this case upon another ground. The testatrix says, 'I declare that this will annuls all the others . . . and that it shall thus be considered in England the same as in France.' I think that that amounts to a declaration by the testatrix that she meant the will to operate as her last will in England as well as in France. I think it is indicated upon the face of the will that she wrote it with reference to the law of England as well as the law of France. Therefore I think that I am entitled to apply the rules of construction which would by English law be applied to a will expressed in the same terms and of the same date as that annexed to the letters of administration, including the rule of construction introduced by s. 27 of the Wills Act.

No question arises between Monsieur Forfillier and the daughter of his wife by her first marriage, who by the law of France might have a claim if this fund had been part of Madame Forfillier's property; for she appears and supports the claim of Monsieur Forfillier.

In my opinion, therefore, the husband, Monsieur Forfillier, is entitled to the fund.

A general bequest in the will of a testator domiciled abroad exercises a general power of appointment conferred by an English instrument unless a contrary intention appears in the will.

A testator has capacity to exercise by will a power of appointment over movables conferred by an English instrument if he has testamentary capacity by the law of his domicile at the time of making his will.

In re LEWAL'S SETTLEMENT TRUSTS [1918] 2 Ch. 391
(Chancery Division)

By an antenuptial settlement made in 1907 upon the marriage of Gertrude Loyd, an infant aged 19, to the defendant Maxime Lewal, an officer in the French Army, certain property belonging to the intended wife was settled after her death, and in the event (which happened) of there being no child of the marriage, upon trust for such person or persons as the wife should by deed or will (executed in such manner as to be valid by the law of her domicile) appoint, with a gift over in default of appointment. The settlement contained a statement that it should be construed, and that the rights of all parties claiming thereunder should in all respects be regulated, according to English law. The settlement was duly sanctioned by the court under the Infant Settlements Act 1855. The marriage was solemnized on 15 April 1907. The husband was at all material times a French citizen domiciled in France.

In re
LEWAL'S
SETTLEMENT
TRUSTS.

Immediately after the marriage the wife, then 19 years of age, signed at Versailles an unattested French holograph will as follows: 'J'institue mon mari pour mon légataire universel.' The wife died in June 1917 in the lifetime of the husband. Letters of administration with the French will annexed were granted in England to the wife's mother as attorney for the husband.

The trustees of the settlement took out a summons to determine whether and to what extent the will exercised the general power of appointment given to the wife by the settlement.

The evidence showed that the will was in point of form a valid will according to French law, and that as the wife at the time of making the will was over 16 but under 21 years of age, she was, under French law, competent to dispose by will of one-half of the property which she could have disposed of if she had been 21 years of age.

PETERSON J.: . . . It was contended, in the first place, that as she was, when she made her will, under twenty-one years of age, she could not thereby exercise the power of appointment at all, and reliance was placed on the provision that the rights of all parties claiming under the settlement were to be regulated by the law of England in the same way as if both husband and wife had throughout been domiciled in England. It could not be disputed that a holograph French will might operate as an exercise of the power, as it was expressly within the terms of the settlement, and if it had not been expressly provided for it would, on the authorities, be a will which was recognised in England as valid and therefore a will capable of exercising the power. But it was urged that the provisions in the settlement only related to the form of this will and did not affect the question of testamentary capacity, and that this question must be determined by English law, as the rights under the settlement were to be regulated by English law as if the husband and wife had been domiciled in England. This argument, in my opinion, is unsound. The settlement expressly enables the power of appointment to be exercised by Madame Lewal by a will executed in such manner as to be valid according to the law of her actual domicile as well as by a will executed in such manner as to be valid as such according to the law of England. It obviously contemplated that she should be able to exercise the power by a French will which might not comply with the requirements as to wills of the English law. Nor do I think that this provision related merely to the form of the will and to the presence or absence of attesting witnesses. What the settlement contemplated was a will which should be valid according to French law or a will which would be valid according to English law. This will is a good will according to French law notwithstanding the fact that Madame Lewal was under twenty-one years of age when she made it. This objection therefore, in my opinion, fails.

The next objection was that the will did not, in fact, exercise the power. It does not refer to the settlement or to the property comprised in the settlement, and it was said that s. 27 of the Wills Act cannot be invoked for the purpose of interpreting a French will. This contention has given rise to a considerable difference in judicial opinion. In *In re D'Este's Settlement Trusts*,[1] Buckley J. held that a will by a domiciled Frenchwoman, which appointed her husband her universal legatee and bequeathed to him all her personal estate, did not operate as an exercise of a general power of appointment, and that reference could not be made to s. 27 of the Wills Act for the purpose of interpreting the will, as the section was intended as a statutory rule for the interpretation of English wills and could not be applied to the interpretation of foreign wills, which must be construed according to the law of the domicile. This decision was followed by Kekewich J. in *In re Scholefield*.[2] These two cases were, however, subjected to a very destructive criticism by Neville J. in *In re Simpson*,[3] where it was held that an unattested holograph will of a British subject domiciled in France, by which she disposed of all the property and rights comprised in her estate, effectually exercised a general power of appointment which she had over the trust funds under the English settlement, the learned judge expressly dissenting from the decisions in the two earlier cases. In *In re Wilkin-*

---

[1] [1903] 1 Ch. 898.   [2] [1905] 2 Ch. 408.   [3] [1916] 1 Ch. 502.

son's Settlement,[1] Sargant J. (although the point seems to have been unnecessary for the decision of that case) agreed with the opinion of Neville J. and added some further reasons for disagreeing with the view of Buckley J. and Kekewich J. In these circumstances I am at liberty to express my own opinion. The judgment of Buckley J. is summarized in the following passage from his judgment: 'Then it is said that I must take this French document and read it, not as a will in the sense in which I have explained, but as if the directions contained in it were introduced into the instrument which contained the power. That is quite right: but how must I read it? I have, referentially, to introduce into the instrument which contains the power a foreign document. I have to see whether the power was exercised, and therefore to find out the meaning of what is expressed by the donee of the power. Now how am I to ascertain the meaning of the donee of the power? I must ascertain it according to the law of the place applicable to the document executed by the donee and to the domicile of that person, and that law is to be taken as the law governing its construction. If I do that, I have to read the French will and say what its meaning is according to the principle of French construction, excluding, therefore, s. 27, which is a rule for English construction.' With all respect to the learned judge, it appears to me that his conclusion does not necessarily follow from his premisses. If the French will was to be interpreted according to the principles of French construction it did not follow that s. 27 of the Wills Act was to be excluded. As pointed out by Neville J., the French court does not know anything of powers of appointment and would require to be informed what a general power of appointment was and in what manner it might be exercised, and the answer to this question must involve the effect of s. 27. A further argument indicated, I think, by Sargant J. in *In re Wilkinson's Settlement*, against the view of Buckley J. may be put in this way. Prior to the Wills Act the exercise of a general power of appointment by will had to refer either to the power or to the property subject to the power. After that Act the power could be exercised by a will which disposed of the personal estate of the appointor. This, in effect, amounted to a provision that every general power of appointment by will should be read as a power to appoint by a will which referred to the power, or to the property subject to the power, or disposed of the personal estate of the appointor in general words. The result then would in

In re
LEWAL'S
SETTLEMENT
TRUSTS.
—
Peterson J.

[1] [1917] 1 Ch. 620.

469

the present case be that the power authorised the appointment by a valid French will which disposed of the appointor's estate in general terms and the will of Madame Lewal would be an exercise of the power. I agree with the opinions of Neville J. and Sargant J., and therefore hold that the general power of appointment was exercised by the will of Madame Lewal.

I may add that in the present case there seems to be an additional reason why a French court, on being asked to determine whether the will operated as an exercise of the power of appointment, would be bound to ascertain what the English law on the subject was. In order to determine the question it would be necessary to refer to the settlement which contained the power in order to see what was authorised by the power, and it would then be found that the settlement contained a provision that the rights of all parties claiming under it should be regulated in the same way as if the husband and the wife were and continued to be domiciled in England—a clear reference to English law.

The question, however, remains whether the will of Madame Lewal effectively appoints the whole of the fund subject to the power. On the evidence Madame Lewal, when she made her will, had only a limited testamentary capacity. She could only dispose of one-half of the property which she could have disposed of if she had been twenty-one. It appears to me that I am not concerned with the fact that one-quarter of her property went to her mother under art. 14 of the Civil Code. Her mother cannot claim a share of the settled funds unless they have been appointed to her or she takes under the settlement in default of appointment.

The result, in my opinion, is that, as Madame Lewal's testamentary capacity was limited in the way which I have mentioned, her will only operated on one-half of the funds which were subject to the power, and that the other half goes as in default of appointment.

The material or essential validity of an exercise by will of a power of appointment over movables depends in the case of a special power on the law governing the instrument of creation, and in the case of a general power on the law governing the instrument of appointment (at any rate if the donee intended to take the appointed property out of the instrument creating the power for all purposes).

In re PRYCE [1911] 2 Ch. 286 (Court of Appeal)

Thomas Pryce died in 1904 domiciled in England and having by his will given a share of residue on certain trusts for his daughter Jane Pryce and her children if any, but if no child should attain a vested interest, then for such persons as Jane should by will appoint, and in default of appointment for the persons who would have been entitled if she had died intestate and a spinster.

In January 1908 Jane Pryce married G. H. O. Geertsema, a Dutch subject domiciled in the Netherlands. There was no issue of the marriage, and she died in October 1909, having by her will, which was dated in September 1909 and made in the Dutch language and form, appointed her husband as her 'sole heir of the whole of the estate of which the law in force at the time of her death should allow her to dispose of in his favour'.

According to Dutch law the exercise of the power had the effect of making the appointed property the assets of the testatrix for all purposes; but the testatrix's mother was entitled to one-eighth of her property and her husband to seven-eighths only.

The executor of Thomas Pryce took out an originating summons for the determination of the question who was entitled to the property subject to the power. Parker J. held that the husband was entitled to the whole of such property. The testatrix's mother appealed.

COZENS-HARDY M.R.: . . . It has not been, and it cannot be, seriously denied that the power has been fully exercised in this sense, that the persons entitled in default of appointment are completely cut out. The real question is whether the testatrix had such complete disposing power as the law of England gives, or only such as the law of Holland gives. Parker J. has held that the husband is beneficially entitled to the whole fund. . . .

In the present case I think the lady has exercised the power in such a manner as to make the property her assets for all purposes. If so it seems to me to follow that her power of disposition over this property is neither greater nor less than over that which was strictly her own property. That power of disposition must depend upon the law of Holland, by which she could not beneficially dispose of more than seven-eighths.

Parker J. based his judgment on three cases which it is necessary for me to consider. The first is *In re Bald*,[1] a decision of Byrne J. It is very shortly reported and no authority is cited. A general power of appointment given by a Scottish instrument was executed by an English will. Under English law the appointed fund would be assets for payment of the appointor's debts, but under Scotch law it would not. Byrne J. held apparently that the appointment was specific and not such as to make the fund the appointor's own assets for all purposes, and accordingly he held that the fund went to the appointees, and was not assets of the appointor for the benefit of his creditors. The second case is *Pouey* v. *Hordern*,[2] a decision of Farwell J. There the power was special and not general. The learned judge held, and, if I may respectfully say so, with perfect accuracy, that the will exercising the power was not a disposition of her own property, but was only a nomination of the persons whose names were to be inserted in the English settlement creating the power. But there are some observations which led me, in *In re Mégret*,[3] to suppose, as Parker J. supposed, that Farwell J.'s view was that the same principle applied to a general as to a special power. If this statement is taken without any qualification, I think it is too wide. But on further consideration I am satisfied that the observations of Farwell J. were addressed only to a case where the appointment under the general power is direct to the object of the appointor's bounty, and not in such a manner as to make the fund part of her own estate to be dealt with in one mass. The third case is *In re Mégret*, the facts of which are distinguishable from the facts in the present case. The appointment there was specific, in this sense, that it did not operate to make the fund a part of her own property for all purposes. My decision was, I think, correct on that view.

The proposition deduced from those cases in Dicey on Domicil,[4] 2nd ed. p. 705, seems to me to be too widely stated. It should ex-

---

[1] (1897) 76 L.T. 462.   [2] [1900] 1 Ch. 492.   [3] [1901] 1 Ch. 547.
[4] *Sic*: Dicey's *Conflict of Laws* was really meant.

clude cases in which the power has been so exercised as to throw the appointed fund into the appointor's own estate and to deal with the whole as one mass.

The present case seems to me to fall within the excepted class. The appointed fund is thrown into one mass with the appointor's own property. In this respect the English law is the same as the law of Holland.

With great respect to Parker J. I am unable to concur in his view, and I think this appeal must be allowed.

I prefer to base my judgment on the above reasons rather than upon the peculiar terms of the gift to the husband.

BUCKLEY L.J.: . . . It is not necessary to consider whether *In re Mégret* was rightly decided or not. The present case is distinguishable inasmuch as the property the subject of the power was in *In re Mégret* the only property dealt with, while in the present case all the property of which the testatrix had power to dispose is dealt with in one mass. . . .

KENNEDY L.J. concurred.

Appeal allowed.

NOTE W: EXERCISE BY WILL OF POWERS OF APPOINTMENT

AT first sight it might be supposed that the validity of a will exercising a power of appointment depended on the same considerations as the validity of any other will. But for two reasons it may be necessary to look not only at the law governing the instrument of appointment but also at the law governing the instrument of creation (which in all the English cases is English law). In the first place, the laws of many foreign countries do not recognize powers of appointment at all; hence if the donee dies domiciled in such a country the law of his domicile cannot determine whether his will is a valid exercise of the power. In the second place, the donee of the power is strictly speaking not disposing of his own property, but that of the donor. This is true in theory of general powers and true in substance as well as theory of special powers. Evidently, there is more justification for looking to the law governing the instrument of creation in the case of special powers than there is in the case of general powers. It is necessary to consider separately (1) formalities, (2) construction, (3) essential validity, (4) revocation, and (5) capacity. The English cases have disclosed some remarkable differences of judicial opinion.

1. *Formalities.* Under s. 1 of the Wills Act 1963 (*ante*, p. 457) a will exercising a power of appointment will be treated as properly executed if its execution conformed to the internal law in force in the country where it was executed, or in the country where, at the time of its execution or

of the testator's death, he was domiciled or had his habitual residence, or in a state of which, at either of those times, he was a national.

S. 2 (i) (*d*) of the Act confirms a line of English cases (see the cases cited on p. 465, *ante*, and *Murphy* v. *Deichler* [1909] A.C. 446) which decided that a will exercising a power was well executed if its execution conformed to English domestic law as being the law governing the instrument of creation, even though it did not conform to the law of the donee's domicile.

S. 2 (2) of the Act abolishes a troublesome and unnecessary distinction by providing that compliance with any formal requirements contained in the instrument creating the power shall not be necessary.

2. *Construction*. The rules laid down in the preceding note indicate when a will is capable of exercising a power as a matter of form: they do not indicate when a will does execute a power as a matter of construction. The general rule is that the question whether the will was intended to exercise the power must be determined by the law which governs the construction of the will, that is, in the absence of indications to the contrary, the law of the donee's domicile at the time when the will was made. Thus, if a special power is created by an English instrument, and alleged to be exercised by the will of a testator domiciled in Scotland, Scots law will prima facie determine whether the words used by the testator are sufficient to exercise the power: *Re McMorran* [1958] Ch. 624. Conversely, if a general power is created by an English or Scottish instrument, and alleged to be exercised by the will of a testator domiciled in South Africa, South African law will prima facie determine whether the words used are sufficient to exercise the power: *Durie's Trustees* v. *Osborne*, 1960 S.C. 444.

On the other hand, the effect of a line of English cases is that if there are indications in the will that the testator intended it to be construed in accordance with the law governing the instrument creating the power, or if powers of appointment are unknown to the law of the testator's domicile, the question whether the will was intended to exercise the power will be determined in accordance with the law governing the instrument of creation. If this is English law, then under s. 27 of the Wills Act 1837, a general decree or bequest will amount to an exercise of a general (but not a special) power. This is so notwithstanding the fact that the will fails to comply with the formalities prescribed by ss. 9 and 10 of the Wills Act 1837: *Re Price* (*ante*, p. 462); *Re Simpson* [1916] 1 Ch. 502; *Re Lewal's Settlement* (*ante*, p. 466); *Re Strong* (1925) 95 L.J. Ch. 22; *Re Waite's Settlement* [1958] Ch. 100.

3. *Essential validity*. Even if the requisite formalities have been complied with and the will exercises the power as a matter of construction, the appointment may still be invalid if it contravenes some rule of the law of the donee's domicile: for example, the rule found in many civil law countries that he must leave a fixed portion of his estate (legitima portio) to his wife and family. Do such rules apply to property subject to a power of appointment created by an English instrument? If the power is special, they do not: *Pouey* v. *Hordern* [1900] 1 Ch. 492; and this is logical, because the donee is not dealing with his own property but is regarded as an agent carrying out the wishes of the donor. If the power is general, a distinction must be drawn between (*a*) cases where the donee makes a specific appointment and keeps the appointed property separate from his own property, and (*b*) cases where

the donee deals with the appointed property and his own property as one mass so as to take the appointed property out of the instrument creating the power for all purposes. If the donee dies domiciled in a country where the rule is that he must leave a legitima portio to his wife and family, the rule does not apply in case (a) (Re Mégret [1901] 1 Ch. 547), but does apply in case (b) (Re Pryce, ante, p. 471; the contrary decision of Danckwerts J. in Re Waite's Settlement [1958] Ch. 100 is manifestly erroneous: see 73 L.Q.R. 459; Dicey, pp. 624–5); and it was not followed in Re Khan's Settlement [1966] Ch. 567. This is also logical, because in case (a) the donee can be regarded, like the donee of a special power, as the agent of the donor, while in case (b) he is in substance dealing with his own property.

4. *Revocation.* A testamentary exercise of a power which is valid by a foreign lex domicilii may be revoked in a manner sufficient by that law though insufficient by English law, e.g. by destroying the will by the testator's direction but not in his presence: *Velasco* v. *Coney* [1934] P. 143; or by a later will which complies with s. 2 (1) (c) of the Wills Act 1963 (ante, p. 458).

5. *Capacity.* To the extent that the appointor has capacity by the law of his domicile at the time of making his will, to that extent the will may be a good exercise of the power: *Re Lewal's Settlement Trusts* (ante, p. 466). There is no authority as to what the position would be if he had capacity by English law but not by the law of his domicile at the time of making his will.

PART V

FOREIGN JUDGMENTS

Chapter 19

FOREIGN JUDGMENTS

Section A: JURISDICTION

No action lies in England on a foreign judgment in personam unless the defendant either submitted to the jurisdiction or was present in the foreign country at the date of the issue of the writ.

SCHIBSBY
v.
WESTEN-
HOLZ.

SCHIBSBY *v.* WESTENHOLZ (1870) L.R. 6 Q.B. 155 (Court of Queen's Bench)

Blackburn
J.

THE judgment of the court (Blackburn, Mellor, Lush, and Hannen JJ.) was delivered by

BLACKBURN J.: This was an action on a judgment of a French tribunal given against the defendants for default of appearance.

The pleas to the action were, amongst others, a plea of never indebted, and, thirdly, a special plea asserting that the defendants were not resident or domiciled in France, or in any way subject to the jurisdiction of the French court, nor did they appear; and that they were not summoned, nor had any notice or knowledge of the pending of the proceedings, or any opportunity of defending themselves therefrom. On these pleas issue was joined.

On the trial before me the evidence of a French avocat was given, by which it appeared that by the law of France a French subject may sue a foreigner, though not resident in France, and that for this purpose an alien, if resident in France, was considered by the French law as a French subject. The mode of citation in such a case, according to the French law, is by serving the summons on the

Procureur Impérial. If the foreign defendant thus cited does not within one month appear, judgment may be given against him, but he may still, at any time within two months after judgment, appear and be heard on the merits. After that lapse of time the judgment is final and conclusive. The practice of the imperial government is, in such a case, to forward the summons thus served to the consulate of the country where the defendant is resident, with directions to intimate the summons, if practicable, to the defendant; but this, as was explained by the avocat, is not required by the French law, but is simply done by the imperial government voluntarily from a regard to fair dealing.

It appeared by other evidence that the plaintiff in this case was a Dane resident in France. The defendants were also Danes, resident in London and carrying on business there. A written contract had been made between the plaintiff and defendants, which was in English, and made in London. By this contract the defendants were to ship in Sweden a cargo of Swedish oats free on board a French or Swedish vessel for Caen, in France, at a certain rate for all oats delivered at Caen. The plaintiff asserted, and the defendants denied, that the delivery at Caen was short of the quantity for which the plaintiff had paid, and the plaintiff made some other complaints as to the condition of the cargo which were denied by the defendants. The plaintiff very plainly told the defendants that if they would not settle the claim he would sue them in the French courts. He did issue process in the manner described, and the French consulate in London served on the defendants a copy of the citation.

The following admissions were then made, namely: that the judgment was regular according to French law; that it was given in favour of the plaintiff, a foreigner domiciled in France, against the defendants, domiciled in England, and in no sense French subjects, and having no property in France.

I then ruled that I could not enter into the question whether the French judgment was according to the merits, no fraud being alleged or shewn.

I expressed an opinion (which I have since changed) that, subject to the third plea, the plaintiff was entitled to the verdict, but reserved the point.

The jury found that the defendants had notice and knowledge of the summons and the pendency of the proceedings in time to have appeared and defended the action in the French court. I then directed the verdict for the plaintiff, but reserved leave to enter the verdict for the defendants on these facts and this finding.

A rule was accordingly obtained by Sir George Honyman, against which cause was shewn in the last term and in the sittings after it before my brothers Mellor, Lush, Hannen, and myself. During the interval between the obtaining of the rule and the shewing cause the case of *Godard* v. *Gray*,[1] on which we have just given judgment, was argued before my brothers Mellor, Hannen, and myself, and we had consequently occasion to consider the whole subject of the law of England as to enforcing foreign judgments.

My brother Lush, who was not a party to the discussions in *Godard* v. *Gray*, has, since the argument in the present case, perused the judgment prepared by the majority in *Godard* v. *Gray* and approves of it; and, after hearing the argument in the present case, we are all of opinion that the rule should be made absolute.

It is unnecessary to repeat again what we have already said in *Godard* v. *Gray*.

We think that, for the reasons there given, the true principle on which the judgments of foreign tribunals are enforced in England is that stated by Parke B., in *Russell* v. *Smyth*,[2] and again repeated by him in *Williams* v. *Jones*,[3] that the judgment of a court of competent jurisdiction over the defendant imposes a duty or obligation on the defendant to pay the sum for which judgment is given, which the courts in this country are bound to enforce; and consequently that anything which negatives that duty, or forms a legal excuse for not performing it, is a defence to the action.

We were much pressed on the argument with the fact that the British legislature has, by the Common Law Procedure Act 1852, ss. 18 and 19,[4] conferred on our courts a power of summoning foreigners, under certain circumstances, to appear, and in case they do not, giving judgment against them by default. It was this consideration principally which induced me at the trial to entertain the opinion which I then expressed and have since changed. And we think that if the principle on which foreign judgments were enforced was that which is loosely called 'comity', we could hardly decline to enforce a foreign judgment given in France against a resident in Great Britain under circumstances hardly, if at all, distinguishable from those under which we, mutatis mutandis, might give judgment

---

[1] (1870) L.R. 6 Q.B. 139; *post*, p. 492.   [2] (1842) 9 M. & W. 810, 819.
[3] (1845) 13 M. & W. 628, 633.   [4] Now R.S.C., Ord. 11, r. 1 (1) (*Ed.*).

against a resident in France; but it is quite different if the principle be that which we have just laid down.

Should a foreigner be sued under the provisions of the statute referred to, and then come to the courts of this country and desire to be discharged, the only question which our courts could entertain would be whether the Acts of the British legislature, rightly construed, gave us jurisdiction over this foreigner, for we must obey them. But if, judgment being given against him in our courts, an action were brought upon it in the courts of the United States (where the law as to the enforcing foreign judgments is the same as our own), a further question would be open, viz., not only whether the British legislature had given the English courts jurisdiction over the defendant, but whether he was under any obligation which the American courts could recognize to submit to the jurisdiction thus created. This is precisely the question which we have now to determine with regard to a jurisdiction assumed by the French jurisprudence over foreigners.

Again, it was argued before us that foreign judgments obtained by default, where the citation was (as in the present case) by an artificial mode prescribed by the laws of the country in which the judgment was given, were not enforceable in this country because such a mode of citation was contrary to natural justice, and if this were so, doubtless the finding of the jury in the present case would remove that objection. But though it appears by the report of *Buchanan* v. *Rucker*[1] that Lord Ellenborough in the hurry of nisi prius at first used expressions to this effect, yet when the case came before him in banco in *Buchanan* v. *Rucker*,[2] he entirely abandoned what (with all deference to so great an authority) we cannot regard as more than declamation, and rested his judgment on the ground that laws passed by our country were not obligatory on foreigners not subject to their jurisdiction. 'Can', he said, 'the island of Tobago pass a law to bind the rights of the whole world?'

The question we have now to answer is, Can the empire of France pass a law to bind the whole world? We admit, with perfect candour, that in the supposed case of a judgment, obtained in this country against a foreigner under the provisions of the Common Law Procedure Act, being sued on in a court of the United States, the question for the court of the United States would be, Can the Island of Great Britain pass a law to bind the whole world? We think in each

[1] (1807) 1 Camp. 63.   [2] (1808) 9 East 192.

case the answer should be, No, but every country can pass laws to bind a great many persons; and therefore the further question has to be determined whether the defendant in the particular suit was such a person as to be bound by the judgment which it is sought to enforce.

Now on this we think some things are quite clear on principle. If the defendants had been at the time of the judgment subjects of the country whose judgment is sought to be enforced against them, we think that its laws would have bound them.[1] Again, if the defendants had been at the time when the suit was commenced resident in the country, so as to have the benefit of its laws protecting them, or, as it is sometimes expressed, owing temporary allegiance to that country, we think that its laws would have bound them.

If at the time when the obligation was contracted the defendants were within the foreign country, but left it before the suit was instituted, we should be inclined to think the laws of that country bound them;[2] though before finally deciding this we should like to hear the question argued. But every one of those suppositions is negatived in the present case.

Again, we think it clear, upon principle, that if a person selected, as plaintiff, the tribunal of a foreign country as the one in which he would sue, he could not afterwards say that the judgment of that tribunal was not binding upon him.

In the case of *General Steam Navigation Company* v. *Guillou*,[3] on a demurrer to a plea, Parke B., in delivering the considered judgment of the Court of Exchequer, then consisting of Lord Abinger C.B., Parke, Alderson, and Gurney BB., thus expresses himself: 'The substance of the plea is that the cause of action has been already adjudicated upon, in a competent court, against the plaintiffs, and that the decision is binding upon them, and that they ought not to be permitted again to litigate the same question. Such a plea ought to have had a proper commencement and conclusion. It becomes, therefore, unnecessary to give any opinion whether the pleas are bad in substance; but it is not to be understood that we feel much doubt on that question. They do not state that the plaintiffs were French subjects, or resident, or even present in France when the suit began,

[1] As to this, see *post*, p. 483, n. 1.
[2] It has since been held that the foreign court has no jurisdiction in such a case: *Sirdar Gurdyal Singh* v. *Rajah of Faridkote* [1894] A.C. 670; *Emanuel* v. *Symon* [1908] 1 K.B. 302, *post*, p. 482. (*Ed.*)
[3] (1843) 11 M. & W. 877, 894

so as to be bound by reason of allegiance or temporary presence by
the decision of a French court, and they did not select the tribunal
and sue as plaintiffs, in any of which cases the determination might
have possibly bound them. They were mere strangers, who put forward the negligence of the defendant as an answer, in an adverse
suit in a foreign country, whose laws they were under no obligation
to obey.'

It will be seen from this that those very learned judges, besides
expressing an opinion conformable to ours, also expressed one to
the effect that the plaintiffs in that suit did not put themselves under
an obligation to obey the foreign judgment, merely by appearing to
defend themselves against it. On the other hand, in *Simpson* v.
Fogo,[1] where the mortgagees of an English ship had come into the
courts of Louisiana, to endeavour to prevent the sale of their ship
seized under an execution against the mortgagors, and the courts of
Louisiana decided against them, the Vice-Chancellor and the very
learned counsel who argued in the case seem all to have taken it for
granted that the decision of the Court in Louisiana would have
bound the mortgagees, had it not been in contemptuous disregard
of English law. The case of *General Steam Navigation Company* v.
Guillou was not referred to, and therefore cannot be considered as
dissented from; but it seems clear that they did not agree in the
latter part of the opinion there expressed.

We think it better to leave this question open, and to express no
opinion as to the effect of the appearance of a defendant, where it is
so far not voluntary that he only comes in to try to save some property in the hands of the foreign tribunal. But we must observe that
the decision in *De Cosse Brissac* v. *Rathbone*[2] is an authority that
where the defendant voluntarily appears and takes the chance of a
judgment in his favour he is bound.

In *Douglas* v. *Forrest*,[3] the court, deciding in favour of the party
suing on a Scotch judgment, say: 'We confine our judgment to a
case where the party owed allegiance to the country in which the
judgment was so given agaist him, from being born in it, and by the
laws of which country his property was, at the time those judgments
were given, protected. The debts were contracted in the country in
which the judgments were given, whilst the debtor resided in it.'
Those circumstances are all negatived here. We should, however,

[1] (1863) H. & M. 195.   [2] (1861) 6 H. & N. 301.
[3] (1828) 4 Bing. 686, 703.

SCHIBSBY
v.
WESTEN-
HOLZ.
—
Blackburn
J.

point out that, whilst we think that there may be other grounds for holding a person bound by the judgment of the tribunal of a foreign country than those enumerated in *Douglas* v. *Forrest*, we doubt very much whether the possession of property, locally situated in that country and protected by its laws, does afford such a ground. It should rather seem that, whilst every tribunal may very properly execute process against the property within its jurisdiction, the existence of such property, which may be very small, affords no sufficient ground for imposing on the foreign owner of that property a duty or obligation to fulfil the judgment. But it is unnecessary to decide this, as the defendants had in this case no property in France. As to this, see *London and North Western Railway Company* v. *Lindsay*.[1]

We think, and this is all that we need decide, that there existed nothing in the present case imposing on the defendants any duty to obey the judgment of a French tribunal.

Judgment for defendants.

The possession of property in a foreign country is not sufficient to give the courts of that country jurisdiction in personam over the owner thereof.

EMANUEL
v.
SYMON.

EMANUEL *v.* SYMON [1908] 1 K.B. 302 (Court of Appeal)

Appeal from the judgment of Channell J.[2]

In 1895 the defendant, who was then residing and carrying on business in Western Australia, entered into partnership with five other persons, whose interests were now represented by the plaintiffs, for the purpose of working and developing a gold mine situate in that colony and owned by the partnership. The defendant subsequently gave up his business in Western Australia, and in 1899 he left the colony permanently and came to live in England.

In November 1901 a writ was issued by the plaintiffs against the defendant in the Supreme Court of Western Australia, claiming a dissolution of partnership, a sale of the mine, accounts and inquiries, and other relief as in an ordinary partnership action. On 13 November 1901 that writ was served on the defendant in England, but he did not enter an appearance, or take any other step to defend the

[1] (1858) 3 Macq. 99.   [2] [1907] 1 K.B. 235.

action. He was, however, kept informed from time to time of the proceedings in the action.

On 25 July 1902 the Supreme Court of Western Australia, in default of appearance by the defendant, pronounced a decree for the dissolution of the partnership as from that date, and ordered the mine to be sold and the usual accounts to be taken by the taxing officer. The sale was carried out and the accounts were taken, and the taxing officer issued his certificate shewing liabilities of the partnership amounting to a sum of £7,687. 9s. 9d. In May 1903 the final order of the court was pronounced, under which the plaintiffs paid the sum found to be due from the partnership. They subsequently issued the writ in this action to recover from the defendant the sum of £1,281. 4s. 11d. as his share of the sum of £7,687. 9s. 9d. paid by them as aforesaid.

The defendant denied that he was bound by the finding or order of the Colonial Court, on the ground that he was a British subject resident and domiciled in England; that neither at the commencement nor during the continuance of the action was he resident or domiciled in Western Australia, or subject to the jurisdiction of the courts of that colony; and that he had neither appeared to the process nor agreed to submit himself to the jurisdiction of those courts.

Channell J. held that by entering into a partnership in Western Australia relating to real estate in that colony the defendant had impliedly agreed to submit to the jurisdiction of the Colonial Court as to disputes arising during the continuance and on the termination of the partnership, and was therefore bound by the findings of that court. He accordingly gave judgment for the plaintiffs.

The defendant appealed.

BUCKLEY L.J.: In actions in personam there are five cases in which the courts of this country will enforce a foreign judgment: (1) Where the defendant is a subject of the foreign country in which the judgment has been obtained;[1] (2) where he was resident in the foreign country when the action began; (3) where the defendant in the character of plaintiff has selected the forum in which he is afterwards sued;[2] (4) where he has voluntarily appeared; and (5) where

EMANUEL
v.
SYMON.

---

[1] This is supported by a long chain of dicta from 1828 to 1948, but was rejected in *Blóhn* v. *Desser* [1962] 2 Q.B. 116, 123; *Rossano* v. *Manufacturers Life Insurance Co. Ltd.* [1963] 2 Q.B. 352, 382–3 and *Rainford* v. *Newall-Roberts* [1962] I.R. 95. Cf. Dicey, pp. 983–4; Cheshire, pp. 554–5. (*Ed.*)

[2] Query 'as the one in which he would sue'. (*Ed.*)

EMANUEL
v.
SYMON.

Buckley L.J.

he has contracted to submit himself to the forum in which the judgment was obtained. The question in the present case is whether there is yet another and a sixth case. In *Rousillon* v. *Rousillon*,[1] Fry J., after enumerating the five cases above mentioned, added these words, 'and, possibly, if *Becquet* v. *MacCarthy*[2] be right, where the defendant has real estate within the foreign jurisdiction, in respect of which the cause of action arose whilst he was within that jurisdiction'. The principle upon which this court proceeds in enforcing foreign judgments is stated by Blackburn J. in *Schibsby* v. *Westenholz*[3] in these words: (His Lordship read the passage on p. 478, *ante*, beginning 'We think that for the reasons there given' and ending 'as a defence to the action'). In other words, the courts of this country enforce foreign judgments because those judgments impose a duty or obligation which is recognized in this country and leads to judgment here also. Referring to *Becquet* v. *MacCarthy*, Mr. Dicey in his work on the Conflict of Laws has, at p. 373, the following comment: 'But whether this case has reference to the possession of real property by the defendant as a ground of jurisdiction?' That comment is justified, and the doubt there expressed recognized, if indeed a negative answer to the question was not given in a substantive form, and without any doubt, by Lord Selborne in *Sirdar Gurdyal Singh* v. *Rajah of Faridkote*.[4] *Becquet* v. *MacCarthy* has been the subject of adverse comment—first, in *Schibsby* v. *Westenholz*,[5] where Blackburn J. said: 'Whilst we think that there may be other grounds for holding a person bound by the judgment of the tribunal of a foreign country than those enumerated in *Douglas* v. *Forrest*,[6] we doubt very much whether the possession of property, locally situated in that country and protected by its laws, does afford such a ground'; secondly, by Fry J. in *Rousillon* v. *Rousillon*, where that learned judge said, 'and possibly, if *Becquet* v. *MacCarthy* be right, where the defendant has real estate within the foreign jurisdiction, in respect of which the cause of action arose whilst he was within that jurisdiction'; and, thirdly, by Lord Selborne in *Sirdar Gurdyal Singh* v. *Rajah of Faridkote*, where he said: 'Of *Becquet* v. *MacCarthy* it was said by great authority in *Don* v. *Lippmann*[7] that it "had been supposed to go to the verge of the law"; and it was explained (as their Lordships think correctly) on the ground that

---

[1] (1880) 14 Ch. D. 351, 371.   [2] (1831) 2 B. & Ad. 951.
[3] (1870) L.R. 6 Q.B. 155; *ante*, p. 476.   [4] [1894] A.C. 670.
[5] *Ante*, p. 482.   [6] (1828) 4 Bing. 686, 703.   [7] (1837) 5 Cl. & F. 1.

"the defendant held a public office in the very Colony in which he was originally sued". He still held that office at the time when he was sued; the cause of action arose out of, or was connected with it; and, though he was in fact temporarily absent, he might, as the holder of such an office, be regarded as constructively present in the place where his duties required his presence, and therefore amenable to the Colonial jurisdiction. If the case could not be distinguished on that ground from that of any absent foreigner who, at some previous time, might have been in the employment of a Colonial Government, it would, in their Lordships' opinion, have been wrongly decided; and it is evident that Fry L.J. in *Rousillon* v. *Rousillon* took that view.' Lord Selborne then goes on to discuss the question whether it makes any difference that the defendant, at the time when the obligation was contracted, was resident in the foreign country, but left it before the suit was instituted; and, after observing that Blackburn J., delivering the opinion of the Court of Queen's Bench in *Schibsby* v. *Westenholz*, inclined to the view that the laws of the foreign country would bind the defendant, though he declined to decide that point without further argument, Lord Selborne said: 'Their Lordships do not doubt that, if he'—i.e., Blackburn J.—'had heard argument upon the question, whether an obligation to accept the forum loci contractus, as having, by reason of the contract, a conventional jurisdiction against the parties in a suit founded upon that contract for all future time, wherever they might be domiciled or resident, was generally implied, he would have come (as their Lordships do) to the conclusion, that such obligation, unless expressed, could not be implied.' Having regard to these passages, *Becquet* v. *MacCarthy*, if and in so far as it decides that a person, who merely possesses property or enters into a contract in a foreign country, binds himself to submit to the jurisdiction of the foreign country, can, I think, no longer be sustained; and the proposition on which Channell J. based his judgment, namely, that inasmuch as the defendant had become a party to a contract of partnership in Western Australia he must be taken to have bound himself to submit to the jurisdiction of the courts of that colony, is not sound. This appeal must therefore be allowed.

LORD ALVERSTONE C.J. and KENNEDY L.J. delivered judgment to the same effect.

Appeal allowed.

EMANUEL
v.
SYMON.
Buckley L.J.

A defendant who appears by counsel to contest the jurisdiction of a court does not thereby voluntarily submit to its jurisdiction.

In re
DULLES'
SETTLE-
MENT
(No. 2).
—
Denning
L.J.

In re DULLES' SETTLEMENT (No. 2) [1951] Ch. 842 (Court of Appeal)

Appeal from Romer J.

DENNING L.J.: On December 23, 1930, in Paris, Mrs. Dulles, an Englishwoman, married the respondent, who was an American then domiciled in France. On May 5, 1940, a son was born to them. On May 28, 1946, the husband obtained in the French courts a decree of divorce against the wife. On September 5, 1947, the mother brought the child to England, and she has remained here with him ever since. The father afterwards obtained an order from the French courts giving him the custody of the child, but this order has never been put into operation, because on February 6, 1948, an action was brought in England in the Chancery Division by the infant (by his mother as his next friend), against his maternal grandparents, claiming to become a ward of the court.

On June 28, 1948, the infant (by his mother as his next friend) took out a summons in that action asking for the mother to be given the custody of the child and also 'that such provision may be made for the maintenance of the said infant as to this court may seem meet'. A copy of that summons was sent to the father's solicitors and they acknowledged it. It is to be noted that in that summons no direct claim was made on the father for maintenance. He was no party to the action: and he was only given notice of the application so that he could attend if he wished. The father himself had by this time gone back to America. He is a very rich man and is said to have assets in England worth £40,000.

When the summons came on for hearing the father, by his counsel, attended and strongly contested the wife's claim for custody, relying on the order which he had obtained from the French courts; but nevertheless the wife was awarded the custody. The judge must have been of opinion that that was best in the interests of the child: see *In re B's Settlement;*[1] *McKee* v. *McKee.*[2]

So far as maintenance of the child was concerned, the father by his counsel vigorously opposed any order for maintenance being made against him. He said that the court had no jurisdiction to make an

[1] [1940] Ch. 54.   [2] [1951] A.C. 352.

order against him. The judge upheld this view, but the Court of Appeal reversed his decision, holding that the English courts had power to order maintenance against him if he had voluntarily submitted to the jurisdiction in that respect: see *In re Dulles' Settlement No. 1*.[1] The Court of Appeal therefore referred the case back to the judge to see if the father had submitted to the jurisdiction. The judge has held that the father has not submitted to the jurisdiction, and I agree with his decision.

I cannot see how anyone can fairly say that a man has voluntarily submitted to the jurisdiction of a court when he has all the time been vigorously protesting that it has no jurisdiction. If he does nothing and lets judgment go against him in default of appearance, he clearly does not submit to the jurisdiction. What difference in principle does it make, if he does not merely do nothing, but actually goes to the court and protests that it has no jurisdiction? I can see no distinction at all. I quite agree, of course, that if he fights the case, not only on the jurisdiction, but also on the merits, he must then be taken to have submitted to the jurisdiction, because he is then inviting the court to decide in his favour on the merits; and he cannot be allowed, at one and the same time, to say that he will accept the decision on the merits if it is favourable to him and will not submit to it if it is unfavourable. But when he only appears with the sole object of protesting against the jurisdiction, I do not think that he can be said to submit to the jurisdiction: see *Tallack* v. *Tallack*,[2] per Lord Merrivale P.

It may be said that in this case the father did more than protest against the jurisdiction, because he contested the issue of custody. But in that respect he was only seeking to protect the order for custody which he himself had obtained in the French courts. That is not sufficient to amount to a submission to jurisdiction in the maintenance claim. So also it is said that he did more than protest against the jurisdiction, because he took the technical objection that the application was not made by the mother, but that was not an objection on the merits: it was another objection going to jurisdiction, and was not sufficient to amount to a submission to the jurisdiction.

Harris v. *Taylor*[3] appears at first sight to conflict with the views which I have expressed, but a careful examination of that case

In re
DULLES'
SETTLE-
MENT
(No. 2).

Denning
L.J.

---

[1] [1951] Ch. 265.   [2] [1927] P. 211, 222.
[3] [1915] 2 K.B. 580.

In re
DULLES'
SETTLE-
MENT
(No. 2).

Denning
L.J.

shows that it is quite distinguishable. The plaintiff there sued the defendant in the Isle of Man for a tort committed there. The defendant was not in the island, but the Manx court gave leave to serve him out of the jurisdiction of that court, on the ground that the cause of action was founded on a tort committed within their jurisdiction. The defendant entered a conditional appearance in the Manx court and took the point that the cause of action had not arisen within the Manx jurisdiction. That point depended on the facts of the case, and it was decided against him; whence it followed that he was properly served out of the Manx jurisdiction in accordance with the rules of the Manx court. Those rules correspond with the English rules for service out of the jurisdiction contained in Order 11; and I do not doubt that our courts would recognize a judgment properly obtained in the Manx courts for a tort committed there, whether the defendant voluntarily submitted to the jurisdiction or not;[1] just as we would expect the Manx courts in a converse case to recognize a judgment obtained in our courts against a resident in the Isle of Man, on his being properly served out of our jurisdiction for a tort committed here. *Harris* v. *Taylor* is an authority on res judicata in that the defendant was not allowed in our courts to contest the service on him out of Manx jurisdiction; because that was a point that he had raised unsuccessfully in the Manx court, and he had not appealed against it. To that extent he had submitted to the jurisdiction of the Manx court and was not allowed to go back on it. But the case is no authority on what constitutes a submission to jurisdiction generally.

Relieved of *Harris* v. *Taylor*, I think it is plain that the father here did not voluntarily submit to the jurisdiction of the Court of Chancery in regard to the claim for maintenance. He appeared and protested vigorously against it. It would be contrary to the facts to say that he submitted to it. . . .

The appeal therefore fails. I must say that I regret it, because it only fails on a technicality. I would willingly overcome it if I could, but I do not see how to do it, having regard to all that has happened.

---

[1] Can this suggestion be reconciled with the case of *Schibsby* v. *Westenholz* (*ante*, p. 476), and in particular with the observations of the court (*ante*, p. 478) on service of the writ out of the jurisdiction under ss. 18 and 19 of the Common Law Procedure Act 1852, the precursor of Order 11 of the R.S.C.? The suggestion was adversely criticized in *Sharps Commercials Ltd.* v. *Gas Turbines Ltd.* [1956], N.Z.L.R. 819, 823, and was not adopted in *Société Co-operative Sidmetal* v. *Titan International Ltd.* [1966] 1 Q.B. 828. See Dicey, p. 984–6; contrast Cheshire, p. 558 (*Ed.*). See also *Indyka* v. *Indyka*, *ante*, p. 124.

The process of the court can only be exercised against a person who is properly made a party to the proceedings and is properly served. EVERSHED M.R. delivered a concurring judgment.

Appeal dismissed.

In re
DULLES'
SETTLE-
MENT
(No. 2).
—
Denning
L.J.

Section B: FINALITY OF JUDGMENTS

A foreign judgment cannot be sued on in England unless it is final and conclusive.

NOUVION *v*. FREEMAN (1889) 15 App. Cas. 1 (House of Lords)

Appeal from a decision of the Court of Appeal (Cotton, Lindley, and Lopes L.JJ.)[1] reversing a judgment of North J.[2]

In 1878 the plaintiff obtained judgment against the defendant in Spain for a large sum of money. The judgment was a 'remate' judgment and the proceedings were summary or 'executive'. In such proceedings the defendant could plead such defences as payment or waiver, but could not set up any defence denying the validity of the contract. Either plaintiff or defendant, if unsuccessful in the 'executive' proceedings, might take separate and independent proceedings in the same Spanish court called 'ordinary' or 'plenary' proceedings, in which the 'remate' judgment could not be pleaded as res judicata or otherwise made use of. In such 'plenary' proceedings all defences and the whole merits of the matter might be gone into.

The plaintiff brought an action in England on the 'remate' Spanish judgment. The Court of Appeal held that the action failed. The plaintiff appealed.

LORD HERSCHELL: . . . My Lords, there can be no doubt that in the courts of this country effect will be given to a foreign judgment. It is unnecessary to inquire upon what principle the courts proceed in giving effect to such a judgment, and in treating it as sufficient to establish the debt. Reliance was placed upon a dictum by Parke B. and Alderson B. in the case of *Williams* v. *Jones*,[3] where the law is thus stated: 'Where a court of competent jurisdiction has adjudicated a certain sum to be due from one person to another, a legal obligation arises to pay that sum, on which an action of debt to

---

[1] 37 Ch. D. 244.   [2] 35 Ch. D. 704.
[3] (1845) 13 M. & W. 628, 633.

enforce the judgment may be maintained.' But it was conceded, and necessarily conceded, by the learned counsel for the appellant, that a judgment, to come within the terms of the law as properly laid down, must be a judgment which results from an adjudication of a court of competent jurisdiction, such judgment being final and conclusive. I shall of course have something to say upon the meaning which must be given to those words, but the general proposition in that form is not disputed by the learned counsel for the appellant. They contend that this judgment is final and conclusive, and no doubt in a certain sense that must be conceded. It puts an end to and absolutely concludes that particular action. About that there can be no manner of doubt—in that sense it is final and conclusive. But the same may be said of some interlocutory judgments upon which there can be no question that an action could not be maintained; they do settle and conclude the particular proceeding, the interlocutory proceeding, in which the judgment is pronounced. It is obvious, therefore, that the mere fact that the judgment puts an end to and finally settles the controversy which arose in the particular proceeding, is not of itself sufficient to make it a final and conclusive judgment upon which an action may be maintained in the courts of this country, when such judgment has been pronounced by a foreign court.

My Lords, I think that in order to establish that such a judgment has been pronounced it must be shewn that in the court by which it was pronounced it conclusively, finally, and for ever established the existence of the debt of which it is sought to be made conclusive evidence in this country, so as to make it res judicata between the parties. If it is not conclusive in the same court which pronounced it, so that notwithstanding such a judgment the existence of the debt may between the same parties be afterwards contested in that court, and upon proper proceedings being taken and such contest being adjudicated upon, it may be declared that there existed no obligation to pay the debt at all, then I do not think that a judgment which is of that character can be regarded as finally and conclusively evidencing the debt, and so entitling the person who has obtained the judgment to claim a decree from our courts for the payment of that debt.

The principle upon which I think our enforcement of foreign judgments must proceed is this: that in a court of competent jurisdiction, where according to its established procedure the whole merits of the case were open, at all events, to the parties, however much they may have failed to take advantage of them, or may have waived any of their rights, a final adjudication has been given that a debt or obligation exists which cannot thereafter in that court be disputed, and can only be questioned in an appeal to a higher tribunal. In such a case it may well be said that giving credit to the courts of another country we are prepared to take the fact that such adjudication has been made as establishing the existence of the debt or obligation. But where, as in the present case, the adjudication is consistent with the non-existence of the debt or obligation which it is sought to enforce, and it may thereafter be declared by the tribunal which pronounced it that there is no obligation and no debt, it appears to me that the very foundation upon which the courts of this country would proceed in enforcing a foreign judgment altogether fails.

It has been suggested that a judgment obtained in an 'executive' action may be regarded as analogous to a judgment obtained in a common law action in the time prior to the Judicature Act, the execution of which might be restrained by a Court of Equity, so as to prevent the plaintiff who had succeeded in such an action from obtaining the fruits of his judgment. I do not think that such an analogy is a complete one; but even if it were more complete than I think it to be, it appears to me that it would afford very little assistance to your Lordships unless we could know what had been the course adopted with regard to such judgments in countries in whose system of law the same force and effect are given to foreign judgments as are given in the courts of this country. Upon that point we have had no information whatsoever.

Then, my Lords, it is said that such a judgment is analogous to a judgment which has been obtained upon which a suit may be instituted in the courts of this country, even although an appeal may be pending. It appears to me that there is a vital distinction between the two cases. Although an appeal may be pending, a court of competent jurisdiction has finally and conclusively determined the existence of a debt, and it has none the less done so because the right of appeal has been given whereby a superior court may overrule that decision. There exists at the time of the suit a judgment which must be assumed to be valid until interfered with by a higher tribunal, and which conclusively establishes the existence of the debt which is sought to be recovered in this country. That appears

NOUVION
v.
FREEMAN.

Lord
Herschell.

491

NOUVION
v.
FREEMAN.
―
Lord
Herschell.

to me to be in altogether a different position from a 'remate' judgment, where the very court which pronounced the 'remate' judgment (not the Court of Appeal) may determine, if proper proceedings are taken, that the debt for which this 'remate' judgment is sought to be used as conclusive evidence has no existence at all.

My Lords, the plaintiff in such a suit, an executive suit, is not, by the decision which is now under appeal, deprived of his rights. He may still sue upon the original cause of action. Of course it may happen, as in this particular case, that such a suit is barred by lapse of time, but that is an accident. The right of the plaintiff to sue on his original cause of action is not at all interfered with by the judgment which has been pronounced; and in such an action, if it were brought, all questions upon which the rights of the parties depend, and by the solution of which the obligation to pay must ultimately be determined, would be open to consideration and could be dealt with by the courts, and finally and conclusively settled. I do not, therefore, see that there is any wrong or any hardship done by holding that a judgment which does not conclusively and for ever as between the parties establish the existence of a debt in that court cannot be looked upon as sufficient evidence of it in the courts of this country. . . .

For these reasons I move your Lordships that the judgment appealed from be affirmed, and the appeal dismissed with costs.

LORDS WATSON, BRAMWELL, and ASHBOURNE delivered judgments to the same effect.

Appeal dismissed.

Section *C*: DEFENCES

A foreign judgment cannot be impeached on its merits even if the foreign tribunal has proceeded on a mistaken view of English law.

GODARD
v.
GRAY.
―
Blackburn
J.

GODARD *v.* GRAY (1870) L.R. 6 Q.B. 139 (Court of Queen's Bench)

BLACKBURN J.: In this case the plaintiffs declare on a judgment of a French tribunal, averred to have jurisdiction in that behalf.

The question arises on a demurrer to the second plea, which sets out the whole proceedings in the French court. By these it appears that the plaintiffs, who are Frenchmen, sued the defendants, who are Englishmen, on a charterparty made at Sunderland, which charterparty contained the following clause: 'Penalty for non-performance of this agreement, estimated amount of freight'. The French court below, treating this clause as fixing the amount of liquidated damages, gave judgment against the defendants for the amount of freight on two voyages. On appeal, the superior court reduced the amount to the estimated freight of one voyage, giving as their reason that the charterparty itself 'fixait l'indemnité à laquelle chacune des parties aurait droit pour inexécution de la convention par la faute de l'autre; que moyennant paiement de cette indemnité chacune des parties avait le droit de rompre la convention', and the tribunal proceeds to observe that the amount thus decreed was after all more than sufficient to cover all the plaintiffs' loss.

GODARD
v.
GRAY.
Blackburn
J.

All parties in France seem to have taken it for granted that the words in the charterparty were to be understood in their natural sense; but the English law is accurately expressed in Abbott on Shipping,[1] and had that passage been brought to the notice of the French tribunal, it would have known that in an English charterparty, as is there stated, 'Such a clause is not the absolute limit of damages on either side; the party may, if he thinks fit, ground his action upon the other clauses or covenants, and may, in such action, recover damages beyond the amount of the penalty, if in justice they shall be found to exceed it. On the other hand, if the party sue on such a penal clause, he cannot, in effect, recover more than the damage actually sustained.' But it was not brought to the notice of the French tribunal that according to the interpretation put by the English law on such a contract, a penal clause of this sort was in fact idle and inoperative. If it had been, they would, probably, have interpreted the English contract made in England according to the English construction. No blame can be imputed to foreign lawyers for not conjecturing that the clause was merely a brutum fulmen. The fault, if any, was in the defendants, for not properly instructing their French counsel on this point.

Still the fact remains that we can see on the face of the proceedings that the foreign tribunal has made a mistake on the construction of an English contract, which is a question of English law; and that, in consequence of that mistake, judgment has been given for an amount probably greater than, or, at all events, different from that for which it would have been given if the tribunal had been correctly informed what construction the English contract bore according to English law.

[1] 5th ed., p. 170.

The question raised by the plea is, whether this is a bar to the action brought in England to enforce that judgment, and we are all of opinion that it is not, and that the plaintiff is entitled to judgment.

The following are the reasons of my brother Mellor and myself. My brother Hannen, though agreeing in the result, qualifies his assent to these reasons to some extent, which he will state for himself.

It is not an admitted principle of the law of nations that a state is bound to enforce within its territories the judgment of a foreign tribunal. Several of the continental nations (including France) do not enforce the judgments of other countries, unless where there are reciprocal treaties to that effect. But in England and in those states which are governed by the common law, such judgments are enforced, not by virtue of any treaty, nor by virtue of any statute, but upon a principle very well stated by Parke B., in *Williams* v. *Jones*:[1] 'Where a court of competent jurisdiction has adjudicated a certain sum to be due from one person to another, a legal obligation arises to pay that sum, on which an action of debt to enforce the judgment may be maintained. It is in this way that the judgments of foreign and colonial courts are supported and enforced.' And taking this as the principle, it seems to follow that anything which negatives the existence of that legal obligation, or excuses the defendant from the performance of it, must form a good defence to the action. It must be open, therefore, to the defendant to shew that the court which pronounced the judgment had not jurisdiction to pronounce it, either because they exceeded the jurisdiction given to them by the foreign law, or because he, the defendant, was not subject to that jurisdiction; and so far the foreign judgment must be examinable. Probably the defendant may shew that the judgment was obtained by the fraud of the plaintiff, for that would shew that the defendant was excused from the performance of an obligation thus obtained; and it may be that where the foreign court has knowingly and perversely disregarded the rights given to an English subject by English law, that forms a valid excuse for disregarding the obligation thus imposed on him; but we prefer to imitate the caution of the present Lord Chancellor, in *Castrique* v. *Imrie*,[2] and to leave those questions to be decided when they arise, only observing that in the present case, as in that, 'the whole of the facts appear to have been inquired into by the French courts, judicially, honestly, and

[1] (1845) 13 M. & W. 628, 633.   [2] (1870) L.R. 4 H.L. 414, 445.

with the intention to arrive at the right conclusion, and having heard the facts as stated before them they came to a conclusion which justified them in France in deciding as they did decide'. . . .

The decisions of the Court of Queen's Bench in *Bank of Australasia* v. *Nias*,[1] of the Court of Common Pleas in *Bank of Australasia* v. *Harding*,[2] and of the Court of Exchequer in *De Cosse Brissac* v. *Rathbone*,[3] seem to us to leave it no longer open to contend, unless in a court of error, that a foreign judgment can be impeached on the ground that it was erroneous on the merits; or to set up as a defence to an action on it, that the tribunal mistook either the facts or the law.

But there still remains a question which has never, so far as we know, been expressly decided in any court.

It is broadly laid down, by the very learned author of Smith's Leading Cases, in the original note to *Doe* v. *Oliver*,[4] that 'it is clear that if the judgment appear on the face of the proceedings to be founded on a *mistaken notion* of the English law', it would not be conclusive. . . . We think that the defendant can no more set up as an excuse, relieving him from the duty of paying the amount awarded by the judgment of a foreign tribunal having jurisdiction over him and the cause, that the judgment proceeded on a mistake as to English law, than he could set up as an excuse that there had been a mistake as to the law of some third country incidentally involved, or as to any other question of fact.

It can make no difference that the mistake appears on the face of the proceedings. That, no doubt, greatly facilitates the proof of the mistake; but if the principle be to inquire whether the defendant is relieved from a prima facie duty to obey the judgment, he must be equally relieved, whether the mistake appears on the face of the proceedings or is to be proved by extraneous evidence. Nor can there be any difference between a mistake made by the foreign tribunal as to English law, and any other mistake. No doubt the English court can, without arrogance, say that where there is a difference of opinion as to English law, the opinion of the English tribunal is probably right; but how would it be if the question had arisen as to the law of some of the numerous portions of the British dominions where the law is not that of England? The French tribunal, if incidentally inquiring into the law of Mauritius, where French law prevails,

GODARD
v.
GRAY.

Blackburn
J.

---

[1] (1851) 16 Q.B. 717.   [2] (1850) 9 C.B. 661.   [3] (1861) 6 H. & N. 301.
[4] (1829) 2 Sm. L.C. (2nd ed.) p. 448.

GODARD
v.
GRAY.

Blackburn
J.

would be more likely to be right than the English court; if inquiring into the law of Scotland it would seem that there was about an equal chance as to which took the right view. If it was sought to enforce the foreign judgment in Scotland, the chances as to which court was right would be altered. Yet it surely cannot be said that a judgment shewn to have proceeded on a mistaken view of Scotch law could be enforced in England and not in Scotland, and that one proceeding on a mistaken view of English law could be enforced in Scotland but not in England.

If, indeed, foreign judgments were enforced by our courts out of politeness and courtesy to the tribunals of other countries, one could understand its being said that though our courts would not be so rude as to inquire whether the foreign court had made a mistake, or to allow the defendant to assert that it had, yet that if the foreign court itself admitted its blunder they would not then act: but it is quite contrary to every analogy to suppose that an English court of law exercises any discretion of this sort. We enforce a legal obligation, and we admit any defence which shews that there is no legal obligation or a legal excuse for not fulfilling it; but in no case that we know of is it ever said that a defence shall be admitted if it is easily proved, and rejected if it would give the court much trouble to investigate it. Yet on what other principle can we admit as a defence that there is a mistake of English law apparent on the face of the proceedings, and reject a defence that there is a mistake of Spanish or even Scotch law apparent in the proceedings, or that there was a mistake of English law not apparent on the proceedings, but which the defendant avers that he can shew did exist?

The whole law was much considered and discussed in *Castrique* v. *Imrie*, where the French tribunal had made a mistake as to the English law, and under that mistake had decreed the sale of the defendant's ship. The decision of the House of Lords was, that the defendant's title derived under that sale was good, notwithstanding that mistake: Lord Colonsay pithily saying, 'It appears to me that we cannot enter into an inquiry as to whether the French courts proceeded correctly, either as to their own course of procedure or their own law, nor whether under the circumstances they took the proper means of satisfying themselves with respect to the view they took of the English law. Nor can we inquire whether they were right in their views of the English law. The question is, whether under the circumstances of the case, dealing with it fairly, the original tribunal did proceed against the ship, and did order the sale of the ship.'

The question in *Castrique* v. *Imrie* was as to the effect on the property of a judgment ordering a ship, locally situate in France, to be sold, and therefore was not the same as the question in this case as to what effect is to be given to a judgment against the person. But at least the decision in *Castrique* v. *Imrie* establishes this, that a mistake as to English law on the part of a foreign tribunal does not operate in all cases so as to prevent the courts of this country from giving effect to the judgment. . . .

For these reasons we have come to the conclusion that judgment should be given for the plaintiffs.

HANNEN J., while expressing no final opinion on the question whether the French judgment might not be impeached on the ground that it appeared on its face to have proceeded on an incorrect view of English law, agreed in the result on the ground that the defendants should have taken steps to bring the English law to the notice of the French tribunal.

Judgment for the plaintiff.

GODARD
v.
GRAY.

Blackburn
J.

A foreign judgment given by a court having jurisdiction is not void in England merely because the court mistook or misapplied its own procedure.

PEMBERTON *v.* HUGHES [1899] 1 Ch. 781 (Court of Appeal)

This was an action by Mrs. Pemberton who claimed to be the widow of Francis Pemberton asking for a declaration that under a deed poll executed by him in 1891 she was entitled to a jointure or rentcharge of £200 p.a. issuing out of certain lands in Cambridge-shire. The lands were settled by the will of a testator who died in 1850 on Francis Pemberton for life with remainders over, with power for every tenant for life in possession by deed to appoint a rentcharge to any woman whom he should marry or have married, to commence from the death of such tenant for life. Francis Pemberton died in 1892.

The defence was that the plaintiff was married to one Holmes Erwin in Florida in 1884, both parties being domiciled in Florida;

PEMBERTON
v.
HUGHES.

497

PEMBERTON
v.
HUGHES.

that in 1888 Erwin obtained a divorce from a Florida court on the ground of the plaintiff's violent and ungovernable temper; that this divorce was invalid because the rules of the Florida court required that ten days should intervene between the day on which process was issued and the day on which it was returnable, whereas in the present case only nine clear days had intervened; that Erwin was still living when the plaintiff went through a ceremony of marriage with Francis Pemberton; and that therefore the plaintiff's marriage with Francis Pemberton was void and she was not within the power of jointuring conferred by the settlement.

Kekewich J. held that the Florida divorce was void and dismissed the action with costs.

The plaintiff appealed.

LINDLEY M.R. (after stating the facts, and holding that the Florida court had jurisdiction because the plaintiff and Erwin were domiciled in Florida, and stating that he was not satisfied on the evidence that the alleged defect of procedure rendered the divorce void in Florida, continued:) Assuming that the defendants are right, and that the decree of divorce is void by the law of Florida, it by no means follows that it ought to be so regarded in this country. It sounds paradoxical to say that a decree of a foreign court should be regarded here as more efficacious or with more respect than it is entitled to in the country in which it was pronounced. But this paradox disappears when the principles on which English courts act in regarding or disregarding foreign judgments are borne in mind. If a judgment is pronounced by a foreign court over persons within its jurisdiction and in a matter with which it is competent to deal, English courts never investigate the propriety of the proceedings in the foreign court, unless they offend against English views of substantial justice. Where no substantial justice, according to English notions, is offended, all that English courts look to is the finality of the judgment and the jurisdiction of the court, in this sense and to this extent—namely, its competence to entertain the sort of case which it did deal with, and its competence to require the defendant to appear before it. If the court had jurisdiction in this sense and to this extent, the courts of this country never inquire whether the jurisdiction has been properly or improperly exercised, provided always that no substantial injustice, according to English notions, has been committed.

There is no doubt that the courts of this country will not enforce the decisions of foreign courts which have no jurisdiction in the sense above explained—i.e., over the subject-matter or over the persons brought before them: *Schibsby* v. *Westenholz*;[1] *Rousillon* v. *Rousillon*;[2] *Price* v. *Dewhurst*;[3] *Buchanan* v. *Rucker*;[4] *Sirdar Gurdyal Singh* v. *Rajah of Faridkote*.[5] But the jurisdiction which alone is important in these matters is the competence of the court in an international sense—i.e., its territorial competence over the subject-matter and over the defendant. Its competence or jurisdiction in any other sense is not regarded as material by the courts of this country. This is pointed out by Mr. Westlake[6] and by Foote[7], and is illustrated by *Vanquelin* v. *Bouard*.[8] That was an action on a judgment obtained in France on a bill of exchange. The court was competent to try such actions, and the defendant was within its jurisdiction. He let judgment go by default, and in the action in this country on the judgment he pleaded that by French law the French court had no jurisdiction, because the defendant was not a trader and was not resident in a particular town where the cause of action arose. In other words, the defendant pleaded that the French action was brought in the wrong court (see the 13th plea). The Court of Common Pleas held the plea bad, and that the defence set up by it should have been raised in the French action. The French action in *Vanquelin* v. *Bouard* was an action in personam, and the parties to the action in France were also the parties to the action brought in this country on the French judgment. The decision, therefore, does not exactly cover the present case, but it goes far to show that the defendants' contention in this case cannot be supported.

The defendants' contention entirely ignores the distinction between the jurisdiction of tribunals from an international and their jurisdiction from a purely municipal point of view. But that distinction rests on good sense, and is recognised by modern writers on private international law. . . .

It may be safely said that, in the opinion of writers on international law, and for international purposes, the jurisdiction or the competency of a court does not depend upon the exact observance of its own rules of procedure. The defendants' contention is based upon the assumption that an irregularity in procedure of a foreign

PEMBERTON
v.
HUGHES.

Lindley
M.R.

---

[1] (1870) L.R. 6 Q.B. 155 ; *ante*, p. 476.   [2] (1880) 14 Ch. D. 351.
[3] (1838) 4 My. & Cr. 76.   [4] (1808) 9 East 192
[5] [1894] A.C. 670.   [6] Private International Law, 3rd ed., s. 328.
[7] Private International Jurisprudence, 2nd ed., p. 547.   [8] (1863) 15 C.B. N.S. 341.

court of competent jurisdiction in the sense above explained is a matter which the courts of this country are bound to recognise if such irregularity involves nullity of sentence. No authority can be found for any such proposition; and, although I am not aware of any English decision exactly to the contrary, there are many which are so inconsistent with it as to show that it cannot be accepted.

A judgment of a foreign court having jurisdiction over the parties and subject-matter—i.e., having jurisdiction to summon the defendants before it and to decide such matters as it has decided—cannot be impeached in this country on its merits: *Castrique* v. *Imrie*[1] (in rem); *Godard* v. *Gray*[2] (in personam); *Messina* v. *Petrococchino*[3] (in personam). It is quite inconsistent with those cases, and also with *Vanquelin* v. *Bouard*, to hold that such a judgment can be impeached here for a mere error in procedure. And in *Castrique* v. *Imrie* Lord Colonsay said that no inquiry on such a matter should be made.

A decree for divorce, altering as it does the status of the parties and affecting, as it may do, the legitimacy of their afterborn children, is much more like a judgment in rem than a judgment in personam: see *Niboyet* v. *Niboyet*.[4] And where there are differences between the two, the decisions on foreign judgments in rem are better guides for the determination of this case than decisions on foreign judgments in personam. The leading cases on foreign judgments in rem are *Doglioni* v. *Crispin*;[5] *Castrique* v. *Imrie*; *In re Trufort*.[6] There is nothing, however, in the decisions in these cases to assist the defendants. On the contrary, the judgments delivered in them are, in my opinion, adverse to the defendants' contention. . . .

RIGBY and VAUGHAN WILLIAMS L.JJ. delivered judgments to the same effect.

Appeal allowed.

---

[1] (1870) L.R. 4 H.L. 414.   [2] (1870) L.R. 6 Q.B. 139; *ante*, p. 492.
[3] (1872) L.R. 4 P.C. 144.   [4] (1878) 4 P.D. 1; *ante*, p. 107.
[5] (1866) L.R. 1 H.L. 301.   [6] (1887) 36 Ch. D. 600.

A foreign judgment can be impeached on the ground of fraud, even if (a) the fraud alleged is such that it cannot be proved without retrying the questions adjudicated upon by the foreign court, or (b) the defendant could have taken the point in the foreign court, but did not.

SYAL *v.* HEYWARD [1948] 2 K.B. 443 (Court of Appeal)

Interlocutory appeal from Jones J.

In February 1947 the plaintiff, an Indian moneylender, obtained judgment against the defendants, two English lieutenant-colonels, from a court at Saharanpur, India, on a plaint in which he alleged that the defendants had borrowed 20,000 rupees from him in October 1946, and had executed a promissory note for that amount. The defendants did not defend this action. In November 1947 this judgment was ordered to be registered in the High Court pursuant to the Foreign Judgments (Reciprocal Enforcement) Act 1933 (*post*, p. 507). The defendants applied for an order that the registration of the judgment should be set aside under s. 4 (1) (*a*) (iv) of the Act on the ground that the judgment had been obtained by fraud. They alleged that the amount which they had borrowed from the plaintiff was not 20,000 rupees but only 10,800 rupees, the difference being made up in part of commission and in part of interest; and that the plaintiff had deceived the Indian court by pretending that he had lent 20,000 rupees, whereas in fact he had lent only 10,800 rupees, thereby concealing from the court the possibility that the defendants might have a defence under the Indian Usurious Loans Act 1918.

The master dismissed the defendants' application on the ground that all the facts on which they relied were known to them at all material times and could have been raised by way of defence in the Indian proceedings. Jones J. reversed this decision and directed an issue to be tried. The plaintiff appealed.

The judgment of the court (Scott, Cohen and Wrottesley L.JJ.) was read by

COHEN L.J.: Mr. Foot [counsel for the plaintiff] submitted that: (1) The fraud contemplated by s. 4 of the Foreign Judgments (Reciprocal Enforcement) Act 1933 is fraud on the court. Unless the court has been deceived, the section is not applicable. (2) An appli-

SYAL
v.
HEYWARD.

Cohen L.J.

cation under s. 4 should be treated in the same way as, before the Act of 1933 came into force, an action to set aside a judgment would have been treated. (3) Precisely the same tests apply whether the judgment sought to be set aside is a foreign judgment or an English judgment. (4) Where a judgment is sought to be set aside on the ground of fraud, the fraud must have been discovered by the applicants since the date of the judgment. (5) It was plain that the facts relied on in the present case were all known to the defendants before the date of the Indian judgment.

[Counsel for the defendants] agreed with the first of these propositions and he did not, we think, dispute the second. The third is supported by the observations of Lindley L.J. in *Vadala* v. *Lawes*,[1] where he said: 'First of all, there is the rule which is perfectly well established and well known, that a party to an action can impeach the judgment in it for fraud. Whether it is the judgment of an English court or of a foreign court does not matter; using general language, that is a general proposition unconditional and undisputed.' It is unnecessary for us on this appeal to consider how far those observations go.

The fifth proposition is also plainly correct if Mr. Foot means only that the defendants knew they were being sued for a sum in excess of 10,800 rupees and that in the plaint, verified by affidavit, the plaintiff was alleging that they had borrowed 20,000 rupees, but there is no evidence that they knew that the plaint so verified would be the only evidence before the court if in fact that was the position.

Be that as it may, Mr. Foot's real difficulty is in his fourth proposition. For it he relied on *Boswell* v. *Coaks (No. 2)*,[2] a decision of the House of Lords applied in *Birch* v. *Birch*.[3] These cases, no doubt, establish that in proceedings to set aside an English judgment, the defendants cannot ask for a re-trial of the issue of fraud as between them and the plaintiff on facts known to them at the date of the earlier judgment; but in cases under s. 4 of the Act of 1933, the question is not one of fraud on the plaintiff,[4] but of fraud on the court, and it seems to us to be clearly established by authority binding on us, that if the defendant shows a prima facie case that the court was deceived, he is entitled to have that issue tried even though in trying it the court may have to go into defences which

[1] (1890) 25 Q.B.D. 310, 316.   [2] (1894) 86 L.T. 365, n.
[3] [1902] P. 130.
[4] *Sic* in the report : evidently a misprint for defendant. (*Ed.*)

could have been raised at the first trial. See *Abouloff* v. *Oppen-* *heimer*,[1] as explained in *Vadala* v. *Lawes*, where Lindley L.J., immediately after the passage we have already cited, says: 'Another general proposition which, speaking in equally general language, is perfectly well settled, is, that when you bring an action on a foreign judgment, you cannot go into the merits which have been tried in the foreign court. But you have to combine those two rules and apply them in the case where you cannot go into the alleged fraud without going into the merits. Which rule is to prevail? That point appears to me to have been one of very great difficulty before the case of *Abouloff* v. *Oppenheimer*. At the time when that case was decided, namely, in 1882, there was a long line of authorities including *Bank of Australasia* v. *Nias*,[2] *Ochsenbein* v. *Papelier*,[3] and *Cammell* v. *Sewell*,[4] all recognizing and enforcing the general proposition, that in an action on a foreign judgment you cannot re-try the merits. But until *Abouloff's* case the difficulty of combining the two rules and saying what ought to be done where you could not enter into the question of fraud to prove it without reopening the merits, had never come forward for explicit decision. That point was raised directly in the case of *Abouloff* v. *Oppenheimer*, and it was decided. I cannot fritter away that judgment, and I cannot read the judgments without seeing that they amount to this: that if the fraud upon the foreign court consists in the fact that the plaintiff has induced that court to come to a wrong conclusion, you can reopen the whole case even although you will have in this court to go into the very facts which were investigated and which were in issue in the foreign court. The technical objection that the issue is the same is technically answered by the technical reply that the issue is not the same, because in this court you have to consider whether the foreign court has been imposed upon. That, to my mind, is only meeting technical argument by a technical answer, and I do not attach much importance to it; but in that case the court faced the difficulty that you could not give effect to the defence without re-trying the merits. The fraud practised on the court, or alleged to have been practised on the court, was the misleading of the court by evidence known by the plaintiff to be false. That was the whole fraud. The question of fact, whether what the plaintiff had said in the court below was or was not false, was the very question of fact

SYAL
v.
HEYWARD.

Cohen L.J.

---

[1] (1882) 10 Q.B.D. 295. [2] (1851) 16 Q.B. 717.
[3] (1873) L.R. 8 Ch. App. 695. [4] (1860) 5 H. & N. 728; *ante*, p. 353.

that had been adjudicated on in the foreign court; and, notwithstanding that was so, when the court came to consider how the two rules, to which I have alluded, could be worked together, they said: "Well, if that foreign judgment was obtained fraudulently, and if it is necessary, in order to prove that fraud, to re-try the merits, you are entitled to do so according to the law of this country." I cannot read that case in any other way.'

In the present case it is plain that the defendants are alleging a fraud on the court and it is, therefore, immaterial that to establish their allegation they will have to adduce evidence which was available to them before the date of the Indian judgment.

As a subsidiary point, Mr. Foot contended that the defendants had failed to establish a prima facie case of fraud. We are unable to accede to this argument. It may well be that the plaintiff will rebut that prima facie case, but we think that the evidence filed by the defendants discloses sufficient evidence of a case to entitle them to an issue.

Appeal dismissed.

NOTE X: DEFENCES TO ACTIONS ON FOREIGN JUDGMENTS

1. *What are not defences*

(a) *Errors of fact or law.* The general principle is that it is no defence that the foreign judgment was wrong either on the facts or on the law. The merits cannot be reopened in England: interest rei publicae ut sit finis litium. Still less can the defendant in England allege that he has discovered fresh evidence the production of which in the foreign court would have led to a decision in his favour. It is his business to take all possible defences in the foreign court: *Ellis* v. *McHenry* (1871) L.R. 6 C.P. 228; *Re Trufort* (1887) 36 Ch. D. 600. Nor is it any defence that the foreign court, purporting to apply English law, made an obvious mistake in doing so: *Castrique* v. *Imrie* (1870) L.R. 4 H.L. 414; *Godard* v. *Gray* (ante, p. 492); *Re Trufort, supra.* It would seem to follow that it is no defence that the foreign court applied its own domestic law when according to English conflict of laws rules it should have applied English domestic law. In *Simpson* v. *Fogo* (1863) 1 H. & M. 195, Page-Wood V.-C. declined to enforce a Louisiana judgment on the ground that it showed on its face a perverse and deliberate refusal to recognize the law of England. But this case has never been followed, and has been doubted by Scrutton L.J. in *Luther* v. *Sagor* (ante, p. 375) and by the House of Lords in *Carl Zeiss Stiftung* v. *Rayner & Keeler Ltd.* (*No. 2*) [1967] 1 A.C. 853, 917–18, 922, 978.

(b) *Defects of procedure.* It is no defence that the foreign court mistook or misapplied its own rules of procedure: *Pemberton* v. *Hughes* (ante, p. 497).

(c) *Lack of internal competence.* Is it a defence that though the foreign court had jurisdiction in the international sense, it lacked competence in the internal sense? This is a difficult question, and the authorities are in confusion.

In *Vanquelin* v. *Bouard* (1863) 15 C.B. N.S. 341, the defendant was sued in England on a French judgment in respect of a bill of exchange. The French court had jurisdiction according to the English rules of the conflict of laws and the subject-matter of the action (bills of exchange) was within its internal competence. But the defendant pleaded that the particular French court had no internal competence over him because he was not a trader. This plea was overruled.

On the other hand, in *Castrique* v. *Imrie* (1870) L.R. 4 H.L. 414, 429, 448, Lord Chelmsford, adopting a statement of Blackburn J. in the same case, regarded it as material 'whether the sovereign authority of that state has conferred on the court jurisdiction to decide as to the disposition of the thing, and the Court has acted within its jurisdiction'. In that case the foreign judgment was a judgment in rem. And in *Pemberton* v. *Hughes* (*ante*, p. 498) Lindley M.R. said that 'all that English courts look to are the finality of the judgment and the jurisdiction of the court, in this sense and to this extent, namely its competence to entertain the sort of case which it did deal with and its competence to require the defendant to appear before it'. In that case the foreign judgment was a divorce decree which is analogous to a judgment in rem. If by 'competence' the learned Master of the Rolls meant internal competence, then his statement supports that of Blackburn J. without being inconsistent with *Vanquelin* v. *Bouard*. In *Bater* v. *Bater* [1906] P. 209, another case of divorce, Sir Gorell Barnes P., having held that the husband and wife were domiciled in New York at the date of the proceedings there, seemed to think it was his duty to inquire whether the wife was resident in New York within the meaning of a New York statute so as to give the New York Court internal competence to grant her a divorce: but this seems contrary to principle. And in *Papadopoulos* v. *Papadopoulos* [1930] P. 55 one reason for refusing to recognize a Cyprus decree of nullity was that the court had no internal competence to annul a marriage.

It is submitted that the best way of reconciling the authorities is to say that the English court will inquire whether the foreign judgment was irregular, that is, valid until set aside; or a complete nullity, having no effect at all in the foreign country. In the former case the judgment will be held valid in England unless and until it is set aside in the foreign country. In the latter case it will be held invalid in England. A foreign judgment is, of course, much more likely to be irregular than void.

2. *What are defences*

(a) *Fraud.* It is settled that a foreign judgment, like any other, can be impeached for fraud. Such fraud may be either fraud on the part of the court, as where it is interested in the subject-matter of the suit; or fraud on the part of the successful party, as where he suppresses evidence or produces forged or perjured evidence; or fraud on the part of both court and party, as where one party bribes the court.

The difficult question is whether a foreign judgment can be impeached for fraud if, in order to prove the fraud, it is necessary to reopen the merits which have already been decided by the foreign court. Two principles are here in conflict, the principle that foreign judgments are impeachable for fraud, and the principle that the merits cannot be reopened. In this situation, four decisions of the Court of Appeal lay down in the clearest terms that it is the former principle which prevails: *Abouloff* v. *Oppenheimer* (1882) 10 Q.B.D. 295; *Vadala* v. *Lawes* (1890) 25 Q.B.D. 310; *Ellerman Lines* v. *Read* [1928] 2 K.B. 144 (a judgment in rem); and *Syal* v. *Heyward* (*ante*, p. 501). In *Abouloff* v. *Oppenheimer* and *Vadala* v. *Lawes* the defendant argued unsuccessfully in the foreign court that the plaintiff was deceiving it. In *Syal* v. *Heyward* he did nothing and allowed judgment to go against him by default, although aware of the facts which (as he alleged) constituted fraud on the plaintiff's part. Yet in each case the defendant was allowed to raise the plea of fraud in England. *Syal* v. *Heyward* is criticized by Cowen in 65 L.Q.R. 82 (1949). It is difficult to reconcile it with the principle that the defendant ought to take all possible defences in the foreign court.

(*b*) *Contrary to public policy.* An action on a foreign judgment, like any other action based on foreign facts, will fail if the enforcement of the plaintiff's claim would be contrary to English public policy. Naturally, the limits of the doctrine are somewhat ill defined. Well-recognized grounds on which enforcement is refused are that the foreign judgment was enforcing a contract in restraint of trade: *Rousillon* v. *Rousillon* (1880), 14 Ch. D. 351; or was penal: *Huntingdon* v. *Attrill* (*ante*, p. 25); or for taxes: *Government of India* v. *Taylor* (*ante*, p. 30). In *Re Macartney* [1921] 1 Ch. 522, an affiliation order made in Malta against a dead man's estate, granting maintenance to the mother of his illegitimate child without any provision for termination when the child reached the age of 16, was refused recognition in England on three grounds: (1) it was contrary to public policy to give an illegitimate child perpetual maintenance; (iii) the making of posthumous affiliation orders was unknown to English law; (iii) the order was not final and conclusive since it could be varied by the Maltese court in accordance with changes in the child's circumstances. It is submitted that the second ground, that the cause of action was unknown to English law, is an inadequate reason for refusing recognition of a foreign judgment. In *Burchell* v. *Burchell* (1926) 58 Ont. L.R. 515 an Ontario court enforced a judgment of an Ohio divorce court for a lump-sum payment by a wife for the support of her husband, although by the law of Ontario a husband could not have obtained alimony from his wife.

(*c*) *Contrary to natural justice.* This conception is even vaguer than that of public policy. A foreign judgment is not contrary to natural justice merely because it is obviously wrong. A foreign judgment might be impeachable on the ground that the defendant did not receive notice of the proceedings in sufficient time to enable him to defend them or was unfairly prevented from putting his case to the foreign court: but reported instances are practically non-existent. The Foreign Judgments (Reciprocal Enforcement) Act 1933 does not mention the requirement of natural justice, but does insist that the defendant should have received sufficient notice of the proceedings to enable him to defend them: s. 4 (1) (*a*) (iii).

Section D: DIRECT ENFORCEMENT

Foreign Judgments (Reciprocal Enforcement) Act 1933

An Act to make provision for the enforcement in the United Kingdom of judgments given in foreign countries which accord reciprocal treatment to judgments given in the United Kingdom, for facilitating the enforcement in foreign countries of judgments given in the United Kingdom, and for other purposes in connection with the matters aforesaid.

Part I

Registration of Foreign Judgments

1.—(1) His Majesty, if he is satisfied that, in the event of the benefits conferred by this Part of this Act being extended to judgments given in the superior courts of any foreign country, substantial reciprocity of treatment will be assured as respects the enforcement in that foreign country of judgments given in the superior courts of the United Kingdom, may by Order in Council direct—

(a) that this Part of this Act shall extend to that foreign country;[1] and

(b) that such courts of that foreign country as are specified in the Order shall be deemed superior courts of that country for the purposes of this Part of this Act.

(2) Any judgment of a superior court of a foreign country to which this Part of this Act extends, other than a judgment of such a court given on appeal from a court which is not a superior court, shall be a judgment to which this Part of this Act applies, if—

(a) it is final and conclusive as between the parties thereto; and

(b) there is payable thereunder a sum of money, not being a sum payable in respect of taxes or other charges of a like nature or in respect of a fine or other penalty; and

(c) it is given after the coming into operation of the Order in Council directing that this Part of this Act shall extend to that foreign country.

[1] Orders in Council have been made under this s. applying Part I of the Act to Austria, Belgium, France, Norway, West Germany, and Berlin. In 1964 a convention was signed with Italy, but has not yet been implemented by Order in Council. See also *post*, p. 511, n. 1.

(3) For the purposes of this section, a judgment shall be deemed to be final and conclusive notwithstanding that an appeal may be pending against it, or that it may still be subject to appeal, in the courts of the country of the original court.

2.—(1) A person, being a judgment creditor under a judgment to which this Part of this Act applies, may apply to the High Court at any time within six years after the date of the judgment, or, where there have been proceedings by way of appeal against the judgment, after the date of the last judgment given in those proceedings, to have the judgment registered in the High Court, and on any such application the court shall, subject to proof of the prescribed matters and to the other provisions of this Act, order the judgment to be registered:

Provided that a judgment shall not be registered if at the date of the application—

(*a*) it has been wholly satisfied; or

(*b*) it could not be enforced by execution in the country of the original court.

(2) Subject to the provisions of this Act with respect to the setting aside of registration—

(*a*) a registered judgment shall, for the purposes of execution, be of the same force and effect; and

(*b*) proceedings may be taken on a registered judgment; and

(*c*) the sum for which a judgment is registered shall carry interest; and

(*d*) the registering court shall have the same control over the execution of a registered judgment;

as if the judgment had been a judgment originally given in the registering court and entered on the date of registration:

Provided that execution shall not issue on the judgment so long as, under this Part of this Act and the Rules of Court made thereunder, it is competent for any party to make an application to have the registration of the judgment set aside, or, where such an application is made, until after the application has been finally determined.

3. (*Power to make rules of Court.*)

4.—(1) On an application in that behalf duly made by any party against whom a registered judgment may be enforced, the registration of the judgment—

(*a*) shall be set aside if the registering court is satisfied—

(i) that the judgment is not a judgment to which this Part of this Act applies or was registered in contravention of the foregoing provisions of this Act; or

(ii) that the courts of the country of the original court had no jurisdiction in the circumstances of the case; or

(iii) that the judgment debtor, being the defendant in the proceedings in the original court, did not (notwithstanding that process may have been duly served on him in accordance with the law of the country of the original court) receive notice of those proceedings in sufficient time to enable him to defend the proceedings and did not appear; or

(iv) that the judgment was obtained by fraud; or

(v) that the enforcement of the judgment would be contrary to public policy in the country of the registering court; or

(vi) that the rights under the judgment are not vested in the person by whom the application for registration was made;

(b) may be set aside if the registering court is satisfied that the matter in dispute in the proceedings in the original court had previously to the date of the judgment in the original court been the subject of a final and conclusive judgment by a court having jurisdiction in the matter.

(2) For the purposes of this section the courts of the country of the original court shall, subject to the provisions of subsection (3) of this section, be deemed to have had jurisdiction—

(a) in the case of a judgment given in an action in personam—

(i) if the judgment debtor, being a defendant in the original court, submitted to the jurisdiction of that court by voluntarily appearing in the proceedings otherwise than for the purpose of protecting, or obtaining the release of, property seized, or threatened with seizure, in the proceedings or of contesting the jurisdiction of that court; or

(ii) if the judgment debtor was plaintiff in, or counterclaimed in, the proceedings in the original court; or

(iii) if the judgment debtor, being a defendant in the original court, had before the commencement of the proceedings agreed, in respect of the subject matter of the proceedings, to submit to the jurisdiction of that court or of the courts of the country of that court; or

    (iv) if the judgment debtor, being a defendant in the original court, was at the time when the proceedings were instituted resident in, or being a body corporate had its principal place of business in, the country of that court; or

    (v) if the judgment debtor, being a defendant in the original court, had an office or place of business in the country of that court and the proceedings in that court were in respect of a transaction effected through or at that office or place;

(b) in the case of a judgment given in an action of which the subject matter was immovable property or in an action in rem of which the subject matter was movable property, if the property in question was at the time of the proceedings in the original court situate in the country of that court;

(c) in the case of a judgment given in an action other than any such action as is mentioned in paragraph (a) or paragraph (b) of this sub-section, if the jurisdiction of the original court is recognized by the law of the registering court.

(3) Notwithstanding anything in sub-section (2) of this section, the courts of the country of the original court shall not be deemed to have had jurisdiction—

(a) if the subject matter of the proceedings was immovable property outside the country of the original court; or

(b) except in the cases mentioned in sub-paragraphs (i), (ii) and (iii) of paragraph (a) and in paragraph (c) of sub-section (2) of this section, if the bringing of the proceedings in the original court was contrary to an agreement under which the dispute in question was to be settled otherwise than by proceedings in the courts of the country of that court; or

(c) if the judgment debtor, being a defendant in the original proceedings, was a person who under the rules of public international law was entitled to immunity from the jurisdiction of the courts of the country of the original court and did not submit to the jurisdiction of that court.

5.—(1) If, on an application to set aside the registration of a judgment, the applicant satisfies the registering court either that an appeal is pending, or that he is entitled and intends to appeal, against the judgment, the court, if it thinks fit, may, on such terms as it may think just, either set aside the registration or adjourn the application to set aside the registration until after the expiration of such period as appears to the court to be reasonably sufficient to enable the applicant to take the necessary steps to have the appeal disposed of by the competent tribunal.

(2) Where the registration of a judgment is set aside under the last foregoing subsection, or solely for the reason that the judgment was not at the date of the application for registration enforceable by execution in the country of the original court, the setting aside of the registration shall not prejudice a further application to register the judgment when the appeal has been disposed of or if and when the judgment becomes enforceable by execution in that country, as the case may be.

(3) Where the registration of a judgment is set aside solely for the reason that the judgment, notwithstanding that it had at the date of the application for registration been partly satisfied, was registered for the whole sum payable thereunder, the registering court shall, on the application of the judgment creditor, order judgment to be registered for the balance remaining payable at that date.

6. No proceedings for the recovery of a sum payable under a foreign judgment, being a judgment to which this Part of this Act applies, other than proceedings by way of registration of the judgment, shall be entertained by any court in the United Kingdom.

7.—(1) His Majesty may by Order in Council direct that this Part of this Act shall apply to His Majesty's dominions outside the United Kingdom and to judgments obtained in the courts of the said dominions as it applies to foreign countries and judgments obtained in the courts of foreign countries, and, in the event of His Majesty so directing, this Act shall have effect accordingly and Part II of the Administration of Justice Act, 1920, shall cease to have effect except in relation to those parts of the said dominions to which it extends at the date of the Order.[1]

(2) If at any time after His Majesty has directed as aforesaid an Order in Council is made under section one of this Act extending Part 1 of this Act to any part of His Majesty's dominions to which the said Part II extends as aforesaid, the said Part II shall cease to have effect in relation to that part of His Majesty's dominions.

(3) References in this section to His Majesty's dominions outside the United Kingdom shall be construed as including references to any territories which are under His Majesty's protection and to any

---

[1] Orders in Council have been made under this s. applying Part I of the Act to India, Pakistan, and the Australian Capital Territory.

territories in respect of which a mandate under the League of Nations has been accepted by His Majesty.

PART II

Miscellaneous and General

8.—(1) Subject to the provisions of this section, a judgment to which Part I of this Act applies or would have applied if a sum of money had been payable thereunder, whether it can be registered or not, and whether, if it can be registered, it is registered or not, shall be recognised in any court in the United Kingdom as conclusive between the parties thereto in all proceedings founded on the same cause of action and may be relied on by way of defence or counterclaim in any such proceedings.

(2) This section shall not apply in the case of any judgment—

(*a*) where the judgment has been registered and the registration thereof has been set aside on some ground other than—

   (i) that a sum of money was not payable under the judgment; or

   (ii) that the judgment had been wholly or partly satisfied; or

   (iii) that at the date of the application the judgment could not be enforced by execution in the country of the original court; or

(*b*) where the judgment has not been registered, it is shown (whether it could have been registered or not) that if it had been registered the registration thereof would have been set aside on an application for that purpose on some ground other than one of the grounds specified in paragraph (*a*) of this subsection.

(3) Nothing in this section shall be taken to prevent any court in the United Kingdom recognising any judgment as conclusive of any matter of law or fact decided therein if that judgment would have been so recognised before the passing of this Act.

9.—(1) If it appears to His Majesty that the treatment in respect of recognition and enforcement accorded by the courts of any foreign country to judgments given in the superior courts of the United Kingdom is substantially less favourable than that accorded by the courts of the United Kingdom to judgments of the superior courts of that country, His Majesty may by Order in Council apply this section to that country.

(2) Except so far as His Majesty may by Order in Council under this section otherwise direct, no proceedings shall be entertained in any court in the United Kingdom for the recovery of any sum alleged to be payable under a judgment given in a court of a country to which this section applies.

10. (*Power of High Court to issue certified copies of foreign judgments.*)

11.—(1) (*Definitions.*)

(2) For the purposes of this Act, the expression 'action in personam' shall not be deemed to include any matrimonial cause or any proceedings in connection with any of the following matters, that is to say, matrimonial matters, administration of the estates of deceased persons, bankruptcy, winding up of companies, lunacy, or guardianship of infants.

12. (*Application to Scotland.*)

13. (*Application to Northern Ireland.*)

14. This Act may be cited as the Foreign Judgments (Reciprocal Enforcement) Act 1933.

PART VI

LAW OF PROCEDURE

Chapter 20

JURISDICTION TO STAY ACTIONS

The English courts have jurisdiction to stay or restrain an English or foreign action where the defendant is sued in England as well as abroad by the same plaintiff, or where the defendant in England is plaintiff abroad, but will exercise it only where the double proceedings are vexatious and oppressive.

COHEN *v.* ROTHFIELD [1919] 1 K.B. 410 (Court of Appeal)

APPEAL from a decision of Shearman J.

SCRUTTON L.J.: This is an appeal by one Rothfield, a moneylender, from an order of Shearman J. in chambers, staying Rothfield from proceeding with an action brought by him as plaintiff against one Cohen in Scotland, on the ground that its substance is included in an action brought by Cohen, another moneylender, against Rothfield in England. Cohen carried on a business as moneylender in the north of England and Scotland, and Rothfield was his manager on the terms of getting one-fourth of the profits and paying one-fourth of the losses. Rothfield demanded accounts; Cohen alleged the receipt by Rothfield of secret commissions. Rothfield, through his solicitor, threatened an action in Scotland in respect of the Scotch business if accounts were not rendered in a week. Cohen within the week issued his English writ for an account as agent and for damages for misconduct as agent. Rothfield then issued his Scotch writ for an account of the Scotch business. Rothfield has got his Scotch action to the stage when it is nearly ready to be set down for trial. Cohen has done nothing in his English action. Cohen then applied in England to restrain Rothfield from proceeding with his Scotch action on the ground that it was vexatious, and Shearman J. granted him an injunction and gave leave to appeal. Rothfield now appeals.

Where it is proposed to stay an action on the ground that another is pending, and the action to be stayed is not in the court asked to make the order, the same result is obtained by restraining the person who is bringing the second action from proceeding with it. But, as the effect is to interfere with proceedings in another jurisdiction, this power should be exercised with great caution to avoid even the appearance of undue interference with another court.

Where an English court is asked to stay an action commenced in a foreign jurisdiction—that is, one outside the British Empire—on the ground that the plaintiff in the foreign action is also plaintiff in an English action, the burden is on the person asking for relief from the English court to satisfy it that the plaintiff in the foreign court cannot obtain any advantage from the foreign procedure that he would not obtain in the English court. It is not prima facie vexatious for the same plaintiff to commence two actions relating to the same subject-matter, one in England and one abroad. The applicant must prove a substantial case of vexation resulting from the identity of proceedings, remedies, and benefits, or from the existence of some motive other than a bona fide desire to determine disputes. Within the English courts two actions by the same plaintiff relating to the same subject-matter may be prima facie vexatious, but this prima facie case does not exist where one action is out of the King's dominions, and the court is not necessarily aware of the advantages of the foreign procedure. This appears to be the result of the judgments in *McHenry* v. *Lewis*[1] and *Hyman* v. *Helm*.[2] Where the plaintiff in the foreign action is not plaintiff, but defendant, in the English action, the case against interference is even stronger, for the person to be stayed has not himself initiated two proceedings. He has initiated one, and has been compelled to appear in another over which he has, as defendant, no control. When Cotton L.J. in 1883 in *Hyman* v. *Helm* asked if there was any case in which a defendant sued here has before decree been restrained from commencing an action abroad, no case was produced. When, in 1909, in *Vardopulo*

---

[1] (1882) 22 Ch. D. 397.　　[2] (1883) 24 Ch. D. 531.

v. *Vardopulo*,[1] a similar question was asked, again no case was produced. In *In re Connolly Brothers*[2] Cozens-Hardy M.R., who had asked the question in *Vardopulo v. Vardopulo*, again referred to the matter, and he then pointed out that there was one case in which a defendant had been restrained before decree. That case was *Bushby* v. *Munday*,[3] in which the plaintiff, who was suing to set aside a bond alleged to have been given for a gaming debt, succeeded in restraining the defendant from suing on the bond in Scotland by proving that, owing to the superior powers of discovery possessed by the English court, there would be more likelihood of the facts being correctly ascertained in England. While, therefore, there is jurisdiction to restrain a defendant from suing abroad, it is a jurisdiction very rarely exercised, and to be resorted to with great care and on ample evidence produced by the applicant that the action abroad is really vexatious and useless.

COHEN
v.
ROTHFIELD.
—
Scrutton
L.J.

Does the same rule of procedure apply where the action to be stayed is not abroad but in another court in the King's dominions, as in Scotland, Ireland, or the Colonies? In *McHenry* v. *Lewis*, though it was not necessary to decide the question, Jessel M.R. expressed the view that in the case of the same plaintiff bringing two actions in two parts of the Empire, as there were facilities for enforcing the English judgment in other parts of the Empire, the case was more like concurrent actions in the same jurisdiction, though, as he pointed out, if the remedies were different, the case altered. It is obvious, for instance, that an action in South Africa, where the Dutch procedure prevails, in Mauritius or Quebec, where French procedure exists, in Malta with its peculiar law, or in Scotland with its Roman procedure, may produce quite different results from an English action. It appears to me that unless the applicant satisfies the court that no advantage can be gained by the defendant by proceeding with the action in which he is plaintiff in another part of the King's dominions, the court should not stop him from proceeding with the only proceedings which he, as plaintiff, can control. The principle has been repeatedly acted upon. Thus on similar grounds the court has declined to stay proceedings in Scotland in *In re Derwent Rolling Mills Co.*,[4] in which case it was pointed out that by the arrestment in Scotland the plaintiff got a charge on the property arrested taking priority from the date of the judgment and

---

[1] (1909) 25 T.L.R. 518.   [2] [1911] 1 Ch. 731, 745.   [3] (1821) 5 Madd. 297.
[4] (1904) 21 T.L.R. 81, 701.

had no similar advantage in England, and also in *In re Warrand*,[1] and has refused to stay an action in England, the only reason given being that proceedings were pending in Ireland between the same parties for the same relief: *Carter* v. *Hungerford*.[2] In *Jopson* v. *James*,[3] the Court of Appeal reversed an order of the Vice-Chancellor of the Palatine Court, who had restrained a partnership action in Nova Scotia on the ground of a partnership action pending in England in his court. In *Thornton* v. *Thornton*,[4] the court refused to restrain a wife from proceeding in England for restitution of conjugal rights because her husband was already bringing divorce proceedings against her in India; and the explanation of this case given in *In re Norton's Settlement*[5] does not at all detract from its authority. In the last case, as in several of the others, the decision or discretion of the judge below was overruled.

Applying these principles to the present case, Rothfield has brought a perfectly proper action in Scotland to take the accounts of a business carried on in Scotland, and by arrestment has obtained a charge on certain funds. He announced his intention of bringing this action before Cohen commenced his action in England, and has prosecuted it with much greater diligence than Cohen has in England. Cohen gives no evidence to show that Rothfield will obtain no advantage by the Scotch action, and, so far as the English action relates to Scotch affairs, the evidence can more easily be taken in Scotland than in England. In my view the applicant did not in any way support the burden imposed on him by the principles I have stated, and on those principles there was no evidence which justified Shearman J. in staying the defendant from proceeding with his action in Scotland. His order must be set aside, and the appeal allowed with costs here and below.

EVE J. delivered judgment to the same effect.

Appeal allowed.

---

[1] (1892) 93 L.T. Jo. 82.   [2] (1915) 59 S.J. 428.   [3] (1908) 77 L.J. Ch. 824.
[4] (1886) 11 P.D. 176.   [5] [1908] 1 Ch. 471.

If a contract provides that all disputes between the parties are to be referred to the exclusive jurisdiction of a foreign tribunal, prima facie the English court will stay proceedings instituted in England in breach of such agreement; but the court may in its discretion allow them to continue.

THE FEHMARN [1958] 1 W.L.R. 159 (Court of Appeal)

Appeal by the defendants from a decision of Willmer J.

LORD DENNING: In September 1955, a Russian company loaded about 500 tons of turpentine in bulk on a German ship then at a port in the Baltic. The Russian shippers presented to the master a bill of lading for signature. One half of the face of the bill of lading was in Russian and the corresponding half in English. All the conditions on the back were in the English language. The bill of lading said that these goods were shipped in apparent good order and condition on the vessel and that they were to be delivered subject to the conditions on the bill of lading. Amongst the conditions was one that the shipowners were bound to make the ship seaworthy before and at the beginning of the voyage. At the end of these conditions there were two clauses which I must read. Condition 26 says: 'All claims and disputes arising under and in connection with this bill of lading shall be judged in the U.S.S.R.' Condition 27 says: 'All questions and disputes not mentioned in this bill of lading shall be determined according to the Merchant Shipping Code of the U.S.S.R.'

The turpentine was duly shipped in bulk, I suppose by being pumped on board the ship, at the port of Ventspils in the Baltic. The Fehmarn was owned by German owners in Hamburg. She made her journey to London, and the Russian shippers sold the goods to English buyers, who became holders of the bill of lading.

After the turpentine was unloaded in England, the English importers made complaint of short delivery and contamination. They say (as it now appears from the statement of claim) that there were some three tons short on delivery and that the turpentine was contaminated owing to the failure of the shipowners to make the ship seaworthy and fit for the reception of the turpentine. They say the tanks of the ship had previously carried linseed oil or other vegetable oils on previous voyages and they had not been properly cleaned out before the turpentine was loaded, with the result that there was a skin of linseed oil on the inside of the tanks, which dissolved and so contaminated the turpentine.

The solicitors to the English importers wrote a letter to the German owners making a claim for some £5,000 and intimating that, as the ship was a frequent visitor to this country, it might be necessary to take steps to arrest the vessel when she next came to this country in order that their claim should be settled. The German owners instructed English solicitors to deal with the claim. The solicitors to the English importers spoke on the telephone to the solicitors for the German owners and told them that, if they did not receive an undertaking for security to be given, they would arrest the ship when she next arrived in this country. Thereupon the solicitors for the German owners, after two months' interval, on November 15, 1956, wrote: 'We understand there will be no objection by our clients to a submission to a private arbitrator, but having regard to clauses 26 and 27 of the bill of lading our clients are not prepared to give security to meet your claim.' Clauses 26 and 27 are those which I have already read.

So the parties were at issue. Eventually the English importers, the owners of the cargo, brought an action against the German owners of the ship in the Admiralty Division of the High Court claiming damages. Thereupon the German owners moved to set aside the writ on the ground that the English courts had no jurisdiction or alternatively that by the agreement the parties had agreed that all the disputes should be adjudged in the courts of Russia and not in this country.

As to the first point, it is not now suggested that the Court of Admiralty has not jurisdiction. By s. 1 (1) (g) of the Administration of Justice Act 1956 (following previous statutes), it is plain that the Court of Admiralty in England has jurisdiction to deal with such a claim as this.

Then the next question is whether the action ought to be stayed because of the provision in the bill of lading that all disputes are to be judged by the Russian courts. I do not regard this provision as equal to an arbitration clause, but I do say that the English courts are in charge of their own proceedings: and one of the rules they apply is that a stipulation that all disputes should be judged by the tribunals of a particular country is not absolutely binding. It is a matter to which the courts of this country will pay much regard and to which they will normally give effect, but it is subject to the over-riding principle that no one by his private stipulation can oust these courts of their jurisdiction in a matter that properly belongs to them.

I would ask myself therefore: Is this dispute a matter which properly belongs to the courts of this country? Here are English importers who, when they take delivery of the goods in England, find them contaminated. The goods are surveyed by surveyors on both sides, with the result that the English importers make a claim against the German shipowners. The vessel is a frequent visitor to this country. In order to be sure that their claim, if substantiated, is paid by the shipowners, the English importers are entitled by the procedure of our courts of Admiralty to arrest the ship whenever she comes here in order to have security for their claim. There seems to me to be no doubt that such a dispute is one that pro-perly belongs for its determination to the courts of this country. But still the question remains: Ought these courts in their discretion to stay this action?

It has been said by Mr. Roche that this contract is governed by Russian law and should be judged by the Russian courts, who know that law. And the dispute may involve evidence from witnesses in Russia about the condition of the goods on shipment. Then why, says Mr. Roche, should it not be judged in Russia as the condition says?

I do not regard the choice of law in the contract as decisive. I prefer to look to see with what country is the dispute most closely concerned. Here the Russian element in the dispute seems to me to be comparatively small. The dispute is between the German owners of the ship and the English importers. It depends on evidence here as to the condition of the goods when they arrived here in London and on evidence of the ship, which is a frequent visitor to London. The correspondence leaves in my mind, just as it did in the judge's mind, the impression that the German owners did not object to the dispute being decided in this country but wished to avoid the giving of security.

I think the dispute is more closely connected with England than Russia, and I agree with the judge that sufficient reason has been shown why the proceedings should continue in these courts and should not be stayed. I would therefore dismiss the appeal.

HODSON and MORRIS L.JJ. delivered judgments to the same effect.

Appeal dismissed.

Chapter 21

SUBSTANCE AND PROCEDURE

Foreign statutes of limitation are substantive if they extinguish the plaintiff's right, but procedural if they merely bar his remedy.

HUBER *v.* STEINER.

HUBER *v.* STEINER (1835) 2 Bing. (N.C.) 202 (Court of Common Pleas)

ASSUMPSIT on a promissory note made by the defendant in France on the 12th of May 1813, and payable to the order of the plaintiff 10th of May 1817.

The defendant pleaded (1) the general issue; (2) the Statute of Limitations; (3) and (4) the French law of prescription. The effect of these pleas appears fully from the judgment.

TINDAL C.J.: The answer which the defendant has set up against this action is twofold: first, he relies upon the English Statute of Limitations; and, secondly, upon the French Law of Prescription, as stated in his third and fourth pleas. As the plea of the Statute of Limitations has been disposed of, by reason that the replication of the plaintiff's being beyond sea from the time of the cause of action accruing has been found in his favour, the only ground of defence which it will be necessary to consider will be that which arises from the plea of the French law.

It becomes necessary to consider the general question in the cause; whether, by the law of France, the contract made by the defendant in his promissory note, is altogether extinguished and made null and void in that country, by reason of the doctrine of prescription, which holds in the French law; or whether, under the doctrine of prescription, the contract itself is not annulled and extinguished, but the remedy only barred in the French courts of law. For we take it to be clearly established, and recognised as part of the law of England, by various decisions, that if the prescription of the French law, which has been opposed to the plaintiff in the present case, is no more than a limitation of the time within which the action upon the note must be brought in the French courts, it will not form a bar to the right of action in our English courts; but that the question whether the action is brought within due and proper time must be governed by the English statute. The distinction between that part of the law of the foreign country where a personal contract is made, which is adopted, and that which is not adopted by our English courts of law, is well known and established; namely, that so much of the law as affects the rights and merit of the contract, all that relates 'ad litis decisionem', is adopted from the foreign country; so much of the law as affects the remedy only, all that relates 'ad litis ordinationem', is taken from the 'lex fori' of that country where the action is brought; and that in the interpretation of this rule, the time of limitation of the action falls within the latter division, and is governed by the law of the country where the action is brought, and not by the lex loci contractûs, is evident from many authorities. . . .

Such being the general rule of law, a distinction has been sought to be engrafted on it by the learned counsel for the defendant; that 'where the statutes of limitation of a particular country not only extinguish the right of action, but the claim or title itself, ipso facto, and declare it a nullity after the lapse of the prescribed period, that in such case the statute may be set up in any other country to which the parties remove, by way of extinguishment'. This distinction is stated to be adopted from a work entitled Commentaries on the Conflict of Laws, p. 487, by Joseph Story LL.D.; a work which it would be unjust to mention without at the same time paying a tribute to the learning, acuteness, and accuracy of its author. And undoubtedly the distinction, when taken with the qualification annexed to it by the author himself, appears to be well founded. That qualification is, 'that the parties are resident within the jurisdiction during all that period, so that it has actually operated upon the case'; and with such restriction, it does indeed appear but reasonable that the part of the lex loci contractûs which declares the contract to be absolutely void at a certain limited time, without any intervening suit, should be equally regarded by the foreign country, as the part of the lex loci contractûs which gives life to and regulates the construction of the contract; both parts go equally 'ad valorem contractûs', both 'ad decisionem litis'.

So much, however, being conceded to the defendant, it remains for him to set up and establish to the satisfaction of the court the proposition for which he contends, that the French law of prescrip-

HUBER
v.
STEINER.

Tindal C.J.

tion which applies to the present case, is one which extinguishes not only the remedy, but the right or contract itself; for unless it has this effect in France, the case falls within the larger and more general rule, that the time of limitation of the action must be governed by the law of the country where the action is brought.

Before, however, we come to the argument on this point, it may be expedient to advert to the facts of the present case, to which the rule of the French law is proposed to be applied.

The action is brought on a promissory note, made at Mulhausen, which at that time was subject to the law of France, where both the plaintiff and the defendant may be taken to have been then domiciled. The promissory note was made and bore date on the 12th of May 1813, and was payable to the order of the plaintiff, on the 10th of May 1817. In the course of 1813, very shortly after the making of the note and nearly four years before it became due, both parties quitted Mulhausen; the plaintiff going to Switzerland, the defendant to England, where he has ever since resided and been domiciled.

Under such a state of facts, the defendant seeks to apply the 189th article of the Code de Commerce as a bar to the present action; on the ground that it operates as an annulling of the contract, as an extinguishment of the claim and right of action in that country. That article is found in the division of the Code de Commerce which relates to bills of exchange, and is contained in the following words, viz.:—

'Sect. 3, of Prescription.—All actions relative to letters of exchange and to bills to order, subscribed by tradesmen, merchants, and bankers, or for matters of commerce, "prescribe themselves" by five years, reckoning from the day of protest, or from the last suing out any judicial process, if there hath been no judgment, or if the debt hath not been acknowledged by any separate act.'

'Nevertheless, the pretended debtors shall be held, if required, to affirm upon oath that they no longer owe the money. And their widows, heirs, &c., that they bonâ fide believe there is nothing more due.'

Now, the question is, whether the defendant has made out, affirmatively, to the satisfaction of the court, that this prescription has the necessary force of extinguishing and annulling the contract upon the note, ipso facto, after a lapse of five years from the time it becomes due: for unless the prescription has this force, it

operates on the remedy only; which, upon the general principle before laid down and acknowledged, will be governed by the lex fori,
and not by the lex loci contractûs.

And, after giving every attention to the authorities cited on both
sides, we think the French law is not shewn to have the force contended for by the defendant. The defendant has brought different
passages in the Code de Commerce, and by contrasting them with
others which are found in the Code Civil, has shewn it possible that
such may be the force and effect of the article in question; but he
has produced no distinct authority that the contract is intended to
be annulled; whereas, on the contrary, the very terms of the article
itself, the authorities of text writers, and the reason of the thing, do
so far outweigh, as it appears to us, the inference drawn from the
comparison of different parts of the French law, that we cannot but
hold the section relied upon amounts only to a limitation of the
remedy in the French courts, to the space of five years, and not to
an utter avoidance of the contract itself at the end of that period.

The article itself begins by stating, that 'all actions prescribe
themselves', not 'that the contract is prescribed or gone'. The exception, that the 'action is not prescribed, if the debt is acknowledged by a separate writing'; the power given to the creditor to put
the debtor to his oath, that he owes nothing, called in the French
law 'le serment décisoire';—all these circumstances agree with the
notion that it is the action, not the debt, which is prescribed by the
law. . . .

But, from the ground of reason and expediency, the inference is
still more strong that the prescription limits the action only, and
does not destroy the debt; for if the debt itself is absolutely gone by
reason of the lapse of five years, without any reference to the power
of the plaintiff to sue in the meantime, what would be the condition
of the creditor whose debtor quits the country, where this law
applies, before the day of payment arrives,—that is before there
is a possibility of maintaining the action,—and never returns to it
again?

To maintain a position so contrary to reason, very strong authority must be expected; but none is shewn; on the contrary, the very
text of the book from which the distinction is first taken (Story,
p. 487) annexes to it the condition, that the debtor and creditor
have remained within the jurisdiction during the time of the prescription.

In the case before us, both were absent: it would be enough, how-ever, to say that the debtor was absent, to call in aid the maxim of the French, no less than of the civil law, 'contra non valentem agere, non currit prescriptio.'

We do therefore think, that the law set up on the part of the defendants amounts to no more than a limitation of the time for bringing the action, not to an extinction of the contract; that, consequently, it is no bar in itself under any circumstances; still less, where the debtor ceased to reside in the country where the law prevails during the whole period of time that the debt was owing and due.

We therefore think the verdict must be entered for the plaintiff, upon the general issue, as well as upon the issues arising on the special pleas.

Judgment for the plaintiff.

Remoteness of damage is a question of substance, governed by the proper law of the contract. The measure of damages is a question of procedure, governed by the lex fori.

D'ALMEIDA
ARAUJO
LDA.
v.
SIR
FREDERICK
BECKER
& CO.
LTD.

D'ALMEIDA ARAUJO LDA. *v.* SIR FREDERICK BECKER & CO. LTD.
[1953] 2 Q.B. 329 (Queen's Bench Division)

On 20 March 1947 the plaintiffs, a firm of merchants carrying on business in Lisbon, agreed to sell to the defendants, an English company carrying on business as merchants in the City of London, 500 tons of palm oil at 14.20 escudos a kilogramme f.o.b. Angora, Portuguese West Africa, payment to be by open credit to be opened by 24 March. The proper law of the contract was Portuguese.

On the same date the plaintiffs had contracted with one Mourao for the purchase of 500 tons of palm oil which was designed to implement the plaintiffs' contract with the defendants. This contract provided that payment was to be by open credit to be opened by 24 March. The contract also provided that in the event of breach by either party the party in default should pay to the other as indemnity for the damages an amount corresponding to 5 per cent. of the total value of the contract. Mourao had entered into a similar contract with one Guimeraes for the purchase of the oil.

The defendants had agreed to resell the palm oil, payment for which was to be made by credit in their favour in Lisbon, but the sub-purchasers failed to open the credit, with the result that the

D'ALMEIDA
ARAUJO
LDA.
v.
SIR
FREDERICK
BECKER
& CO.
LTD.

defendants were unable to open the credit in favour of the plaintiffs. The plaintiffs were ready to complete the sale, if the defendants opened the credit, at least up to 12 April. On 14 April the plaintiffs advertised the palm oil for sale in a Lisbon newspaper against immediate opening credit, but were unable to sell it.

On 18 April Guimeraes cabled that if the credit was not opened on that day his contract would be cancelled.

The defendants having failed to open the credit in the plaintiffs' favour, the plaintiffs were unable to open the credit in favour of Mourao, and accordingly under their contract with him were bound to pay him the indemnity, which amounted to £3,500, and they did so pay him.

The plaintiffs claimed damages for the defendants' breach of contract under two heads, (1) £1,000 for the loss of profit which they would have made on the resale; and (2) £3,500 which they had had to pay Mourao for breach of their contract with him.

PILCHER J. (having held that there was a contract and that the defendants had broken it and that the only remaining point was what damages, if any, the plaintiffs were entitled to recover, continued:) While it was common ground between the parties that the substantive contract between them was governed by Portuguese law, the plaintiffs contended that the damages which they were entitled to recover in the particular circumstances of the case were also to be determined in accordance with the principles of Portuguese law. The defendants, on the contrary, submitted that even in a case where the substantive contract was governed by foreign law, procedural or remedial questions, which included the question of damages, ought to be determined according to the lex fori, in this case, the law of England. Subject to the question of the obligation of an innocent party to mitigate the damages, to which I will refer in a moment, the question of the proper law to be applied in regard to the damages in this case has importance, because the plaintiffs are seeking to recover from the defendants the £3,500 as one head of damage—that being, of course, the sum which they had to pay to Mourao for failing to carry out their contract with him.

The loss sustained by the plaintiffs in paying that sum was clearly not a loss which was foreseeable by the defendants at the time when they negotiated this contract with the plaintiffs, and it is clear that under English law this sum of £3,500 would be irrecoverable by the

D'ALMEIDA
ARAUJO
LDA.
v.
SIR
FREDERICK
BECKER
& CO.
LTD.

Pilcher J.

plaintiffs from the defendants. It was argued by Mr. Mocatta, on behalf of the plaintiffs, that they would, under Portuguese law, have been entitled to include this sum in their damages if damages were assessed on the principles of Portuguese law. While I feel no certainty that the plaintiffs' right to recover damages in this case will turn out in the end to be any different whether the principles of English or Portuguese law are applied, it is none the less desirable that I should state my view on the point.

I was referred to a number of textbooks on the particular point whether in a foreign contract which has to be determined by the lex loci contractus the issue of damages is, in the words of some of the textbook writers, 'a procedural or remedial matter' such as falls to be determined in accordance with the lex fori, or whether, on the other hand, it is part of the substantive contract between the parties and so to be determined in accordance with the lex loci contractus. I propose to read certain passages from the textbooks, because there is very little authority on this particular topic in English law. In Dicey's Conflict of Laws, 6th ed., pp. 649–50, this passage occurs: 'A further difficulty is created by the problem of how to distinguish between the effect of the contract and the remedies which are available for its enforcement. Whether a contract gives rise to a claim for performance or to a claim for damages, whether, in the event of a breach of contract, the other party has a right to rescind it, whether interest is payable on a debt—all these are matters which, on a proper analysis, should be regarded as affecting the rights and obligations to which the contract gives rise. While it is clear that, in the view of the English courts, the liability to pay contractual interest and the rate of such interest are determined by the proper law, it appears to be a generally accepted view that the measure of damages is, in an English court, governed by English law, whatever be the proper law of the contract. This principle is apt to deprive a party of rights he would have enjoyed under the proper law or to confer upon him an uncovenanted benefit merely owing to the fact that he happened to be able to invoke the jurisdiction of an English court. Its rigour could be mitigated if, following Cheshire's suggestion, the courts could separate from the question of the measure of damages that known as "remoteness of damage" and hold that it was one of the effects of a contract to determine what events may and must be taken into account in assessing the damages for which a party is liable.'

On p. 862, under the head 'Procedure, Rule 193', the following passage occurs: 'While there is little authority, it appears that English courts, contrary to the prevailing American practice, tend to hold that damages are a matter of procedure in an action based on a foreign tort. In contract, there is no direct English authority, but it is submitted that questions of remoteness of damage should be determined by the proper law of the contract, and should not be treated as a matter of procedure', and a reference is then given to a case decided in the Supreme Court of Canada, *Livesley* v. *Horst*,[1] to which I will refer. 'The rate of interest to be allowed (if any) for breach of a foreign contract must depend on its proper law.' Those are the relevant passages in Dicey.

D'ALMEIDA
ARAUJO
LDA.
v.
SIR
FREDERICK
BECKER
& CO.
LTD.

Pilcher J.

There are also certain passages in Cheshire's Private International Law, 4th ed., to which I must refer. After considering the principles on which damages are recoverable in this country in actions founded respectively in contract and tort, the author states at pp. 659–60: 'The truth would appear to be that judicial pronouncements and the statements in textbooks are unintelligible unless two entirely different questions are segregated. In brief, remoteness of liability or remoteness of damage must be distinguished from measure of damages. The rules relating to remoteness indicate what kind of loss actually resulting from the commission of a tort or from breach of contract is actionable; the rules for the measure of damages show the method by which compensation for an actionable loss is calculated. Damage may be, but damages can never be, too remote. In tort the rule of remoteness established by the *Polemis* case[2] is that a tortfeasor is responsible for all the direct consequences of his wrongful act, even though they could not reasonably have been anticipated. The analogous rule in contracts, however, is different. The breach of a contract, like the commission of a tort, causes material loss, and it is that loss to which the rule in *Hadley* v. *Baxendale*[3] applies. In other words, it is impossible to claim monetary compensation in respect even of an admitted loss unless it arose naturally and in the ordinary course of things from the breach of contract. But the rule that regulates the measure of damages is the same for contracts as it is for torts. It requires restitutio in integrum. In torts compensation must be paid for the

---

[1] [1925] 1 D.L.R. 159.
[2] [1921] 3 K.B. 560. See now *The Wagon Mound* (*No. 1*) [1961] A.C. 388 (Ed.).
[3] (1854) 9 Exch. 341.

D'ALMEIDA
ARAUJO
LDA.
v.
SIR
FREDERICK
BECKER
& CO.
LTD.

Pilcher J.

whole of the direct loss; in contracts, as *Robinson* v. *Harman*[1] insists, compensation must be paid for the whole of the natural or foreseeable loss.

'Alive to the distinction between remoteness of liability and measure of damages we can now attempt to state the relevant principles of private international law.

'There can be no doubt, at least on principle, that remoteness of liability must be governed by the proper law of the obligation that rests upon the defendant. Not only the existence, but also the extent, of an obligation, whether it springs from a breach of contract or the commission of a wrong, must be determined by the system of law from which it derives its source. The proper law admittedly determines the nature and content of the right created by a contract, and it is clear that the kind of loss for which damages are recoverable upon breach forms part of that contract. Both the nature and the content of a contractual right depend in part upon the question whether certain consequential loss that may ensue if the contract is unperformed will be too remote in the eye of the law. If the proper law determines what constitutes a breach, it is also entitled to determine the consequences of a breach.'

That passage from Professor Cheshire's book seems to me to be very closely reasoned and to offer considerable help in deciding this problem, which is not an easy one. The conclusion at which he arrives would seem to be that questions of remoteness of damage should be governed by the proper law of the contract, whereas the quantification of damage, which according to the proper law is not too remote, should be governed by the lex fori.

I must also refer to *Livesley* v. *Horst*, the headnote of which reads: 'The right to damages for breach of a contract made in a foreign country and to be executed there is governed by the lex loci contractus and not by the lex fori.' (After quoting from that case at considerable length, his Lordship continued:)

The question which I have to determine here really depends, if I accept and adopt, as I do, the analysis given by Professor Cheshire, on whether the £3,500 which the plaintiffs have had to pay to Mourao is a head of damage which is recoverable or not on principles of remoteness of damage, or whether it is to be regarded as a mere established quantification of a part of the loss the plaintiffs have in fact sustained. While the decision in the Canadian case is

[1] (1848) 1 Exch. 850.

not binding on me, and while the facts of that case can be distinguished from those of the present case, it is none the less a decision which I must, and do, treat with respect. I confess that in the absence of any direct authority I was attracted by the reasoning in the passage I have quoted from Professor Cheshire's work.

D'ALMEIDA
ARAUJO
LDA.
v.
SIR
FREDERICK
BECKER
& CO.
LTD.
—
Pilcher J.

Fortified by the decision of the Supreme Court of Canada, I conclude that the question whether the plaintiffs are entitled to claim from the defendants the £3,500 which they have paid to Mourao, depends on whether such damage is or is not too remote. In my view, the question here is one of remoteness, and therefore falls to be determined in accordance with Portuguese law. Whether the plaintiffs are entitled to recover this sum under Portuguese law is, however, quite another matter.

(His Lordship proceeded to review the evidence of Portuguese law. He concluded that under that law, unlike English law, it was possible to recover unforseeable damages, but that, as in English law, the plaintiff was under a duty to mitigate his damage. Assuming that the £3,500 could have been recovered under Portuguese law apart from this duty, his Lordship held that the plaintiffs could reasonably have mitigated their damage by reselling the palm oil on the Lisbon Produce Exchange at a price which would have been at least as high as, and almost certainly higher than, the contract price. He therefore awarded nominal damages of 40s. only.)

Judgment for the plaintiffs with costs up to the time of payment into court of £5 by the defendants, thereafter the defendants to have three-quarters of their costs.

Note. In *N.V. Handel Maatschappij J. Smits Import-Export* v. *English Exporters Ltd.* [1955] 2 Ll. L. Rep. 69, 72 (affirmed ibid. 317), McNair J. said that he had 'the greatest possible difficulty in appreciating the distinction' drawn by Pilcher J. in the above case between remoteness of damage and quantification of damages.

In *Boys* v. *Chaplin* [1967] 3 W.L.R. 266, an action in England on a tort committed in Malta, Milmo J. assessed the damages in the same way as he would have done if the case had been governed wholly by English law.

The English presumption of survivorship is substantive, not procedural.

In re COHN [1945] Ch. 5 *(ante, p. 1)*

PRINTED IN GREAT BRITAIN
AT THE UNIVERSITY PRESS, OXFORD
BY VIVIAN RIDLER
PRINTER TO THE UNIVERSITY

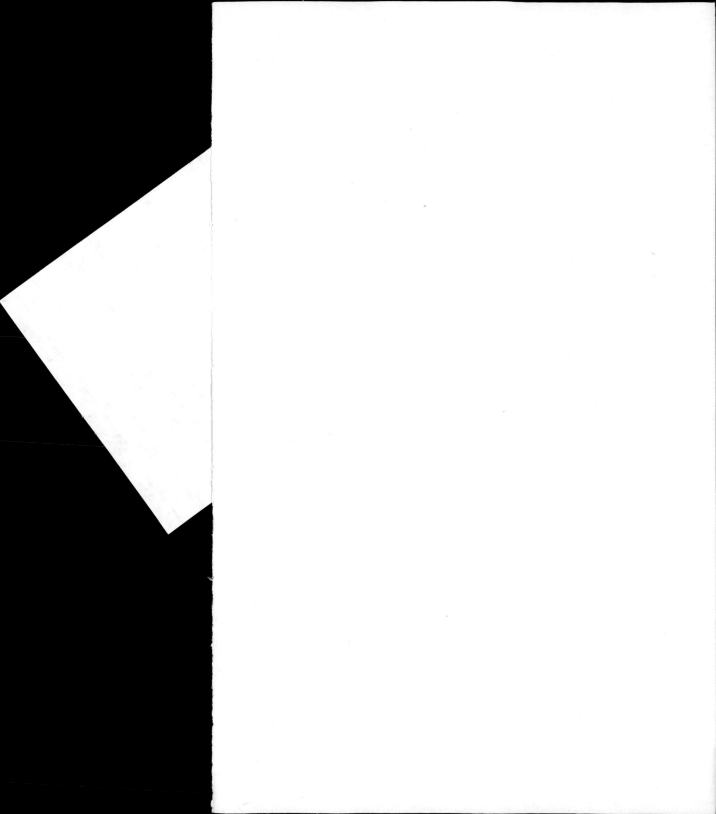

RENEWALS

APR 10

APR 14

GAYLORD

PRINTED IN U.S.A
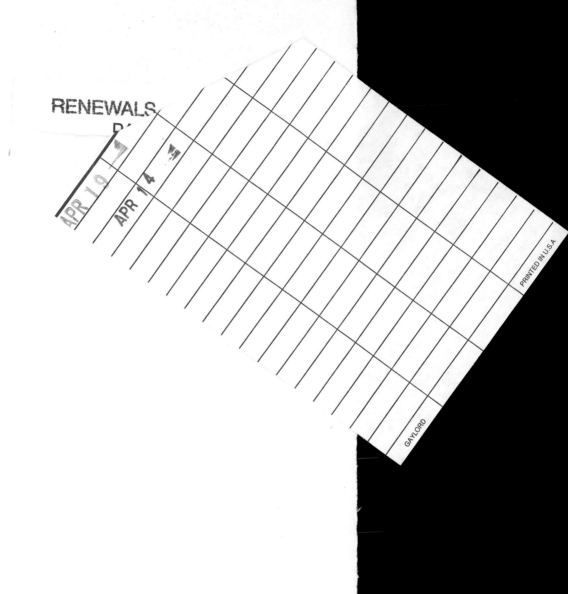